MALT
WHISKY
YEARBOOK
2021

First published in Great Britain in 2020 by
MagDig Media Limited

© MagDig Media Limited 2020

ISBN 978-0-9576553-7-9

MagDig Media Limited
1 Brassey Road
Old Potts Way, Shrewsbury
Shropshire SY3 7FA
ENGLAND

E-mail: info@maltwhiskyyearbook.com
www.maltwhiskyyearbook.com

Contents

Introduction

Writing this year's edition of the Malt Whisky Yearbook has been an unusual experience. With the covid-19 pandemic raging across the world, the gathering of information has been challenging to say the least. All my travels from March on were suspended and many producers around the world have been preoccupied with mitigating the effects of the virus. Some of them have been furloughed for months which meant that finding information was harder than ever. But I realize that I am one of the lucky ones. The troubles I have encountered working on the book are nothing compared to the economic nightmare many of the smaller whisky companies, as well as companies in other sectors, have had to endure. Not to mention those who have lost loved ones to the disease. The world of whisky will most probably have to live with the consequences of the current situation for a couple of years but the industry has seen both wars and depressions in the past and managed to bounce back. No doubt that will be the case this time too.

On a more positive note – in this year's edition I have managed to fulfill a dream I've had for a couple of years. I present interviews with some of the true legends of the Scotch whisky industry. These seven icons share a total of 358 years of whisky experience between them! They all deserve at least ten pages each (or an entire book), but the Yearbook format has its limitations so I hope you will enjoy their condensed words of wisdom and experience.

As usual, my excellent team of whisky writers have excelled themselves this year and have contributed with some fascinating articles:

It's very simple – without malted barley there is no malt whisky. Charles MacLean tells the fascinating story of starch, enzymes and hidden sugars.

The new distillers in Scotland are keen to leave their own mark on whisky production. Joel Harrison has asked some of them what makes their whisky stand out.

If you consider yourself an objective and experienced whisky taster, this article will make you think again. Ian Wisniewski explains all the tricks our brains are playing when we evaluate a whisky.

Were the whiskies from days gone better than the ones made today? Neil Ridley thinks it isn't as black and white as many enthusiasts claim.

The course of history can sometimes be changed by a single person, or a single whisky for that matter. Gavin D Smith has selected ten malts that broke the mould.

Right now, a new category of single malts is developing. Jonny McCormick went across the Atlantic and found himself in the middle of an American revolution.

In Malt Whisky Yearbook 2021 you will also find the unique, detailed and much appreciated section on Scottish malt whisky distilleries. It has been thoroughly revised and updated, not just in text, but also including numerous, new pictures, new distilleries and tasting notes for all the core brands. The chapter on distilleries from the rest of the world has been hugely expanded. You will also find a list of more than 150 of the best whisky shops in the world with their full details and suggestions on where to find more information on the internet. The Whisky Year That Was provides a summary of all the significant events during the year. Finally, the very latest statistics gives you all the answers to your questions on production and consumption.

Thank you for buying Malt Whisky Yearbook 2021. I hope that you will have many enjoyable moments reading it and I can assure you that I will be back with a new, updated edition next year.

Malt Whisky Yearbook 2022 will be published in October 2021.
If you need any of the previous fifteen volumes of Malt Whisky Yearbook,
some of them are available for purchase (in limited numbers) from the website
www.maltwhiskyyearbook.com

Acknowledgements

First of all I wish to thank the writers who have shared their great specialist knowledge on the subject in a brilliant and entertaining way – Joel Harrison, Charles MacLean, Jonny McCormick, Neil Ridley, Gavin D. Smith and Ian Wisniewski.

A special thanks goes to Gavin who put in a lot of effort nosing, tasting and writing notes for more than 100 different whiskies.

I am also deeply grateful to Stefan van Eycken who keeps us all up to date on Japanese whiskies and to Philippe Jugé for his valuable input on French distilleries.

The following persons have also made important photographic or editorial contributions and I am grateful to all of them:

Asa Abraham, Iain Allan, Alasdair Anderson, Russel Anderson, Lukas Andrlik, Alexander Atha, Duncan Baldwin, Sanjeev Banga, Adam Barber, Emma Battat, Laura Beadell, Richard Beattie, Marilena Bidaine, Graham Bowie, Ben Bradley, Lauren Braithwaite, Keith Brian, Henrik Brinks, Ross Bremner, Andrew Brown, David Brown, Rory Brown, Alex Bruce, Gordon Bruce, Alex Buck, Neil Bulloch, Stephen Burnett, Pär Caldenby, Ian Chang, Ashok Chokalingam, Marcus Christensson, David Clark, Suzanne Clark, Francis Conlon, Alexandra Cook, Lois Cope, Jason Craig, Andrew Crook, Ewa Czernecka, Alasdair Day, Paul Dempsey, Scott Dickson, Patricia Dillon, Alex Driver, Chris Dumont, Lukasz Dynowiak, Gavin Edwards, Michael Elliot, Simon Erlanger, Graham Eunson, Allan Findlay, Andy Fiske, Robert Fleming, John Fordyce, Callum Fraser, Kathrin Furst, Calum Gee, Archie Gillies, Colin Gordon, Stephen Gould, Pierrick Guillaume, Gary Haggart, Chloe Hall, Andy Hannah, Soichiro Harada, Wendy Harries Jones, Mickey Heads, Kieran Healey-Ryder, Erik Hirschfeld, Fraser Hughes, Robbie Hughes, Caryn Inglis, Sandy Jamieson, John Jarvis, Holly Johnstone, Bart Joosten, Luke Juranek, Pramod Kashyap, Davin de Kergommeaux, Kim King, Andrew Laing, Emily Lineham, David Livingstone, Graham Logan, Alistair Longwell, Barry Macaffer, Iain McAlister, Tommy Macarthur, Brian MacAulay, Des McCagherty, Robert McEachern, Alistair McDonald, John MacDonald, Jim McEwan, Frank McHardy, Sandy Macintyre, Doug McIvor, Connal Mackenzie, Joanne McKerchar, Jaclyn McKie, Julia Mackillop, Paul Mclean, Ian MacMillan, Kevin MacPherson, James MacTaggart, Ian McWilliam, Dennis Malcolm, Graham Manson, Neil Mathieson, Jack Mayo, Kwanele Mdluli, Ibon Mendiguren, Norbert Merics, Santiago Mignone, Gary Mills, Rune Molvik, Carol More, Jes Mosgaard, Katy Muggeridge, Cristina Munoz, Neil Murphy, Kate Newton, Tim Nicholson, Sietse Offringa, Edel O´Keffe, Emily Ooi, Gemma Paterson, Hannah Peebles, Wouter Peeters, Sean Phillips, Colin Poppy, Rupert Ponsonby, Simon Proud, Lars Ragnå, Struan Grant Ralph, Joanne Reavley, Ian Renwick, David Robertson, Jackie Robertson, Stuart Robertson, Jenny Rogerson, Colin Ross, Colette Savage, Lila and Nestor Serenelli, Steven Shand, Matthew Simpson, Daniel Smith, Derrick Smith, Kris Smyth, Greig Stables, Marie Stanton, Scott Steele, Duncan Tait, Stephanie Talbot, Eddie Thom, Annabel Thomas, Phil Thompson, Kirsty Thomson, Laura Thomson, Ruth Thomson, Kaitlyn Tsai, David Turner, Sandrine Tyrbas de Chamberet, Perry Unger, Michael Urquhart, Stewart Walker, Mark Watson, Ranald Watson, Mark Watt, Andy Watts, Emily Webster, Thuli Weerasena, Iain Weir, Nick White, Ronald Whiteford, Anthony Wills, Alan Winchester, Jamie Winfield, Gordon Winton, Kristoffer Wittström, Stephen Woodcock, Allison Young, Derek Younie and Lasse Öznek.

Finally, to my wife Pernilla and our daughter Alice, thank you for your patience and your love and to Vilda, our labrador and my faithful companion in the office during long working hours.

Ingvar Ronde
Editor
Malt Whisky Yearbook

The sweet story of Malting

by Charles MacLean

The fundamentals of any production of spirit
is transforming sugar into alcohol. Different types of spirit
require different methods. In the case of whisky making it is a story
of activating enzymes to get access to the hidden sugars.
It is the story of malting.

Barley and wheat were the first food crops in the world, domesticated from wild strains in the Fertile Crescent (Middle East) during the Neolithic period at the dawn of agriculture, around 7000BC. Chemical tests on ancient pottery reveal that barley also provided these early farmers with their first alcoholic drink, ale, and by the fifth millennium BC it was the staple cereal in Egypt, providing both bread and beer. Artefacts in the Cairo Museum show that by the third millennium BC barley cultivation was systematic and disciplined.

Whisky is, of course, a distillate of ale (correctly defined as un-hopped beer) and ale may be made from any cereal grain, but at least a portion of the grain must be malted in order to activate enzymes within the grains which will convert the starch into sugar, which in turn will be converted into alcohol by yeast.

The malting process is described in detail below; essentially it is controlled germination and was in all likelihood discovered accidentally, as was the fact that of all cereals barley is best for supplying the required enzymes.

As well as Egypt, the malting process was known in China (by 2100BC, it is said), Sumeria (ale features in the Epic of Gilgamesh, c.2010BC) and in northern Europe before the first century AD. Julius Caesar found that in Britain: "…they drink a high and mighty liquor, different from that of any other nation, made of barley and water. The drink is not so subtle in its effects as wine, but it is warming, even more nourishing…"

Ale soon superseded mead and cider as the most favoured drink in England; such was its popularity that in 970AD villages were permitted only one ale-house. The term 'malt-house' is first attested in c.1050 (as mealthus), 'maltman' in 1408 and 'malting' ('maltyn or make malt…') in c.1440.

It was soon discovered that some cereals – wheat, rye and oats, for example – rot very quickly after they have been harvested, unless they are thoroughly dried, owing to bacteria penetrating their outer skins or husks. Wheat and rye have no husk at all – they are termed 'naked grains' and successful malting of such grains is a constant fight against mould and bacterial attack. Oats are slightly better covered, but their husks are only loosely attached to the grain, so split and rub off unless they are carefully handled, allowing the bugs in. What's more, their loose structure allows water in, which causes the grain to swell and the husk to drop off. In Scotland, oats were described as 'food crop' and were the stable diet in the Highlands. Barley, on the other hand, called 'drink crop', is covered with material which Diageo's former Director of Malt Distilling, Brian Higgs, described to me as "nature's equivalent of Kevlar".

"This armour plated outer casing can cope with significant mechanical abuse and provides the young embryo with a head start on the opportunistic moulds and bacteria…"

"So the domination (not total but certainly significant) of barley as the starting point for malt production arose because of its husk. The protection that this thin layer afforded the barleycorn allowed malting techniques to be developed which would be able to meet the ever-increasing demand for beer and grain based spirits. It would be many years before the introduction of pneumatically controlled malting plants [see below], with techniques that could suppress the mould growth on the likes of wheat. By which time the common practice of using barley for malt production and the generic term 'malt' (instead of malted barley) had been established. Even when the grain distillers developed their techniques to produce potable spirit from the cheaper un-malted cereals, they had – and have – to use a portion of malted barley to provide the enzyme source. Un-malted cereals do not contain the enzymes required to convert the starch into sugar."

Most seeds, including barley, have two parts: the embryo (which takes up about a third of the seed's volume) is the living structure that will grow into a new plant, and the endosperm, a store of starch which will feed the young plant until it can fend for itself. The starch is secured in a matrix of small cells, divided by walls made of protein – think of each grain as being like a bag of sweets, where the bag itself is the husk and the starch cells the individual sweets, each tightly wrapped. In effect, malting unwraps the sweets, to allow access to the starch and its conversion into soluble sugars (during mashing) and thence to alcohol (during fermentation).

Yeast does not feed on starch, it feeds on sugar, so these enzymes are essential for the creation of alcohol – and according to the legal definition of Scotch whisky they have to be 'endogenous' (they must be produced within the grains and cannot be artificially created and added). The enzymes in malted barley are capable of converting starch in unmalted cereals into soluble sugar, however, and this is what happens in mixed mash-bills for Scotch grain whisky and most Irish and American whiskeys.

Malting is controlled germination. During germination the barleycorn produces the required enzymes, principally cytase, which breaks down the cell walls and make the starch accessible to feed the growing plant, and amylase, which converts the starch into soluble sugar.

The craft of the maltster is to allow germination to progress to a point where the cell walls have been broken down, but before the starch begins to be used by the growing plant. He stops the growth by drying the "green malt" (i.e. after it has germinated) in a kiln.

This is how it's done;

Screening

The first stage, before the truck bringing the barley to the maltings is even unloaded, is to check that it is capable of germination by making sure the embryo is still alive. Then it is checked for moisture content and sensitivity to water, nitrogen content and absence of mold, following which it is dried (if necessary) to under 13°C to prevent it germinating accidentally during storage.

Finally it is 'dressed' to remove any small stones, straw, chaff, dust and small corns. This is done by rotating and shaking sieves, which also have magnets attached to remove any fragments of metal. This is essential since when the malt is milled they might

Floor malting at Highland Park
Photo: Soren Solkjaer

Port Ellen drum maltings in 2012

cause a spark, which would lead to a dust explosion. Many distilleries have been severely damaged by this over the years.

Now the barley is ready to be stored until required for malting.

Steeping

The 'active malting' process begins with 'awakening the dormant grain', which many claim to be the most important stage in the whole process.

Dry barley has less than 12% moisture. This must be raised to 46% for the enzymes to be activated. This is done by immersion in water (called 'wet stand'), then drained and rested ('dry stand'). During the wet stands air is periodically bubbled up through the grains to ensure equal uptake of water and avoid 'clumping', and also to clean the corns further. If the maltster under-steeps he can spray the grain, but this leads to an uneven water uptake. If he over-steeps, the grain can be dried out by a tumble-drying process.

Steeping lasts for two to three days – the actual length of time depends upon the barley variety, the temperature of the water, the ambient temperature, the size of the grains, their nitrogen level and capacity for absorption.

Germinating

In traditional floor maltings, the damp grain is then spread out on a concrete floor to a depth of about 30cm and soon each grain sprouts a tiny rootlet. This generates heat, particularly close to the floor, so the barley has to be turned twice a day with wooden shovels and rakes to keep the temperature even and prevent the little roots becoming entangled.

The task is called 'turning the piece', and goes on day and night for about a week, or less in warm weather. It is hard and monotonous work, and malt-men often developed a repetitive strain injury called 'monkey shoulder' – wittily used by William Grant & Sons for their blended malt.

The grains lose moisture at the rate of 0.5% each day, and are spread out more thinly until the rootlets begin to wither and the grain – now referred to as 'green malt' – becomes mealy. Maltsters call this 'modification', and can gauge the progress made by biting the grain to taste its sweetness and rubbing it to assess its texture – if the grain is chalky and smooth it is ready, if lumps remain it is under-mo-dified. The degree of modification may make a difference to the overall flavour of the whisky, although maltsters argue that the number of under-modified and over-modified grains balance out.

Kilning

In the kiln the green malt is spread out evenly on a perforated metal floor with a furnace below. There are two kinds of modern kilns; direct fired from below, where the gases of combustion pass through the malt bed, and indirect fired, where the air is heated by oil-fired burners or steam-heated radiators, before it passes through the malt. The kilns have tapering roofs to draw out the heat from the furnace and since the late-nineteenth century they have been capped with the pagoda-style roofs which have become the architectural motif of malt whisky distilleries.

The first stage of the kilning process is the 'free drying phase', which evaporates moisture on the surface of the green malt. Hot air at 60°C to 65°C is driven through the layer of malt (the volume of air is more important than the temperature). When peat is used, it is thrown into the furnace at this stage. The temperature must be kept below 60°C or the phenols in the peat which lend the whisky its smoky characteristics will be destroyed. The lower the temperature is, the higher the level of peatiness communicated to the malt.

Next there is the 'forced drying phase', during which the temperature is increased to 70°C to 75°C and the air flow reduced. By now the moisture content of the malt will have reduced to about 5%.

Finally there may be a cooling phase, where the temperature is lowered to about 30°C to prevent further curing of the malt. The whole exercise takes between 20 and 48 hours, depending on what type of kilning process is being used, the size of the kiln and the amount of malt.

The fuel used during the kilning process can make a significant contribution to the flavour of the whisky. In the Highlands, peat was the only fuel, and,

depending on how hot the kiln was run, gave varying degrees of smokiness to the whisky – indeed it was universally accepted that this was what distinguished Highland from Lowland whiskies. Historically, the Highland region included what we now call 'Speyside', which took off in the 1890s by producing very lightly peated malts for blending. When Alfred Barnard visited in the mid-1880s he found only two distilleries which mixed peat with coke (which was called 'silent coal').

Sir Walter Gilbey wrote in 1904: "Barley of the best quality is made into Malt with water running from the heather-clad hills, dried in a kiln with peat dug in the neighbourhood; it is this combination which accounts for the fine flavour of Whisky produced in the Highlands of Scotland."

But this is not to say that all Highland malts were as peaty as those from Lagavulin and Laphroaig today. Indeed, when Speyside took off in the 1890s the distilleries' key customers, the blending houses, wanted mildly peated whiskies. This is not a problem, even if you are kilning over a peat fire, if you run the furnace hot, and was greatly facilitated by the invention in 1889 of the 'Doig Ventillator' [aka the pagoda roofed kiln] by the great distillery architect, Charles Chree Doig, which made it possible to control the flow of draft through the bed of green malt by the use of adjustable louvres, in order to expel smoke rapidly, if desired.

Pneumatic malting

Having your own maltings allows for greater control of the flavour sought. The process is slower and more natural and does not force germination. Bowmore, Laphroaig, Springbank, Balvenie and Highland Park all swear by it. The last experimented with using commercial maltsters on mainland Scotland, supplying them with Orkadian peat, but this was not a success. All make around 20% of their requirement, and buy in the rest, malted to their own specification and usually un-peated, to be blended with their home-made malt.

There are several problems associated with floor malting, however. First, the limitation it necessarily imposes upon the amount of malt that can be made at a time. Second, the labour intensive nature of the process and third, the variable nature of the malt created. For these reasons, floor maltings have been replaced by pneumatic malting systems – the term simply means that air is passed through the grain while it is germinating, to control its temperature, and by doing this the batch size can be greatly increased.

Port Ellen floor maltings from the 1970s

Glen Ord Saladin maltings in 1968

There are three pneumatic systems: Saladin Boxes, Rotary Drums and Steep, Germinate and Kilning Vessels (SGKVs).

The Saladin box system was named after its inventor, the Belgian Jules Alphonse Saladin, and comprises a long concrete or metal trench fitted with helical screws, attached to a horizontal bar which passes up and down the trench two or three times a day, driven by belts and pulleys. The screws revolved alternatively in opposite directions to raise the germinating grain from the bottom of the bed to the top, separating the corns and preventing them matting together. It also made for more even germination throughout the bed by moving the corns from the cooler layers to the warmer, and vice versa, assisted by cool, humidified air being blown through the bed. Typically the Saladin system can process 200 tonnes per batch.

Although it was invented in the 1880s, the Saladin system was not widely adopted by the Scotch whisky industry – the first to install it, in 1948, was North British (grain) Distillery, and only six more followed suit between then and 1962. Tamdhu Distillery, which installed Saladin boxes in 1949, retained them until 2010, when the maltings closed. They were removed in 2018.

By the late 1960s Saladin boxes were superseded by rotary drum malting.

The 'drums' themselves are huge cast-iron cylinders, mounted horizontally, holding from nine to 50 tonnes of barley, at its original weight, 65 tonnes at

45% moisture content. Once loaded with damp grain from the steeps, the drum slowly rotates to create an even bed; it will be rotated again every eight hours to prevent the rootlets becoming matted. Humidity and temperature are controlled by internal sprays and by blowing cool air through the grain. Temperature must be carefully controlled to ensure that the enzymes within the corns are not damaged. In 4-6 days the grain will be completely modified into 'green malt' and is ready to be sent for kilning.

SGKVs were developed in the late 1970s at Moray Firth Maltings in order to achieve the whole malting operation in a single vessel. In this case, when steeping and germination is complete, the humidified air is replaced by heated air.

Because of their huge size, drums are best suited to large, centralized, maltings, supplying many distilleries. Scottish Malt Distillers, the Distillers' Company's production division, built maltings at Burghead (1966 with 24 drums, expanded to 48 in 1971 – the largest drum maltings in Europe), Glenesk (1968), Port Ellen (1973 with seven drums, the largest in the U.K.) and Roseisle (1980, with SGKVs), and added a drum to the existing Saladin box at Ord Maltings in 1968 (the latter was removed in 1983). Other specialist maltsters like Kilgours, Bairds, Simpson's and Moray Firth, expanded their operations, so that by 1980 only a handful of distilleries were malting their own barley, and most of these producing only around 20% of their requirement.

Around 1.5 million tonnes of malt is produced in the U.K. each year by seven large and seven smaller maltings. Around 48% of this goes to British distilleries, 40% to breweries, 3% to the food industry and the remaining 9% to overseas whisky distilleries.

Flavour

The closure of individual distillery floor maltings in favour of pneumatic systems and centralised drum maltings during the 1960s and '70s was one of several significant changes in the production of malt whisky in the post-war era, in the interest of increasing capacity to meet the burgeoning demand for Scotch, increasing efficiency and consistency of spirit character. Although these 'plant modifications' were mostly made cautiously, they were driven by chemists and accountants, and there is no doubt that the flavour of the whisky made before the modifications is different from that made after – richer and heavier in texture, often more smoky and waxy.

What contribution, if any, did malting make to 'flavour drift', as blenders term it? After all, the early stages of production – malting, milling and mashing

– impact more on yield (the amount of alcohol produced per tonne of malt) than on flavour.

It is beyond the remit of this essay to consider the contribution to flavour made by the barley variety – the given wisdom of the industry is that the variety makes no difference, although some would question this. Diageo's boffins maintain that "barley varieties influence yield but not quality of spirit".

What is certain is that the use of peat in kilning decreased substantially post 1945, although it was once the acknowledged hallmark of Highland malts, and by the late 1950s most of the malt used by mainland distilleries was classified as 'lightly peated' or specified as unpeated. In 1967 Professor R.J.S. McDowell wrote in The Whiskies of Scotland:

"The peaty flavour of some malt whiskies is specially prominent, for example Tomatin, Glenfiddich, Dufftown, Clynelish and Laphroaig…[an interesting choice of 'peaty' whiskies!]… some distillers are beginning to question the necessity for peat, especially since labour costs have greatly increased its price…I am assured that many distillers in the last few years have tended to reduce the amount of smokiness to make whiskies taste less heavy…[But] it would take a particularly good whisky to do entirely without it."

Some mourn the passing of floor maltings – probably not those who had to 'turn the piece' day and night! – and claim it was the variability of the malt made in such which added 'character'. More than one retired distillery operator I spoke to maintained that the uniform consistency of the malt supplied by centralised maltings was at the expense of flavour.

Let Neil Gunn, novelist and former excise officer, have the last word:

"In all this malting process, skilled judgement is needed, for the goodness of the malt determines not only the quantity of alcohol that may result from its fermentation, but the quality of the ultimate distillate itself." Whisky and Scotland (1935).

Charles MacLean has been writing about Scotch whisky for 39 years, and has published eighteen books on the subject. He was the founding editor of Whisky Magazine, writes regularly for several international magazines and is a frequent commentator on TV and radio. He was chief presenter of the TV channel www.singlemalt.tv and starred in Ken Loach's film The Angels' Share, which won the Jury Prize at the Cannes Film Festival in 2012. In 2009 he was elected Master of the Quaich, in 2012 won the I.W.S.C.'s 'Outstanding Achievement Award', in 2016 was inducted into the Whisky Hall of Fame and in 2019 was named 'International Ambassador of the Year' at the Spirit of Speyside Festival.

Steven Kersley, distillery manager at Brew Dog distillery

The quest for your own whisky profile

by Joel Harrison

While building on a foundation that was formed centuries ago, the new distillers in Scotland are definitely keen to leave their own mark on whisky production today. Find out how they intend to make their whiskies relevant to the consumers of tomorrow.

On the face of it single malt whisky is a pretty simple product. Drawing on some sound scientific principals, it marries the concept of fermentation with distillation to produce a spirit that was given the moniker 'the water of life'.

These principals remain the foundation of today's whisky production, and provides a tangible handshake back through the ages, to Friar John Corr and beyond. I'm sure if the fabled monk appeared at the new Macallan distillery today, he would have at least a tacit understanding of the production process, albeit agog at the size and scale of the single malt's subterranean process.

Ever since the first drops of a barley based spirit ran from a still, mankind has been working to refine the stages of whisky-making. And, as whisky focused as much on finances as it did flavour, including the way each and every element of production worked towards the dual goals of efficiency and yield, the age of the 'shareholder single malt' was born, and profit over palate became the order of the day.

Individual maltings were lost in favour of mass-produced malt. Out went speciality strains of barley; in came cleverly crossed varieties with high starch content and an even higher resistance to pests. Wormtubs, a key flavour-driver in the production of spirit, were replaced with shell-and-tube condensers.

Everything that Ian Palmer does at InchDairnie is driven by flavour

Yet this refined process is more than just an echo of the Big Bang from the genesis of whisky-making. It is still, despite all the modern-day renovations, a traditional process at heart.

Across Scotland's many single malt distilleries, custodians captain historic distilleries, as aware of the past as they are of the future. And these ancient grandfathers of the industry are still the benchmark for today's new up-starts, either to take inspiration from and try to replicate, or to use as a point of reference to zig where the heritage distilleries zag.

One such distillery that zigs where others zag, and is entirely designed to move with the times, embracing modern technology, is InchDairnie. Founded by Ian Palmer 2015 with 'flavour, innovation and experimentation' as their motto, the resulting spirit falls very much under the classification of a Scotch single malt.

With a sideways look at single malt production, using a hammer mill, a mash filter and double condensers on Italian-made stills, that sit alongside a six-plate Lomond style still, there was always an element of risk to build a distillery which is so unusual in set-up, especially with one eye on the whisky business's appetite for traditional malts to include in blends.

"We've never stopped since we started, running at full capacity since about the middle of 2016, so we are very please with everything. It's been quite a smooth ride so far, really", Palmer says with a smile.

InchDairnie is a distinctly different distillery, and it is easy to be different for the sake of being different. So what was the driver for Palmer and his team to choose the unique set up that they have?

"We started with a blank sheet of paper. We didn't look at historical productions methods. What we did know was that we wanted to produce a Scotch whisky, and there are legal definitions for that, so that was the first lead on the paper, knowing the definition of the product we wanted to make. This was the first box to tick off", Palmer notes.

"The second box to tick was to look at the business element of it and the development of a brand that can have a long life. We didn't have heritage to fall back on. All we had was the contents of the bottle."

"Taking those two stages into account" Palmer continues, "I wanted to do something quite different, that was driven by flavour. So we looked at what technology would give us a flavour difference".

Palmer's passion for flavour is obvious, and this core belief in driving as much flavour and personality into the spirit has led to his obsession with focusing on the individual parts of the process, to ensure the result is a team effort from the individual production stages.

"Our approach was about building in different levers to give us different flavours," he says.

"The starting point was a focus on the spirit, working backwards from there. We needed to be able to modify the flavours that we wanted, and we looked at the technology that allowed us to make those changes".

And thus a pilgrimage for production parts started.

"One of the things about flavour is the raw material. Cereal is the foundation of the flavour and we wanted the technology to be able to work with more difficult cereals. The hammer mill is a direct result of this conversation. The mash filter allows us to modify the clarity of the wort, another lever in our ability to change the flavour of the spirit," Palmer reflects.

With most distillers choosing to make their malt whisky from spring barley, Palmer decided to buck this trend and look elsewhere for his cereal.

"We asked ourselves, 'why does everyone use spring barley, and do we have to use it?'. It was an important question for us at the start," Palmer notes.

"The answer was 'no'. Everyone uses spring barley because it is easy to use, and easy to use through a traditional distillery set up. It also gives you yield. The one thing that is missing from the list of reasons to use spring barley, is flavour."

"Our approach was that we wanted to build a brand that was based on flavour," Palmer says.

Of course one the advantages of building a distillery from scratch is the ability to not only produce single malt, but other styles of whisky too. And at InchDairnie the inclusion of the hammer mill and mash filter means hardier grains can be used.

"We are now thinking about putting a product in the market, which will be our grain whisky made from rye, and that's the project that I'm focusing on now," says Palmer. Their Ryelaw brand is almost ready to hit the market.

A wide variety of flavours

One man who knows a thing or two about being a custodian of single malts is David Robertson, the former Master Distiller at The Macallan, and one of the founders of the Holyrood distillery in Edinburgh, the first malt distillery to open in the city for nearly a century.

"It's a tiny distillery, but what we have done, by making it small, is we've made it super flexible," Robertson says.

Continuing a theme started by Palmer above, Robertson continues to explain that, "what we've decided to do is not just having a low cost, high yield offering, but a more complex, smaller, distillery producing tiny batch sizes which are flexible flavour-wise.

"We have started a custom cask programme where customers can come in and design a recipe that they want - not that we want - which is incredible," says Robertson.

It is the small, flexible set up that has allowed this level of bespoke whisky making to occur. With just a one ton mash, and six small (5,000 litre) washbacks, each of the washbacks fills their 5,000 litre wash still, and the second distillation takes place in their 3,750 spirit still. The only element that isn't small, is the height of their stills which stand just one meter shorter than those at Glenmorangie, coming in at a whopping 7 meters tall.

Unlike at InchDairnie, Holyrood has chosen a traditional set up, relying on a more manageable set up, and their decades of distilling expertise to make more unusual spirit styles.

"This bespoke approach hasn't really been supported by technology, or plant and equipment led; it's been more about quality of selection and the way that we process through the distillery.

"We are looking at malted barley, looking at a huge amount of different styles, to see how that changes and effects flavour. We don't do tweaks just to get marketing copy. These are fundamental changes based on flavour," Robertson says with passion in his voice.

"The aim is not to have a vertical range across, say, 10, 12, 15, 21 year olds and up. We are trying to take a leaf out the craft brewers' book and make everything affordable and accessible, but with a wide range of flavours and styles," he notes.

If this is the case, how would Robertson describe the distillery house style? His answer is simple:

"Well, we don't really have one!"

They do have four key styles of spirit maturing in

David Robertson and Rob Carpenter - founders of Holyrood Distillery in Edinburgh

oak, including a smoky spirit, which will be used for future releases when the team feel they are ready.

"We only started filling into wood at the end of September 2019, so they are still very young. The aim is for the public to come to the distillery and taste these, and let us know what they like and we can focus on those styles more," Robertson says.

Despite both Holyrood and InchDairnie weighing in as Lowland distilleries, neither Palmer nor Robertson feel the need to tow the party line of the region's assumed style, although Robertson does lean towards experiment with the lighter style of spirit which often defines Lowland whisky.

"We are planning to do some triple distilled spirit as a nod to being in the Lowlands, but that's not what has driven us to be based in Edinburgh. We just want to be easy to find and easy to access," he says.

Further north, the Isle of Raasay distillery on the island of the same name opened in 2017. Located off the eastern tip of Skye, it is another small operation, boasting a one ton mash tun, six washbacks and two small copper pot stills coming in at 5,000 litres and

3,600 litres respectively.

In setting up the distillery, co-founder Alasdair Day was delighted to start with a blank sheet of paper.

"We knew we were setting up on a Hebridean island, so that informed a lot of our thinking when we were looking at the style of spirit we wanted to make," he reflects.

"We thought that it should be lightly peated. This isn't Islay but it is an island and so that played a lot into our thinking, in terms of how and where we draw our inspiration from for the set-up.

"The other thing that has always fascinated me is the discussion around the 1970's and 1980's Bowmore and where those fruity and floral flavours came from. That's why we ended up with a lightly peated, fruity flavour," Day adds.

The big challenge for start-up distilleries is the lengthy wait for mature spirit, and the commercial need to sell younger whisky was at the forefront of the team's mind when designing their processes.

"We knew we were going to have to sell young whisky," says Day.

"So we worked with some chemical engineers to look at our process and how we can deliver a quality to allow our spirit to be great at a young age.

"This included things like having stainless washbacks, and cooling jackets on them too. This is really unusual in Scotch and it gives us control over the fermentation. For example when we are making our peated spirit we don't use the cooling jackets. This allows for more complex flavours to build up. We also do up to five days fermentation too. This gives us different styles of wash, which is very exiting," Day explains.

Their attention to detail extends to their water source, which is mineral rich with manganese aiding the development of yeast. The wash still feature a cooling jacket on its lyne arm too, allowing even more tunes to be played, and the spirit still has a small six plate copper purifier that can be used, turning it from a traditional pot still into a quasi Carter-Head still.

And Day lets us into a little secret.

"Our core single malt should be released in April 2021, which will draw on a six cask maturation policy," he says. With such a malleable distillery set up, it is going to be fascinating to see the resulting mature spirit and how it has reacted to time in oak."

Designed for doing the unusual

One of the more esoteric set-ups in Scotland is to be found in Ellon, just outside of Aberdeen, at the Brew Dog distillery, formerly know as Lone Wolf Distillery and the experimental spirits site of the well-known brewery.

Head Distiller Steven Kersley has a passion for all types of spirit, from gin to vodka and of course whisky. With a background at distilling giants Diageo, Kersley has been happy to find a home where he can experiment, and has done so in whisky with both single malt and rye distillates at Brew Dog where the equipment is designed for doing the unusual; as such it typifies a modernist set-up that eschews the past and forgoes tradition.

"Our 'triple bubble' still, as we've come to call it, is such an integral part of our still house," Kersley says.

"When it comes to whisky creation we have the opportunity to use this still to make many different styles of new make spirit.

"The still comprises of three large bubbles between the pot and the lyne arm, these massively increase the surface area of copper available for the spirit vapour to interact with as it makes its way to the 8 plate rectification column or condenser, depending

Isle of Raasay Distillery

BrewDog distillery - formerly known as Lone Wolf

on the style of spirit we're making," he explains.

This built-in purifier, if you like, allows Brew Dog to utilise a stainless steel condenser instead of copper, and was devised by Kersley and BrewDog co-founder Martin Dickie, sketched onto the back of a receipt from a cocktail bar, and brought to life by the still-makers Arnold Holstein.

Despite this very unusual still design, Kersley still leans into traditional distilling methods to make whisky.

"I suppose the significant difference is that we insist on more control over those processes and pre, during and post distillation," Kersley says.

"As an example we use specific yeast strains and then tailor the fermentation profile via temperature and pressure to manage the yeasts performance to create flavours we like. We use a temperature and humidity controlled warehouse to control the environment that the casks are maturing in; currently our warehouse is at 32ºC and 55% humidity."

"We use these traditional processes but experiment within their confines," Kersley concludes.

Ian Palmer noted that, 'a distillery is often a reflection of when it was built' and this is very much the case with the esoteric Brew Dog, the innovative Isle of Raasay, the flexible Holyrood and, of course the Willy Wonka's chocolate factory that is InchDairnie.

When the whisky writers of the future visit these distillers and read about their history, these sites will indeed reflect the current whisky-boom, and the production techniques available to those building anew.

If this is this case, then older distillery set-ups must reflect the moment they were born?

Across Scotland this seems to be the case (to which anyone who has visited some of the more brutalist constructions of the mid-20th century can attest).

Founded in 1775, Glenturret fights with a small group of distilleries for the crown as 'Scotland's oldest'. Having held a licence to make whisky since 1818, under then-owner John Drummond, it should be a true reflection of that era of distilling, and is today still a truly agricultural distillery where most of the processes are done by hand.

However, General Manager John Laurie says that these early-style production processes were actually retro-fitted in the mid-1950s.

"We have been looking a lot recent at the history and heritage of the distillery," Laurie says.

"We think we are the last commercial distillery doing a hand mashing, with all others doing theirs mechanically. In fact, when Alfred Barnard visited in 1880 he noted that the mash tun was mechanically

roused, powered by a water-jetty. So, in terms of production technology, we are actually further back now than we were in 1880".

This time-consuming process can only really be done at small distilleries, and Laurie feels that the size and history add important dimensions to a distillery's production process and style.

"We are very much a farmhouse distillery," Laurie says.

"You have to respect the space you've got and work within those spaces. For me a distillery is the product of the building that it is in; the environment it is in, the local area and how people view it; how the owners have respected it over time."

"Like anything, as you go through time the soul is developed, the spirit of that site is developed and it gets to a point where that is so strong, that it is palpable. It all builds in the character."

Laurie is right, of course. Scotch distilleries are a snapshot of their time. Yet they are so much more, and this additional 'maturation' element, not of the spirit in cask, but of the process itself, is one that is often forgotten in the wider world of whisky.

As expensive as Japanese whisky has become; as award-winning as Taiwanese malt is; as sleek as Scandi single malt has become; as competitive as English, Australian, American, French, and a host of other malt distillers now are… none have the assured wisdom rooted in centuries of production, that Scotch owns.

It is these grey hairs on the head of Scotch which gives it the wisdom to educate and inform not only those over-seas looking to replicate the house style of Scottish whisky, but also the newer, more versatile, often boundary-pushing distilleries closer to home.

Scotch is both the shepherd and the flock; the master and the apprentice, and that is what keeps it so exciting in the world of whisky.

Joel Harrison is an award winning author, communicator and industry consultant, whose work has been published in over 20 countries, across 16 different languages. His writing work can be seen in publications such as The Wall Street Journal India and The Daily Telegraph in the UK. Harrison also appears regularly on British television across a number of shows as a whisky specialist. He sits as a judge for the International Wine and Spirits Competition (IWSC) where today he holds the role of a Trophy Judge and Chairman across Scotch whisky and other spirits. In 2013 Harrison was made a Keeper of the Quaich

The Whisky Brain

by Ian Wisniewski

Assessing and rating a whisky without prejudice
is much harder than it seems. Our brain is playing all kinds of tricks
to stop us from being objective. Learn about the intricate relationship between
aromas, flavours, perceptions and emotional responses
and become a better whisky taster.

Of course I said yes, the invitation from Gordon & MacPhail was to taste the Mortlach 75 year old. Arriving at Claridge's Hotel, my excitement intensified when I saw the malt being poured. Inhaling deeply then taking a sip, I submitted totally to the experience: only flavour and emotion existed (while I, temporarily, did not).

'What do you think ?' asked my hosts.

'Do you mind if I don't think,' I replied, wanting my feelings to continue. Gradually emerging from a transcendent state, my mind took over: analysing and composing a tasting note. This is the extraordinary power malt whisky has, to create intense emotions, inspire so much thought, and provide supreme fulfilment.

Assessing a malt begins before any nosing and tasting, as the brain is programmed to find clues of what to expect: by studying the design of the bottle, thinking of the retail price, the age, or an enticing production story (which I find highly emotive). This inevitably creates a sense of expectation, and if it's not fulfilled I feel my trust has been betrayed. How ridiculous ! I should blame myself for judging a malt against my expectations, rather than on its own merits. That's why I try to stop my brain from conducting any detective work before tasting.

I also try to banish any emotions, so that my starting point is 'neutral.'

"The emotions and mood people have coming into a tasting can be influential, as the way you think about a whisky is contextual. Mood is a case of maintenance or management, either maintaining a good mood, or managing the mood by changing it.

Both scenarios impact how analytical or sensitive you might be, and the way you process information when tasting whisky," says Jordan LeBel, who specializes in designing sensory experiences as a Professor and National Teaching Fellow at Concordia University, Montreal.

Just as our mood can influence perception of a malt, a malt can influence our mood, even evoking specific emotions.

"Aromas reminiscent of ripe fruit in an orchard on a summer's day, which are present in BenRiach for example, are stimulating and lively. Meanwhile, a weighty, robust malt with walnuts, dates and dried fruit, such as Sherry cask Glendronach, creates a more reflective, contemplative feeling," says Rachel Barrie, Master Blender, BenRiach Distillery Company.

The relationship between aromas, flavours, perceptions and emotional responses can be readily summarised.

"Sensory inputs cause us to draw blocks of information, largely in the form of concepts, from our memory of previous product experiences. Concepts are the building blocks of the emotions that we conjure-up when we interact with brands and products, and emotions, in turn, are the fundamental basis of product satisfaction (or otherwise)," says David Thomson, Founder, MMR Research Worldwide, where he specialises in sensory and consumer research.

But exactly how various parts of the brain process information, individually and collectively, is only partially understood. I also think of the feelings malt whisky evokes as emanating from the heart, the traditional symbol of emotion. This isn't simply my fantasy. Research shows that the heart and brain engage in meaningful dialogue. Alterations in the heart rate for example indicate emotions which are identified by the brain.

Research has not confirmed my hope that a large nose would give me an advantage when assessing aromas. Dimensions are irrelevant, it's the contents that matter. Specifically olfactory receptors within the olfactory epithelium, at the summit of each nasal cavity. Whether nostrils below the olfactory epithelium contribute to aroma detection is uncertain, but they have a fascinating dynamic.

"At any time, one nostril has a greater rate of air flow than the other, which enhances the delivery of odours to the olfactory receptors in that nostril, but this greater rate of air flow switches from one nostril to the other every 30 minutes. Nosing with an open mouth may draw air across the receptors in both directions, and breathing out through the nose with the mouth closed boosts the experience," says Professor Barry Smith, Director of the Centre for the Study of the Senses, University of London.

Olfactory receptors divide up into about 400 different groups, each with varying capabilities. An individual aroma can stimulate numerous groups of receptors, though most respond to more than one aroma. Different groups of receptors also work together in various permutations, which extends the range of aromas they respond to.

The aroma is the overture

How aromas are perceived depends of course on our individual capability. We all have varying levels of sensitivity and insensitivity to every aroma and flavour. Three characteristics eliciting the broadest range of sensitivity/insensitivity are phenolics (peaty, smokey notes), coconut and cork taint. Some people are so sensitive to cork taint it would dominate a malt's aromas, while others would only detect malt whisky aromas oblivious of cork taint.

As aroma is the first direct interaction with a malt whisky it's a major event, but this is often treated (merely) as a preview of the flavours to follow. Again, this creates expectations, though intense aromas can lead to mellow flavours, or vice-versa, causing surprise or disappointment. That's why I approach the aroma as a separate experience from the palate, and only think about their relationship subsequently.

"Aroma and palate are interwoven, the aroma is the overture and the palate is the crescendo. I'm always looking to exceed expectations on the palate, and it's vital to achieve a crescendo of flavour, even with a lighter style of malt," says Rachel Barrie.

The palate's star performer is the tongue, with supporting roles for the soft palate (including gums, cheeks and back of the roof of the mouth), and the retro-nasal passage (at the back of the throat, connecting the mouth to the olfactory epithelium).

The tongue is equipped with papillae, structures containing taste buds. An average tongue totals between 2,000-5,000 taste buds, which identify the primary characteristics: sweetness, sourness, salt, umami and bitterness.

"Genetics may influence the number of taste buds. Some (though not all) studies suggest that super-tasters tend to have more taste papillae. Regardless, that would be an average tendency and not true of all super-tasters," says Dr Paul Wise, Associate Member, Monell Chemical Senses Centre in Philadelphia.

Taste buds have a porous surface through which

Rachel Barrie, Master Blender BenRiach Distillery Company

liquid and flavour compounds pass, reaching receptor cells within. A single taste bud contains up to 150 different taste receptors, with each receptor detecting either an individual characteristic or range of characteristics. Each taste bud may also contain a higher proportion of receptors that detect a particular taste, such as sweetness.

The soft palate (so-called as bones are absent) identifies characteristics rather than flavours. The roof of the mouth does contain taste receptors, but the gums and cheeks rely on the underlying nervous system to assess smoothness, dryness, pepperiness and astringency.

Mouthfeel is gauged by the nervous system in the tongue, with the gums and cheeks assisting. There's plenty to discern as texture varies enormously among malts, from delicate to thicker and creamier, and from elegant to fuller-bodied, and so a significant element of a malt's individuality.

But even when malt whisky is present on the palate the olfactory sense plays a vital role, as volatile compounds evaporate from the liquid and waft through the retro-nasal passage. This passage doesn't

conduct any detection work, it's simply a conduit for vapours to reach olfactory receptors. Evaporation of volatile compounds, such as phenols (peaty, smokey notes), vanillin (vanilla) and esters (fruitiness), is promoted by the palate warming whisky from the ambient to body temperature (37 degrees centigrade).

"Most of what contributes to the sense of taste are aroma molecules. The aromas that go from the glass to the nose, also go from the palate to the nose. The brain interprets flavour as though it's happening on the tongue, but this is an illusion," says Professor Barry Smith.

A few compounds that vaporise from the palate are also detected by taste receptors in the tongue. This includes acids, characterised by a sour aroma and taste. Similarly, alcohol produces sharp, peppery aromas, and although alcohol dries out the palate this is perceived as 'burn' rather than dryness. Additionally, alcohol provides the sense of weight and body on the palate, not to mention intensity, though alcohol can also curtail the experience.

"Holding malt whisky on the palate for longer may

Bill Lumsden - Glenmorangie´s Director of Distillin
Whisky Creation & Whisky Stocks

enable you to discover more, but alcohol is also an irritant, which becomes evident the longer it's present on the palate," says Jacob Lahne, Assistant Professor, Department of Food Science and Technology, Virginia Tech in the USA.

The second sip

The extent to which alcohol is detected on the tongue compared to the olfactory sense is determined by alcoholic strength. The higher the strength the greater the proportion of alcohol vaporising. However, a higher abv (alcohol by volume) can temporarily overwhelm and 'shut down' olfactory and taste receptors, which require recovery time before resuming normal service.

Alcohol should also be considered in conjunction with saliva. As saliva comprises 99.5% water, this may seem the equivalent of adding water to a glass of malt, in the sense that alcoholic strength is reduced. As the abv is one factor that determines a malt's flavour profile, this raises the question of whether saliva may lower the abv sufficiently to alter the flavour profile. This in turn depends on practicalities such as the size of the sip and saliva rates, which are variable (the faster the rate the greater the dilution effect).

Saliva has other significant benefits, keeping the palate moist, fresh and consequently comfortable, while also 'transporting' flavour compounds to taste buds. Consequently, lower levels of saliva reduce the ability to taste, and make the palate less comfortable.

A fascinating aspect of tasting malt whisky is the extent to which the flavour profile can evolve, partly due to the warming and diluting effect of the palate. Correspondingly, malt whisky alters the environment across the palate, which means the second sip can be significantly different to the first. This is due to the palate acclimatising to alcohol for example, and flavours such as sweetness accruing. But it's also a case of the brain adjusting.

"The first sip results in flavour notes playing in the brain in a more cacophonous way than the second sip, which is easier for the brain to focus on and process as it already has a head start," says Professor Barry Smith.

Jacob Lahne continues, "The strongest characteristics are most apparent in the first sip, subtler sensations become more evident in the second sip. The brain is better at registering differences than absolute levels of intensity, so sequential sips may highlight different flavours."

The second sip is definitely the focus for professionals.

"When tasting I first take one small sip and work it around the palate then dispose of it, I call this the mouthwash. Then I take a larger sip and hold it for a few seconds, really thinking of the primary flavours, the flavour development and the finish," says Dr Bill Lumsden, Glenmorangie's Director of Distilling, Whisky Creation & Whisky Stocks.

Richard Paterson, Whyte & Mackay's Master Blender, advises, "Take a sip, hold it then let it go down, and go back for a second time. The second

sip, not the first, is when you really get to know that whisky."

How we get to know a whisky depends on messages conveyed to the brain by the central nervous system from the soft palate, and more specifically, by two separate cranial nerves, one at the front and the other at the back of the tongue, and by the first cranial nerve (olfactory nerve) from olfactory receptors. This also means that messages initially cruise separate pathways within the brain. Even messages from each nostril travel independently.

"Messages from receptors in the left nostril go to the left hemisphere of the brain, and from the right nostril to the right hemisphere of the brain, both reaching the olfactory bulb," says Professor Barry Smith.

The olfactory bulb plays a role in assessing aroma, but also refines and reinforces signals before sending them onto other parts of the brain, including the piriform cortex, which identifies and encodes aromas. The identification process poses two questions: 'what is this aroma, and what does this aroma mean to me ?'

Olfactory and palate messages meet in different parts of the brain, including the orbitofrontal cortex which is involved in flavour perception, as well as emotion and decision making, for example 'is this flavour enjoyable ?'

Sensory messages are also relayed back and forth between the piriform cortex and amygdala, which computes emotional responses. Meanwhile, the hippocampus converts experiences into memories, and stores them along with acquired knowledge.

"When learning new information it's tagged at the front end of the hippocampus, and during the night the back end of the hippocampus takes these tags and finds a place to store them in the long term memory. Once stored it can be 'relocated' within the long term memory for up to 7 years, until a final place is found," says Jordan LeBel.

Knowledge of aromas and flavours, and the associations they hold for us, reside in the memory, though explaining this further is a challenge.

"Understanding how memory works, how we correlate and categorise memories, and apply positive and negative emotions to them, is such a complex and evolving area that it's only partially understood. But a characteristic of great tasters is that they can access memory better, rather than having superior tasting skills," says Greg Tucker, Consumer Psychologist, The Marketing Clinic.

The process used by the mind to identify and categorise flavours is referred to as schema (a set of

Brian Kinsman - Master Blender at Wm Grants

understood criteria).

"There are three principal ways of referencing schema. One is on the basis of aroma and flavour. A second is a visual aspect and appreciation of it, with a third being emotional kinaesthesia and how it makes you feel. Most people use a combination of these three schemas, in varying orders of priority and ratios, which are determined by genetics, nature, conditioning and environment," adds Greg Tucker.

The way of the Masters

How this works for a Master of the Art depends of course on who you ask.

"I think in terms of words, physical sensation, emotional connection and colours. Ardbeg Corryv-

Defining the flavour of a malt entails a very different approach.

"Writing tasting notes is a combination of analysis and instinct. I keep going back to a malt, nosing and tasting over a few hours, jotting down a few words each time then turning it into sentences. I wonder how do I tell the story of this expression, and I like to communicate how a malt makes me feel," adds Brian Kinsman.

This raises another question: the relationship between the tasting experience and the vocabulary we each use to express it. Can acquiring more specific descriptors also help us improve our ability to discern subtler nuances ?

"The Whorfian hypothesis holds that language shapes our thoughts and perception, not vice-versa, though I think it can be a bit of both," says Jordan LeBel.

Another vital influence is experience.

"The vocabulary used when tasting definitely changes in the course of a career. It's like writing a book at the age of 20 compared to 50, you have richer levels of experience to write from, more layers and a deeper understanding," says Rachel Barrie.

The concept, and the content, of tasting notes has also evolved significantly.

"When I started in the business describing a single malt was a case of light, medium or heavy-bodied, together with elegant, rounded and strong. Descriptors have become far more specific, 'orange' for example gives a direction but you have to convey exactly what the flavour is, is it sweet or zesty, succulent or over-ripe," says Richard Paterson, who has 50 years experience in the Scotch whisky industry.

So, where does that leave us ? Our understanding of the tasting process combines some certainties, possibilities and variables. Assessing a malt whisky is definitely a case of variables, as this is influenced by our mood and physiology, which frequently change, while our perspectives and preferences evolve with experience. This means reactions to the same malt will inevitably vary on different occasions. We are, after all, only human, though malt whisky can make us feel that we are so much more.

Richard Paterson, Whyte & Mackay's Master Blender

reckan for example is deep, deep Burgundy, almost mahogany brown. I see Ardbeg 10 year old as stripes of black, white and green, while Ardbeg 19 year old Traigh Bhan is yellow," says Dr Bill Lumsden.

Professionals essentially have two tasting scenarios: assessing samples (checking for faults), and sensory appraisals when creating new expressions and writing tasting notes.

"When assessing samples I'm in a particular frame of mind and can put aside emotions and become instinctive, samples are either right or wrong. Instinct is very important, there are times in the sample room when the instant I try a sample an alarm bell goes off, I might go back to it several times and not find what alarmed me, but I'd still put that sample to one side," says Brian Kinsman, Master Blender, William Grant & Sons.

Ian Wisniewski is a freelance drinks writer focusing on spirits, particularly Scotch whisky. He contributes to various publications including Whisky Magazine and is the author of eleven books, the latest being The Whisky Dictionary published in September, 2019. He regularly visits distilleries in Scotland, in order to learn more about the production process, which is of particular interest to him.

Picture of Ian Wisniewski courtesy of Finlandia vodka

They don't make 'em like they used to ...or do they?

by Neil Ridley

Was whisky a better product in the decades gone by?
It's a debate which has raged deeply amongst the community for at least a decade now - and one, which Neil Ridley feels is perhaps not quite as black or white as the impassioned few like to make out.

Readers of a certain age will no doubt be familiar with the phrase 'I remember when it was all green fields over there.'

For those of you who aren't that familiar, the premise is pretty straight forward. It's usually uttered wistfully by a grandfather to his wide-eyed grandchild, as they both gaze down onto a brand new estate of gleaming modern four-bedroom houses; back in time, to the place where cows once roamed, horses whinnied, children merrily played on makeshift rope swings and - rather stereotypically - everything and everyone was apparently far better and happier than today.

This nostalgic haven of memories sounds idillic, especially when it is accompanied by stories which, like Chinese whispers, have conveniently become separated from the facts, concealing the ugly truth: that the muddy puddles once playfully trodden in barefoot were actually deposited there by a cow's backside - and that the arthritis in grandpa's left leg is down to when the pitifully thin rope swing snapped mid-air, with only a rusty iron gate and a bed of stinging nettles breaking his fall…and his knee. Deep down, the hazy, sepia-tinged nostalgia of the yesteryear can suppress a multitude of horrors too.

That, my friends, is where we currently find ourselves in the world of the historically-indentured whisky enthusiast: part luscious green field, inconveniently littered with cow pats.

Explore new ways but keep an eye on the past says Bill Lumsden

freely. Phrases like 'not as good as I remember' and 'hit-and-miss' caused brows to furrow slightly and - in the case of the old Glenlivet 12 - 'lacking the freshness of the modern equivalent' (this was from me, by the way) gave everyone pause for thought.

Comparing old to new

So is 'Old vs New' even a comparable debate? It felt like the time was right to wheel in a few genuine heavyweights for their two pennies'worth.

"I think that 'New vs Old' makes for a very lively debate indeed," laughs Dr Bill Lumsden, Director of Distilling, Whisky Creation & Whisky Stocks for Glenmorangie and Ardbeg. "While the main results of my work over many years in the Scotch whisky industry would suggest that I sit firmly on the side of 'New', I have to say that I frequently take inspiration and guidance from the 'Old', and like to think that all of my whisky creations have a little bit of the romance associated with the olden days in them. So while I am all for exploring new, uncharted territories, I think it is important not to lose sight of the guiding principles of Scotch whisky which were established many years ago."

Wise words from a very wise man indeed. I wondered then, if they were shared by his younger whisky making partner-in-crime, Brendan McCarron?

"The bottom line is that great whisky is great whisky," he succinctly concludes. "Some are from the old, some are from the new. The same rules apply to bad whisky."

I'm keen to canvas as wide a view on this 'lively debate' as possible, so who better than to shake up the proceedings than whisky's original enfant terrible, Mr Mark Reynier - the man who very much put the 'lad' in Bruichladdich and is now applying his characteristically unconventional approach to single malt over at the newly established Waterford distillery in Ireland.

"Old vs New? Not any more. We've all seen the casks of 30 year old Glen McSporren that are as clear as water - the fatal combo of exhausted wood and industrial spirit; nothing a bucket or two of E150 won't disguise or the imposition of some fancy French chateau won't finish!'"

Ok. This is getting interesting...

"Look, perhaps in some distilleries, with their rushed spirit and tired wood, when the whisky needs a long time until it's ready, then sure", he continues. "But there are new distilleries who find that process abhorrent; I know I do. I think we are making the very best spirit possible at Waterford. I am used to

I've seen this coming for some time, but no where did I both fear and relish it the most than earlier this year in Helsinki, where I was hosting a tasting event at the fabulous Uisge festival. My topic was Old vs New: looking at historical whiskies, as well as a few others from distilleries who make modern whisky, but in a relatively old fashioned way.

Once the room filled up and I unveiled the bottles: (a White Horse blend, an independently released Glen Mhor and a proprietary Glenlivet 12 year old - all from the 1970s, alongside a Tamdhu Batch Strength, a Springbank Cask Strength and a Kilchoman Loch Gorm.) I took a show of hands on who in the room felt the older whiskies would be 'better'. I gave no more description than that.

Unsurprisingly, at least 80% of the attendees thought the older whiskies would be better, with words like 'character', 'depth' and 'personality' being thrown around the room. They were not wrong.

However, by the end of the tasting, a different story had emerged. Words like 'inconsistent' roamed

erford Distillery´s owner. Mark Reynier, sees no reason why whiskies from the old should be better than the ones produced today

state of the art machinery. Bruichladdich was in 1881; Waterford is in 2015. But here we have an artisanal approach on a serious scale."

"Sadly, It's a debate that I've been priced out of," exclaims Steven Kersley, Director of Distilling Operations for Brewdog and a man, who is very much at the cutting edge of modern Scotch whisky making techniques at the distillery in Ellon.

"The majority of old bottlings are out of most people's price range so it's super tough debate to enter into with the right amount of knowledge required to have any authority. What I would say is there's a perception amongst some that a few distilleries have sacrificed the quality of their liquid in order to facilitate demand i.e. releasing spirit that doesn't quite reach the high bar of old. That said there are plenty of distillers releasing fantastic liquid today, these are very easy to find and very affordable. I don't doubt that there's credible arguments on both sides but realistically, there's no clear winner.'"

Perhaps there's a better way of framing this debate.

Taking 'age' out of the equation, which is of course, a subjective concept in maturing whisky, I wonder if the romance of the past has slightly skewed our perception of whiskies made decades ago. Is it naive and nostalgic to think that distilling in the past was better?

"Today's equipment and data control means that technically and - if the will is there - distilling should be better", smiles Mr Reynier. "It's a question of resources, motivation and vision as to how one uses the tools one has though."

"The past is the past. We need to hold on to it and continue to learn from it," explains Richard Paterson, a man with perhaps more living insight into the working practices in whisky than any other.

"However, we should never forget the consumer. That's what has changed beyond recognition in the last 50 years. The whisky knowledge the consumer has today is incredible. They expect fantastic whiskies, and that's what we as whisky makers need to deliver."

Bigger organisations today sometimes make less room for a personal touch says Tamdhu Distillery Manager Sandy McIntyre

"I admire those who went before us and what they achieved with fewer resources, but I'm also delighted to see the variety now available," thinks Alan Winchester, another living legend, whose whisky making career at The Glenlivet began over four decades ago.

"In the 1970's very few single malts were available, now we can taste the likes of Glen Keith, Braeval and Caperdonich."

Over at Ian MacLeod's Tamdhu, Distillery Manager Sandy McIntyre believes that it's not just the distillation techniques of the time that played a huge part in the style of whisky making which many regard as some how 'better', pointing also to the people who made it too.

"I think that because some of the characters are no longer in the industry and a lot of the camaraderie has gone, a great deal of things have changed. Also now that the companies operating distilleries are less likely to be small or independently-minded, the personalities of the people running them no longer shine through. They're effectively part of a massive organisation now that makes people just small cogs in a big system."

"There are different ways to view this," thinks Fraser Hughes at the newly established Ardnahoe distillery on Islay.

"We will always look back nostalgically but it is naïve to think it was better to distil then. However, today there is more emphasis in regards working safely and rightly so. We have made distilleries a better environment to work in with advancement in systems such as CIP (cleaning in place), digital gauge and monitors, the list goes on. Back in the not too distant past the operators had to climb into the wash still to clean the coils and pans with caustic soda. They also had to enter the mash tun twice a week to lift and clean the plates [some still do today]. There was also a number of other practices which made it more challenging to mash and distil in the past as opposed to a more operator environment-friendly experience we have nowadays."

"Ultimately it's human nature to always look back at things through rose tinted spectacles, and we all do this when considering various topics in the past," continues Dr Lumsden. "But what I would say here is that our production today is far more consistent and hygienic than it ever was, but deep down I

...i Banik (far right) from Copper Rivet distillery sees a come-back for some of the old techniques thanks to small, artisan producers

can't help thinking that the drive towards increased production and efficiency has led to a certain extent to a degree of bland uniformity. Certainly when I am creating my whiskies consistency is a bad word and I love (and aim for) batch-to-batch variation."

More consistency today

The good Dr has certainly hit the nail on the head here with the C Word: Consistency. A more divisive subject I can barely think of, and something really very much at the heart of this debate. To the majority of the industry, consistency is an essential part of the fundamentals in modern whisky-making, somewhat highlighted by the relative inconsistency of some whiskies in the past. Open a bottle of Glenxxxx 12 year old and you should expect the same experience time and time again. However, as Dr Bill alludes to, there's a school of thought that actively celebrates a modern - engineered inconsistency, as opposed to the happy and more-often-than-not, unhappy accidents of old.

Perhaps it's a leading question, but I'm keen to find out from a range of today's whisky makers - both older and younger, whether they felt that whiskies distilled decades before have more 'character' or... less consistency?

"I would say less consistency," thinks Sandy McIntyre. "Nowadays we assess so many parameters – scientific assessments, comparing spirit runs, the nose of the new make, the cut points, wort quality measurements, cask assessments and traceability etc etc. We are trying to give the consumer the consistent product they expect and, like any other industry, taking measurements or assessing quality throughout that process can only help to improve that outcome. Whisky has always had character – in the past that was perhaps driven out by blending whisky and the lack of consistency from batch to batch was easier to hide that way. However people are moving towards single malts and that is where consistency has a higher level of importance as variations are difficult to hide."

"The whiskies I've worked with and tasted that are older have all varied in quality this is why we can't say with any certainty that old is best," reckons Steven Kersley. "Character is subjective as it can encompass a whole host of flavours, however I would

Glenmorangie's Brendan McCarron thinks that scientific breakthroughs like gas chromotography give distillers of today an advant

say that consistency was more variable in older whiskies. I wouldn't call this out as a major problem though, we've become a lot more refined in our cask management over the last few decades and taking out the variability swings between casks has driven a more consistent spirit throughout maturation."

Over on the south east coast of England newcomers The Copper Rivet distillery, led by head distiller Abhi Banik have a slightly different take on the subject of character vs consistency.

"The modern world has brought with it an industri-alisation to all spirits including whisky," points out Banik. "With that, we've lost some [of the old] cha-racter and charm, but that's where craft and artisan producers come in. For example, with industrialisa-tion, the idea of traceability – knowing where your whisky started life as a grain – has gone from most of the market, but this is something that we, with our Masthouse Whisky, are bringing back. This is one of the beauties of English whisky – just now, there's no set expectation of a flavour profile or character. So we get to define it for ourselves. I am sure this will evolve, but for now, it's a really fascinating space for connoisseurs to begin to explore."

"I have to say that my answer to this is both," concludes Lumsden. "In the past with the use of longer fermentations, longer germination time, slower distillation etc, overall I think there was the potential to have superior flavour. These and many other aspects of production have had to change due to ever increasing demand. The other side of the coin of course is that back in the day it wasn't all 'sweet-ness and light' and along with some of the real gems distilled, I believe that there would have also been a lot of inconsistent rubbish produced. These views are certainly backed up with my few experiences of tasting really old bottlings of whisky: where I have had some absolute beauties …and some which were well - nigh undrinkable!"

Can we learn from the past?

To throw in some hypothetical sideways thinking for a second, imagine we were blessed with the ability to travel through time. Aside from obviously hoarding all the Malt Mill, Port Ellen and Karuizawa they could lay their hands on I wondered what techniques our distillers would take back to the past and, if appropriate, which things that were perhaps lost to today's modern industrialism would they bring back to resurrect?

Brendan McF̶l̶y̶Carron: the keys to the DeLorian are all yours and the clock is ticking….!

"There have been a lot of scientific breakthroughs that I am sure could be used in the past, for example Gas Chromotography and a better understanding of various parts of maturation and distillation" he points out, "but they made great whisky back then as we do now, so perhaps they don't need to know about the new technology from today! In truth, perhaps the best information from the future would be the sales levels for every year. The overproduction periods, particularly the one that lead to the mass closure of distilleries in the 1980s, simply didn't need to happen and the effects were devastating on the mostly rural communities where these distilleries disappeared from."

With McCarron's turn at the wheel complete, I fling the keys over The Doc for his thoughts.

"I would take back the science of better hygiene and how to combat infection," explains Lumsden, "because way back in the day there was all sorts of health issues and fermentation infections, which we now know how to deal with. What I would bring back from the future is the sense that not everything revolves around money (cost, returns, profit etc) and that sometimes just making a great product: one made with love, care and pride, is enough."

"The loss of direct fired stills could be a great revival," thinks Copper Rivet's Abhi Banik. "It's not so much that we left the knowledge or the desire to use them behind, more that workplace health and safety (and myriad other issues) have made them impractical. Conversely, we know that distilling can use a lot of the energy and resources. I'd love to take back some of the technology we have today to save energy historically."

Evidently, there's never going to be a definitive conclusion to this story. What is great is that the industry is still clearly blessed with people who care deeply about trying to make the very best whisky they can with the resources they have in front of them: from large organisations and independent set ups. There's no doubt that modern whiskies are more consistent by their nature and perhaps an element of 'vanilla' has crept in to some of the global giants, where alcohol yield, higher demand and share price dictate the proceedings. However the

very same technology and a greater understanding of working practices have helped eliminate many of the unknowns: a place which allows for 'positive inconsistency' to drive more flavour variables into different expressions where the whisky maker feels it is appropriate.

As for those who insist that their older bottlings of whiskies still readily produced today are superior, that may be the case for a few of them and in truth, the feeling of discovering something truly remarkable is like opening a time capsule. However, for every great find, there must be an acknowledgement that not everything can possibly live up to that level of expectation.

It's a little like a vinyl records fanatic steadfastly sticking to their belief that modern music formats like digital streaming have taken the music industry in a totally undesirable, homologised direction. There comes a stage where that listener ceases to actually hear and appreciate the music, but prefers pointing out the faults and idiosyncrasies of everything else. The bottom line is that doesn't sound like fun at all to me.

I'll leave it to Richard Paterson for the final word.

"Technology will continue to play an important role. In truth we can continue to learn across the whisky making process. However, the craft and the art of the whisky maker will always be at the heart of it."

Amen to that.

Neil writes about whisky and other fine spirits for a number of publications globally, including The Daily and Sunday Telegraph. He is a Keeper Of The Quaich and a Liveryman in the Worshipful Company Of Distillers. Neil regularly presents a drinks feature on the popular TV food and drink show, Channel Four Sunday Brunch. His first book, (written with Gavin D. Smith) 'Let Me Tell You About Whisky' was published in 2013 and since then, he has co-authored five further books including 'Distilled', with Joel Harrison, which is now printed in 14 languages. His latest book, The World Atlas Of Gin has been shortlisted for the prestigious Tales Of The Cocktail Spirited award.

Ten Malts That Broke The Mould

by Gavin D Smith

In the same way it sometimes takes a single person
to change the course of history, there are whiskies that pave the way
for others. Often by being innovative and unique in combination with clever
marketing but occasionally by simply being in the right place at the
right time. Here are ten single malts that broke the mould.

Every competitive industry innovates: to improve upon what already exists, to stay ahead of the crowd and to maintain the interest of consumers. Not surprisingly then, the history of whisky is filled with stories of innovation, and of individuals who dared to be different, who sometimes refused to accept conventional wisdom and trod their own paths. As the great 'Whisky Baron' Tommy Dewar once declared, "Minds, like parachutes, only function when they are open."

Many of what we think of today as the 'norms' of malt whisky were quite radical at the time of their development and implementation. The world of Scotch whisky has tended to be relatively conservative in its views, and certain malts stand out from the crowd for bringing something new to the whisky party. But there are also whiskies from other parts of the world that have challenged the general conception. What all ten malts on the following pages have in common is that they were pioneers, they were the ones that triggered the consumers´ interest in their respective categories – in short they broke the mould.

Glenfiddich Straight Malt
– the first single malt to go global

While the Stand Fast Scotch blend accounted for the vast majority of William Grant & Sons' sales around 1960, Glenfiddich Pure Malt was also available; selling modestly in a number of countries. Indeed, company records show sales to Canada in 1904, just two years after Glenfiddich was first bottled.

With the same sort of foresight that had helped pull the firm through lean times in the past and added to profits when trading conditions were good, Grant's made the bold decision in 1960 to market a version of Glenfiddich, under the name Glenfiddich Straight Malt, throughout the UK.

The first case was bottled on 3rd April 1961, and export sales began two years later, with existing distribution networks meaning that the new product was immediately available across 110 different countries.

In a wide range of markets, Glenfiddich soon became the bestselling single malt, a position it has retained in many instances to this day. 2019 saw the brand sell 18 million bottles worldwide, compared to chief rival Glenlivet's 15,6 million bottles.

The late Chairman of William Grant & Sons Ltd Charles Gordon noted that "There was a lot of malt whisky being sold in small quantities by people like Gordon & MacPhail of Elgin, but the big distillers were not interested in single malts. For the first 20 years we had Glenfiddich on sale, nobody bothered us about it! That was the reason we got such a head start on all our competitors."

Glenfiddich was introduced into the USA in 1963, and its launch was accompanied by an advertising campaign with the headline 'Sit when you drink Glenfiddich, you may never stand for a blended Scotch again.' The text explained what a straight malt was – 'Glenfiddich is straight. Unblended. A single malt whisky every drop from the same distillery' – and described it as '…a man's drink mellowed 10 years.'

The Glenlivet 12 year old
– the single malt that cracked America

In 1921 Captain Bill Smith Grant took charge of the family-owned company George & JG Smith Ltd, proprietors of Glenlivet distillery. These were hard times for the Scotch whisky industry as economies floundered in the wake of the First World War, and Prohibition was in force across the USA (1920-33).

Although blended Scotch was dominant, Smith Grant decided to promote Glenlivet as a single malt, in order to insulate the distillery from the whims of hard-pressed blenders.

Glenlivet had the advantage of being a famous name with strong historical credentials, and Smith Grant enjoyed some success in the UK, with the prestigious White's Club and the International Sportsmen's Club in London stocking the whisky. However, with the repeal of Prohibition, he knew that the USA offered potentially great opportunities, and turned his attention across the Atlantic.

In 1933 an agreement was reached with the Wine & Spirit Import Corp. of New York City, granting them sole agency in the United States, and shipping orders during the early years were around 100 cases per time. 1933 also saw Smith Grant sign a deal with the Pullman Rail Company to offer two-ounce miniatures of whisky to passengers in its sleeping and dining cars, a move that was notably instrumental in getting Glenlivet known by a much wider audience.

Passengers were typically affluent business professionals, and having Glenlivet listed on the dining car beverages menus alongside blended Scotches was a real coup for the distiller. The word 'unblended' was noted alongside 'Geo. & J G Smith's The Glenlivet' in bold type.

Initially, sales in the USA were of 10 year old whisky, but some customers expressed a preference for it at 12, with both ages selling until the late 1940s, when the 12 year old became the standard expression. By 1950 Glenlivet accounted for half the single malt Scotch sold in the US, and the brand's position as the best-selling single malt in the country has been retained ever since.

Laphroaig 10 year old
– the malt that gave peatreek to the world

Today, heavily-peated single malts are highly desirable, with an almost fanatical following all around the world. But it was not always so. As recently as the 1980s, several Islay distilleries – including Ardbeg and Bruichladdich – were silent, with little sign that there would ever be a justification for re-opening them.

Independent bottlers and distillers themselves had long offered modest quantities of single malt from Islay distilleries, but the key word is 'modest,' and they enjoyed a niche appeal. One Islay single malt was, however, different from the rest, and it was Laphroaig. In 1908 Ian Hunter took over running of the family owned distillery and terminated its agency agreement with Mackie & Co, proprietors of neighbouring Lagavulin distillery. From that year onwards, Laphroaig began to market its own whisky, and market it with serious intent.

Hunter headed abroad and made inroads into the USA before the onset of Prohibition in 1920. The story goes that he managed to continue selling Laphroaig while the USA was 'dry' as whisky was allowed to be sold and consumed for medicinal purposes. Nobody nosing or tasting Laphroaig believed it could be drunk for pleasure!

With Prohibition repealed in 1933, Ian Hunter began to travel once again to the USA and to the Caribbean selling Laphroaig, and he registered the Laphroaig trademark in the USA during 1934. The 10 year old was launched in the 1940s, and after the Second World War, America's love affair with its singular charms endured.

Laphroaig, with its high-profile uncompromising character and lengthy pedigree, led the current growth of interest in Islay single malts as a genre from the 1990s onwards and today it remains the leading Islay single malt and the 7th best selling single malt in the world, with sales of almost four million bottles during 2018.

Glen Grant 5 year old
– Italy's favourite single malt

Back in 1961 Douglas Mackessack, descendant of the Grant brothers who established Glen Grant distillery in 1840, met Italian businessman Armando Giovinetti who was visiting Speyside. So impressed was Giovinetti by Glen Grant that on his return home he began to import the single malt, starting with a 100-case order. This led to a firm friendship between the Italian entrepreneur and Mackessack and a long-standing love affair between the Rothes distillery and Italian whisky drinkers.

The Italians had been drinking Scotch whisky for many years prior to this, however, with the Genoese firm of Wax & Vitale being appointed agents for Johnnie Walker in 1906, but almost all the Scotch they consumed was blended, with the exception, perhaps, of Glenmorangie, which was being exported to Italy during the 1930s.

Armando Giovinetti was intent on offering his customers something different to the numerous blends available in his home country, hence his choice of Glen Grant single malt, and at the youthful age of five it seemed particularly suited to Italian palates.

Starting in high-end hotel bars, Giovinetti expanded sales of Glen

Grant through the medium of television commercials, and Italy was soon the leading export market for the brand, helped by the fact that it sold for almost the same price as a bottle of blended Scotch. By the 1970s Italy was the third-largest importer of Scotch whisky, and rather remarkably, the leading export market for single malts.

Sales of single malt to Italy fell from the late 1990s onwards, and have subsequently fluctuated, with 1.31m lpa being exported in 2018, representing 35.1% of the 'bottled in Scotland' whisky total. Since 2006, Glen Grant distillery has been owned by Milan-based Gruppo Campari.

Locke's
– Scotch-style Irish malt whiskey

Back in 1987, the Irish Distillers Group (IDG) enjoyed a total monopoly over Irish whiskey production, with distilleries at Bushmills in County Antrim and Midleton in County Cork. The Group produced triple-distilled single malt at Bushmills, and triple-distilled 'pure' pot still and grain spirit at Midleton, making it entirely self-sufficient when it came to popular blends such as Jameson, Powers and Paddy.

But in that year, Irish entrepreneur John Teeling decided to challenge the IDG stranglehold on Irish whiskey, buying the former Ceimici Teoranta potato spirit distillery at Riverstown on the Cooley peninsula, near Dundalk. Remarkably, it was the first time in 100 years that a new distillery had been founded in Ireland.

Teeling renamed the distillery Cooley, and supplemented the existing column stills with a pair of pot stills sourced from the closed Old Comber distillery near Newtonards, and in 1992 launched the first single malt from Cooley – Locke's Single Malt Irish Whiskey.

In so doing he was resurrecting an old and cherished Irish distilling name, as Locke's Kilbeggan distillery had been founded in 1757, only closing almost two centuries later. Teeling was also creating something consciously different to IDGs offerings, as Locke's was a double-distilled single malt, very much in the Scottish style.

According to John Teeling, "Cooley had a number of outcomes. It broke the monopoly and offered choice. By building column stills it offered the possibility of producing blended whiskeys. Irish Distillers was the sole column still producer and it did not sell to third parties. Cooley also produced single malt, while Irish Distillers was mainly a pot still producer, though Bushmills malt was distilled and was used in blends.

"Additionally, by offering 'retail own label' and 'private label' bottlings it helped create an Irish category. Too often Irish was a single bottle on a shelf at the end of an aisle of Scotch. Cooley whiskeys were lighter and slightly sweeter than those from Irish Distillers – something new, young drinkers wanted. Cooley broke the mould."

Glenmorangie 1963 Vintage
– the earliest cask-finished single malt

Cask-finished single malts have become such a ubiquitous part of the whisky repertoire that it is easy to think they have been around for much longer than is actually the case. In the past, whisky maturing in leaking or ineffective casks must have been transferred to other casks from time to time, and inevitably some will have had a different previous content.

However, deliberate 'cask-finishing' began in the 1980s, and although Balvenie makes a case for its 1983 Classic – rebranded a decade later as Double-Wood – as the first, that honour probably belongs to Glenmorangie, courtesy of its 1963 Vintage expression, available from 1985 to 1987.

It was first bottled as a 22 year old, having spent 21 years in ex-Bourbon wood, before a final year in former oloroso sherry casks. According to Brendan McCarron, Glenmorangie's Head of Maturing Whisky Stocks, "Glenmorangie 1963 Vintage was the first whisky ever deliberately 'finished' and proclaiming the fact on the label. It was transferred from one cask to another to create a different flavour and experience. We put it into an oloroso sherry cask to deliberately make it something different."

McCarron declares that "Glenmorangie spirit really suits ex-bourbon wood, and filling it straight into sherry cask would allow the sherry characteristics to dominate, but we worked out a way of getting it to take on classic sherry style without overwhelming the distillery character. Bill Lumsden (now Director of Distilling, Whisky Creation & Whisky Stocks) arrived at the company after this had started, and he saw the potential to do a lot more. He saw it as a category changer, and he set out to perfect and drive it.

"Bill did lots of work with fortified and big, meaty red wine casks. Glenmorangie suits finishing, as it quite quickly takes on the character of other casks. That 1980s bottling led to everything we've done with cask finishing since, right up to our current finished expressions."

Yamazaki 12 year old
– Japanese malt makes its presence felt

The earliest Japanese whisky was distilled around 1870, but in 1924, the country's first dedicated whisky distillery opened at Yamazaki, on the outskirts of Kyoto. It was created by entrepreneur Shinjiro Torii, whose company was ultimately renamed Suntory.

After several decades of creating blended whiskies, Suntory broke into the single malt market during the 1980s, when Japan was enjoying a period of sustained economic growth. As a Suntory spokesperson explains, "A malt whisky with a strong character was preferred, and so 'Yamazaki' was born. It was a whole new step forward for Japanese whisky and for Master Blender Keizo Saji, who sensed the mood of the era."

Yamazaki 12 launched in 1984, which marked the 60th anniversary of the Yamazaki distillery first making whisky, and according to Liam Hiller, Head of Content at specialist Japanese whisky retailer

dekanta, "The Yamazaki 12 is a ground-breaking masterpiece, which is as perfectly balanced and complex a whisky as you will find."

He notes that "It was the first Japanese whisky to win an international whisky award, picking up a Gold Medal at the International Spirits Challenge in 2003. That really set the ball rolling for the Japanese whisky industry, as people around the world started to sit up and take notice of the incredible expressions being produced around Japan."

"There are a few others that helped propel Japanese whisky to the lofty heights it enjoys today, like the Yamazaki 25 year old (the first Japanese whisky to win 'World's Best Single Malt', in 2012) and the Hibiki 21 year old (winner of World's Best Blended Whisky in six of the last 10 years), but it was the Yamazaki 12 that started it all. It has become a staple of the Japanese whisky aficionado and is probably the Japanese expression best known to drinkers around the world."

Amrut Single Malt
– India's first single malt whisky

Today, single malt whiskies from Asia are highly regarded. Apart from those made in Japan, the best-known is probably Taiwan's Kavalan, while other distillers such as Milk & Honey and Golani in Israel, Murree in Pakistan, and John Distilleries and Rampur in India represent Asia internationally in the single malt sector.

However, the whisky that started it all was created by another Indian distiller, in Bangalore, southern

India. Amrut Single Malt Whisky was officially launched by Amrut Distilleries Ltd in Glasgow, Scotland on 24th August 2004. The firm had been established in 1948 by J N Radhakrishna Rao Jagdale but did not begin distilling malt whisky until 1987, initially for blending purposes.

As Head of International Operations Ashok Chokalingam explains, "The emergence of Japanese whiskies combined with our current Managing Director studying for his MBA in Newcastle upon Tyne and writing a thesis on 'The Potential for Indian Single Malt Whisky to be sold in Europe' led us to launch India's first single malt whisky for the global market."

The launch took place in Glasgow because Amrut decided to focus its marketing at the Indian restaurant sector, and Glasgow was the acknowledged 'curry capital' of Scotland. Prior to the official launch, a number of blind tastings were carried out at the city's whisky-centric Pot Still bar, and the feedback was very positive.

However, as Chokalingam recalls, "Initially the response was poor in the general market and it was an uphill task. People could not get their heads around with the concept of a single malt whisky coming from India. We changed the trajectory and focused more on whisky specialists and whisky-related events, and global sales grew. Now, the Indian market has tremendous growth potential for us and it is overwhelming."

As for the legacy of Amrut's move into single malts on other Asian distillers, Chokalingam says, "I am sure that the success of Amrut has encouraged other distillers from India to come forward with single malts and also encouraged Kavalan in Taiwan."

Monkey Shoulder
– the trendiest mixing malt

Blended malts – or vatted malts as they used to be known – have enjoyed a somewhat checkered history, seeming to lack the cachet of single malts, despite the undoubtedly high quality of the best of them.

One blended malt that has proved a great commercial success, however, is Monkey Shoulder, produced by William Grant & Sons Ltd, and launched in 2005. Monkey Shoulder has become the cocktail bartender's go-to Scotch, with a striking name and presentation to back up the liquid.

According to the Global Monkey Shoulder Team, "The starting point from day one was that our whisky was made for mixing, going against the typical perceptions at the time of how you should drink Scotch."

"The liquid is smooth, accessible and of such high quality that we encourage drinkers to be adventurous and not play by the rules. For example, our lazy-old fashioned or cocktails on draught demonstrate how we're pushing perceptions of how blended malts can be enjoyed. We set out to create a great-tasting whisky that could stand up to other malts but also be incredibly versatile in drinks."

When it comes to the actual liquid that makes up the blended malt, Master Blender Brian Kinsman notes that "Monkey Shoulder has been blended in combinations of three Speyside single malts (Glenfiddich, Balvenie and Kininvie). For each batch, we select various combinations from our warehouses, and marry them together to achieve exactly the same quality and flavour profile since the original flavour was selected back in 2004."

According to the 2019 Brands Report, compiled by industry magazine Drinks International, from a worldwide survey of leading bartenders, owners and managers, Monkey Shoulder was the 'best-selling and trendiest' Scotch whisky. It was named the preferred Scotch at 22% of bars, with Johnnie Walker recording 17%. In 2019, 5,8 million bottles were sold, representing a year on year compound annual growth rate of 18%.

Macallan 12 year old
– Taiwan's love affair with single malt

When it comes to malt Scotch whisky imports, Taiwan punches far above its weight. Remarkably, this state with a population of 23.8 million people is the third-largest consumer of malt Scotch in the world in both volume and value terms, behind only the USA and France. 2019 saw a near 25% increase in the value of single malt sales.

So how and why did Taiwan develop this love for the produce of Scotland's pot stills? According to the Taiwanese Master of the Quaich and Single Malt Ambassador Ho-Cheng Yao, aka 'Kingfisher,'

"It probably started with Macallan when they put out an advertising campaign using Michael Jackson's description of Macallan as 'the Rolls Royce of whiskies in the late 1990s."

"As Macallan actually goes very well with Chinese food, it soon became the premium spirit brand, and people started to learn about single malt. Back in those days there were only Sherry Oak expressions, and the majority that was sold

in Taiwan was 12 year old, but the 18 year old was certainly quite popular."

Yao explains that "Macallan had the number one position from the early 2000s and actually in some years it was not only the leading brand in single malt but also the leading brand if compared with blended whisky. Its sales have gradually decreased in the past few years due to the brand strategy worldwide to increase its price. Now Singleton (of Glen Ord) is the best-selling single malt in Taiwan. For about 10 years, we were unique in the world, as the single malt market was bigger than the blended whisky market until last year."

It was not until 1990, that the Taiwanese government allowed competition in the spirits market, and, as Yao notes, "Before that, spirits consumers drank Chinese white liquor – Kaoliang or sorghum liquor – and this is still the leading spirit today. When the market first opened, the best-selling brown spirit was cognac, but it changed to whisky around 1995. Before Macallan took off, the major whisky brands being drunk were blends, such as Johnnie Walker, Royal Salute, and Chivas Regal."

In their very different ways, the malts explored above have been innovative, whether introducing the joys of the genre to new audiences, or augmenting, rejuvenating and even challenging existing styles and characteristics. The result has been the enrichment of the world of malt whisky, and long may the industry's parachutes remain open.

Gavin D Smith is one of Scotland's leading whisky writers and Contributing Editor Scotland for Whisky Magazine. He regularly undertakes writing commissions for leading drinks companies and produces articles for a wide range of publications, including Whisky Magazine, Whisky Magazine & Fine Spirits – France, Whisky Etc, Whisky Advocate, Whiskeria, The Keeper, Irish Whiskey Magazine, Unfiltered and Whisky Quarterly.

He is the author and co-author of some 30 books, and recent publications include The Microdistillers' Handbook, Ardbeg: Heavenly Peated and World of Whisky (with David Wishart and Neil Ridley). His latest title (co-written with Charles MacLean) is A History of Whisky in One Hundred Objects.

HOUSE SPIRITS
DISTILLERY
#2 5-12 (jug fill: 6·13·12
WHISKEY

2   5-12 (36m)

Miles Munroe - Head Distiller at Westward Whiskey

The American Revolution

by Jonny McCormick

There is an American whisky revolution underway. New distillers are looking to define what American single malt whiskey should (and should not) be. For many of them, sipping a Scotch was their ticket into the world of spirits. Today, as producers, they are determined to create their own, American take on single malts.

There are three things to know about American single malt whiskey; it's new, it's growing, and it's unregulated (but it's trying to go legit). Trust me, few articles on the subject will tell you more. This is a newborn whiskey style with all the fierce defiance and invincibility of youth, yet one that is still finding its feet and learning from its mistakes. Its greatest fortune perhaps, is that all possibilities lie ahead of it. Americans are known for making bourbon and rye and their penchant for drinking good Scotch, but this essay explores the frontier of an American whiskey revolution, one that is pushing single malt into new territories.

The laziest accusation levelled at any fledgling single malt nation is the implication that they are peddling imitation Scotch. This notion about wanna-be Scotch whisky persisted in the mainstream understanding of single malts from Japan and elsewhere in the latter part of the 20th century, but fortunately, mainstream coverage of Japanese whisky these days is much better informed: articles now highlight their quality and collectability.

Quite frankly, I've never met a distiller making single malt outside of Scotland whose ambitions ran no higher than pumping out burlesqued Scotch to the undiscerning. New single malt whisky producers have always run the gauntlet of cautious suspicion and curiosity in order to gain wider recognition in their aspiring quest for parity with classic single

House Spirits, home of Westward Single Malt, wedged in between the Interstate 5 and the Union Pacific Railroad

malt brands. At the minute, American single malt whiskey is a counter-culture movement within American distilling. The early pioneers were Clear Creek Distillery on their McCarthy's Oregon Single Malt, joined later by St. George Spirits, Stranahan's, and Balcones, however, liquor stores often failed to differentiate them from bourbons and ryes on their shelf.

Arguably, for some producers, this is a creative rejection of bourbon driven by non-conformist distillers more inspired by American craft brewers or the whisky makers of Islay than their forebears in Kentucky and Tennessee. Others rejoice in making every type of American spirit they can. It's akin to pioneering musical styles such as blues, jazz, country, soul, rock n' roll, and hip-hop that have been adopted by others musicians around the world and refashioned for their own purposes: American single malt is just another example of cultural exchange

While it's not legal for Scots to reciprocate and start making Caledonian bourbon, neither are distillers in the U.S. working with a picture of Talisker Distillery scotch taped above the controls of their stills in place of an instruction manual. This is a vibrant area of whiskey worthy of your attention for its ability to reinterpret the received wisdom on Scotch by filtering it through a spirit of unrestricted expe-

rimentalism. The American single malt movement escalates the global popularity of single malts from the backyard of bourbon, tuning into sensibilities that are more blue sky than blue collar. Without the encumbrance of the history, nostalgia, or the weighty traditions of Scotch, these distilleries are innovating and inventing their own rules, actions that distance themselves from other styles of American whiskey. Are these the true rebels of American whiskey?

In the final four months of 2019, I made four trips from Scotland to the U.S. and as we progressed through 2020, I cherished ever more dearly the friends, new and old, that I met on those travels; the bottles we emptied by the glasses we raised, the camaraderie over a good dinner, and all the highs and lows of every flight, bus journey, cab ride, and subway trip that made it all possible. Few Europeans will have had the opportunity to tour many U.S. distilleries this year, so to compensate, we will begin to explore the meaning of American single malt through the prism of an American distillery.

The Distillery Row

It's early one morning in late September 2019, and I find myself standing in the rain in Pioneer Square in Portland, Oregon in the Pacific Northwest.

Fat droplets of rain drum against the canvas of the seating area parasols while rivulets cascade down the red brick steps into the deserted square. A car sloshes through the puddles bearing a scuffed 'Keep Portland Weird' bumper sticker. In my experience, it seems to rain here every morning; swirling clouds of grey misty drizzle on good days, but apocalyptic downpours that drench the streets if you're unlucky and the rain sets in.

Westward Whiskey is part of Portland's Distillery Row, a collective of craft distillers scattered either side of the Willamette River. The Row is less about the physical proximity of a whiskey neighbourhood and more about a state of mind. It's born out of the same spirit of mutual support and belief in making something honest and authentic that bonds the food cart to those shop owners roasting and brewing great coffee in the shadow of corporate America.

House Spirits Distillery, where Westward Whiskey is made, is wedged between the I-5, the lengthy west coast highway that runs between the Mexican and Canadian borders, and the Union Pacific Railroad, where powerful freight locomotives crawl interminably past the distillery doors blasting their air horns over the ding ding ding of the railroad crossing. For-mer brewer Christian Krogstad founded the distillery in 2002 that has since become known for Westward Whiskey and Aviation American Gin (another spirit devised to open up new territory). Given the profusion of breweries in this part of the world, brewers make up the majority of the production staff and epitomise a philosophy of making whisky from good beer (in a brewery with a distillery attached).

Westward American Single Malt Whiskey is a cop-per-coloured dram launched in 2017 with a sweet, viscous mouthfeel offering peaches, dried fruit, and later stone fruits, while unspooling flavours of baking spices, vanilla, and desiccated coconut with a herbal finish.

Miles Munroe, head distiller at Westward Whiskey, uses a craft brewer's set-up with a closed fermentation system. They buy ale malt from Great Western Malting in Washington State, an enormous regional facility just over the Columbia River that dwarf the maltings in Scotland. It's a high colour base malt kilned at a higher temperature which roasts the grains to produce more toasty flavours, though Munroe also experiments with rye malt, chocolate malt, and single origin malted barleys sourced from a small floor maltings in Eastern Oregon.

Westward still room

Westland Distillery in Seattle

The mash tun is filled from one continuous sparge, then left to rest so the hot water can extract the sugars from the milled grains. The soft water has a low minerality and is drawn from the Bull Run Lake, which gathers surface water from the environs of Mount Hood (after my early morning soaking, I'm in no doubt there is a plentiful supply). Intriguingly, the worts are pasteurised in a kettle for ten minutes after mashing. This kills off any native bacteria that could sour the batch and derail the development of flavours from the yeast.

Munroe uses the Sierra Nevada pale ale yeast in the main, which generates a beer with plenty of fruity character, lots of pear and banana, with rose petal and jasmine notes, though they have run batches with other brewer's yeasts. Certainly, distiller's yeast would be more efficient for its ability to handle more complex sugars, as brewer's yeast mainly works on monosaccharides and disaccharides. The workaround is to add dextrinase as the wort comes out of the kettle, enabling the yeast to get straight to work in their temperature-controlled fermenters. Set to 24°C, the alcohol slowly rises to 8.5%–9% over the next four to five days, creating a beer which is delicious enough to drink. Afterwards, the fermen-

ters are fastidiously cleaned to try to control the development of bacteria in the next batch.

Taking care of the flavours

Protecting the flavours of the grain and the fruit flavours created during fermentation guides Westward's entire approach to distillation. Obviously, distillation concentrates and purifies the alcohol, but the skill lies in capturing the right fraction to frame the flavours desired. As stillrooms go, the first thing that strikes you at House Spirits is there's a lot more stainless steel than copper on display. From ground level up, the spindly swan neck on the high wines still looks almost decorative; I've seen worm tubs with more copper, but as Munroe explains, its idiosyncratic shape is purposeful and calculated.

It's pot still distillation, but with a light touch: they don't want to strip out the good flavours from the wash. Think of it like the alembic equivalent of a chef letting good quality ingredients shine, rather than overcooking them and disguising the fiasco with a heavy sauce.

The House Spirits wash still has a stainless steel

cone topped by a stubby copper stovepipe barely a metre tall: it's not pretty, but it's a tried and true part of Westward Whiskey. This trustworthy vessel was transferred when they outgrew the original distillery and relocated to the Buckman neighbourhood. In the early days when Munroe was the sole distiller, this was the only still and work was laborious. The breweries around town would make him a wash, but he had to toil over three consecutive wash distillations to generate sufficient low wines for a new make run in the same still. These days, 11,000 litres are pumped into the pot, though the diminutive copper tube deliberately leaves very little headspace to minimise reflux.

The neck is stuffed with sacrificial copper wool, which refines the vapours by reducing the sulphur compounds. The first 4-5 litres are discarded completely; a tiny fraction of the whole, mainly diverted to exclude any impurities from the previous run. With 2,300 litres of low wines collected at 35% ABV for the new make run, the residual boiling hot pot ale is pumped into an insulated thermal tank to keep for warming the beer wash through a heat exchanger at the start of tomorrow's run.

The steam-heated high wines still, built by Vendome, has a large stainless steel pot with no visible copper below the neck. The small copper boil ball at the base can be visualised as a giraffe that's swallowed a car tyre from a Mini Cooper. Again, this is deliberately compact to discourage reflux, yet sufficiently functional to condense certain highly volatile vapours.

The copper swan neck is short and narrow, tipping over into a steeply angled lyne arm that plummets into a shotgun condenser, Munroe's name for his shell and tube. The distiller tastes through the heads until they identify the heart then makes the cut with the Westward flavour profile in mind; it's not done by proof, it doesn't involve a timer. Westward sacrifice a great deal of efficiency in their pursuit of flavour, and with just 1,000 litres of new make, they only have enough to fill four or five barrels per run.

Every Westward Whiskey begins maturation in a brand new American white oak cask for at least two years, a concession to the conventional profile of other American whiskeys. You could say it's produced like Scotch but aged like bourbon. Casks are ordered from cooperages in Kentucky and from the Ozarks in southern Missouri, specifying no toasting and a low to medium level 2 char. The new oak yields plenty of colour in the first few weeks, but as their core whiskey is aged for 4–5 years, they rack it into alternative casks after 2 years to avoid overpowering the fermentation characteristics.

Westward is matured at the Jenny Barrel House, a 28,000 square foot warehouse facility in Clackamas, 10 miles southeast of Portland. The warehouse isn't temperature controlled nor open and exposed to the elements like a Kentucky rickhouse, but it keeps an ambient temperature. The casks are aged upright on pallets, lashed together with steel bands, and stacked four high: Portland sits in a high seismic zone and this helps to keep everything stable in the event of a big earthquake.

Plenty of innovators

Westland is a prime example of the potential for distilleries making American single malt whiskeys to innovate and grow. Look at Sante Fe Spirits, where Colin Keegan is using mesquite smoked malt and apple brandy cask finishing on his Colkegan line, the restless enthusiasm of Paul Hletko at F.E.W. spirits and Darek Bell at Corsair using fruit woods to produce different triple smoke single malts, Matt Hofmann at Westland using local peat from Labrador tea plants, experimenting with different barley species and filling native Garry oak casks, or Gareth Moore at the Virginia Distilling Co. eschewing new oak in favour of imported sherry casks and finishing in port, chardonnay, and cider barrels, not to mention the widespread collaborations on single malt beer cask finishing taking place around the country.

Terroir is an often misunderstood and misappropriated term in whiskey, extrapolated from viticulture to cover environmental variables, whether that's soil, climate, aspect, or microbiological factors and their ability to influence the final flavour profile of the drink. Distilleries such as Bruichladdich and Waterford use it correctly to look at the aspects of their barley source from different farms.

For American single malt whiskey, cultural ergonomics, a discipline that encompasses the human factors and performance within systems, might be a more appropriate framework for innovation than terroir. The inventiveness of American single malt whiskey is based on the experiences and preferences of the distiller, the chosen raw materials, and the distillery set-up. All the on-the-job learning at a distillery and the evolution of the culture of the team helps producers to perfect the profile of their whiskeys, making it impossible for others to replicate at another location.

Supporting local independent producers has been another lesson from 2020, whether that's buying a bottle of American single malt whiskey from a nearby craft distillery or the best egg sandwich you ever ate. Consistency is the result of optimising the performance of each distillery through the fusion

Colin Keegan, founder and owner of Santa Fe Spirits and Darek Bell, co-founder of Corsair Artisan Distillery

of raw materials, distillery apparatus, and human factors. With such momentum behind American single malt, the natural next step for producers was to campaign for greater recognition.

Pioneers of American single malt banded together to form the American Single Malt Whiskey Commission (ASMWC) in 2016 and membership now encompasses over 160 distilleries in 42 different states.

Under President Steve Hawley of Westland Distillery, the ASMWC has written a Standard of Identity of American Single Malt Whiskey which serves three purposes; firstly, to educate consumers, secondly, to lobby the authorities, and thirdly, to open the doors to greater international trade.

If you've not looked at their webpage by now, (www.americansinglemaltwhiskey.org) the six standards for American Single Malt Whiskey are i) made from 100% malted barley ii) distilled at one distillery iii) mashed, distilled, and matured in the U.S.A. iv) matured in oak casks not exceeding 700 litres v) distilled to no higher than 80% ABV vi) bottled at 40% ABV or more.

The standards are a well-balanced industry consensus founded on the consumer understanding of single malt whiskey designed for the smoothest passage through the hands of the legislators. If ratified by the U.S. Federal Government, American Single Malt Whiskey would take its place amongst other spirits legally recognised by the Alcohol and Tobacco Tax and Trade Bureau (TTB) giving producers a basic standard to help educate consumers. Five harvests have passed since the commission was founded, and although undaunted, they have learned how hard it is to change the labelling categories in the TTB's Beverage Alcohol Manual.

Undeniably, the standards leave ample scope for innovation, differentiation, and flexibility, though that becomes more apparent when you scrutinize the areas where practice isn't controlled. Remember, these are standards, not detailed regulations such as exist in Ireland and Scotland.

Barley does not need to be American grown (just as single malt Scotch doesn't require barley grown in Scotland), but it does specify 100% malted barley, ruling out any mixed mashes of malted cereals. No restrictions on barley types, roast levels, or peat are stipulated.

Gareth and Maggie Moore from Virginia Distilling Company

Notice the separation of points ii) and iii), which at first glance could have been one single standard; only specifying that distillation has to be done at one distillery leaves distillers the option to mash and ferment at other locations. Susannah Skiver Barton, my colleague at Whisky Advocate, broke the news of Brendan Coyle at High West in Utah (not an ASMWC member) blending single malt whiskeys on their High West High Country American Single Malt produced at the company's two distillery facilities: an example that currently falls outside the proposals.

The standards don't comment on still types; column, hybrid, or pot stills are all fine. The distillation strength of 80% ABV matches the Federal Standards of Identity for Distilled Spirits used for bourbon, rather than 94.8% ABV specified in the Scotch whisky and Irish whiskey regulations.

The casks must be oak, but they need not be American oak, or new oak, and filling strength has not been set, giving plenty of room for innovation.

No minimum age before bottling is specified, though this is eminently sensible given the climactic variations across the country, which results in a greater range of maturation rates. The Scotch whisky and Irish whiskey regulations outline the suitability of maturation warehouse environments and permit additives of water and spirit caramel before bottling, but there is no mention of that here, nor any insistence for bottling to take place in the U.S.

Obviously, it has to taste different from bourbon and rye to earn recognition as a distinctive drink, but the great strength of the ASMWC's Standards of Identity are that they are relatively unchallenging and exclude very few producers. In my view, they should be widely acceptable to whiskey lovers and lawmakers alike.

There are three things to know about American single malt whiskey; it's new, it's growing, and it's unregulated (but it's trying to go legit). Trust me, few articles on the subject will tell you more.

Whisky writer and photographer Jonny McCormick is Contributing Editor of Whisky Advocate magazine and one of their leading whisky reviewers. He is known as a specialist in the field of rare and collectable whiskies, and his prolific writing on the topic has made him an authority on the secondary market. He is a Keeper of the Quaich and has presented Scotch whisky tastings in Europe, North America, and Asia.

Malt distilleries

Including the subsections:
Scottish distilleries | New distilleries | Closed distilleries
Distilleries around the globe

Explanations

Owner: Name of the owning company, sometimes with the parent company within brackets.

Region/district: There are five protected whisky regions or localities in Scotland today; Highlands, Lowlands, Speyside, Islay and Campbeltown. Where useful we mention a location within a region e.g. Orkney, Northern Highlands etc.

Founded: The year in which the distillery was founded is usually considered as when construction began. The year is rarely the same year in which the distillery was licensed.

Status: The status of the distillery's production. Active, mothballed (temporarily closed), closed (but most of the equipment still present), dismantled (the equipment is gone but part of or all of the buildings remain even if they are used for other purposes) and demolished.

Visitor centre: The letters (vc) after status indicate that the distillery has a visitor centre. Many distilleries accept visitors despite not having a visitor centre. It can be worthwhile making an enquiry.

Address: The distillery´s address.

Tel: This is generally to the visitor centre, but can also be to the main office.

Website: The distillery's (or in some cases the owner's) website.

Capacity: The current production capacity expressed in litres of pure alcohol (LPA).

History: The chronology focuses on the official history of the distillery and independent bottlings are only listed in exceptional cases.

Tasting notes: For all the Scottish distilleries that are not permanently closed we present tasting notes of what, in most cases, can be called the core expression (mainly their best selling 10 or 12 year old).

We have tried to provide notes for official bottlings but in those cases where we have not been able to obtain them, we have turned to independent bottlers.

The whiskies have been tasted either by Gavin D Smith (GS), a well-known whisky authority and author of 20 books on the subject or by Ingvar Ronde (IR). All notes have been prepared especially for Malt Whisky Yearbook 2021.

Aberfeldy

[ah•bur•fell•dee]

Owner:
John Dewar & Sons
(Bacardi)

Region/district:
Southern Highlands

Founded: | **Status:** | **Capacity:**
1896 | Active (vc) | 3 400 000 litres

Address: Aberfeldy, Perthshire PH15 2EB

Website:
aberfeldy.com

Tel:
01887 822010 (vc)

Known as the backbone of Dewar's blended Scotch since the late 1800s, the single malt from Aberfeldy has made an impressive journey on its own merits in the last decade.

Since the relaunch in 2014/2015, sales figures have increased by 200% and if we go back ten years, when the brand was number 33 on the sales list of all Scotch malts, the rise is an impressive 600%. It now resides in place 21, selling 1,5 million bottles per year.

The distillery lies in the southern Highlands. Driving north on the A9, 10 minutes before you reach Pitlochry, you take the A827 heading west. After 15 minutes you reach the distillery and it's definitely worth a detour. There is an excellent visitor centre with different tours to choose from attracting more than 40,000 visitors per year.

The equipment consists of a 7.5 ton stainless steel, full lauter mash tun, eight washbacks made of larch (two of them replaced in February 2019) and three made of stainless steel with an average fermentation time of 72 hours, and four stills. Working a seven-day week with 23 mashes, the plan for 2020 is to make 3.4 million litres of alcohol. The owners have also invested £1.2m in a biomass boiler and recently commissioned an upgrade of the effluent treatments plant.

The core range consists of **12, 16** and **21 years old**. For the duty free market there are two widely available expressions; a **16 year old** and a **21 year old** both of them finished for up to 12 months in madeira casks (ex-Bual and ex-Malvasia Malmsey respectively). Another range aimed at selected airports around the world is the Exceptional Cask Series. Recent releases in that range are an **18 year old finished in PX casks**, and a **19 year old** and a **24 year old**, both fully matured in first fill sherry butts. Recent limited releases include a **15 year old** finished in Pomerol casks and the first of three **40 year olds** which can be hand-filled at the distillery or ordered by their website.

History:

1896 John and Tommy Dewar embark on the construction of the distillery, a stone's throw from the old Pitilie distillery which was active from 1825 to 1867. Their objective is to produce a single malt for their blended whisky - White Label.

1898 Production starts in November.

1917 The distillery closes.

1919 The distillery re-opens.

1925 Distillers Company Limited (DCL) takes over.

1972 Reconstruction takes place, the floor maltings is closed and the two stills are increased to four.

1991 The first official bottling is a 15 year old in the Flora & Fauna series.

1998 Bacardi buys John Dewar & Sons from Diageo at a price of £1,150 million.

2000 A visitor centre opens and a 25 year old is released.

2005 A 21 year old is launched in October, replacing the 25 year old.

2009 Two 18 year old single casks are released.

2010 A 19 year old single cask, exclusive to France, is released.

2011 A 14 year old single cask is released.

2014 The whole range is revamped and an 18 year old for duty free is released.

2015 A 16 year old is released.

2018 A 16 year old and a 21 year old madeira finish are released for duty free.

2020 A limited 15 year old finished in Pomerol casks is released.

Tasting notes Aberfeldy 12 years old:

GS – Sweet, with honeycombs, breakfast cereal and stewed fruits on the nose. Inviting and warming. Mouth-coating and full-bodied on the palate. Sweet, malty, balanced and elegant. The finish is long and complex, becoming progressively more spicy and drying.

12 years old

Aberlour

[ah•bur•lower]

Owner: | **Region/district:**
Chivas Brothers Ltd | Speyside
(Pernod Ricard)

Founded: | **Status:** | **Capacity:**
1879 | Active (vc) | 3 800 000 litres

Address: Aberlour, Banffshire AB38 9PJ

Website: | **Tel:**
aberlour.com | 01340 881249

It looks like Aberlour distillery is due for a major upgrade in coming years. A building application was submitted to Moray council in July 2017, but was later withdrawn. A new one was submitted in December 2019 and is now awaiting approval.

The first phase is to upgrade the evaporator and effluent treatment systems as well as the boiler. According to the owners, any expansion of the capacity or distillation equipment is still awaiting an internal review and decision. However, according to the available drawings it could mean a doubling of the capacity with a new still house, tun room and mash house including an additional four stills and another 16 washbacks.

The distillery is currently equipped with a 12 ton semi-lauter mash tun, six stainless steel washbacks and two pairs of large and wide stills in a spacious still room. To achieve the desired character of the newmake, which is fruity, the operators run a very slow distillation. With a 7.5 hour spirit cycle, the middle cut (73-63%) takes two hours to complete.

The core range of Aberlour includes **12, 16** and **18 year olds** – all matured in a combination of ex-bourbon and ex-sherry casks. Another core expression is **Casg Annamh** matured in ex-oloroso casks (both European and American oak) as well as ex-bourbon. A new **14 year old** has also been announced but not confirmed. Finally there is **Aberlour a'bunadh**, matured in ex-Oloroso casks. It is always bottled at cask strength and up to 67 different batches have been released by summer 2020. Exclusively available in the American market, **a'bunadh Alba** was recently released matured in American oak. For select markets (mainly France) another three expressions are available; **12 year old** un chill-filtered, **15 year old Select Cask Reserve** and **White Oak Millennium 2004**. Two exclusives are available for duty free – a **12 year old Sherry Cask** and a **15 year old Double Cask**. There are also five cask strength bottlings in the Distillery Reserve Collection, available at all Chivas' visitor centres – from **17** to **21 years old**.

History:
1879 The local banker James Fleming founds the distillery.
1892 The distillery is sold to Robert Thorne & Sons Ltd who expands it.
1896 A fire rages and almost totally destroys the distillery. The architect Charles Doig is called in to design the new facilities.
1921 Robert Thorne & Sons Ltd sells Aberlour to a brewery, W. H. Holt & Sons.
1945 S. Campbell & Sons Ltd buys the distillery.
1962 Aberlour terminates floor malting.
1973 Number of stills are increased from two to four.
1974 Pernod Ricard buys Campbell Distilleries.
2000 Aberlour a'bunadh is launched.
2001 Pernod Ricard buys Chivas Brothers and merges Chivas Brothers and Campbell Distilleries under the brand Chivas Brothers.
2002 A new, modernized visitor centre is inaugurated in August.
2008 The 18 year old is also introduced outside France.
2013 Aberlour 2001 White Oak is released.
2014 White Oak Millenium 2004 is released.
2018 Casg Annamh is released.
2019 A'bunadh Alba is released.

12 years old

Tasting notes Aberlour 12 year old:
GS – The nose offers brown sugar, honey and sherry, with a hint of grapefruit citrus. The palate is sweet, with buttery caramel, maple syrup and eating apples. Liquorice, peppery oak and mild smoke in the finish.

Allt-a-Bhainne

[alt a•vain]

Owner:
Chivas Brothers Ltd
(Pernod Ricard)

Region/district:
Speyside

Founded: 1975
Status: Active
Capacity: 4 200 000 litres

Address: Glenrinnes, Dufftown, Banffshire AB55 4DB

Website: -
Tel: 01542 783200

While Allt-a-Bhainne is a comparatively new distillery, it lies in surroundings that are steeped in whisky history dating back to the 1700s.

The B9009 is a beautiful road stretching for 17 kilometres from Dufftown to Auchbreck. Halfway, you will find a building on your right hand side that definitely doesn't resemble a distillery. Four tiny and ornamental pagoda roofs might give it away, but apart from that Allt-a-Bhainne could be any industrial building from the 1970s. A geographical landmark that is impossible to miss in these parts of Speyside – the Ben Rinnes mountain, rises behind it. From the mountain's summit you can see eight counties and – on a clear day – even the Moray coast. At the end of the B9009, near Glenlivet, lies the closed Aucherachan distillery. Opened around 1780 it operated for a time under the name Glenlivat. The connection with the world famous distillery is even tighter than that. Captain William Grant, the last owner of Aucherachan which closed in 1852, married Margaret Smith, the daughter of Glenlivet´s founder George Smith. Their son, George Smith Grant, eventually became the owner of Glenlivet.

Allt-a-Bhainne single malt has been an important part of the Scotch blend The 100 Pipers for many years. The brand, which sells around 17 million bottles per year, has its biggest markets in Asia and especially in Thailand and India. The soft, yet distinctive smoky, note in the whisky comes from the fact that Allt-a-Bhainne for a number of years have been distilling peated whisky for part of the year. Usually it constitutes 30-50% of the total production and has a phenol specification in the barley between 10 and 20ppm.

The equipment consists of 9 ton lauter mash tun, eight stainless steel washbacks with a fermentation time of 48-50 hours and two pairs of stills. The distillery is currently working seven days a week with 25 mashes resulting in 4 million litres of alcohol.

Official bottlings are few. A lightly peated **Allt-a-Bhainne NAS** was launched in 2018 and there is also a **14 year old cask strength** distilled in 2005 in the Distillery Reserve Collection, available at all Chivas´ visitor centres.

History:

1975 The distillery is founded by Chivas Brothers, a subsidiary of Seagrams, in order to secure malt whisky for its blended whiskies. The total cost amounts to £2.7 million.

1989 Production has doubled.

2001 Pernod Ricard takes over Chivas Brothers from Seagrams.

2002 Mothballed in October.

2005 Production restarts in May.

2018 An official, lightly peated bottling is released.

Allt-a-Bhainne NAS

Tasting notes Allt-a-Bhainne NAS:

IR – Subtle smokiness is mixed with butterscotch, honey, apples and a touch of pepper. Sweet peat on the palate, oranges, ginger, melon, more pepper and vanilla.

Ardbeg

[ard•beg]

Owner:
The Glenmorangie Co
(Moët Hennessy)

Region/district:
Islay

Founded: 1815
Status: Active (vc)
Capacity: 2 400 000 litres

Address: Port Ellen, Islay, Argyll PA42 7EA

Website:
ardbeg.com

Tel:
01496 302244 (vc)

It is probably an understatement to say that Ardbeg single malt has many loyal followers. The Committee which celebrates its 20th anniversary this year has more than 120,000 members worldwide.

Chairman of the committee is Mickey Heads who is also the distillery manager. In the last 13 years he has become well-known to every Ardbeg fan for his passion and his conviviality whether you met him at the Feis Ile on Islay or at tastings or whisky shows around the world. In March 2020 it was announced that he was to retire in October. This marks the end of a more than 40 year long career in the whisky industry, including eight years as the manager of Jura distillery. His succesor as distillery manager will be Colin Gordon who has been managing Lagavulin for the past few years and Port Ellen maltings before that.

A much anticipated expansion of the distillery is currently underway. Another two stills and five more washbacks arrived at the distillery in spring 2019, a completely new still house was built and the old tun room, still house and fuel store were refurbished to accommodate the new equipment. Due to the corona virus the commissioning of the new stills were postponed until later in 2020. With the new equipment, Ardbeg currently has a 5 ton stainless steel semi lauter mash tun and eleven washbacks (currently eight of them are in use) made of Oregon pine with a fermentation time of 60 hours. Furthermore, there are two pairs of stills with the spirit stills being fitted with purifiers to help create the special fruity character of the spirit. The plan for 2020 is to do 16-17 mashes per week and 1.4 million litres of pure alcohol.

The core range, all of them non-chill filtered, consists of the **10 year old**, a mix of first and re-fill bourbon casks, **Uigeadail**, a marriage of bourbon and sherry casks and bottled at cask strength, **Corryvreckan**, also a cask strength and a combination of bourbon casks and new French oak, **An Oa**, a vatting of whiskies matured in several types of casks that have been married together for a minimum of three months in three huge vats (14,000 and 30,000 litres respectively) and the 19 year old **Traigh Bhan** (batch 2 released in October 2020) which has been matured in a combination of American oak and ex-oloroso sherry casks and is bottled at 46,2%. A sixth member of the range was added in spring 2020 by way of the 5 year old **Wee Beastie**, matured in a combination of bourbon and oloroso casks.

Fairly recent limited expressions include a **21 year old** and **Ardbeg Twenty Something** – a 23 year old made from spirit distilled in the mid-nineties. It was then followed up in autumn 2018 by a **22 year old** matured in ex-bourbon casks. The Ardbeg Day expression for 2020 was **Blaaack**, matured in ex-bourbon barrels and then finished for three years in pinot noir casks from New Zealand. A Committee version was launched in March, bottled at 50.7% with a general release in early June, bottled at 46%. A special bottling to honour the retiring Mickey Heads has been rumoured but without an official confirmation at the time of writing,

History:

1794 First record of a distillery at Ardbeg. It was founded by Alexander Stewart.

1798 The MacDougalls, later to become licensees of Ardbeg, are active on the site through Duncan MacDougall.

1815 The current distillery is founded by John MacDougall, son of Duncan MacDougall.

1853 Alexander MacDougall, John's son, dies and sisters Margaret and Flora MacDougall, assisted by Colin Hay, continue the running of the distillery. Colin Hay takes over the licence when the sisters die.

1888 Colin Elliot Hay and Alexander Wilson Gray Buchanan renew their license.

1900 Colin Hay's son takes over the license.

1959 Ardbeg Distillery Ltd is founded.

1973 Hiram Walker and Distillers Company Ltd jointly purchase the distillery for £300,000 through Ardbeg Distillery Trust.

1977 Hiram Walker assumes single control of the distillery. Ardbeg closes its maltings.

1979 Kildalton, a less peated malt, is produced over a number of years.

1981 The distillery closes in March.

1987 Allied Lyons takes over Hiram Walker and thereby Ardbeg.

Mickey Heads retired after 13 years as distillery ma

History continued:

1989 Production is restored. All malt is taken from Port Ellen.

1996 The distillery closes in July.

1997 Glenmorangie plc buys the distillery for £7 million. Ardbeg 17 years old and Provenance are launched

1998 A new visitor centre opens.

2000 Ardbeg 10 years is introduced and the Ardbeg Committee is launched.

2001 Lord of the Isles 25 years and Ardbeg 1977 are launched.

2002 Ardbeg Committee Reserve and Ardbeg 1974 are launched.

2003 Uigeadail is launched.

2004 Very Young Ardbeg (6 years) and a limited edition of Ardbeg Kildalton are launched.

2005 Serendipity is launched.

2006 Ardbeg 1965 and Still Young are launched. Almost There (9 years old) and Airigh Nam Beist are released.

2007 Ardbeg Mor, a 10 year old in 4.5 litre bottles is released.

2008 The new 10 year old, Corryvreckan, Rennaissance, Blasda and Mor II are released.

2009 Supernova is released, the peatiest expression from Ardbeg ever.

2010 Rollercoaster and Supernova 2010 are released.

2011 Ardbeg Alligator is released.

2012 Ardbeg Day and Galileo are released.

2013 Ardbog is released.

2014 Auriverdes and Kildalton are released.

2015 Perpetuum and Supernova 2015 are released.

2016 Dark Cove and a Twenty Something 21 year old are released.

2017 An Oa, Kelpie and Twenty Something 23 year old are released.

2018 Grooves and Twenty Something 22 year old are released.

2019 Drum and Traigh Bhan are released.

2020 Blaaack, Wee Beastie and Traigh Bhan batch 2 are released.

Tasting notes Ardbeg 10 year old:

GS – Quite sweet on the nose, with soft peat, carbolic soap and Arbroath smokies. Burning peats and dried fruit, followed by sweeter notes of malt and a touch of liquorice in the mouth. Extremely long and smoky in the finish, with a fine balance of cereal sweetness and dry peat notes.

Wee Beastie   Blaaack   Traigh Bhan Batch 2

10 years old   Uigeadail   Corryvreckan

Ardmore

[ard•moor]

Owner:	**Region/district:**
Beam Suntory	Highland
Founded: **Status:**	**Capacity:**
1898 Active	5 550 000 litres

Address: Kennethmont, Aberdeenshire AB54 4NH

Website:	**Tel:**
ardmorewhisky.com	01464 831213

For many years Ardmore was a distillery which staunchly produced single malt whisky to become part of some of the best known blends in the business including Teachers.

The owners showed little or no interest in promoting Ardmore as a single malt. Today the main part of the production is still intended for blends but after Jim Beam Brands took over as owners, more and more single malt has been bottled. The increase in sales in the last six years is a staggering 275% and close to 700,000 bottles are sold yearly. In the same period of time sales of Teachers have gone down by almost 20% and the volume now lies around 20 million bottles.

The distillery is equipped with a 12 ton, cast iron, semi-lauter mash tun with a copper dome, 14 Douglas fir washbacks (four large and ten smaller ones), as well as four pairs of stills. At the moment, Ardmore is working a seven-day week with 23 mashes per week resulting in 4.5 million litres of alcohol. Traditionally, Ardmore has been the only distillery in the region consistently producing peated whisky with a phenol specification of the barley at 12-14 ppm. For blending purposes, they also produce the unpeated Ardlair (around 45% of the yearly output in 2020). The fermentation time for Ardlair is longer than for regular Ardmore – 70 hours compared to 55 hours.

Plans for a visitor centre have not yet come to fruition but when they do, the owners come well prepared. Long time distillery manager and today responsible for all five distilleries in the group, Alistair Longwell, has gathered and preserved old equipment over the years, production records and ledgers, ads and photos – all of which will serve as important components of a future visitor centre.

The core range of Ardmore single malt is made up of **Legacy**, a mix of 80% peated and 20% unpeated malt, and a **12 year old Port Finish**. **Tradition** and **Triple Wood** are eclusive to travel retail. A new release in 2017 was a **20 year old**, double matured in a mix of first- and second-fill bourbon casks and a second batch was launched in 2018 together with a **30 year old**.

History:

1898 Adam Teacher, son of William Teacher, starts the construction of Ardmore Distillery which eventually becomes William Teacher & Sons' first distillery. Adam Teacher passes away before it is completed.

1955 Stills are increased from two to four.

1974 Another four stills are added, increasing the total to eight.

1976 Allied Breweries takes over William Teacher & Sons and thereby also Ardmore. The own maltings (Saladin box) is terminated.

1999 A 12 year old is released to commemorate the distillery's 100th anniversary. A 21 year old is launched in a limited edition.

2002 Ardmore is one of the last distilleries to abandon direct heating (by coal) of the stills in favour of indirect heating through steam.

2005 Jim Beam Brands becomes new owner when it takes over some 20 spirits and wine brands from Allied Domecq for five billion dollars.

2007 Ardmore Traditional Cask is launched.

2008 A 25 and a 30 year old are launched.

2014 Beam and Suntory merge. Legacy is released.

2015 Traditional is re-launched as Tradition and a Triple Wood and a 12 year old port finish are released.

2017 A 20 year old, double matured is released.

2018 A 30 year old is released.

Tasting notes Ardmore Legacy:

GS – Vanilla, caramel and sweet peat smoke on the nose, while on the palate vanilla and honey contrast with quite dry peat notes, plus ginger and dark berries. The finish is medium to long, spicy, with persistently drying smoke.

Legacy

Whisky Legends

Ian MacMillan
47 years in the Whisky business

Glancing through Ian MacMillan´s career, it strikes me that this is a man who enjoys challenges. When he sees a distillery that is run down and forgotten by most, he recognizes that as an excellent opportunity to create something great. And Ian has clearly come across a number of distilleries that were in need of good care.

Ian has whisky distillers in his family but his path into the industry was more coincidental. During a term recess from college he began a summer job at Glengoyne distillery in 1973. It developed into a full time position as a mashman/stillman and he stayed on for three years. He moved to Glasgow to learn about grain distilling at Port Dundas and also spent a short spell at Caledonian. His next stop was London and five years of working with gin distillation before he returned to Scotland.

He managed Glenturret distillery for two years before he started a 25 year long career with Burn Stewart Distillers as distillery director and master blender. The same year he started, the company had bought the run-down Deanston distillery and lay on Ian's shoulders to revive it. Three years later they acquired Tobermory on Mull which also needed substantial refurbishing. A third distillery, Bunnahabhain, completed the trio in 2003 and now Ian focused on changing the distilling regime as well as the maturation of all three single malts.

He was determined to recreate the traditional character of the whiskies, a character that had been lost over the years, not least due to ceasing with chill filtration for the entire range. When he left Burn Stewart in 2015 he did exactly the same thing with the sadly neglected and closed Bladnoch in the Lowlands.

Today he is working as an independent consultant involved in several new distillery projects in Scotland, Ireland, Myanmar and Macau. He also consults on a number of qualitative assessment projects of new-make spirit and mature whiskies in Scotland and overseas.

I ask Ian if he sees any major differences in Scotch whisky production from when he started until today.

" There is a remarkable difference in the overall quality of malted barley compared to what I was using 40 years ago. The development of reliable, consistent yeast strains has also assisted in achieving undeviating quality of product. I have never been in agreement on the total automation of distillery operations, as I believe that this destroys the myth of Scotch being hand produced recognizing traditional methods. The availability today of all the excellent quality casks, of all styles, has in my view been the greatest contributor to the increased consistent quality of all whisky in general."

Ian describes himself as a traditionalist when it comes to whisky making and so it comes as no surprise that he thinks the Scotch Whisky Association is doing a good job protecting the identity of Scotch. As he himself puts it;

" For many years the recognition of the production practices utilized in the Scotch Whisky industry have been the blueprint for

many global distilleries. We have always been told that imitation is the greatest form of flattery !"

There is one aspect however where he would like to see a further relaxation of the rules and that concerns the types of wood that can be used for maturation.

" There is already historical references of other types of wood being used to manufacture casks for the maturation of Scotch Whisky."

One thing that has definitely changed over the years, says Ian, is the consumers´ approach to whisky. They have a greater desire to understand how the spirit is produced and they are much more knowledgable about the product and the different expressions available. And the greater acceptance of whiskies in cocktails has created a whole new audience.

I am curious to know if he thinks that whiskies produced 50-60 years ago were better than the ones we enjoy today.

" We must remember that whiskies distilled during the 1950`s and 60`s were all made in completely manually operated distilleries mostly utilizing direct fired stills. I have experienced some quite majestic complex drams created during these decades, but I have also sampled some not so memorable. The industry of today benefits from much increased quality control and raw ingredients distilling a more consistent distillate. Not necessarily better, just different."

In the last decade the combined production capacity for the Scottish malt distilleries has increased by more than 40%. Will there be a demand for that much whisky in the near future?

" During my time in the industry I have been unfortunate to have experienced a number of periods of over production which ultimately led to the closure of many distilleries. I believe that the industry of today is much more aligned to the supply and demand for Scotch globally and move forward with a cautious optimism, able to react to any indications of a downturn which would avoid the unhappy closure of further distilleries. "

With a huge number of new malt distilleries opening up all over the world, there is a discussion about Scotch being challenged and potentially standing the risk of losing market shares to these global producers. While Ian is sometimes impressed by the innovation and quality displayed by some of these whisky makers he really doesn't see it as a competition.

" For me comparing Scotch Whisky to a whisky produced in another country is like comparing an apple to a banana, they are both fruits but taste totally different."

Ian may describe himself as a traditionalist but as most veterans in the whisky business, he is very openminded about how people enjoy their dram. There is no wrong way of drinking it – there is only the way you drink it which is the right way.

"I remember being in South Africa and being convinced to drink whisky with milk. A good measure of blended whisky, ice, and topped up with full fat milk – it has to be full fat. It's really quite nice. It's a lovely breakfast drink."

Auchentoshan

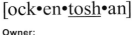

[ock•en•tosh•an]

Owner:
Beam Suntory

Region/district:
Lowlands

Founded: **Status:**
1823   Active (vc)

Capacity:
2 000 000 litres

Address: Dalmuir, Clydebank, Glasgow G81 4SJ

Website:
auchentoshan.com

Tel:
01389 878561

Since 2010, sales of Auchentoshan single malt have increased by an impressive 200% and it now sells around 1,7 million bottles yearly. But apparently the owners wont settle for this.

In November 2019 the entire Auchentoshan range received a new look that, according to the owners, was aimed at "connecting with a younger generation of drinker". The new identity is supposed to position Auchentoshan as an urban malt and this is well emphasized on the packaging showing the Glasgow city skyline. Auchentoshan is situated on the western outskirts of Glasgow right on the A82 and the proximity to the city is important to the distillery which attracts more than 20,000 people every year to their excellent visitor centre.

Auchentoshan is one of few Scottish distilleries practicing triple distillation and the only one that uses it for the entire production. Their middle cut during the spirit run starts at 82% and stops at 80%, which is long before any other distillery starts collecting.

The equipment consists of a semi-lauter mash tun with a 6.8 ton mash charge, four Oregon Pine washbacks and three made of stainless steel, all 38,000 litres, and with a fermentation time of 50 to 120 hours. There are three stills; wash still (17,500 litres), intermediate still (8,200 litres) and spirit still (11,500 litres). The 2020 plan is to mash 10 to 15 mashes per week and 1.5 million litres of alcohol.

The core range consists of **American Oak**, without age statement and matured in ex-bourbon barrels, **12 years, Three Woods, 18 years** and **21 years**. The duty free range is made up of **Blood Oak**, matured in a combination of bourbon and red wine casks and two new expressions launched in autumn 2019; **American Oak Reserve** matured in first fill bourbon and **Dark Oak** which is a vatting of whiskies matured in ex-bourbon, PX and oloroso casks. The previous expressions, Heartwood and Springwood, have recently been discontinued. A limited **29 years old 1988 Vintage** finished in PX casks appeared in early 2019 and this was followed later that year by a bottling, matured in ex-bourbon and **finished in sauvignon blanc barriques**.

History:

1817 First mention of the distillery Duntocher, which may be identical to Auchentoshan.

1823 The distillery is founded by John Bulloch.

1823 The distillery is sold to Alexander Filshie.

1878 C.H. Curtis & Co. takes over.

1903 The distillery is purchased by John Maclachlan.

1941 The distillery is severely damaged by a German bomb raid.

1960 Maclachlans Ltd is purchased by the brewery J. & R. Tennent Brewers.

1969 Auchentoshan is bought by Eadie Cairns Ltd who starts major modernizations.

1984 Stanley P. Morrison, eventually becoming Morrison Bowmore, becomes new owner.

1994 Suntory buys Morrison Bowmore.

2002 Auchentoshan Three Wood is launched.

2004 More than a £1 million is spent on a new, refurbished visitor centre. The oldest Auchentoshan ever, 42 years, is released.

2006 Auchentoshan 18 year old is released.

2007 A 50 year old, the oldest ever Auchentoshan to be bottled, was released.

2008 New packaging as well as new expressions - Classic, 18 year old and 1988.

2010 Two vintages, 1977 and 1998, are released.

2011 Two vintages, 1975 and 1999, and Valinch are released.

2012 Six new expressions are launched for the Duty Free market.

2013 Virgin Oak is released.

2014 American Oak replaces Classic.

2015 Blood Oak and Noble Oak are released for duty free.

2017 Bartender's Malt is launched.

2018 Bartender's Malt 2 and 1988 PX Cask are released.

2019 American Oak Reserve and Dark Oak are released for the travel retail market.

Tasting notes Auchentoshan 12 year old:
IR – Green and herbal on the nose with notes of pine needles, citrus and fresh oak. Quite dry on the palate with spicy notes coming through (nutmeg, clove and bay leaf) as well as vanilla and roasted nuts and sunflower seeds.

12 years old

Auchroisk

[ar•thrusk]

Owner:
Diageo

Region/district:
Speyside

Founded: | **Status:** | **Capacity:**
1974 | Active | 5 900 000 litres

Address: Mulben, Banffshire AB55 6XS

Website: | **Tel:**
malts.com | 01542 885000

When Auchroisk started production in 1974, it was a time of great optimism in the Scotch whisky industry. For three decades after the Second World War, Scotch had become the favourite spirit in Europe and, not least, America.

From 1970-75, seven new distilleries were built and another 15 were sizably expanded. Historically, there had been two similar 5-year periods. One was in 1895-1900 when close to 20 new distilleries opened, but the happy days ended with the Pattison crash. A much larger expansion happened between 1823 and 1828 when no less than 203 new distilleries were registered. The amazing figure is easily explained though. The Excise Act of 1823 called for whisky distilleries to obtain a license and the vast majority of these more than 200 distilleries, which had previously been working as illicit stills, were now entered into the rolls. Of the 203, only 14 are still working today, nearly 200 years later.

The equipment consists of a 12 ton stainless steel semi-lauter mash tun, eight stainless steel washbacks with a fermentation time of 53 hours and four pairs of stills. The washbacks are large (holding 50,000 litres each) and one washback can serve all four wash stills which hold 12,700 litres each. Auchroisk is working 24/7 with 24 mashes per week, producing 5.8 million litres of alcohol per year, currently with a nutty/malty character. The character has changed over the years, which is not unusual for distilleries that produce malt mainly for blends, and not so long ago the style was green/grassy. For a number of years Auchroisk was also the backup distillery for Gordon´s gin, should any problems occur at the Cameronbridge distillery in Fife.

The first, widely available release of Auchroisk single malt was in 1986 under the name Singleton. That particular name is now reserved for another three distilleries in the Diageo range – Dufftown, Glendullan and Glen Ord. In 2001, it was replaced by a **10 year old** in the Flora & Fauna range. The most recent limited bottling was released in October 2016 – a **25 year old** from 1990.

History:

1972 Building of the distillery commences by Justerini & Brooks (which, together with W. A. Gilbey, make up the group IDV) in order to produce blending whisky. In February the same year IDV is purchased by the brewery Watney Mann which, in July, merges into Grand Metropolitan.

1974 The distillery is completed and, despite the intention of producing malt for blending, the first year's production is sold 12 years later as single malt thanks to the high quality.

1986 The first whisky is marketed under the name Singleton.

1997 Grand Metropolitan and Guinness merge into the conglomerate Diageo. Simultaneously, the subsidiaries United Distillers (to Guinness) and International Distillers & Vintners (to Grand Metropolitan) form the new company United Distillers & Vintners (UDV).

2001 The name Singleton is abandoned and the whisky is now marketed under the name of Auchroisk in the Flora & Fauna series.

2003 Apart from the 10 year old in the Flora & Fauna series, a 28 year old from 1974, the distillery's first year, is launched in the Rare Malt series.

2010 A Manager´s Choice single cask and a limited 20 year old are released.

2012 A 30 year old from 1982 is released.

2016 A 25 year old from 1990 is released.

10 years old

Tasting notes Auchroisk 10 year old:

GS – Malt and spice on the light nose, with developing nuts and floral notes. Quite voluptuous on the palate, with fresh fruit and milk chocolate. Raisins in the finish.

Aultmore

[ault•moor]

Owner:
John Dewar & Sons
(Bacardi)

Region/district:
Speyside

Founded: **Status:** **Capacity:**
1896 Active 3 200 000 litres

Address: Keith, Banffshire AB55 6QY

Website: **Tel:**
aultmore.com 01542 881800

Although built in 1896, the Aultmore we see today is the result of an unprecedented refurbishing and rebuilding of whisky distilleries in Scotland during the 1960s and 1970s.

This was a time when the Scotch whisky industry was in the midst of its second golden age which had started after the second world war. At least twelve new distilleries were built and a huge number of older distilleries were in need of reconstruction. The biggest producer, DCL, owned 45 distilleries (including Aultmore) and all of them were rebuilt or refurbished during the 1960s and 1970s. Starring in this scheme was Leslie Darge, chief architect in an in-house engineering team. He joined the company in 1953 and stayed on for 28 years. One of the main trends during these decades was the rebuild of still houses and the glass curtains that could be rolled up to ease the replacement of large pieces of equipment became a distinguishing feature. They were also perfect for dissipating heat from the very hot still rooms. And of course, for whisky enthusiasts it gave the opportunity to admire the stills from outside,

The distillery is equipped with a 10 ton Steinecker full lauter mash tun, six washbacks made of larch with a minimum fermentation time of 56 hours and two pairs of stills. Since 2008 production has been running seven-days a week, which for 2020 means 16 mashes per week and just over 3 million litres of alcohol.

The core range includes a **12 year old** and an **18 year old**. The 25 year old, released a few years back, has now been discontinued. For the duty free market there is a **21 year old** and this has also been released for the domestic US market. In 2018, Dewars launched a collection of rare single malts, The Exceptional Cask Series, destined to be sold in the duty free market. Part of that range were three bottlings released at Heathrow in spring 2019; all three were **22 years old** with the final eleven years having been extra matured in casks that had held **Super Tuscan wine**, **Châteauneuf-du-Pape** and **Moscatel** wine respectively. Later in the year a **17 year old** with a finish in several types of casks, including palo cortado, was released.

History:

1896 Alexander Edward, owner of Benrinnes and co-founder of Craigellachie Distillery, builds Aultmore.

1897 Production starts.

1898 Production is doubled; the company Oban & Aultmore Glenlivet Distilleries Ltd manages Aultmore.

1923 Alexander Edward sells Aultmore for £20,000 to John Dewar & Sons.

1925 Dewar's becomes part of Distillers Company Limited (DCL).

1930 The administration is transferred to Scottish Malt Distillers (SMD).

1971 The stills are increased from two to four.

1991 United Distillers launches a 12-year old Aultmore in the Flora & Fauna series.

1996 A 21 year old cask strength is marketed as a Rare Malt.

1998 Diageo sells Dewar's and Bombay Gin to Bacardi for £1,150 million.

2004 A new official 12 year old bottling is launched

2014 Three new expressions are released – 12, 25 and 21 year old for duty free.

2015 An 18 year old is released.

2019 Three 22 year old single casks with different second maturations are released for duty free.

12 years old

Aultmore 12 years old:

GS – A nose of peaches and lemonade, freshly-mown grass, linseed and milky coffee. Very fruity on the palate, mildly herbal, with toffee and light spices. The finish is medium in length, with lingering spices, fudge, and finally more milky coffee.

Balblair

[bal•blair]

Owner:
Inver House Distillers
(Thai Beverages plc)

Region/district:
Northern Highlands

Founded: 1790

Status: Active (vc)

Capacity: 1 800 000 litres

Address: Edderton, Tain, Ross-shire IV19 1LB

Website: balblair.com

Tel: 01862 821273

During the past two decades the owners of Balblair have tested a number of different branding strategies for their single malt. It started in 2000 with the new core range opening with a no age statement expression called Elements.

The name referred to one of the four elements, air and on the bottle it said "Distilled where the air is said to be the purest in Scotland". A 10 and a 16 year old were also in the range as well as a number of older whiskies aged 33 years or more. In 2007 a bold step was taken when the entire range of ten expressions was transformed into three vintages – a step that only Glenrothes had taken previously. The presentation, both bottle and label, was also changed in a major way to stand out in the crowd. Admittedly, the new range was appreciated by many Balblair fans but it became a bit of a struggle to reach a wider audience. The owners finally decided in 2019 to change the direction once again. A classic range of four bottlings with age statements was launched but retaining the highly original bottle.

The distillery is equipped with a stainless steel, 4.4 ton semi lauter mash tun, six Oregon pine washbacks and one pair of stills. The distillery recently went from a five-day week to a seven-day week and the plan for 2020 is to make 19 mashes per week, which means a target of 1.5 million litres for the full year. It also entails that fermentation time is now 60 hours instead of mixing short (60 hours) and long (90 hours) fermentations. A very elegant and contemporary visitor centre/shop was opened in late 2011.

The new core range from Balblair consists of **12 year old** matured in ex-bourbon and double-fired American oak, the **15 year old** matured in ex-bourbon casks followed by time in Spanish oak sherry butts, the **18 year old** with the same maturation as the previous and the **25 year old** which starts in ex-bourbon casks and is finished in ex-oloroso sherry casks. All the new expressions are also available in travel retail with the exception of the 18 year old, which has been replaced by a **17 year old** finished in first fill sherry butts in the duty free line-up.

12 years old

History:

1790 The distillery is founded by James McKeddy.

1790 John Ross takes over.

1836 John Ross dies and his son Andrew Ross takes over with the help of his sons.

1872 The distillery is moved to the present location.

1873 Andrew Ross dies and his son James takes over.

1894 Alexander Cowan takes over and rebuilds the distillery

1911 Cowan is forced to cease payments and the distillery closes.

1941 The distillery is put up for sale.

1948 Robert Cumming buys Balblair for £48,000.

1949 Production restarts.

1970 Cumming sells Balblair to Hiram Walker.

1988 Allied Distillers becomes the new owner through the merger between Hiram Walker and Allied Vintners.

1996 The distillery is sold to Inver House Distillers.

2000 Balblair Elements and the first version of Balblair 33 years are launched.

2001 Thai company Pacific Spirits (part of the Great Oriole Group) takes over Inver House.

2004 Balblair 38 years is launched.

2005 12 year old Peaty Cask, 1979 (26 years) and 1970 (35 years) are launched.

2006 International Beverage Holdings acquires Pacific Spirits UK.

2007 Three new vintages replace the former range.

2008 Vintage 1975 and 1965 are released.

2009 Vintage 1991 and 1990 are released.

2011 Vintage 1995 and 1993 are released.

2012 Vintage 1975, 2001 and 2002 are released. A visitor centre is opened.

2013 Vintage 1983, 1990 and 2003 are released.

2014 Vintage 1999 and 2004 are released for duty free.

2016 Vintage 2005 is released.

2019 A new range with age statements is launched.

Tasting notes Balblair 12 year old:

IR – Sugary and malty on the nose with herbal and earthy notes coming through. Rich, creamy and sweet on the palate, grilled corn cobs, caramel, honey and some bitter, oaky notes.

Balmenach

[bal•men•ack]

Owner:
Inver House Distillers
(Thai Beverages plc)

Region/district:
Speyside

Founded: 1824
Status: Active
Capacity: 2 800 000 litres

Address: Cromdale, Moray PH26 3PF

Website:
inverhouse.com

Tel:
01479 872569

Balmenach lies on the outskirts of Speyside at the foot of the Cromdale Hills. Three kilometres to the west is Grantown-on-Spey and the nearest distillery, ten kilometres to the southeast, is Tomintoul.

In terms of distillery bagging, this means that Balmenach is not a distillery you just stumble upon travelling the Speyside area. The same goes for the whisky. With no official release you have to rely on independent bottlers to be able to try the single malt. There is a good reason however for the owners´ reluctance to brand it: Balmenach represents a dying breed of malt that can make wonders with any blend. They produce old school whisky in the same way as Benrinnes and Mortlach. A long fermentation, a quick distillation in small stills and condensing the spirit vapours using worm tubs results in a meaty and heavy newmake which after a long maturation is a blessing to a blended Scotch.

Balmenach is equipped with an eight ton stainless steel semi-lauter mash tun with an old copper canopy. There are six washbacks made of Douglas Fir and with a 5-day production there are 7 short fermentations (56 hours) and 7 long (over 90 hours). Finally there are three pairs of stills connected to worm tubs. The production plan for 2020 is to do 14 mashes per week which translates to 1.9 million litres of alcohol. A new biogas plant was installed at Balmenach last year to treat whisky co-products such as pot ale and spent lees. About 130 m³ of these will be processed by the plant daily and through anaerobic digestion it will be turned into 2,000 m³ of biogas.

For the past decade, Caorunn gin has also been part of the production at Balmenach. Purchased neutral spirit is pumped through a vaporizer and then to a copper berry chamber where the vapours travel upwards passing five trays with different kinds of botanicals.

There used to be a 12 year old from the previous owners but the last time an official bottling of Balmenach turned up was in 2002 when a 25 year old was launched to celebrate the Queen´s Golden Jubilee. Aberko though, has been working with the distillery for a long time and has released Balmenach under the name Deerstalker. The current expression is a 12 year old.

History:

1824 The distillery is licensed to James MacGregor who operated a small farm distillery by the name of Balminoch.

1897 Balmenach Glenlivet Distillery Company is founded.

1922 The MacGregor family sells to a consortium consisting of MacDonald Green, Peter Dawson and James Watson.

1925 The consortium becomes part of Distillers Company Limited (DCL).

1930 Production is transferred to Scottish Malt Distillers (SMD).

1962 The number of stills is increased to six.

1964 Floor maltings replaced with Saladin box.

1992 The first official bottling is a 12 year old.

1993 The distillery is mothballed in May.

1997 Inver House Distillers buys Balmenach from United Distillers.

1998 Production recommences.

2001 Thai company Pacific Spirits takes over Inver House at the price of £56 million. The new owner launches a 27 and a 28 year old.

2002 To commemorate the Queen's Golden Jubilee a 25-year old Balmenach is launched.

2006 International Beverage Holdings acquires Pacific Spirits UK.

2009 Gin production commences.

Tasting notes Deerstalker 12 years old:

IR – The nose is sweet and fruity, with green garden notes and sweet liquorice coming through. Sweet, fruity barley on the palate with notes of honey, custard, apricots, peaches and slightly bitter notes from the oak.

Deerstalker 12 years old

Balvenie

[bal•ven•ee]

Owner: **Region/district:**
William Grant & Sons   Speyside

Founded: **Status:**   **Capacity:**
1892   Active (vc)   7 000 000 litres

Address: Dufftown, Keith, Banffshire AB55 4DH

Website: **Tel:**
thebalvenie.com   01340 820373

Like few other distilleries, Balvenie has recently made the connection with its history and the past twenty years of innovation in malting, distillation and maturation clearer.

The result has been brought forward by way of a new range of bottlings called The Balvenie Stories. The various backgrounds to the whiskies are excellently presented on the distillery website where global brand ambassador Gemma Paterson interacts with many of the people involved in the whiskies over the years

The distillery is equipped with an 11.8 ton full lauter mash tun, nine wooden and five stainless steel washbacks with a fermentation time of 68 hours, five wash stills and six spirit stills. For 2020, the production plan is 30 mashes per week and 7 million litres of alcohol. The main part is unpeated but each year one week of production comes from peated barley (20-40 ppm).

The core range consists of **Doublewood 12 years, Doublewood 17 years, Caribbean Cask 14 years, Single Barrel 12 years First Fill, Single Barrel 15 years Sherry Cask, Portwood 21 years, 30 years** and **40 years old**. The Single Barrel 25 years Traditional Oak will be replaced by a **21 year old** version in late 2020. Recent limited releases include batch 7 of **Tun 1509**, batch 7 of the **Tun 1858**, chapter five of **The Balvenie DCS Compendium** and a new **50 year old**. A new, limited range named The Balvenie Stories was launched in May 2019 with the **12 year old The Sweet Toast of American Oak**, the **14 year old A Week of Peat** and a **26 year old** called **A Day of Dark Barley**. A fourth expression, **The Edge of Burnhead Wood 19 years old**, was added in spring 2020, made from barley grown on the estate and then malted using heather from Burnhead Wood to add a different flavour. The current Duty Free range with the **Triple Cask series**, a 21 year old Madeira Cask and the **14 year old Peated Triple Cask** will be replaced in late 2020 or beginning of 2021 by three new Stories; **The Creation of a Classic, The Week of Peat 17 year old** and **The Second Rose 21 year old**. Later on, a Madeira 15 year old and a PX 18 year old will also be added.

History:

1892 William Grant rebuilds Balvenie New House to Balvenie Distillery.

1893 The first distillation takes place in May.

1957 The two stills are increased by another two.

1965 Two new stills are installed.

1971 Another two stills are installed and eight stills are now running.

1973 The first official bottling appears.

1982 Founder's Reserve is launched.

1996 Two vintage bottlings and a Port wood finish are launched.

2001 The Balvenie Islay Cask is released.

2002 A 50 year old is released.

2004 The Balvenie Thirty is released.

2005 A 14 year old rum finish is released.

2006 The Balvenie New Wood 17 years old, Roasted Malt 14 years old and Portwood 1993 are released.

2007 Vintage Cask 1974 and Sherry Oak 17 years old are released.

2008 Signature, Vintage 1976, Balvenie Rose and Rum Cask 17 year old are released.

2009 Vintage 1978, 17 year old Madeira finish, 14 year old rum finish and Golden Cask 14 years old are released.

2010 A 40 year old, Peated Cask and Carribean Cask are released.

2011 Second batch of Tun 1401 is released.

2012 A 50 year old and Doublewood 17 years old are released.

2013 Triple Cask 12, 16 and 25 years are launched for duty free.

2014 Single Barrel 15 and 25 years, Tun 1509 and two new 50 year olds are launched.

2015 The Balvenie DCS Compendium is launched.

2016 A 21 year old madeira finish is released.

2017 The Balvenie Peat Week 2002 and Peated Triple Cask are released.

2018 A limited 25 year old is released.

2019 The Balvenie Stories is launched.

2020 A 21 year old is released together with a fourth instalment in the Balvenie Stories series.

Doublewood 12 years old

Tasting notes Balvenie Doublewood 12 years:

GS – Nuts and spicy malt on the nose, full-bodied, with soft fruit, vanilla, sherry and a hint of peat. Dry and spicy in a luxurious, lengthy finish.

Ben Nevis

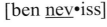

[ben nev•iss]

Owner:
Ben Nevis Distillery Ltd
(Nikka, Asahi Breweries)

Region/district:
Western Highlands

Founded: **Status:** **Capacity:**
1825 Active (vc) 2 000 000 litres

Address: Lochy Bridge, Fort William PH33 6TJ

Website: **Tel:**
bennevisdistillery.com 01397 702476

A true whisky icon was retired in autumn 2019 after 55 years in the industry. Colin Ross started his career in 1965 as a trainee manager with Chivas Brothers.

Six years later he was appointed head brewer at Tormore where he stayed for 12 years. In 1983 he became distillery manager at Ben Nevis, and except for a two-year stint at Laphroaig, he held that position until 2019. Over the years, he tirelessly promoted Ben Nevis single malt at whisky shows and tastings and became a well-known face to many malt enthusiasts. He was also inducted into the Whisky Hall of Fame. Colin Ross was succeeded by Soichiro Harada as Managing Director.

One of Ben Nevis' more eccentric owners was Joseph Hobbs who installed a Coffey still so the distillery could produce both malt and grain spirit. He also conducted a most unusual experiment with concrete washbacks. Apart from releasing small amounts of single malt, the owners since 1989, Nikka, use the distillery as a supplier of newmake for their hugely popular blend Black Nikka. Up to 75% of the production is shipped to Japan every year. The current whisky legislation in Japan allows foreign whisky in a product that still can be labelled Japanese whisky.

Ben Nevis is equipped with a ten ton full lauter mash tun made of stainless steel, six stainless steel washbacks and two made of Oregon pine with a 48 hour fermentation as well as two pairs of stills. The plan for 2020 is to make 13 mashes in a five-day week and 2 million litres of alcohol. Around 50,000 litres of this will be heavily peated with a phenol specification of 40ppm in the barley.

The range is currently reviewed by the owners and new packaging is due end of 2020. The core range consists of **MacDonald's Ben Nevis 10 year old** and the peated **MacDonald's Traditional Ben Nevis**. The latter is an attempt to replicate the style of Ben Nevis single malt from the 1880s. In 2018, a limited version of the 10 year old was released under the name **Ben Nevis 10 years old Batch No. 1** but this has now been discontinued. Very old versions of Ben Nevis have occurred and three vintages from **1966**, **1967** and **1968** were released in Taiwan in 2019.

History:

1825 The distillery is founded by 'Long' John McDonald.
1856 Long John dies and his son Donald P. McDonald takes over.
1878 Demand is so great that another distillery, Nevis Distillery, is built nearby.
1908 Both distilleries merge into one.
1941 D. P. McDonald & Sons sells the distillery to Ben Nevis Distillery Ltd headed by the Canadian millionaire Joseph W. Hobbs.
1955 Hobbs installs a Coffey still which makes it possible to produce both grain and malt whisky.
1964 Joseph Hobbs dies.
1978 Production is stopped.
1981 Joseph Hobbs Jr sells the distillery back to Long John Distillers and Whitbread.
1984 After restoration and reconstruction totalling £2 million, Ben Nevis opens up again.
1986 The distillery closes again.
1989 Whitbread sells the distillery to Nikka Whisky Distilling Company Ltd.
1990 The distillery opens up again.
1991 A visitor centre is inaugurated.
1996 Ben Nevis 10 years old is launched.
2006 A 13 year old port finish is released.
2010 A 25 year old is released.
2011 McDonald's Traditional Ben Nevis is released.
2014 Forgotten Bottlings are introduced.
2015 A 40 year old "Blended at Birth" single blend is released.
2018 Ben Nevis 10 years old Batch No. 1 is released.

Tasting notes Ben Nevis 10 years old:

GS – The nose is initially quite green, with developing nutty, orange notes. Coffee, brittle toffee and peat are present on the slightly oily palate, along with chewy oak, which persists to the finish, together with more coffee and a hint of dark chocolate.

10 years old

Benriach

[ben•ree•ack]

Owner:
BenRiach Distillery Company
(Brown Forman)

Region/district:
Speyside

Founded: 1897
Status: Active (vc)
Capacity: 2 800 000 litres

Address: Longmorn, Elgin, Morayshire IV30 8SJ

Website: benriachdistillery.com
Tel: 01343 862888

The owners of BenRiach distillery describes it as both unconventional and progressive. These are not just marketing buzzwords – the huge range includes unusually, at least for Speyside, heavily peated whiskies and also triple-distilled spirit.

Add to that wood finishes in a variety of unusual cask types. But there is also a very traditional side to BenRiach. They are one of only sixteen distilleries still using a traditional mash tun with rakes instead of the more common lauter tuns. And in 2013 they resurrected their floor malting – a time-consuming and cost-inefficient method abandoned by the vast majority of distilleries.

The distillery is equipped with a 5.8 ton traditional cast iron mash tun with a stainless steel shell, eight washbacks made of stainless steel with short (55 hours) and long fermentations (+100 hours) and two pairs of stills. Recent production plans have been 1.8 million litres of pure alcohol which includes peated spirit at 35ppm as well as 15,000 litres of triple-distilled spirit. In 2013, the owners revamped the malting floor but it is only used sporadically, typically once or twice a year.

The range of BenRiach is currently being revamped with new bottlings being launched sometime during autumn 2020. The new range will include The Original Ten, The Smoky Ten, The Twelve, The Smoky Twelve, The Twenty One, The Twenty Five and The Thirty. A limited expression called Smoke Season will also be released.

The current core range, due to be replaced, consists of **Heart of Speyside, Cask Strength, 10, 12, 21, 25** and **30 year old**. Peated varieties include **Birnie Moss, Peated Cask Strength, Curiositas 10 year old, Temporis 21 year old** and **Authenticus 30 year old**. Currently, there are three different wood finishes, all of them 22 years old – **Dark Rum, Dunder** and the peated **Albariza**. Exclusive to the travel retail segment are **10 year old Triple-distilled** as well as duty-free versions of **Classic Quarter Cask** and **Peated Quarter Cask**. Finally, batch 16 of the **Cask Bottlings** (single casks) was launched in July 2019.

History:

1897 John Duff & Co founds the distillery.

1900 The distillery is closed.

1965 The distillery is reopened by the new owner, The Glenlivet Distillers Ltd.

1972 Production of peated Benriach starts.

1978 Seagram Distillers takes over.

1985 The number of stills is increased to four.

1998 The maltings is decommissioned.

2002 The distillery is mothballed in October.

2004 Intra Trading, buys Benriach together with the former Director at Burn Stewart, Billy Walker.

2004 Standard, Curiositas and 12, 16 and 20 year olds are released.

2005 Four different vintages are released.

2006 Sixteen new releases, i.a. a 25 year old, a 30 year old and 8 different vintages.

2007 A 40 year old and three new heavily peated expressions are released.

2008 New expressions include a peated Madeira finish, a 15 year old Sauternes finish and nine single casks.

2009 Two wood finishes (Moscatel and Gaja Barolo) and nine single casks are released.

2010 Triple distilled Horizons and heavily peated Solstice are released.

2011 A 45 year old and 12 vintages are released.

2012 Septendecim 17 years is released.

2013 Vestige 46 years is released. The maltings are working again.

2015 Dunder, Albariza, Latada and a 10 year old are released.

2016 Brown Forman buys the company for £285m. BenRiach cask strength and Peated Quarter Cask are launched.

2017 10 year old Triple Distilled and Peated Cask Strength are released.

2018 A 12 and a 21 year old as well as Temporis 21 year old and Authenticus 30 year old are released.

2019 Batch 16 of the Cask Bottlings is released.

2020 The entire core range is relaunched with seven new expressions.

Tasting notes BenRiach 10 year old:

GS – Earthy and nutty on the early nose, with apples, ginger and vanilla. Smooth and rounded on the palate, with oranges, apricots, mild spice and hazelnuts. The finish is medium in length, nutty and spicy.

10 years old

Benrinnes

[ben rin•ess]

Owner: Diageo   **Region/district:** Speyside

Founded: 1826   **Status:** Active   **Capacity:** 3 500 000 litres

Address: Aberlour, Banffshire AB38 9NN

Website: malts.com   **Tel:** 01340 872600

Speyside is one of the official whisky regions recognized by the SWA and you can still hear distillers and whisky-drinkers referring to whiskies from this area as typical Speysiders in terms of flavour.

If there ever was an indistinguishable character to these malts, things have definitely changed. Today the whiskies from the 50 plus distilleries situated in Speyside come in all shapes and forms. One small camp of whiskies could best be described as heavy and meaty and Benrinnes together with Mortlach and Dailuaine are excellent representatives of this style. There are different ways of achieving this character and in Benrinnes' case it starts with a quick distillation where the spirit is forced through the stills at a fast rate. This will give it less time to get in touch with the copper in the stills and creates a sulphury newmake. At the same time the middle cut is allowed to go as low as 58% to catch some of the heavier flavour compounds. The next step, cooling the vapours, takes place in worm tubs which per definition creates a more robust spirit compared to using shell and tube condensers.

There are no visible remains of the original Benrinnes distillery dating back to 1826. The current distillery is in fact a creation from the 1950s. The equipment consists of an 8.5 ton semi-lauter mash tun, eight washbacks made of Oregon pine with a fermentation time ranging from 65 to 100 hours. There are also two wash stills and four spirit stills. From 1966 until 2009, these were run three and three with a partial triple distillation. This system has now been abandoned and one wash still now serves two spirit stills. In the last couple of years, Benrinnes has been alternating between a seven-day production week and a five-day with either 21 or 15 mashes per week.

Most of the production goes into blended whiskies – J&B, Johnnie Walker and Crawford's 3 Star – and there is currently only one official single malt, the **Flora & Fauna 15 year old**. In 2010 a **Manager's Choice** from 1996 was released and in autumn 2014 it was time for a **21 year old Special Release** bottled at 57%.

History:

1826 Lyne of Ruthrie distillery is built at Whitehouse Farm by Peter McKenzie.

1829 A flood destroys the distillery and a new distillery is constructed by John Innes a few kilometres from the first one.

1834 John Innes files for bankruptcy and William Smith & Co takes over.

1864 William Smith & Co goes bankrupt and David Edward becomes the new owner.

1896 Benrinnes is ravaged by fire which prompts major refurbishment. Alexander Edward takes over.

1922 John Dewar & Sons takes over ownership.

1925 John Dewar & Sons becomes part of Distillers Company Limited (DCL).

1956 The distillery is completely rebuilt.

1964 Floor maltings is replaced by a Saladin box.

1966 The number of stills doubles to six.

1984 The Saladin box is taken out of service and the malt is purchased centrally.

1991 The first official bottling from Benrinnes is a 15 year old in the Flora & Fauna series.

1996 United Distillers releases a 21 year old cask strength in their Rare Malts series.

2009 A 23 year old is launched as a part of this year´s Special Releases.

2010 A Manager´s Choice 1996 is released.

2014 A limited 21 year old is released.

15 years old

Tasting notes Benrinnes 15 years old:

GS – A brief flash of caramel shortcake on the initial nose, soon becoming more peppery and leathery, with some sherry. Ultimately savoury and burnt rubber notes. Big-bodied, viscous, with gravy, dark chocolate and more pepper. A medium-length finish features mild smoke and lively spices.

Benromach

[ben•ro•mack]

Owner:
Gordon & MacPhail

Region/district:
Speyside

Founded: 1898

Status: Active (vc)

Capacity: 700 000 litres

Address: Invererne Road, Forres, Morayshire IV36 3EB

Website: benromach.com

Tel: 01309 675968

There is remarkably little information about the history of Benromach on the official website, despite the distillery's foundation as long back as over 120 years ago. The timeline more or less starts in 1993.

That was the year when Gordon & MacPhail, the current owner, bought the distillery and, in all honesty, that was when Benromach received the attention it deserved. A combination of several owners, bankruptcies and extended periods of silence characterized the first 40 years of the distillery's operation. When Joseph Hobbs, a native Scot who had returned to Scotland from Canada, took over the distillery it was through a company called Associated Scottish Distilleries which was a subsidiary of Train & McIntyre which in its turn was owned by National Distillers of America. In 1953 it vanished into the giant conglomerate called DCL and not until 1998, following five years of careful refurbishing, was the distillery re-opened by Gordon & MacPhail. Since then Benromach single malt has finally become a brand respected by the whisky aficionados.

The distillery is equipped with a 1.5 ton semi-lauter mash tun with a copper dome and 13 washbacks made of larch with a fermentation time of 67-115 hours. There is also one pair of stills with the condensers outside. The barley is predominantly peated to a phenol specification of 12ppm. The cut points for the middle cut are 72%-60% but they are lower when producing heavily peated spirit. The 2020 plan entails 14 mashes per week for 44 weeks and 400,000 litres of pure alcohol including 11,000 litres of peated spirit.

The core range consists of the re-launched **10 and 15 year old** and **Cask Strength Vintage 2009**. Recent limited releases include a **1978 single cask**, a **2009 Triple Distilled** and a **20th Anniversary** bottling. In spring 2019, two vintage expressions (**1972 and 1977**) were released as part of the Heritage Collection. There are also special editions; **Organic 2012** and **Peat Smoke 2009**. A special version of the latter is **Peat Smoke Sherry Cask Matured** which was released in 2019. Recent wood finishes include **Chateau Cissac 2010** and **Sassicaia 2011**. In October 2019, a **50 year old**, distilled in 1969 was released.

History:

1898 Benromach Distillery Company starts the distillery.

1911 Harvey McNair & Co buys the distillery.

1919 John Joseph Calder buys Benromach and sells it to Benromach Distillery Ltd.

1931 The distillery is mothballed.

1937 The distillery reopens.

1938 Joseph Hobbs buys Benromach and sells it on to National Distillers of America (NDA).

1953 NDA sells Benromach to Distillers Company Ltd.

1966 The distillery is refurbished.

1968 Floor maltings is abolished.

1983 Benromach is mothballed.

1993 Gordon & McPhail buys Benromach.

1998 The distillery is once again in operation.

1999 A visitor centre is opened.

2004 The first bottle distilled by the new owner is 'Benromach Traditional'.

2005 A Port Wood finish, a Vintage 1968 and Classic 55 years ar released.

2006 Benromach Organic is released.

2007 Peat Smoke, the first heavily peated whisky from the distillery, is released.

2008 Benromach Origins Golden Promise is released.

2009 Benromach 10 years old is released.

2011 New edition of Peatsmoke, a 2001 Hermitage finish and a 30 year old are released.

2014 Three new bottlings are launched; a 5 year old, 100 Proof and Traveller's Edition.

2015 A 15 year old and two wood finishes (Hermitage and Sassicaia) are released.

2016 A 35 year old and 1974 single cask are released.

2017 A 1976 single cask and a 2009 Triple Distilled are released.

2018 A 20th Anniversary bottling and a Sassicaia 2010 are released.

2019 Peat Smoke Sherry Cask Matured and a 50 year old are released.

2020 New versions of Cissac and Sassicaia are released.

Tasting notes Benromach 10 year old:

GS – A nose that is initially quite smoky, with wet grass, butter, ginger and brittle toffee. Mouth-coating, spicy, malty and nutty on the palate, with developing citrus fruits, raisins and soft wood smoke. The finish is warming, with lingering barbecue notes.

10 years old

Bladnoch

[blad•nock]

Owner:
David Prior

Region/district:
Lowlands

Founded: 1817

Status: Active (vc)

Capacity: 1 500 000 litres

Address: Bladnoch, Wigtown, Wigtonshire DG8 9AB

Website:
bladnoch.com

Tel:
01988 402605

When David Prior took over Bladnoch in 2015 the run-down distillery had to be completely refurbished. In fact, the only piece of equipment that could be used was the mill.

But in Prior's plans was also a completely new and stylish visitor centre. Whisky production started already in summer 2017 but it wasn't until July 2019 that visitors were welcomed and on the 11th September that year the visitor centre was officially opened by Prince Charles.

The distillery is equipped with a five ton stainless steel semi-lauter mash tun and six Douglas fir washbacks. Fermentations used to be a combination of short (76 hours) and long (100 hours) ones, but due to increased production it is now at 60-80 hours. There is also two pairs of stills. The original plan for 2020 is to produce 1,2 million litres of pure alcohol. A small part of heavily peated production (60-80ppm) started already in 2017 and will continue in 2020 with 100,000 litres.

When the new owner took over, the deal included several thousand casks of whisky dating back to the 1980s. Whisky veteran Ian MacMillan, who used to work for Burn Stewart, was hired not only to oversee the reconstruction of the distillery but also to sample every cask. Where needed, he re-filled whiskies from inferior casks into quality wood and in November 2016, the first new whiskies were released. MacMillan left in 2018 and Nick Savage, who was the Macallan master distiller for three years, is responsible for the blending today. At the same time Neil Bulloch took over as distillery manager.

The core range today consists of **10, 11** and **17 year old**. There are also **Samsara** with no age statement and matured in ex-bourbon and casks that had contained Californian red wine, the 15 year old **Adela** matured in ex-oloroso casks and three versions of **Talia** (25, 26 and 27 year old) with different finishes. Limited releases occcur frequently, for example a **14 year old** in summer 2020.

History:

1817 Founded by Thomas and John McClelland.

1878 John McClelland's son Charlie reconstructs and refurbishes the distillery.

1905 Production stops.

1911 Dunville & Co. buys T. & A. McClelland Ltd. Production is intermittent until 1936.

1937 Dunville & Co. is liquidated and Bladnoch is wound up. Ross & Coulter from Glasgow buys the distillery after the war. The equipment is dismantled and shipped to Sweden.

1956 A. B. Grant (Bladnoch Distillery Ltd.) takes over and restarts production with four new stills.

1964 McGown and Cameron becomes new owners.

1973 Inver House Distillers buys Bladnoch.

1983 Arthur Bell and Sons take over.

1985 Guiness Group buys Arthur Bell & Sons which, from 1989, are included in United Distillers.

1988 A visitor centre is built.

1993 United Distillers mothballs Bladnoch in June.

1994 Raymond Armstrong buys Bladnoch in October.

2000 Production commences in December.

2003 The first bottles from Armstrong are launched, a 15 year old cask strength from UD casks.

2008 First release of whisky produced after the takeover in 2000 - three 6 year olds.

2009 An 8 year old of own production and a 19 year old are released.

2014 The distillery is liquidated.

2015 The distillery is bought by David Prior.

2016 Samsara, Adela and Talia are released.

2017 Production starts again and a Vintage 1988 is released.

2018 A 10 year old is released.

2019 A visitor centre is opened.

2020 Limited bottlings, including a 14 year old, are released.

10 years old

Tasting notes Bladnoch 10 year old:

IR – Fresh and grassy on the nose with sweet notes of honey and lilac, citrus, vanilla and a hint of cardamom. Rich and herbal on the palate with eucalyptus, ginger, pineapple, liquorice and milk chocolate coming through. Lovely mouthfeel.

Blair Athol

[blair ath•ull]

Owner:	**Region/district:**
Diageo	Southern Highlands

Founded:	**Status:**	**Capacity:**
1798	Active (vc)	2 800 000 litres

Address: Perth Road, Pitlochry, Perthshire PH16 5LY

Website:	**Tel:**
malts.com	01796 482003

Blair Athol is an excellent example of a single malt distillery and a blended whisky having a relationship that goes back many years. In fact it started already in 1896 when Bell's blend was first released.

The connection was strengthened when Arthur Bell & Sons bought the distillery in 1933. The success for Bell's continued and in 1970 it became the best selling whisky in Scotland. Eight years later it was the number one seller in the entire UK, a position it managed to hold until 2011 when Famous Grouse took the lead. It remains number two in the UK with a 16% market share but nowadays it's not even on the global Top Ten list. In 2019 sales dropped by 15% – more than any other of the big blends – to 23 million bottles. While still a substantial volume, it remains to be seen if the owners kan revitalize the brand by finding new markets. This has worked very well in recent years for classic brands such as Black & White and VAT 69.

Blair Athol is by far the most visited of all the Diageo distilleries and number four in Scotland. Almost 90,000 people travel here every year. The distillery has its location as an advantage: in Pitlochry, just off the bustling A9 with lots of travelers going from Edinburgh north to the Highlands. A new feature introduced a couple of years ago is a used mash tun from Clynelish which has been turned into a whisky tasting bar!

The equipment of Blair Athol distillery consists of an 8.2 ton semi-lauter mash tun, six washbacks made of stainless steel and two pairs of stills. The part of the spirit which goes into Bell's is matured mainly in bourbon casks, while the rest is matured in sherry casks. The last couple of years, the distillery has been working a five-day week with 12 mashes per week and around two million litres of alcohol. This also means a scheme of short (46 hours) and long (104 hours) fermentations. A very cloudy wort gives Blair Athol newmake a nutty and malty character.

The only official bottling is the **12 year old Flora & Fauna** and, available only at the distillery, a **no age statement expression** matured in rejuvenated casks and ex-bourbon.

History:

1798 John Stewart and Robert Robertson found Aldour Distillery, the predecessor to Blair Athol. The name is taken from the adjacent river Allt Dour.

1825 The distillery is expanded by John Robertson and takes the name Blair Athol Distillery.

1826 The Duke of Atholl leases the distillery to Alexander Connacher & Co.

1860 Elizabeth Connacher runs the distillery.

1882 Peter Mackenzie & Company Distillers Ltd of Edinburgh (future founder of Dufftown Distillery) buys Blair Athol and expands it.

1932 The distillery is mothballed.

1933 Arthur Bell & Sons takes over by acquiring Peter Mackenzie & Company.

1949 Production restarts.

1973 Stills are expanded from two to four.

1985 Guinness Group buys Arthur Bell & Sons.

1987 A visitor centre is built.

2003 A 27 year old cask strength from 1975 is launched in Diageo's Rare Malts series.

2010 A distillery exclusive with no age statement and a single cask from 1995 are released.

2016 A distillery exclusive without age statement is released.

2017 A 23 year old is released as part of the Special Releases.

12 years old

Tasting notes Blair Athol 12 years old:

GS – The nose is mellow and sherried, with brittle toffee. Sweet and fragrant. Relatively rich on the palate, with malt, raisins, sultanas and sherry. The finish is lengthy, elegant and slowly drying.

Bowmore

[bow•moor]

Owner:
Beam Suntory

Region/district:
Islay

Founded: 1779
Status: Active (vc)
Capacity: 2 000 000 litres

Address: School Street, Bowmore, Islay, Argyll PA43 7GS

Website: bowmore.com

Tel: 01496 810441

For the last five years, Bowmore has been in a constant battle with Lagavulin for second place among best selling Islay malt after the undisputed number one, Laphroaig. The latest sales figure for Bowmore is around two million bottles.

The distillery has a lot of features that would please any marketeer. Conveniently located in the largest town on Islay, it is the only distillery on the island currently working that was established in the 1700s. It is one of three on the island having their own floor maltings. Thirty percent of the malt requirement is produced in-house and the green malt is dried for 18 hours using peat and then for 42 hours with dry air. The remaining part is bought from Simpson's. Both parts have a phenol specification of 25-30 ppm and are always mixed on a ratio of 2.5 tons in house malt and 5.5 tons of malt from Simpsons before mashing. At least until 2016. From that year on, a small amount has been made every year exclusively using malt from their own floors. To finish off the list of unique selling points: Bowmore has the oldest existing whisky warehouse in Scotland – the famous Vault No. 1.

Bowmore is equipped with an eight ton stainless steel semi-lauter mash tun with a copper lid which was previously in use at Jura distillery. There are also two magnificent and unusual hot water tanks made of copper to feed the mash tun. The six washbacks are made of Oregon pine, with both short (60 hours) and long (90 hours) fermentations and have all been named after previous owners of the distillery. One washback will feed one of the two wash stills and is then in its turn split between the two spirit stills. The foreshots are 35 minutes and the cut points for the middle cut are 74%-61%. The 27,000 casks are stored in two dunnage and one racked warehouse. In 2020, the plan is to do 15 mashes per week which amounts to 2 million litres of alcohol.

The domestic core range includes **No. 1, 12 years, 15 years, 18 years** and **25 years**. Starting in 2016, a new range highlighting the influence from the famous warehouse Vault No. 1 was launched. The latest installment was named **Peat Smoke**. Another new range, focusing on how wine casks interact with Bowmore single malt, was introduced in 2017. The first two bottlings in the Vintner's Trilogy were the **18 year old Double Matured Manzanilla** and a **26 year old** which had received a second maturation in ex-wine barriques. The third expression, a **27 year old port finish**, was released in 2018. The **36 year old Dragon Edition**, an exclusive to China was launched in 2019 and was followed by the **37 year old Fenghuang Edition** in August 2020. The duty free range consists of **10 year old** (Dark and Intense), **15 year old** (Golden and Elegant) and **18 year old** (Deep and Complex). Limited releases for duty free also occur, the latest being a **21 year old**. Another limited release in August 2020 was the **Black Bowmore DBS**. Distilled in 1964 it was launched in collaboration with Aston Martin. With the Feis Ile 2020 interrupted by the pandemic, Bowmore decided not to launch a festival bottling.

History:

1779 Bowmore Distillery is founded by David Simpson and becomes the oldest Islay distillery.

1837 The distillery is sold to James and William Mutter of Glasgow.

1892 After additional construction, the distillery is sold to Bowmore Distillery Company Ltd, a consortium of English businessmen.

1925 J. B. Sheriff and Company takes over.

1929 Distillers Company Limited (DCL) takes over.

1950 William Grigor & Son takes over.

1963 Stanley P. Morrison buys the distillery and forms Morrison Bowmore Distillers Ltd.

1989 Japanese Suntory buys a 35% stake in Morrison Bowmore.

1993 The legendary Black Bowmore is launched.

1994 Suntory now controls all of Morrison Bowmore.

1996 A Bowmore 1957 (38 years) is bottled at 40.1% but is not released until 2000.

1999 Bowmore Darkest with three years finish on Oloroso barrels is launched.

2000 Bowmore Dusk with two years finish in Bordeaux barrels is launched.

2001 Bowmore Dawn with two years finish on Port pipes is launched.

2002 A 37 year old Bowmore from 1964 and matured in fino casks is launched in a limited edition of 300 bottles (recommended price £1,500).

2003 Another two expressions complete the wood trilogy which started with 1964 Fino - 1964 Bourbon and 1964 Oloroso.

2005 Bowmore 1989 Bourbon (16 years) and 1971 (34 years) are launched.

History continued:

2006 Bowmore 1990 Oloroso (16 years) and 1968 (37 years) are launched.

2007 An 18 year old is introduced. 1991 (16yo) Port and Black Bowmore are released.

2008 White Bowmore and a 1992 Vintage with Bordeaux finish are launched.

2009 Gold Bowmore, Maltmen´s Selection, Laimrig and Bowmore Tempest are released.

2010 A 40 year old and Vintage 1981 are released.

2011 Vintage 1982 and new batches of Tempest and Laimrig are released.

2012 100 Degrees Proof, Springtide and Vintage 1983 are released for duty free.

2013 The Devil´s Casks, a 23 year old Port Cask Matured and Vintage 1984 are released.

2014 Black Rock, Gold Reef and White Sands are released for duty free.

2015 New editions of Devil´s Cask, Tempest and the 50 year old are released as well as Mizunara Cask Finish.

2016 A 9 year old, a 10 year old travel retail exclusive and Bowmore Vault Edit1on are released as well as the final batch of Black Bowmore.

2017 No. 1 is released together with three new expressions for travel retail.

2018 Vintner´s Trilogy is launched.

2019 Vault Edit1on Peat Smoke, a 21 year old for duty free and the 36 year old Dragon Edition are released.

2020 Black Bowmore DBS is launched.

Tasting notes Bowmore 12 year old:

GS – An enticing nose of lemon and gentle brine leads into a smoky, citric palate, with notes of cocoa and boiled sweets appearing in the lengthy, complex finish.

Vintner´s Trilogy
27 year old Port Cask

18 years old
Travel Retail

Vault Edition
Peat Smoke

No. 1

12 years old

25 years old

Braeval

[bre•vaal]

Owner: **Region/district:**
Chivas Brothers (Pernod Ricard)   Speyside

Founded: **Status:**   **Capacity:**
1973   Active   4 200 000 litres

Address: Chapeltown of Glenlivet, Ballindalloch, Banffshire AB37 9JS

Website: **Tel:**
-                               01542 783042

Braeval and its sister distillery, Allt-a-Bhainne, which is a 20-minute drive to the north, appear quite different as regards their exteriors, yet the two were built in the same era, the mid 1970s, when Chivas Brothers was owned by the Canadian drinks giant Seagram's.

While some think that Allt-a-Bhainne resembles an East German housing complex, Braeval has often been described in more positive words. The white-washed walls and beautiful windows, together with the pastoral location, give you the feeling of an Italian monastery. Both were mothballed in 2002 by new owners Pernod Ricard, just before today's Scotch whisky boom took off. Subsequently, when new markets got interested in Scotch, the distilleries were re-opened – Allt-a-Bhainne in 2005 and Braeval three years later.

The equipment at Braeval consists of a 9 ton stainless steel, full lauter mash tun. Even though the distillery was built in the mid 1970s when a lauter mash tun would have been the obvious choice, a traditional tun with rakes was installed. It wasn't until 2016, that a full lauter gear with a 9 ton mash was installed. There are 13 stainless steel washbacks with a fermentation time of 70 hours and six stills. Two of them are wash stills with aftercoolers and four are spirit stills, and with the possibility of doing 26 mashes per week, the distillery can now produce 4.2 million litres per year.

It took until 2017 before the first official bottling saw the light of day: a 16 year old single cask available only at Chivas' visitor centres. Then, in July 2019, a new range called The Secret Speyside Collection was launched - a total of 15 bottlings from four different distilleries where Braeval was one. Initially they were reserved for travel retail but were later rolled out to domestic markets as well. The three from Braeval are **25, 27** and **30 year old**, all matured in ex-bourbon barrels and hogsheads. The first two are bottled at 48% and the 30 year old is a cask strength (50.3%). Finally there is an **18 year old** available in the Distillery Reserve Collection available at the visitor centres.

History:
1973   The distillery is founded by Chivas Brothers (Seagram's) and production starts in October.
1975   Three stills are increased to five.
1978   Five stills are further expanded to six.
1994   The distillery changes name to Braeval.
2001   Pernod Ricard takes over Chivas Brothers.
2002   Braeval is mothballed in October.
2008   The distillery starts producing again in July.
2017   The first official bottling, a 16 year old single cask, is released.
2019   Three new official bottlings in a new range, The Secret Speyside Collection, are released.

25 years old

Tasting notes Braeval 16 year old:
GS – Marzipan, milk chocolate-coated Turkish Delight and orange peel on the nose. The palate is sweet and fruity, with stewed apples, sugared almonds, nutmeg and ginger. Medium to long in the finish, consistently sugary and spicy.

Whisky Legends

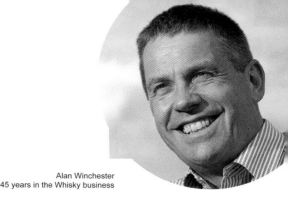

Alan Winchester
45 years in the Whisky business

My first meeting with Alan Winchester was a pure coincidence. I had arrived at Glenallachie distillery to take some exterior images for a book. With no appointment, I was careful not to walk around the premises – I just parked the car, got out and started to take photographs.

Suddenly I saw a tall man coming out from the distillery and was prepared to be scolded for trespassing. Instead he courteously asked if he could help and we ended up having a two-hour walk around the distillery. This was long ago and I have met Alan Winchester many times since then but this first encounter was typical of him – always eager to tell the story of whisky and its history.

Alan started at Glenfarclas as a tour guide in 1975 and four years later joined The Glenlivet Distillers but it would take a few years before he actually started working at the distillery that is now intricably linked with his name – The Glenlivet. Instead he spent a couple of years at the cooperage and warehouses at Glen Grant and Caperdonich. He trained to become a brewer at Glen Keith and Strathisla and then had spells at a few of the other Chivas Brothers' distilleries. In 2002, he became the Chivas Brothers Distilling Manager which meant he had production responsibilities for no less than 17 distilleries! In 2018 he stepped back from production and distilling duties but is still with the company as The Glenlivet Master Distiller.

I ask him to name some of the greatest achievements of his career. His role representing the iconic The Glenlivet around the world as Master Distiller is definitely one of them. And on the production side, Alan mentions being part of the team that oversaw the two expansions of The Glenlivet, the reopening of Glen Keith and the construction of Dalmunach distillery.

I remain on the production track and ask what changes he has seen during his career.

"The understanding of raw materials and the development of large commercial maltings from the 1960s onwards have allowed for the expansion of distilling. This was a long evolution and replaced many of the floor maltings, but it supported local farming. One modern process that revolutionized the whisky business was adopting cooling towers which allowed us to distil when burn and river levels were lower."

"In broader terms, the use of digital technology changed everything from process control to stock control and the advent of the internet helped increase knowledge sharing about whisky and how it can be consumed. Energy use and conservation have also seen big advances. For example, all electricity from the Dalmunach distillery [built by Chivas in 2014] comes from renewable hydro and wind sources in Scotland."

So with all these changes in whisky production, is there a notable difference to be seen in the actual whiskies today compared to the bottlings from 50 years ago?

"I would say better control of distillation has helped greatly in consistency. We know the early blenders tried to achieve a consistent style from their distilleries, but there were many outside factors that could influence the consistency of the whiskies. But nowadays consistency is achieved thanks to new controls in place during the distillation processes."

Alan welcomes the recent relaxations in SWAs (Scotch Whisky Association) rule book concerning different types of casks being allowed.

" The new regulations have allowed us to experiment with a variety of different cask types to stretch the category and bring new flavours to consumers. Take for example The Glenlivet Caribbean Reserve or the recent Chivas Extra 13 Tequila Cask Finish."

Yet at the same time he acknowledges the importance of the SWA and their regulatory role.

"... these strict regulations also ensure all Scotch producers are all operating from a level playing field and protect our consumers, by making sure they're always getting that same consistent quality with every bottle they buy."

Alterations in whisky production is one thing but have there been changes in the last decades how the consumers enjoy their whisky?

" In the past few years, a new generation of drinkers looking for new experiences has enabled us to stretch the boundaries of what Scotch whisky can be. This has meant a great deal of change in the production and marketing of whisky, as we aim to make it more relevant to an evolving audience with changing values and interests."

For Alan, these changes involve flavour innovation and experimentation but also interacting with bars and mixologists to build a presence in the expanding cocktail side of the whisky business. As an example Alan mentions The Glenlivet Capsule Collection that attracted a lot of attention when it was launched last year at London Cocktail Week.

I know that Alan has a huge interest in and profound knowledge of the heritage and the history of Scotch whisky so I ask him if that is still relevant when addressing younger consumers today?

"Provenance and heritage are at the heart of Scotch whisky and are embedded naturally in our brands. Interestingly, younger consumers are often choosing brands with heritage and provenance and they are putting history, craft and ethos above price, for example. "

"Whilst we acknowledge the growing consumer interest in quality and provenance, it's important as well that we speak younger consumers' language and ensure our brands fit into their lifestyles."

Towards the end of the interview, I remind him of one of our meetings at The Glenlivet where we walked in the surroundings of the distillery. Alan told me stories about smugglers and illicit stills, about George Smith (the founder of The Glenlivet) and the Jacobite rising. It was obvious that he was profoundly proud of Scotch whisky and of being a Scot but at the same time Alan is open minded and he has no problem highlighting the work that other whisky makers around the globe are putting into their products.

" I was recently in New Zealand and saw lovely whisky which was smoked by Manuka. It was fascinating and showcases that there is always something new to learn in the whisky world. We're lucky at Chivas Brothers, as our parent company Pernod Ricard has many different subsidiary whisky producers around the world, so there is always something interesting to see and taste!"

Bruichladdich

[brook•lad•dee]

Owner:
Rémy Cointreau

Region/district:
Islay

Founded: 1881
Status: Active (vc)
Capacity: 1 500 000 litres

Address: Bruichladdich, Islay, Argyll PA49 7UN

Website:
bruichladdich.com

Tel:
01496 850221

Ever since the resurrection of Bruichladdich in 2001, the distillery has chosen its own path when it comes to the barley they are using and their belief in what impact this may have on the final flavour of the whisky.

That way of thinking was implemented by the people who bought the distillery at the time but it is interesting that this direction has continued even after the distillery was bought by a mega player such as Rémy Cointreau. In fact, a couple of years ago they purchased the croft beside the distillery with the aim of starting R&D with their own barley growing using more heritage varieties and by applying sustainable agricultural practices.

The distillery is equipped with a 7 ton cast iron, open mash tun with rakes, six washbacks made of Oregon pine with a fermentation time between 60 and 105 hours and two pairs of stills. All whisky produced is based on Scottish barley. Around half comes from Islay and 5% is organically grown. During 2020, the plan is to mash 9-10 times per week and one make million litres of alcohol. The breakdown of the three whisky varieties will be 50% Bruichladdich, 40% Port Charlotte and 10% Octomore.

The malting floors at Bruichladdich were closed in 1961 but the decision has now been taken to start up own maltings again within the next two to four years. Instead of traditional floor malting, Saladin boxes will be installed. The main reason for this is to keep up the consistency of the spirit since Baird's, their current malt supplier, are using that same technique. The malting will be located in one of the current warehouses.

Bruichladdich has three product lines; unpeated Bruichladdich, heavily peated Port Charlotte and ultra-heavily peated Octomore. The only core expressions, in the sense that they are widely available and not released by vintage, are **The Classic Laddie** and **Port Charlotte 10 year old**. The following appear every year with new batches/vintages; for Bruichladdich there are **Islay Barley 2011**, **Bere Barley 2010** and **The Organic 2010** and for Port Charlotte, **Islay Barley 2012** and the new **OLC:01**. The latter has an interesting maturation story; first filled in 2010 into an array of ex-bourbon, ex-syrah and ex-vin doux naturel casks it was then finished in ex-oloroso hogsheads.

The duty free range is made up of **The Laddie Eight, Bruichladdich 1990** and **Port Charlotte MC:01**. The mysterious **Black Art 8** is due to be released in late 2020. In October 2020, another batch of the heavily peated Octomore was released; **11.1** matured in first fill bourbon casks, **11.2** matured in a combination of ex-bourbon and Bordeaux wine casks and **11.3** made from barley grown on the Octomore farm and matured in first fill ex-bourbon. All three are 5 years old. Finally there is a **10 year old** with a phenol specification of 208ppm that had matured in American and virgin oak. The special bottling for Feis Ile 2020 was a **16 year old Port Charlotte** with a complex maturation story involving ex-bourbon, ex.sauternes, ex-sherry and virgin oak.

History:

1881 Barnett Harvey builds the distillery with money left by his brother William III to his three sons William IV, Robert and John Gourlay.

1886 Bruichladdich Distillery Company Ltd is founded and reconstruction commences.

1929 Temporary closure.

1936 The distillery reopens.

1938 Joseph Hobbs, Hatim Attari and Alexander Tolmie purchase the distillery through the company Train & McIntyre.

1952 The distillery is sold to Ross & Coulter.

1960 A. B. Grant buys Ross & Coulter.

1961 Own maltings ceases.

1968 Invergordon Distillers take over.

1975 The number of stills increases to four.

1983 Temporary closure.

1993 Whyte & Mackay buys Invergordon Distillers.

1995 The distillery is mothballed in January.

1998 In production again for a few months.

2000 Murray McDavid buys the distillery from JBB Greater Europe for £6.5 million.

2001 The first distillations of Port Charlotte and Bruichladdich starts in July.

2002 Octomore, the world's most heavily peated whisky (80ppm) is distilled.

2004 Second edition of the 20 year old (nick-named Flirtation) and 3D, also called The Peat Proposal, are launched.

2005 Several new expressions are launched - the second edition of 3D, Infinity, Rocks, Legacy Series IV, The Yellow Submarine and The Twenty 'Islands'.

2006 The first official bottling of Port Charlotte; PC5.

2007 New releases include Redder Still, Legacy 6, PC6 and an 18 year old.

History continued:

2008 New expressions include the first Octomore, Bruichladdich 2001, PC7 and Golder Still.

2009 New releases include Classic, Organic, Black Art, Infinity 3, PC8, Octomore 2 and X4+3 - the first quadruple distilled single malt.

2010 PC Multi Vintage, Organic MV, Octomore/3_152, Bruichladdich 40 year old are released.

2011 The first 10 year old from own production is released as well as PC9 and Octomore 4_167.

2012 Ten year old versions of Port Charlotte and Octomore are released as well as Laddie 16 and 22, Bere Barley 2006, Black Art 3 and DNA4. Rémy Cointreau buys the distillery.

2013 Scottish Barley, Islay Barley Rockside Farm, Bere Barley 2nd edition, Black Art 4, Port Charlotte Scottish Barley, Octomore 06.1 and 06.2 are released.

2014 PC11 and Octomore Scottish Barley are released.

2015 PC12, Octomore 7.1 and High Noon 134 are released.

2016 The Laddie Eight, Octomore 7.4 and Port Charlotte 2007 CC:01 are released.

2017 Black Art 5 and 25 year old sherry cask are launched. The limited Rare Cask series is launched.

2018 The Port Charlotte range is revamped and a 10 year old and Islay Barley 2011 are released.

2019 Bere Barley 10, Organic 10, Black Art 7 and Octomore 10.1, 10.2, 10.3 and 10.4 are released.

2020 Port Charlotte OLC:01, Port Charlotte 16 year old and four new Octomore are released.

Tasting notes Bruichladdich Scottish Barley:

GS – Mildly metallic on the early nose, then cooked apple aromas develop, with a touch of linseed. Initially very fruity on the gently oily palate. Ripe peaches and apricots, with vanilla, brittle toffee, lots of spice and sea salt. The finish is drying, with breakfast tea.

Tasting notes Port Charlotte Scottish Barley:

GS – Wood smoke and contrasting bonbons on the nose. Warm Tarmac develops, with white pepper. Finally, fragrant pipe tobacco. Peppery peat and treacle toffee on the palate, with a maritime note. Long in the finish, with black pepper and oak.

Tasting notes Octomore Scottish Barley:

GS – A big hit of sweet peat on the nose; ozone and rock pools, supple leather, damp tweed. Peat on the palate is balanced by allspice, vanilla and fruitiness. Very long in the finish, with chilli, dry roasted nuts and bonfire smoke.

Black Art 7

Port Charlotte
Feis Ile 2020

The Organic 2010

The Classic Laddie Scottish Barley

Port Charlotte
OLC:01 2010

Port Charlotte
10 year old

Bunnahabhain

[buh•nah•hav•enn]

Owner:	**Region/district:**
Distell International Ltd.	Islay
Founded: **Status:**	**Capacity:**
1881 Active (vc)	2 700 000 litres
Address: Port Askaig, Islay, Argyll PA46 7RP	
Website:	**Tel:**
bunnahabhain.com	01496 840646

If one looks at the latest sales figures, Bunnahabhain is in place number six of the eight Islay distilleries that have yet released their own single malts. Around 600,000 bottles were sold in the last year.

In the last ten years however, sales have increased by 160% which is more than for any other Islay brand except Ardbeg. A substantial part of that increase occurred after Distell took over the distillery in 2013. The new owner has also invested heavily in the distillery itself in recent years, not least by the construction of a brand new and long overdue visitor centre with a plan to open it in autumn 2020.

The distillery is equipped with a 12.5 ton traditional stainless steel mash tun with a copper lid, six washbacks made of Oregon pine and two pairs of stills. Two of the washbacks were replaced in spring 2019. The fermentation time varies between 55 and 110 hours. The production plan for 2020 is 1,8 million litres, split between 35% peated and 65% unpeated. The peating level has increased during the last years and the barley now has a phenol specification of 35-45ppm.

The core range consists of **12, 18, 25** and a **40 year old**. The peated side of Bunnahabhain is represented by **Toiteach a Dha** without age statement and matured in both bourbon and sherry casks and **Stiùireadair**, matured in first and re-fill sherry casks. Recent limited releases include the first in the new **Elements series** - a **39 year old**, launched in June 2019, that was finished for 6 months in a Spanish sherry octave. Only 26 decanters were produced. July 2020 saw five bottlings being released; a **2008 manzanilla matured**, a **1997 PX finish**, a **2005 burgundy finish** (distillery exclusive) and two releases for Feis Ile 2020 - a **2010 Amontillado** and a **2002 Madeira**. Finally, there are three travel retail exclusives – **Cruach-Mhòna** which comprises of young, heavily peated Bunnahabhain, **Eirigh Na Greine**, a vatting of whisky from bourbon, sherry and red wine casks and the sherry-matured **An Cladach**.

History:

1881 William Robertson founds the distillery together with the brothers William and James Greenless.

1883 Production starts in January.

1887 Islay Distillers Company Ltd merges with William Grant & Co. in order to form Highland Distilleries Company Limited.

1963 The two stills are augmented by two more.

1982 The distillery closes.

1984 The distillery reopens. A 21 year old is released to commemorate the 100th anniversary.

1999 Edrington takes over Highland Distillers and mothballs Bunnahabhain but allows for a few weeks of production a year.

2001 A 35 year old from 1965 is released during Islay Whisky Festival.

2002 Auld Acquaintance 1968 is launched at the Islay Jazz Festival.

2003 Edrington sells Bunnahabhain and Black Bottle to Burn Stewart Distilleries for £10 million. A 40 year old from 1963 is launched.

2004 The first limited edition of the peated version is a 6 year old called Moine.

2005 Three limited editions are released - 34 years old,18 years old and 25 years old.

2006 14 year old Pedro Ximenez and 35 years old are launched.

2008 Darach Ur is released for the travel retail market and Toiteach (a peated 10 year old) is launched on a few selected markets.

2009 Moine Cask Strength is released.

2010 The peated Cruach-Mhòna and a limited 30 year old are released.

2013 A 40 year old is released.

2014 Eirigh Na Greine and Ceobanach are released.

2017 Moine Oloroso, Stiùireadair and An Cladach are released.

2018 Toiteach a Dha and a 20 year old Palo Cortado are released.

2019 A 2007 brandy finish and a 1988 marsala finish are released.

2020 A 2008 manzanilla, a 1997 PX finish and a 2005 burgundy finish are released.

Tasting notes Bunnahabhain 12 years old:

GS – The nose is fresh, with light peat and discreet smoke. More overt peat on the nutty and fruity palate, but still restrained for an Islay. The finish is full-bodied and lingering, with a hint of vanilla and some smoke.

12 years old

Caol Ila

[cull eel•a]

Owner:
Diageo

Region/district:
Islay

Founded: **Status:** **Capacity:**
1846 Active (vc) 6 500 000 litres

Address: Port Askaig, Islay, Argyll PA46 7RL

Website: **Tel:**
malts.com 01496 302760

Calling a distillery a workhorse because it mainly produces large volumes of single malt whisky to become part of various blends may sound degrading. Well it's not. A good and versatile malt is the backbone of any successful blend.

The owners of Caol Ila, Diageo, have to a high degree built their success in the whisky business on quality blends such as Johnnie Walker and J&B. The secret behind that is of course blending skills but also availability of good malt whiskies. Caol Ila is one, providing character to many blends, not least Johnnie Walker Black Label. Since 2002 the owners have also tried to establish the whisky as a stand-alone single malt brand. While popular by the whisky aficionados the whisky hasn't really hit it off with the general consumer. Sales figures have been more or less constant during the last decade. A significant reason for that is probably the fierce competition they are facing from some of the other, more well-known Islay single malts. Perhaps the anonymity the brand is experiencing will diminish once a new visitor centre is up and running. It is part of a greater plan involving new visitor centres also at Glenkinchie, Cardhu and Clynelish as well as a huge investment in a Johnnie Walker experience in Edinburgh.

Caol Ila is equipped with a 12.5 ton full lauter mash tun, eight wooden washbacks and two made of stainless steel and three pairs of stills. In recent years, the distillery has either been working a seven-day week with 26 mashes or a five-day week with 16 mashes. On a five-day week production, there is a mix of short (55 hours) and long (120 hours) fermentations. Caol Ila is known for its peated whisky but unpeated new-make is also produced.

The core range consists of **Moch** without age statement, **12**, **18** and **25 year old**, **Distiller's Edition** with a moscatel finish and **Cask Strength**. The release for Feis Ile 2020 was a **16 year old**, bottled at 53,9%, that had been matured in refill American oak hogsheads and finished in amoroso casks. In July 2020, a **35 year old**, matured in a refill sherry butt and bottled at 50,8% was part of the new Prima & Ultima range.

History:
1846 Hector Henderson founds Caol Ila.
1852 Henderson, Lamont & Co. is subjected to financial difficulties and Henderson is forced to sell Caol Ila to Norman Buchanan.
1863 Norman Buchanan sells to the blending company Bulloch, Lade & Co. from Glasgow.
1879 The distillery is rebuilt and expanded.
1920 Bulloch, Lade & Co. is liquidated and the distillery is taken over by Caol Ila Distillery.
1927 DCL becomes sole owners.
1972 All the buildings, except for the warehouses, are demolished and rebuilt.
1974 The renovation, which totals £1 million, is complete and six new stills are installed.
1999 Experiments with unpeated malt.
2002 The first official bottlings since Flora & Fauna/ Rare Malt appear; 12 years, 18 years and Cask Strength (c. 10 years).
2003 A 25 year old cask strength is released.
2006 Unpeated 8 year old and 1993 Moscatel finish are released.
2007 Second edition of unpeated 8 year old.
2009 The fourth edition of the unpeated version (10 year old) is released.
2010 A 25 year old, a 1999 Feis Isle bottling and a 1997 Manager's Choice are released.
2011 An unpeated 12 year old and the unaged Moch are released.
2012 An unpeated 14 year old is released.
2013 Unpeated Stitchell Reserve is released.
2014 A 15 year old unpeated and a 30 year old are released.
2016 A 15 year old unpeated is released.
2017 An 18 year old unpeated is released.
2018 Two bottlings in the Special Releases - a 15 year old and a 35 year old.
2020 A 35 year old is released as part of the new Prima & Ultima range.

Tasting notes Caol Ila 12 year old:
GS – Iodine, fresh fish and smoked bacon feature on the nose, along with more delicate, floral notes. Smoke, malt, lemon and peat on the slightly oily palate. Peppery peat in the drying finish.

12 years old

Cardhu

[car•doo]

Owner: Diageo	**Region/district:** Speyside
Founded: 1824	**Status:** Active (vc)	**Capacity:** 3 400 000 litres

Address: Knockando, Aberlour, Moray AB38 7RY

Website: malts.com	**Tel:** 01479 874635

A substantial investment from Diageo in new visitor centres for some of their distilleries as well as a completely new Johnnie Walker Experience in Edinburgh is currently underway.

In the same way that Clynelish will become the Highland home of Johnnie Walker, Cardhu will be the Speyside home of the world famous brand. In 1893, Cardhu was the first distillery to be acquired by John Walker & Sons. The planning permission for Cardhu was granted in July 2019 but the covid pandemic has delayed work, which will include substantial landscaping and a completely new warehouse experience. Currently the distillery attracts 15,000 visitors yearly.

Cardhu single malt is one of the most important components of Johnnie Walker. But, at the same time, it is one of the Top Ten single malt brands in the world. Cardhu is Diageo's third best selling single malt after The Singleton and Talisker with more than 3 million bottles sold in 2019.

The distillery is equipped with an eight ton stainless steel full lauter mash tun with a copper top, ten washbacks (eight of wood and two of stainless steel in a separate room), all with a fermentation time of 75 hours, and three pairs of stills. Four of the wooden washbacks are new and made of Oregon pine, having replaced four old ones made of larch. The production plan for 2020 is a seven-day week with 21 mashes per week and a production of 3.4 million litres of alcohol.

The core range from the distillery is **12, 15** and **18 year old** and two expressions without age statement – **Amber Rock** and **Gold Reserve**. There is also a **Special Cask Reserve** matured in rejuvenated bourbon casks. In spring 2019, **Cardhu Gold Reserve House Targaryen** was released in the Game of Thrones series. A **14 year old** was released in autumn 2019 in the Rare by Nature series and this was followed in autumn 2020 by an **11 year old** bottled at 56%.

History:

1824 John Cumming applies for and obtains a licence for Cardhu Distillery.
1846 John Cumming dies and his wife Helen and son Lewis takes over.
1872 Lewis dies and his wife Elizabeth takes over.
1884 A new distillery is built to replace the old.
1893 John Walker & Sons purchases Cardhu for £20,500.
1908 The name reverts to Cardow.
1960 Reconstruction and expansion of stills from four to six.
1981 The name changes to Cardhu.
1998 A visitor centre is constructed.
2002 Diageo changes Cardhu single malt to a vatted malt with contributions from other distilleries in it.
2003 The whisky industry protests sharply against Diageo's plans.
2004 Diageo withdraws Cardhu Pure Malt.
2005 The 12 year old Cardhu Single Malt is relaunched and a 22 year old is released.
2009 Cardhu 1997, a single cask in the new Manager's Choice range is released.
2011 A 15 year old and an 18 year old are released.
2013 A 21 year old is released.
2014 Amber Rock and Gold Reserve are launched.
2016 A distillery exclusive is released.
2019 A 14 year old appears in the Special Releases and Cardhu is also part of the Game of Thrones series.
2020 An 11 year old Rare by Nature bottling is released.

Amber Rock

Tasting notes Cardhu 12 years old:

GS – The nose is relatively light and floral, quite sweet, with pears, nuts and a whiff of distant peat. Medium-bodied, malty and sweet in the mouth. Medium-length in the finish, with sweet smoke, malt and a hint of peat.

Websites to watch

There are a lot of great blogs and websites
to be found on the internet and, to be honest, some not so great.
These are the ones I follow frequently and while they are all well worth
visiting, the ones marked with * are my personal favourites.

allthingswhisky.com *

angelshare.it

bestshotwhiskyreviews.com *

blog.thewhiskyexchange.com *

canadianwhisky.org *

edinburghwhiskyblog.com *

greatdrams.com *

insidethecask.com *

jason-scotchreviews.blogspot.com

maltandoak.com

malted.blog

maltermagasin.se *

maltfascination.com

maltimpostor.com

malt-review.com *

masterofmalt.com/blog *

meleklerinpayi.com

scotchmaltwhisky.co.uk *

scotchnoob.com

scotchwhisky.com *

scotch-whisky.org.uk

speller.nl

spiritedmatters.com

spiritsjournal.klwines.com

spiritsnews.se

taswhiskytrail.com

thedramble.com

thewhiskeyjug.com

thewhiskeywash.com *

thewhiskylady.net

thewhiskyphiles.com

thewhiskyviking.blogspot.com

thewhiskywire.com *

timeforwhisky.com

tjederswhisky.se *

tomswhiskyreviews.com

topwhiskies.com

whiskeyapostle.com

whisky.buzz

whiskyandwisdom.com

whiskyboys.com

whiskycast.com *

whiskycritic.com

whisky-distilleries.net *

whiskyfacile.com

whiskyfanblog.de

whiskyforeveryone.blogspot.com *

whiskyfun.com *

whiskyintelligence.com *

whiskyisrael.co.il *

whiskymonster.com

whiskymylife.wordpress.com

whisky-news.com *

whiskynotes.be *

whiskeyreviewer.com

whiskyreviews.net

whiskysaga.com *

whiskysponge.com *

whiskywaffle.com

wordsofwhisky.com

Clynelish

[cline•leash]

Owner: Diageo

Region/district: Northern Highlands

Founded: 1967

Status: Active (vc)

Capacity: 4 800 000 litres

Address: Brora, Sutherland KW9 6LR

Website: malts.com

Tel: 01408 623003 (vc)

Clynelish is a bustling place at the moment. The distillery, a little more than a one hour drive north of Inverness, is about to have a substantial upgrade of its visitor centre. But that's not all. On the same site a sleeping distillery is about to be awakened.

The current Clynelish distillery was built in 1967, next to Brora which had been operating as Clynelish ever since 1819. The two distilleries worked in tandem for a few years until the old one closed in 1983. Even though some of the equipment was left, the hopes of ever producing again were slim until Diageo announced in 2017 that it was to be rebuilt with a re-opening planned for 2021. At the same time, the current Clynelish visitor centre is in for a major upgrade. Planning permission was granted in July 2019 and includes a bar and tasting area with a view of the Sutherland coast and an upper floor telling the story of the distillery and its connection to the Johnnie Walker blend.

Following a year-long upgrade which was completed in June 2017, Clynelish is now equipped with a 12.5 ton full lauter mash tun, eight wooden washbacks and two made of stainless steel. The still room, with its three pairs of stills, has stunning views towards the village of Brora and the North Sea. Clynelish is usually operational seven-days a week, producing around 4.8 million litres of alcohol. Approximately 6,000 casks of Clynelish are stored in the two old Brora warehouses next door, but most of the production is matured elsewhere.

Official bottlings include a **14 year old** and a **Distiller's Edition**, with an Oloroso Seco finish. In spring 2019, Clynelish was also part of the series of eight single malts named after houses in the popular Tv series Game of Thrones. **Clynelish House of Tyrell** was launched without age statement and bottled at 51.6%. Recent limited bottlings include a **26 year old** matured in refill American oak which was part of the new Prima & Ultima range launched in July 2020. There is also a **distillery exclusive** matured in a combination of American ex-bourbon and rejuvenated casks.

History:

1819 The 1st Duke of Sutherland founds a distillery called Clynelish Distillery.

1827 The first licensed distiller, James Harper, files for bankruptcy and John Matheson takes over.

1846 George Lawson & Sons become new licensees.

1896 James Ainslie & Heilbron takes over.

1912 James Ainslie & Co. narrowly escapes bankruptcy and Distillers Company Limited (DCL) takes over together with James Risk.

1916 John Walker & Sons buys a stake of James Risk's stocks.

1931 The distillery is mothballed.

1939 Production restarts.

1960 The distillery becomes electrified.

1967 A new distillery, also named Clynelish, is built adjacent to the first one.

1968 'Old' Clynelish is mothballed in August.

1969 'Old' Clynelish is reopened as Brora and starts using a very peaty malt.

1983 Brora is closed in March.

2002 A 14 year old is released.

2006 A Distiller´s Edition 1991 finished in Oloroso casks is released.

2009 A 12 year old is released for Friends of the Classic Malts.

2010 A 1997 Manager´s Choice single cask is released.

2014 Clynelish Select Reserve is released.

2015 Second version of Clynelish Select Reserve is released.

2017 The distillery produces again after a year long closure for refurbishing.

2019 Clynelish House Tyrell is released as part of the Game of Thrones series.

2020 A 26 year old Prima & Ultima is released.

14 years old

Tasting notes Clynelish 14 year old:

GS – A nose that is fragrant, spicy and complex, with candle wax, malt and a whiff of smoke. Notably smooth in the mouth, with honey and contrasting citric notes, plus spicy peat, before a brine and tropical fruit finish.

Cragganmore

[crag•an•moor]

Owner: Diageo   **Region/district:** Speyside

Founded: 1869   **Status:** Active (vc)   **Capacity:** 2 200 000 litres

Address: Ballindalloch, Moray AB37 9AB

Website: malts.com   **Tel:** 01479 874700

Cragganmore single malt has always been known as one of the more complex malts coming from Speyside. The reason behind this is to be found in the distillation process.

The style of the newmake is characterized as heavy and sulphury. The large size of the wash stills could indicate a delicate spirit but sharply descending lyne arms allow for little reflux. The spirit stills are considerably smaller with boil balls and long, slightly descending lyne arms, facilitating more copper contact and thus producing a lighter character. The spirit finally ends up in worm tubs which, by definition, gives a robust flavour which is even more true at Cragganmore, where the worms are only 15 metres but very thick.

The whisky from Cragganmore was chosen by United Distillers in 1988 to become one of the original Classic Malts, representing Speyside. Despite that promotion, it has never really become one of the more prominent single malts. In fact, with around 300,000 bottles sold yearly, only Glenkinchie out of the six original Classics sells less. Nevertheless, the brand has its die hard devotees and the distillery has a small but elegant visitor centre with a number of tours to choose from.

Cragganmore is equipped with a 6.8 ton stainless steel full lauter mash tun with a copper canopy and six washbacks made of Oregon pine. Since they are working a five-day week in 2020 there will be six short (60 hours) and six long (90 hours) fermentations. There are two wash stills and two spirit stills, all attached to worm tubs for cooling the spirit vapours. In 2020, the production will amount to around 1.65 million litres of alcohol.

Cragganmore single malt plays an important part in the Old Parr blend which was first introduced in 1909 and is very popular in Japan and Latin America. The official core range of Cragganmore is made up of a **12 year old** and a **Distiller's Edition** with a finish in port pipes. In July 2020, a **48 year old**, matured in first fill sherry (the last remaining cask from when Cragganmore used coal fired stills) was part of the new Prima & Ultima range and in the Rare by Nature series in autumn 2020 a **20 year old appeared**.

History:
- 1869 John Smith, who already runs Glenfarclas distillery, founds Cragganmore.
- 1886 John Smith dies and his brother George takes over operations.
- 1893 John's son Gordon, at 21, is old enough to assume responsibility for operations.
- 1901 The distillery is refurbished and modernized with help of the famous architect Charles Doig.
- 1912 Gordon Smith dies and his widow Mary Jane supervises operations.
- 1917 The distillery closes.
- 1918 The distillery reopens and Mary Jane installs electric lighting.
- 1923 The distillery is sold to the newly formed Cragganmore-Glenlivet Distillery Co. where Mackie & Co. and Sir George Macpherson-Grant of Ballindalloch Estate share ownership.
- 1927 White Horse Distillers is bought by DCL which thus obtains 50% of Cragganmore.
- 1964 The number of stills is increased from two to four.
- 1965 DCL buys the remainder of Cragganmore.
- 1988 Cragganmore 12 years becomes one of six selected for United Distillers´ Classic Malts.
- 1998 Cragganmore Distillers Edition Double Matured (port) is launched for the first time.
- 2002 A visitor centre opens in May.
- 2006 A 17 year old from 1988 is released.
- 2010 Manager´s Choice single cask 1997 and a limited 21 year old are released.
- 2014 A 25 year old is released.
- 2016 A Special Releases vatting without age statement and a distillery exclusive are released.
- 2019 A 12 year bottled at cask strength appears in the Special Releases series.
- 2020 A 48 year old and a 20 year old are released.

Tasting notes Cragganmore 12 years old:

GS – A nose of sherry, brittle toffee, nuts, mild wood smoke, angelica and mixed peel. Elegant on the malty palate, with herbal and fruit notes, notably orange. Medium in length, with a drying, slightly smoky finish.

12 years old

Craigellachie

[craig•ell•ack•ee]

Owner:
John Dewar & Sons
(Bacardi)

Region/district:
Speyside

Founded: 1891 | **Status:** Active | **Capacity:** 4 100 000 litres

Address: Aberlour, Banffshire AB38 9ST

Website: craigellachie.com | **Tel:** 01340 872971

Of the five malt distilleries owned by Dewar's, Craigellachie is the only one using worm tubs to condense the spirit vapours.

A worm tub is a large vat filled with water with a sometimes more than 100 metres long copper spiral (the worm) fitted inside. The spirit vapours run through the spiral and are condensed by the surrounding water. This is the traditional way of cooling the vapours and only 17 distilleries in Scotland continue this practice today. Invented in Germany at around 1540, worm tubs were installed in every distillery until the 1880s when the first shell and tube condenser appeared. With this device, the cooling water runs through copper tubes surrounded by the spirit vapours inside a copper shell. This new technique did not get its break through until after the second world war and, after the mid 1960s, only two distilleries in Scotland have installed worm tubs, namely Ballindalloch and Ardnahoe. The use of worm tubs generally creates a heavier and more sulphury newmake which requires a longer maturation time.

Craigellachie distillery is equipped with a Steinecker full lauter mash tun, installed in 2001, which replaced the old, open cast iron mash tun. There are also eight 47,000 litre washbacks made of larch with a fermentation time of 56-60 hours and two pairs of stills. Both stills are attached to worm tubs. The old cast iron tubs were exchanged for stainless steel in 2014 and the existing copper worms were moved to the new tubs. The production plan for 2020 is 21 mashes per week and 3.9 million litres of alcohol.

The core range, introduced in 2014, consists of **13, 17** and **23 year old**. A **33 year old**, released for duty free, was later rolled out onto the US domestic market. Recent (autumn 2019) limited cask strength releases in the Exceptional Cask series include a **19 year old** matured in a sherry butt and a **23 year old** matured in first fill oloroso. In the beginning of 2020 a **39 year old** single cask, exclusively available at London Heathrow Airport, was launched.

History:

1890 The distillery is built by Craigellachie–Glenlivet Distillery Company which has Alexander Edward and Peter Mackie as part-owners.

1891 Production starts.

1916 Mackie & Company Distillers Ltd takes over.

1924 Peter Mackie dies and Mackie & Company changes name to White Horse Distillers.

1927 White Horse Distillers are bought by Distillers Company Limited (DCL).

1930 Administration is transferred to Scottish Malt Distillers (SMD), a subsidiary of DCL.

1964 Refurbishing takes place and two new stills are bought, increasing the number to four.

1998 United Distillers & Vintners (UDV) sells Craigellachie together with Aberfeldy, Brackla and Aultmore and the blending company John Dewar & Sons to Bacardi Martini.

2004 The first bottlings from the new owners are a new 14 year old which replaces UDV's Flora & Fauna and a 21 year old cask strength from 1982 produced for Craigellachie Hotel.

2014 Three new bottlings for domestic markets (13, 17 and 23 years) and one for duty free (19 years) are released.

2015 A 31 year old is released.

2016 A 33 year old and a 1994 Madeira single cask are released.

2018 A 24 year old and and a 17 year old palo cortado finish are released for duty free and the oldest official Craigellachie so far, 51 years old, is launched.

2019 A 19 and a 23 year old are released.

2020 A 39 year old is launched.

13 years old

Tasting notes Craigellachie 13 years old:

GS – Savoury on the early nose, with spent matches, green apples and mixed nuts. Malt join the nuts and apples on the palate, with sawdust and very faint smoke. Drying, with cranberries, spice and more subtle smoke.

Dailuaine

[dall•yoo•an]

Owner:
Diageo

Region/district:
Speyside

Founded: | **Status:** | **Capacity:**
1852 | Active | 5 200 000 litres

Address: Carron, Banffshire AB38 7RE

Website: | **Tel:**
malts.com | 01340 872500

Not being particularly well-known to whisky consumers today, there was a time when Dailuaine enjoyed a much more prominent place in the Scotch whisky industry.

Founded by William Mackenzie, his son Thomas eventually took over and in 1898 this Speyside distillery amalgamated with another distillery in the far west, namely Talisker on Skye. Other components in the Dailuaine-Talisker Distilleries Ltd were also Imperial distillery and the North of Scotland grain distillery. In a geographical sense perhaps not the most likely conglomerate but the constellation was thriving. In the 1914 edition of Who's Who in Business, the company is described as "believed to be the largest distillers of Pure Malt Whisky in the world"!

The following years however proved to be a challenge. When Thomas Mackenzie died in 1915 leaving no heirs, the company was bought by a consortium of other distillers in 1916 and in 1917 Dailuaine was raged by a fire and forced to close temporarily.

Today, the distillery is equipped with a stainless steel, 11.25 ton full lauter mash tun, eight washbacks made of Douglas fir plus two stainless steel ones placed outside and three pairs of stills. All the condensers are made of copper as usual but, until a few years ago, some were made of stainless steel to help achieve a sulphury style of new make. In 2015, the fermentation time was changed to produce a more waxy character to the spirit. The reason for that change was that Clynelish distillery had been closed for refurbishing. That is the only Diageo distillery so far that has accounted for this style which is so important for some blends. The plan for 2020 is to do four short (80 hours) and eight long fermentations (107 hours) per week amounting to 2.6 million litres of pure alcohol.

Dailuaine is one of many distilleries whose main task is producing malt whisky which is to become part of blended Scotch. The only core bottling is the **16 year old Flora & Fauna**. In 2015, a **34 year old** from 1980 was launched as part of the Special Releases.

History:

1852 The distillery is founded by William Mackenzie.

1865 William Mackenzie dies and his widow leases the distillery to James Fleming, a banker from Aberlour.

1879 William Mackenzie's son forms Mackenzie and Company with Fleming.

1891 Dailuaine-Glenlivet Distillery Ltd is founded.

1898 Dailuaine-Glenlivet Distillery Ltd merges with Talisker Distillery Ltd and forms Dailuaine-Talisker Distilleries Ltd.

1915 Thomas Mackenzie dies without heirs.

1916 Dailuaine-Talisker Company Ltd is bought by the previous customers John Dewar & Sons, John Walker & Sons and James Buchanan & Co.

1917 A fire rages and the pagoda roof collapses.

1920 The distillery reopens.

1925 Distillers Company Limited (DCL) takes over.

1960 Refurbishing. The stills increase from four to six and a Saladin box replaces the floor maltings.

1965 Indirect still heating through steam is installed.

1983 On site maltings is closed down and malt is purchased centrally.

1991 The first official bottling, a 16 year old, is launched in the Flora & Fauna series.

1996 A 22 year old cask strength from 1973 is released as a Rare Malt.

1997 A cask strength version of the 16 year old is launched.

2000 A 17 year old Manager's Dram matured in sherry casks is launched.

2010 A single cask from 1997 is released.

2012 The production capacity is increased by 25%.

2015 A 34 year old is launched as part of the Special Releases.

16 years old

Tasting notes Dailuaine 16 years old:

GS – Barley, sherry and nuts on the substantial nose, developing into maple syrup. Medium-bodied, rich and malty in the mouth, with more sherry and nuts, plus ripe oranges, fruitcake, spice and a little smoke. The finish is lengthy and slightly oily, with almonds, cedar and slightly smoky oak.

Dalmore

[dal•moor]

Owner:
Whyte & Mackay Ltd
(Emperador Inc)

Region/district:
Northern Highlands

Founded: 1839

Status: Active (vc)

Capacity: 4 300 000 litres

Address: Alness, Ross-shire IV17 0UT

Website: thedalmore.com

Tel: 01349 882362

It can be said that Dalmore single malt has had a market presence in two different camps for many years; one where it was selling decent volumes to the general consumer and the other where it was selling extremely rare whiskies to the rich and fortunate.

Ten years ago, the brand wasn't even in the Top 30 of single malts in terms of sales volume. In 2019 it had climbed to sixteenth place with an increase during the decade of no less than a staggering 600%! The only other Scotch single malt that has accomplished this leap is Aberfeldy. The markets in China and the Far East have been important in this development and there the owners have managed to grow the brand from being mainly considered ultra prestige for the few to a point where the core range has become interesting to the average whisky drinker.

Dalmore has an excellent location in Alness next to the busy A9 going from Inverness north to Thurso. With a completely refurbished visitor centre, including a museum that was opened in June 2019, the owners expect to grow the annual number of visitors (14,000 in 2018) substantially.

The distillery is equipped with a 10.4 ton stainless steel, semi-lauter mash tun, eight washbacks made of Oregon pine with a fermentation time of 50 hours and four pairs of stills. The spirit stills are equipped with water jackets, which allow cold water to circulate between the reflux bowl and the neck of the stills, thus increasing the reflux. The owners expect to mash 22 times per week during 2020, producing close to 4 million litres.

The core range consists of **12, 15, 18** and **25 year old, 1263 King Alexander III, Cigar Malt Reserve** and **Port Wood Reserve**. In autumn 2019, the entire travel retail range was replaced by three new bottlings, **The Trio, The Quartet** and **The Quintet**, finished in three, four and five casks respectively. Recent limited bottlings include **35, 40 and 45 year old**, a range called **Vintage Port Collection** with three different expressions and a **60 year old**. In spring 2020 a **51 year old** matured in a combination of ex-bourbon, port and sherry casks was released.

History:
1839 Alexander Matheson founds the distillery.

1867 Three Mackenzie brothers run the distillery.

1891 Sir Kenneth Matheson sells the distillery for £14,500 to the Mackenzie brothers.

1917 The Royal Navy moves in to start manufacturing American mines.

1920 The Royal Navy moves out and leaves behind a distillery damaged by an explosion.

1922 The distillery is in production again.

1956 Floor malting replaced by Saladin box.

1960 Mackenzie Brothers (Dalmore) Ltd merges with Whyte & Mackay.

1966 Number of stills is increased to eight.

1982 The Saladin box is abandoned.

1990 American Brands buys Whyte & Mackay.

1996 Whyte & Mackay changes name to JBB (Greater Europe).

2001 Through management buy-out, JBB (Greater Europe) is bought from Fortune Brands and changes name to Kyndal Spirits.

2002 Kyndal Spirits changes name to Whyte & Mackay.

2007 United Spirits buys Whyte & Mackay. A 15 year old, and a 40 year old are released.

2008 1263 King Alexander III is released.

2009 New releases include an 18 year old, a 58 year old and a Vintage 1951.

2010 The Dalmore Mackenzie 1992 is released.

2011 More expressions in the River Collection and 1995 Castle Leod are released.

2012 The visitor centre is upgraded and Constellaton Collection is launched.

2013 Valour is released for duty free.

2014 Emperador Inc buys Whyte & Mackay.

2016 Three new travel retail bottlings are released as well as a 35 year old and Quintessence.

2017 Vintage Port Collection is launched.

2018 The Port Wood Reserve is released.

2019 A new travel retail range is launched.

2020 A 51 year old is released.

Tasting notes Dalmore 12 years old:
GS – The nose offers sweet malt, orange marmalade, sherry and a hint of leather. Full-bodied, with a dry sherry taste though sweeter sherry develops in the mouth along with spice and citrus notes. Lengthy finish with more spices, ginger, Seville oranges and vanilla.

12 years old

Dalwhinnie

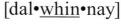
[dal•**whin**•nay]

Owner: Diageo	**Region/district:** Speyside
Founded: 1897	**Status:** Active (vc)	**Capacity:** 2 200 000 litres

Address: Dalwhinnie, Inverness-shire PH19 1AB

Website: malts.com	**Tel:** 01540 672219 (vc)

Dalwhinnie is probably the most easily spotted distillery in Scotland. Nobody travelling by car on the busy A9 between Perth and Inverness will be able to miss it when the road reaches its highest point (462 metres), Drumochter Summit, in the Cairngorms.

But instead of going by car there is an alternative way of reaching the distillery. You can catch The Caledonian Sleeper around nine in the evening from Euston Station in London and ten hours later you get off the train at Dalwhinnie station. Built in 1863, the station is only a five minute walk from the distillery. The distillery itself is the second highest in Scotland after Braeval.

The distillery is equipped with a 7.3 ton full lauter mash tun and six wooden washbacks with the fermentation split into four short sessions of 60 hours and six long, fermenting over the weekend, of 110 hours. There is one pair of stills, replaced in 2018, attached to worm tubs which were replaced with new ones in 2015. The production plan for 2020 is a five-day production week which means 10 mashes per week resulting in 1.4 million litres of alcohol in the year.

Dalwhinnie was chosen as one of the six original Classic Malts in 1988 representing the Highlands. Today it is one of Diageo's best selling single malts and comes in at sixth place with around one million bottles. It is also a key malt in two major Scotch blends – Buchanans and Black & White. The latter has increased sales by no less than 90% since 2014 and now sells 32 million bottles, mainly in Brazil, Mexico and Colombia.

The core range is made up of a **15 year old, Distiller's Edition** with a finish in oloroso casks and **Dalwhinnie Winter's Gold**. In 2018, **Lizzie's Dram**, a distillery exclusive was launched. In spring 2019, Dalwhinnie was also part of the series named after the popular TV series Game of Thrones. Dalwhinnie **Winter's Frost**, representing House Stark was matured in ex-bourbon barrels. In autumn 2020, a 30 year old bottled at 51,9% was launched in the Rare by Nature range.

15 years old

History:

1897 John Grant, George Sellar and Alexander Mackenzie commence building the facilities. The first name is Strathspey.

1898 The owner encounters financial troubles and John Somerville & Co and A P Blyth & Sons take over and change the name to Dalwhinnie.

1905 Cook & Bernheimer in New York, buys Dalwhinnie for £1,250 at an auction.

1919 Macdonald Greenlees & Williams Ltd headed by Sir James Calder buys Dalwhinnie.

1926 Macdonald Greenlees & Williams Ltd is bought by Distillers Company Ltd (DCL) which licences Dalwhinnie to James Buchanan & Co.

1930 Operations are transferred to Scottish Malt Distilleries (SMD).

1934 The distillery is closed after a fire in February.

1938 The distillery opens again.

1968 The maltings is decommissioned.

1987 Dalwhinnie 15 years becomes one of the selected six in United Distillers´ Classic Malts.

1991 A visitor centre is constructed.

1992 The distillery closes and goes through a major refurbishment costing £3.2 million.

1995 The distillery opens in March.

2002 A 36 year old is released.

2006 A 20 year old is released.

2012 A 25 year old is released.

2014 A triple matured bottling without age statement is released for The Friends of the Classic Malts.

2015 Dalwhinnie Winter´s Gold and a 25 year old are released.

2016 A distillery exclusive without age statement is released.

2018 Lizzie´s Dram, a distillery exclusive bottling, is released.

2019 Dalwhinnie Winter´s Frost, part of the Game of Thrones series, is released as well as a 30 year old in the annual Special Releases.

2020 A 30 year old is released as part of the Rare by Nature series.

Tasting notes Dalwhinnie 15 years old:

GS – The nose is fresh, with pine needles, heather and vanilla. Sweet and balanced on the fruity palate, with honey, malt and a very subtle note of peat. The medium length finish dries elegantly.

Deanston

[deen•stun]

Owner:
Distell International Ltd.

Region/district:
Southern Highlands

Founded: 1965

Status: Active (vc)

Capacity:
3 000 000 litres

Address: Deanston, Perthshire FK16 6AG

Website:
deanstonmalt.com

Tel:
01786 843010

In 1785, the Buchanan brothers built a cotton mill and a weavery on the shores of the river Leith. Over time it turned into a a major workplace for over a thousand people who needed somewhere to live.

A small city, Deanston, grew up around the weavery and it even had its own currency minted, which could be used in the local shops. Over time, competition from low-salary countries intensified and the weavery was closed in 1965. The owners, James Findlay & Co, decided that the premises could be used for something else and – joining forces with Brodie Hepburn, a whisky broker in Glasgow – they turned the site into a whisky distillery. For many years the distillery produced single malt for blends and it wasn't until the master blender at the time, Ian MacMillan, refined the production and the recipe that the whisky found its way into the single malt market. Today, under the ownership of Distell International, the brand is slowly gaining recognition from malt whisky enthusiasts.

Deanston is equipped with a new 10.5 ton traditional open top, stainless steel mash tun and eight stainless steel washbacks. In 2019 the distillery worked 7 days per week producing 2,4 million litres but for 2020 they have decided to go for a 5-day week with both short and long fermentations with an average fermentation time of 85 hours. There are also two pairs of stills with ascending lyne arms. Having started in 2000, organic spirit is produced every year. Due to the demand for "traditional" Deanston single malt, the volume of organic spirit has been reduced to around 10,000 litres per year.

The core range is a **12** and an **18 year old,** the **Virgin Oak** matured in ex-bourbon and with a finish in virgin oak casks and the **15 year old Organic**. Recent limited bottlings, released in July 2020, include a **1991 Muscat finish,** a **2002 Organic Pedro Ximenez** and a **2002 Pinot Noir finish**. The only available duty-free exclusive is a **10 year old Bordeaux red wine cask finish**. Finally, there are two recent distillery exclusives - a **2002 Port finish** and a **2007 Calvados finish**.

History:

1965 A weavery from 1785 is transformed into Deanston Distillery by James Findlay & Co. and Brodie Hepburn Ltd. Brodie Hepburn also runs Tullibardine Distillery.

1966 Production commences in October.

1971 The first single malt is named Old Bannockburn.

1972 Invergordon Distillers takes over.

1974 The first single malt bearing the name Deanston is produced.

1982 The distillery closes.

1990 Burn Stewart Distillers from Glasgow buys the distillery for £2.1 million.

1991 The distillery resumes production.

1999 C L Financial buys an 18% stake of Burn Stewart.

2002 C L Financial acquires the remaining stake.

2006 Deanston 30 years old is released.

2009 A new version of the 12 year old is released.

2010 Virgin Oak is released.

2012 A visitor centre is opened.

2013 Burn Stewart Distillers is bought by South African Distell Group for £160m.

2014 An 18 year old cognac finish is released in the USA.

2015 An 18 year old is released.

2016 Organic Deanston is released.

2017 A 40 year old and Vintage 2008 are released.

2018 A 10 year old Bordeaux finish is released for duty free.

2019 A number of limited releases including 1997 Palo Cortado finish, 2006 Cream Sherry finish and a 2012 Beer finish.

2020 A 1991 Muscat finish, a 2002 Organix PX and a 2002 Pinot Noir finish are released.

12 years old

Tasting notes Deanston 12 years old:

GS – A fresh, fruity nose with malt and honey. The palate displays cloves, ginger, honey and malt, while the finish is long, quite dry and pleasantly herbal.

Dufftown

[duff•town]

Owner:
Diageo

Region/district:
Speyside

Founded: **Status:**   **Capacity:**
1896   Active   6 000 000 litres

Address: Dufftown, Keith, Banffshire AB55 4BR

Website:
malts.com
thesingleton.com

Tel:
01340 822100

Of the 28 malt distilleries owned by Diageo, Dufftown is the fifth largest in terms of capacity. In fact, before Roseisle opened in 2009, it was the biggest together with Caol Ila. For the past 13 years it has been working 24/7 producing 6 million litres yearly.

From early days, Dufftown single malt was an important part of the Bell´s blended whisky and the distillery was actually bought by Arthur Bell & Sons in 1933. It has remained a component of Bell´s and many other blends but already in the late 1970s it was sold as an 8 year old under the name Dufftown-Glenlivet. The major break-through as a single malt, however, came in 2006 when it was launched as one of the three Singleton malts together with Glen Ord and neighbouring Glendullan.

Dufftown distillery is equipped with a 13 ton full lauter mash tun, 12 stainless steel washbacks and three pairs of stills. Furthermore, all stills have sub coolers. The style of Dufftown single malt is green and grassy which is achieved by a clear wort and long fermentation (75 hours minimum). In a seven-day week, no less than 165 still runs are completed (110 in the wash stills and 55 in the spirits stills) which clearly shows what a busy distillery it is. Dufftown has been working 24/7 since 2007 and during 2020 the plan is to produce 6 million litres of alcohol.

The distillery lies in a cul-de-sac right by the river Dullan and 500 metres to the west are the warehouses and a filling station on the same spot where the now demolished Pittyvaich distillery used to be.

The core range consists of **The Singleton of Dufftown 12, 15** and **18 year old**. A new expression was added to the line-up two years ago – **Malt Master's Selection**. Without age statement, the whisky has been matured in a combination of bourbon and sherry casks with a high proportion of refill casks. A range for duty-free was introduced in 2013 and now consists of **Trinité, Liberté** and **Artisan**. In July 2020, a **30 year old**, matured in refill American oak was part of the new Prima & Ultima range and in the autumn, a **17 year old**, matured in refill casks was part of the Rare by Nature series.

History:

1895   Peter Mackenzie, Richard Stackpole, John Symon and Charles MacPherson build the distillery Dufftown-Glenlivet in an old mill.

1896   Production starts in November.

1897   The distillery is owned by P. Mackenzie & Co., who also owns Blair Athol in Pitlochry.

1933   P. Mackenzie & Co. is bought by Arthur Bell & Sons for £56,000.

1968   The floor maltings is discontinued and malt is bought from outside suppliers. The number of stills is increased from two to four.

1974   The number of stills is increased from four to six.

1979   The stills are increased by a further two to eight.

1985   Guinness buys Arthur Bell & Sons.

1997   Guinness and Grand Metropolitan merge to form Diageo.

2006   The Singleton of Dufftown 12 year old is launched as a special duty free bottling.

2008   The Singleton of Dufftown is made available also in the UK.

2010   A Manager´s Choice 1997 is released.

2013   A 28 year old cask strength and two expressions for duty free - Unité and Trinité - are released.

2014   Tailfire, Sunray and Spey Cascade are released.

2016   Two limited releases are made - a 21 year old and a 25 year old.

2018   Malt Master´s Selection is released.

2020   A 30 year old Prima & Ultima and a 17 year old Rare by Nature are released.

Singleton of Dufftown 12 year

Tasting notes Dufftown 12 years old:

GS – The nose is sweet, almost violet-like, with underlying malt. Big and bold on the palate, this is an upfront yet very drinkable whisky. The finish is medium to long, warming, spicy, with slowly fading notes of sherry and fudge.

Edradour

[ed•ra•<u>dow</u>•er]

Owner:
Signatory Vintage
Scotch Whisky Co. Ltd

Region/district:
Southern Highland

Founded: **Status:** **Capacity:**
1825 Active (vc) 260 000 litres

Address: Pitlochry, Perthshire PH16 5JP

Website: **Tel:**
edradour.com 01796 472095

Four years of expansion and refurbishing at Edradour have now come to an end. The major task during these years has been to build Edradour #2, an entirely new distillery next to the existing one.

But it didn't stop there. The better part of 2018 and into 2019 saw the rekitting of Edradour 1 where all equipment was replaced like for like with the exception of the old Morton refrigerator and one of the worms. The combined equipment for the two distilleries now consists of two open, traditional cast iron mash tuns with a mash size of 1.1 tons, two Morton refrigerators to cool the wort and eight washbacks made of Oregon pine, with enough room left to install more in the future. The two stills in each distillery are attached to a worm tub on the outside and new warehouses have also been erected next to the new still house

The plan for 2020 is to do 5 mashes per week at each distillery with three short at 48 hours and two long at 96 hours. This will equate to 200,000 litres of alcohol during 2020. Due to rapidly increasing demand for the unpeated Edradour, the amount of peated production has diminished in the last couple of years with only around 13,000 litres being distilled per year. Peated production now only takes place in the old distillery.

The core range consists of a **10 year old** and the **12 year old Caledonia Selection**. Both are vattings of 1st and 2nd fill Oloroso casks and in the future, these will be darker and more intense in the flavour due to the fact that more active casks have been used since 2009. In the range are also **Cask Strength Sherry 12 year old** and **Cask Strength Bourbon 11 year old**. There is also the peated **Ballechin 10 year old**. matured in a combination of ex-bourbon and ex-oloroso. The Straight From The Cask range are all fully matured in different casks. Some of the latest include **Ballechin 2009 Oloroso, 2008 Bourbon, 2007 Bordeaux** and **Edradour 2009 Sherry**. Recent wood finishes include **Edradour 19 year old Bordeaux** and **Edradour 18 year old Barolo**. A limited release is the interesting **8 year old vatting** of sherry-matured Edradour and bourbon-matured Ballechin.

History:

1825 Probably the year when a distillery called Glenforres is founded by farmers in Perthshire.

1837 The first year Edradour is mentioned.

1841 The farmers form a proprietary company, John MacGlashan & Co.

1886 John McIntosh & Co. acquires Edradour.

1933 William Whiteley & Co. buys the distillery.

1982 Campbell Distilleries (Pernod Ricard) buys Edradour and builds a visitor centre.

1986 The first single malt is released.

2002 Edradour is bought by Andrew Symington from Signatory for £5.4 million. The product range is expanded with a 10 year old and a 13 year old cask strength.

2003 A 30 year old and a 10 year old are released.

2004 A number of wood finishes are launched as cask strength.

2006 The first bottling of peated Ballechin is released.

2007 A Madeira matured Ballechin is released.

2008 A Ballechin matured in Port pipes and a 10 year old Edradour with a Sauternes finish are released.

2009 Fourth edition of Ballechin (Oloroso) is released.

2010 Ballechin #5 Marsala is released.

2011 Ballechin #6 Bourbon and a 26 year old PX sherry finish are released.

2012 A 1993 Oloroso and a 1993 Sauternes finish as well as the 7th edition of Ballechin (Bordeaux) are released.

2013 Ballechin Sauternes is released.

2014 The first release of a 10 year old Ballechin.

2015 Fairy Flag is released.

2017 New releases include an 8 year old vatting of Edradour and Ballechin.

2018 The new distillery is commissioned.

EDRADOUR

The Distillery Edition
HIGHLAND SINGLE MALT SCOTCH WHISKY

10

10 years old

Tasting notes Edradour 10 years old:

GS – Cider apples, malt, almonds, vanilla and honey ar present on the nose, along with a hint of smoke and sherry. The palate is rich, creamy and malty, with a persistent nuttiness and quite a pronounced kick of slightly leathery sherry. Spices and sherry dominate the medium to long finish.

Fettercairn

Whisky enthusiasts can sometimes be quite conservative. If they've sampled a malt they dislike they rarely give it another chance a few years later to see if the whisky, or indeed their own palate, has changed.

Quite often they also distribute their opinions to other whisky drinkers and eventually a certain brand has been deemed mediocre even by people who haven't tried it. There are a few good examples of that in the Scotch whisky business and one of them is Fettercairn or Old Fettercairn as the whisky was called until 2002. Over the years very little attention was put into the brand and it was mainly used as a filler for blends. But during the last years, a re-racking programme, similar to what was done with Jura twenty years ago and what is going on at Tamnavulin now, has been implemented. Re-racking basically means putting maturing whisky into better wood. This scheme has worked wonders and with a completely new range, Fettercairn single malt is now deservedly getting the attention from more whisky lovers.

Fettercairn distillery is equipped with a traditional, five ton cast iron mash tun and eleven washbacks with a fermentation time of 60 hours. There are two pairs of stills with an unusual feature. When collecting the middle cut, cooling water is allowed to trickle along the outside of the spirit still necks in order to increase reflux and thereby produce a lighter spirit. The production goal for 2020 is 18 mashes per week and 1.5 million litres of alcohol.

The core range consists of a **12 year old** and a **28 year old**, both matured in ex-bourbon casks. A new addition was made in June 2020 – a **16 year old** made from chocolate malt and finished for two years in both sherry and port casks and this was followed up in July by a **22 year old**, matured in first fill ex-bourbon and bottled at 47%. Recent limited releases include a **46 year old**, distilled in 1973 and finished in tawny port pipes. In 2019 there was the release of a **12 year old PX sherry finish** exclusive to duty-free and this was followed up in 2020 by a one litre version of the **16 year old** as well as a **23 year old**.

[fett•er•cairn]

Owner:	**Region/district:**
Whyte & Mackay (Emperador)	Eastern Highlands
Founded: **Status:**	**Capacity:**
1824 Active (vc)	3 200 000 litres

Address: Fettercairn, Laurencekirk, Kincardineshire AB30 1YB

Website:	**Tel:**
fettercairnwhisky.com	01561 340205

History:

1824 Sir Alexander Ramsay founds the distillery.

1830 Sir John Gladstone buys the distillery.

1887 A fire erupts and the distillery is forced to close for repairs.

1890 Thomas Gladstone dies and his son John Robert takes over. The distillery reopens.

1912 The company is close to liquidation and John Gladstone buys out the other investors.

1926 The distillery is mothballed.

1939 The distillery is bought by Associated Scottish Distillers Ltd. Production restarts.

1960 The maltings discontinues.

1966 The stills are increased from two to four.

1971 The distillery is bought by Tomintoul-Glenlivet Distillery Co. Ltd.

1973 Tomintoul-Glenlivet Distillery Co. Ltd is bought by Whyte & Mackay Distillers Ltd.

1974 The mega group of companies Lonrho buys Whyte & Mackay.

1988 Lonrho sells to Brent Walker Group plc.

1989 A visitor centre opens.

1990 American Brands Inc. buys Whyte & Mackay for £160 million.

1996 Whyte & Mackay and Jim Beam Brands merge to become JBB Worldwide.

2001 Kyndal Spirits buys Whyte & Mackay from JBB Worldwide.

2002 The whisky changes name to Fettercairn 1824.

2003 Kyndal Spirits changes name to Whyte & Mackay.

2007 United Spirits buys Whyte & Mackay. A 23 year old single cask is released.

2009 24, 30 and 40 year olds are released.

2010 Fettercairn Fior is launched.

2012 Fettercairn Fasque is released.

2015 Emperador Inc buys Whyte & Mackay.

2018 A new range is launched; 12, 28, 40 and 50 year old.

2019 A 12 year old PX finish is released for duty free.

2020 A 16 year old and a 22 year old are added to the core range.

Tasting notes Fettercairn 12 years old:

IR – A delicious combination of pineapple, banana and mango together with coffee beans, cured ham and dried flowers. Still fruity on the palate but also becomes more spicy and malty and with a bit of mint at the end.

12 years old

Glenallachie

[glen•alla•key]

Owner: **Region/district:**
The Glenallachie Distillers Co.   Speyside

Founded: **Status:**   **Capacity:**
1967   Active (vc)   4 000 000 litres

Address: Aberlour, Banffshire AB38 9LR

Website: **Tel:**
www.theglenallachie.com   01236 422120

In 1960, the architect William Delmé Evans joined forces with Mackinlay McPherson and resurrected Jura distillery. A few years later the same constellation built Glenallachie.

This was to become Delmé-Evans project from beginning to end. He was entrusted with finding the right spot in the Highlands and then he not only designed the buildings but all of the equipment by himself. He also fulfilled a life long dream of his – a gravity fed distillery

The distillery is equipped with a 9.4 ton semi-lauter mash tun, six washbacks made of mild steel, but lined with stainless steel, plus another two washbacks made from stainless steel which were brought in from Caperdonich when that was demolished. The latter two have now been converted to low wines and feints vessels for peated and unpeated spirit to facilitate the switch between the two styles. There are also two pairs of unusually wide stills with horizontal condensers. Distilling 700,000 litres in a distillery built to make 4 million litres allows for very long fermentations – in GlenAllachie's case up to 160 hours. 100,000 litres of heavily peated spirit with an 80ppm phenol specification is also made. The owners fill the newmake into casks at three different strengths to achieve different flavour profiles – 63.5%, 68% and 72%.

Under Chivas' regime, Glenallachie single malt was a key ingredient in one of the top selling blends – Clan Campbell. With the new owners, a range of single casks was released in March 2018. A few months later a core range was unveiled; a **10 year old cask strength, 12, 18** and **25 year old**. In September 2019, a **15 year old** was added to the range. Recent limited releases appeared in 2019; **8 year old Koval finish, 10 year old port finish** and a **12 year old PX sherry finish**. These were followed in April 2020 by a **9 year old Rye finish,** an **11 year old Port finish** and an **11 year old Moscatel finish**. Various single cask bottlings have also been released for selected markets. Finally there is a range of peated, blended malts called MacNair's Lum Reek.

History:

1967   The distillery is founded by Mackinlay, McPherson & Co., a subsidiary of Scottish & Newcastle Breweries Ltd. William Delmé Evans is architect.

1985   Scottish & Newcastle Breweries Ltd sells Charles Mackinlay Ltd to Invergordon Distillers which acquires both Glenallachie and Isle of Jura.

1987   The distillery is decommissioned.

1989   Campbell Distillers (Pernod Ricard) buys the distillery, increases the number of stills from two to four and takes up production again.

2005   The first official bottling for many years is a Cask Strength Edition from 1989.

2017   Glenallachie Distillery Edition is released and the distillery is sold to The Glenallachie Consortium.

2018   A series of single casks is released followed by a core range consisting of 12, 18 and 25 year old.

2019   A range of wood finishes is launched as well as a 15 year old core bottling. A visitor centre is opened.

2020   Three new wood finishes are launched; rye, port and moscatel.

12 years old

Tasting notes Glenallachie 12 years old:

IR – Baked apples with almonds and custard, lemon zest and pine needles on the nose. Rich and lively on the palate, sweet spices, ginger, bananas, liquorice, raisins and hints of pepper.

Glenburgie

[glen•bur•gee]

Owner:
Chivas Brothers
(Pernod Ricard)

Region/district:
Speyside

Founded: 1810 | **Status:** Active | **Capacity:** 4 250 000 litres

Address: Glenburgie, Forres, Morayshire IV36 2QY

Website: - | **Tel:** 01343 850258

At least since the late 1920s, Glenburgie single malt has been intricably linked to Ballantine´s blended Scotch. The connection between the two can be contributed to one of the largest profiles of the Scotch whisky industry – Jimmy Barclay.

Barclay started his career at Benrinnes and in 1909 he moved to Glasgow to work with Peter Mackie – creator of White Horse and owner of Lagavulin. Ten years later he, together with R. A. McKinlay, acquired the Ballantines brand from the family. The timing was terrible with prohibition hitting the USA just a couple of months later. Jimmy however was a true entrepreneur and quickly saw ways of getting the whisky into the illegal US market via Canada and the West Indies. He joined forces with Jack Kriender and Charlie Berns, owners of several speakeasys in New York and later founders of the legendary 21 Club. When prohibition was repealed in 1933, Ballantines had become known to whisky drinkers as a brand of great quality. Barclay and McKinlay sold the brand to Hiram Walker in 1935 but continued to work in the company. After a couple of years, Barclay went on to work with Chivas Brothers developing yet another blended whisky, Chivas Regal, into a global mega brand.

For slightly more than two decades, 1958-1981, two Lomond stills were operative at Glenburgie. Instead of the traditional swan neck, they had columns with a number of adjustable plates inside. The whisky from these stills is known as Glencraig.

Glenburgie is equipped with a 7.5 ton full lauter mash tun, 12 stainless steel washbacks with a 52 hour fermentation time and three pairs of stills. The majority of the production is filled into bourbon casks and a part thereof is matured in four dunnage, two racked and two palletized warehouses.

Since 2017 there are two official bottlings of Glenburgie - **15** and **18 year old** both aged in ex-bourbon casks and bottled at 40%. A **17 year old cask strength** in the range The Distillery Reserve Collection is also available at Chivas' visitor centres.

History:

1810 William Paul founds Kilnflat Distillery. Official production starts in 1829.

1870 Kilnflat distillery closes.

1878 The distillery reopens under the name Glenburgie-Glenlivet, Charles Hay is licensee.

1884 Alexander Fraser & Co. takes over.

1925 Alexander Fraser & Co. files for bankruptcy and the receiver Donald Mustad assumes control of operations.

1927 James & George Stodart Ltd (owned by James Barclay and R A McKinlay since 1922) buys the distillery which by this time is inactive.

1930 Hiram Walker buys 60% of James & George Stodart Ltd.

1936 Hiram Walker buys Glenburgie Distillery in October. Production restarts.

1958 Lomond stills are installed producing a single malt, Glencraig. Floor malting ceases.

1981 The Lomond stills are replaced by conventional stills.

1987 Allied Lyons buys Hiram Walker.

2002 A 15 year old is released.

2004 A £4.3 million refurbishment and reconstruction takes place.

2005 Chivas Brothers (Pernod Ricard) becomes the new owner through the acquisition of Allied Domecq.

2006 The number of stills are increased from four to six in May.

2017 A 15 year old is released.

2019 An 18 year old is released.

15 years old

Tasting notes Glenburgie 15 years old:

IR – Very fruity on the nose with notes of pears, apple pie, honey, marzipan and roasted nuts. The palate reveals tropical fruits, white chocolate, marmalade, vanilla and caramel.

Glencadam

[glen•ka•dam]

Owner: **Region/district:**
Angus Dundee Distillers   Eastern Highlands

Founded: **Status:**   **Capacity:**
1825   Active   1 300 000 litres

Address: Brechin, Angus DD9 7PA

Website: **Tel:**
glencadamwhisky.com   01356 622217

For a distillery that is celebrating its 200th anniversary five years from now, one would think that there are some amazing stories to be told about Glencadam and its single malts.

This couldn't be further from the truth. In fact when Alfred Barnard, the first "whisky tourist", came here in 1886 he was less than impressed and the half of the one page he devoted to the distillery in his famous book was about the history of Brechin where the distillery is situated. Glencadam´s recent fame started in earnest in 2003 when Angus Dundee bought the distillery. They rapidly created a broad and interesting range of whiskies and in order to create a wider awareness of the brand a visitor centre is now being built. The current office building will be extended with a shop and visitor centre on the ground floor and a café and outdoor terrace on the first floor.

Glencadam distillery is equipped with a traditional, 4.9 ton cast iron mash tun, six stainless steel washbacks with a fermentation time of 52 hours and one pair of stills. The external heat exchanger on the wash still is from the fifties and is perhaps the first in the business. On site, two dunnage warehouses from 1825, three from the 1950s and one modern racked can be found. The distillery is currently working a 7-day week, which enables 16 mashes per week and 1.3 million litres of alcohol. The owners also produce a large number of blends. These are blended in 16 huge steel tanks next to the distillery. From here the spirit is sent to the bottling plant in Coatbridge east of Glasgow.

The extensive core range from Glencadam shows no sign of diminishing. On the contrary – yet another bottling was added in spring 2020, the **Reserva Andalucia**. Matured in a combination of bourbon and sherry it was then finished in oloroso casks before being bottled at 46%. Apart from that the core range consists of **Origin 1825, 10, 13, 15, 18, 21** and **25 year old**. Two wood finishes are also in the range; a **17 year old port finish** and a **19 year old oloroso finish**. Rare single cask bottlings are also regularly released, usually aged between 25 and 35 years old.

History:

1825   George Cooper founds the distillery.

1827   David Scott takes over.

1837   The distillery is sold by David Scott.

1852   Alexander Miln Thompson becomes the owner.

1857   Glencadam Distillery Company is formed.

1891   Gilmour, Thompson & Co Ltd takes over.

1954   Hiram Walker takes over.

1959   Refurbishing of the distillery.

1987   Allied Lyons buys Hiram Walker Gooderham & Worts.

1994   Allied Lyons changes name to Allied Domecq.

2000   The distillery is mothballed.

2003   Allied Domecq sells the distillery to Angus Dundee Distillers.

2005   The new owner releases a 15 year old.

2008   A re-designed 15 year old and a new 10 year old are introduced.

2009   A 25 and a 30 year old are released in limited numbers.

2010   A 12 year old port finish, a 14 year old sherry finish, a 21 year old and a 32 year old are released.

2012   A 30 year old is released.

2015   A 25 year old is launched.

2016   Origin 1825, 17 year old port finish, 19 year old oloroso finish, an 18 year old and a 25 year old are released.

2017   A 13 year old is released.

2019   The 15 year old is back in the range and batch two of the 25 year old is released.

2020   Reserva Andalucia is released.

Tasting notes Glencadam 10 years old:

GS – A light and delicate, floral nose, with tinned pears and fondant cream. Medium-bodied, smooth, with citrus fruits and gently-spiced oak on the palate. The finish is quite long and fruity, with a hint of barley.

10 years old

GlenDronach

[glen•dro•nack]

Owner:
Benriach Distillery Co
(Brown Forman)

Region/district:
Highlands

Founded: 1826   **Status:** Active (vc)   **Capacity:** 1 400 000 litres

Address: Forgue, Aberdeenshire AB54 6DB

Website:
glendronachdistillery.com

Tel:
01466 730202

Travelling on the A96 from Aberdeen towards Keith, you will find GlenDronach 10 kilometres northeast of Huntly, surrounded by Aberdeenshire's flourishing agricultural lands. It wouldn't be fair to call it secluded but you won't stumble on it by chance.

Nearest neighbours are Knockdhu and Glen Garioch but in this area you will not find the abundance of distilleries like in Speyside an hour's drive to the west. But the single malt has devoted fans and almost 10,000 people travel here every year, a number that will surely increase with the newly refurbished visitor centre.

The distillery equipment consists of a 3.7 ton cast iron mash tun with rakes, nine washbacks made of larch with a fermentation time of 60 to 90 hours and two pairs of stills. The distillery usually produces 1.2 million litres per year. The visitor centre was completely renovated in early 2020 and includes a new tasting room, whisky bar, lounge area and a shop. There is also a display with old and rare bottles including the distillery's oldest bottle of GlenDronach from 1913.

The core range is **The Hielan 8 years, Original 12 years, Revival 15 years, Allardice 18 years, Parliament 21 years** and **Peated** (first introduced in 2015). The latter has been matured in bourbon casks and then finished in a combination of oloroso and PX sherry casks. In November 2019 it was replaced by **Traditionally Peated** with a maturation in oloroso, PX and port casks. Unusually, the peat was added to towards the end of the kilning to create a more earthy and less medicinal smoky flavour. Recent limited releases include **Cask Strength Batch 7,** the **27 year old Grandeur, Peated Port Wood, Master Vintage 1993** (a combination of oloroso and PX casks) and **GlenDronach Port Wood.** The latter, released in summer 2019, was matured in ex-sherry wood followed by a second maturation in ex-port pipes. In July 2019, batch 17 of the **Cask Bottlings** was launched. The first GlenDronach for duty free appeared in autumn 2018 when 10 year old **Forgue** was launched followed in May 2019 by the 16 year old **Boynsmill** where port pipes had been used to complement the sherried profile.

History:

1826   The distillery is founded by a consortium with James Allardes as one of the owners.

1837   Parts of the distillery is destroyed in a fire.

1852   Walter Scott (from Teaninich) takes over.

1887   Walter Scott dies and Glendronach is taken over by a consortium from Leith.

1920   Charles Grant buys Glendronach for £9,000.

1960   William Teacher & Sons buys the distillery.

1966   The number of stills is increased to four.

1976   Allied Breweries takes over William Teacher & Sons.

1996   The distillery is mothballed.

2002   Production is resumed on 14th May.

2005   The distillery closes to rebuild from coal to indirect firing by steam. Reopens in September. Chivas Brothers (Pernod Ricard) becomes new owner through the acquisition of Allied Domecq.

2008   Pernod Ricard sells the distillery to the owners of BenRiach distillery.

2009   Relaunch of the whole range including 12, 15 and 18 year old.

2010   A 31 year old, a 1996 single cask and a total of 11 vintages and four wood finishes are released. A visitor centre is opened.

2011   The 21 year old Parliament and 11 vintages are released.

2012   A number of vintages are released.

2013   Recherché 44 years and a number of new vintages are released.

2014   Nine different single casks are released.

2015   The Hielan, 8 years old, is released.

2016   Brown Forman buys the distillery. Peated GlenDronach and Octaves Classic are released.

2017   A range of new single casks is released.

2018   Two bottlings for duty free are released - 10 year old Forgue and 16 year old Boynsmill.

2019   Port Wood, Traditionally Peated and batch 17 of the Cask Bottlings are released.

Tasting notes GlenDronach 12 years old:

GS – A sweet nose of Christmas cake fresh from the oven. Smooth on the palate, with sherry, soft oak, fruit, almonds and spices. The finish is comparatively dry and nutty, ending with bitter chocolate.

12 years old Original

Glendullan

[glen•dull•an]

Owner:
Diageo

Region/district:
Speyside

Founded: **Status:** **Capacity:**
1897 Active 5 000 000 litres

Address: Dufftown, Keith, Banffshire AB55 4DJ

Website: **Tel:**
www.thesingleton.com 01340 822100

In the late 1800s, Campbeltown was considered the whisky capital of the world with its more than 30 distilleries. These days are long gone and today the small town of Dufftown in Speyside is well suited to lay claim to the same title.

This small town with 1,700 people not only has six working distilleries with a combined production capacity making up 12% of the total Scotch malt whisky production. It is also the home to two of the largest Scotch brands in the world, Glenfiddich and Balvenie, and is also the centre of the best known whisky gathering in the world – the Spirit of Speyside Whisky Festival – every year in May. No less than nine distilleries (six of them still working) were established here. First to open, in 1823, was Mortlach followed by Glenfiddich 63 years later. Glendullan was one of five distilleries founded in the first golden era of Scotch whisky – the 1890s. The distillery we see today is of a much later date. Built in 1972, it worked in tandem with the old distillery for thirteen years.

Glendullan distillery is situated just one minute drive east of Glenfiddich near a river which, in spite of the distillery's name isn't Dullan, but Fiddich. The confluence of the two rivers lies a mile to the south of Glendullan.

The distillery is equipped with a 12 ton full lauter stainless steel mash tun, 8 washbacks made of larch and two made of stainless steel with a fermentation time of 75 hours to promote a green/grassy character of the whisky, as well as three pairs of stills. In 2020 the distillery will be doing 21 mashes per week, producing 5 million litres of alcohol.

The core range consists of **12, 15** and **18 year old**. The Singleton Reserve Collection with **Classic** (American oak), **Double Matured** (American and European oak and then married together) and **Master's Art** (Muscat finish) is exclusive to duty free. Recent limited expressions include a **40 year old** released in 2018 followed by a **41 year old** the year after. With **House Tully**, Glendullan was also a part of the Game of Thrones series launched in early 2019.

History:

1896 William Williams & Sons, a blending company with Three Stars and Strahdon among its brands, founds the distillery.

1902 Glendullan is delivered to the Royal Court and becomes the favourite whisky of Edward VII.

1919 Macdonald Greenlees buys a share of the company and Macdonald Greenlees & Williams Distillers is formed.

1926 Distillers Company Limited (DCL) buys Glendullan.

1930 Glendullan is transferred to Scottish Malt Distillers (SMD).

1962 Major refurbishing and reconstruction.

1972 A brand new distillery is constructed next to the old one and both operate simultaneously during a few years.

1985 The oldest of the two distilleries is mothballed.

1995 The first launch of Glendullan in the Rare Malts series is a 22 year old from 1972.

2005 A 26 year old from 1978 is launched in the Rare Malts series.

2007 Singleton of Glendullan is launched in the USA.

2013 Singleton of Glendullan Liberty and Trinity are released for duty free.

2014 A 38 year old is released.

2015 Classic, Double Matured and Master´s Art are released.

2018 The Forgotten Drops 40 years old is released.

2019 House of Tully, part of the Game of Thrones series, as well as a 41 year old are released

12 years old

Tasting notes Singleton of Glendullan 12 years

GS – The nose is spicy, with brittle toffee, vanilla, new leather and hazelnuts. Spicy and sweet on the smooth palate, with citrus fruits, more vanilla and fresh oak. Drying and pleasingly peppery in the finish.

Glen Elgin

[glen el•gin]

Owner:
Diageo

Region/district:
Speyside

Founded: **Status:**
1898   Active

Capacity:
2 700 000 litres

Address: Longmorn, Morayshire IV30 8SL

Website:
malts.com

Tel:
01343 862100

With more than 50 distilleries, Speyside is a haven for any whisky lover. Many of them can easily be spotted from the main roads and at least sixteen are open to visitors.

But there are also the ones that are quite difficult to find even if you know the location. One such is Glen Elgin. It lies in a small hamlet called Fogwatt which is on the busy A941 between Elgin and Rothes. It takes 30 seconds to drive through Fogwatt and it is not possible to spot the distillery from the road. There are two streets leading from the main road to the distillery but since this is a working plant with a no visitor policy it is recommended you park your car on one of the side roads and walk a couple of minutes to reach the distillery. Take your pictures when you've reached the distillery office but avoid walking onto the premises. Health and safety regulations are nowadays not taken lightly at most distilleries.

When you know about the secluded location it appears well-founded that the owners launched the whisky in 2002 in a range called The Hidden Malts together with Caol Ila, Clynelish and Glen Ord. That particular range is now history and three of them are part of the extended Classic Malts range while Glen Ord became one of three distilleries in the successful Singleton family.

The distillery is equipped with an 8.4 ton Steinecker full lauter mash tun from 2001, nine washbacks made of larch (two of them replaced in 2018) and six small stills. The distillery alternates between 12 and 16 mashes per week. The stills are connected to six wooden worm tubs in which the spirit vapours are condensed. Although worm tubs might indicate a heavy and perhaps sulphury newmake, the long fermentation (between 80 and 120 hours) and the slow distillation produce a fruity spirit with depth, perfect for a blended whisky. The production plan for 2020 is a five-day week, producing 1.8 million litres of alcohol.

The only official bottling is a **12 year old**, but a limited **18 year old**, matured in ex-bodega European oak butts was one of the Special Releases in 2017.

History:

1898 The former manager of Glenfarclas, William Simpson and banker James Carle found Glen Elgin.

1900 Production starts in May but the distillery closes just five months later.

1901 The distillery is auctioned for £4,000 to the Glen Elgin-Glenlivet Distillery Co. and is mothballed.

1906 The wine producer J. J. Blanche & Co. buys the distillery for £7,000 and production resumes.

1929 J. J. Blanche dies and the distillery is put up for sale again.

1930 Scottish Malt Distillers (SMD) buys it and the license goes to White Horse Distillers.

1964 Expansion from two to six stills plus other refurbishing takes place.

1992 The distillery closes for refurbishing and installation of new stills.

1995 Production resumes in September.

2001 A 12 year old is launched in the Flora & Fauna series.

2002 The Flora & Fauna series malt is replaced by Hidden Malt 12 years.

2003 A 32 year old cask strength from 1971 is released.

2008 A 16 year old is launched as a Special Release.

2009 Glen Elgin 1998, a single cask in the new Manager´s Choice range is released.

2017 An 18 year old is launched as part of the Special Releases.

12 years old

Tasting notes Glen Elgin 12 years old:

GS – A nose of rich, fruity sherry, figs and fragrant spice. Full-bodied, soft, malty and honeyed in the mouth. The finish is lengthy, slightly perfumed, with spicy oak.

Glenfarclas

[glen•fark•lass]

Owner:	**Region/district:**
J. & G. Grant	Speyside

Founded:	**Status:**	**Capacity:**
1836	Active (vc)	3 500 000 litres

Address: Ballindalloch, Banffshire AB37 9BD

Website:	**Tel:**
glenfarclas.com	01807 500257

The interest in old and rare Scotch single malts has grown at an astonishing rate in the past decade, not least in the Far East and especially in China, Taiwan and Singapore.

Certain brands are sought after – Macallan, Dalmore, Glenfiddich and Glenfarclas – and these bottlings often cost five-digit sums in pounds. These expressions have not just age in common, but a maturation in sherry casks is often preferred as well as, of course, a bottle that stands out. A crystal decanter, preferably encrusted with gemstones, is a given. No matter how unobtainable these releases are to the general whisky enthusiast, they will get their share of attention. In 2016 three Glenfarclas bottlings in the Pagoda Reserve series (43, 48 and 59 years old) were released in a collaboration with The Whisky Corporation in Singapore. This was followed up in spring 2020 with the 62 year old Pagoda Ruby and later in the year with the 63 year old Pagoda Sapphire. All five whiskies had been distilled from the distillery's floor malted barley – a practice that stopped in 1972.

Glenfarclas is one of few family-owned distilleries (now in its sixth generation) still remaning in Scotland. Sales of the single malt have increased substantially in the last few years and currently it sells 2.3 million bottles yearly which makes it the twelfth most sold single malt in the world.

The distillery is equipped with a 16.5 ton semi-lauter mash tun, the largest in Scotland, and twelve stainless steel washbacks with a minimum fermentation time of 60 hours but with a current average of 102 hours. There are three pairs of directly fired stills and the wash stills are equipped with rummagers. The production plan for 2020 is to mash around 8-9 times a week which means 2 million litres of pure alcohol. A number of new dunnage warehouses have recently been built and the owners can now store 105,000 casks on site in 38 warehouses.

The Glenfarclas core range consists of **8, 10, 12, 15, 21** and **25 year old,** as well as the lightly sherried **Heritage** which comes without an age statement and the **105 Cask Strength.** The latter was the first commercially available cask strength single malt in the industry. There is also a **17 year old** destined for the USA, Japan and Sweden. The **30** and **40 year olds** are limited but new editions occur regularly. An 18 year old exclusive to travel retail was launched in 2014 but has now been discontinued. The owners quite often produce spectacular limited releases and the rarity of the expressions clearly show the impressive selection that they have available in their warehouses. Apart from the Pagoda Reserve series mentioned above, they have released a series of bottlings called **The Generations Range** which included whiskies made in the 1950s in the last few years! The owners also continue to release bottlings in their **Family Casks** series with vintages ranging from **1954** to **2004.** Finally, in May 2019, the **Glenfarclas Trilogy** was released with three bottlings aged **14, 20** and **27 years,** matured in ex-oloroso casks.

History:

1836 Robert Hay founds the distillery on the original site since 1797.

1865 Robert Hay passes away and John Grant and his son George buy the distillery. They lease it to John Smith at The Glenlivet Distillery.

1870 John Smith resigns in order to start Cragganmore and J. & G. Grant Ltd takes over.

1889 John Grant dies and George Grant takes over.

1890 George Grant dies and his widow Elsie takes over the license while sons John and George control operations.

1895 John and George Grant take over and form The Glenfarclas-Glenlivet Distillery Co. Ltd with the infamous Pattison, Elder & Co.

1898 Pattison becomes bankrupt. Glenfarclas encounters financial problems after a major overhaul of the distillery but survives by mortgaging and selling stored whisky to R. I. Cameron, a whisky broker from Elgin.

1914 John Grant leaves due to ill health and George continues alone.

1948 The Grant family celebrates the distillery's 100th anniversary, a century of active licensing. It is 9 years late, as the actual anniversary coincided with WW2.

1949 George Grant senior dies and sons George Scott and John Peter inherit the distillery.

1960 Stills are increased from two to four.

1968 Glenfarclas is first to launch a cask-strength single malt. It is later named Glenfarclas 105.

1972 Floor maltings is abandoned and malt is purchased centrally.

1973 A visitor centre is opened.

1976 Enlargement from four stills to six.

2002 George S Grant dies and is succeeded as company chairman by his son John L S Grant.

History continued:

2003 Two new gift tins are released (10 years old and 105 cask strength).

2005 A 50 year old is released to commemorate the bi-centenary of John Grant's birth.

2006 Ten new vintages are released.

2007 Family Casks, a series of single cask bottlings from 43 consecutive years, is released.

2008 New releases in the Family Cask range. Glenfarclas 105 40 years old is released.

2009 A third release in the Family Casks series.

2010 A 40 year old and new vintages from Family Casks are released.

2011 Chairman's Reserve and 175th Anniversary are released.

2012 A 58 year old and a 43 year old are released.

2013 An 18 year old for duty free is released as well as a 25 year old quarter cask.

2014 A 60 year old and a 1966 single fino sherry cask are released.

2015 A 1956 Sherry Cask and Family Reserve are released.

2016 40 year old, 50 year old, 1981 Port and 1986 cask strength are released.

2018 A 22 year old version of the 105 Cask Strength is released.

2019 Glenfarclas Trilogy is released.

2020 Pagoda Ruby Reserve 62 and 63 years old are released.

Tasting notes Glenfarclas 10 year old:

GS – Full and richly sherried on the nose, with nuts, fruit cake and a hint of citrus fruit. The palate is big, with ripe fruit, brittle toffee, some peat and oak. Medium length and gingery in the finish.

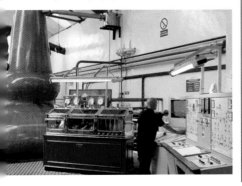

105 Cask Strength   50 years old

18 years old   Family Cask 1959

12 years old   21 years old   40 years old

Glenfiddich

[glen•fidd•ick]

Owner:
William Grant & Sons

Region/district:
Speyside

Founded: 1886

Status: Active (vc)

Capacity: 13 700 000 litres

Address: Dufftown, Keith, Banffshire AB55 4DH

Website:
glenfiddich.com

Tel:
01340 820373 (vc)

Glenfiddich continues to be the most popular single malt in the world with no less than 18 million bottles sold in 2019 – an increase of 9% compared to the previous year.

A lot of the past year's success can be contributed to a rise in sales in the USA. Admittedly, this is a market where Glenfiddich is "only" third after Glenlivet and Macallan but the growth has been impressive. However, the positive view of Glenfiddich on the American market came to a halt in October 2019. That was when the American government imposed a 25% tariff on single malt imported from Scotland and Northern Ireland as a response to the subsidies to Airbus by European governments. The final quarter of 2019 saw a 25% value decline of Scotch export to USA.

Nonetheless, the owners of Glenfiddich have been preparing for larger sales volumes in the years to come. In December 2015 planning approval was granted for a major expansion of the distillery. The expansion includes a new tun room and a new still house and the added equipment will be two new mash tuns, 16 washbacks made of Douglas fir, five wash stills and ten spirit stills. This means an additional 7 million litres to the annual capacity. The expansion has taken longer than expected, not least due to delays caused by the corona virus, and it remains to be seen if the new distillery will be commissioned in 2020 as planned.

Currently, Glenfiddich is equipped with two, stainless steel full lauter mash tuns – both with a ten ton mash. There are 32 washbacks made of Douglas fir with a minimum fermentation time of 68 hours. Two still rooms hold a total of 11 wash stills and 20 spirit stills. All the stills in still house number 2 (5 wash stills and 10 spirit stills) are directly fired using gas. Last year the production was 68 mashes per week and 13.65 million litres of pure alcohol.

The core range consists of **12, 15, 18, 21, 30, 40** and **50 years old**. A new addition to the core range appeared in September 2019 with **Grand Cru 23 year old**, finished in champagne casks and this was followed in 2020 by the **Grande Couronne 26 years old** with a cognac finish. A **14 year old** bourbon matured is available only in the USA , Canada, France and Israel and for China and Taiwan there is the newly released **Gran Cortes 22 years old**.

Recent limited releases include **Glenfiddich The Original,** the **38 year old Glenfiddich Ultimate** and a **50 year old**. In the Experimental Series, **IPA Experiment** and **Project XX** are ongoing items. A third bottling, the 21 year old **Winter Storm**, was released in 2018 followed by **Fire & Cane**. Two bottlings exclusive to Taiwan were released in August 2019, **Black Queen** and **Ice Breaker**, both finished in Taiwan wine casks and in spring 2020, two **1975 Vintages 44 years old** from the Rare Collection were released in the US. Included in the duty free range is the Cask Collection with **Select Cask, Reserve Cask, Vintage Cask** and **Finest Solera**. Another duty free exclusive is **Glenfiddich Rare Oak 25 years**. Finally, a **15 year old Distillery Edition** is available both in duty-free and at the distillery.

History:

1886 The distillery is founded by William Grant.

1887 The first distilling takes place on Christmas Day.

1892 William Grant builds Balvenie.

1898 The blending company Pattisons, largest customer of Glenfiddich, files for bankruptcy and Grant decides to blend their own whisky. Standfast becomes one of their major brands.

1903 William Grant & Sons is formed.

1957 The famous, three-cornered bottle is introduced.

1958 The floor maltings is closed.

1963 Glennfiddich becomes the first whisky to be marketed as single malt in the UK and the rest of the world.

1964 A version of Standfast's three-cornered bottle is launched for Glenfiddich in green glass.

1969 Glenfiddich becomes the first distillery in Scotland to open a visitor centre.

1974 16 new stills are installed.

2001 1965 Vintage Reserve is launched in a limited edition of 480 bottles. Glenfiddich 1937 is bottled (61 bottles).

2002 Glenfiddich Gran Reserva 21 years old, Caoran Reserve 12 years and Glenfiddich Rare Collection 1937 (61 bottles) are launched.

2003 1973 Vintage Reserve (440 bottles) is launched.

2004 1991 Vintage Reserve (13 years) and 1972 Vintage Reserve (519 bottles) are launched.

2005 Circa £1.7 million is invested in a new visitor centre.

2006 1973 Vintage Reserve, 33 years (861 bottles) and 12 year old Toasted Oak are released.

History continued:

2007 1976 Vintage Reserve, 31 years is released.

2008 1977 Vintage Reserve is released.

2009 A 50 year old and 1975 Vintage Reserve are released.

2010 Rich Oak, 1978 Vintage Reserve, the 6th edition of 40 year old and Snow Phoenix are released.

2011 1974 Vintage Reserve and a 19 year old Madeira finish are released.

2012 Cask of Dreams and Millenium Vintage are released.

2013 A 19 year old red wine finish and 1987 Anniversary Vintage are released. Cask Collection with three different expressions is released for duty free.

2014 The 26 year old Glenfiddich Excellence, Rare Oak 25 years and Glenfiddich The Original are released.

2015 A 14 year old for the US market is released.

2016 Finest Solera is released for travel retail. Two expressions in the Experimental Series are launched; Project XX and IPA Experiment.

2017 Winter Storm is released.

2018 Fire & Cane is released.

2019 Grand Cru 23 year old and Rare Collection Cask No. 20050 are released.

2020 Gran Cortes 22 year old, Grande Couronne 26 year old and two 1975 Vintages are released.

Tasting notes Glenfiddich 12 year old:

GS – Delicate, floral and slightly fruity on the nose. Well mannered in the mouth, malty, elegant and soft. Rich, fruit flavours dominate the palate, with a developing nuttiness and an elusive whiff of peat smoke in the fragrant finish.

Project XX

Grand Cru

IPA Experiment

Reserve Cask

Grande Couronne 26 years

Our Original Twelve

Our Solera Fifteen

Our Small Batch Eighteen

Glen Garioch

[glen gee•ree]

Owner:	**Region/district:**
Beam Suntory	Eastern Highlands
Founded: **Status:**	**Capacity:**
1797 Active (vc)	1 370 000 litres

Address: Oldmeldrum, Inverurie, Aberdeenshire
AB51 0ES

Website:	**Tel:**
glengarioch.com	01651 873450

Glen Garioch is currently going through a major re-furbishment with renewal of much equipment. This is nothing unusual – whisky production is a wear and tear business and distillation takes its toll.

What sticks out this time though, is that the distillery's wash still is replaced by one that will be directly fired. This was the common way many years ago but these days virtually all stills in Scotland are heated with pans or coils inside the still. The only distilleries using directly fired stills are Springbank, Glenfarclas, Glenfiddich (some of the stills) and Dornoch. The owners of Glen Garioch say that heating the wash still using a direct gas fire will add to the spirits character. Using a directly fired wash still also mean you have to use a rummager, a chain going round the bottom of the still, to prevent burnt solids from getting stuck.

The distillery is equipped with a four ton full lauter mash tun, nine stainless steel washbacks (one new installed in 2020) with a fermentation time of 72 hours, one wash still and one spirit still (replaced in 2016). A redundant third still was removed in 2020. The spirit is tankered to Glasgow, filled into casks and returned to the distillery's four warehouses. The production plan for 2020 is to do 14 mashes per week before the summer shutdown and 18 mashes after the upgrade with a total of 850,000 litres being produced.

The core range is the **1797 Founder's Reserve** (without age statement) and a **12 year old**, both of them bottled at 48%. A limited **15 year old** matured in oloroso casks was launched, mainly for the duty free market, in 2018. Since 2013 there is also **Virgin Oak**, fully matured in virgin American white oak. Recent limited releases include a selection of **Vintage** expressions with **1978, 1990, 1994, 1997** and **1998**. The first chapter of a new range of cask strength bottlings called Glen Garioch Renaissance Collection was released in 2014 with a 15 year old and the fourth and final installment came in 2018 by way of an **18 year old**.

History:

1797 John Manson founds the distillery.

1798 Thomas Simpson becomes licensee.

1825 Ingram, Lamb & Co. bcome new owners.

1837 The distillery is bought by John Manson & Co.

1884 The distillery is sold to J. G. Thomson & Co.

1908 William Sanderson buys the distillery.

1933 Sanderson & Son merges with the gin maker Booth's Distilleries Ltd.

1937 Booth's Distilleries Ltd is acquired by Distillers Company Limited (DCL).

1968 Glen Garioch is decommissioned.

1970 It is sold to Stanley P. Morrison Ltd.

1973 Production starts again.

1978 Stills are increased from two to three.

1994 Suntory controls all of Morrison Bowmore Distillers Ltd.

1995 The distillery is mothballed in October.

1997 The distillery reopens in August and from now on, it is using unpeated malt.

2004 Glen Garioch 46 year old is released.

2005 15 year old Bordeaux Cask Finish is launched. A visitor centre opens in October.

2006 An 8 year old is released.

2009 Complete revamp of the range - 1979 Founders Reserve (unaged), 12 year old, Vintage 1978 and 1990 are released.

2010 1991 vintage is released.

2011 Vintage 1986 and 1994 are released.

2012 Vintage 1995 and 1997 are released.

2013 Virgin Oak, Vintage 1999 and 11 single casks are released.

2014 Glen Garioch Renaissance Collection 15 years is released.

2018 The fourth and final installment of the Rennaisance Collection is released.

12 years old

Tasting notes Glen Garioch 12 years old:

GS – Luscious and sweet on the nose, peaches and pineapple, vanilla, malt and a hint of sherry. Full-bodied and nicely textured, with more fresh fruit on the palate, along with spice, brittle toffee and finally dry oak notes.

Whisky Legends

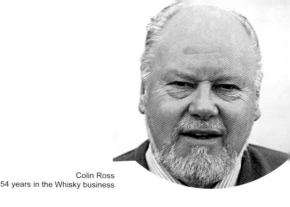

Colin Ross
54 years in the Whisky business

Even though they may have spent their career working for several distilleries, some managers become intricably linked with just the one and that seems to be the case with Colin Ross. To many whisky enthusiasts he is Ben Nevis personified which is no surprise. His two terms as distillery manager at the distillery in Fort William amount to 34 years!

But let's start at the beginning. At the age of 17 Colin was desperate to leave school and an interview for a trainee manager's position with a fish processing company was scheduled. The day before however, his father delivered a couple of Ailsa Craig curling stones to Jim Morrison, manager of all Chivas sites in Keith. He discovered that there was an opening as a trainee distillery manager at Strathisla. Colin applied and got the job. The duties involved everything from working at the barley intake, building wooden washbacks and working in the warehouse team. He learned the mashing and distillation processes and helped setting up the distillery laboratory at Strathislay. After six years in Keith he became head brewer at Tormore and stayed there for twelve years as assistant manager. The owner of Tormore also had Ben Nevis under their umbrella and in 1983 he moved there to become distillery manager. Except for a two-year spell when he managed Laphroaig he remained at Ben Nevis until autumn 2019 when he was retired.

When I asked the question what he thought were his two greatest achievements, I have to admit I didn't expect the answer I received considering his long career.

" My two greatest achievements during my career has to be keeping Tormore distillery producing, during the two haulage strikes during the 1970's when all around were closed and staff had signed on for unemployment benefit. Similarly, in the late 1980's when at Laphroaig the ferries went on strike and we managed to get yeast delivered thanks to the help from local fishermen."

At least to me that shows a dedicated person who is determined to keep the production going no matter what. When pressed for yet another example, Colin admits that having Ben Nevis regarded as a top quality malt whisky compared to when he first went there in 1983 when it was a third class spirit, is something that makes him proud.

The biggest change in production since Colin started in 1965 is definitely about manual versus automated work.

"With a few exceptions, no more emptying the mash tun by hand, no more going inside wooden wash backs to scrub them clean then sweeten with lime solution, very little having to go inside to scrub clean the stills with wire brushes and hot caustic solution and similarly cleaning the inside of the hot liquor tanks. Even jobs like having to go inside and chip the scale from inside the boiler, cleaning the flues around the coal fired stills, handling of casks without the use of forklifts. Yes, the operators have considerably less manual involvement now compared to when I started in the industry."

So were the whiskies better in those days? There is more consistency in the product today, says Colin, but he is not sure that the whiskies of today are as good as the ones produced 50-60 years ago.

"In the 1970's, accountants were running the whisky businesses and we had to produce at the lowest possible cost. This meant increasing production levels, shorter fermentation times and faster distillation times, which had to be at the expense of quality."

"I had the very good fortune to taste some Malt Mill whisky while I was on Islay. We were told that the whisky had been produced prior to the First World War but was not bottled until the 1920's. I have to say that this was the finest, smoothest whisky I had ever tasted, and this long before computers entered the industry."

Colin sees himself as a traditionalist so when I ask him whether or not the SWA should lighten up the rules surrounding Scotch whisky production, the answer is not surprising.

"I believe that the SWA does a fantastic job in protecting Scotch whisky and the rules should not be tampered with."

He has one objection though.

"Nikka had developed a system to allow whisky to mature more quickly by removing the sulphur content by filtration and applied to the SWA seeking approval. In Nikka's mind, what they were suggesting was not so different to chill-filtering which obviously has their approval, but they would not consider such an application from Nikka. My feeling is that other companies in other countries with less rigorous rules could use such a system helping to make their whiskies much better at 5 years old than the equivalent Scotch whisky of the same age."

In the last 30-40 years, sales of single malts have increased substantially and Colin thinks one of the reasons could be that whisky writers in the mid to late 1980s started to focus on that category. It was good for the promotion, marketeers jumped on the train and readers and consumers were led to believe that a single malt was a far superior product compared to a blend.

"I do not know how the blenders must feel about such marketing, but there definitely is an art in producing a great blended whisky and we should not be doing a disservice to their work."

A number of new distilleries have opened up in the past decades and old distilleries have increased their capacity. Are we about to create a new whisky loch of surplus whisky like in the early 1980s? Colin is not completely convinced that there are new, untapped markets that can absorb all this whisky but he is clearly impressed by the longevity of the current golden era for Scotch.

"In my 50 odd years of working in this industry I have witnessed a number of peaks and troughs in production levels but none has ever been sustained for as long as this current trend."

My final question for Colin is if he sees any whiskies from other countries challenging Scotch. He mentions Japan and reminds me of the Yoichi single malt that was awarded world's best malt some years ago. His theory why this came about includes a tribute to forgotten production methods in Scotland.

"Was it because the Yoichi stills are externally heated by coal fires, mashing is done in an old cast iron tun and the casks are matured in low dunnage warehouses, harking back to a time when the distilleries in Scotland in the 1950's and 60's were producing and maturing their whiskies? Need I say more?"

Glenglassaugh

[glen•gla•ssa]

Owner:
Glenglassaugh Distillery Co
(BenRiach Distillery Co.)

Region/district:
Highlands

Founded: 1875

Status: Active (vc)

Capacity: 1 100 000 litres

Address: Portsoy, Banffshire AB45 2SQ

Website:
glenglassaugh.com

Tel:
01261 842367

It's not easy being the lesser known third of a trio of distilleries in which the other two are cherished by whisky aficionados. That was the role of Glen Moray before it stepped out of the shadow of Glenmorangie and Ardbeg, and such is the case of Glenglassaugh.

Stablemates BenRiach and GlenDronach both enjoy brand recognition while Glenglassaugh is struggling for attention. There are two important reasons for this. One is that the distillery was closed for more than half of the time since it was opened in 1873 - not the best prerequistite for building a brand. Secondly, and as a consequence of the long-time closure, the new owners do not have a large stock of old whisky to show off to consumers. So, except for a tiny stock of whiskies 30 years or older, the owners have to rely on what they have produced since 2008. This means a core range of no age statement expressions plus spirit filled into octaves – 50 litre casks that allow for a quick maturation.

The equipment of the distillery consists of a 5.2 ton Porteus cast iron mash tun with rakes, four wooden washbacks and two stainless steel ones, with a fermentation time between 54 and 80 hours, and one pair of stills. The production is around 800,000 litres of pure alcohol, and usually 5% is is peated (30ppm). The main part (85%) is filled to be used as single malt while the rest is sold externally.

The core range is **Revival**, finished in oloroso casks, **Evolution,** matured in American oak and the peated **Torfa** without age statement. Limited releases include **30, 40** and **51** year old, as well as single casks in the **Rare Cask Series** where batch three was released in autumn 2018. The second release of **Octaves Classic** and **Octaves Peated**, matured around seven years in small casks holding 50-60 litres, appeared at the same time. Autumn 2017 saw the first release of a wood finish series from the distillery – **Port, PX Sherry, Peated Port** and **Peated Virgin oak**. All expressions started out in ex-bourbon casks and were bottled at 46%.

History:

1873 The distillery is founded by James Moir.

1887 Alexander Morrison embarks on renovation work.

1892 Morrison sells the distillery to Robertson & Baxter. They in turn sell it on to Highland Distilleries Company for £15,000.

1908 The distillery closes.

1931 The distillery reopens.

1936 The distillery closes.

1957 Reconstruction takes place.

1960 The distillery reopens.

1986 Glenglassaugh is mothballed.

2005 A 22 year old is released.

2006 Three limited editions are released - 19 years old, 38 years old and 44 years old.

2008 The distillery is bought by the Scaent Group for £5m. Three bottlings are released - 21, 30 and 40 year old.

2009 New make spirit and 6 months old are released.

2010 A 26 year old replaces the 21 year old.

2011 A 35 year old and the first bottling from the new owners production, a 3 year old, are released.

2012 A visitor centre is inaugurated and Glenglassaugh Revival is released.

2013 BenRiach Distillery Co buys the distillery and Glenglassaugh Evolution and a 30 year old are released.

2014 The peated Torfa is released as well as eight different single casks and Massandra Connection (35 and 41 years old).

2015 The second batch of single casks is released.

2016 Octaves Classic and Octaves Peated are released.

2017 Three wood finishes are released.

2018 Batch three in the Rare Cask series and the second release of Octaves are released.

Tasting notes Glenglassaugh Evolution:

GS – Peaches and gingerbread on the nose, with brittle toffee, icing sugar, and vanilla. Luscious soft fruits dipped in caramel figure on the palate, with coconut and background stem ginger. The finish is medium in length, with spicy toffee.

Evolution

Glengoyne

[glen•goyn]

Owner:
Ian Macleod Distillers

Region/district:
Southern Highlands

Founded: 1833
Status: Active (vc)
Capacity: 1 100 000 litres

Address: Dumgoyne by Killearn, Glasgow G63 9LB

Website:
glengoyne.com

Tel:
01360 550254 (vc)

In autumn 2020, the second chapter in the Legacy Series was released. The range is all about highlighting people that were instrumental in bringing the Glengoyne brand to where it is today.

The first chapter celebrated the late 1800s when distillery manager Cochrane Cartwright introduced the slow distillation that to this day is Glengoyne´s hallmark. The second chapter is dedicated to Peter Russell who, at the age of 92, still is the chairman of Ian Macleod Distillers. His father Leonard started as a whisky broker in 1936 and when he died 20 years later, Peter joined the company and started a transformation towards blending and bottling. Peter's son Leonard, who is now the managing director, started in the company in 1989 and father and son soon realized that there was something missing in the company - their own distillery. Glengoyne was acquired in 2003 and in later years another two have been added, Tamdhu and the soon to be reopened Rosebank. Peter Russell was inducted into the Whisky hall of Fame in 2016.

The distillery is equipped with a 3.84 ton semi lauter mash tun. There are also six Oregon pine washbacks, as well as the rather unusual combination of one wash still and two spirit stills. Both short (56 hours) and long (110 hours) fermentations are practiced. The production plan for 2020 is a combination of 12 and 16 mashes per week and 920,000 litres of alcohol

The core range consists of **10, 12, 18, 21** and **25 year old**. There is also batch eight of the **Cask Strength**. Recent limited releases include a new series called **Glengoyne Legacy. Chapter Two** was launched in autumn 2020 and is a whisky predominantly matured in ex-bourbon casks which also contains a proportion of refill sherry casks. Other limited releases are a **30 year old**, batch 7 of the popular **The Teapot Dram**, and the **17 year old Duncan's Dram**. The latter is a single cask selected by the assistant distillery manager Duncan McNicoll. The line-up for duty free consists of four expressions; **Cuartillo** (American oak oloroso), **Balbaine** (European oak oloroso), **28 year old** (a combination of American and European oak oloroso) and **Glengoyne PX** (American and European oak with a finish in PX casks).

History:

1833 The distillery is licensed under the name Burnfoot Distilleries by the Edmonstone family.

1876 Lang Brothers buys the distillery and changes the name to Glenguin.

1905 The name changes to Glengoyne.

1965 Robertson & Baxter takes over Lang Brothers and the distillery is refurbished. The stills are increased from two to three.

2001 Glengoyne Scottish Oak Finish (16 years old) is launched.

2003 Ian MacLeod Distillers Ltd buys the distillery plus the brand Langs from the Edrington Group for £7.2 million.

2005 A 19 year old, a 32 year old and a 37 year old cask strength are launched.

2006 Nine "choices" from Stillmen, Mashmen and Manager are released.

2007 A new version of the 21 year old, two Warehousemen´s Choice, Vintage 1972 and two single casks are released.

2008 A 16 year old Shiraz cask finish, three single casks and Heritage Gold are released.

2009 A 40 year old, two single casks and a new 12 year old are launched.

2010 Two single casks, 1987 and 1997, released.

2011 A 24 year old single cask is released.

2012 A 15 and an 18 year old are released as well as a Cask Strength with no age statement.

2013 A limited 35 year old is launched.

2014 A 25 year old is released.

2018 A new range for duty free is released – Cuartillo, Balbaine, a 28 year old and Glengoyne PX.

2019 Glengoyne Legacy is launched.

2020 Glengoyne Legacy Chapter Two is released.

12 years old

Tasting notes Glengoyne 12 years old:

GS – Slightly earthy on the nose, with nutty malt, ripe apples, and a hint of honey. The palate is full and fruity, with milk chocolate, ginger and vanilla. The finish is medium in length, with milky coffee and soft spices.

Glen Grant

[glen grant]

Owner: Campari Group

Region/district: Speyside

Founded: 1840

Status: Active (vc)

Capacity: 6 200 000 litres

Address: Elgin Road, Rothes, Banffshire AB38 7BS

Website: glengrant.com

Tel: 01340 832118

The owners of Glen Grant single malt have been struggling for quite some time now to raise the brand's sales figures and strengthen its presence in the market. In 2002, it was the second largest Scotch malt in the world but recently it slid off the Top Ten list.

Why this has happened is no secret. The brand became too dependent on one market, Italy, where consumption of Scotch hasn't grown in the past 15 years. And when other producers shifted to older and more expensive expressions, Glen Grant relied heavily on unaged malt. Campari, the owners, now have a plan where future focus is shifted towards the aged whiskies in their range. However, an entry-level expression to bring consumers in for the first time is also needed. So far it has been Major's Reserve (around 3 years old) but in May 2020 a new bottling was launched – first in Australia but rolling out in other markets in the autumn. Arboralis has no age statement but it is said that the whisky is between five and ten years old. In the range it will sit between the 5 year old and the 10 year old.

Arboralis means "light from within the trees" and the name ties in well with one of Glen Grant distillery's attractions – The Major's Garden. Covering 22 acres of the glen behind the distillery the Victorian garden was founded in 1886 by the owner at the time, Major James Grant. With its beautiful orchards, lawns and flowerbeds it is a must for any visitor to the distillery.

The distillery is equipped with a 12.3 ton semi-lauter mash tun, ten Oregon pine washbacks with a minimum fermentation time of 48 hours and four pairs of stills. The wash stills are peculiar in that they have vertical sides at the base of the neck and all eight stills are fitted with purifiers. This gives an increased reflux and creates a light and delicate whisky. An extremely efficient £5m bottling hall was inaugurated in 2013. It has a capacity of 12,000 bottles an hour and Glen Grant is alone among the larger distillers bottling the entire production on site. In 2015 a second line for the premium range was installed. The production plan for 2020 shows a 55% increase in volume (in spite of Covid) compared to the previous year. For 30 weeks there will be 22 mashes per week which will amount to 3.1 million litres of pure alcohol.

The Glen Grant core range consists of **Major's Reserve** with no age statement, a **5 year old** sold in Italy, the new **Arboralis,** matured in a combination of ex-bourbon and ex-sherry, a **10 year old,** a **12 year old** matured in both bourbon and sherry casks and an **18 year old** bourbon matured. There are two expressions for the duty free market – one **without age statement** and a **12 year old.** In 2018, a **15 year old,** matured in first fill bourbon was launched for the American market as well as for duty free. The current distillery exclusive bottlings, available only at the distillery, are a **10 year port finish** and a **12 year old Apleton rum finish**. Older expressions are rarely released by the owners but can from time to time be found in the range from Gordon & MacPhail.

History:

1840 The brothers James and John Grant, managers of Dandelaith Distillery, found the distillery.

1861 The distillery becomes the first to install electric lighting.

1864 John Grant dies.

1872 James Grant passes away and the distillery is inherited by his son, James junior (Major James Grant).

1897 James Grant decides to build another distillery across the road; it is named Glen Grant No. 2.

1902 Glen Grant No. 2 is mothballed.

1931 Major Grant dies and is succeeded by his grandson Major Douglas Mackessack.

1953 J. & J. Grant merges with George & J. G. Smith who runs Glenlivet distillery, forming The Glenlivet & Glen Grant Distillers Ltd.

1961 Armando Giovinetti and Douglas Mackessak found a friendship that leads to Glen Grant becoming the most sold malt whisky in Italy.

1965 Glen Grant No. 2 is back in production, but renamed Caperdonich.

1972 The Glenlivet & Glen Grant Distillers merges with Hill Thompson & Co. and Longmorn-Glenlivet Ltd to form The Glenlivet Distillers.

1973 Stills are increased from four to six.

1977 The Chivas & Glenlivet Group (Seagrams) buys Glen Grant Distillery. Stills are increased from six to ten.

2001 Pernod Ricard and Diageo buy Seagrams Spirits & Wine, with Pernod acquiring Chivas Group.

History continued:

2006 Campari buys Glen Grant for €115m.

2007 The entire range is re-packaged and re-launched and a 15 year old single cask is released. Reconstruction of the visitor centre.

2008 Two limited cask strengths - a 16 year old and a 27 year old - are released.

2009 Cellar Reserve 1992 is released.

2010 A 170th Anniversary bottling is released.

2011 A 25 year old is released.

2012 A 19 year old Distillery Edition is released.

2013 Five Decades is released and a bottling hall is built.

2014 A 50 year old and the Rothes Edition 10 years old is released.

2015 Glen Grant Fiodh is launched.

2016 A 12 year old and an 18 year old are launched and a 12 year old non chill-filtered is released for travel retail.

2017 A 15 year old is released for the American market.

2018 A 15 year old is released for the duty free market.

2020 Arboralis with no age statement is released.

Tasting notes Glen Grant 12 year old:

GS – A blast of fresh fruit – oranges, pears and lemons – on the initial nose, before vanilla and fudge notes develop. The fruit carries over on to the palate, with honey, caramel and sweet spices. Medium in length, with cinnamon and soft oak in the finish.

12 years old   Arboralis   18 years old

10 years old   The Major´s Reserve

Glengyle

[glen•gajl]

Owner:	**Region/district:**
Mitchell's Glengyle Ltd	Campbeltown
Founded: **Status:**	**Capacity:**
2004 Active	750 000 litres

Address: Glengyle Road, Campbeltown, Argyll PA28 6LR

Website:	**Tel:**
kilkerran.com	01586 551710

Founded by William Mitchell in 1872, Glengyle distillery was dormant for 79 years until Hedley Wright, owner of Springbank and related to the founder, brought it back to life.

One of the reasons for Wright's interest in reviving the old distillery, was that the Scotch Whisky Association in 1998 had decided to stop referring to Campbeltown as a whisky region. Two distilleries (Springbank and Glen Scotia) were simply not enough. Hedley Wright noted that with only three distilleries, Lowland was at that time considered a region so he decided to resurrect Glengyle to get the numbers up. In 2004, Campbeltown once again became a region of its own and Wright had proved his point.

The distillery is equipped with a 4.5 ton semi-lauter mash tun, two washbacks made of boat skin larch and two made of Douglas fir. The fermentation varies between 72 and 110 hours. There is also one set of stills. Malt is obtained from the neighbouring Springbank and operations are managed by the same staff. The capacity is 750,000 litres, but considerably smaller amounts have been produced over the years. However, production has increased in later years and the plan for 2020 is to mash five times per week between September and December. This will amount to 94,000 litres with 80% made up of "regular" Kilkerran and the rest of heavily peated spirit. Over the years, the owners have been conducting some interesting experimental production at Glengyle including quadruple distillation.

After many years of "work in progress" bottlings, the first core **12 year old** was launched in 2016. It was a vatting of bourbon- (70%) and sherry-matured (30%) whisky. In spring 2017, an **8 year old cask strength** was added to the range with a new batch in autumn 2019. The first batch of **Kilkerran Heavily Peated** was released in spring 2019 followed by a second batch in autumn. The word "heavily" is no exaggeration – the phenol specification of the barley was a staggering 84ppm! The main event in terms of new releases however, came in autumn 2020 when a **16 year old**, the oldest Kilkerran so far, was launched. Matured primarily in ex-bourbon it will be a part of the core range going forward.

History:

1872 The original Glengyle Distillery is built by William Mitchell.

1919 The distillery is bought by West Highland Malt Distilleries Ltd.

1925 The distillery is closed.

1929 The warehouses (but no stock) are purchased by the Craig Brothers and rebuilt into a petrol station and garage.

1941 The distillery is acquired by the Bloch Brothers.

1957 Campbell Henderson applies for planning permission with the intention of reopening the distillery.

2000 Hedley Wright, owner of Springbank Distillery and related to founder William Mitchell, acquires the distillery.

2004 The first distillation after reconstruction takes place in March.

2007 The first limited release - a 3 year old.

2009 Kilkerran "Work in progress" is released.

2010 "Work in progress 2" is released.

2011 "Work in progress 3" is released.

2012 "Work in progress 4" is released.

2013 "Work in progress 5" is released and this time in two versions - bourbon and sherry.

2014 "Work in progress 6" is released in two versions - bourbon and sherry.

2015 "Work in progress 7" is released in two versions - bourbon and sherry.

2016 Kilkerran 12 years old is released.

2017 Kilkerran 8 year old cask strength is released.

2019 Kilkerran Heavily Peated is released.

2020 A 16 year old is released.

Tasting notes Kilkerran 12 year old:

GS – Initially, quite reticent on the nose, then peaty fruit notes develop. Oily and full on the palate, with peaches and more overt smoke, plus an earthy quality. Castor oil and liquorice sticks. Slick in the medium-length finish, with slightly drying oak and enduring liquorice.

12 years old

Whisky Legends

Frank McHardy
57 years in the Whisky business

You have to search hard to find a person who's held leading positions both at a Scottish and an Irish distillery. Frank McHardy is one of few. But let's start at the beginning when Frank was 18 years old. He took a job at Invergordon distillery in 1963 with "no real interest in distilling. Instead it was just to make money so that I could go out and enjoy myself at the weekend."

Three years later he went on to Tamnavulin. The distillery gave its staff the opportunity to take part in all processes carried out to produce the spirit followed by preparing, filling and warehousing the casks. For Frank it was a golden opportunity to learn about production and maturation of malt spirit.

After seven years there he spent four years at Bruichladdich as a working brewer before he became the assistant manager and, a year later, manager at Springbank distillery. In 1986 he moved to Ireland to assume the role of Master Distiller at Bushmills with responsibilities for production and warehousing before he went back to Campbeltown and Springbank as distillery manager.

The latter role is the one most of today's whisky enthusiasts associate with Frank. Many of us have met him in Campbeltown or at tastings around the world when he relentlessly and with huge enthusiasm and humour has preached the gospel of whisky. He retired from full-time employment in 2013 but was still involved with the Springbank Whisky School until 2017. Today he is acting as a consultant to various whisky companies who wish to take advantage of his vast experience in whisky production. Living not far from Springbank and Glengyle he is also called upon to carry out special tours of both J & A Mitchell distilleries from time to time.

From a long and diverse career such as Frank's it must be hard to pick one achievement that could be labelled ones greatest but Frank is quick to respond – the reawakening of Glengyle Distillery.

"Mr Hedley Wright, Chairman of J & A Mitchell granted permission for my plans to lay out the distillery equipment. The restarting of Glengyle meant that there were three distilleries in Campbeltown thus giving it Whisky producing region status in its own right."

Frank has seen a lot of improvements in whisky production since the early 1960s. Many of them have had to do with a higher yield due to better barley but also more efficient equipment and better hygiene. But yield isn't everything and Frank is eager to highlight today's cask quality.

"In the old days, little attention was paid to how many times a cask was used. I always say that the cask will produce up to 60% of the quality and flavour of the Whisky. At the end of the day, in the quest for higher yields and more efficiency, we must not lose sight of the traditional way of producing spirit and fill it into quality wood."

Another big change is the way that most distilleries encourage visitors to come and experience the making of whisky. Frank recalls an incident where the distillery more or less locked its doors.

"I remember at Tamnavulin when we were told that there were some oriental visitors staying in Tomintoul, 7 miles from the distil-

lery. We were ordered that if they turned up, they were not to be allowed in as they would "steal all our secrets"."

Frank welcomes the recent alleviation in legislation regarding what types of casks you can use for maturation of Scotch but adds that although innovation is okey up to a point, the producers should never forget the history and the basic principals of creating whisky.

He calls himself "old fashioned" and relates whisky to Scotland's heritage and terroir. Especially single malts should be connected with the region and the people who make the product. "Having said that I can understand that not everyone sees it that way and marketeers will look to promote the product in a way that it appeals to new and current drinkers."

When I ask Frank if the thinks the whiskies available in the 1950s and 1960s were of a higher quality, he is not convinced.

"Not sure that all whisky in the 1950's and 60's was better than it is at present. There were some interesting individual casks but none as far as I know were bottled as single cask. Can remember some fantastic Sherry casks with branded names on like Harvey's Bristol Cream and Williams & Humbert to name a couple. These were fresh sherry but most of the wood used was tired."

In the last decade the combined production capacity for the Scottish malt distilleries has increased by more than 40% while the volume of exported Scotch has only gone up by 18%. I want to know if Frank thinks that the Scotch industry is being overly optimistic?

"As you say production facilities continue to grow while at present, sales figures would suggest that supply will outstrip the demand and create another whisky loch. [But] remember that a lot of the increased production is not available for use at present. By the time it has matured the analysts forecast that new markets will be found for the product and there will be an increase in people who want to buy the product."

So, obviously single malt Scotch seems to have a bright future but what about blended malts? More and more producers seem to take an interest in this forgotten category.

"I do not like the wording "Blended Malt" I still think that it can be confusing for people who associate the word "Blend "with a mixture of grain and malt whisky. Vatted is much better. Mind you in the near future people will not be confused. Yes, I think that there is a place for vatted/blended malt in bottle."

My final question is whether or not Frank sees any competition for Scotch whisky in the future?

"Scotch whisky is a unique product and will always remain as such. There are other Single Malt Whiskies made in various parts of the world which can be extremely good quality but will never compete with Scotch Whisky. Irish whiskey in my mind, certainly provides stiff competition. Of course there are lots of other spirits with which Scotch Whisky has to compete but I think that the uniqueness of the product and it's growing appeal throughout the world will ensure that it will remain popular in years to come."

It's clear that Frank thinks that Scotch whisky and the the whisky world as a whole is in a healthy state at the moment and with 57 years of experience, he as a consultant will continue to be a part of its success.

Glen Keith

[glen keeth]

Owner:	**Region/district:**
Chivas Brothers	Speyside
(Pernod Ricard)	
Founded: **Status:**	**Capacity:**
1957 Active	6 000 000 litres

Address: Station Road, Keith, Banffshire AB55 3BU

Website:	**Tel:**
-	01542 783042

Keith, with its 5,000 inhabitants and ancestry from the 12th century, is best known in whisky circles for accommodating Speyside's oldest distillery Strathisla.

But there is more to it than meets the eye. A mere kilometre south of Strathisla, right by the river Isla, lies Strathmill – a working distillery producing malt mainly for the J&B blend. The town is also the home to some of Chivas Brothers largest whisky warehouses and blending facilities and five kilometres to the west lies Mulben with even more warehouses and space for more than one million casks. And then there is Glen Keith distillery. Built as late as in 1957 by Chivas Brothers (the current owners) it soon became a testing plant where trials with triple distillation and peated production were carried out.

From the very start, the malt from Glen Keith was supposed to be a part of one of the new blended Scotch of the time – 100 Pipers. The brand is still very much a part of the international whisky scene and even though sales have decreased by 40% in the past decade it sold 17 million bottles in 2019, mainly in Brazil and Mexico.

Reopened in 2013, following 13 years of silence, Glen Keith is equipped with a Briggs 8 ton full lauter mash tun and six stainless steel washbacks. In the old building there are nine washbacks made of Oregon pine and six, old but refurbished stills. The distillery has the capacity to make 6 million litres with the possibility of producing 40 mashes per week.

The only officila core bottling from the distillery is the **Distillery Edition**. In July 2019, Chivas launched The Secret Speyside Collection with 15 bottlings from four distilleries (Glen Keith, Longmorn, Braeval and Caperdonich). They were first available in the duty-free segment before being rolled out to domestic markets. The three Glen Keith expressions, **21, 25** and **28 years old**, were all matured in American oak. Finally, there is a **21 year old** cask strength bottling, distilled in 1998, in the Distillery Reserve Collection, available at all Chivas´ visitor centres.

History:
1957 The Distillery is founded by Chivas Brothers (Seagrams).
1958 Production starts.
1970 The first gas-fuelled still in Scotland is installed, the number of stills increases from three to five.
1976 Own maltings (Saladin box) ceases.
1983 A sixth still is installed.
1994 The first official bottling, a 10 year old, is released as part of Seagram's Heritage Selection.
1999 The distillery is mothballed.
2001 Pernod Ricard takes over Chivas Brothers from Seagrams.
2012 The reconstruction and refurbishing of the distillery begins.
2013 Production starts again.
2017 A Distillery Edition is launched.
2019 Three bottlings in The Secret Speyside Collection are launched.

Distillery Edition

Tasting notes Glen Keith Distillery Edition:
IR – Sweet and fruity on the nose with notes of toffee and apples. Smooth on the palate, vanilla, tropical fruits, marzipan, sponge cake, honey, pears and a hint of dry oak in the finish.

Glenkinchie

[glen•kin•chee]

Owner:
Diageo

Region/district:
Lowlands

Founded: **Status:**   **Capacity:**
1837   Active (vc)   2 500 000 litres

Address: Pencaitland, Tranent,
East Lothian EH34 5ET

Website:
malts.com

Tel:
01875 342004

Glenkinchie is sitting in a part of the country known as East Lothian. It takes its name after Lot, the alleged ruler of southeast Scotland in ancient times and the brother-in-law of King Arthur. It is also often referred to as Scotland's garden county.

With more hours of sunshine than anywhere else in Scotland, the farmland with its abundance of meadows, groves and gardens is striking. Sometimes Diageo call Glenkinchie "the garden distillery" which will be emphasized in the new visitor centre that currently is in construction. Buildings have been torn down to give way for a large landscaped garden leading up to the distillery. In June 2020 they also partnered with a local honey manufacturer and put up three bee hives in the garden, containing 65,000 bees. The proximity to Edinburgh and the possibility of taking a designated shuttle bus from the City to the distillery makes it perfect for a day trip while visiting Edinburgh.

The character of the matured Glenkinchie single malt is, if using the term carelessly, typical Lowland – elegant, floral and citrusy. The newmake on the other hand has a completely different character. Clear wort and fermentations up to 100 hours indicate fruitiness but the declining lyne arms from the stills do not support any reflux back to the copper pots. The worm tubs finally compensate for what estery notes came from the wash and the newmake ends up grainy and sulphury requiring a lengthy maturation to take away the edges.

The distillery is equipped with a full lauter mash tun (nine tons) and six wooden washbacks. There are two stills where the wash still has the biggest charge in Scotland – 21,000 litres (the actual capacity is 32,000 litres). The production plan for 2020 is a five-day week with 10 mashes, producing just under 2 million litres of alcohol.

The core range consists of a **12 year old** and a **Distiller's Edition** with a finish in amontillado sherry casks. There is also a **limited version**, which was released in 2019 together with The Royal Edinburgh Military Tattoo, matured in rejuvenated hogsheads and ex-bourbon barrels and available only at the distillery.

History:

1825   A distillery known as Milton is founded by John and George Rate.

1837   The Rate brothers are registered as licensees of a distillery named Glenkinchie.

1853   John Rate sells the distillery to a farmer by the name of Christie who converts it to a sawmill.

1881   The buildings are bought by a consortium from Edinburgh.

1890   Glenkinchie Distillery Company is founded. Reconstruction and refurbishment is on-going for the next few years.

1914   Glenkinchie forms Scottish Malt Distillers (SMD) with four other Lowland distilleries.

1939-
1945   Glenkinchie is one of few distilleries allowed to maintain production during the war.

1968   Floor maltings is decommissioned.

1969   The maltings is converted into a museum.

1988   Glenkinchie 10 years becomes one of selected six in the Classic Malt series.

1998   A Distiller's Edition with Amontillado finish is launched.

2007   A 12 year old and a 20 year old cask strength are released.

2010   A cask strength exclusive for the visitor centre, a 1992 single cask and a 20 year old are released.

2016   A 24 year old and a distillery exclusive without age statement are released.

2019   A limited version is released in connection with The Royal Edinburgh Military Tattoo.

Tasting notes Glenkinchie 12 years old:

GS – The nose is fresh and floral, with spices and citrus fruits, plus a hint of marshmallow. Notably elegant. Water releases cut grass and lemon notes. Medium-bodied, smooth, sweet and fruity, with malt, butter and cheesecake. The finish is comparatively long and drying, initially rather herbal.

12 years old

Glenlivet

THE GLENLIVET

[glen•liv•it]

Owner:
Chivas Brothers
(Pernod Ricard)

Region/district:
Speyside

Founded: 1824
Status: Active (vc)
Capacity: 21 000 000 litres

Address: Ballindalloch, Banffshire AB37 9DB

Website: theglenlivet.com
Tel: 01340 821720 (vc)

Until the expansion of Glenfiddich distillery has been completed, Glenlivet remains by far the biggest malt distillery in Scotland. When their second unit was commissioned in 2018, it meant that between the two, they had the capacity to do 21 million litres.

Glenlivet is the second best selling single malt after Glenfiddich and sold almost 16 million bottles in 2019. Around 40% of that volume went to the USA where Glenlivet has been No. 1 for decades. Last year the brand also made a name for itself when a set of three whisky cocktail capsules (citrus, wood and spice) were introduced with Glenlivet as the main ingredient. The capsules, made from seaweed extract, contained 23ml and the idea was to simply pop them in the mouth and swallow (including the capsule itself). The capsules were a limited release available only during London Cocktail Week in October. The purpose with that release, which was later followed by a global marketing campaign named Original by Tradition, was to show that a whisky producer that had been around since 1823 was not foreign to innovation.

With the new distillery in 2018, Glenlivet is now equipped with two Briggs full lauter mash tuns, each with a 13.5 ton charge. The 16 wooden washbacks have been augmented by another 16 of stainless steel. Fourteen pairs of stills are divided with four pairs in the oldest still room, three in the beautiful room that was built in 2010 and another seven in the third and latest still room.

The core range is made up of **Founder's Reserve, Captain's Reserve** (with a finish in cognac casks), **12 year old, 15 year old French oak Reserve, 18 year old, 21 year old Archive** and **Glenlivet XXV**. As an exclusive to the American market, a **14 year old cognac finish** was released in 2019. This was followed by **Carribean Reserve** finished in rum casks. A special range of non-chill filtered whiskies called **Nàdurra** include: **Oloroso Cask Strength, First Fill Selection Cask Strength** and **Peated Whisky Cask Finish**. All three are available at cask strength but also bottled at 48% for duty free. The smoky notes in the latter come from a finish in casks that had previously held peated Scotch whisky. The travel retail range includes **Triple Cask Distiller's Reserve, Triple Cask White Oak Reserve** and **Triple Cask Rare Cask**. All three are basically the same whiskies as the three in the previous Master Distiller's Reserve range, but with new names. In 2014 a 50 year old became the first bottling in a new range, The Winchester Collection (named after Master Distiller Alan Winchester) with a third edition, **Vintage 1967**, released in 2018. Over the years, the owners have released bottlings where very little has been revealed about the content. The fifth and latest expression in this series was a three-bottle set called **Spectra**, released in spring 2020. Spectra challenges the consumer to use their senses before using a QR code in the box which will reveal the facts through a digital experience. Finally, there are ten cask strength bottlings in the Distillery Reserve Collection, available at all Chivas´ visitor centres – from **8** to **25 years old**.

History:

1817 George Smith inherits the farm distillery Upper Drummin from his father Andrew Smith who has been distilling on the site since 1774.

1840 George Smith buys Delnabo farm near Tomintoul and leases Cairngorm Distillery.

1845 George Smith leases three other farms, one of which is situated on the river Livet and is called Minmore.

1846 William Smith develops tuberculosis and his brother John Gordon moves back home to assist his father.

1858 George Smith buys Minmore farm and obtains permission to build a distillery.

1859 Upper Drummin and Cairngorm close and all equipment is brought to Minmore which is renamed The Glenlivet Distillery.

1871 George Smith dies and his son John Gordon takes over.

1880 John Gordon Smith applies for and is granted sole rights to the name The Glenlivet.

1890 A fire breaks out and some of the buildings are replaced.

1896 Another two stills are installed.

1901 John Gordon Smith dies.

1904 John Gordon's nephew George Smith Grant takes over.

1921 Captain Bill Smith Grant, son of George Smith Grant, takes over.

1953 George & J. G. Smith Ltd merges with J. & J. Grant of Glen Grant Distillery and forms the company Glenlivet & Glen Grant Distillers.

1966 Floor maltings closes.

1970 Glenlivet & Glen Grant Distillers Ltd merges with Longmorn-Glenlivet Distilleries Ltd and Hill Thomson & Co. Ltd to form The Glenlivet Distillers Ltd.

1978 Seagrams buys The Glenlivet Distillers Ltd. A visitor centre opens.

History continued:

2000 French Oak 12 years and American Oak 12 years are launched

2001 Pernod Ricard and Diageo buy Seagram Spirits & Wine. Pernod Ricard thereby gains control of the Chivas group.

2004 This year sees a lavish relaunch of Glenlivet. French Oak 15 years replaces the previous 12 year old.

2005 Two new duty-free versions are introduced – The Glenlivet 12 year old First Fill and Nadurra. The 1972 Cellar Collection (2,015 bottles) is launched.

2006 Nadurra 16 year old cask strength and 1969 Cellar Collection are released.

2007 Glenlivet XXV is released.

2009 Four more stills are installed and Nadurra Triumph 1991 is released.

2010 Another two stills are commissioned and capacity increases to 10.5 million litres. Glenlivet Founder's Reserve is released.

2011 Glenlivet Master Distiller's Reserve is released for the duty free market.

2012 1980 Cellar Collection is released.

2013 The 18 year old Batch Reserve and Glenlivet Alpha are released.

2014 Nadurra Oloroso, Nadurra First Fill Selection, The Glenlivet Guardian's Chapter and a 50 year old are released.

2015 Founder's Reserve is released as well as two new expressions for duty free; Solera Vatted and Small Batch.

2016 The Glenlivet Cipher and the second edition of the 50 year old are launched.

2018 Captain's Reserve and Code are released. A new distillery is commissioned.

2019 Enigma and a 14 year old cognac finish are released.

2020 Spectra and Carribean Reserve are released.

Tasting notes Glenlivet 12 year old:
GS – A lovely, honeyed, floral, fragrant nose. Medium-bodied, smooth and malty on the palate, with vanilla sweetness. Not as sweet, however, as the nose might suggest. The finish is pleasantly lengthy and sophisticated.

Tasting notes Glenlivet Founder's Reserve:
GS – The nose is fresh and floral, with ripe pears, pineapple, tangerines, honey and vanilla. Medium-bodied, with ginger nuts, soft toffee and tropical fruit on the smooth palate. Soft spices and lingering fruitiness in the finish.

Distiller's Reserve   White Oak Reserve   Carribean Reserve

18 years old   Nàdurra Oloroso

Founder's Reserve   Captain's Reserve   12 years old

Glenlossie

[glen•loss•ee]

Owner:	**Region/district:**
Diageo	Speyside
Founded: **Status:**	**Capacity:**
1876 Active	3 700 000 litres

Address: Birnie, Elgin, Morayshire IV30 8SS

Website:	**Tel:**
malts.com	01343 862000

In the first half of the 1800s, distilleries were usually founded by a single farmer or landowner. Towards the end of the century, local businessmen and blenders often joined forces to open a new distillery.

That was the case with Glenlossie and the people involved is a virtual "who-is-who" of the Scotch whisky industry at that time. The best known was John Duff who had a background as manager of Glendronach. After ten years at Glenlossie he went abroad for a few years and, unsuccessfully, tried to build distilleries in South Africa and Kentucky. When he returned to Scotland he, together with two of his Glenlossie colleagues (George Thomson and Charles Shirres), founded Longmorn distillery and four years later BenRiach as well. Alexander Grigor Allan left Glenlossie to become part owner of Talisker (and later Dailuaine) together with Roderick Kemp who later bought Macallan. John Hopkins, a bottler and blender from Glasgow, took over Tobermory in 1890 and later founded Speyburn distillery and H M S MacKay became president of the Malt Distillers' Association of Scotland.

Glenlossie was closed for an upgrade from January 2018 until June 2019. During the 18 months of closure, huge improvements were made. To mention but a few; new yeast house, new compressor room and new CIP (cleaning in place) . On top of that all electrical equipment, cables, pumps and pipework were replaced and a general upgrade of buildings also took place. Finally, two new, external washbacks were installed and the old cast iron low wines receiver and feints receiver were replaced with stainless steel vessels.

The equipment consists of an eight ton stainless steel full lauter mash tun, eight washbacks made of larch and two made of stainless steel with a fermentation time of 65 and 106 hours. There are three pairs of stills with the spirit stills equipped with purifiers. The production plan for 2020 is to do 12 mashes per week producing 2 million litres of alcohol.

Glenlossie is one of the major contributors to the Haig Gold Label blend and the only official bottling of Glenlossie single malt available today is a **10 year old Flora & Fauna**.

History:

1876 John Duff, former manager at Glendronach Distillery, founds the distillery. Alexander Grigor Allan (to become part-owner of Talisker Distillery), the whisky trader George Thomson and Charles Shirres (both will co-found Longmorn Distillery some 20 years later with John Duff) and H. Mackay are also involved in the company.

1895 The company Glenlossie-Glenlivet Distillery Co. is formed. Alexander Grigor Allan passes away.

1896 John Duff becomes more involved in Longmorn and Mackay takes over management of Glenlossie.

1919 Distillers Company Limited (DCL) takes over the company.

1929 A fire breaks out and causes considerable damage.

1930 DCL transfers operations to Scottish Malt Distillers (SMD).

1962 Stills are increased from four to six.

1971 Another distillery, Mannochmore, is constructed by SMD on the premises. A dark grains plant is installed.

1990 A 10 year old is launched in the Flora & Fauna series.

2010 A Manager´s Choice single cask from 1999 is released.

10 years old

Tasting notes Glenlossie 10 years old:

GS – Cereal, silage and vanilla notes on the relatively light nose, with a voluptuous, sweet palate, offering plums, ginger and barley sugar, plus a hint of oak. The finish is medium in length, with grist and slightly peppery oak.

Whisky Legends

Jim McEwan
57 years in the Whisky business

During my interview with Jim McEwan, one expression comes up several times so let's address that once and for all – "We are the chosen race". You could probably argue that these days saying something like that is all but politically correct but even though Jim has always been known to be outspoken I know him well enough to assure you that there is nothing xenophobic in that statement. It's just Jim's way of declaring his everlasting love for Scotch. To put it simple – there are no other spirits that can compete with Scotch. The Scots were chosen to produce the world's best drink!

He was born in Bowmore in 1948 and at the age of 15 he started working at Bowmore distillery. This was the same year that the distillery was taken over by the famous Stanley P Morrison who later went on to buy also Auchentoshan and Glen Garioch. There were plenty of opportunities for a young lad in the company and Jim decided to qualify as a cooper and later moved on to become Head Warehouseman. Eager to learn more about the business, he moved to the company's headquarters in Glasgow to work on the blending side and soon became Morrison & Bowmore's Chief Blender.

It was at that time he received the offer he couldn't refuse – to move back to his native Islay and take on the role as Distillery Manager at Bowmore. This was in 1984, the very infancy of the whisky boom we are in the middle of now, but Bowmore single malt was already known to whisky enthusiasts.

Going back to these days in the early 80s, I pose the question if perhaps the quality of Scotch was better than compared to today, but Jim doesn't agree.

"The quality of new spirit has never been better and there is more consistency in the barley varieties with higher yield. More distilleries have installed computer software and that's as it should be." And he continues; "The quality of the casks used today has never been higher."

Jim soon combined his work as distillery manager with the role of global brand ambassador travelling around the world promoting Bowmore single malt. Thousands of people have sat down to his tastings and experienced his knowledge, passion and humour. Soon he had become one of Scotch whisky's most familiar faces. Jim was Bowmore in the same way that Bowmore was Jim and eyebrows were raised considerably when he moved across the bay to Bruichladdich in 2001.

Mark Reynier, who recently had acquired the closed distillery with his business partners, realized they needed all the experience they could muster to be able to start production again. This was also a catalyst for Jim in his working career. He does not hesitate when I ask him about his two greatest achievements in his career:

"Getting Bruichladdich back into production and creating the Botanist gin."

As Production Director and Master Distiller at Bruichladdich, Jim worked closely with Mark Reynier – a man who was known for walking his own way, sometimes challenging the rules and regulations of the industry much to the annoyance of the Scotch Whisky Association (SWA). Jim however has nothing but good to say about the SWA.

"I believe in innovation and I also believe the industry is in great shape and that is due largely to the SWA working closely with the distilleries. The SWA have got it absolutely right. Without their guidance it would become a free for all."

Jim spent fifteen exciting and inspirational years with Bruichladdich and his fame amongst whisky enthusiasts grew even bigger. In 2015 he retired from company but not from the world of whisky. He sat up his own company, The Cask Whisperer, working in whisky consultancy and bottling and selling his own casks.

One of his first assignments was to assist Hunter Laing when they were establishing the ninth distillery on Islay – Ardnahoe. Another job took him across the world to Australia to help build a gin distillery in Byron Bay. In 2019 he returned there starting up also single malt production.

As previously mentioned, Jim is fiercely proud of Scotch whisky and he thinks the product speaks for itself.

"The days of Highland warriors and stags on the hill have gone. This is a spirit that requires no props."

Yet at the same time he's not mincing his words when it comes to the important connection between the country and the spirit.

"People love Scotland as a nation and not just as a producer of whisky. Whisky is part of our heritage. The Good Lord bestowed this gift upon us as he knew we would cherish it. Toning down the heritage would be an insult to our forefathers."

Jim has an optimistic mind and when I mention the possible risk of a new whisky loch because malt production capacity has gone up by 40% in the last decade while sales volumes "only" increased by 18%, he's not worried.

"The increase in production is due to opening new markets around the globe and there are still many markets to be discovered and educated."

And the last word is important to Jim. Educating the consumer about the quality of Scotch either through a brand ambassador at a tasting or opening up visitor centres is the key.

"A huge wave of teaching for the consumer has developed and it's working really well. There is a transparency on all aspects of production, maturation and cask selection. There has never been a better time to be a single malt consumer."

Scotch single malt is made from three ingredients; barley, water and yeast but talking to Jim it becomes so obvious that without a fourth part, passion, there would be no whisky. That passion is not just a part of the whisky making but also of how you present it to the consumer and Jim McEwan is the living proof of that.

Glenmorangie

[glen•mor•run•jee]

Owner:
The Glenmorangie Co
(Moët Hennessy)

Region/district:
Northern Highlands

Founded: | **Status:** | **Capacity:**
1843 | Active (vc) | 6 500 000 litres

Address: Tain, Ross-shire IV19 1PZ

Website: | **Tel:**
glenmorangie.com | 01862 892477 (vc)

For decades Glenmorangie has been known as a distillery that doesn't shy away from innovation, whether it is the use of unusual types of wood for maturation or experiments with different types of yeast.

This quest for new styles of single malt has been spearheaded by Bill Lumsden, Director of Distilling, Whisky Creation & Whisky Stocks. What has been missing though for him and his team was the possibility of experimental distillation that did not interfere with the on-going production of Glenmorangie single malt which is the fourth best selling single malt in the world.

Thus, the Lighthouse project was embarked on during 2018. The idea is to construct a new, standalone still house which will incorporate two stills of exactly the same size and shape as the already existing stills. Furthermore a separate building, using reclaimed stone from some of the distillery warehouses, will incorporate more mashing and fermentation facilities. The aim is to have the Lighthouse project up and running some time in 2021 and it will add another million litres to the distillery capacity.

The distillery is currently equipped with a full lauter mash tun with a charge of 10,3 tons, 12 stainless steel washbacks with a fermentation time of 52 hours and six pairs of stills – the tallest in Scotland. The production plan for 2020 is to make around 6,2 million litres of pure alcohol.

The core range consists of **Original** (10 year old) and **18 year old**. The 25 year old has now been discontinued. There are three wood finishes: **Quinta Ruban**, which used to be a 12 year old but is now a 14 year old that has been finished in a combination of 225 litre ruby barriques and 670 litre ruby pipes. **Lasanta** is 12 year old with a finish in a combination of oloroso casks (75%) and PX sherry casks (25%). Finally, there is **Nectar D'Or** with no age statement that has been finished in Sauternes casks. Added to the core range is **Signet**, an unusual piece of work with 20% of the whisky made using chocolate malt. A series of bottlings, called Private Edition, started in 2009 with the release of Sonnalta PX. This has been followed up once a year where **Allta**, made from wild yeast, was the last, at least for the time being. The old range exclusive to duty-free was replaced in spring 2020 by three new expressions: 12 year old **The Accord** which is a vatting of ex-bourbon and ex oloroso, 14 year old **The Elementa** matured in ex-bourbon casks and finished in new charred oak and 16 year old **The Tribute** which is a mix of slightly peated and unpeated Glenmorangie. Exclusive to the travel retail market is also **Grand Vintage 1995** released in April 2020.

Recent limited releases include the 26 year old **Truffle Oak** and **The Cadboll Estate**, only available in North America. There is also the **Grand Vintage Malt 1996**, a 23 year old that has been matured in the same type of wood from the Ozark Mountains in Missouri that has previously been used for the Astar bottlings. Finally, in October 2020, **A Tale Of Cake** with a finish in Tokaji wine casks was released.

History:

1843 William Mathesen applies for a license for a farm distillery called Morangie, which is rebuilt by them. Production took place here in 1738, and possibly since 1703.

1849 Production starts in November.

1887 The distillery is rebuilt and Glenmorangie Distillery Company Ltd is formed.

1918 40% of the distillery is sold to Macdonald & Muir Ltd and 60 % to the whisky dealer Durham. Macdonald & Muir takes over Durham's share by the late thirties.

1931 The distillery closes.

1936 Production restarts in November.

1980 Number of stills increases from two to four and own maltings ceases.

1990 The number of stills is doubled to eight.

1994 A visitor centre opens. Glenmorangie Port Wood Finish is released.

1995 Glenmorangie´s Tain I´Hermitage is launched.

1996 Two different wood finishes are launched, Madeira and Sherry. Glenmorangie plc is formed.

2001 Cask strength port wood finish, Cote de Beaune Wood Finish and Three Cask (ex-Bourbon, charred oak and ex-Rioja) are launched.

2002 A 20 year old Sauternes finish is launched.

2003 Burgundy Wood Finish and cask strength Madeira-matured are released.

2004 Glenmorangie buys the Scotch Malt Whisky Society. The Macdonald family decides to sell Glenmorangie plc (including the distilleries Glenmorangie, Glen Moray and Ardbeg) to Moët Hennessy at £300 million. A new version of Glenmorangie Tain I´Hermitage (28 years) is released as well as Glenmorangie Artisan Cask.

History continued:

2005 A 30 year old is launched.

2007 The entire range gets a complete makeover with 15 and 30 year olds being discontinued and the rest given new names as well as new packaging.

2008 An expansion of production capacity is started. Astar and Signet are launched.

2009 The expansion is finished and Sonnalta PX is released for duty free.

2010 Glenmorangie Finealta is released.

2011 28 year old Glenmorangie Pride is released.

2012 Glenmorangie Artein is released.

2013 Glenmorangie Ealanta is released.

2014 Companta, Taghta and Dornoch are released.

2015 Túsail and Duthac are released.

2016 Milsean, Tayne and Tarlogan are released.

2017 Bacalta, Astar and Pride 1974 are released.

2018 Spios, Cadboll and Grand Vintage Malt 1989 and 1993 are released.

2019 Allta, Cask 1784 and Grand Vintage Malt 1991 are launched.

2020 A new range of travel retail exclusives is released as well as the 26 year Truffle Oak, Grand Vintage Malt 1996 and A Tale of Cake.

The Tribute   Vintage 1996   Nectar D´Or

Tasting notes Glenmorangie Original 10 year old:

GS – The nose offers fresh fruits, butterscotch and toffee. Silky smooth in the mouth, mild spice, vanilla, and well-defined toffee. The fruity finish has a final flourish of ginger.

Original 10 years old   Truffle Oak Reserve   A Tale of Cake

Glen Moray

[glen mur•ree]

Owner:
La Martiniquaise (COFEPP)

Region/district:
Speyside

Founded: 1897

Status: Active (vc)

Capacity: 5 700 000 litres

Address: Bruceland Road, Elgin,
Morayshire IV30 1YE

Website:
glenmoray.com

Tel:
01343 542577

In October 2019 Graham Coull, distillery manager and master blender, left after fifteen years at the distillery. His successor however, at least on the blending side, is certainly not wet behind the ears.

Kirstie McCallum has 20 years experience in the whisky business and spent several years at Burn Stewart as master blender responsible for the Bunnahabhainn, Deanston and Tobermory ranges as well as the blend Black Bottle. As Head of Whisky Creation and Stock at Glen Turner she will not just oversee the Glen Moray single malt range but will also be in charge of three major blends – Cutty Sark, Label 5 and Sir Edward's.

Having spent the many years owned by Glenmorangie Company, in the shadow of Glenmorangie and Ardbeg, Glen Moray single malt has increased sales in the last decade by 150% and now sells 1,5 million bottles annually.

Glen Moray is equipped with an 11 ton full lauter mash tun. Recently though, they have dropped to a 10,1 ton mash to increase efficiency but also to get a higher gravity fermentation. There are 14 stainless steel washbacks placed outside with a fermentation time of 60 hours and nine stills (3 wash and 6 spirit). The current capacity is 5.7 million litres of alcohol, but the owners have the option of reintroducing the old mash tun, adding a few more washbacks and two more wash stills which would increase the capacity to 8.9 million litres. In 2020, the owners plan to mash 27 times per week and produce 5 million litres of alcohol. A small batch of peated newmake (48ppm) was made for ten days in March.

The core range consists of **Classic, Classic Port Finish, Classic Chardonnay Finish, Classic Sherry Finish, Classic Cabernet Sauvignon Finish** and **Classic Peated** as well as **10 year old Fired Oak, 12, 15** and **18 year old**. Limited releases include a **25 year old portwood finish**, a **30 year old sherry finish**, a **Rhum Agricole finish** and (released in May 2020 and exclusive to the UK) the **13 year old Madeira Cask** with a full maturation in madeira casks. Finally, there are three **15 year olds** to be found at the distillery; all fully matured in **chenin blanc, chardonnay** and **burgundy** casks respectively.

History:

1897 Elgin West Brewery, dated 1830, is reconstructed as Glen Moray Distillery.

1910 The distillery closes.

1920 Financial troubles force the distillery to be put up for sale. Buyer is Macdonald & Muir.

1923 Production restarts.

1958 A reconstruction takes place and the floor maltings are replaced by a Saladin box.

1978 Own maltings are terminated.

1979 Number of stills is increased to four.

1996 Macdonald & Muir Ltd changes name to Glenmorangie plc.

1999 Three wood finishes are introduced - Chardonnay (no age) and Chenin Blanc (12 and 16 years respectively).

2004 Louis Vuitton Moët Hennessy buys Glenmorangie plc and a 1986 cask strength, a 20 and a 30 year old are released.

2006 Two vintages, 1963 and 1964, and a new Manager's Choice are released.

2007 New edition of Mountain Oak is released.

2008 The distillery is sold to La Martiniquaise.

2009 A 14 year old Port finish and an 8 year old matured in red wines casks are released.

2011 Two cask finishes and a 10 year old Chardonnay maturation are released.

2012 A 2003 Chenin Blanc is released.

2013 A 25 year old port finish is released.

2014 Glen Moray Classic Port Finish is released.

2015 Glen Moray Classic Peated is released.

2016 Classic Chardonnay Finish and Classic Sherry Finish are released as well as a 15 and an 18 year old.

2017 Glen Moray Mastery is launched.

2018 10 year old Fired Oak is released.

2019 Glen Moray Rhum Agricole is released.

2020 A 13 year old Madeira Cask is released.

12 years old

Tasting notes Glen Moray 12 years old:

GS – Mellow on the nose, with vanilla, pear drops and some oak. Smooth in the mouth, with spicy malt, vanilla and summer fruits. The finish is relatively short, with spicy fruit.

Glen Ord

[glen ord]

Owner:	**Region/district:**
Diageo	Northern Highlands
Founded: **Status:**	**Capacity:**
1838 Active (vc)	11 000 000 litres

Address: Muir of Ord, Ross-shire IV6 7UJ

Website:	**Tel:**
malts.com	01463 872004 (vc)

Since 2006, Glen Ord single malt has been selling impressive volumes under the umbrella brand name The Singleton. Already in the 1980s, however, the whisky was sold under a variety of names: apart from Glen Ord also Ord, Ordie and Muir of Ord.

But we need to go back further to seek the very first bottlings of Glen Ord single malt. In his book The Whisky Distilleries of the United Kingdom from 1887, Alfred Barnard points out Singapore and South Africa as markets for the whisky. He also mentions something interesting from his visit to the distillery. The cooling of the vapours is done by a combination of shell and tube condensers as well as worm tubs. While not unique, it was usually either or when it came to condensing. To my knowledge, the only distillery today that uses a combination of the two techniques is Knockdhu.

Since 2011, Glen Ord distillery has been expanded rapidly in several stages and with its latest expansion in 2015, the distillery now has a capacity of 11 million litres. The complete set of equipment comprises of two stainless steel mashtuns, each with a 12.5 ton mash. There are 22 wooden washbacks with a fermentation time of 75 hours and no less than 14 stills. There are also drum maltings on-site providing a number of Diageo distilleries with malted barley. The barley is soaked for two days in 18 steeping vessels and then germinated for four days in the 18 drums. There are four kilns to dry the malt – two that are always used for unpeated production and two where they exchange between using peat and hot air. The total capacity is 45,000 tons per year

The core range is the **Singleton of Glen Ord 12, 15 and 18 year old**. A sub-range, The Singleton Reserve Collection, is exclusive to duty free and consists of **Signature, Trinité, Liberté** and **Artisan**. The Forgotten Drops Series is made up of old and limited releases. The most recent, and final release, was a **43 year old** in July 2019, matured in two types of sherry casks and then finished both in ex-muscat casks and small firkin casks. An **18 year old** also appeared in the 2019 Special Releases. Finally, there is a bottling available exclusively at the distillery.

History:

1838 Thomas Mackenzie founds the distillery.

1855 Alexander MacLennan and Thomas McGregor buy the distillery.

1870 Alexander MacLennan dies and the distillery is taken over by his widow who marries the banker Alexander Mackenzie.

1877 Alexander Mackenzie leases the distillery.

1878 Alexander Mackenzie builds a new still house and barely manages to start production before a fire destroys it.

1896 Alexander Mackenzie dies and the distillery is sold to James Watson & Co. for £15,800.

1923 John Jabez Watson, James Watson's son, dies and the distillery is sold to John Dewar & Sons. The name changes from Glen Oran to Glen Ord.

1961 A Saladin box is installed.

1966 The two stills are increased to six.

1968 Drum maltings is built.

1983 Malting in the Saladin box ceases.

1988 A visitor centre is opened.

2002 A 12 year old is launched.

2003 A 28 year old cask strength is released.

2004 A 25 year old is launched.

2005 A 30 year old is launched as a Special Release from Diageo.

2006 A 12 year old Singleton of Glen Ord is launched.

2010 A Singleton of Glen Ord 15 year old is released in Taiwan.

2011 Two more washbacks are installed, increasing the capacity by 25%.

2012 Singleton of Glen Ord cask strength is released.

2013 Singleton of Glen Ord Signature, Trinité, Liberté and Artisan are launched.

2015 The Master's Casks 40 years old is released.

2017 A 41 year old reserved for Asia is released.

2018 A 14 year old triple-matured is launched as part of the Special Releases.

2019 A 43 year old is released as well as an 18 year old in the Special Releases.

Tasting notes Glen Ord 12 years old:

GS – Honeyed malt and milk chocolate on the nose, with a hint of orange. These characteristics carry over onto the sweet, easy-drinking palate, along with a biscuity note. Subtly drying, with a medium-length, spicy finish.

12 years old

Glenrothes

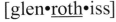

[glen•roth•iss]

Owner:
The Edrington Group

Region/district:
Speyside

Founded: **Status:**
1878   Active

Capacity:
5 600 000 litres

Address: Rothes, Morayshire AB38 7AA

Website:
theglenrothes.com

Tel:
01340 872300

The last couple of years, the owners of Glenrothes have released a special Halloween edition each autumn. The inspiration for this may very well have come from the distillery's nearest neighbour – the Rothes cemetery.

It is an unusual setting and there are literally only a few metres between the distillery buildings and the tombstones. Many of the headstones have been blackened over the years by the whisky fungus (*Baudoinia compniacensis*) which feeds on on the vapours of the alcohol that is being distilled at the nearby distillery. The Glenrothes is a well-respected single malt known for its vintages until quite recently when the owners returned to bottlings with age statements. Around 600,000 bottles were sold in 2019.

The distillery is equipped with a 5.5 ton stainless steel full lauter mash tun. Twelve washbacks made of Oregon pine are in one room, whilst an adjacent tun room houses eight stainless steel washbacks – all of them with a 58 hour fermentation time. The magnificent still house has five pairs of stills performing a very slow distillation. In 2019 the distillery made 44 mashes per week, producing just over 4 million litres of alcohol. There is also a major cooperage on site with four coopers and two apprentices. Together they repair 6,000-6,500 butts per year for Glenrothes and the other Edrington distilleries.

The entire core range was replaced a couple of years ago by Soleo Collection which is based on whiskies that have matured 100% in sherry casks. The range consists of **10 year old, 12 year old, Whisky Maker's Cut, 18 year old** and **25 year old**. There is also Aqua Collection including **Whisky Maker's Dram** and a **12 year old** which will be sold on-line. Exclusive to travel retail are **Robur Reserve, Manse Reserve, Elder's Reserve, Minister's Reserve** and the 25 year old **Ancestor's Reserve**. Recent limited releases include a **13 year old Halloween Edition** from October 2019 which has received a finish in casks that previously held peated whisky. Exceptionally old expressions, **40** and **50 years old**, have also recently been released.

History:

1878 James Stuart & Co. begins planning the new distillery with Robert Dick, William Grant and John Cruickshank as partners.

1879 Production starts in December.

1884 The distillery changes name to Glenrothes-Glenlivet.

1887 William Grant & Co. joins forces with Islay Distillery Co. and forms Highland Distillers Company.

1897 A fire ravages the distillery.

1903 An explosion causes substantial damage.

1963 Expansion from four to six stills.

1980 Expansion from six to eight stills.

1989 Expansion from eight to ten stills.

1999 Edrington and William Grant & Sons buy Highland Distillers.

2002 Four single casks from 1966/1967 are launched.

2005 A 30 year old is launched together with Select Reserve and Vintage 1985.

2008 1978 Vintage and Robur Reserve are launched.

2009 The Glenrothes John Ramsay, Alba Reserve and Three Decades are released.

2010 Berry Brothers takes over the brand.

2011 Editor´s Casks are released.

2013 2001 Vintage and the Manse Brae range are released.

2014 Sherry Cask Reserve and 1969 Extraordinary Cask are released.

2015 Glenrothes Vintage Single Malt is released.

2016 Peated Cask Reserve and Ancestor´s Reserve are released.

2017 The brand returns to Edrington and The Glenrothes Wine Merchant´s Collection is introduced.

2018 The entire range is revamped and four new bottlings with age statements are introduced.

2019 A 40 year old and a 50 year old are released.

12 years old

Tasting notes Glenrothes Soleo 12 year old:

IR – Fresh and fruity on the nose with notes of strawberries/raspberries and a hint of cinnamon. The taste if fruity and spicy with notes of pear, cinnamon, nutmeg, lemon zest and, in the finish, brown sugar and a little ginger.

Whisky Legends

Michael Urquhart
39 years in the Whisky business

Some people say being second or third generation of a family company should be easy. Someone before you built the company and the "only" thing you have to do is to take care of it. My feeling is that it must be quite the opposite. What a daunting experience it must be to step into someone else's shoes. People around you will inevitably compare you to your predecessor (not to mention your own comparisons) and you inherit a legacy, not only to protect but to build upon so that you can pass it on, in a hopefully more prosperously state, to the next generation.

While most whisky companies and distilleries in Scotland are part of big conglomerates, there are a handful of old family companies left. Gordon & MacPhail is one of them. In 1895 James Gordon and John Alexander MacPhail opened up a grocery store in Elgin which included blending and sale of whisky. That same year John Urquhart was hired as an apprentice and in 1915 he became a senior partner.

Today the company is wholly owned by the Urquhart family. Michael Urquhart is part of the third generation and after having worked as a chartered accountant for a couple of years, he joined the company in 1981 to become finance director. Over the years he also added international sales to his duties and eventually became managing director.

In 2014, Michael retired at the age of sixty, just as his siblings had done, with the management of the business passing onto the next generation along with other non family directors, one of whom has spent all his working career at Gordon & MacPhail.

The company isn't well served by family members hanging on to their seats and the company, not the individual, is paramount! There are now five of the fourth generation working in the company and it's owned by a mix of third and fourth generation of the Urquhart family.

Michael became a Master of the Quaich in 2012 and a year later he joined the management committee of the Keepers of the Quaich. He is also secretary to the Scottish Committee of the Worshipful Company of Distillers – a London Livery Company dating back to 1638.

There was a time when most of the whisky produced went into blends. In due course the distillers discovered that there was a market for single malt as well. This was something that Gordon & MacPhail had realized for a long time and often they became the "official bottler" of many distilleries. Their contribution to the interest in single malt Scotch that we see today can not be overrated. Gordon & MacPhail has a solid reputation as one of the best (some say the best) independent bottlers in the business. A huge range of single malts is available and quite often extremely rare bottlings are launched, like the 75 year old Mortlach a few years ago – the oldest Scotch single malt ever released!

But Gordon & MacPhail has also taken the step into production.

When I ask Michael to name his greatest achievements during his whisky career, he says;

"Being part of the team that bought Benromach distillery in 1993, taking it back to life and recommencing distilling in 1998."

Benromach distillery had been dormant for ten years when Gordon & MacPhail bought it. After five years it was producing again and in the last two decades, Benromach has become a whisky that is mentioned with respect and Gordon & MacPhail are now planning to build a new distillery at Craggan in Cairngorms National Park.

Another achievement that Michael mentions is "being part of the movement that educated the world in the intricacies of single malt Scotch whisky with the resulting growth in sales worldwide."

Education and sharing of knowledge is obviously something close to Michael's heart. He often refers to the consumers´ thirst for more information and eagerness to learn "whether it be online forums, books, magazines, tastings, whisky festivals or visiting distilleries themselves" as one of the biggest changes in the whisky world during the past decades.

Wouldn't it be good to see a development where rules and regulations regarding Scotch whisky were less strict?, I ask, but Michael is not overwhelmed.

"I think it is important to keep the integrity, and hence regulation, of Scotch whisky as tight as possible so it can continue to be held in high esteem and understood by consumers around the world. I would say the innovation that we have today is about right."

We talk about the increased production capacity in the Scotch whisky industry in recent years and I ask him if he thinks there is a risk of overproduction and a new whisky loch like that in the late 70s and early 80s.

"It is always very difficult, if not impossible, for a distiller to know what the correct level of production should be remembering the spirit will not be bottled for 3, 5, 10, 21, possibly 50 or 75 years time. A good yardstick is make what you can afford to make and mature in good quality casks."

What about the heritage of Scotch whisky? Doesn't the message of history and provenance sometimes gets lost in the marketing?

"It is important to make Scotch whisky open to all ages. If heritage was the dominant message it might not be so appealing to younger consumers who are potentially more interested in the dynamics of the taste and aromas of what is in their glass,"

When we come to the end of the interview I can't help but think that if it was me, just because there's a family tradition in the company stating you have to pass the baton when you're sixty, I wouldn't really be that comfortable with it. I would have liked to continue and do more.

That doesn't seem to bother Michael and perhaps that's the secret of Gordon & MacPhail's greatness. Never during the interview do I hear Michael say "I did this" but rather "I was part of a team that did this."

This year they are celebrating their 125th anniversary and judging by their pole position in the whisky industry their formula seems to be a winning one.

Glen Scotia

[glen sko•sha]

Owner:
Loch Lomond Group
(Hillhouse Capital Management)

Region/district:
Campbeltown

Founded: 1832
Status: Active (vc)
Capacity: 800 000 litres

Address: High Street, Campbeltown, Argyll PA28 6DS

Website: glenscotia.com
Tel: 01586 552288

The demise of more than 30 distilleries in Campbeltown, once known as the whisky capital of the world, in the late 1800s and early 1900s is a story that keeps fascinating people.

Only two distilleries managed to remain until contemporary times: Springbank, probably saved by being family-owned since the start in 1828, and Glen Scotia surviving by the skin of its teeth after closure in 1930. Three years later, the blender and broker Bloch Brothers from Glasgow took over and restarted the production. The company was spearheaded by Sir Maurice Bloch who remained the owner until 1954 when he sold his business, set up a trust with assets of more than £400,000 and devoted the rest of his life to charity. The Bloch connection with Glen Scotia however went on for another three decades until 1986 through Sir Maurice's nephew David Wolfe who was partner/director in two of the owning companies, A. Gillies and ADP.

Glen Scotia is equipped with a traditional 2.8 ton cast iron mash tun, nine washbacks made of stainless steel with an average fermentation time of 128 hours and one pair of stills. The shortest fermentation time is 70 hours and the longest up to 140 hours. The cut points for the middle cut are 73%-63% and slightly lower for the peated version. The production plan for 2020 is ten mashes per week resulting in 520,000 litres of pure alcohol. The peated share of the production is around four weeks of lightly peated (19ppm) and medium peated (25ppm).

The core range consists of **Double Cask, 15, 18** and **25 year old** and the gently peated **Victoriana** which has been bottled at cask strength. There is also **Glen Scotia Harbour**, a 100% first fill bourbon, which is an exclusive to Waitrose and Tesco Scotland as well as a **10 year old** peated sold only in USA and Germany. The duty free range is made up of Glen Scotia **Campbeltown 1832** finished in PX sherry casks, a **16 year old** and a **vintage 1991**. Recent limited releases include a **14 year old** peated tawny port finish, a **30 year old** and a **45 year old** – both bourbon-matured.

History:

1832 The families of Stewart and Galbraith start Scotia Distillery.

1895 The distillery is sold to Duncan McCallum.

1919 Sold to West Highland Malt Distillers.

1924 West Highland Malt Distillers goes bankrupt and Duncan MacCallum buys back the distillery.

1930 The distillery closes and Duncan MacCallum commits suicide.

1933 Bloch Brothers Ltd take over and production restarts.

1954 Hiram Walker takes over.

1955 A. Gillies & Co. becomes new owner.

1970 A. Gillies & Co. becomes part of Amalgamated Distilled Products.

1979 Reconstruction takes place.

1984 The distillery closes.

1986 Amalgamated Distilled Products is taken over by Gibson International.

1989 Production starts again.

1994 Glen Catrine Bonded Warehouse Ltd takes over and the distillery is mothballed.

1999 The distillery re-starts under Loch Lomond Distillery supervision using staff from Springbank.

2000 Loch Lomond Distillers runs operations with its own staff from May onwards.

2005 A 12 year old is released.

2006 A peated version is released.

2012 A new range (10, 12, 16, 18 and 21 year old) is launched.

2014 A 10 year old and one without age statement are released - both heavily peated.

2015 A new range is released; Double Cask, 15 year old and Victoriana.

2017 A 25 year old and an 18 year old as well as two bottlings for duty-free are released.

2019 The distillery is sold to Hillhouse Capital Management. A 2003 Vintage and a 45 year old are released.

Tasting notes Glen Scotia Double Cask:

GS – The nose is sweet, with bramble and redcurrant aromas, plus caramel and vanilla. Smooth mouth-feel, with ginger, sherry and more vanilla. The finish is quite long, with spicy sherry and a final hint of brine.

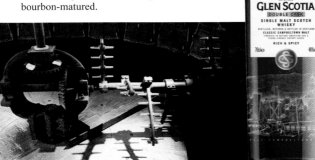

Double Cask

Glen Spey

Photo: © Raymond MacDonald

[glen spey]

Owner:
Diageo

Region/district:
Speyside

Founded: **Status:** **Capacity:**
1878 Active 1 400 000 litres

Address: Rothes, Morayshire AB38 7AU

Website: **Tel:**
malts.com 01340 831215

There are currently 126 malt whisky distilleries operating in Scotland. The vast majority are represented by official bottlings and the whisky from many of them is also available from independent bottlers.

But there is a handful that rarely get any attention at all. Glen Spey is one of them. The distillery sits in the centre of Rothes – a true whisky town – but three neighbouring distilleries outshine it; Glen Grant, Glenrothes and Speyburn. Even The Scotch Malt Whisky Society, established in 1983, has only released 14 expressions. The distillery is the third smallest in terms of capacity in the Diageo group of 28 malt distilleries and considering its size and the fact that it has virtually no presence in the single malt market its future might be questionable.

However, it is still an important part of the blend J&B together with Auchroisk, Knockando and Strathmill, Ten years ago it was still the third biggest blend in the world selling 64 million bottles. Today, sales have dropped to sixth place with 35 million bottles. Part of the decline is due to the fact that whisky sales in some of its primary markets, such as Spain, has declined for a long time now.

The distillery is equipped with a 4.4 ton semi-lauter mash tun, eight stainless steel washbacks with both short (46 hours) and long (100 hours) fermentations and two pairs of stills. Usually, heating the stills is done by using internal coils or pans but the wash stills at Glen Spey have radiators. The two spirit stills are equipped with purifiers which add reflux and also help eliminate the heavier esters. Due to a cloudy wort, the Glen Spey new make is nutty and slightly oily. Even though a new control room was installed in 2017, Glen Spey is still run largely as a manual distillery. The production plan for 2020 is 18 mashes per week (ten short and eight long) and 1.5 million litres of pure alcohol in the year.

The only official single malt is the **12 year old Flora & Fauna** bottling. In 2010, two limited releases were made – a **1996 single cask** from new American oak and a **21 year old** with maturation in ex-sherry American oak.

History:

1878 James Stuart & Co. founds the distillery which becomes known by the name Mill of Rothes.

1886 James Stuart buys Macallan.

1887 W. & A. Gilbey buys the distillery for £11,000 thus becoming the first English company to buy a Scottish malt distillery.

1920 A fire breaks out and the main part of the distillery is re-built.

1962 W. & A. Gilbey combines forces with United Wine Traders and forms International Distillers & Vintners (IDV).

1970 The stills are increased from two to four.

1972 IDV is bought by Watney Mann which is then acquired by Grand Metropolitan.

1997 Guiness and Grand Metropolitan merge to form Diageo.

2001 A 12 year old is launched in the Flora & Fauna series.

2010 A 21 year old is released as part of the Special Releases and a 1996 Manager´s Choice single cask is launched.

12 years old

Tasting notes Glen Spey 12 years old:

GS – Tropical fruits and malt on the comparatively delicate nose. Medium-bodied with fresh fruits and vanilla toffee on the palate, becoming steadily nuttier and drier in a gently oaky, mildly smoky finish.

Glentauchers

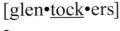
[glen•tock•ers]

Owner: **Region/district:**
Chivas Brothers   Speyside
(Pernod Ricard)

Founded:	**Status:**	**Capacity:**
1897	Active	4 200 000 litres

Address: Mulben, Keith, Banffshire AB55 6YL

Website: **Tel:**
-                                       01542 860272

There are some striking historic similarities between Glentauchers and Imperial. Both were founded in the last shivering years of the 19th century and both suffered badly, like most of the industry, almost immediately due to the Pattison crash.

The two distilleries came under DCL ownership around 1925 and remained under that umbrella for sixty years when they were mothballed. At least they weren't closed, a destiny affecting many distilleries in the mid eighties. In 1989, United Distillers (the successor of DCL) sold the two distilleries to Allied Distillers who decided to reopen them in 1991/1992. After this date their destinies took different turns: While Imperial was mothballed again in 1998, Glentauchers continued to produce. Pernod Ricard became new owners in 2005 and later demolished Imperial to build Dalmunach on the same grounds. Glentauchers on the other hand is still thriving doing the same thing it's always done, namely producing malt whisky for blends. It is one of the cornerstones in the mega brand Ballantines and has until recently been almost completely unknown to malt whisky drinkers.

The distillery is equipped with a 12.2 ton stainless steel full lauter mash tun. There are six washbacks made of Oregon pine and three pairs of stills. The distillery is now doing 18 mashes per week and a total of 4 million litres per year. In February 2020, Pernod Ricard announced that they had plans to turn Glentauchers into their first carbon-neutral distillery by using biofuel within two years. The plan is part of a grander scheme where the emission of greenhouse gases for all of their plants will be reduced by a further 20%.

Glentauchers´role has always been to produce malt whisky for blends – Buchanan´s Black & White, Teachers and today it is Ballantines. Official bottlings have been scarce but in 2017 a **15 year old** was launched as a part of the Ballantine's Single Malt Series. There are also three cask strength bottlings in the Distillery Reserve Collection, available at all Chivas´ visitor centres – **12, 13** and **20 years old.**

History:

1897 James Buchanan and W. P. Lowrie, a whisky merchant from Glasgow, found the distillery.

1898 Production starts.

1906 James Buchanan & Co. takes over the whole distillery and acquires an 80% share in W. P. Lowrie & Co.

1915 James Buchanan & Co. merges with Dewars.

1923 Mashing house and maltings are rebuilt.

1925 Buchanan-Dewars joins Distillers Company Limited (DCL).

1930 Glentauchers is transferred to Scottish Malt Distillers (SMD).

1965 The number of stills is increased from two to six.

1969 Floor maltings is decommissioned.

1985 DCL mothballs the distillery.

1989 United Distillers (formerly DCL) sells the distillery to Caledonian Malt Whisky Distillers, a subsidiary of Allied Distillers.

1992 Production recommences in August.

2000 A 15 year old Glentauchers is released.

2005 Chivas Brothers (Pernod Ricard) become the new owner through the acquisition of Allied Domecq.

2017 A 15 year old is released in the Ballantine´s Single Malt Series.

Tasting notes Glentauchers 15 years old:

IR – Delicious on the nose, both floral and fruity, vanilla, pastry, heather and honey. Still fruity on the palate with additional notes of roasted nuts, toffee and milk chocolate..

15 years old

Glenturret

[glen•turr•et]

Owner:
Lalique Group/Hansjörg Wyss

Region/district:
Southern Highlands

Founded: 1775
Status: Active (vc)
Capacity: 340 000 litres

Address: The Hosh, Crieff, Perthshire PH7 4HA

Website:
theglenturret.com

Tel:
01764 656565

Glenturret is not only one of the smallest distilleries in Scotland – it is also one of the oldest, in fact some say the oldest. For almost 30 years it was owned by Edrington who made it into the spiritual home of the blend Famous Grouse.

In 2018 it was sold to Lalique, a Swiss company specializing in luxury products such as crystal glassware, jewelry and furniture. In the end of 2019, the new owners announced that they were planning for a revamp of the entire site including the construction of new warehouses. The total investment is worth around £12m.

The fact that the distillery is even producing today, can be contributed to the whisky enthusiast James Fairlie who roused the distillery from its 30-year long slumber in 1957. His intention was to make a malt whisky using traditional methods and in that sense he was very much a pioneer of today's craft movement.

The distillery is equipped with a 1.05 ton stainless steel, open mash tun which is the only one left in Scotland where the mash is stirred by hand. There are eight Douglas fir washbacks with a fermentation time of up to 120 hours and one pair of stills. The production target for 2020 pre-Covid with 8-10 mashes per week was 215,000 litres of pure alcohol but this has now been reduced to 150,000 litres. A small part of the production is usually made up of the heavily peated (80ppm) Ruadh Maor and in 2019 10,000 litres were produced. The new owners plan to increase production, without adding any new equipment, to 500,000 litres within the next couple of years.

New products will be introduced in 2020 or 2021 under supervision of the former Macallan master blender Bob Dalgarno. The current core range consists of **10 year old, Glenturret Sherry, Glenturret Triple Wood** and **Glenturret Peated**. Recent limited releases include two 29 year olds – **Cameron's Cut** and **Jamieson's Jigger Edition** – as well as the **Peated Drummond Edition,** a 100% peated Glenturret, bottled at cask strength and available only at the distillery. In April 2020 a limited **15 year old** was released in connection with this year's Whisky Magazine Awards.

History:

1775 Whisky smugglers establish a small illicit farm distillery named Hosh Distillery.

1818 John Drummond is licensee until 1837.

1826 A distillery in the vicinity is named Glenturret, but is decommissioned before 1852.

1852 John McCallum is licensee until 1874.

1875 Hosh Distillery takes over the name Glenturret Distillery and is managed by Thomas Stewart.

1903 Mitchell Bros Ltd takes over.

1921 Production ceases and the buildings are used for whisky storage only.

1929 Mitchell Bros Ltd is liquidated, the distillery dismantled and the facilities are used as storage for agricultural needs.

1957 James Fairlie buys the distillery and re-equips it.

1959 Production restarts.

1981 Remy-Cointreau buys the distillery and invests in a visitor centre.

1990 Highland Distillers takes over.

1999 Edrington and William Grant & Sons buy Highland Distillers for £601 million. The purchasing company, 1887 Company, is a joint venture between Edrington (70%) and William Grant (30%).

2002 The Famous Grouse Experience, a visitor centre costing £2.5 million, is inaugurated.

2003 A 10 year old Glenturret replaces the 12 year old as the distillery´s standard release.

2007 Three new single casks are released.

2013 An 18 year old bottled at cask strength is released as a distillery exclusive.

2014 A 1986 single cask is released.

2015 Sherry, Triple Wood and Peated are released.

2016 Fly´s 16 Masters is released.

2017 Cameron´s Cut, Jamieson´s Jigger Edition and Peated Drummond Edition are launched.

2019 Lalique Group and Hansjörg Wyss buy the distillery.

2020 A limited 15 year old is released.

Tasting notes Glenturret 10 years old:

GS – Nutty and slightly oily on the nose, with barley and citrus fruits. Sweet and honeyed on the full, fruity palate, with a balancing note of oak. Medium length in the sweet finish.

10 years old

Highland Park

[hi•land park]

Owner:	**Region/district:**
The Edrington Group	Highlands (Orkney)

Founded:	**Status:**	**Capacity:**
1798	Active (vc)	2 500 000 litres

Address: Holm Road, Kirkwall, Orkney KW15 1SU

Website:	**Tel:**
highlandparkwhisky.com	01856 874619

Highland Park is an oldtimer amongst Scottish distilleries, having been founded in the late 18th century. It is also a single malt that has had a solid reputation for being a high-class whisky, not least for blending purposes.

In 1924 the famous blending firm George Ballantine & Sons considered it second only to Glen Grant and for many years it was an important cornerstone of blends such as Cutty Sark and Famous Grouse. In the late 1970s the owners decided to invest heavily in promoting Highland Park as a brand and today it is estimated that 75-80% of the production is sold as single malts. In the last seven years sales have almost doubled to 2,2 million bottles in 2019.

The distillery is equipped with a 12 ton semi-lauter mash tun (filled at 50%), twelve Oregon pine washbacks with a fermentation time between 50 and 80 hours, and two pairs of stills. In the last couple of years there has been 22 mashes per week which means a total of 2.5 million litres of alcohol. Highland Park is malting 30% of its malt themselves and there are five malting floors with a capacity of almost 36 tons of barley. The phenol content is 30-40 ppm in its own malt and the malt which has been bought from Simpson's is unpeated. There are also 19 dunnage warehouses and four racked on site.

The distillery has an excellent visitor centre attracting 15,000 people every year and recently the owners opened a shop right in the centre of Kirkwall. Apart from selling Highland Park whisky, the shop will house a gallery and an education area for the distillery's community training programme.

The core range of Highland Park consists of **10 year old Viking Scars, 12 year old Viking Honour, 18 year old Viking Pride** as well as **21, 25, 30** and **40 year olds**. The 21 year old is new since 2019. In autumn 2020 a **Cask Strength** was added to the range and included are also **Dragon Legend** and **Viking Tribe**. The duty free range, called the Warrior Series, has been around for several years now and the more expensive ones, **Sigurd, Ragnvald** and **Thorfinn**, are still available. The rest, however, were replaced in autumn 2018 by **Spirit of the Bear** (matured mainly in American Oak ex-sherry), **Loyalty of the Wolf** (14 years old, matured in a combination of American Oak ex-sherry and ex-bourbon), **Wings of the Eagle** (16 years old, predominantly from European Oak ex-sherry) and a duty free version of the **18 year old Viking Pride** bottled at the higher strength of 46%.

Recent limited expressions include a new edition of the **50 year old**, the 16 year old **Twisted Tattoo** which was partly matured in ex-Rioja casks, the third installment in the Viking Legend series, **Valfather**, a **26 year old** matured in ex-sherry and first fill bourbon honouring the photographer Soren Solkjaer, **Ness of Brodgar's Legacy** and **Ballet**, available only at the distillery and **Triskelion**. The latter, released in late 2019, was created by the distillery's current master whisky maker Gordon Motion together with his predecessors John Ramsay and Max McFarlane.

History:

1798 David Robertson founds the distillery. The local smuggler and businessman Magnus Eunson previously operated an illicit whisky production on the site.

1816 John Robertson, an Excise Officer who arrested Magnus Eunson, takes over production.

1826 Highland Park obtains a license and the distillery is taken over by Robert Borwick.

1840 Robert's son George Borwick takes over but the distillery deteriorates.

1869 The younger brother James Borwick inherits Highland Park and attempts to sell it as he does not consider the distillation of spirits as compatible with his priesthood.

1895 James Grant (of Glenlivet Distillery) buys Highland Park.

1898 The distillery is expanded from two to four stills.

1937 Highland Distilleries buys Highland Park.

1979 Highland Distilleries invests considerably in marketing Highland Park as single malt which increases sales markedly.

1986 A visitor centre, considered one of Scotland's finest, is opened.

1997 Two new Highland Park are launched, an 18 year old and a 25 year old.

1999 Highland Distillers are acquired by Edrington Group and William Grant & Sons.

2000 Visit Scotland awards Highland Park "Five Star Visitor Attraction".

2005 Highland Park 30 years old is released. A 16 year old for the Duty Free market and Ambassador's Cask 1984 are released.

2006 The second edition of Ambassador's Cask, a 10 year old from 1996, is released.

History continued:

2007 The Rebus 20, a 21 year old duty free exclusive, a 38 year old and a 39 year old are released.

2008 A 40 year old and the third and fourth editions of Ambassador´s Cask are released.

2009 Two vintages and Earl Magnus 15 year are released.

2010 A 50 year old, Saint Magnus 12 year old, Orcadian Vintage 1970 and four duty free vintages are released.

2011 Vintage 1978, Leif Eriksson and 18 year old Earl Haakon are released.

2012 Thor and a 21 year old are released.

2013 Loki and a new range for duty free, The Warriors, are released.

2014 Freya and Dark Origins are released.

2015 Odin is released.

2016 Hobbister, Ice Edition, Ingvar and King Christian I are released.

2017 Valkyrie, Dragon Legend, Voyage of the Raven, Shiel, Full Volume, The Dark and The Light are released.

2018 New bottlings in the duty free range include Spirit of the Bear, Loyalty of the Wolf and Wings of the Eagle. The limited Valknut is also released.

2019 Twisted Tattoo, Valfather, Triskelion and a 21 year old are released.

2020 A cask strength is added to the core range.

Tasting notes Highland Park 12 year old:

GS – The nose is fragrant and floral, with hints of heather and some spice. Smooth and honeyed on the palate, with citric fruits, malt and distinctive tones of wood smoke in the warm, lengthy, slightly peaty finish.

21 years old   Twisted Tattoo   Triskelion

12 years old

Cask Strength

Loyalty of the Wolf

Inchgower

[inch•gow•er]

Owner:		Region/district:
Diageo		Speyside

Founded:	Status:	Capacity:
1871	Active	3 200 000 litres

Address: Buckie, Banffshire AB56 5AB

Website:	Tel:
malts.com	01542 836700

When Arthur Bell & Sons bought Inchgower from Buckie Town Council it must have been considered a bargain for both parties. The town had taken over the distillery by the end of 1936 when the original owners went bankrupt.

They paid £1,000 for it and sold it just a few months later to Bell's for £6,000. Bell's, of course, were happy with the price and so was the town council. They made a profit of £5,000 but, more importantly, they still had the water rights that were part of the original deal. Just four years earlier, Bell's had paid £56,000 for Blair Athol and Dufftown distilleries. One of Bell's less successful ventures on the distillery front was building Pittyvaich on the outskirts of Dufftown. The distillery was inaugurated in 1974 and less than 30 years thereafter, it was closed for good but, by then, Bell's was long since acquired by Diageo.

Inchgower is an ideal choice as one of the signature malts for Bells blended Scotch (together with Blair Athol). With a nutty and waxy newmake it makes for a spicy and rather robust whisky after a decade or more in ex-bourbon barrels. As the owners wish to avoid the fruity esters, the middle cut starts at 70% abv. On the other hand, they are eager to catch the heavier compounds at the end of the spirit distillation and come off spirit as low as 55%.

The distillery is equipped with an 8.4 ton stainless steel semilauter mash tun where the cloudy wort adds to the spirit character. Six washbacks made from Oregon pine with an average fermentation time of 48-53 hours are complemented by two pairs of stills. The production plan for 2020 is a five-day operation which means short (42 hours) and long (90 hours) fermentations and a total production of 2 million litres of pure alcohol.

Besides the official **Flora & Fauna 14 year old**, there have also been a few limited bottlings of Inchgower single malt. The most recent was a **27 year old** in autumn 2018 which was part of the yearly Special Releases.

History:

1871 Alexander Wilson & Co. founds the distillery. Equipment from the disused Tochineal Distillery, also owned by Alexander Wilson, is installed.

1936 Alexander Wilson & Co. becomes bankrupt and Buckie Town Council buys the distillery and the family's home for £1,600.

1938 The distillery is sold on to Arthur Bell & Sons for £3,000.

1966 Capacity doubles to four stills.

1985 Guinness acquires Arthur Bell & Sons.

1987 United Distillers is formed by a merger between Arthur Bell & Sons and DCL.

1997 Inchgower 1974 (22 years) is released as a Rare Malt.

2004 Inchgower 1976 (27 years) is released as a Rare Malt.

2010 A single cask from 1993 is released.

2018 A 27 year old is launched as part of the Special Releases.

14 years old

Tasting notes Inchgower 14 years old:

GS – Ripe pears and a hint of brine on the light nose. Grassy and gingery in the mouth, with some acidity. The finish is spicy, dry and relatively short.

Jura

Todays' fans of Jura single malt owe a great deal to two Jura landowners, one brewery and a Welsh architect. It is quite possible that without the commitment from that constellation, the distillery had not existed today.

Jura closed in 1901 and over the decades, it was left in an increasingly dilapidated state. In 1960 Tony Riley-Smith who owned Jura House and Robin Fletcher, the owner of Ardlussa Estate, presented a suggestion how to resurrect the distillery to Scottish & Newcastle, a brewery also involved in the whisky business. The idea was accepted and William Delmé-Evans was brought in as the architect. Three years later, the distillery was producing again.

Jura distillery has a 5 ton semi-lauter mash tun, six stainless steel washbacks with a fermentation time of 54 hours and two pairs of stills – the second tallest in Scotland. The production plan for 2020 is 28 mashes per week and 2.1 million litres of alcohol which will include two weeks of peated production (at 45ppm).

The core range consists of **Journey, 10 year old**, **12 year old**, **Seven Wood** (a vatting of whiskies matured in seven types of French oak as well as ex-bourbon barrels) and **18 year old** (finished in red wine casks). All the expressions have an amount of peated Jura in the recipe. Four expressions available for duty-free include **The Sound, The Road, The Loch** and **The Paps** – all of them finished in PX casks. Exclusive to travel retail in Asia are the 12 year old **The Bay** and, released in April 2020, **Vintage 1975**. One more expression was added to the duty free range in summer 2019 when the 21 year old **Jura Time**, finished in ex-peated malt casks, was launched. Recent limited releases include a **Vintage 1988** finished in port pipes, a **Vintage 1989**, the **21 year old Jura Tide** with a finish in virgin American oak casks, **French Oak** finished in French oak casks and the 13 year old **Two-One-Two** which was finished in casks made of Chinkapin oak. In May 2020 **Red Wine Cask**, the first in a new series called Cask Editions, was released and it was then followed in September by **Winter Edition** finished in sherry casks.

[joo•rah]

Owner:
Whyte & Mackay
(Emperador Inc)

Region/district:
Highlands (Jura)

Founded: 1810

Status: Active (vc)

Capacity: 2 400 000 litres

Address: Craighouse, Isle of Jura PA60 7XT

Website: isleofjura.com

Tel: 01496 820240

History:

1810 Archibald Campbell founds a distillery named Small Isles Distillery.

1853 Richard Campbell leases the distillery to Norman Buchanan from Glasgow.

1867 Buchanan files for bankruptcy and J. & K. Orr takes over the distillery.

1876 Licence transferred to James Ferguson & Sons.

1901 Ferguson dismantles the distillery.

1960 Charles Mackinlay & Co. extends the distillery. Newly formed Scottish & Newcastle Breweries acquires Charles Mackinlay & Co.

1963 The first distilling takes place.

1985 Invergordon Distilleries acquires Charles Mackinlay & Co. from Scottish & Newcastle.

1993 Whyte & Mackay (Fortune Brands) buys Invergordon Distillers.

1996 Whyte & Mackay changes name to JBB (Greater Europe).

2001 The management buys out the company and changes the name to Kyndal.

2002 Isle of Jura Superstition is launched.

2003 Kyndal reverts back to its old name, Whyte & Mackay. Isle of Jura 1984 is launched.

2006 The 40 year old Jura is released.

2007 United Spirits buys Whyte & Mackay. The 18 year old Delmé-Evans and an 8 year old heavily peated expression are released.

2008 A series of four different vintages, called Elements, is released.

2009 Prophecy and Paps of Jura are released.

2012 The 12 year old Jura Elixir is released.

2013 Camas an Staca, 1977 Juar and Turas-Mara are released.

2014 Whyte & Mackay is sold to Emperador Inc.

2016 The 22 year old "One For The Road" is released.

2017 The limited One and All is released.

2018 A new core range is released; 10, 12 and 18 year old as well as Journey and Seven Wood.

2019 A new range for duty-free is released.

2020 Red Wine Cask and Winter Edition are released.

Tasting notes Jura 10 years old:

GS – Resin, oil and pine notes on the delicate nose. Light-bodied in the mouth, with malt and drying saltiness. The finish is malty, nutty, with more salt, plus just a wisp of smoke.

12 years old

Kilchoman

[kil•ho•man]

Owner:
Kilchoman Distillery Co.

Region/district:
Islay

Founded: **Status:** **Capacity:**
2005 Active (vc) 480 000 litres

Address: Rockside farm, Bruichladdich, Islay PA49 7UT

Website: **Tel:**
kilchomandistillery.com 01496 850011

Of the currently nine whisky distilleries on Islay, seven are owned by multinational companies. Only two stand out as privately owned – Kilchoman and the newly opened Ardnahoe.

Anthony Wills, the founder and owner of Kilchoman, made a bold move in 2005 when he opened his distillery as the first on Islay for 124 years. Not only because Islay is sacred ground for whisky enthusiasts from all over the world and any new whisky from that island will be thoroughly scrutinized. Wills also decided to open a farm distillery, growing part of his own barley and malt it on site – the only one on the island to do so.

Fifteen years on, sales of Kilchoman single malt has now forced the owners to increase production. A second distillery, mirroring the existing one, was commissioned in 2019 and with the recent expansion the equipment now consists of two 1.2 ton stainless steel semi-lauter mash tuns, 12 stainless steel, 6,000 litre washbacks with an average fermentation time of 90 hours and two pairs of stills. In 2020, the plan is to produce close to 350,000 litres. A new malting floor and kiln has also been opened which means that the distillery is now able to produce 30% of their malt requirement themselves, typically with a phenol content of 20ppm. The rest (50ppm) is bought from Port Ellen.

The core range consists of **Machir Bay** and **Sanaig**. Limited, but regular releases are **Loch Gorm** and **100% Islay** made from 100% barley grown and malted on the island. Other limited releases during 2020 include **Am Burach** ("the mess" in Gaelic), which is the result of a serendipitous mix of Machir Bay and port matured Kilchoman during vatting, in May and a **fino sherry cask** matured in September as well as the bottling intended for Feis Ile 2020, a **12 year old bourbon matured** bottled at cask strength. For the UK duty free market there is **Coull Point** and for global duty free, **Saligo Bay** is available. The first bottling of unpeated Kilchoman (7 years old and matured in a sherry hogshead) was released by Berry Brothers in early 2020. This was the result of a breakdown of the kiln in late 2012 and a total of 75 casks were filled.

History:

2002 Plans are formed for a new distillery at Rockside Farm on western Islay.

2005 Production starts in June.

2006 A fire breaks out in the kiln causing a few weeks' production stop but malting has to cease for the rest of the year.

2007 The distillery is expanded with two new washbacks.

2009 The first single malt, a 3 year old, is released on 9th September followed by a second release.

2010 Three new releases and an introduction to the US market. John Maclellan from Bunnahabhain joins the team as General Manager.

2011 Kilchoman 100% Islay is released as well as a 4 year old and a 5 year old.

2012 Machir Bay, the first core expression, is released together with Kilchoman Sherry Cask Release and the second edition of 100% Islay.

2013 Loch Gorm and Vintage 2007 are released.

2014 A 3 year old port cask matured and the first duty free exclusive, Coull Point, are released.

2015 A Madeira cask maturation is released and the distillery celebrates its 10th anniversary.

2016 Sanaig and a Sauternes cask maturation are released.

2017 A Portuguese red wine maturation and Vintage 2009 are released.

2018 Original Cask Strength and 2009 Vintage are released.

2019 Capacity is doubled with two more stills. A limited STR Cask Matured is released.

2020 Am Burach and a fino sherry cask are released.

BARLEY GROWING FOR KILCHOMAN 100% ISLAY

Tasting notes Kilchoman Machir Bay:

GS – A nose of sweet peat and vanilla, undercut by brine, kelp and black pepper. Filled ashtrays in time. A smooth mouth-feel, with lots of nicely-balanced citrus fruit, peat smoke and Germolene on the palate. The finish is relatively long and sweet, with building spice, chili and a final nuttiness.

Machir Bay

Kininvie

[kin•in•vee]

Owner:
William Grant & Sons

Region/district:
Speyside

Founded: **Status:**
1990   Active

Capacity:
4 800 000 litres

Address: Dufftown, Keith, Banffshire AB55 4DH

Website:
kininvie.com

Tel:
01340 820373

Kininvie basically consists of a tin shed hidden away between two iconic distilleries – Glenfiddich and Balvenie but there is definitely more to it than meets the eye. It was built 30 years ago to provide malt whisky for the company's blends.

In the last 7-8 years much experimental distillation has been going on at Kininvie while at the same time the distillery has continued to traditionally distil malt whisky for Grants blends and for Monkey Shoulder. A new range under the name Kininvie Works was launched in autumn 2019 including triple distilled malt whisky as well as whisky made from a combination of malted barley and malted rye. These exciting new whiskies are the most recent results of an innovation team led by Kevin Abrook. Other exciting projects launched by Abrook and his co-workers are the first releases of Ailsa Bay, Girvan Patent Still grain whisky and the release of Ladyburn single malt. Having spent 30 years in whisky marketing and innovation, Kevin Abrook left the industry in 2019 to devote more time to his other passion in life – art.

Kininvie distillery consists of one still house with three wash stills and six spirit stills. There is a 9.6 ton stainless steel full lauter mash tun which is placed next to Balvenie's in the Balvenie distillery and ten Douglas fir washbacks with a minimum fermentation time of 75 hours can be found in two separate rooms. In 2020, production will be about 20 mashes per week and just under four million litres of pure alcohol.

The first official bottling appeared in 2013 and end of 2015 saw the release of a 23 year old core bottling and a 17 year old became available for duty free. Both have now been discontinued. In October 2019, three experimental whiskies were launched under the name Kininvie Works. The **KVSM001** is a 5 year old triple distilled single malt while the **KVSG002** is a whisky with a mash bill of 11% malted rye and 89% malted barley and then matured in virgin American oak for three years. Finally, there is **KVSB003** which is a blend of traditionally double distilled malt and the aforementioned rye/barley whisky.

History:

1990   Kininvie distillery is inaugurated and the first distillation takes place on 25th June.

1994   Another three stills are installed.

2006   The first expression of a Kininvie single malt is released as a 15 year old under the name Hazelwood.

2008   In February a 17 year old Hazelwood Reserve is launched at Heathrow's Terminal 5.

2013   A 23 year old Kininvie is launched in Taiwan.

2014   A 17 year old and batch 2 of the 23 year old are released.

2015   Batch 3 of the 23 year old is released and later in the year, the batches are replaced by a 23 year old signature bottling. Three 25 year old single casks are launched.

2019   Three expressions in the Kininvie Works series are released.

Kininvie KVSB003

Tasting notes Kininvie 17 years old:

GS – The nose offers tropical fruits, coconut and vanilla custard, with a hint of milk chocolate. Pineapple and mango on the palate, accompanied by linseed oil, ginger, and developing nuttiness. The finish dries slowly, with more linseed, plenty of spice, and soft oak.

Knockando

[nock•an•doo]

Owner:		Region/district:
Diageo.		Speyside
Founded:	**Status:**	**Capacity:**
1898	Active	1 400 000 litres

Address: Knockando, Morayshire AB38 7RT

Website:	**Tel:**
malts.com	01340 882000

There are 50 distilleries in what is known as the Speyside region which, in terms of whisky, consists of the entire Moray Council and the Badenoch and Strathspey ward of the Highland Council.

Many of them are easily found and can often be spotted from the main roads with the pagoda roofs giving them away. Knockando is different. To say that it is remote is probably a bit far fetched. Secluded is a better word. The B9102 is a beautiful road which takes you from Craigellachie to Grantown-on-Spey. If you wish to drive close to river Spey this road is the perfect choice. Just after you have passed Cardhu, going west, there is a narrow turnoff on your left. It will lead you first to the historic Knockando Woolmill, then past Tamdhu distillery until you finally reach Knockando distillery which lies just a few metres from the Spey. No need continuing on the road because here is where it ends. This is a good spot for exterior pictures but unfortunately the distillery has never been opened to visitors.

The distillery is equipped with a small (4.4 ton), semi-lauter mash tun, eight Douglas fir washbacks and two pairs of stills. Knockando has always worked a five-day week with 16 mashes per week, 8 short fermentations (50 hours) and 8 long (100 hours). The nutty character of the newmake, a result of the cloudy worts coming from the mash tun, has given it its fame. However, in order to balance the taste, the distillers also wish to create the typical Speyside floral notes by using boiling balls on the spirit stills to increase reflux. The distillery was closed due to a major refurbishment in December 2017 and it is highly unlikely that the distillery will start producing at least until some time in 2021.

Even though Knockando is a vital part of the J&B blend, it is also Diageo's 8th most sold single malt (around 600,000 bottles) and has for many years been popular in, especially, France, Spain and Greece. The core range consists of **12 year old, 15 year old Richly Matured, 18 year old Slow Matured** and the **21 year old Master Reserve**. In 2011 a **25 year old** matured in first fill European oak was released as part of the Special Releases.

History:

1898 John Thompson founds the distillery. The architect is Charles Doig.

1899 Production starts in May.

1900 The distillery closes in March and J. Thompson & Co. takes over administration.

1903 W. & A. Gilbey purchases the distillery for £3,500 and production restarts in October.

1962 W. & A. Gilbey merges with United Wine Traders (including Justerini & Brooks) and forms International Distillers & Vintners (IDV).

1968 Floor maltings is decommissioned.

1969 The number of stills is increased to four.

1972 IDV is acquired by Watney Mann who, in its turn, is taken over by Grand Metropolitan.

1978 Justerini & Brooks launches a 12 year old Knockando.

1997 Grand Metropolitan and Guinness merge and form Diageo; simultaneously IDV and United Distillers merge to United Distillers & Vintners.

2010 A Manager´s Choice 1996 is released.

2011 A 25 year old is released.

Tasting notes Knockando 12 years old:

GS – Delicate and fragrant on the nose, with hints of malt, worn leather, and hay. Quite full in the mouth, smooth and honeyed, with gingery malt and a suggestion of white rum. Medium length in the finish, with cereal and more ginger.

12 years old

Knockdhu

[nock•doo]

Owner:
Inver House Distillers
(Thai Beverages plc)

Region/district:
Highland

Founded: 1893
Status: Active (vc)
Capacity: 2 000 000 litres

Address: Knock, By Huntly, Aberdeenshire AB54 7LJ

Website: ancnoc.com
Tel: 01466 771223

John Morrison is sometimes mentioned as the founder of Knockdhu. It is true that he had bought the land in 1892 and discovered a high quality water source which he sent for analysis with distilling purposes in mind.

That is however as far as he became involved. Instead he sold the land to DCL which built the distillery. DCL was the largest player in the industry and their influence would strengthen over the years. The founders of the company, in 1877, were seven grain distilleries in the Lowlands. Their expansion strategy was focussed on acquiring operational distilleries but Knockdhu was the first and one of few which they built themselves.

Knockdhu distillery is equipped with a 5 ton stainless steel lauter mash tun, eight washbacks made of Oregon pine (two of them used as intermediate vats), with fermentation time now increased to 65 hours and one pair of stills with worm tubs. Oddly enough there is also a shell and tube condenser fitted on the wash still just before the worm tub. In 2019, they've moved from a five-day week to seven-days and the plan is to repeat that during 2020 which means 20 mashes per week and a total of 1.7 million litres of pure alcohol in the year. Around 400,000 litres will be heavily peated (45ppm). Two of the dunnage warehouses were knocked down last year and there are now one dunnage and one racked warehouse on site.

The core range consists of **12, 18** and **24 years old**. In addition to that there is the smoky **Peatheart** made from 40ppm barley which has now become a part of the core range. A 35 year old has been discontinued but can still be found. Every year a new vintage is released and in spring 2017 it was a **2002**. More recent limited bottlings, launched in September 2019 to commemorate the 125th anniversary of the distillery, were a **16 year old cask strength** bottled at 56,3% and matured in ex-bourbon barrels and **Peat**, a smoky expression (40ppm) with an extra maturation in Spanish oak sherry butts. For the duty-free market there are **Black Hill Reserve** and the peated (20ppm) **Rùdhan** both having been matured in bourbon casks.

History:
1893 Distillers Company Limited (DCL) starts construction of the distillery.
1894 Production starts in October.
1930 Scottish Malt Distillers (SMD) takes over production.
1983 The distillery closes in March.
1988 Inver House buys the distillery from United Distillers.
1989 Production restarts on 6th February.
1990 First official bottling of Knockdhu.
1993 First official bottling of anCnoc.
2001 Pacific Spirits purchases Inver House Distillers at a price of $85 million.
2003 Reintroduction of anCnoc 12 years.
2004 A 14 year old from 1990 is launched.
2005 A 30 year old from 1975 and a 14 year old from 1991 are launched.
2006 International Beverage Holdings acquires Pacific Spirits UK.
2007 anCnoc 1993 is released.
2008 anCnoc 16 year old is released.
2011 A Vintage 1996 is released.
2012 A 35 year old is launched.
2013 A 22 year old and Vintage 1999 are released.
2014 A peated range with Rutter, Flaughter, Tushkar and Cutter is introduced.
2015 A 24 year old, Vintage 1975 and Peatlands are released as well as Black Hill Reserve and Barrow for duty free.
2016 Vintage 2001, Blas and Rùdhan are released.
2017 Vintage 2002 and Peatheart are released.
2019 A 16 year old cask strength is released.

Tasting notes anCnoc 12 years old:
GS – A pretty, sweet, floral nose, with barley notes. Medium bodied, with a whiff of delicate smoke, spices and boiled sweets on the palate. Drier in the mouth than the nose suggests. The finish is quite short and drying.

12 years old

Lagavulin

[lah•gah•**voo**•lin]

Owner:		Region/district:
Diageo		Islay

Founded:	Status:	Capacity:
1816	Active (vc)	2 600 000 litres

Address: Port Ellen, Islay, Argyll PA42 7DZ

Website:	Tel:
malts.com	01496 302749 (vc)

For a whisky novice, the character of most malts from Islay may come out as being pretty similar – they are simply smoky! Peat freaks however can spend hours discussing and comparing the differences between The Kildalton Three.

This is the collective name for the three classic distilleries within miles from each other on the Kildalton coast on southeast Islay – Ardbeg, Laphroaig and Lagavulin. All three use malted barley peated at roughly the same phenol level, an average of 45-55 ppm, so the secret clearly lies in the equipment and the production itself and to some degree in the maturation regime. While the newmake from Ardbeg often is described as sooty and the one from Laphroaig as tarry, Lagavulin often carries notes of a bonfire. With a 30 minute foreshots, some sweet, fruity notes come through but not as much as with Ardbeg (10 minute foreshots) but way more than Laphroaig (45 minutes). For the middle cut, all three start at 72% collecting some of the early esters while Lagavulin comes off low (59%) to catch the heavier phenols and a fairly slow distillation at Lagavulin adds sweeter notes.

With Laphroaig being the most sold of the Islay malts, it is a tight race between Bowmore and Lagavulin in second place, both currently selling around 2 million bottles yearly.

The distillery is equipped with a 4.4 ton stainless steel full lauter mash tun and ten washbacks made of larch with a 55 hour fermentation cycle. There are two pairs of stills where the spirit stills are actually larger than the wash stills. The newmake is, almost without exception, filled into ex-bourbon hogsheads. There are only 5,000 casks maturing at the distillery and all of the new production is now shipped to the mainland for maturation. The production plan for 2020 is a 7-day week with 29 mashes per week and close to 2.6 million litres of alcohol.

The core range of Lagavulin consists of an **8 year old** (added to the range in 2017), a **12 year old cask strength** which actually forms part of the yearly Rare by Nature series (formerly known as Special Releases), a **16 year old** and the **Distiller's Edition**, a Pedro Ximenez sherry finish. Recent limited bottlings include three bottlings in 2016 to celebrate the distillery's bicentenary – an **8 year old** (later to become part of the core range), a **25 year old** bottled at cask strength and matured in sherry casks and a single cask **Lagavulin 1991**. In spring 2019, a **9 year old House Lannister** was released as part of the Game of Thrones series and in August 2019 a **10 year old** was released exclusively for duty-free. In November 2019 as an exclusive to the US, the **11 year old Lagavulin Offerman Edition**, made in collaboration with the actor Nick Offerman and matured in a mixture of refill and rejuvenated bourbon casks, was released. The Islay Festival special release for 2020, bottled at 54%, was a **20 year old** matured in a combination of refill casks and PX/oloroso hogsheads. Finally, in July 2020, a **28 year old**, matured in refill American oak was part of the new Prima & Ultima range.

History:

1816 John Johnston founds the distillery.

1825 John Johnston takes over the adjacent distillery Ardmore.

1836 John Johnston dies and the two distilleries are merged and operated under the name Lagavulin. Alexander Graham, a wine and spirits dealer from Glasgow, buys the distillery.

1861 James Logan Mackie becomes a partner.

1867 The distillery is acquired by James Logan Mackie & Co. and refurbishment starts.

1878 Peter Mackie is employed.

1889 James Logan Mackie passes away and nephew Peter Mackie inherits the distillery.

1890 J. L. Mackie & Co. changes name to Mackie & Co. Peter Mackie launches White Horse onto the export market with Lagavulin included in the blend.

1908 Peter Mackie uses the old distillery buildings to build a new distillery, Malt Mill, on the site.

1924 Peter Mackie passes away and Mackie & Co. changes name to White Horse Distillers.

1927 White Horse Distillers becomes part of Distillers Company Limited (DCL).

1930 The distillery is administered under Scottish Malt Distillers (SMD).

1952 An explosive fire breaks out and causes considerable damage.

1962 Malt Mills distillery closes and today it houses Lagavulin's visitor centre.

1974 Floor maltings are decommisioned and malt is bought from Port Ellen instead.

1988 Lagavulin 16 years becomes one of six Classic Malts.

1998 A Pedro Ximenez sherry finish is launched as a Distillers Edition.

History continued:

2002 Two cask strengths (12 years and 25 years) are launched.

2006 A 30 year old is released.

2007 A 21 year old from 1985 and the sixth edition of the 12 year old are released.

2010 A new edition of the 12 year old, a single cask exclusive for the distillery and a Manager´s Choice single cask are released.

2011 The 10th edition of the 12 year old cask strength is released.

2012 The 11th edition of the 12 year old cask strength and a 21 year old are released.

2013 A 37 year old and the 12th edition of the 12 year old cask strength are released.

2014 A triple matured for Friends of the Classic Malts and the 13th edition of the 12 year old cask strength are released.

2015 The 14th edition of the 12 year old cask strength is released.

2016 An 8 year old and a 25 year old are launched.

2017 A new edition of the 12 year old cask strength is released.

2018 An 18 year old is released for Feis Ile.

2019 A 19 year old is released for Feis Ile, a 9 year old House Lannister in the Game of Thrones series and a 10 year old for duty free.

2020 The 11 year old Offerman Edition, the 1991 Prima & Ultima and a 20 year old for Feis Ile are released.

Tasting notes Lagavulin 16 year old:

GS – Peat, iodine, sherry and vanilla merge on the rich nose. The peat and iodine continue on to the expansive, spicy, sherried palate, with brine, prunes and raisins. Peat embers feature in the lengthy, spicy finish.

Offerman Edition
11 years old

20 years old
Feis Ile 2020

Rare by Nature
12 year old c.s.

16 years old

8 years old

Distiller´s Edition

Laphroaig

[lah•**froyg**]

Owner:
Beam Suntory

Region/district:
Islay

Founded: **Status:** **Capacity:**
1815 Active (vc) 3 300 000 litres

Address: Port Ellen, Islay, Argyll PA42 7DU

Website: **Tel:**
laphroaig.com 01496 302418

Back in the days when peat was abundant and coal and coke was used for the general industry, all Scotch whiskies had at least a touch of smoke in their flavour.

Going forward, this character became a signum of whiskies made on Islay and a few other islands. It alone was not a taste desired by many whisky drinkers but as a part of a blend it made a great contribution. Come the 1980s, and an increasing number of whisky aficionados started searching for these challengingly flavoured single malts. The smoky category was spearheaded by Laphroaig which, thanks to the previous owner Ian Hunter, had built a reputation going back to the days of the American prohibition. The Laphroaig trademark was registered in the USA as early as in 1934. The rest is history and peat freaks can now be found all over the world.

The distillery is equipped with a 5.5 ton stainless steel full lauter mash tun and six stainless steel washbacks with an average fermentation time of 53-55 hours. The distillery uses an unusual combination of three wash stills, three smaller spirit stills and a fourth, double the size. All stills are fitted with ascending lyne arms and foreshots are unusually long – 45 minutes. The middle cut starts at 72% and goes down to 60%. It is one of very few distilleries with its own maltings which, using two malting floors, produces 15% of its requirements. The malt is dried for 12-15 hours using peat and then for another 10 hours on hot air. The in-house malt has a phenol specification of 50-60ppm, while the remaining malt from Port Ellen or the mainland lies between 35 and 45ppm. On the refurbishing side, some new stills replacing the ones where the copper is becoming thin have been ordered and a new cooling tower will be installed during 2020. The distillery is running at full capacity which means 34 mashes per week and 3.3 million litres. Around 70% of the production is destined to be bottled as single malt and the rest is used for blends.

The core range consists of **Select** without age statement, **10 year old, 10 year old cask strength, Quarter Cask, Triple Wood, Lore** and a **25 year old**. The travel retail range consists of **Four Oak**, the **1815 Edition** and **PX Cask**. Also a part of the duty free range is the newly launched **Bessie Williamson Story 25 years old**. The bottle was released in honour of the distillery's first (and so far only) female manager back in the 1950s and 60s

Recent limited releases include the Cairdeas range encompassing bottlings exclusively for the Friends of Laphroaig; **Quarter Cask, Fino, 15 year old** and **Triple Wood**. In the same way that Bessie Williason was recognized, the legendary Ian Hunter, the last of the Johnston family to own Laphroaig, is remembered by way of an entire "book of whisky" where **Chapter One**, a **30 year old**, was released in autumn 2019 followed by **Chapter 2** (also 30 years) in autumn 2020. The Feis Ile bottling for 2020 was a **Port & Wine Casks** matured in a combination of ex-bourbon, ex-ruby port and ex-red wine casks.

History:

1815 Brothers Alexander and Donald Johnston found Laphroaig.
1836 Donald buys out Alexander and takes over.
1837 James and Andrew Gairdner found Ardenistiel a stone's throw from Laphroaig.
1847 Donald Johnston is killed in an accident in the distillery. The Manager of neigh-bouring Lagavulin, Walter Graham, takes over.
1857 Operation is back in the hands of the Johnston family when Donald's son Dougald takes over.
1877 Dougald, being without heirs, passes away and his sister Isabella, married to their cousin Alexander takes over.
1907 Alexander Johnston dies and the distillery is inherited by his two sisters Catherine Johnston and Mrs. William Hunter (Isabella Johnston).
1908 Ian Hunter arrives in Islay to assist his mother and aunt with the distillery.
1924 The two stills are increased to four.
1927 Catherine Johnston dies and Ian Hunter takes over.
1928 Isabella Johnston dies and Ian Hunter becomes sole owner.
1950 Ian Hunter forms D. Johnston & Company
1954 Ian Hunter passes away and management of the distillery is taken over by Elisabeth "Bessie" Williamson.
1967 Seager Evans & Company buys the distillery through Long John Distillery, having already acquired part of Laphroaig in 1962. The number of stills is increased from four to five.
1972 Bessie Williamson retires. Another two stills are installed bringing the total to seven.
1975 Whitbread & Co. buys Seager Evans (now renamed Long John International) from Schenley International.

Bessie Williamson

History continued:

1989 The spirits division of Whitbread is sold to Allied Distillers.

1991 Allied Distillers launches Caledonian Malts. Laphroaig is one of the four malts included.

1994 The Friends of Laphroaig is founded.

1995 A 10 year old cask strength is launched.

2001 A 40 year old is released.

2004 Quarter Cask is launched.

2005 Fortune Brands becomes new owner.

2007 A vintage 1980 (27 years old) and a 25 year old are released.

2008 Cairdeas, Cairdeas 30 year old and Triple Wood are released.

2009 An 18 year old is released.

2010 A 20 year old for French Duty Free and Cairdeas Master Edition are launched.

2011 Laphroaig PX and Cairdeas - The Ileach Edition are released.

2012 Brodir and Cairdeas Origin are launched.

2013 QA Cask, An Cuan Mor, 25 year old cask strength and Cairdeas Port Wood Edition are released.

2014 Laphroaig Select and a new version of Cairdeas are released.

2015 A 21 year old, a 32 year old sherry cask and a new Cairdeas are released and the 15 year old is re-launched.

2016 Lore, Cairdeas 2016 and a 30 year old are released.

2017 Four Oak, The 1815 Edition and a 27 year old are released.

2018 A 28 year old and Cairdeas Fino are released.

2019 A 30 year old is the first release in a new series named The Ian Hunter Story.

2020 The Ian Hunter Story chapter 2 and Cairdeas Port & Wine Casks are released.

Select

Quarter Cask

25 years old

Tasting notes Laphroaig Select:

GS – The nose offers chocolate and malt notes set against peat, citrus fruit and iodine. Citrus fruit is most apparent on the relatively light palate, along with ginger, cinnamon and dried fruits. The peat is muted. The finish offers bright spices, new oak and medicinal notes.

Tasting notes Laphroaig 10 year old:

GS – Old-fashioned sticking plaster, peat smoke and seaweed leap off the nose, followed by something a little sweeter and fruitier. Massive on the palate, with fish oil, salt and plankton, though the finish is quite tight and increasingly drying.

Ian Hunter Chapter 2

The 1815 Edition

10 years old

Triple Wood

Cairdeas
Port & Wine Casks

Linkwood

[link•wood]

Owner: Diageo

Region/district: Speyside

Founded: 1821

Status: Active

Capacity: 5 600 000 litres

Address: Elgin, Morayshire IV30 8RD

Website: malts.com

Tel: 01343 862000

Elgin is the largest town in that whisky hot spot of Scotland that is called Speyside. Even though there are more than 50 distilleries in the region, there are only two in Elgin – Glen Moray in the centre and Linkwood on the southern outskirts.

While Glen Moray is a popular visitor's destination with a single malt that sells 1,5 million bottles yearly, Linkwood is closed to visitors and single malt sales are a mere trickle compared to its neighbour. Linkwood's greatness can be found in its ability to elevate a blend to new levels. In a blender's list from 1924 (and several more after that), Linkwood is ranked one of twelve in the top group together with icons such as Macallan, Glenlivet, Glenfiddich and Highland Park. These malts were, and to a great extent still are, used as top dressers in a blend to add depth and complexity. Other malts further down the list are considered fillers and packers contributing texture and balance to the blend. It is important to realize that this or other similar lists should not be seen as a quality ranking per se but rather a testament to its performance in a blend.

The old part of the distillery worked in tandem with the new site (built in 1971) but stopped producing in 1996. In connection with an upgrade in 2013, the old buildings from the 1800s facing Linkwood Road were demolished and an extension of the current still house, which houses two of the stills and the tunroom, was conducted. The only original buildings from 1872 left standing are No. 6 warehouse and the redundant, old kiln with the pagoda roof. The set up of equipment is one 12.5 ton full lauter mash tun, 11 wooden washbacks and three pairs of stills. The fermentation time during a five-day week production varies between 65 and 105 hours. Production during the last couple of years has varied between 3.6 and 5.6 million litres of alcohol, depending on having a five or seven-day production week.

The only official core bottling is a **12 year old Flora & Fauna**. In 2016, a **37 year old** distilled in 1978 and bottled at 50.3%, was launched as part of the Special Releases.

History:

1821 Peter Brown founds the distillery.

1868 Peter Brown passes away and his son William inherits the distillery.

1872 William demolishes the distillery and builds a new one.

1897 Linkwood Glenlivet Distillery Company Ltd takes over operations.

1902 Innes Cameron, a whisky trader from Elgin, joins the Board and eventually becomes the major shareholder and Director.

1932 Innes Cameron dies and Scottish Malt Distillers takes over in 1933.

1962 Major refurbishment takes place.

1971 The two stills are increased by four. Technically, the four new stills belong to a new distillery referred to as Linkwood B.

1985 Linkwood A (the two original stills) closes.

1990 Linkwood A is in production again for a few months each year until 1996.

2002 A 26 year old from 1975 is launched as a Rare Malt.

2005 A 30 year old from 1974 is launched as a Rare Malt.

2008 Three different wood finishes (all 26 year old) are released.

2009 A Manager´s Choice 1996 is released.

2013 Expansion of the distillery including two more stills.

2016 A 37 year old is released.

12 years old

Tasting notes Linkwood 12 years old:

GS – Floral, grassy and fragrant on the nutty nose, while the slightly oily palate becomes increasingly sweet, ending up at marzipan and almonds. The relatively lengthy finish is quite dry and citric.

Loch Lomond

[lock low•mund]

Owner:
Loch Lomond Group
(Hillhouse Capital Management)

Region/district:
Western Highlands

Founded: 1965

Status: Active

Capacity: 5 000 000 litres

Address: Lomond Estate, Alexandria G83 0TL

Website: lochlomondwhiskies.com

Tel: 01389 752781

Sold under various names, the range from the distillery has sometimes been confusing for the consumer. Refreshing the brand in 2020 will make it simpler to understand Loch Lomond.

The names Inchmurrin and Inchmoan, both having been used as brand names, will henceforth be used to differentiate distinctive Loch Lomond styles (fruity & sweet and smoky & spicy) with Loch Lomond being the overall brand name.

Loch Lomond has an extremely unusual equipment setup. Founded in 1966, one pair of straight neck pot stills were installed. Yet another pair were installed in 1990 and four years later a grain distillery with two continuous stills was opened. One pair of traditional swan neck pot stills were installed in 1998 and in 2007 a single grain coffey still was added. Complemented with a third pair of straight neck stills the distillery now has 11 stills of four different kinds! Of the 5 million litres on the malt side, 70% is distilled in the Coffey still with Loch Lomond Single Grain (actually a single malt but not accepted as such by the SWA) being the big seller. The Loch Lomond is distilled in the traditional pot stills but mixed before bottling with whisky from the straight neck stills. Inchmurrin comes from the straight neck stills and so does the heavily peated Inchmoan. The rest of the equipment consists of a 9.5 ton full lauter mash tun, 21 stainless steel washbacks (with a fermentation time of 92 to 160 hours) for the malt side of the production and another 18 for the grain side. The plan for 2020 is to make 2,8 million litres of malt spirit and 2 million litres of grain

From 2020 the core range will consist of **Loch Lomond Classic, Original, 10, 12** and **18 year old** with another three launched in July; **14, 21** and **30 year old**. Furthermore there is **Loch Lomond Inchmurrin 12 year old** and **Loch Lomond Inchmoan 12 year old**. For duty-free there is **Original, Madeira Wood Finish** (former Inchmurrin), **12 year old, 14 year old Peated** and **18 year old** (former Inchmurrin). Recent limited releases include a **50 year old** and the **12 year old Open Special Edition** which had been produced using Chardonnay yeast. Finally, there are two core grain expressions, the **Single Grain** and the **Single Grain Peated**.

History:

1965 The distillery is built by Littlemill Distillery Company Ltd owned by Duncan Thomas and American Barton Brands.

1966 Production commences.

1971 Duncan Thomas is bought out.

1984 The distillery closes.

1985 Glen Catrine Bonded Warehouse Ltd buys Loch Lomond Distillery.

1987 The distillery resumes production.

1993 Grain spirits are also distilled.

1997 A fire destroys 300,000 litres of maturing whisky.

1999 Two more stills are installed.

2005 Inchmoan and Craiglodge as well as Inchmurrin 12 years are launched.

2006 Inchmurrin 4 years, Croftengea 1996 (9 years), Glen Douglas 2001 (4 years) and Inchfad 2002 (5 years) are launched.

2010 A peated Loch Lomond with no age statement is released as well as a Vintage 1966.

2012 New range for Inchmurrin released – 12, 15, 18 and 21 years.

2014 The distillery is sold to Exponent Private Equity. Organic versions of 12 year old single malt and single blend are released.

2015 Loch Lomond Original Single Malt is released together with a single grain and two blends, Reserve and Signature.

2016 A 12 year old and an 18 year old are launched.

2017 This year´s releases include Inchmoan 12 year old and Inchmurrin 12 and 18 year old.

2018 A 50 year old Loch Lomond is released.

2019 The distillery is sold to Hillhouse Capital Management and a 50 year old is released.

2020 The core range is revamped and expanded.

Tasting notes Loch Lomond 12 years old:

IR – Starts out malty on the nose followed by pears, apple pie with custard and digestive. Herbal at first on the palate with cinnamon and thyme, roasted root vegetables and nuts, caramel, vanilla and a hint of peat.

Loch Lomond 12 year old

Lochranza

[lock•ran•sa]

Owner:
Isle of Arran Distillers

Region/district:
Highlands (Arran)

Founded: 1993

Status: Active (vc)

Capacity: 1 200 000 litres

Address: Lochranza, Isle of Arran KA27 8HJ

Website: arranwhisky.com

Tel: 01770 830264

With Arran Distillers now operating two distilleries on the island it was inevitable that the first distillery was in need for a new name and it has now been changed from Arran to Lochranza after the village where it is situated.

It became equally important to have a distillery manager on each site. With Graham Omand already the manager at Lagg, David Livingstone, with a history from Laphroaig and Ardnahoe, is the new manager at Lochranza since autumn 2019. This means that James MacTaggart, who has been with the company since 2007, now is Production and Operations Director in the company. MacTaggart started his career in the industry at Bowmore in 1975.

Lochranza is equipped with a 2.5 ton semi-lauter mash tun, six Oregon pine washbacks with an average fermentation time of 60 hours and four stills. The production plan for 2020 is to make 13 mashes per week and 500,000 litres of pure alcohol, all unpeated. The distillery is by far the most visited distillery in Scotland with well over 100,000 people coming here annually.

The core range consists of **10, 18** and **21 year old, Barrel Reserve** and **Robert Burns**. Also included are **Quarter Cask The Bothy** and **Sherry Cask The Bodega** both bottled at cask strength. A new addition to the range, a **25 year old**, is due to be released in October 2020. Finally, the peated side of Arran is represented by **Machrie Moor** bottled both at 46% and at cask strength as well as the limited **Machrie Moor Fingal's Cut** with three varieties; single cask, quarter cask finish and sherry finish.

A range of limited wood finishes include **Amarone, Port** and **Sauternes** and every year a number of single casks are released. The third install- ment in the Explorer's Series, first launched in 2018, appeared in June 2020 in the shape of **Kildonan & Pladda**, a 21 year old matu- red in sherry butts and puncheons followed by a finish in ruby port pipes. Finally, **Master of Distilling II** honouring the company's master distiller James MacTaggart, was released in autumn 2019. This time it was a 12 year old matured in palo cortado sherry casks.

History:

1993 Harold Currie founds the distillery.

1995 Production starts in full on 17th August.

1998 The first release is a 3 year old.

1999 The Arran 4 years old is released.

2002 Single Cask 1995 is launched.

2003 Single Cask 1997, non-chill filtered and Calvados finish is launched.

2004 Cognac finish, Marsala finish, Port finish and Arran First Distillation 1995 are launched.

2005 Arran 1996 and two finishes, Ch. Margaux and Grand Cru Champagne, are launched.

2006 After an unofficial launch in 2005, Arran 10 years old is released as well as a couple of new wood finishes.

2007 Four new wood finishes and Gordon's Dram are released.

2008 The first 12 year old is released as well as four new wood finishes.

2009 Peated single casks, two wood finishes and 1996 Vintage are released.

2010 A 14 year old, Rowan Tree, three cask finishes and Machrie Moor (peated) are released.

2011 The Westie, Sleeping Warrior and a 12 year old cask strength are released.

2012 The Eagle and The Devil's Punch Bowl are released.

2013 A 16 year old and a new edition of Machrie Moor and released.

2014 A 17 year old and Machrie Moor cask strength are released.

2015 A 18 year old and The Illicit Stills are released.

2017 The Exciseman is released.

2018 A 21 year old and Brodick Bay are released.

2019 The core range is revamped and the limited Lochranza Castle is released.

2020 A 25 year old and the 21 year old Kildonan & Pladda are released.

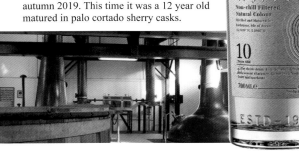

10 years old

Tasting notes Arran 14 year old:

GS – Very fragrant and perfumed on the nose, with peaches, brandy and ginger snaps. Smooth and creamy on the palate, with spicy summer fruits, apricots and nuts. The lingering finish is nutty and slowly drying.

Longmorn

[long•morn]

Owner: **Region/district:**
Chivas Brothers   Speyside
(Pernod Ricard)

Founded: **Status:**   **Capacity:**
1894   Active   4 500 000 litres

Address: Longmorn, Morayshire IV30 8SJ

Website: **Tel:**
-                01343 554139

Although popular with both blenders and independent bottlers, Longmorn is a single malt that has always been overshadowed by its stablemates in the Chivas group – Glenlivet and Aberlour.

There is a small range of official bottlings which have received a particular interest from the Japanese market. One of the reasons for this is probably the fact that Masataka Taketsuru, often called the father of Japanese whisky making, spent a week at the distillery in April 1919. He had been sent to Scotland by his employer to learn how to make whisky and made a short internship at Longmorn. Back in Japan he helped build the Yamazaki distillery and a few years later he founded his own, Yoichi, which in many ways was inspired by what he saw at Longmorn.

Longmorn distillery is equipped with a modern 8.5 ton Briggs full lauter mash tun which replaced the old, traditional tun in 2012. At the same time, seven of the eight, old stainless steel washbacks were moved to the new tun room and an additional three were installed. The eight, onion-shaped stills with declining lyne arms are big and fitted with sub-coolers and the wash stills have external heat exchangers. The production capacity was also increased in 2012 by 30% to 4.5 million litres. Currently, the production runs for five days per week with 18 mashes. This means roughly 3 million litres of alcohol over the year. The style of the newmake is fruity yet robust.

The core range consists of **The Distiller's Choice** (with no age statement), a **16 year old** and a **23 year old**. In July 2019, another three bottlings appeared in the new Chivas series named The Secret Speyside Collection. Two of them, **18** and **23 year old**, had been matured in American oak barrels and hogsheads and were bottled at 48%. The third, a **25 year old**, had been filled into a combination of ex-bourbon and ex-sherry and was bottled at 52.2%. All three are available for the first year in duty-free and will then be made available to domestic markets in 2020. Finally, there are four cask strength bottlings in the Distillery Reserve Collection, available at all Chivas' visitor centres – from **14** to **23 years old**.

History:

1893 John Duff & Company, which founded Glenlossie already in 1876, starts construction. John Duff, George Thomson and Charles Shirres are involved in the company. The total cost amounts to £20,000.

1894 First production in December.

1897 John Duff buys out the other partners.

1898 John Duff builds another distillery next to Longmorn which is called Benriach (at times aka Longmorn no. 2). Duff declares bankruptcy and the shares are sold by the bank to James R. Grant.

1970 The distillery company is merged with The Glenlivet & Glen Grant Distilleries and Hill Thomson & Co. Ltd. Own floor maltings ceases.

1972 The number of stills is increased from four to six. Spirit stills are converted to steam firing.

1974 Another two stills are added.

1978 Seagrams takes over through The Chivas & Glenlivet Group.

1994 Wash stills are converted to steam firing.

2001 Pernod Ricard buys Seagram Spirits & Wine together with Diageo and Pernod Ricard takes over the Chivas group.

2004 A 17 year old cask strength is released.

2007 A 16 year old is released replacing the 15 year old.

2012 Production capacity is expanded.

2015 The Distiller's Choice is released.

2016 A 16 year old and a 23 year old are released.

2019 Three expressions in the new The Secret Speyside Collection are released.

Tasting notes Longmorn Distiller's Choice:

GS – Barley sugar, ginger, toffee and malt on the sweet nose. The palate reveals caramel and milk chocolate, with peppery Jaffa orange. Toffee, barley and a hint of spicy oak in the medium-length finish.

Distiller's Choice

Macallan

[mack•al•un]

Owner: Edrington Group

Region/district: Speyside

Founded: 1824

Status: Active (vc)

Capacity: 15 000 000 litres

Address: Easter Elchies, Craigellachie, Morayshire AB38 9RX

Website: themacallan.com

Tel: 01340 871471

In terms of value, Macallan is the best selling malt whisky today (it is number three in terms of volume) but it's road to fame started quite late, in the 1970s. It was then that the owners began focusing on maturation in ex-sherry casks.

The preferred casks were those that had held oloroso sherry but in 2002 Elegancia was launched where fino casks also were used. Two years later a much discussed deviation from the sherry track occurred when the Fine Oak range was introduced, where whisky matured in bourbon casks were blended with "traditional" Macallan. The range definitely had some success but now, 16 years later it seems that Edrington are ready to go back to its roots with Macallan. The only Fine Oak (known as Triple Cask) that will remain for the time being is the 12 year old while the 15 and 18 year old are being discontinued. With more than 97% of the casks used for maturation being seasoned with sherry, it is clear that the owners now want to focus as much as possible on sherry casks as the foundation for Macallan.

The distillery is equipped with a full lauter mash tun with a 17 ton mash and 21 washbacks made of stainless steel with a fermentation time of 60 hours. There are 12 wash stills and 24 spirit stills. The capacity is 15 million litres of pure alcohol per year and last year, before the pandemic, they mashed 35-40 times per week resulting in 11-11.5 million litres of alcohol. The old distillery has been closed since December 2018 and has no plans to reopen. The equipment is still in place though, two mash tuns, 22 stainless steel washbacks and six made of wood, seven wash stills and 14 spirit stills. The capacity when working was 11 million litres.

The core range of Macallan consists of three styles. **Sherry Oak** (100% maturation in sherry casks) is represented by **12, 18, 25, 30** and **40 years old**. **Triple Cask** (formerly known as Fine Oak) is a combination of whisky matured in ex-bourbon and ex-sherry casks and is represented by a **12 year old**. **Double Cask**, finally, is the youngest addition to the range and is currently made up of **Gold** without age statement, **12, 15** and **18 year old**. The latter two were launched in July 2020. In this case, Double Cask means a mix of sherry casks from both American and European Oak. Finally, in 2019 a new core release, **Macallan Estate** made from barley grown on the Macallan estate, was launched.

The Macallan Quest Collection is reserved for duty-free including **Quest, Lumina, Terra** and **Enigma**. A fifth member is **Aurora**, released exclusively for Taiwan. Another duty-free bottling appeared in late 2019 when **Concept No. 2**, the second in a new range, was released. A range of prestige bottlings called The Macallan Masters Decanter Series includes **Reflexion, No 6, M Rare Cask** and **M Black**. Recent limited releases include **Edition No. 5, Classic Cut** and **Genesis**. Macallan holds an impressive stock of old whiskies and in 2018 a **72 year old Genesis Decanter** and a **52 year old** were released. Finally, there is the **Fine and Rare Collection** with single casks from 1926 to 1991.

History:

1824 The distillery is licensed to Alexander Reid under the name Elchies Distillery.

1847 Alexander Reid passes away and James Shearer Priest and James Davidson take over.

1868 James Stuart takes over the licence. He founds Glen Spey distillery a decade later.

1886 James Stuart buys the distillery.

1892 Stuart sells the distillery to Roderick Kemp from Elgin. Kemp expands the distillery and names it Macallan-Glenlivet.

1909 Roderick Kemp passes away and the Roderick Kemp Trust is established to secure the family's future ownership.

1965 The number of stills is increased from six to twelve.

1966 The trust is reformed as a private limited company.

1968 The company is introduced on the London Stock Exchange.

1974 The number of stills is increased to 18.

1975 Another three stills are added, now making the total 21.

1984 The first official 18 year old single malt is launched.

1986 Japanese Suntory buys 25% of Macallan-Glenlivet plc stocks.

1996 Highland Distilleries buys the remaining stocks. 1874 Replica is launched.

1999 Edrington and William Grant & Sons buys Highland Distilleries for £601 million through The 1887 Company with 70% held by Edrington and 30% by William Grant & Sons. Suntory still holds 25% in Macallan.

2000 The first single cask from Macallan (1981) is named Exceptional 1.

2001 A new visitor centre is opened.

Gold | Sherry Oak 12 years | Triple Cask 12 years

History continued:

2002 Elegancia replaces 12 year old in the duty-free range. 1841 Replica, Exceptional II and Exceptional III are also launched.

2003 1876 Replica and Exceptional IV, single cask from 1990 are released.

2004 Exceptional V, single cask from 1989 is released as well as Exceptional VI, single cask from 1990. The Fine Oak series is launched.

2005 New expressions are Macallan Woodland Estate, Winter Edition and the 50 year old.

2006 Fine Oak 17 years old and Vintage 1975 are launched.

2007 1851 Inspiration and Whisky Maker´s Selection are released as a part of the Travel Retail range.

2008 Estate Oak and 55 year old Lalique are released.

2009 The mothballed No. 2 stillhouse is re-opened. The Macallan 1824 Collection and a 57 year old Lalique bottling is released.

2010 Oscuro is released for Duty Free.

2011 Macallan MMXI is released for duty free.

2012 Macallan Gold, the first in the new 1824 series, is launched.

2013 Amber, Sienna and Ruby are released.

2014 1824 Masters Series (with Rare Cask, Reflexion and No. 6) is released.

2015 Rare Cask Black is released.

2016 Edition No. 1 and 12 year old Double Cask are released.

2017 Folio 2 is released. The new distillery is commissioned.

2018 Fine Oak changes name to Triple Cask, The Quest Collection is released for duty free and Macallan M Black and Genesis are launched. Concept No. 1 and a 72 and a 52 year old are released.

2019 Macallan Estate, Edition No. 5 and Concept No. 2 are released.

2020 Double Cask 15 and 18 year old are released.

Tasting notes Macallan 12 year old Sherry oak:

GS – The nose is luscious, with buttery sherry and Christmas cake characteristics. Rich and firm on the palate, with sherry, elegant oak and Jaffa oranges. The finish is long and malty, with slightly smoky spice.

Tasting notes Macallan 12 year old Triple Cask:

GS – The nose is perfumed and quite complex, with marzipan and malty toffee. Expansive on the palate, with oranges, marmalade, milk chocolate and oak. Meidum in length, balanced and comparatively sweet.

Enigma | 52 years old | Double Cask 18 year old

Double Cask 12 years | Macallan Estate | Rare Cask Black | Rare Cask Batch 2

Macduff

[mack•duff]

Owner:
John Dewar & Sons Ltd
(Bacardi)

Region/district:
Highlands

Founded: 1960

Status: Active

Capacity: 3 400 000 litres

Address: Banff, Aberdeenshire AB45 3JT

Website: lastgreatmalts.com

Tel: 01261 812612

When you cross the river Deveron going from the Banff side to the Macduff side, you find the distillery on your right. The location is stunning and you would think that this distillery has been there for ages. Well it hasn't.

In fact it was built in the early 1960s, celebrating its 60th anniversary in September 2020, riding on the wave of Scotch whisky popularity at the time. The distillery spearheaded whisky production. They were pioneers when it came to heating the stills using internal steam coils and instead of a worm tub to cool the spirit vapours, they introduced shell and tube heat exchangers. Built by Scots it soon came under Italian ownership when Martini & Rossi bought it in the early 1970s. This was a time when Italians, already familiar with blended Scotch, had fallen in love with single malt starting with the huge success for Glen Grant in the 1960s. Almost a decade before Martini & Rossi took over Macduff they had acquired the William Lawson's Scotch blend brand and it didn't take long until the single malt from Macduff became an integral part of that blend. It remains so to this day. William Lawson's is currently number five on the Top Ten list of Scotch whiskies and sold 40 million bottles in 2019.

Macduff is equipped with a 6.75 ton stainless steel semi-lauter mash tun and nine washbacks (29,800 litres) made of stainless steel with a fermentation time of 55 hours. There is also a rather unusual set-up of five stills – two wash stills and three spirit stills. In order to fit the stills into the still room, the lyne arms on four of the stills are bent in a peculiar way and on one of the wash stills it is U-shaped. In 2020, the plan is to mash 26 times per week for 48 weeks, producing 3.3 million litres of alcohol.

Since 2015, the core range from the distillery is known under the name The Deveron and consists of a **10 year old**, exclusive to France, as well as a **12** and **18 year old**. For duty free, a range first launched in 2013, is available named Glen Deveron encompassing a **16**, a **20** and a **30 year old**.

History:

1960 The distillery is founded by Marty Dyke, George Crawford, James Stirrat and Brodie Hepburn (who is also involved in Tullibardine and Deanston). Macduff Distillers Ltd is the name of the company.

1964 The number of stills is increased from two to three.

1967 Stills now total four.

1968 The first bottling from the distillery is launched - the 5 year old Macduff Pure Highland Malt Scotch Whisky.

1972 William Lawson Distillers, part of General Beverage Corporation which is owned by Martini & Rossi, buys the distillery from Glendeveron Distilleries.

1990 A fifth still is installed.

1993 Bacardi buys Martini Rossi (including William Lawson) and eventually transfered Macduff to the subsidiary John Dewar & Sons.

2013 The Royal Burgh Collection (16, 20 and 30 years old) is launched for duty free.

2015 A new range is launched - 10, 12 and 18 years old.

12 years old

Tasting notes The Deveron 12 years old:

GS – Soft, sweet and fruity on the nose, with vanilla, ginger, and apple blossom. Medium-bodied, gently spicy, with butterscotch and Brazil nuts. Caramel contrasts with quite dry spicy oak in the finish.

Mannochmore

[man•och•moor]

Owner:		Region/district:
Diageo		Speyside

Founded:	Status:	Capacity:
1971	Active	6 000 000 litres

Address: Elgin, Morayshire IV30 8SS

Website:	Tel:
malts.com	01343 862000

Mannochmore was built in 1971 by DCL, the predecessor of Diageo, at a time when interest in Scotch whisky was booming. At the same time another four distilleries opened in the Speyside area.

DCL was at that time dominating the Scotch whisky industry. It had already been founded in 1877 and for a large part of the 20th century the company had dominated the market. By 1982 it owned 46 of the 119 malt distilleries and 5 of the 12 grain distilleries. In terms of ownership, it was even more dominant than Diageo is today. But the large number of distilleries didn't tell the whole story. Since the 1960s, the company had steadily lost market shares. It was run in traditional but inefficient ways and there was an imminent threat from its competitors. As the whisky market started deflating towards the beginning of the 1980s, the company became a target for buyers and in 1986 DCL was acquired by the giant brewer, Guinness.

On the same site as Mannochmore lies Glenlossie which was built almost 100 years earlier. There is also a dark grains plant which converts pot ale into cattle feed, as well as a biomass burner which generates draff into steam which powers the entire site.

Since 2013 the distillery is equipped with an 11.1 ton Briggs full lauter mash tun, eight wooden washbacks and another eight external made of stainless steel and four pairs of stills. Clear wort and long fermentations (up to 100 hours) create a new-make spirit with a fruity character and the distillery is currently running a seven-day production.

Mannochmore is the signature malt for Haig, a brand first introduced in the late 1880s and which today sells almost 5 million bottles per year. The Haig family belonged to the elite of Scottish whisky aristocracy and had been involved in distilling since the middle of the 17th century.

The only current official bottling is a **12 year old Flora & Fauna**. In autumn 2016, a **25 year old** distilled in 1990 and bottled at 53.4%, was launched as part of the Special Releases.

History:

1971 Distillers Company Limited (DCL) founds the distillery on the site of their sister distillery Glenlossie. It is managed by John Haig & Co. Ltd.

1985 The distillery is mothballed.

1989 In production again.

1992 A Flora & Fauna series 12 years old becomes the first official bottling.

2009 An 18 year old is released.

2010 A Manager's Choice 1998 is released.

2013 The number of stills is increased to eight.

2016 A 25 year old cask strength is released.

Tasting notes Mannochmore 12 years old:

GS – Perfumed and fresh on the light, citric nose, with a sweet, floral, fragrant palate, featuring vanilla, ginger and even a hint of mint. Medium length in the finish, with a note of lingering almonds.

12 years old

Miltonduff

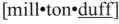
[mill•ton•duff]

Owner:
Chivas Brothers
(Pernod Ricard)

Region/district:
Speyside

Founded: 1824

Status: Active

Capacity: 5 800 000 litres

Address: Miltonduff, Elgin, Morayshire IV30 8TQ

Website:
-

Tel:
01343 547433

Chivas Brothers can't seem to do anything wrong at the moment with their biggest Scotch whisky brand – Ballantines. The sales growth during the past decade is impressive to say the least.

In the last five years the growth in sales is 25% with more than 92 million bottles sold in 2019. Only Johnnie Walker, with a 4,5% increase in sales during that same period, is selling more and of the Top Ten Scotch blends only Black & White exceed recent years' growth. The situation was different in 2012 when sales figures for Ballantines were the lowest since the new millenium started. The problem was that the brand's biggest strongholds at the time, Spain and South Korea, showed rapidly declining numbers due to struggling local economies. The solution was to relaunch it in Latin America and Eastern Europe, not least by way of a new global music platform called True Music.

Miltonduff is, since at least 1936 when Hiram Walker, the owner of the Ballantines brand at the time, bought the distillery, one of the signature malts for Ballantines blend. Official bottlings of the single malt were rare until 2017 when Miltonduff, together with Glenburgie and Glentauchers, were released in a new range called Ballantine's Single Malt Series.

The distillery is equipped with an eight ton full lauter mash tun with a copper dome, 16 stainless steel washbacks with a fermentation time of 56 hours and six, large stills. The lyne arms are sharply descending which allows for very little reflux. This makes for a robust and oily new make in contrast to the lighter and more floral Glenburgie. In 1964, two Lomond stills were installed at Miltonduff. They were equipped with columns with adjustable plates with the intention of distilling different styles of whisky from the same still. They were dismantled in 1981 but the special whisky produced, Mosstowie, can still, with a bit of luck, be found.

The official bottling is a **15 year old**. There is also a **19 year old** exclusive to Taiwan and a **12 year old cask strength** distilled in 2007 in the Distillery Reserve Collection, available at all Chivas' visitor centres.

History:

1824 Andrew Peary and Robert Bain obtain a licence for Miltonduff Distillery. It has previously operated as an illicit farm distillery called Milton Distillery but changes name when the Duff family buys the site it is operating on.

1866 William Stuart buys the distillery.

1895 Thomas Yool & Co. becomes new part-owner.

1936 Thomas Yool & Co. sells the distillery to Hiram Walker Gooderham & Worts. The latter transfers administration to the newly acquired subsidiary George Ballantine & Son.

1964 A pair of Lomond stills is installed to produce the rare Mosstowie.

1974 Major reconstruction of the distillery.

1981 The Lomond stills are decommissioned and replaced by two ordinary pot stills, the number of stills now totalling six.

1986 Allied Lyons buys 51% of Hiram Walker.

1987 Allied Lyons acquires the rest of Hiram Walker.

1991 Allied Distillers follow United Distillers´ example of Classic Malts and introduce Caledonian Malts in which Tormore, Glendro-nach and Laphroaig are included in addition to Miltonduff. Tormore is later replaced by Scapa.

2005 Chivas Brothers (Pernod Ricard) becomes the new owner through the acquisition of Allied Domecq.

2017 A 15 year old is released.

15 years old

Tasting notes Miltonduff 15 years old:

IR – Fresh citrus and honey on the nose together with heather, ginger and peaches. More spicy on the palate with cinnamon and clove, vanilla, honey, red berries and liquorice.

Mortlach

[mort•lack]

Owner: Diageo	**Region/district:** Speyside
Founded: 1823	**Status:** Active	**Capacity:** 3 800 000 litres

Address: Dufftown, Keith, Banffshire AB55 4AQ

Website: mortlach.com, malts.com

Tel: 01340 822100

Not every launch of a new whisky range turns into a commercial success and when the opposite happens, most whisky producers are reluctant to comment on their failure.

That is why Diageo's candid way of dealing with the aftermaths of the Mortlach re-launch in 2014 was both unusual and refreshing. The distillery's whisky, at that time officially available only as a hard-to-find 16 year old, was known mostly to hardcore fans of Scotch single malt. The owners decided not only to launch an entirely new range but also to rebuild the distillery, doubling the production capacity. It soon became apparent that the four new expressions, presented in 50 cl bottles, were too expensive for a wider audience. In connection with that, a general downturn of sales of Scotch whisky made Diageo cautious and they took the decision to put the distillery expansion on hold. Just four years later, the company more or less openly declared that the new range had not matched the consumers' expectations and yet a new, more competitively priced, range was introduced with a substantial increase of sales as the result.

The distillery is equipped with a 12 ton full lauter mash tun and six washbacks made of Douglas fir, currently with six short fermentations (55 hours) and six long (110 hours). There are three wash stills and three spirit stills working in a highly unique way which can at best be described as a 2,81 time distillation. All the stills are attached to worm tubs for cooling the spirit vapours. The production plan for 2020 is a five-day week with 12 mashes per week with a target of making 2.6 million litres.

The core range consists of **12 year old Wee Witchie, 16 year old Distiller's Dram, 20 year old Cowie's Blue Seal** and, for duty-free, the **14 year old Alexander's Way**. In 2019, the first in Mortlach's Singing Stills series appeared when a **47 year old** was released. In July 2020, a **25 year old**, matured in a first fill PX/oloroso butt was part of the new Prima & Ultima range and later in the year a **21 year old** appeared in the Rare by Nature series. There is also the **15 year old** The Six Kingdoms (Game of Thrones).

History:

1823 The distillery is founded by James Findlater.

1824 Donald Macintosh and Alexander Gordon become part-owners.

1831 The distillery is sold to John Robertson for £270.

1832 A. & T. Gregory buys Mortlach.

1837 James and John Grant of Aberlour become part-owners. No production takes place.

1842 The distillery is now owned by John Alexander Gordon and the Grant brothers.

1851 Mortlach is producing again after having been used as a church and a brewery for some years.

1853 George Cowie joins and becomes part-owner.

1867 John Alexander Gordon dies and Cowie becomes sole owner.

1896 Alexander Cowie joins the company.

1897 The number of stills is increased from three to six.

1923 Alexander Cowie sells the distillery to John Walker & Sons.

1925 John Walker becomes part of Distillers Company Limited (DCL).

1964 Major refurbishment.

1968 Floor maltings ceases.

1996 Mortlach 1972 is released as a Rare Malt.

1998 Mortlach 1978 is released as a Rare Malt.

2004 Mortlach 1971, a 32 year old cask strength is released.

2014 Four new bottlings are released - Rare Old, Special Strength, 18 year old and 25 year old.

2018 A new range is presented; 12 year old Wee Witchie, 16 year old Distiller's Dram and 20 year old Cowie's Blue Seal.

2019 The oldest official Mortlach bottling ever, 47 years, is released and a 26 year old appears in the Special Releases.

2020 A 25 year old Prima & Ultima is released followed by a 21 year old Rare by Nature.

Tasting notes Mortlach 12 years old:

IR – Fresh and intense on the nose with notes of sherry, apple cider, dark plums, tobacco and toffee. The palate is robust with orange marmalade, dark chocolate, espresso and chili pepper.

12 years old

Oban

[oa•bun]

Owner: Diageo		**Region/district:** Western Highlands
Founded: 1794	**Status:** Active (vc)	**Capacity:** 870 000 litres

Address: Stafford Street, Oban, Argyll PA34 5NH

Website: malts.com	**Tel:** 01631 572004 (vc)

In terms of production capacity, Oban may be the second smallest distillery within the Diageo group. Of the 28 malt distilleries only Royal Lochnagar is producing less volumes on a yearly basis.

On the other hand, Oban single malt is a brand the owners go all-in for. It all started in 1988 when Oban became one of the six original Classic Malts representing Western Highlands. Together with its five "team mates" it suddenly became available in thousands of pubs and bars all over the UK. At the same time the whisky also established a genuine fan base in the USA. Currently it is the fifth best seller of all the Diageo malts and in the last decade sales figures have more than doubled to 1,5 million bottles. The only other Diageo malts that have achieved similar sales growths are The Singleton (which consists of three sub brands) and Talisker.

The equipment consists of a seven ton traditional stainless steel mash tun with rakes. The four wooden washbacks used to be made from European larch but, by November 2020 all of them will have been replaced by washbacks made from Oregon pine. There is one pair of stills that is attached to a rectangular, stainless steel, double worm tub to condense the spirit vapours. Worm tubs usually result in a heavy newmake but the fact that they run the worms hot means that the condensation takes longer than usual providing more copper contact. This gives a soft and citrusy newmake. The fruity character of Oban single malt is also dependent on long fermentations, hence they can only manage six mashes per week with five long (110 hours) and one short (65 hours). The production plan for 2020 is to do around 840,000 litres.

The core range consists of **Little Bay, a 14 year old,** an **18 year old** (exclusive to USA) and a **Distiller's Edition** with a montilla fino sherry finish. In spring 2019, the **Night's Watch - Oban Bay Reserve** was released as part of the Game of Thrones series and in summer the same year, **Oban Old Teddy,** a distillery exclusive matured in ex-bodega sherry casks was released. The whisky was named after Teddy Maclean who worked as a master distiller at Oban in the 1950s. Both his son and grandson are currently working at the distillery.

History:
- 1793 John and Hugh Stevenson found the distillery.
- 1820 Hugh Stevenson dies.
- 1821 Hugh Stevenson's son Thomas takes over.
- 1829 Bad investments force Thomas Stevenson into bankruptcy. His eldest son John takes over.
- 1830 John buys the distillery from his father's creditors for £1,500.
- 1866 Peter Cumstie buys the distillery.
- 1883 Cumstie sells Oban to James Walter Higgins who refurbishes and modernizes it.
- 1898 The Oban & Aultmore-Glenlivet Co. takes over with Alexander Edwards at the helm.
- 1923 The Oban Distillery Co. owned by Buchanan-Dewar takes over.
- 1925 Buchanan-Dewar becomes part of Distillers Company Limited (DCL).
- 1931 Production ceases.
- 1937 In production again.
- 1968 Floor maltings ceases and the distillery closes for reconstruction.
- 1972 Reopening of the distillery.
- 1979 Oban 12 years is on sale.
- 1988 United Distillers launches Classic Malts and Oban 14 year old is included.
- 1998 A Distillers' Edition is launched.
- 2002 The oldest Oban (32 years) so far is launched.
- 2004 A 1984 cask strength is released.
- 2009 Oban 2000, a single cask, is released.
- 2010 A no age distillery exclusive is released.
- 2013 A limited 21 year old is released.
- 2015 Oban Little Bay is released.
- 2016 A distillery exclusive without age statement is released.
- 2018 A 21 year old is launched as a part of the Special Releases.
- 2019 Night´s Watch - Oban Bay Reserve and Oban Old Teddy are released.

Tasting notes Oban 14 years old:
GS – Lightly smoky on the honeyed, floral nose. Toffee, cereal and a hint of peat. The palate offers initial cooked fruits, becoming spicier. Complex, bittersweet, oak and more gentle smoke. The finish is quite lengthy, with spicy oak, toffee and new leather.

14 years old

Pulteney

[poolt•ni]

Owner:
Inver House Distillers
(Thai Beverages plc)

Region/district:
Northern Highlands

Founded: 1826
Status: Active (vc)
Capacity: 1 800 000 litres

Address: Huddart St, Wick, Caithness KW1 5BA

Website: oldpulteney.com
Tel: 01955 602371

During the time when Pulteney was owned by Allied, the single malt produced was mainly destined for a part of the Ballantines blend. It wasn't until the current owners, Inver House, took over that the brand was promoted on its own merits.

They have worked hard making Old Pulteney available in markets all over the world and last year it sold almost 600,000 bottles. In older days the single malt was known as "the manzanilla of the north" in order to describe the dry, briny and slightly salty character of the spirit. Lately, the owners are instead using "The maritime malt" in their marketing which makes sense with fewer people today knowing what a manzanilla sherry is or tastes like.

Pulteney is located in Wick and not only was the distillery closed between 1930 and 1951, but the entire town was dry. A law gave communities in Scotland the right to implement prohibition similar to the one that was enforced in the USA, provided a majority of the people voted for it. The ban came into place in 1922 and it took 25 years until pubs were allowed to serve alcohol again.

The distillery is equipped with a stainless steel semi-lauter mash tun with a copper canopy. There are seven washbacks made of stainless steel with a fermentation time between 50 and 110 hours. The wash still is equipped with a huge boil ball and a very thick lye pipe. Both stills use stainless steel worm tubs for condensing the spirit. Around 1.6 million litres of alcohol are produced yearly.

The core range is made up of **12 years old**, matured in ex-bourbon casks and bottled at 40%, the smoky **Huddart** without age statement and **15, 18** and **25 years old**, all three matured in a combination of ex-bourbon and ex-sherry casks. For the travel retail market there is a **10 year old** matured in ex-bourbon barrels, a **16 year old** with a finish ex-oloroso casks and a **Vintage 2006** which had spent time in first fill ex-bourbon barrels. A number of limited single casks have also occured with a **34 year old sherry finish** for the Chinese market in May 2020 as one of the most recent.

History:
1826 James Henderson founds the distillery.
1920 The distillery is bought by James Watson.
1923 Buchanan-Dewar takes over.
1930 Production ceases.
1951 In production again after being acquired by the solicitor Robert Cumming.
1955 Cumming sells to James & George Stodart, a subsidiary to Hiram Walker & Sons.
1958 The distillery is rebuilt.
1959 The floor maltings close.
1961 Allied Breweries buys James & George Stodart Ltd.
1981 Allied Breweries changes name to Allied Lyons.
1995 Allied Domecq sells Pulteney to Inver House Distillers.
1997 Old Pulteney 12 years is launched.
2001 Pacific Spirits (Great Oriole Group) buys Inver House at a price of $85 million.
2004 A 17 year old is launched.
2005 A 21 year old is launched.
2006 International Beverage Holdings acquires Pacific Spirits UK.
2010 WK499 Isabella Fortuna is released.
2012 A 40 year old and WK217 Spectrum are released.
2013 Old Pulteney Navigator, The Lighthouse range (3 expressions) and Vintage 1990 are released.
2014 A 35 year old is released.
2015 Dunnet Head and Vintage 1989 are released.
2017 Three vintages (1983, 1990 and 2006) are released together with a 25 year old.
2018 A completely new core range is launched; 12 years old, Huddart, 15 years old and 18 years old.
2020 A limited 34 year old is released.

12 years old

Tasting notes Old Pulteney 12 years old:
GS – The nose presents pleasingly fresh malt and floral notes, with a touch of pine. The palate is comparatively sweet, with malt, spices, fresh fruit and a suggestion of salt. The finish is medium in length, drying and decidedly nutty.

Royal Brackla

[royal brack•lah]

Owner: **Region/district:**
John Dewar & Sons   Highlands
(Bacardi)

Founded: **Status:**   **Capacity:**
1812   Active   4 100 000 litres

Address: Cawdor, Nairn, Nairnshire IV12 5QY

Website: **Tel:**
lastgreatmalts.com   01667 402002

Royal Brackla is one of five malt distilleries in the Dewar's group, which has been owned since 1998 by Bacardi. That same year Stephanie Macleod joined the company and in 2006 she was appointed master blender and malt master.

She became the seventh master blender in the company and her main responsibilities were to maintain the quality and develop new versions of the company's two blends – Dewar's and Lawson's. Both are in the Top 10 global Scotch so it was obviously a huge task. At the same time the five malt brands had been more or less neglected. In 2007 she introduced single cask bottlings from Aberfeldy and in 2014/2015, together with her team, she made an un-precedented re-launch of all the company's malts. With more than 15 new expressions, the series became known as The Last Great Malts and even though some of the whiskies can still be hard to come by in certain markets, new bottlings continue to be released.

Royal Brackla is equipped with a 12.6 ton full lauter mash tun. There are six wooden washbacks and another two made of stainless steel which have been placed outside – all with a fermentation time of 70 hours. Finally, there are also two pairs of stills. In 2020, the production plan is 17 mashes per week which translates to 3.97 million litres of alcohol which is more or less the full capacity of the distillery. With a mash tun producing a clear wort, long fermentations, long foreshots (30 minutes), a slow distillation and lots of reflux from the stills due to ascending lyne arms – the house style of Brackla is elegant and fruity.

The core range consists of a **12, 16 and 21 year old**. In autumn 2019, the range for travel retail was revamped and now consists of a **12 year old** finished in oloroso casks, an **18 year old** with a palo cortado sherry finish and a **20 year old** finished in a blend of PX, oloroso and palo cortado sherry casks. There is also the limited Exceptional Cask Series with two **20 year olds** having been finished for 11 years in **moscatel** and **French red wine** casks respectively.

History:

1812   The distillery is founded by Captain William Fraser.

1833   Brackla becomes the first of three distilleries allowed to use 'Royal' in the name.

1852   Robert Fraser & Co. takes over the distillery.

1897   The distillery is rebuilt and Royal Brackla Distillery Company Limited is founded.

1919   John Mitchell and James Leict from Aberdeen purchase Royal Brackla.

1926   John Bisset & Company Ltd takes over.

1943   Scottish Malt Distillers (SMD) buys John Bisset & Company Ltd and thereby acquires Royal Brackla.

1964   The distillery closes for a big refurbishment
-1966 and the number of stills is increased to four. The maltings closes.

1970   Two stills are increased to four.

1985   The distillery is mothballed.

1991   Production resumes.

1993   A 10 year old Royal Brackla is launched in United Distillers´ Flora & Fauna series.

1997   UDV spends more than £2 million on improvements and refurbishing.

1998   Bacardi–Martini buys Dewar´s from Diageo.

2004   A new 10 year old is launched.

2014   A 35 year old is released for Changi airport in Singapore.

2015   A new range is released; 12, 16 and 21 year old.

2019   A new range for travel retail, including 12, 18 and 20 year olds, is launched.

12 years old

Tasting notes Royal Brackla 12 years old:

GS – Warm spices, malt and peaches in cream on the nose. The palate is robust, with spice and mildly smoky soft fruit. Quite lengthy in the finish, with citrus fruit, mild spice and cocoa powder.

Royal Lochnagar

[royal loch•nah•gar]

Owner: Diageo

Region/district: Eastern Highlands

Founded: 1845

Status: Active (vc)

Capacity: 500 000 litres

Address: Crathie, Ballater, Aberdeenshire AB35 5TB

Website: malts.com

Tel: 01339 742700

For many years, the single malt from Lochnagar has been an integral part of what was once the best selling Scotch blend in South Korea – Windsor. But the brand, introduced in 1996, has been on a slippery slope for the past 7-8 years.

Sales have dropped by 75% in the last nine years. In 2005, Korea was the fourth biggest market for Scotch whisky. Fifteen years later it has fallen to place 24 with sales deteriorating by 77%. An economy downturn is one of the reasons as is a newly implemented antigraft law, similar to what happened in China some years ago. A third reason is a recent change in taxation of spirits where it is now based on alcoholic content rather than price. This on the other hand has prompted the owners, Diageo, to successfully launch a low-alcohol version of Windsor called W. Royal Lochnagar is set in beautiful surroundings with Royal Deeside and the imposing Lochnagar Mountain situated to the south and Balmoral, the Queen's summer residence, just a stone's throw to the north,

The distillery is equipped with a 5.4 ton open, traditional stainless steel mash tun. There are two wooden washbacks (a third that hadn't been used for years has now been removed), with short fermentations of 70 hours and long ones of 110 hours. The two stills are quite small with a charge in the wash still of 6,100 litres and 4,000 litres in the spirit still and the spirit vapours are condensed in cast iron worm tubs. The whole production is filled on site with 1,000 casks being stored in its only warehouse, while the rest is sent to Glenlossie. Four mashes per week during 2020 will result in 450,000 litres of pure alcohol.

The official core range of single malts consists of the **12 year old** and **Selected Reserve**. The latter is a vatting of casks, usually around 18-20 years of age. In 2015 one of the oldest bottlings from the distillery was launched, a **36 year old** single cask. Recent limited releases include the **12 year old** House Baratheon, part of Diageo's Gane of Thrones series in 2019 as well as a **distillery exclusive** matured in a combination of ex-bourbon and ex-sherry and bottled at 48%

History:

1823 James Robertson founds a distillery in Glen Feardan on the north bank of River Dee.

1826 The distillery is burnt down by competitors but Robertson decides to establish a new distillery near the mountain Lochnagar.

1841 This distillery is also burnt down.

1845 A new distillery is built by John Begg, this time on the south bank of River Dee. It is named New Lochnagar.

1848 Lochnagar obtains a Royal Warrant.

1882 John Begg passes away and his son Henry Farquharson Begg inherits the distillery.

1896 Henry Farquharson Begg dies.

1906 The children of Henry Begg rebuild the distillery.

1916 The distillery is sold to John Dewar & Sons.

1925 John Dewar & Sons becomes part of Distillers Company Limited (DCL).

1963 A major reconstruction takes place.

2004 A 30 year old cask strength from 1974 is launched in the Rare Malts series (6,000 bottles).

2008 A Distiller's Edition with a Moscatel finish is released.

2010 A Manager's Choice 1994 is released.

2013 A triple matured expression for Friends of the Classic Malts is released.

2016 A distillery exclusive without age statement is released.

2019 House Baratheon is released as part of the Game of Thrones series.

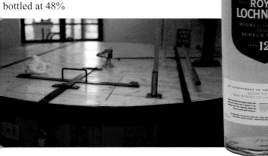

12 years old

Tasting notes Royal Lochnagar 12 years old:

GS – Light toffee on the nose, along with some green notes of freshly-sawn timber. The palate offers a pleasing and quite complex blend of caramel, dry sherry and spice, followed by a hint of liquorice before the slightly scented finish develops.

Scapa

[ska•pa]

Owner:
Chivas Brothers
(Pernod Ricard)

Region/district:
Highlands (Orkney)

Founded: **Status:** **Capacity:**
1885 Active 1 300 000 litres

Address: Scapa, St Ola, Kirkwall, Orkney KW15 1SE

Website: **Tel:**
scapawhisky.com 01856 876585

One of only two whisky distilleries in the Orkneys, Scapa down by the coast has always played the part of little brother to Highland Park located in Kirkwall a mere kilometre away.

Highland Park was founded in the 1700s, almost a century before Scapa and it has had the same owners for almost one hundred years. Scapa on the other hand, with new owners coming and going, has an excellent location overlooking Scapa Flow. This is a sheltered bay which was used by the Royal Navy as a naval base during both world wars. The links between the distillery and the navy, however, are not merely geographical. During the First World War, the distillery was used by Admiral Jellicoe as his base and he also saved the distillery from a fire during his tenure. In May 1916, Jellicoe led his fleet against the Germans in the Battle of Jutland near the coast of Denmark. It was the largest naval battle of the war and to commemorate the centenary, a special single cask Scapa was launched a couple of years ago.

The equipment consists of a 2.9 ton semi-lauter mash tun with a copper dome, twelve washbacks and two stills. Until recently, there were eight washbacks with four of them made from Corten steel. With the Corten replaced by stainless steel and another four added, there are now twelve made of stainless steel. At the same time, the boiler was also replaced. Due to increased production, fermentation time was down to 52 hours from the previous 160 but with the additional washbacks, it is now possible to increase fermentation time again. The wash still, sourced from Glenburgie distillery in 1959, is only one of two surviving Lomond stills in the industry but on the Scapa still, the adjustable plates were removed in 1979.

The core range consists of **Skiren** with no age statement (released in 2015) and matured in first fill bourbon as well as **Glansa**, matured in American oak and then finished in casks that previously held peated whisky. Currently there are also no less than nine different cask strength bottlings in the Distillery Reserve Collection, available at all Chivas' visitor centres from **10** to **19 years old** – three from sherry butts and the rest matured in first or second fill ex-bourbon barrels.

History:

1885 Macfarlane & Townsend founds the distillery with John Townsend at the helm.

1919 Scapa Distillery Company Ltd takes over.

1934 Scapa Distillery Company goes into voluntary liquidation and production ceases.

1936 Production resumes.

1936 Bloch Brothers Ltd (John and Sir Maurice) takes over.

1954 Hiram Walker & Sons takes over.

1959 A Lomond still is installed.

1978 The distillery is modernized.

1994 The distillery is mothballed.

1997 Production takes place a few months each year using staff from Highland Park.

2004 Extensive refurbishing takes place at a cost of £2.1 million. Scapa 14 years is launched.

2005 Production ceases in April and phase two of the refurbishment programme starts. Chivas Brothers becomes the new owner.

2006 Scapa 1992 (14 years) is launched.

2008 Scapa 16 years is launched.

2015 The distillery opens for visitors and Scapa Skiren is launched.

2016 The peated Glansa is released.

Tasting notes Scapa Skiren:

GS – Lime is apparent on the early nose, followed by musty peaches, almonds, cinnamon, and salt. More peaches on the palate, with tinned pear and honey. Tingling spices in the drying finish, which soon becomes slightly astringent.

Scapa Skiren

Speyburn

Owner:
Inver House Distillers
(Thai Beverages plc)

Region/district:
Speyside

Founded: 1897 **Status:** Active **Capacity:** 4 500 000 litres

Address: Rothes, Aberlour, Morayshire AB38 7AG

Website: speyburn.com **Tel:** 01340 831213

Being strangely unknown, except for in a few markets, Speyburn single malt sells around 300,000 bottles every year which is on par of brands that are more renowned such as Glendronach and Glengoyne.

However, there is one thing with this distillery in Rothes that makes the whisky enthusiast's heart skip a beat. It was the first whisky distillery in Scotland to make use of a completely new way of malting the barley. Malting is the stage where enzymes in the barley are activated – enzymes that give the distillers access to the soluble sugars that are then turned into alcohol. For centuries floor malting was the common process but in 1898, the first pneumatic malting in Scotland was installed at Speyburn. The drum maltings, as they were called, was an invention by the Frenchman Nicholas Galland and the German Julius Henning and it was a far more efficient method than turning the sprouting barley by hand three times a day for a week. The drums were used for the last time in 1968 but are still to be seen in the distillery.

An impressive expansion of the distillery was completed in 2015 and it is now equipped with a 6.25 ton stainless steel mash tun. There are four wooden washbacks and 15 made of stainless steel. Finally, there is one large wash still with a shell and tube condenser and two spirit stills that are connected to a worm tub. The distillery has recently changed to a five-day week with both short (72 hours) and long fermentations (120 plus hours) and are looking to produce 2,8 million litres of alcohol during 2020.

The core range consists of a **10 year old**, a **15 year old**, an 18 year old and **Bradan Orach** without age statement. Limited to USA is **Arranta Casks** as well as **Companion Cask**, a series of single casks matured in first fill ex Buffalo Trace bourbon casks. Three bottlings are available in travel retail; a **10 year old** (ex-bourbon and ex-sherry), the **Hopkins Reserve** that has been matured in casks that previously held a peated whisky and a **16 year old** aged in ex-bourbon barrels.

History:

1897 Brothers John and Edward Hopkins and their cousin Edward Broughton found the distillery through John Hopkins & Co. They already own Tobermory. The architect is Charles Doig. Building the distillery costs £17,000 and the distillery is transferred to Speyburn-Glenlivet Distillery Company.

1916 Distillers Company Limited (DCL) acquires John Hopkins & Co. and the distillery.

1930 Production stops.

1934 Productions restarts.

1962 Speyburn is transferred to Scottish Malt Distillers (SMD).

1968 Drum maltings closes.

1991 Inver House Distillers buys Speyburn.

1992 A 10 year old is launched as a replacement for the 12 year old in the Flora & Fauna series.

2001 Pacific Spirits (Great Oriole Group) buys Inver House for $85 million.

2005 A 25 year old Solera is released.

2006 Inver House changes owner when International Beverage Holdings acquires Pacific Spirits UK.

2009 The un-aged Bradan Orach is introduced for the American market.

2012 Clan Speyburn is formed.

2014 The distillery is expanded.

2015 Arranta Casks is released.

2017 A 15 year old and Companion Casks are launched.

2018 Two expressions for duty free are released - a 10 year old and Hopkins Reserve. A core 18 year old is launched.

10 years old

Tasting notes Speyburn 10 years old:

GS – Soft and elegant on the spicy, nutty nose. Smooth in the mouth, with vanilla, spice and more nuts. The finish is medium, spicy and drying.

Speyside

[spey•side]

Owner:
Speyside Distillers Co.

Region/district:
Speyside

Founded: **Status:**
1990 Active

Capacity:
600 000 litres

Address: Glen Tromie, Kingussie, Inverness-shire
PH21 1NS

Website:
speysidedistillery.co.uk

Tel:
01540 661060

This lovely, small distillery set in beautiful and quite remote surroundings just a few kilometres east of Kingussie does unfortunately not cater to visitors except for rare occasions.

The owners, however, opened up a visitor experience a few years ago in nearby Aviemore. Named The Snug after a local pub, the centre is selling the distillery´s range and also arranges tastings. The distillery lived a modest existance during the first 20 years but with new owners since 2012 sales and the number of different expressions have increased considerably and the single malt is especially popular in Taiwan. A distribution deal with a Chinese distributor, Luzhou Laojiao, from last year will safeguard an increased presence in the growing Chinese market.

Speyside distillery is equipped with a 4.2 ton semi-lauter mash tun, four stainless steel washbacks with a 70-120 hour fermentation time and one pair of stills. For the last couple of years they have been working a six-day week with a total production of 600,000 litres of alcohol. There are no warehouses on site. Instead, the spirit is tankered away to the company's warehouses in Glasgow. Since 2017, gin has also been produced and recently a dedicated gin still was installed.

The core range of Spey single malt is made up of **Tenné** (with a 6 months port finish), **Trutina** which is a 100% bourbon maturation, **Fumare**, similar to Trutina but distilled from peated barley, **Chairman's Choice** and **Royal Choice**. The latter two are multi-vintage marriages from both American and European oak. Also part of the core range is **Beinn Dubh** which replaced the black whisky Cu Dubh. The sherry-matured 18 year old has now been discontinued. Recent limited releases include the second batch of **cask strength versions** of Tenné, Trutina and Fumare (with a third batch planned for autumn 2020 or maybe early 2021), a **10 year old bourbon/port marriage**, a **12 year old peated** and, in summer 2020, a **12 year old port cask**.

History:

1956 George Christie buys a piece of land at Drumguish near Kingussie.

1957 George Christie starts a grain distillery near Alloa.

1962 George Christie (founder of Speyside Distillery Group in the fifties) commissions the drystone dyker Alex Fairlie to build a distillery in Drumguish.

1986 Scowis assumes ownership.

1987 The distillery is completed.

1990 The distillery is on stream in December.

1993 The first single malt, Drumguish, is launched.

1999 Speyside 8 years is launched.

2000 Speyside Distilleries is sold to a group of private investors including Ricky Christie, Ian Jerman and Sir James Ackroyd.

2001 Speyside 10 years is launched.

2012 Speyside Distillers is sold to Harvey´s of Edinburgh.

2014 A new range, Spey from Speyside Distillery, is launched (NAS, 12 and 18 year old).

2015 The range is revamped again. New expressions include Tenné, 12 years old and 18 years old.

2016 "Byron´s Choice - The Marriage" and Spey Cask 27 are released.

2017 Trutina and Fumare are released.

2019 Cask strength versions of Tenné, Trutina and Fumare are released.

2020 A 10 year old bourbon/port, a peated 12 year old and a 12 year old port cask are released.

Trutina

Tasting notes Spey Trutina:

IR – A floral nose, with lemon, granola, shortbread and dried grass. A sweet start on the palate, honey, white chocolate, sweet red apples and then ends with a dry, oaky note.

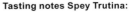

Whisky Legends

Dennis Malcolm
59 years in the Whisky business

If a person says "I was born at a distillery" it is likely he or she means they've had a relationship with whisky from early on in the same way as they could have said "I've got whisky in my blood." But when it comes to Dennis Malcolm, you should take it literally. He was actually born on the Glen Grant distillery site in 1946.

His father was working at the distillery at the time, employed by Douglas MacKessack, great grandson of James Grant, one of the founders. Dennis himself started as an apprentice cooper at Glen Grant when he was 15 years old. Having serviced his apprenticeship he spent the next six years working in all areas including malting, mashing, fermentation and distillation. He was promoted to the position of brewer, which today could be called production process manager, and also took on the responsibility for Glen Grant's sister distillery across the street – Caperdonich.

In the 1960s and early 1970s, Glen Grant single malt had become hugely popular in Italy and it was one of the best selling Scotch whiskies in the world. Dennis was very much a part of this expansive period.

"My first memorable achievement was to double the production capacity of Glen Grant from 1973-1976 to enable the distillery to produce in excess of six million litres of alcohol per year and not stop the production whilst doing so."

Things changed, both for Glen Grant and Dennis, when the distillery together with Glenlivet was taken over by Seagrams in 1978. The new owners' main interest lay in the mega blend Chivas Regal and the focus shifted from producing Glen Grant to be bottled as single malt to become part of blended whisky. For Dennis the career went on with the role of distillery manager at Glenlivet and then heading back to managing Glen Grant. With more than thirty years of experience under his belt, he was asked to take over the responsibility for all nine distilleries in the Chivas group in 1992.

Eight years later, he was contemplating early retirement when he received a phone call from Inver House asking if he would be interested in re-opening and managing the closed Balmenach distillery which they had just bought. Dennis took the job and stayed for six years. When I visited Balmenach just after Dennis had left, the distillery workers were still talking about how he had enthusiastically swept in through the doors in 2000, inspiring everyone to do their best to bring the distillery back on its feet. One person especially mentioned his obsession with cleanliness, a characteristic that Dennis himself is well aware of. In his own words "...there is no excuse for a distillery not to be clean." and that "cleanliness is next to godliness."

With mission accomplished at Balmenach in 2006, Dennis was again thinking of ending his whisky career when he all of a sudden found himself back at Glen Grant as distillery manager. The distillery had been bought by Campari and the Italians had great plans. This suited Dennis who knew the potential of the brand, a potential that hadn't come to full glory during almost three decades under the previous owners. Backed by the new owners, Dennis began the work of transforming Glen Grant back to its former glory, a work he is immensely proud of.

"One of my greatest achievements was when Campari bought the distillery in 2006 which allowed me to expand and premiumize our range of expressions for all to enjoy. Campari's commitment to the brand has seen huge investments such as purchase and refurbishment of 11 maturation warehouses and construction of a state of the art bottling plant which allows us to produce/mature and bottle on site giving us complete control of quality."

When it comes to the increased usage of computers in the whisky production, Dennis is not a traditionalist.

"Some 40 years ago there were five people operating the production process per 8 hour shift. Now we have one operator who controls all areas of the production process per 8 hour shift. This is only possible due to the computerization of the control process which is in my view an excellent way to achieve consistent quality and protect the process parameters. However automation alone is not the answer – it requires the passion and commitment of knowledgeable operators."

I want to know if he sees any change in the consumers' attitudes towards whisky compared to when he got involved.

"I think when I started almost 60 years ago most people were of the mind that single malts were for more mature people and were to be enjoyed as a late after dinner drink. It was almost unheard of to put anything other than water or a small cube of ice in your drink. I do not think this is the case today where people of all ages have turned to single malts and are more inquisitive as to why your single malt is different from others."

My first of many meetings with Dennis was in 2016 when I visited Glen Grant. I had just begun my work with the Malt Whisky Yearbook and few people knew who I was. I was welcomed by Dennis in the office and was prepared for a quick tour through the distillery. After all he was a busy man and I was a rookie. But Dennis didn't head for the still house. Instead we jumped into a golf cart and drove through the Major's garden to that famous safe imbedded in the cliff. A bottle of Glen Grant was opened and we cut our whisky with water from the burn. Standing on a small bridge enjoying our drams, Dennis told me stories about the Grant family, about Rothes and Scotland in general. Eventually we made it into the distillery and a planned one hour visit became an incredible encounter lasting for three hours. This sums up Dennis pretty accurately as a person who is always willing to share his passion with and devote his time to another person who simply wants to learn more.

" I think it is very important to be proud of where you come from, what you make and how you make it. The people with the pride and passion that make it – that is brand heritage to me."

Dennis current role at Glen Grant is master distiller and he is also on the company's board. A few years ago he became the 20th inductee in the Whisky Magazine Hall of Fame and in 2016 he was awarded an OBE on the Queen´s birthday and even though he appreciated the recognition of all the work he has put into developing and promoting Scotch whisky for six decades, he somehow couldn't see the reason for all the fuss. As he himself puts it:

"It's not been a job but a way of life"

Springbank

[spring•bank]

Owner:
Springbank Distillers
(J & A Mitchell)

Region/district:
Campbeltown

Founded: 1828
Status: Active (vc)
Capacity: 750 000 litres

Address: Well Close, Campbeltown, Argyll PA28 6ET

Website: springbankwhisky.com
Tel: 01586 551710

In one of Charles Maclean's books, Springbank is described as "Arguably the most archaic of Scotland's malt whisky distilleries." In some industries, a company with that label would struggle to survive but not in the whisky business.

On the contrary – Springbank's way of sticking to traditional production methods, distilling sustainable volumes and avoiding costly marketing campaigns has rendered them a place in many malt whisky enthusiasts personal hall of fame. Add to that the fact that the distillery has been family-owned since the start and you have a cult whisky. The downside, if there is one, is that with a strategy like that the brand will never get into the Top 50 single malts in terms of sales, but that has never been the goal. Survival no matter what and, more important, making a lasting difference in the community of Campbeltown has always been paramount.

The distillery is equipped with a 3.5 ton open cast iron mash tun, six washbacks made of Scandinavian larch with a fermentation time of up to 110 hours, one wash still and two spirit stills. The wash still is unique in Scotland, as it is fired by both an open oil-fire and internal steam coils. Ordinary condensers are used to cool the spirit vapours, except in the first of the two spirit stills, where a worm tub is used. Springbank is also the only distillery in Scotland that malts its entire need of barley using own floor maltings. Currently there are ten warehouses on site (dunnage and racked) shared between Spingbank and its sister distillery Glengyle. The latest, with the capacity for 7,000 hogsheads, was built in 2020 as was a new tasting bar for visitors to enjoy their whisky.

Springbank produces three distinctive single malts with different phenol contents in the malted barley. Springbank is distilled two and a half times (12-15ppm), Longrow is distilled twice (50-55 ppm) and the unpeated Hazelburn is distilled three times. When Springbank is produced, the malted barley is dried using 6 hours of peat smoke and 30 hours of hot air, while Longrow requires 48 hours of peat smoke. In the last couple of years, the production volumes have increased and 280,000 litres were planned for 2020. However due to the corona virus the owners are now aiming for 120,000 litres of which 10% is Longrow and 10% Hazelburn.

The core range is **Springbank 10, 15** and **18 year old**, as well as **12 year old cask strength** (latest batch in February 2020). There are also limited but yearly releases of a **21 year old** and a **25 year old.** Other recent limited releases include **Springbank Local Barley 10 years old,** a **15 year old Springbank rum wood** and a **17 year old madeira finish** scheduled for autumn 2020. Longrow is represented by **Longrow without age statement** and the **18 year old**. A limited yet annual release is **Longrow Red** with a **13 year old Cabernet Sauvignon finish** released in February 2020 being the latest. A limited, unusually old Longrow (**21 years**) was released in November 2019. For Hazelburn, the core expression is a **10 year old** complemented by limited annual releases. In April 2019 it was a **Hazelburn 14 year old** matured in oloroso casks.

History:

1828 The Reid family, in-laws of the Mitchells (see below), founds the distillery.

1837 The Reid family encounters financial difficulties and John and William Mitchell buy the distillery.

1897 J. & A. Mitchell Co Ltd is founded.

1926 The depression forces the distillery to close.

1933 The distillery is back in production.

1960 Own maltings ceases.

1979 The distillery closes.

1985 A 10 year old Longrow is launched.

1987 Limited production restarts.

1989 Production restarts.

1992 Springbank takes up its maltings again.

1997 First distillation of Hazelburn.

1998 Springbank 12 years is launched.

1999 Dha Mhile (7 years), the world's first organic single malt, is launched.

2000 A 10 year old is launched.

2001 Springbank 1965 'Local barley' (36 years), 741 bottles, is launched.

2002 Number one in the series Wood Expressions is a 12 year old with five years in rum casks.

2004 Springbank 10 years 100 proof is launched as well as Longrow 14 years old, Springbank 32 years old and Springbank 14 years Port Wood.

2005 Springbank 21 years, the first version of Hazelburn (8 years) and Longrow Tokaji Wood Expression are launched.

2006 Longrow 10 years 100 proof, Springbank 25 years, Springbank 9 years Marsala finish, Springbank 11 years Madeira finish and a new Hazelburn 8 year old are released.

2007 Springbank Vintage 1997 and a 16 year old rum wood are released.

History continued:

2008 The distillery closes temporarily. Three new releases of Longrow - CV, 18 year old and 7 year old Gaja Barolo.

2009 Springbank Madeira 11 year old, Springbank 18 year old, Springbank Vintage 2001 and Hazelburn 12 year old are released.

2010 Springbank 12 year old cask strength and a 12 year old claret expression together with new editions of the CV and 18 year old are released.

2011 Longrow 18 year old and Hazelburn 8 year old Sauternes wood expression are released.

2012 Springbank Rundlets & Kilderkins, Springbank 21 year old and Longrow Red are released.

2013 Longrow Rundlets & Kilderkins, a new edition of Longrow Red and Springbank 9 year old Gaja Barolo finish are released.

2014 Hazelburn Rundlets & Kilderkins, Hazelburn 10 year old and Springbank 25 years old are launched.

2015 New releases include Springbank Green 12 years old and a new edition of the Longrow Red.

2016 Springbank Local Barley and a 9 year old Hazelburn barolo finish are released.

2017 Springbank 14 year old bourbon cask and Hazelburn 13 year old sherrywood are released.

2018 Local Barley 10 year old, 14 year old Longrow Sherry Wood and a new Longrow Red are released.

2019 Springbank 25, Hazelburn 14 and a 21 year old Longrow are released.

2020 Springbank Local Barley 10 years old, a 17 year old madeira finish and Longrow Red Cabernet Sauvignon are released.

Longrow 18 years

Springbank 18 years

Hazelburn 10 years

Springbank 10 years

Springbank 25

Longrow Red

Springbank 12 years c.s.   Longrow NAS

Tasting notes Springbank 10 years old:

GS – Fresh and briny on the nose, with citrus fruit, oak and barley, plus a note of damp earth. Sweet on the palate, with developing brine, nuttiness and vanilla toffee. Coconut oil and drying peat in the finish.

Tasting notes Longrow NAS:

GS – Initially slightly gummy on the nose, but then brine and fat peat notes develop. Vanilla and malt also emerge. The smoky palate offers lively brine and is quite dry and spicy, with some vanilla and lots of ginger. The finish is peaty with persistent, oaky ginger.

Tasting notes Hazelburn 10 years old:

GS – Pear drops, soft toffee and malt on the mildly floral nose. Oiliness develops in time, along with a green, herbal note and ultimately brine. Full-bodied and supple on the smoky palate, with barley and ripe, peppery orchard fruits. Developing cocoa and ginger in the lengthy finish.

Strathisla

[strath•eye•la]

Owner:
Chivas Bros (Pernod Ricard)

Region/district:
Speyside

Founded: 1786

Status: Active (vc)

Capacity: 2 450 000 litres

Address: Seafield Avenue, Keith, Banffshire AB55 5BS

Website: chivas.com

Tel: 01542 783044

Not only is Strathisla considered to be the oldest working distillery in the Speyside area. The sheer look of it gives you the impression that this is a distillery that sticks to traditional methods.

The distillery is equipped with wooden washbacks and, more importantly, the mash tun is of the traditional style equipped with rakes and ploughs rather than the knives that cut through the mash in the more modern lauter tuns that were first introduced in Scotland in 1974 at Tomatin. In fact, there are only 16 of the currently 126 operating Scotch malt whisky distilleries that have a traditional mash tun.

Strathisla is the key malt in the blended Scotch Chivas Regal, which is currently the third biggest blend in the world having surpassed Grant's during 2019 with 53 million bottles being sold. A while ago, the owners launched a blending kit containing 6 miniature bottles. One with the Chivas Regal 12 year old, one with a blended grain whisky and four others with single malts with different characteristics (fruity, citrus, creamy and smoky). The idea was for the consumer to try their hand at creating a blended Scotch similar to Chivas Regal.

Strathisla is equipped with a 5.12 ton traditional mash tun with a raised copper canopy, seven washbacks made of Oregon pine and three of larch – all with a 54 hour fermentation cycle. There are two pairs of stills in a cramped, but very charming stillroom. The wash stills are of lantern type with descending lyne arms and the spirit stills have boiling balls with the lyne arms slightly ascending. Most of the spirit produced at Strathisla is piped to nearby Glen Keith distillery for filling or to be tankered away.

The only core expression is the **12 year old** but currently there are also no less than six cask strength bottlings in the Distillery Reserve Collection, available at all Chivas´ visitor centres. Three of them, **13, 16 and 23 year old** were matured in sherry butts while the other three, **12, 27 and 28 year old**, came from either bourbon hogsheads of barrels.

History:

1786 Alexander Milne and George Taylor found the distillery under the name Milltown, but soon change it to Milton.

1823 MacDonald Ingram & Co. purchases the distillery.

1830 William Longmore acquires the distillery.

1870 The distillery name changes to Strathisla.

1880 William Longmore retires and hands operations to his son-in-law John Geddes-Brown. William Longmore & Co. is formed.

1890 The distillery changes name to Milton.

1942 Jay Pomeroy acquires a majority of the shares in William Longmore & Co. Pomeroy is jailed as a result of dubious business transactions and the distillery goes bankrupt in 1949.

1950 Chivas Brothers buys the run-down distillery at a compulsory auction for £71,000 and starts restoration.

1951 The name reverts to Strathisla.

1965 The number of stills is increased from two to four.

1970 A heavily peated whisky, Craigduff, is produced but production stops later.

2001 The Chivas Group is acquired by Pernod Ricard.

2019 Chivas Distillery Collection Strathisla 12 year old is released.

Tasting notes Strathisla 12 years old:

GS – Rich on the nose, with sherry, stewed fruits, spices and lots of malt. Full-bodied and almost syrupy on the palate. Toffee, honey, nuts, a whiff of peat and a suggestion of oak. The finish is medium in length, slightly smoky and with a final flash of ginger.

12 years old

Strathmill

[strath•mill]

Owner:
Diageo

Region/district:
Speyside

Founded: **Status:**   **Capacity:**
1891   Active   2 600 000 litres

Address: Keith, Banffshire AB55 5DQ

Website: **Tel:**
malts.com   01542 883000

Morayshire in northwest Scotland is definitely the epicentre of Scotch and a must-visit destination for any whisky tourist. The towns of Dufftown and Rothes have ten distilleries together but in the eastern parts there is also the sometimes forgotten Keith.

This is where you will find Strathmill, Strathisla and Glen Keith distilleries and also one of the terminal stops of the heritage Keith and Dufftown Railway, also known as the Whisky Line. A lesser known fact is that Keith is one of the towns in Scotland where you will have a good chance of hearing doric being spoken. This is an ancient Scottish dialect which used to be common in Aberdeenshire and Morayshire and if you are generally having difficulties understanding Scots, doric will definitely be a challenge.

Whereas Strathisla is one of the main attractions along the Whisky Trail, Strathmill is hidden away on a side road right by the river Isla and with no visitor facilities. For many years, Strathmill single malt has been a key ingredient in the J&B Scotch blend. Until 2007, this was the second best selling blend in the world but since then sales have dropped by almost 50% and it now resides in place number five with around 37 million bottles sold in 2019.

The equipment at Strathmill consists of a 9.1 ton stainless steel semi-lauter mash tun and six stainless steel washbacks. Currently, the distillery is working a five-day week which means both short (65 hours) and long (120 hours) fermentations, producing around two million litres of pure alcohol in the year. There are two pairs of stills and Strathmill is one of few distilleries still using purifiers on the spirit stills. This device is mounted between the lyne arm and the condenser and acts as a mini-condenser, allowing the lighter alcohols to travel towards the condenser and forcing the heavier alcohols to go back into the still for another distillation. The result is a lighter spirit. In Strathmill's case both purifiers and condensers are fitted on the outside of the still house to optimize energy savings.

The only official bottling is the **12 year old Flora & Fauna**, but a limited **25 year old** was launched in 2014 as part of the Special Releases.

History:

1891 The distillery is founded in an old mill from 1823 and is named Glenisla-Glenlivet Distillery.

1892 The inauguration takes place in June.

1895 The gin company W. & A. Gilbey buys the distillery for £9,500 and names it Strathmill.

1962 W. & A. Gilbey merges with United Wine Traders (including Justerini & Brooks) and forms International Distillers & Vintners (IDV).

1968 The number of stills is increased from two to four and purifiers are added.

1972 IDV is bought by Watney Mann which later the same year is acquired by Grand Metropolitan.

1993 Strathmill becomes available as a single malt for the first time since 1909 as a result of a bottling (1980) from Oddbins.

1997 Guinness and Grand Metropolitan merge and form Diageo.

2001 The first official bottling is a 12 year old in the Flora & Fauna series.

2010 A Manager's Choice single cask from 1996 is released.

2014 A 25 year old is released.

Tasting notes Strathmill 12 years old:

GS – Quite reticent on the nose, with nuts, grass and a hint of ginger. Spicy vanilla and nuts dominate the palate. The finish is drying, with peppery oak.

12 years old

Talisker

[tal•iss•kur]

Owner: Diageo	**Region/district:** Highlands (Skye)

Founded: 1830	**Status:** Active (vc)	**Capacity:** 3 300 000 litres

Address: Carbost, Isle of Skye, Inverness-shire IV47 8SR

Website: malts.com	**Tel:** 01478 614308 (vc)

Fifteen years ago, Diageo decided to give their distillery on Skye a lot more attention. The goal was to push the brand into the Top 10 single malts in the world. That was achieved in 2014 and the sales growth in the last decade stands at almost 140%.

It is Diego's third best selling single malt and definitely the one that has the most expressions in the core range (8) with an additional two in the travel retail range and a number of yearly limited bottlings. The distillery is also the seventh most visited distillery in Scotland with more than 60,000 people travelling here in 2019. The visitor centre is excellent and the fact that Talisker is on Skye, a major tourist destination, doesn't make things worse.

The distillery is equipped with a stainless steel lauter mash tun with a capacity of 8 tonnes and eight washbacks made of Oregon pine. Before mashing, the malted barley is mixed to a ratio of 25% unpeated and 75% peated which has a phenol specification of 20-25ppm. There are five stills – two wash stills and three spirit stills. Two of the spirit stills were replaced in February 2019. The wash stills are equipped with a special type of "purifiers" or, more specifically, return pipes, which use the colder outside air, and there is also a u-bend in the lyne arms. The return pipes and the peculiar bend of the lyne arms allow for more copper contact and increases the reflux during distillation. All of the stills are connected to wormtubs and Talisker has an unusual system where seawater can be used to cool down the hot water in the tubs. The fermentation time is quite long (60-65 hours) and the middle cut from the spirit still is collected between 76% and 65% which, together with the phenol specification, gives a medium peated spirit. The number 1 wash still and number 3 spirit still were replaced in February 2020 due to age as were the wooden worm tubs on spirit stills 2 and 3. The production plan for 2020 is 20 mashes per week which accounts for 3.3 million litres of alcohol.

Talisker's core range consists of **Skye** and **Storm**, both without age statement, **10, 18, 25** and **30 year old, Distiller's Edition** with an Amoroso sherry finish and **Port Ruighe**, finished in ruby port casks. Talisker 57° North which was introduced in 2008 and released yearly in small batches has now been discontinued. There is also **Dark Storm**, the peatiest Talisker so far, which is exclusive to duty free together with **Neist Point**. A new range of limited bottlings was introduced in summer 2018 – the Bodega Series which will explore the impact of different sherry cask finishes. The second installment, released in July 2019, was a **41 year old** finished in Manzanilla casks that were over 100 years old. This was also the oldest expression ever released from the distillery. **Talisker Select Reserve House Greyjoy** was released in spring 2019 as part of the Game of Thrones series and in July 2020, a 31 year old, matured in refill American oak was part of the new Prima & Ultima range. Finally, in autumn 2020, an unusual **8 year old** that had been finished in Caribbean rum casks and bottled at 57,9%. was part of the yearly Rare by Nature series.

History:

1830 Hugh and Kenneth MacAskill found the distillery

1848 The brothers transfer the lease to North of Scotland Bank and Jack Westland from the ban runs the operations.

1854 Kenneth MacAskill dies.

1857 North of Scotland Bank sells the distillery to Donald MacLennan for £500.

1863 MacLennan experiences difficulties in making operations viable and puts the distillery up for sale.

1865 MacLennan, still working at the distillery, nominates John Anderson as agent in Glasgow.

1867 Anderson & Co. from Glasgow takes over.

1879 John Anderson is imprisoned after having sold non-existing casks of whisky.

1880 New owners are now Alexander Grigor Allan and Roderick Kemp.

1892 Kemp sells his share and buys Macallan Distillery instead.

1894 The Talisker Distillery Ltd is founded.

1895 Allan dies and Thomas Mackenzie, who has been his partner, takes over.

1898 Talisker Distillery merges with Dailuaine-Glenlivet Distillers and Imperial Distillers to form Dailuaine-Talisker Distillers Company.

1916 Thomas Mackenzie dies and the distillery is taken over by a consortium consisting of, among others, John Walker, John Dewar, W. P. Lowrie and Distillers Company Limited (DCL).

1928 The distillery abandons triple distillation.

1960 On 22nd November the distillery catches fire and substantial damage occurs.

1962 The distillery reopens after the fire.

1972 Own malting ceases.

History continued:

1988 Classic Malts are introduced, Talisker 10 years included. A visitor centre is opened.

1998 A new stainless steel/copper mash tun and five new worm tubs are installed. Talisker is launched as a Distillers Edition with an amoroso sherry finish.

2004 Two new bottlings appear, an 18 year old and a 25 year old.

2005 To celebrate the 175th birthday of the distillery, Talisker 175th Anniversary is released.

2006 A 30 year old and the fourth edition of the 25 year old are released.

2007 The second edition of the 30 year old and the fifth edition of the 25 year old are released.

2008 Talisker 57° North, sixth edition of the 25 year old and third edition of the 30 year old are launched.

2009 New editions of the 25 and 30 year old are released.

2010 A 1994 Manager´s Choice single cask and a new edition of the 30 year old are released.

2011 Three limited releases - 25, 30 and 34 year old.

2012 A limited 35 year old is released.

2013 Four new expressions are released – Storm, Dark Storm, Port Ruighe and a 27 year old.

2014 A bottling for the Friends of the Classic Malts is released.

2015 Skye and Neist Point are released.

2016 A distillery exclusive without age statement is released.

2018 A 40 year old, the first in the new Bodega Series, and an 8 year old Special Release are launched.

2019 A 41 year old Bodega Series and House Greyjoy in the Game of Thrones series are released.

2020 A 31 year old Prima & Ultima and an 8 year old rum finish Rare by Nature are released.

Tasting notes Talisker 10 years old:

GS – Quite dense and smoky on the nose, with smoked fish, bladderwrack, sweet fruit and peat. Full-bodied and peaty in the mouthy; complex, with ginger, ozone, dark chocolate, black pepper and a kick of chilli in the long, smoky tail.

Tasting notes Talisker Storm:

GS – The nose offers brine, burning wood embers, vanilla, and honey. The palate is sweet and spicy, with cranberries and blackcurrants, while peat-smoke and black pepper are ever-present. The finish is spicy, with walnuts, and fruity peat.

Port Ruighe — Storm — Skye

Prima & Ultima 1988 — Dark Storm

10 years old

Rare by Nature 8 year old rum finish — Distiller´s Edition

Tamdhu

[tam•doo]

Owner:
Ian Macleod Distillers

Region/district:
Speyside

Founded: **Status:** **Capacity:**
1897   Active   4 000 000 litres

Address: Knockando, Aberlour, Morayshire AB38 7RP

Website:
tamdhu.com

Tel:
01340 872200

Tamdhu has now been in the capable hands of Ian Macleod Distillers for nine years. Once a work horse for blends in the Edrington stable of distilleries, it has been completely renewed and rebranded in recent years.

The new owners carried on with Edrington's dedication to sherry casks for the maturation. That approach came as no surprise as this is exactly what made Glengoyne, the other distillery owned by Ian Macleod, successful. First and second fill oloroso casks made from both European and American Oak is the key to Tamdhu's flavour profile.

The distillery is equipped with an 11.8 ton semilauter mash tun, nine Oregon pine washbacks with a fermentation time of 59 hours and three pairs of stills. There are a total of 24 warehouses (a mix of dunnage, racked and palletized) with the latest four being built in 2019. An on-site cooperage for repairing and testing casks became operational in March 2019. The production plan for 2020 is 16 mashes per week which translates to 3.1 million litres for the entire year.

The core range consists of a **10 year old** exclusive to the UK market, a **12 year old** released globally in August 2018 and the non-chill filtered **Batch Strength** (with the fifth edition launched in September 2020). A limited, but still in the core range, **15 year old** bottling appeared in late 2018. Limited releases include a rare **50 year old**, matured in a first fill European oak sherry butt released in 2017 to celebrate the 120th anniversary of the distillery. Recently, we have seen the release of part three of **Dalbeallie Dram** (the distillery exclusive). The Distillery Manager's Edition, a single cask selected ty Sandy McIntyre who was appointed Manager of the Year 2019 in Whisky Magazine's Icons of Whisky is sold out but was replaced in May 2020 by the 16 year old **Iain Whitecross Single Cask**. Iain is the assistant distillery manager. Since 2019 there are also two travel retail exclusives; **Ámbar 14 year old** and the **Gran Reserva First Edition**.

History:

1896 The distillery is founded by Tamdhu Distillery Company, a consortium of whisky blenders with William Grant as the main promoter. Charles Doig is the architect.

1897 The first casks are filled in July.

1898 Highland Distillers Company, which has several of the 1896 consortium members in managerial positions, buys Tamdhu Distillery Company.

1911 The distillery closes.

1913 The distillery reopens.

1928 The distillery is mothballed.

1948 The distillery is in full production again in July.

1950 The floor maltings is replaced by Saladin boxes when the distillery is rebuilt.

1972 The number of stills is increased from two to four.

1975 Two stills augment the previous four.

1976 Tamdhu 8 years is launched as single malt.

2005 An 18 year old and a 25 year old are released.

2009 The distillery is mothballed.

2011 The Edrington Group sells the distillery to Ian Macleod Distillers.

2012 Production is resumed.

2013 The first official release from the new owners – a 10 year old.

2015 Tamdhu Batch Strength is released.

2017 A 50 year old is released.

2018 A 12 year old, a 15 year old and the Dalbeallie Dram are released.

2019 Two expressions for duty-free - Ámbar and Gran Reserva First Edition.

2020 Iain Whitecross Single Cask is released.

Tasting notes Tamdhu 12 years old:

IR – Distinct sherry notes on the nose with raisins and prunes as well as menthol and green leaves. The taste is wellbalanced with dried fruit, crème brûlée, roasted nuts, bananas and cinnamon.

12 years old

Tamnavulin

[tam•na•<u>voo</u>•lin]

Owner: **Region/district:**
Whyte & Mackay (Emperador)   Speyside

Founded: **Status:**   **Capacity:**
1966   Active   4 000 000 litres

Address: Tomnavoulin, Ballindalloch,
Banffshire AB3 9JA

Website: **Tel:**
www.tamnavulinwhisky.com   01807 590285

Whyte & Mackay owns four malt distilleries but until a few years back, only two of them were promoted as single malt brands – the classic Dalmore and the rising star Jura.

The Fettercairn brand was revamped a decade ago and for the last couple of years, Tamnavulin has had its fair share of attention. This coincides with a shift in ownership in 2014 when Emperador took over, but also a more recent change of strategy where the single malts will take more place within Whyte & Mackay at the expense of blended Scotch and other spirits.

The character of Tamnavulin new make is slightly grassy with a 25 minute foreshot and a middle cut running from 75% down to 60%. In the last couple of years much of the stock in the warehouses has been re-racked into better wood which has improved the quality vastly. A similar programme with the same positive result was implemented at Jura 15-20 years ago.

Tamnavulin distillery is equipped with a full lauter mash tun with an 11 ton charge, nine washbacks made of stainless steel with a fermentation time of 54-60 hours and three pairs of stills. The wash stills, with horizontal lyne arms, are all equipped with sub-coolers while the spirit stills with their descending lyne arms have purifiers. On the environmental side, the distillery is since September 2018 running on LPG (liquefied petroleum gas) rather than heavy fuel oil and a new bioplant has been installed to take care of the residues from the distillation. During 2020, the owners will be mashing 16-19 times per week which means a total of 3 million litres of alcohol. From 2010 to 2013, a small part of the yearly production was heavily peated with a phenol specification of 55ppm. There are two racked warehouses on site, holding 40,000 casks.

The core expression is **Double Cask** with a sherry finish. In 2019 a **Sherry Cask Edition** with a finish in three types of oloroso casks was launched together with a **Tempranillo finish** for duty free. Recent limited bottlings include **four vintages** (from 1970 to 2000) and, released in 2020, three wine cask finishes for select markets - **Cabernet Sauvignon, Grenache** and **Pinot Noir**.

History:

1966 Tamnavulin-Glenlivet Distillery Company, a subsidiary of Invergordon Distillers Ltd, founds Tamnavulin.

1993 Whyte & Mackay buys Invergordon Distillers.

1995 The distillery closes in May.

1996 Whyte & Mackay changes name to JBB (Greater Europe).

2000 Distillation takes place for six weeks.

2001 Company management buy out operations for £208 million and rename the company Kyndal.

2003 Kyndal changes name to Whyte & Mackay.

2007 United Spirits buys Whyte & Mackay. Tamnavulin is opened again in July after having been mothballed for 12 years.

2014 Whyte & Mackay is sold to Emperador Inc.

2016 Tamnavulin Double Cask is released.

2019 Sherry Cask Edition and Tempranillo Finish are released.

2020 Three wine cask finishes are released; cabernet sauvignon, grenache and pinot noir.

Double Cask

Tasting notes Tamnavulin Double Cask:

GS – The nose offers malt, soft toffee, almonds and tangerines. Finally, background earthiness. Smooth on the palate, with ginger nut biscuits, vanilla and orchard fruits, plus walnuts. The finish is medium in length, with lingering fruity spice.

Teaninich

[tee•ni•nick]

Owner:
Diageo

Region/district:
Northern Highlands

Founded: **Status:**
1817   Active

Capacity:
10 200 000 litres

Address: Alness, Ross-shire IV17 0XB

Website:
malts.com

Tel:
01349 885001

If you would make a wish for a versatile distillery that can be used for experimental distillations with different types of grains, then Teaninich would be the perfect choice.

The distillery is equipped with a hammer mill and a mash filter instead of a traditional mill and a mash tun. This facilitates handling for example grains such as rye. Make no mistake though, Teaninich is first and foremost producing malt whisky from barley. But in recent years the distillery has been used by the owners for a variety of innovative production processes to be used in current and future expressions. One such was Johnnie Walker Blender's Batch Espresso Roast, released a few years ago where chocolate malt was used to create a richer flavour

The mashing technique is what sets Teaninich apart from all other Scotch distilleries, except for Inchdairnie. The malted barley is ground into a fine flour without husks in an Asnong hammer mill. This is the basis for a higher spirit yield but also entails that one can use grain varieties that wouldn't mill as well in a traditional Porteus mill with rollers. The grist is mixed with water in a conversion vessel. Once the conversion from starch to sugar is done, the mash passes through a Meura 2001 mash filter which consists of a number of mesh bags. The filter compresses the bags and the wort is collected for the next step – fermentation. The downside of using a mash filter is that it's more expensive, it requires more cleaning and is less flexible when it comes to the size of mash.

Apart from the mash filter, the equipment consists of 18 wooden washbacks and two made of stainless steel – all with a fermentation time of 75 hours and six pairs of stills. A lot of attention has recently been put into sustainability and energy performance. Since July last year, the water efficiency (the amount of water consumed divided by alcohol produced) has been improved by 33%. Teaninich is the third largest malt distillery in the Diageo group.

The only official core bottling is a **10 year old** in the Flora & Fauna series but a limited **17 year old** matured in refill American oak was launched in autumn 2017 as part of the Special Releases.

History:

1817 Captain Hugh Monro, owner of the estate Teaninich, founds the distillery.

1831 Captain Munro sells the estate to his younger brother John.

1850 John Munro, who spends most of his time in India, leases Teaninich to the infamous Robert Pattison from Leith.

1869 John McGilchrist Ross takes over the licence.

1895 Munro & Cameron takes over the licence.

1898 Munro & Cameron buys the distillery.

1904 Robert Innes Cameron becomes sole owner of Teaninich.

1932 Robert Innes Cameron dies.

1933 The estate of Robert Innes Cameron sells the distillery to Distillers Company Limited.

1970 A new distillation unit with six stills is commissioned and becomes known as the A side.

1975 A dark grains plant is built.

1984 The B side of the distillery is mothballed.

1985 The A side is also mothballed.

1991 The A side is in production again.

1992 United Distillers launches a 10 year old Teaninich in the Flora & Fauna series.

1999 The B side is decommissioned.

2000 A mash filter is installed.

2009 Teaninich 1996, a single cask in the new Manager´s Choice range is released.

2015 The distillery is expanded with six new stills and the capacity is doubled.

2017 A 17 year old is launched as part of the Special Releases.

10 years old

Tasting notes Teaninich 10 years old:

GS – The nose is initially fresh and grassy, quite light, with vanilla and hints of tinned pineapple. Mediumbodied, smooth, slightly oily, with cereal and spice in the mouth. Nutty and slowly drying in the finish, with pepper and a suggestion of cocoa powder notes.

Tobermory

[tow•bur•mo•ray]

Owner:
Distell International Ltd.

Region/district:
Highland (Mull)

Founded: 1798
Status: Active (vc)
Capacity: 1 000 000 litres

Address: Tobermory, Isle of Mull, Argyllsh. PA75 6NR

Website:
tobermorydistillery.com

Tel:
01688 302647

Tobermory village on Mull was created in the late 18th century with a very deliberate purpose – to become a fishing harbour. Behind the plans were the British Fisheries Society, the same body that initiated the building of Pulteney town a few years later.

But whereas Pulteney (and Wick) grew to become the largest harbour for herring boats in Europe, Tobermory never managed to build its wealth on fishing but rather on trading and, not least, kelp. The ash from burned kelp was used to make glass and one of the fortunate businessmen of the trade was John Sinclair. He was also the founder of Ledaig distillery (today known as Tobermory) and this year Distell International launched the first whisky in a series called Ledaig Sinclair, celebrating the founder of the distillery. Ledaig, by the way, is a tricky name to pronounce and even native Scots seem divided. One of the most common suggestions is "Let-chick" with emphasis on the first syllable.

Following a two year closure for a substantial refurbishing, the distillery re-opened in July 2019. The equipment consists of a 45 year old traditional five ton cast iron mash tun which is probably due to be replaced like for like in the coming years. There are four, new washbacks made of Oregon pine with a fermentation time of 48 to 100 hours and two pairs of stills. Two of the stills were replaced in 2014 and the other two in summer 2019. The production plan for 2020 is to do 9 mashes per week (800,000 litres of alcohol) with a 50/50 split between the peated Ledaig and the unpeated Tobermory. There is also a recently installed 2,000 litre gin still producing Tobermory Hebridean Gin.

The core range consists of the **12 year old Tobermory** and the **10** and **18 year old Ledaig**. Two additions were made in 2020 – the **23 year old Tobermory oloroso finish** and the NAS **Ledaig Sinclair rioja finish**. Recent limited expressions, from July 2020, include a **Tobermory 2007 port finish**, a **Ledaig 1998 marsala finish** and (exclusive to Germany) a **Ledaig 2007 PX sherry finish**. Available only at the distillery are **Tobermory 2007 PX finish** and **Ledaig 2009** matured in red wine casks.

History:

1798 John Sinclair founds the distillery.

1837 The distillery closes.

1878 The distillery reopens.

1890 John Hopkins & Company buys the distillery.

1916 Distillers Company Limited (DCL) takes over John Hopkins & Company.

1930 The distillery closes.

1972 A shipping company in Liverpool and the sherrymaker Domecq buy the buildings and embark on refurbishment. When work is completed it is named Ledaig Distillery Ltd.

1975 Ledaig Distillery Ltd files for bankruptcy and the distillery closes again.

1979 The estate agent Kirkleavington Property buys the distillery, forms a new company, Tobermory Distillers Ltd and starts production.

1982 No production. Some of the buildings are converted into flats and some are rented to a dairy company for cheese storage.

1989 Production resumes.

1993 Burn Stewart Distillers buys Tobermory.

2002 CL Financial buys Burn Stewart Distillers.

2005 A 32 year old from 1972 is launched.

2007 A Ledaig 10 year old is released.

2008 A Tobermory 15 year old is released.

2013 Burn Stewart Distillers is sold to Distell Group Ltd. A 40 year old Ledaig is released.

2015 Ledaig 18 years and 42 years are released together with Tobermory 42 years.

2018 Two 19 year old Ledaig are released.

2019 A 12 year old Tobermory is released, replacing the 10 year old.

2020 Two additions to the core range; 23 year old Tobermory oloroso finish and Ledaig Sinclair rioja finish.

Tasting notes Tobermory 12 years old:

IR – Butterscotch and heather honey on the nose with peaches and a hint of orange peel. Mouthcoating, rich and malty with notes of fudge, Danish pastry, citrus, pineapple and a hint of pepper. The finish is slightly salty.

Tasting notes Ledaig 10 years old:

GS – The nose is profoundly peaty, sweet and full, with notes of butter and smoked fish. Bold, yet sweet on the palate, with iodine, soft peat and heather. Developing spices. The finish is medium to long, with pepper, ginger, liquorice and peat.

12 years old

Tomatin

[to•mat•in]

Owner:	Region/district:
Tomatin Distillery Co	Highland
(Takara Shuzo Co., Kokubu & Co., Marubeni Corp.)	

Founded:	Status:	Capacity:
1897	Active (vc)	5 000 000 litres

Address: Tomatin, Inverness-shire IV13 7YT

Website:	Tel:
tomatin.com	01463 248144 (vc)

The Scotch whisky industry is full of examples of foreign ownership. Almost fifty percent of the established distilleries, i e those founded before 2000, have owners from other countries outside of the UK.

Some of the first examples of foreign ownership are Hiram Walker in the 1930s, followed by Seagrams in the 1950s. The pace increased from the 1980s with Tomatin as one of the take-overs. Historically the distillery produced spirit for the blended industry and some of their major customers were in Japan. The distillery expanded rapidly and became the largest in Scotland. When the market for whisky dropped, Tomatin was on the verge of bankruptcy and was taken over by two Japanese companies in 1985. The three owners today are well-established companies with a long history; Kokubu is a food and liquor wholesaler founded in 1712, Takara Shuzo, established in 1842 is a major manufacturer of sake and shochu while Marubeni, tracing its roots back to 1858, is the fifth largest sogo shosha (general trading company) in Japan.

The distillery is equipped with a nine ton stainless steel, full lauter mash tun, 12 stainless steel washbacks with a fermentation time from 54 to 110 hours and six pairs of stills. There are also eleven racked warehouses and two dunnage on site. The goal is to produce 1.8 million litres in 2020, including a couple of weeks of peated production at 40ppm.

The core range consists of **Legacy, 12, 18, 30** and **36 year old**. Included are also **Cask Strength, 14 year old port finish** and a **First Fill Bourbon** and a **French Oak finish**, both exclusive to the UK. Recent limited releases include a **2006 amontillado sherry finish** and a **2009 rum finish**. There is also **Five Virtues (Wood, Fire, Earth, Water** and **Metal)** focusing on the effect of different casks and Warehouse 6 Collection, a range of 40-year-old-plus whiskies with **1975 vintage** being the latest. The piece de resistance appeared in late 2018 when a **50 year old** was released. The distillery's duty free range consists of **8, 12, 15, 21** (released in February 2020) and **40 year old** while the smoky side of Tomatin is represented by the relaunched, stand-alone brand **Cù Bòcan** with **Signature, Creation #1** and **Creation #2**.

History:
1897 The distillery is founded by Tomatin Spey Distillery Company.
1906 Production ceases.
1909 Production resumes through Tomatin Distillers.
1956 Stills are increased from two to four.
1958 Another two stills are added.
1961 The six stills are increased to ten.
1974 The stills now total 23 and the maltings closes.
1985 The distillery company goes into liquidation.
1986 Takara Shuzo Co. and Okara & Co., buy Tomatin through Tomatin Distillery Co.
1998 Okara & Co is liquidated and Marubeni buys out part of their shareholding.
2004 Tomatin 12 years is launched.
2005 A 25 year old and a 1973 Vintage are released.
2006 An 18 year old and a 1962 Vintage are launched.
2008 A 30 and a 40 year old as well as several vintages from 1975 and 1995 are released.
2009 A 15 year old, a 21 year old and four single casks (1973, 1982, 1997 and 1999) are released.
2010 The first peated release - a 4 year old exclusive for Japan.
2011 A 30 year old and Tomatin Decades are released.
2013 Cù Bòcan, the first peated Tomatin, is released.
2014 14 year old port finish, 36 year old, Vintage 1988, Tomatin Cuatro, Cù Bòcan Sherry Cask and Cù Bòcan 1989 are released.
2015 Cask Strength and Cù Bòcan Virgin Oak are released.
2016 A 44 year old Tomatin and two Cù Bòcan vintages (1988 and 2005) are released.
2017 New releases include Wood, Fire and Earth as well as a 2006 Cù Bòcan.
2018 A 30 year old and a 50 year old are released.
2019 The entire range of Cù Bòcan is relaunched with three new expressions.
2020 A Vintage 1975 is released.

Tasting notes Tomatin 12 years old:
GS – Barley, spice, buttery oak and a floral note on the nose. Sweet and medium-bodied, with toffee apples, spice and herbs in the mouth. Medium-length in the finish, with sweet fruitiness.

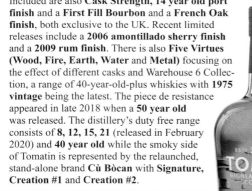

12 years old

Tomintoul

[tom•in•towel]

Owner:
Angus Dundee Distillers

Region/district:
Speyside

Founded: 1965
Status: Active
Capacity: 3 300 000 litres

Address: Ballindalloch, Banffshire AB37 9AQ

Website:
tomintouldistillery.co.uk

Tel:
01807 590274

The Tomintoul Master Distiller is an icon in the Scotch whisky industry. In 2020 Robert Fleming is celebrating his 30th anniversary as the custodian of not only Tomintoul but also its sister distillery Glencadam.

Fleming started his career in the whisky business in 1974, working in the Glenlivet warehouses. He continued for 16 years at various distilleries within the Chivas group until he took on the role as distillery manager for Tomintoul in 1990. Fleming definitely has whisky running through his veins, being the fourth generation of his family making whisky in Speyside.

Tomintoul is equipped with a 12 ton semi lauter mash tun, six stainless steel washbacks with a fermentation time of 54-60 hours and two pairs of stills. There are currently 15 mashes per week, which means that capacity is used to its maximum, and the 13 warehouses (racked and palletized) have a storage capacity of 120,000 casks. The malt used for mashing is unpeated, but every year since 2001, heavily peated (55ppm) spirit is produced. On the site there is also a blending centre with 14 large blending vats.

The major part of the production is used either for the company's own blends or, as part of whiskies specially blended for other companies, so called own-label whiskies.

The core range consists of **Tlàth** without age statement, **10, 14, 16, 18** (launched in 2020), **21** and **25 year old**. There are also two finishes; a **12 year old oloroso sherry cask** and a **15 year old port finish**. The peaty side of Tomintoul is represented by **Peaty Tang**, both without age statement and as a newly released **15 year old**. As a stand-alone range, there is also the heavily peated **Old Ballantruan without age statement** as well as a **10** and **15 year old**. Recent limited releases include **Seiridh** which was launched in March 2020 and is without age statement. The whisky has been matured in ex-bourbon casks and then finished in first fill oloroso butts. During autumn 2020, a number of bottlings known as **Robert Fleming 30th Anniversary** will be released.

History:

1965 The distillery is founded by Tomintoul Distillery Ltd, which is owned by Hay & MacLeod & Co. and W. & S. Strong & Co.

1973 Scottish & Universal Investment Trust, owned by the Fraser family, buys both the distillery and Whyte & Mackay.

1974 The two stills are increased to four and Tomintoul 12 years is launched.

1978 Lonhro buys Scottish & Universal Investment Trust.

1989 Lonhro sells Whyte & Mackay to Brent Walker.

1990 American Brands buys Whyte & Mackay.

1996 Whyte & Mackay changes name to JBB (Greater Europe).

2000 Angus Dundee plc buys Tomintoul.

2002 Tomintoul 10 year is launched.

2003 Tomintoul 16 years is launched.

2004 Tomintoul 27 years is launched.

2005 The peated Old Ballantruan is launched.

2008 1976 Vintage and Peaty Tang are released.

2009 A 14 year old and a 33 year old are released.

2010 A 12 year old Port wood finish is released.

2011 A 21 year old, a 10 year old Ballantruan and Vintage 1966 are released.

2012 Old Ballantruan 10 years old is released.

2013 A 31 year old single cask is released.

2015 Five Decades and a 40 year old are released.

2016 A 40 year old and Tlàth without age statement are launched.

2017 15 year old Peaty Tang and 15 year old Old Ballantruan are launched.

2018 Tomintoul 1965 The Ultimate Cask is released.

2020 Seiridh and a number of bottlings celebrating Robert Fleming's 30th anniversary are released.

Tasting notes Tomintoul 10 years old:

GS – A light, fresh and fruity nose, with ripe peaches and pineapple cheesecake, delicate spice and background malt. Medium-bodied, fruity and fudgy on the palate. The finish offers wine gums, mild, gently spiced oak, malt and a suggestion of smoke.

10 years old

Tormore

[tor•more]

Owner:	**Region/district:**
Chivas Bros (Pernod Ricard)	Speyside
Founded: **Status:**	**Capacity:**
1958 Active	4 800 000 litres

Address: Tormore, Advie, Grantown-on-Spey, Morayshire PH26 3LR

Website:	**Tel:**
tormoredistillery.com	01807 510244

The take-over of Tormore by Pernod Ricard in 2005 was just a tiny detail in a much grander scheme that involved the change-of-hands of dozens of distilleries and mega brands.

The British company Allied Domecq, with roots going back to a conglomerate of breweries formed in 1961, was the second largest spirits producer in the world when Pernod Ricard in spring 2005 offered the owners £7,5bn for the company. The bid was accepted by the board but to comply with the EC Merger Regulations a number of the brands and distilleries had to be sold on, to Fortune Brands in this case. Included in Pernod Ricard´s share of the deal was Tormore and six other malt distilleries but the most important acquisition was Ballantine´s – the second biggest Scotch blend in the world.

For Pernod Ricard, Tormore was "just another" producer of quality malt for their blends and to a large extent it still is. Six years ago, two official single malt bottlings were launched but the whiskies are not that widely spread (mostly sold in the UK and France) and sales volumes are very small.

From the outside, Tormore is without competition the most unusual looking distillery in Scotland, at least until the new Macallan was opened. It is impossible to miss on the right hand side when driving the A95 from Grantown-on-Spey to Craigellachie. Even though the distillery doesn't cater to visitors it is quite easy to park the car on the small road leading to the distillery cottages and take some photos of the stunning building.

Following an upgrade in 2012, Tormore is now equipped with a stainless steel full lauter mash tun, 11 stainless steel washbacks and four pairs of stills. Tormore's fruity and light character is achieved by a clear wort, slow distillation and by using purifiers on all the stills.

The only official bottlings are a **14 year old** bottled at 43% and a **16 year old**, non chill-filtered, bottled at 48%. There are also two cask strength bottlings (**11 and 19 years old**) in the Distillery Reserve Collection, available at all Chivas´ visitor centres.

History:

1958 Schenley International, owners of Long John, founds the distillery.

1960 The distillery is ready for production.

1972 The number of stills is increased from four to eight.

1975 Schenley sells Long John and its distilleries (including Tormore) to Whitbread.

1989 Allied Lyons (to become Allied Domecq) buys the spirits division of Whitbread.

1991 Allied Distillers introduce Caledonian Malts where Miltonduff, Glendronach and Laphroaig are represented besides Tormore. Tormore is later replaced by Scapa.

2004 Tormore 12 year old is launched as an official bottling.

2005 Chivas Brothers (Pernod Ricard) becomes new owners through the acquisition of Allied Domecq.

2012 Production capacity is increased by 20%.

2014 The 12 year old is replaced by two new expressions - 14 and 16 year old.

14 years old

Tasting notes Tormore 14 years old:

GS – Vanilla, butterscotch, summer berries and light spice on the nose. Milk chocolate and tropical fruit on the smooth palate, with soft toffee. Lengthy in the finish, with a sprinkling of black pepper.

Tullibardine

[tully•<u>bar</u>•din]

Owner:
Terroir Distillers
(Picard Vins & Spiritueux)

Region/district:
Highlands

Founded: 1949   **Status:** Active (vc)   **Capacity:** 3 000 000 litres

Address: Blackford, Perthshire PH4 1QG

Website: tullibardine.com   **Tel:** 01764 682252

In the last couple of years, the owners have put in a lot of effort and money to make Tullibardine an attractive distillery to visit. It makes a lot of sense as the distillery is conveniently located on the busy A9 from Stirling to Perth and onwards to the Highlands.

The former owners opted for a combination of a distillery and outlet centre/retail village. For a few years it looked promising but the property crash in 2009 changed everything. The distillery was sold to the French company Picard and the retail area has been transformed into a bottling line, a vatting hall, a small cooperage and more warehouses. The visitor centre received a lot of investment and recently they have also improved the accessibility in the distillery itself which must have been quite a challenge given a very cramped and tight production area. Tullibardine is also the spiritual home to the famous brand, Highland Queen. First launched in 1893 the brand had its heyday in the 1970s when it was popularly sold all over the world. In 2008, it was taken over by the Picard family with Tullibardine single malt being a key component.

The equipment consists of a 6.2 ton stainless steel semi-lauter mash tun, nine stainless steel washbacks with a fermentation of 55-60 hours, two 21,000 litre wash stills and two 16,000 litre spirit stills. During 2020, they will be working 27 mashes per week which will result in 3 million litres of alcohol.

The core range consists of **Sovereign** without age statement, **225 Sauternes finish, 228 Burgundy finish, 500 Sherry finish**, a **20 year old** and a **25 year old**. In spring 2020 a **15 year old** was added to the range. This is the oldest whisky yet released to have been made from spirit distilled after the re-opening in 2003. Custodian's Collection was introduced in 2015 and the latest in that range was **Vintage 1964**. The first cask strength Tullibardine made this century was The Murray 2004 vintage. The latest bottlings are **The Murray Marsala Finish,** released in 2018 and **2007 Cask Strength** launched in 2019. Yet another expression, a **Double Wood finish**, is scheduled for late 2020. Finally, a **Madeira finish** can be found exclusively at the visitor centre.

History:
1949 The architect William Delmé-Evans founds the distillery.
1953 The distillery is sold to Brodie Hepburn.
1971 Invergordon Distillers buys Brodie Hepburn Ltd.
1973 The number of stills increases to four.
1993 Whyte & Mackay buys Invergordon Distillers.
1994 Tullibardine is mothballed.
1996 Whyte & Mackay changes name to JBB (Greater Europe).
2001 JBB (Greater Europe) is bought out from Fortune Brands by management and changes name to Kyndal (Whyte & Mackay from 2003).
2003 A consortium buys Tullibardine for £1.1 million. The distillery is in production again.
2005 Three wood finishes from 1993, Port, Moscatel and Marsala, are launched together with a 1986 John Black selection.
2006 Vintage 1966, Sherry Wood 1993 and a new John Black selection are launched.
2007 Five different wood finishes and a couple of single cask vintages are released.
2008 A Vintage 1968 40 year old is released.
2009 Aged Oak is released.
2011 Three vintages and a wood finish are released. Picard buys the distillery.
2013 A completely new range is launched – Sovereign, 225 Sauternes, 228 Burgundy, 500 Sherry, 20 year old and 25 year old.
2015 A 60 year old Custodian Collection is released.
2016 A Vintage 1970 and The Murray from 2004 are released.
2017 Vintage 1962 and The Murray Chateauneuf-du-Pape are released.
2018 The Murray Marsala Finish is released.
2019 A Vintage 1964 is released.
2020 The Double Wood Finish is released.

Tasting notes Tullibardine Sovereign:
GS – Floral on the nose, with new-mown hay, vanilla and fudge. Fruity on the palate, with milk chocolate, brazil nuts, marzipan, malt, and a hint of cinnamon. Cocoa, vanilla, a squeeze of lemon and more spice in the finish.

Sovereign

David Brown, managing director of John Crabbie & Co. and Marc Watson, head distiller at Bonnington Distillery

New
distilleries

In the first twelve years of the new millennium,
six new malt whisky distilleries opened up in Scotland. In the next six
years, another twentyfour distilleries came on stream and in the last two
years, four more distilleries have been added! The rate of openings seem to
have slowed down in recent years but there are at least another ten
distilleries in different stages of construction or planning.
Read more about them in the chapter
The Year That Was, pages 271-273.

Aberargie

[aber•ar•jee]

Owner:	Region/district:
The Perth Distilling Co.	Lowlands

Founded:	Status:	Capacity:
2017	Active	750 000 litres

Address: Aberargie, Perthshire PH2 9LX

Website:	Tel:
-	01738 787044

The distillery was built on the same grounds in Fife as Morrison & Mackay, independent bottler and producer of Scottish liqueurs, and a company which can trace it´s roots back to 1982.

Founded as John Murray & Co., the company was taken over in 2005 by Kenny Mackay and Brian Morrison, once the chairman of Morrison Bowmore, and his son Jamie. The production of liqueurs, especially Columba Cream, continued while bottling of Scotch single malts (The Carn Mor) was added to the business. Later on, they also took over the Old Perth brand from Whyte & Mackay and relaunched it as a blended malt. The company name was changed to Morrison & Mackay in 2014.

At the same time, the Morrison´s of the company decided to build a distillery on the premises and founded a company

called The Perth Distilling Company. Construction work started in summer 2016 and the first spirit was distilled in November 2017.

The distillery is equipped with a 2 ton semilauter mash tun, six stainless steel washbacks with a fermentation time of 72 hours, one 15,000 litre wash still and one 10,000 litre spirit still. The stills, both with steeply descending lyne arms, were made by Forsyths and are heated with panels instead of coils or pans. With a maturation in a mixture of first fill sherry butts, first fill bourbon barrels and second fill sherry/bourbon casks, the owners are aiming for a fruity character which will be enhanced by occasional peated spirit runs. Different barley varieties are being used, including Golden Promise, and they are all grown in 300 acres of field owned by the Morrison family and that surround the distillery. With the Morrison & Mackay blending and bottling facility next to the distillery, every step of the production (except malting) takes place on site.

Abhainn Dearg

[aveen jar•rek]

Owner:	Region/district:
Mark Tayburn	Highlands (Isle of Lewis)

Founded:	Status:	Capacity:
2008	Active (vc)	c 20 000 litres

Address: Carnish, Isle of Lewis, Na h-Eileanan an Iar HS2 9EX

Website:	Tel:
abhainndearg.co.uk	01851 672429

In September 2008, spirit flowed from a newly constructed distillery in Uig on the island of Lewis in the Outer Hebrides.

This was the first distillery on the island since 1840 when Stornoway distillery was closed. The conditions for new distilleries being built at that time were not improved when James Matheson, a Scottish tradesman, bought the entire island in 1844. Even though he had made his fortune in the opium trade, he was an abstainer and a prohibitionist and did not look kindly on the production or use of alcohol.

The Gaelic name of the new distillery is Abhainn Dearg which means Red River, and the founder and owner is Mark "Marko" Tayburn who was born and raised on the island. There are two 500 kg mash tuns made of stainless steel and two 7,500 litre washbacks made of Douglas fir with a fermentation time of 4 days. The wash still has a capacity of 2,112 litres and the spirit still 2,057 litres. Both

have very long necks and steeply descending lye pipes leading out into two wooden worm tubs. Both bourbon and sherry casks are used for maturation. The plan is to use 100% barley grown on Lewis and in 2013 the first 6 tonnes of Golden Promise (15% of the total requirement) were harvested. Over the years, production has been limited to around 10,000 litres of pure alcohol yearly even though the distillery has the capacity to do more.

The first release from the distillery was The Spirit of Lewis in 2010 and the first single malt was a limited release of a 3 year old in October 2011, followed up by a cask strength version (58%) in 2012. The distillery´s first 10 year old appeared in late 2018 when 10,000 bottles were released, bottled at 46%. At the same time 100 bottles of a limited 10 year old single cask, also bottled at 46% were launched. Since then a number of single casks with different maturations (including madeira and sauternes) have been released for various markets.

Ailsa Bay

[ail•sah bey]

Owner:
William Grant & Sons

Region/district:
Lowlands

Founded: **Status:** **Capacity:**
2007 Active 12 000 000 litres

Address: Girvan, Ayrshire KA26 9PT

Website:
ailsabay.com

Tel:
01465 713091

Commissioned in September 2007, it only took nine months to build this distillery on the same site as Girvan Distillery near Ayr on Scotland´s west coast.

Initially, it was equipped with a 12,1 tonne full lauter mash tun, 12 washbacks made of stainless steel and eight stills. In 2013 however, it was time for a major expansion when yet another mash tun, 12 more washbacks and eight more stills were commissioned, doubling the capacity to 12 million litres of alcohol.

Each washback will hold 50,000 litres and fermentation time is 60 hours for the heavier styles and 72 hours for the lighter "Balveniestyle". The stills are made according to the same standards as Balvenie's and one of the wash stills and one of the spirit stills have stainless steel condensers instead of copper. That way, they have the possibility of

making batches of a more sulphury spirit if desired. To increase efficiency and to get more alcohol, high gravity distillation is used. Maturation for the part that is bottled as single malt starts in small (25-100 litres) ex-bourbon barrels from Tuthilltown distillery and after 6-9 months the spirit is tranferred to regular sized barrels as well as into new oak. The plan for 2020 is to do around 50 mashes per week, producing 10 million litres of alcohol.

Five different types of spirit are produced. The most common is a light and rather sweet spirit. Then there is a heavy, sulphury style and three peated with the peatiest having a malt specification of 50ppm. The production is destined to become a part of Grant´s blended Scotch but in 2016, a peated single malt Ailsa Bay was released. In September 2018 Ailsa Bay Sweet Smoke was launched. Definitely sweeter and slighly smokier, it replaced the inaugural bottling. The ppm on the label (22) is the actual phenol content of the liquid itself and not the barley.

Annandale

[ann•an•dail]

Owner:
Annandale Distillery Co.

Region/district:
Lowlands

Founded: **Status:** **Capacity:**
2014 Active (vc) 500 000 litres

Address: Northfield, Annan, Dumfriesshire DG12 5LL

Website:
annandaledistillery.com

Tel:
01461 207817

In 2010 Professor David Thomson and his wife, Teresa Church, obtained consent from the local council for the building of the new Annandale Distillery in Dumfries and Galloway in the south-west of Scotland.

The old one had been producing since 1836 and was owned by Johnnie Walker from 1895 until it closed down in 1918. From 1924 to 2007, the site was owned by the Robinson family, who were famous for their Provost brand of porridge oats. David Thomson began the restoration of the site in June 2011 with the two, old sandstone warehouses being restored to function as two-level dunnage warehouses. The distillery was in a poor condition and the mash house and the tun room was largely reconstructed while the other buildings were refurbished substantially. The old maltings, with the kiln and original pagoda roof, have been turned into an excellent visitor centre.

Entering the production area you first run into the 2.5 ton semi-lauter mash tun with an elegant copper dome. Then, with three wooden washbacks (a fermentation time of 72-96 hours) on each side, you are guided up to the two spirit stills (4,000 litres). Once you have reached them, you find the wash still (12,000 litres) slightly hidden behind a wall.

The first cask was filled on 15 November 2014 and both unpeated and peated (45ppm) whisky is distilled. In June 2018, two single malts were released, both matured in ex-Buffalo Trace barrels. In both cases the whiskies, the unpeated Man O´Words and the peated Man O´Swords, were bottled at cask strength. More bottlings, all single casks and matured in either bourbon or sherry casks, have followed. Currently whiskies from 2016 make up the Founder´s Selection part of the range while the produce from 2014 and 2015 are part of the Vintage series. The distillery has also launched two blended whiskies – Nation of Scots and Outlaw King and there is also a newmake for sale.

Arbikie

[ar•bi•ki]

Owner:		**Region/district:**	
The Stirling family		Eastern Highlands	
Founded:	**Status:**	**Capacity:**	
2015	Active	200 000 litres	

Address: Inverkeilor, Arbroath, Angus DD11 4UZ

Website:	**Tel:**
arbikie.com	01241 830770

The Stirling family has been farming since the 17th century and the 2000-acre Arbikie Highland Estate in Angus has now been in their possession for four generations.

The three brothers (John, Iain and David) started their careers within other fields but have now returned to the family lands to open up a single-estate distillery. The definition of a single-estate distillery is that, not only does the whole chain of production take place on site, but all the ingredients are also grown on the farm. Ballindalloch is one example but Arbikie is the first to produce both brown and white spirits.

The first vodka from potatoes was distilled in October 2014 which was followed by gin in May 2015. Trials with malt whisky, started in March 2015, went over to full production in October 2015. Responsible for the production side at the distillery is master distiller Kirsty Black.

The barley is grown in fields of their own and then sent to Boorts malt in Montrose. The distillery is equipped with a stainless steel, semi-lauter mash tun with a 0.75 ton charge and four washbacks (two 4,400 litre and two 9,000 litre) with a fermentation time of 96-120 hours. There is also one 4,000 litre wash still and one 2,400 litre spirit still. For the final stage of vodka and gin production, there is a 40 plate rectification column. The Stirlings don't intend to launch their first single malt whisky until 2029/2030.

In common with a few other distilleries in Scotland, Arbikie started trials with rye whisky production in December 2015. It was made from 52% unmalted rye, 33% unmalted wheat and 15% malted barley grown on their own farm. Matured for three years in American oak and finished in ex-PX casks, it was released in December 2018 as the first rye whisky made in Scotland for more than 100 years. It was followed up in January 2020 with a 4 year old second release which had been finished in armagnac casks.

Ardnahoe

[ard•na•hoe]

Owner:		**Region/district:**	
Hunter Laing & Company		Islay	
Founded:	**Status:**	**Capacity:**	
2017	Active (vc)	1 000 000 litres	

Address: Isle of Islay, Port Askaig PA46 7RU

Website:	**Tel:**
ardnahoedistillery.com	01496 840711

Ardnahoe, the newest distillery on Islay, came on stream in November 2018. The location, between Caol Ila and Bunnahabhain and overlooking Jura, is absolutely stunning!

The distillery, owned by independent bottler Hunter Laing, is equipped with a 2.5 ton semi lauter mash tun with a copper lid. The lauter gear is used as little as possible to get a clear wort. There are four washbacks made from Oregon pine with a fermentation time between 60 and 70 hours, one wash still (12,500 litres) and one spirit still (7,500 litres) with a slow distillation, both with extremely long lyne arms (7,5 metres). Actually, these are the longest in Scotland. The distillery is equipped with wooden worm tubs (the only ones on Islay) with a 77 metre copper tube in each. Another unusual piece of equipment is the 4-roller Boby mill from the 1920s which was brought in from

Fettercairn. The aim is to produce a variety of single malts from unpeated to peated whiskies on several levels (from 5ppm up to 40ppm) with the malt being bought from Port Ellen maltings. The distillery has an annual capacity of one million litres of alcohol and the production plan for 2020 was to do 14 mashes per week which amounts to 600,000 litres. Eighty percent of the newmake goes into first fill bourbon and the rest is matured in sherry casks. There is currently one warehouse on site but more will be built – a mix of dunnage and racked.

Ardnahoe is the first new distillery on the island since Kilchoman was opened in 2005 and the 9th on Islay. The distillery visitor centre is surprisingly huge (given the size of the distillery) with a large shop and a café/whisky bar with an excellent view towards the paps of Jura and with Mull in the distance. In the first year (2019), the distillery received 25,000 visitors and was also presented with a Five Star award from Visit Scotland.

Ardnamurchan

[ard•ne•mur•ken]

Owner:		Region/district:
Adelphi Distillery Ltd		Western Highlands
Founded:	**Status:**	**Capacity:**
2014	Active (vc)	500 000 litres

Address: Glenbeg, Ardnamurchan, Argyll PH36 4JG

Website:	Tel:
adelphidistillery.com	01972 500 285

It takes a good 90 minutes to go from Fort William to the distillery on the Ardnamurchan peninsula north of Mull by car but it's well worth the journey.

Winding single track roads beg for careful driving but the stunning scenery it also a good reason for driving slowly. The distillery is owned by independent bottler Adelphi Distillery. In 2007, they realised that the supply of good whisky could become scarce in years to come for those companies not having a distillery of their own. They decided to build one and part of the reason for choosing this remote site was that the land was owned by one of the directors of Adelphi Distillery, Donald Houston.

Ardnamurchan distillery came on stream on 11th July 2014 and is equipped with a two tonne semi lauter mash tun made of stainless steel with a copper canopy, four wooden washbacks and three made of stainless steel. The initial wooden washbacks were made from oak, having been used as cognac vats in France but two of them were exchanged in 2018 to Oregon pine. The fermentation time is 72-96 hours. There is one wash still (10,000 litres) and one spirit still (6,000 litres) with condensers placed outside and quite recently, sub-coolers made from stainless steel were also fitted. Two different styles of whisky are produced; peated and unpeated and for the peated spirit, the barley has a phenol specification of 30-35ppm. The production goal for 2020 is 350,000 litres of alcohol. There are also plans to malt some of their barley themselves and a malting floor is already in place but hasn't been used so far.

Since 2016 they have released spirit from the distillery that is too young to legally be called whisky. The fourth and final bottling, 2019/AD, had been matured in a combination of hogsheads, butts and octaves – all seasoned with oloroso and PX sherry and bottled at 57,4%. Finally, in October 2020, the owners released their inaugural single malt – the AD/09.20:01.

Ardross

[ard•ross]

Owner:		Region/district:
Greenwood Distillers		N Highland
Founded:	**Status:**	**Capacity:**
2019	Active	1 000 000 litres

Address: Ardross Mains, Ardross, Alness

Website:	Tel:
greenwooddistillers.com	-

An old, derelict 19th century farm site north of Inverness, has recently been transformed into one of Scotland's newest distilleries.

The nearest distillery neighbors are Teaninich and Dalmore, some 5 km to the southeast. A planning application was approved in 2017 and behind the project lies Greenwood Distillers Ltd. and that company, in turn, is an affiliate of Vevil International, owner of Ned Hotel and the Wolseley restaurant in London. The CEO of Greenwood Distillers is Barthelemy Brosseau and one of the directors is Andrew Rankin who was Operations Director and Chief Blender at Morrison Bowmore for almost 25 years. As Distillery Manager, the company hired Sandy Jamieson with a long career in the Scotch whisky business, most recently as manager of Speyside Distillery near Kingussie. The company also has a connection in Mexico with a mezcal producer, in France with a producer of armagnac, in Japan with a cooperage making mizunara casks and in Kentucky where Copper Pheasant distillery is about to be built.

The distillery was commissioned in August 2019 and is equipped with a 3 ton semi-lauter mash tun, six wooden washbacks (20,000 litres each and with a fermentation time of 120 hours), one 15,000 litre wash still and one 12,000 litre spirit still. The capacity is an impressive one million litres of pure alcohol and the new make is sent in tankers to the company´s bond in Cumbernauld.

The first release from the distillery was Theodore gin which appeared in August 2019. It features 16 botanicals inspired by those that the Picts may have encountered on their travels to Scotland. The gin will not just be a way of creating cash flow until the future whisky has been released, as a designated gin distillery has been built on the site. Ardross is also said to be on of few distilleries in Scotland to own and manage its own loch (Loch Dubh).

Ballindalloch

[bal•lin•da•lock]

Owner:
The Macpherson-Grant family

Region/district:
Speyside

Founded: **Status:** **Capacity:**
2014 Active (vc) 100 000 litres

Address: Ballindalloch, Banffshire AB37 9AA

Website: **Tel:**
ballindallochdistillery.com 01807 500 331

In the heart of Speyside, the owners of Ballindalloch Castle, the Macpherson-Grant family, decided in 2012 to turn a steading from 1820 into a whisky distillery.

Previous generations of the family had been involved in distilling from the 1860s and from 1923 to 1965, they owned part of Cragganmore distillery, not far away from the castle. The old farm building was meticulously renovated with attention given to every little detail and the result is an amazingly beautiful distillery which can be seen from the A95 between Aberlour and Grantown-on-Spey.

Ballindalloch distillery takes its water from the nearby Garline Springs and all the barley is grown on the Estate. All of the distillery equipment are gathered on the second floor which makes it easy for visitors to get a good view of the production. The equipment consists of an extraordinary 1 ton semi lauter, copper clad mash tun with a copper dome. There are four washbacks made of Oregon pine where the fermentation time was increased a while ago to increase the fruity character of the spirit. There are now four long fermentations (140 hours) and on short (92 hours). Finally there is a 5,000 litre lantern-shaped wash still and a 3,600 litre spirit still with a reflux ball. Both stills are connected to two wooden worm tubs for cooling the spirit vapours. The distillery came on stream in September 2014 and was officially opened 16th April 2015 by Prince Charles. The distillery is working 5 days a week, making 100,000 litres of alcohol. The idea is to produce a robust and bold whisky, enhanced not least by the use of worm tubs. More than 4,000 casks have now been filled since the start in 2014. The first single malt release is expected in 2022.

The distillery is open for visitors by appointment and there is also the opportunity to take part in The Art of Whisky Making, which means spending a day with the crew and learning about whisky from mashing to warehousing.

Bonnington

[bon•ing•tun]

Owner:
John Crabbie & Co. (Halewood)

Region/district:
Lowlands

Founded: **Status:** **Capacity:**
2020 Active 500 000 litres

Address: 21 Graham Street, Edinburgh EH6 5QN

Website: **Tel:**
crabbiewhisky.com 0151 480 8800

The second malt whisky distillery to open up in Edinburgh in recent times could have been the first if archeologists hadn't made some amazing discoveries during construction.

Bonnington is owned by John Crabbie & Co, a subsidiary of Halewood Wines & Spirits, founded in 1978, which is a company that has interests in wines and spirits all over the world. John Crabbie was a co-founder of North British grain distillery in 1885 and a notable whisky blender in his time. When excavations for the distillery began, just a few hundred metres from the original site where John Crabbie matured and blended his whisky, archeologists found the remnants of a whisky distillery from the 1700s but also evidence of Bonnington House, a mansion dating back to the 11th century. The findings meant the time frame for the new distillery was delayed by a year. Construction of the distillery started in January 2019 and was finished in December that year. But, already in 2018 a small pilot distillery was opened in Granton not far away from the current distillery. Producing just one cask a week, here the owners could trial different malts, yeasts, fermentation lengths, cut points and distillation methods before starting at Bonnington.

The first distillation took place in March 2020 and the distillery is equipped with a two ton semi lauter mash tun, six stainless steel washbacks with a fermentation time of 48-70 hours, a 10,500 litre wash still and an 8,000 litre spirit still. The owners managed to find their own production water on site through a borehole to an ancient aquifer. While the main part of the whisky will be unpeated a small portion will be made using peated malt (50ppm). The newmake is filled into a variety of casks (bourbon, sherry, virgin oak, port, marsala and sweet wine). A visitor centre is planned to be opened in 2021.

The Borders

[boar•ders]

Owner:
The Three Stills Co. Ltd.

Region/district:
Lowlands

Founded: | **Status:** | **Capacity:**
2017 | Active (vc) | 1 600 000 litres

Address: Commercial Road, Hawick TD9 7AQ

Website:
thebordersdistillery.com

Tel:
01450 374330

On the 6th of March 2018, the first whisky distillery in the Borders in 180 years started production and the distillery opened to the public a few weeks later.

Behind the Borders Distillery in Hawick is a company called The Three Stills Company which was founded in 2013. The owners include four men who had all previously worked for William Grant & Sons – George Tait, Tony Roberts, John Fordyce and Tim Carton. In 2016, the company started to renovate the beautiful buildings dating from the late 1880s and which used to be an electric company and turned it into a distillery. The river Teviot is running just behind the distillery and like the textile companies that Hawick is renowned for were using the water for dyeing and power, the distillery now uses it for cooling the spirit vapours.

The distillery is equipped with a 5 ton mash tun, eight stainless steel washbacks with a fermentation time of 80 hours, two wash stills (12,500 litres) and two spirit stills (7,500 litres) with all equipment provided by Forsyths. The whisky produced is un-peated and floral. Other spirits are also produced, for instance vodka and gin, where the barley spirit from the pot stills is redistilled in a Carterhead still. The newly released vodka is unique in the way that it is not filtered as a liquid but instead is steamed through charcoal inside the still in order to preserve the character of the barley in the taste. The owners also have plans to install an anaerobic bio plant on the site.

The company has already released a blended Scotch from sourced whisky called Clan Fraser and a blended malt named Lower East Side. The first bottling of spirit actually made at the distillery appeared in July 2018 when William Kerr's Borders Gin was launched and this was later followed by Puffing Billy Steam Vodka.

Brew Dog

[bru•dog]

Owner:
Brewdog plc.

Region/district:
Highlands

Founded: | **Status:** | **Capacity:**
2016 | Active | 450 000 litres

Address: Balmacassie Commercial Park, Ellon, Aberdeenshire AB41 8BX

Website:
brewdog.com

Tel:
01358 724924

In spring 2019, the distillery changed the name from Lone Wolf to Brew Dog in order to tap into the name and fame of the well-known brewery

Founded in 2007 by James Watt and Martin Dickie, Brew Dog grew to become the biggest independent brewery in the UK and in 2014 a decision was taken to open up also a distillery. It is situated next to the brewery in Ellon outside of Aberdeen and as distillery manager, Steven Kearsley who had a background at several Diageo distilleries, was called in. In autumn 2018, David Gates who previously ran Diageo Futures and worked as brand director for Johnnie Walker, joined the company as managing director.

The adjacent brew house provides the wash for the distillery which has the following equipment; one 3,000 litre pot still with an 8 plate rectification column which will be used

for stripping the wash for vodka, whisky and rum, another 3,000 litre still with a 60-plate column is used for the final distillation of vodka and whisky, a 600 litre pot still is dedicated to gin and brandy production, while a 50 litre pot still is used for research and experimentation.

The initial production was gin and vodka and the first bottles were launched in spring 2017. Whisky and rum production has also commenced and while the botanical rum Five Hundred Cuts was recently launched, no whisky has yet been released. In 2017, Lone Wolf became one of the first Scottish distilleries in modern times to distill a rye whisky. In spring 2019, the company entered into a collaboration with three other whisky makers who all designed one whisky each to be paired with Brew Dog beers. The Boilermaker series is made up by Transistor blended Scotch from Compass Box, Torpedo Tulip, a 100% rye whisky from Millstone and a blended Scotch named Skeleton Key from Duncan Taylor.

The Clydeside

[klajdsajd]

Owner:	**Region/district:**
Morrison Glasgow Distillers	Lowlands
Founded: **Status:**	**Capacity:**
2017 Active (vc)	500 000 litres

Address: 100 Stobcross Road, Glasgow G3 8QQ

Website:	**Tel:**
theclydeside.com	0141 2121401

If Tim Morrison, the owner of indepednent bottler AD Rattray. ever wanted to found a distillery he couldn´t have picked a better spot.

The queens Docks in Glasgow oozes of whisky history with ships coming in with barley and coal and going out with barrels of whisky, To add to the picture, Tim´s great grandfather designed the pumphouse which was used to power the hydraulic gates allowing ships in and out of the Queens Dock and which is now the site of Clydeside distillery. Tim Morrison represents the fourth generation of one of Scotland´s best known whisky families. Eventually he took over the independent bottler AD Rattray and expanded the business by opening up a first class shop and whisky centre in Kirkoswald in Ayrshire. Today, Tim´s son Andrew is the managing director of Clydeside Distillery.

The distillery is beautifully situated on the river Clyde with well-known attractions such as the Riverside Museum, Glasgow Science Centre and the SEC Centre as its closest neighbours. The equipment consists of a 1.5 ton semi lauter mash tun made of stainless steel, 8 stainless steel washbacks with a fermentation time of 72 hours, a 7,500 litre wash still and a 5,000 litre spirit still. The foreshots are 15 minutes with a slow distillation and the cutpoints for the spirit run are 76-71%. Production started in autumn 2017 and the aim for 2020 is to produce 440,000 litres of alcohol (up 20% from last year) on 16 mashes per week.

An excellent visitor centre has been constructed within the old Pump House building from 1877 while an adjacent, modern building houses the distillery. Apart from a variety of tours, the distillery shop also offers a wide range of whiskies including new make spirit from the distillery itself. Around 70,000 visitors came here in 2019.

Daftmill

[daf•mil]

Owner:	**Region/district:**
Francis Cuthbert	Lowlands
Founded: **Status:**	**Capacity:**
2005 Active	c 65 000 litres

Address: By Cupar, Fife KY15 5RF

Website:	**Tel:**
daftmill.com	01337 830303

The distillery may be one of the smallest in Scotland but few single malt releases have been more eagerly awaited by the whisky enthusiasts than the inaugural release from Daftmill.

Ever since December 2008, when the spirit legally became whisky, questions to the owners Francis and Ian Cuthbert about when the first whisky would be launched have always been answered by "when it´s ready". In 2017, they signed a distribution agreement with Berry Brothers and in May 2018, a ballot was opened for buying one of the first 629 bottles of a 12 year old matured in ex-bourbon casks. The first release was followed by a Summer Relase in June where seven casks rendered 1665 bottles. More bottlings have followed, including some single casks with one of them sold exclusively to whisky bars in Scotland.

Daftmill´s first distillation was on 16th December 2005

and it is run as a typical farmhouse distillery. The barley is grown on the farm and they also supply other distilleries. The malting is done without peat at Crisp´s in Alloa. The equipment consists of a one tonne semi-lauter mash tun with a copper dome, two stainless steel washbacks with a fermentation between 72 and 100 hours and one pair of stills with slightly ascending lyne arms. The equipment is designed to give a lot of copper contact, a lot of reflux. The wash still has a capacity of 3,000 litres and the spirit still 2,000 litres and around 100 casks are filled very year.

The Cuthbert´s aim is to do a light, Lowland style whisky. In order to achieve this they have very short foreshots (five minutes) and the spirit run starts at 78% to capture all of the fruity esters and already comes off at 73%. Taking care of the farm during spring and autumn obviously prohibits Francis from producing whisky full time. Whisky production is therefore reserved for two months in the summertime and two in the winter.

Dalmunach

[dal•moo•nack]

Owner: Chivas Brothers   **Region/district:** Speyside

Founded: 2015   **Status:** Active   **Capacity:** 10 000 000 litres

Address: Carron, Banffshire AB38 7QP

Website: -   **Tel:** -

One of the newest distilleries in Scotland, and one of the most beautiful, has been built on the site of the former Imperial distillery.

Imperial distillery was founded in 1897, the year of Queen Victoria's Diamond Jubilee and on the top of the roof there was even a large cast iron crown to mark the occasion. The founder was Thomas Mackenzie who at the time already owned Dailuaine and Talisker. The timing was not the best though. One year after the opening, the Pattison crash brought the whisky industry to its knees and the distillery was forced to close. Eventually it came into the hands of DCL who owned it from 1916 until 2005, when Chivas Brothers took over. It was out of production for 60% of the time until 1998 when it was mothballed. The owners probably never planned to use it for distillation again as it was put up for sale in 2005 to become available as residential flats. Soon after, it was withdrawn from the market and, in

2012, a decision was taken to tear down the old distillery and build a new. Demolition of the old distillery began in 2013 and by the end of that year, nothing was left, except for the old warehouses.

Construction on the new Dalmunach distillery started in 2013 and it was commissioned in October 2014. The exceptional and stunning distillery is equipped with an efficient (4 hour mash) 13 ton Briggs full lauter mash tun and 16 stainless steel washbacks charged with 56,000 litres and with a fermentation time of 56-62 hours. There are four pairs of stills of a considerable size – wash stills 28,000 litres and spirits stills 18,000. They are all positioned in a circle with a hexagonal spirit safe in the middle. The distillery, which cost £25m to build, is the company's most ennergy efficient distillery and uses 38% less energy and 15% less water than the industry average. In autumn 2019, the first official release of Dalmunach single malt appeared – a 4 year old bottled at cask strength.

Dornoch

[dor•nock]

Owner: Thompson Bros Distillers   **Region/district:** Northern Highlands

Founded: 2016   **Status:** Active   **Capacity:** 30 000 litres

Address: Castle Street, Dornoch, Sutherland, IV25 3 SD

Website: thompsonbrosdistillers.com   **Tel:** 01862 810 216

Along with their parents, Phil and Simon Thompson have been running the Dornoch Castle Hotel in Sutherland for many years.

The hotel is famous for its outstanding whisky bar and the two brothers are passionate about whisky and other spirits. So passionate in fact that they decided to convert a 135-year old fire station into a distillery. The building is only 47 square metres and the brothers have struggled to fit all the equipment into the limited space. Currently, the distillery is equipped with a 300 kg stainless steel, semi-lauter mash tun from China, six washbacks made of oak with a minimum fermentation time of seven days, a 1,000 litre wash still and a 600 litre spirit still. Both stills, made by Hoga in Portugal, have shell and tube condensers. The stills are directly fired using gas but they are also equipped with steam coils as an alternative heating method. There is also a 2,000 litre still with a column from Holland for

the production of gin and other spirits. The distillery has a yearly capacity of 30,000 litres of pure alcohol of which approximately 15,000 litres are dedicated to whisky. The first distillation was gin in October 2016 and the first cask with whisky-to-be was filled 5th July 2017. A range of experimental batches of the gin were released during spring 2017 and in November the same year, the brothers finally launched their key expression - Thompson Bros Organic Highland Gin. Since then, and inspired by a trip to Japan, they have also released a very limited volume of new make spirit and in autumn 2020 it was time for their first single malt release.

Their interest in "old-style" whiskies produced in the 1960s and earlier also has an influence on the production. All the barley is floor malted, often using old heritage varieties, predominantly Plumage Archer and Maris Otter, and different strains of brewer's yeast is used instead of distiller's yeast.

Eden Mill

[eden mill]

Owner: Paul Miller

Region/district: Lowlands

Founded: 2014

Status: Active (vc)

Capacity: 100 000 litres

Address: St Andrews, Fife, KY16 0UU

Website: edenmill.com

Tel: 01334 834038

In 2012, Paul Miller, the former Molson Coors Sales Director, with a background in the whisky industry, opened up the successful Eden Brewery in Guardbridge, west of St Andrews.

The site was an old paper mill and only 50 metres away, there was a distillery called Seggie which was operative between 1810 and 1860 and owned by the Haig family. As an extension of the brewery, Paul decided to build a distillery called Eden Mill Distillery. The distillery, with a capacity of 80,000 litres per year, mainly produces malt whisky, but gin is also on the map. The distillery is equipped with two wash stills and one spirit still of the alembic type. Made by Hoga in Portugal, all three stills are of the same size – 1,000 litres. Eden Mill is the first combined brewery and distillery in Scotland. The brewery/distillery also has a visitor centre which already attracts 25,000 visitors a year.

Whisky production started in 2014 and the first release of a single malt appeared in 2018. Matured in a combination of French virgin oak, American virgin oak, and Pedro Ximenez casks it sold out instantly. The latest release from 2019 included spirit made from chocolate malt and crystal malt and had been matured in a combination of oloroso, PX and ex-bourbon barrels. Meanwhile a series of seven different 20cl bottlings called the Hip Flask Series has been launched. All of them had been made from different mash-bills and had matured in different types of casks.

In 2018, the owners announced that they had plans to move the entire operation to another building on the same site. As a part of an £8m investment programme, £3.1m has been set aside for an expansion of the production side of the distillery. The new set-up will increase the whisky capacity to 200,000 lpa per year and it is said to become the first carbon neutral distillery in Scotland. The plan is to be up and running end of 2020.

Glasgow

[glas•go]

Owner: Liam Hughes, Ian McDougall

Region/district: Lowlands

Founded: 2015

Status: Active

Capacity: 500 000 litres

Address: Deanside Rd, Hillington, Glasgow G52 4XB

Website: glasgowdistillery.com

Tel: 0141 4047191

When Glasgow Distillery was opened in Hillington Business Park, it became the first new whisky distillery in Glasgow in modern times.

There were stills within the Strathclyde grain distillery producing the malt whisky Kinclaith from 1958-1975 but Liam Hughes, Mike Hayward and Ian McDougall had the intention of building the first proper malt distillery in Glasgow in more than hundred years. Backed up by Asian investors, the distillery was ready to start production in February 2015.

The first distillation of whisky was unpeated but since then peated spirit (50ppm) is also part of the production and since January 2017, triple distillation is also practised one month per year. The distillery is equipped with a one ton mash tun, 14 wash backs (5,400 litres each) with a minimum fermentation of 72 hours, two 2,500 litre wash still,

two 1,400 litre spirit still and one 450 litre gin still - all from Firma Carl in Germany. Two of the stills and seven of the washbacks were installed as late as in November 2019 doubling the capacity to 500,000 litres.

The first product to be bottled was the Makar gin which now exists in several versions. The owners have also bottled old, sourced single malts under the name Prometheus. The fourth and final release in January 2020 was a 30 year old. The first single malt from their own production appeared in June 2018. Aged in ex-bourbon barrels and finished in virgin oak, the whisky was called 1770 Glasgow Single Malt, named after Glasgow's first distillery which was founded at Dundashill in 1770. This was followed by a second edition in spring 2019. The 1770 peated version, matured in ex-sherry butts with a finish in virgin oak was launched in September 2019 with a triple distilled expression released in May 2020.

GlenWyvis

[glen•wivis]

Owner:
GlenWyvis Distillery Ltd.

Region/district:
Highlands

Founded: 2017
Status: Active (vc)
Capacity: 140 000 litres

Address: Upper Docharty, Dingwall IV15 9UF

Website:
glenwyvis.com

Tel:
01349 862005

In 2015, the local farmer John McKenzie, came up with the idea to establish a distillery that was owned by the local people – the first ever 100% community-owned distillery.

A planning application was submitted to the local council in March 2016 and by summer more than £2.5 million had been raised via a community share offer with more than 3,000 people investing. Construction started in January 2017 and later that year, the owners managed to hire one of the most experienced distillers in Scotland as the manager – Duncan Tait – who over the years had been managing several of the Diageo distilleries. In August 2020, Tait left the company to pursue a new career. The first distillation was on the 30th of January 2018 and the production goal for 2020 is to do 35,000 litres of pure alcohol.

The distillery is equipped with a 0.5 ton semi lauter mash tun, six washbacks (4,400 litres each) made of stainless steel with a fermentation time of 96-144 hours, one 2,500 litre wash still and one 1,700 litre spirit still. In October 2019 there was a fire in the distillery´s woodchip store and even though the fire was contained to a small area, it took until March 2020 before they were producing again.

The unpeated spirit, which is mainly filled into American oak, is matured in dunnage warehouse on site. The style of the newmake is a combination o fruity and green/grassy and in November 2019 it was released for sale. A dedicated 400 litre gin still was installed in spring 2018 and the distillery has three types of gin for sale; Good Will Gin, Quercus Alba (matured in bourbon casks) and a recently released third expression matured in first fill oloroso casks.

The distillery is located in Dingwall, north of Inverness but this is not the first distillery in the town. In 1879, Ben Wyvis was founded and it went on producing until 1926 when it was closed.

Harris

[har•ris]

Owner:
Isle of Harris Distillers Ltd.

Region/district:
Highlands (Isle of Harris)

Founded: 2015
Status: Active (vc)
Capacity: 399 000 litres

Address: Tarbert, Isle of Harris,
Na h-Eileanan an Iar HS3 3DJ

Website:
harrisdistillery.com

Tel:
01859 502212

More than ten years ago, Anderson Bakewell had conjured up an idea to build a distillery on the Isle of Harris.

Joining Bakewell, who had been connected to the island for more than 40 years, was Simon Erlanger, a former marketing director for Glenmorangie and now the MD of the new distillery. Construction started in 2014 and the distillery came into production in September 2015. The total cost for the whole project was £11.4m. The distillery, located in Tarbert, was the second distillery after Abhainn Dearg on Lewis to be located in the Outer Hebrides.

The first spirit to be distilled in September 2015 was gin and this was followed by whisky in December. The gin has already been released and apart from traditional botanicals, local ingredients are also used such as sugar kelp.

The equipment consists of a 1.2 tonne semi lauter mash tun made of stainless steel but clad with American oak and 8 washbacks made of Oregon pine with a fermentation time of 72-96 hours. There are also one 7,000 litre wash still and a 5,000 litre spirit still - both with descending lyne arms and made in Italy. From 2016 to 2019, the production increased from 5 to 9 mashes per week and a total of 180,000 litres and that was the initial target also for 2020. The style of the whisky, which will be called Hearach (the Gaelic word for a person living on Harris), will be medium peated with a phenol specification in the barley of 12-14ppm although they have also distilled a few batches of heavily peated malt (30ppm) made with local peat.

Together with three other distilleries (Talisker and Torabhaig on Skye and Isle of Raasay), Harris distillery launched a new whisky route called Hebridean Whisky Trail in August 2018 – www.hebrideanwhisky.com. In 2019, the distillery had no less than 100,000 visitors!

Holyrood

[holly•rude]

Owner:
The Holyrood Distillery Ltd.

Region/district:
Lowlands

Founded: 2019   **Status:** Active (vc)

Capacity: 250 000 litres

Address: 19 St Leonard´s Lane, Edinburgh EH8 9SH

Website:
holyrooddistillery.co.uk

Tel:
0131 2858977

Whether or not it was a deliberate race with other whisky companies, Holyrood eventually became the first whisky distillery for almost 100 years to open up in Edinburgh.

Planning permission was granted in 2016, construction work commenced two years later and in summer 2019 the production started. Behind the project lie whisky veteran David Robertson (ex Macallan master distiller) and the Canadian couple Kelly and Rob Carpenter who together with 60 other investors managed to raise the £7.3m needed for the project. The distillery is located in a listed building from 1835 and as Distillery Manager the company has hired Jack Mayo who used to work for Glasgow Whisky Company. In July 2019 the distillery opened to the public.

The owners are working on five core whisky styles; Floral where wine yeast has been used, with a small spirit cut and

maturing in American and virgin oak, Fruity using three types of yeast and maturing in American oak, ex-wine and ex-sherry casks, Sweet including speciality malt and a mix of yeast and maturation in American oak, Spicy where, again, a mix of yeast (brewers and distillers) are used and maturation takes place in European ex-sherry and finally Smoky where peated newmake is filled into American and European oak. Apart from whisky, the distillery also produces other sprits including gin.

The distillery is equipped with a one ton semi-lauter mash tun and six 5,000 litre washbacks made of stainless steel with a fermentation time of 48-168 hours depending on the style they're making. There are one 5,000 litre wash still and one 3,750 litre spirit still – the latter equipped with a purifier with a water jacket and which, uniquely, can also be charged with liquid to use as a retort tank. Foreshots vary from 6 to 30 minutes, also depending on the spirit style.

InchDairnie

[inch•dairnie]

Owner:
John Fergus & Co. Ltd

Region/district:
Lowlands

Founded: 2015   **Status:** Active

Capacity: 2 000 000 litres

Address: Whitecraigs Rd, Glenrothes, Fife KY6 2RX

Website:
inchdairniedistillery.com

Tel:
01595 510010

For InchDairnie´s distillery manager Ian Palmer there are three key words that govern operation – flavour, innovation and experimentation.

Opened in May 2016, a few miles west of Glenrothes in Fife, the distillery has a capacity of two million litres per year with a possibility of expanding to four million. It is owned by John Fergus & Co. which was founded by Ian Palmer, who has more than 40 years of experience in the Scotch whisky industry, in 2011. Palmer's unorthodox ideas start already with the equipment. The distillery has a hammer mill and a Meura mash filter, instead of a traditional mash tun. There are four washbacks with a fermentation time of 72 hours and one pair of traditional pot stills with double condensers and after-coolers to increase the copper to spirit ratio. The two stills are complemented by a Lomond still with six plates to provide the opportunity for

triple and experimental distillation. A unique yeast recipe is used and high gravity fermentation will create a fruitier character of the newmake. Furthermore, Palmer is working with both the standard spring barley as well as winter barley to give the possibility for a broader palette of flavours.

And it does not stop at that. In November 2017, it was revealed that the distillery was working on a rye whisky which will be called RyeLaw and for the past two years a peated spirit has been distilled which will be named KinGlassie once bottled in 6-8 years from now. These two, together with InchDairnie single malt will form the core range going forward. In June 2019, the first distillation of a whisky made from oat was made. This was the first time in over a century that whisky made from oat was produced in Scotland. Two main styles of whisky are produced. Strathenry (80% of the production both unpeated and peated) will be used for blended whisky while InchDairnie will be sold as a single malt.

Isle of Raasay

[ajl ov rassay]

Owner:
R&B Distillers

Region/district:
Highlands (Raasay)

Founded: **Status:** **Capacity:**
2017 Active (vc) 200 000 litres

Address: Borodale House, Raasay, By Kyle IV40 8PB

Website: **Tel:**
rbdistillers.com 01478 470177

The owners, R&B Distillers, were working on establishing a distillery in The Borders when a new plan surfaced – to build a distillery on the small island of Raasay, east of Skye.

Alasdair Day, with an ancestral interest in Scotch whisky, teamed up with entrepreneur Bill Dobbie and bought Borodale House. With more buildings added for the whisky production, the old Victorian house is now the hotel part of the distillery. With a stunning view towards the Cuillin Mountains on the Isle of Skye, this is now an excellent way of spending a night on Raasay.

The distillery started production in September 2017 and is equipped with a one ton mash tun and six stainless steel (5,000 litre) washbacks with cooling jackets currently with four short fermentations (67 hours) and six long (118 hours) adding up to 192,000 litres of alcohol. The 5,000

litre wash still has a cooling jacket around the lyne arm and there's also a 3,600 litre spirit still with a copper column attached should they want to use it for special runs. The production is a combination of peated (45 ppm) and un-peated spirit. two more warehouses (one dunnage and one palletised) were added in 2019 with the original warehouse now being used for cask filling and bottling.

Meanwhile, the distillery is also working on growing their own barley on the island. So far they've tried four different grains – the classic Golden Promise and three different Scandinavian types including a 6-row barley named Brage.

A wide variety of casks are used for maturation. The inaugural, lightly peated release in November 2020 was matured for two years in first fill bourbon and another year in Bordeaux red wine casks while the core range (available from April 2021) will be a combination including heavily charred *muehlenbergi* American oak, Bordeaux wine casks, ex-rye whiskey casks and virgin oak.

Kingsbarns

[kings•barns]

Owner:
Wemyss family

Region/district:
Lowlands

Founded: **Status:** **Capacity:**
2014 Active (vc) 600 000 litres

Address: East Newhall Farm, Kingsbarns, St Andrews KY16 8QE

Website: **Tel:**
kingsbarnsdistillery.com 01333 451300

The plans for this distillery near St Andrews in Fife, were drafted in 2008 and came to fruition in 2014 when the distillery was opened.

The idea was to restore a derelict farm-steading from the late 18th century and turn it into a modern distillery. Planning permission was received in March 2011 and in 2012, the Scottish government awarded a grant of £670,000. This, in turn, led to the Wemyss family agreeing to inject £3m into the project and becoming the new owners. The company owns and operates the independent bottling company, Wemyss Malts, and also owns other companies in the field of wine and gin.

The distillery is equipped with a 1.5 ton stainless steel mash tun, four 7,500 litre stainless steel washbacks with a fermentation time of 72-120 hours, one 7,500 litre wash still and one 4,500 litre spirit still. A slow distillation and

an early cut are important to achieve the fruity character. Mainly first fill bourbon barrels are used for maturation together with STR casks (wine barriques that have been shaved, toasted and re-charred). The first casks were filled in March 2015 and the current yearly production is 200,000 litres of alcohol.

The first release of Kingsbarns single malt was in 2018 when a limited number of bottles were made available to the members of the Founder's Club. Their first generally available malt, Dream to Dram, was a vatting of 90% ex-bourbon casks and 10% STR red wine barriques and was released in January 2019. In summer 2020 a cask strength version named Family Reserve was released and this was followed in November by the 6 year old Founder's Reserve 2020, the 6 year old Distillery Reserve 2020 with a full maturation in STR casks and the 5 year old Sherry Matured which will become part of the core range going forward.

Lagg

[laag]

Owner:
Isle of Arran Distillers Ltd.

Region/district:
Islands

Founded: 2019
Status: Active (vc)
Capacity: 750 000 litres

Address: Kilmory, Isle of Arran KA27 8PG

Website:
laggwhisky.com
Tel:
01770 870565

The success for Arran distillery, which was opened in 1993, encouraged the owners to open yet another distillery on the island. Work on Lagg distillery began in February 2017 and the first distillation took place in March 2019.

With Arran distillery (now renamed Lochranza) located in the village with the same name on the northern tip of the island, Lagg is situated in the south. Already now, Lochranza is by far the most visited distillery in Scotland with more than 100,000 visitors last year and the owners anticipate that the combined distilleries will see more than 200,000 visitors in a couple of years. For those wanting to do more than just visiting the distillery, there is the possibility of buying entire casks for future bottling.

The distillery is equipped with a four ton semilauter mash tun, four Oregon pine washbacks holding 20,000 litres and with a fermentation time of 72 hours, one wash still (10,000 litres) and one spirit still (7,000 litres). However, there is space for an additional four washbacks and one more pair of stills in the future. All of Arran Distillers´ peated production has now moved from Lochranza to Lagg who uses barley with a phenol specification of 50ppm. The peat used to dry the barley is sourced from different places in Scotland and also from abroad. This is part of the owners ambition to explore the impact of terroir on whisky flavour. Also, Lagg will act as an experimental plant with trials of different yeast strains and types of barley and they have plans to produce their own cider and apple brandy in the future. In spring 2020, newmake from both Lochranza and Lagg were vatted together to eventullay become an Arran blended malt.

The distillery manager for Lagg is Graham Omand, raised on Islay and working as a stillman and mashman at Arran for nearly a decade.

Lindores Abbey

[linn•doors aebi]

Owner:
The Lindores Distilling Co.

Region/district:
Lowlands

Founded: 2017
Status: Active (vc)
Capacity: 225 000 litres

Address: Lindores Abbey House, Abbey Road, Newburgh, Fife KY14 6HH

Website:
lindoresabbeydistillery.com
Tel:
01337 842547

The famous, first written record of whisky was a letter to Friar John Cor, a monk at the Abbey of Lindores, dated 1494 where, by order of King James IV, he was instructed to make "aqua vitae, VIII bolls of malt".

The archeologial and historical evidence for Lindores being the birthplace of Scotch whisky are by no way inconclusive but further excavations of the site may reveal some evidence. Be that as it may, the current owners of the abbey in ruins are Drew and Helen McKenzie Smith and in December 2017 they commissioned a distillery next to the old monastery. The location is stunning and with all the production equipment on one level you have a spectacular view of the surroundings. Behind the washbacks you catch a glimpse of Dundee and from the stills you look down on the abbey ruins with the river Tayne in the background.

Lindores Abbey is one of few producers of a single estate whisky in Scotland. Starting in 2020, all the barley used has been grown in surrounding fields which were under the original ownership of the abbey back in the 15th century. The equipment consists of a 2 ton semi lauter mash tun with a copper lid, four Douglas fir washbacks with a fermentation time between 90 and 115 hours, one 10,000 litre wash still and two 3,500 litre spirit stills. The foreshots are 15-20 minutes and the spirit cut starts at 75% and goes down to 67%. The production goal for 2020 was five mashes per week and 187,500 litres of pure alcohol and during the year, the owners started experimenting with different yeasts and malts. The forthcoming style of the whisky will be light and fruity

An excellent visitor centre with a wide range of activities, including whisky and champagne afternoon teas and an apothecary experience is also a part of the distillery.

Nc'nean

[nook•knee•anne]

Owner:		**Region/district:**
Nc'nean Distillery Ltd.		Western Highlands
Founded:	**Status:**	**Capacity:**
2017	Active (vc)	100 000 litres
Address: Drimnin, By Lochaline PA80 5XZ		
Website:		**Tel:**
ncnean.com		01967 421698

Standing in Tobermory on Mull, you can actually see the distillery on the Morvern peninsula. It's a mere 20 minute trip across the sound but boat connections are very intermittent.

Instead, if you travel from Mull, you have to take the ferry from Fishnish to Lochaline and then drive for 45 minutes to reach the distillery. The reward when you arrive, however, is gratifying. Beautifully situated on the Drimnin estate, the distillery has an astounding view towards Mull. The estate was bought by Derek and Louise Lewis in 2001 and their, daughter, Annabel Thomas, is the founder of the distillery.

One of the fundamentals when it was built was to make it as sustainable as possible. A boiler, fired by wood chips, was brought in from Germany. The ashes from the boiler is used to fertilise the distillery garden. The barley is Scottish and certified organic and the waste heat is recycled through the temperature-controlled warehouse. The distillery came

on stream in March 2017 and is equipped with a one ton semi lauter mash tun. Trials with different types of yeast (champagne, red wine, etc.) to create different flavour profiles is part of the work. There are four stainless steel washbacks and the fermentation time is between 65 and 115 hours. Furthermore there is a 5,000 litre wash still and a 3,500 litre spirit still, both with slightly descending lyne arms and sub coolers. The owner is working on two basic recipes of fruity whisky – "new style" to be enjoyed young and "old style", with lower cut points and destined for a longer maturation. The plan for 2020 is to do five mashes per week and 94,000 litres of pure alcohol.

A botanical spirit including wild herbs and flowers foraged from the surroundings of the distillery, was launched in autumn 2018. The first single malt, Ainnir, matured in red wine and American bourbon barrels, was released in September 2020. In March 2020, a funding of more than €1.9 million was secured to help with the continued growth as well as buying bottling equipment.

Roseisle

[rose•eyel]

Owner:		**Region/district:**
Diageo		Speyside
Founded:	**Status:**	**Capacity:**
2009	Active	12 500 000 litres
Address: Roseisle, Morayshire IV30 5YP		
Website:		**Tel:**
-		01343 832100

Roseisle distillery is located on the same site as the already existing Roseisle maltings just west of Elgin. The distillery has won several awards for its ambition towards sustainable production.

The distillery is equipped with two stainless steel, full lauter mash tuns with a 12.5 tonne charge each. There are 14 huge (112,000 litres) stainless steel washbacks and 14 stills with the wash stills being heated by external heat exchangers while the spirit stills are heated using steam coils. The spirit vapours are cooled through copper condensers but on three spirit stills and three wash stills there are also stainless steel condensers attached, that you can switch to for a more sulphury spirit. The fermentation time for a Speyside style of whisky is 90-100 hours and for a heavier style it is 50-60 hours. The plan for 2020 is to do 23 mashes per week and a total of 12 million litres of alcohol.

The total cost for the distillery was £40m and how to use the hot water in an efficient way was very much a focal point from the beginning. For example, Roseisle is connected by means of two long pipes with Burghead maltings, 3 km north of the distillery. Hot water is pumped from Roseisle and then used in the seven kilns at Burghead and cold water is then pumped back to Roseisle. The pot ale from the distillation will be piped into anaerobic fermenters to be transformed into biogas and the dried solids will act as a biomass fuel source. The biomass burner on the site, producing steam for the distillery, covers 72% of the total requirement. Furthermore, green technology has reduced the emission of carbon dioxide to only 15% of an ordinary, same-sized distillery.

Destined to be used for blends, Roseisle single malt was in autumn 2017, for the first time used in a different role. It was part of the blended malt Collectivum XXVIII where Diageo had used whiskies from all 28 malt distilleries.

Strathearn

[strath•earn]

Owner:
Douglas Laing

Region/district:
Southern Highlands

Founded: **Status:**
2013   Active

Capacity:
c 30 000 litres

Address: Bachilton Farm Steading, Methven PH1 3QX

Website:
strathearndistillery.com

Tel:
01738 840 100

A surprising announcement was made in autumn 2019 that the independent bottler Douglas Laing had bought Strathearn distillery.

It was surprising because at the same time Douglas Laing is working on establishing their own Clutha Distillery on the banks of Clyde in Glasgow. The brainchild of Tony Reeman-Clark, Strathearn, which is situated a couple of miles west of Methven near Perth, was one of the pioneers of Scottish craft distilling. Gin production was started in August 2013 and the first whisky was filled into casks in October that year. The distillery began by using Maris Otter barley which was abandoned by other distillers years ago due to the low yield. Reeman-Clark preferred it though, because of the flavours that it contributes.

All the equipment is fitted into one room and consists of a stainless steel mash tun, two stainless steel washbacks with a fermentation time of 4-5 days, one 1,000 litre wash still and a 500 litre spirit still. Both stills are of the Alambic type with vertical tube copper condensers. The new owners have plans to install more equipment raising the capacity to 200,000 litres. Both peated (35ppm) and un-peated whisky is produced. The distillery has also been experimenting with other types of wood like chestnut, mullberry and cherry. and in order to apply with the SWA rules it was sold as Uisge Beatha, the ancient name for Scotch, rather than whisky

The first single malt Scotch from the distillery was released in December 2016 and when Douglas Laing took over, a version called Batch 001, matured in a combination of virgin European oak and first fill oloroso was launched. The whisky had been distilled in 2013 and 2014 then aged in a combination of European oak and ex-sherry and bottled at 46,6% without chill filtration. Several gins have also been released over the years with Scottish Gin and Heather Rose being the big sellers.

Torabhaig

[tor•a•vaig]

Owner:
Mossburn Distillers

Region/district:
Highlands (Skye)

Founded: **Status:**
2016   Active (vc)

Capacity:
500 000 litres

Address: Teangue, Sleat, Isle of Skye IV44 8RE

Website:
torabhaig.com

Tel:
01471 833447

The idea to build a second distillery on Skye (with Talisker being the first) was presented several years ago by the late Sir Iain Noble.

When he died in 2010, Mossburn Distillers took over and finalised the plans for a distillery. Located in a farmstead from the 1820s, the owners meticulously restored some of the buildings and added new ones in the same style resulting in a distillery with a grand view across the sea to the mainland. Production started in January 2017 and, in March 2018, a visitor centre opened, attracting 12,000 people in its first year.

The entire set of production equipment is situated on one level with a 1.5 ton stainless steel semi lauter mash tun with a copper top. There are eight washbacks made of Douglas fir (10,000 litres) with a fermentation time between 80 and 120 hours, one 8,000 litre wash still and one 5,000 litre spirit still. The production plan for 2020, at least before the corona virus, is 400,000 litres of pure alcohol. The owners produce a heavily peated whisky with a phenol specification of up to 75ppm in the malted barley although coming off spirit at 63%, they are not looking to catch the heaviest phenols. The first single malt from the distillery, 2017. The Legacy Series, was supposed to be released in autumn 2020 but due to the pandemic, it was delayed to February 2021. Made from heavily peated barley (55-60ppm) it had matured in first fill bourbon barrels.

In order to open up for innovation and experiments, an interesting program has been implemented at the distillery called The Journeyman Projects. Different distillers on site are given the chance to create their own designed spirit for a month each. That means laborating with different yeasts and malts but also experimenting with fermentation times, distillation itself and maturation. The only ground rule is – stay within SWA regulations and don´t replicate the standard distillery runs.

Wolfburn

[wolf•burn]

Owner:
Aurora Brewing Ltd.

Region/district:
Northern Highlands

Founded: **Status:**
2013   Active (vc)

Capacity:
135 000 litres

Address: Henderson Park, Thurso,
Caithness KW14 7XW

Website:
wolfburn.com

Tel:
01847 891051

The most northerly distillery on the Scottish mainland, Wolfburn, is situated in an industrial area on the outskirts of Thurso.

The owners have chosen a site that is situated 350 metres from the ruins of the old Wolfburn Distillery. Construction work commenced in August 2012 and the first newmake came off the stills at the end of January 2013. The distillery is equipped with a 1.1 ton semi-lauter stainless steel mash tun with a copper canopy, four stainless steel washbacks with a fermentation time of 70-92 hours, holding 5,500 litres each, one wash still (5,500 litres) and one spirit still (3,600 litres). Wolfburn uses a mix of casks: ex-bourbon quarter casks, ex-bourbon hogsheads as well as barrels and ex-sherry butts.

The main part (80%) of the malt is unpeated but since 2014, a lightly peated (10 ppm) spirit has also been produced. The inaugural bottling from the distillery appeared in early 2016 and had a smoky profile due to the fact that it

had partly been matured in quarter casks from Islay. This limited release was followed by a more widely available bourbon matured whisky which in September 2016 was re-named Northland. At the same time a second bottling appeared, Aurora, which had been partly matured in oloroso sherry casks. The core range was expanded in 2017 with Morven, the distillery's first peated whisky and currently their biggest seller, and September 2018 saw the fourth expression being released - Langskip, matured in ex-bourbon barrels and bottled at 58%. A range of limited bottlings started in 2017 with the lightly peated Batch 128 and was followed in 2018 by the unpeated Batch 270, in spring 2019 by Batch 375 and in February 2020 by Batch 155 with a maturation for almost five years in first fill bourbon and another six months in port hogsheads. Another limited range is Kylver where batch 6 (Kaunaz) was released in April 2020. In August 2020 the lightly peated 5 year old From the Stills, the yearly summer edition, was released together with a limited edition for the Mey Highland Games.

Wolfburn From the Stills, Ardnamurchan AD/09.20:01, Nc'Nean Ainnir and Torabhaig 2017 Legacy Series
- the last three are the inaugural single malt releases from the respective distilleries.

Active distilleries per owner

Diageo
Auchroisk
Benrinnes
Blair Athol
Caol Ila
Cardhu
Clynelish
Cragganmore
Dailuaine
Dalwhinnie
Dufftown
Glendullan
Glen Elgin
Glenkinchie
Glenlossie
Glen Ord
Glen Spey
Inchgower
Knockando
Lagavulin
Linkwood
Mannochmore
Mortlach
Oban
Roseisle
Royal Lochnagar
Strathmill
Talisker
Teaninich

Pernod Ricard
Aberlour
Allt-a-Bhainne
Braeval
Dalmunach
Glenburgie
Glen Keith
Glenlivet
Glentauchers
Longmorn
Miltonduff
Scapa
Strathisla
Tormore

Edrington Group
Glenrothes
Highland Park
Macallan

Inver House (Thai Beverage)
Balblair
Balmenach
Knockdhu
Pulteney
Speyburn

John Dewar & Sons (Bacardi)
Aberfeldy
Aultmore
Craigellachie
Macduff
Royal Brackla

William Grant & Sons
Ailsa Bay
Balvenie
Glenfiddich
Kininvie

Whyte & Mackay (Emperador)
Dalmore
Fettercairn

Jura
Tamnavulin

Beam Suntory
Ardmore
Auchentoshan
Bowmore
Glen Garioch
Laphroaig

Distell International
Bunnahabhain
Deanston
Tobermory

Benriach Dist. Co. (Brown Forman)
Benriach
Glendronach
Glenglassaugh

Loch Lomond Group
Glen Scotia
Loch Lomond

J & A Mitchell
Glengyle
Springbank

Glenmorangie Co. (LVMH)
Ardbeg
Glenmorangie

Angus Dundee Distillers
Glencadam
Tomintoul

Ian Macleod Distillers
Glengoyne
Tamdhu

Campari Group
Glen Grant

Isle of Arran Distillers
Lagg
Lochranza

Signatory
Edradour

Tomatin Distillery Co.
Tomatin

J & G Grant
Glenfarclas

Rémy Cointreau
Bruichladdich

David Prior
Bladnoch

Gordon & MacPhail
Benromach

La Martiniquaise
Glen Moray

Ben Nevis Distillery Ltd (Nikka)
Ben Nevis

Picard Vins & Spiritueux
Tullibardine

Harvey's of Edinburgh
Speyside

Kilchoman Distillery Co.
Kilchoman

Cuthbert family
Daftmill

Mark Tayburn
Abhainn Dearg

Aurora Brewing Ltd
Wolfburn

Douglas Laing
Strathearn

Annandale Distillery Co.
Annandale

Adelphi Distillery Co.
Ardnamurchan

Wemyss
Kingsbarns

Mcpherson-Grant family
Ballindalloch

Paul Miller
Eden Mill

Isle of Harris Distillers
Harris

The Glasgow Distillery Company
Glasgow Distillery

John Fegus & Co. Ltd
Inchdairnie

Stirling family
Arbikie

Brewdog plc
Brew Dog Distillery

Thompson family
Dornoch

Mossburn Distillers
Torabhaig

R & B Distillers
Isle of Raasay

The Lindores Distilling Company
Lindores Abbey

Morrison Glasgow Distillers
Clydeside

Nc'nean Distillery Ltd.
Nc'nean

The Three Stills Co.
The Borders

The Glenallachie Distillers Co.
Glenallachie

The Perth Distilling Company
Aberargie

GlenWyvis Distillery Ltd.
GlenWyvis

Hunter Laing
Ardnahoe

The Holyrood Distillery Ltd.
Holyrood

Greenwood Distillers
Ardross

Lalique Group/Hansjörg Wyss
Glenturret

John Crabbie & Co.
Bonnington

Glenlochy Distillery, closed in 1983 and now demolished

Closed
distilleries

The distilleries on the following pages
have all been closed and some of them even demolished.
One is tempted to say that none of them will ever produce again
but three - Brora, Port Ellen and Rosebank - are actually being re-opened
within the next year or two. As for the rest, the best chances of
finding new bottlings from old stock are probably Caperdonich,
Convalmore, Dallas Dhu, Imperial, Littlemill and Pittyvaich.
There are also a couple of fairly recent releases from
Lochside and North Port. Old bottlings from the others
show up at whisky auctions from time to time
but few, if any, casks remain.

Brora

[bro•rah]

Owner: Diageo
Region/district: Northern Highlands

Founded: 1819
Status: Closed
Capacity: 800,000 litres

Address: Brora, Sutherland KW9 6LR

Of the two Diageo distilleries about to be reopened, Brora will most probably be the first with Port Ellen to follow suit. Planning approval was received from the Highland Council in October 2018 and soon after the work began.

Many of the original buildings can be used as they are but the stillhouse will be demolished and rebuilt brick for brick. The original two stills were in fairly good condition but were sent to Diageo's Abercrombie coppersmiths in Alloa for inspection and refurbishing. Other equipment that was still in place after 35 years was the feints receiver, the spirit receiver and the brass safe. With a capacity of 800,000 litres of alcohol, the plan is to start production at Brora sometime in 2021.

The distillery was built by the Marquis of Stafford who founded it in 1819 and named it Clynelish. The distillery had a chequered history until 1896 when the brewer and whisky broker James Ainslie assumed ownership. He rebuilt the distillery and soon Clynelish single malt enjoyed a good reputation among blenders. In 1967 the owners, DCL, decided to build a new, modern distillery on the same site. This was given the name Clynelish and it was decided the old distillery, with a capacity of 1 million litres of alcohol, should be closed. Shortly after, the demand for peated whisky, especially for the blend Johnnie Walker, increased and the old site re-opened but now under the name Brora and the "recipe" for the whisky was changed to a heavily peated malt.

Brora was closed in 1983 and from 1995 United Distillers regularly released different expressions of Brora in the Rare Malts series. In 2002 a new range was created, Special Releases, and bottlings of Brora appeared yearly in that series until 2018. The latest bottling, in August 2019, was a **40 year old** to celebrate the distillery's 200th anniversary. In October 2019, the most expensive Brora ever was sold at an auction. It was a **40 year old**, distilled in 1972 and released in 2014 at a price of £6,995. When it was sold by Sotheby's it fetched a price of £54,450.

History:

1819 The Marquis of Stafford, 1st Duke of Sutherland, founds the distillery as Clynelish Distillery.

1827 The first licensed distiller, James Harper, files for bankruptcy and John Matheson takes over.

1828 James Harper is back as licensee.

1833 Andrew Ross takes over the license.

1846 George Lawson & Sons takes over.

1896 James Ainslie & Heilbron takes over and rebuilds the facilities.

1912 Distillers Company Limited (DCL) takes over together with James Risk.

1925 DCL buys out Risk.

1930 Scottish Malt Distillers takes over.

1931 The distillery is mothballed.

1938 Production restarts.

1960 The distillery becomes electrified (until now it has been using locally mined coal from Brora).

1967 A new distillery is built adjacent to the first one, it is also named Clynelish and both operate in parallel from August with the new distillery named Clynelish A and the old Clynelish B.

1969 Clynelish B is closed in April but reopened shortly after as Brora and starts using a heavily peated malt until 1973.

1975 A new mashtun is installed.

1983 Brora is closed in March.

1995 Brora 1972 (20 years) and Brora 1972 (22 years) are launched as Rare Malts.

2002 A 30 year old is the first bottling in the Special Releases.

2014 The 13th release of Brora – a 35 year old.

2015 The 14th release of Brora – a 37 year old.

2016 The 15th release of Brora – a 38 year old.

2017 The 16th release of Brora - a 34 year old. Diageo announces that the distillery will re-open in 2020.

2019 A 40 year old is released and the reconstruction of the distillery begins.

40 years old

Port Ellen

[port ell•en]

Owner: Diageo

Region/district: Islay

Founded: 1825

Status: Dismantled

Capacity: -

Address: Port Ellen, Isle of Islay, Argyll PA42 7AJ

The announcement that Port Ellen and Brora distilleries would be reopened, came at the same time in autumn 2017 but while renovation on Brora started in early 2019, the owners did not receive an approval from the council for Port Ellen until December 2019.

Both distilleries stopped producing in 1983 but the main difference between the two is that no equipment remains at Port Ellen and very few of the buildings can be used. A new distillery will be built in the courtyard between the maltings and the old warehouses. The old drawings of the equipment still exist and one pair of stills with shell and tube condensers will be fabricated. There will also be a second, smaller pair with the intention of creating experimental whiskies. The distillery, with an 800,000 litre capacity should be up and running sometime in 2021 and will have a brand home as Diageo calls its visitor centres.

The founder of the distillery, Alexander Mackay, went bankrupt a few months after the distillery had opened and it was a relative of his, John Ramsay, who would run the distillery instead until the late 1800s and he did so with great success. There was no intention of ever bottling the spirit as a single malt – all the production went to blends. In 1930 the distillery was mothballed and didn't reopen until 1967. The final era would last but 16 years and in 1983 the distillery was closed for good (or so it would seem). At its height, Port Ellen was equipped with four stills, producing 1.7 million litres of alcohol.

Port Ellen single malt has been released twice in the Rare Malts range (1998 and 2000). It wasn't until 2001, when the first Port Ellen Special Release turned up that things started to change and the malt became a cult whisky. There is still some stock of old Port Ellen left but going forward, this will not be launched in the Special Releases as it used to be. However, a new range from Diageo, Untold Stories, appeared in spring 2019 with a **39 year old** as the inaugural release. This was followed up by a **40 year old** in 2020 together with another **40 year old** in the Prima & Ultima range. Both were distilled in 1979.

History:

1825 Alexander Kerr Mackay assisted by Walter Campbell founds the distillery. Mackay runs into financial troubles after a few months and his three relatives John Morrison, Patrick Thomson and George Maclennan take over.

1833 John Ramsay, a cousin to John Morrison, comes from Glasgow to take over.

1836 Ramsay is granted a lease on the distillery from the Laird of Islay.

1892 Ramsay dies and the distillery is inherited by his widow, Lucy.

1906 Lucy Ramsay dies and her son Captain Iain Ramsay takes over.

1920 Iain Ramsay sells to Buchanan-Dewar who transfers the administration to the company Port Ellen Distillery Co. Ltd.

1925 Buchanan-Dewar joins Distillers Company Limited (DCL).

1930 The distillery is mothballed.

1967 In production again after reconstruction and doubling of the number of stills from two to four.

1973 A large drum maltings is installed.

1980 Queen Elisabeth visits the distillery and a commemorative special bottling is made.

1983 The distillery is mothballed.

1987 The distillery closes permanently but the maltings continue to deliver malt to all Islay distilleries.

2001 Port Ellen cask strength first edition is released.

2014 The 14th release of Port Ellen - a 35 year old from 1978.

2015 The 15th release of Port Ellen - a 32 year old from 1983.

2016 The 16th release of Port Ellen - a 37 year old from 1978.

2017 The 17th release of Port Ellen - a 37 year old from 1979. Diageo announces that the distillery will re-open in 2020.

2019 A 39 year old is released as the first in a new range – Untold Stories.

2020 Two 40 year olds in the Untold Stories and Prima & Ultima range respectively are released.

40 years old

Rosebank

[rows•bank]

Owner:
Ian Macleod Distillers

Region/district:
Lowlands

Founded: 1840   **Status:** Closed

Capacity: 6-800,000 litres

Address: Falkirk FK1 4DS

Website: rosebank.com

Tel: -

Lovers of the elegant, triple distilled Lowland single malt from Rosebank have had their hopes for a long time that someone would come along och take pity on the closed distillery.

There were several interested parties over the years and there were even rumours that none less than Diageo would re-open it, but no change of state took place. Eventually, in autumn 2017, Ian Macleod (owners of Glengoyne and Tamdhu) bought the property from Scottish Canals, to whom Diageo had sold to in 2002, and acquired the trademark and stock from Diageo. In early 2019, they received planning permission from Falkirk council. Construction work started in December 2019 but stopped in March 2020 due to the covid pandemic. It was later resumed and the plan to open up early autumn 2021 has now been revised and it is more likely that distillation will start some time in 2022. The new distillery, with the iconic chimney being kept, will be equipped with three stills (for triple distillation) and wormtubs with a capacity to produce 1 million litres of pure alcohol per year. The cost for the project is estimated to be £12m.

Established in 1798, Rosebank single malt enjoyed a good reputation during most of its lifespan even though the distillery also produced its fair share of grain whisky which was common especially in the Lowlands at the time. Most of the production went into blends but in 1982, Rosebank 8 year old single malt became a part of the owners Ascot Malt Cellar range together with Lagavulin, Talisker and Linkwood. Six years later, The Classic Malts saw the light of day and when the owners were to decide which malt to represent the Lowlands, their choice was Glenkinchie.

The latest bottling of Rosebank from the previous owners was a 21 year old in the Special Releases autumn 2014. In February 2020, Ian Macleod released **two single casks**, both bottled at cask strength and distilled in 1993, the same year that the distillery closed.

History:

1840 James Rankine founds the distillery.

1845 The distillery is expanded.

1864 Rankine buys Camelon Distillery on the west bank of the Forth-Clyde canal.

1894 Rosebank Distillery Company is formed.

1914 Rosebank, togehter with Clydesdale, Glenkinchie, St. Magdalene and Grange form Scottish malt Distillers (SMD).

1919 SMD becomes a part of Distillers company Limited (DCL).

1982 DCL launches the series The Ascot Malt Cellar with Rosebank, Linkwood, Talisker, Lagavulin and two blendeed malts.

1993 The distillery closes in June.

2002 The buildings are bought by British Waterways.

2008 The stills and other equipment are stolen.

2014 A 21 year old is launched as part of the Special Releases.

2017 The site is bought from Scottish Canals by Ian Macleod Distillers and at the same time they acquire the trademark and stocks from Diageo.

2020 Two single casks distilled in 1993 are released.

1993 single cask

Banff

Owner:	Region:	Founded:	Status:
Diageo	Speyside	1824	Demolished

The distillery has a tragic history of numerous fires, explosions and bombings. The most spectacular incident was when a lone Junkers Ju-88 bombed one of the warehouses in 1941. The distillery was closed in 1983 and the buildings were destroyed in a fire in 1991.

Ben Wyvis

Owner:	Region:	Founded:	Status:
Whyte & Mackay	N Highlands	1965	Dismantled

Built on the same site as Invergordon grain distillery, the distillery was equipped with one mash tun, six washbacks and one pair of stills. The stills are in use today at Glengyle distillery. Production stopped in 1976 and in 1977 the distillery was closed and dismantled.

Caperdonich

Owner:	Region:	Founded:	Status:
Chivas Bros.	Speyside	1897	Demolished

Founded by the owners of Glen Grant. Five years after the opening, the distillery was shut down but was re-opened again in 1965 under the name Caperdonich. In 2002 it was mothballed yet again. Sold in 2010 to Forsyth´s in Rothes and the buildings were demolished.

Coleburn

Owner:	Region:	Founded:	Status:
Diageo	Speyside	1897	Dismantled

Coleburn was used as an experimental workshop where new production techniques were tested. In 1985 the distillery was mothballed and never opened again. Since 2014, the warehouses are used by Aceo Ltd, who owns the independent bottler Murray McDavid.

Convalmore

Owner:	Region:	Founded:	Status:
Diageo	Speyside	1894	Dismantled

This distillery is still intact and can be seen in Dufftown next to Balvenie distillery. The buildings are used by William Grant´s for storage while Diageo still holds the rights to the brand. In the early 20th century, distilling of malt whisky in continuous stills took place. Closed in 1985.

Dallas Dhu

Owner:	Region:	Founded:	Status:
Diageo	Speyside	1898	Closed

The distillery is still intact, equipment and all, but hasn´t produced since 1983. Today it is run by Historic Scotland as a museum which is open all year round. In 2013 a feasibility study was commissioned to look at the possibilities of re-starting production again.

Glen Albyn

Owner:	Region:	Founded:	Status:
Diageo	N Highlands	1844	Demolished

One of three Inverness distilleries surviving into the 1980s. In 1866 the buildings were transformed into a flour mill. but then converted back to a distillery in 1884 and continued producing whisky until 1983 when it was closed. Three years later the distillery was demolished.

Glenesk

Owner:	Region:	Founded:	Status:
Diageo	E Highlands	1897	Demolished

Operated under many names; Highland Esk, North Esk, Montrose and Hillside. In 1968 a large drum maltings was built adjacent to the distillery and the Glenesk maltings still operate today under the ownership of Boortmalt. The distillery building was demolished in 1996.

Glen Flagler

Owner:	Region:	Founded:	Status:
InverHouse	Lowlands	1965	Demolished

Glen Flagler was one of two malt distilleries (Killyloch being the other) that were built on the site of Garnheath grain distillery. Killyloch was closed in the early 1970s, while Glen Flagler continued to produce until 1985. A year later, Garnheath was closed only to be demolished in 1988.

Glenlochy

Owner:	Region:	Founded:	Status:
Diageo	W Highlands	1898	Demolished

Glenlochy was one of three distilleries in Fort William at the beginning of the 1900s. For a period of time, the distillery was owned by Joseph Hobbs who, after having sold the distillery to DCL, bought the second distillery in town, Ben Nevis. Glenlochy was closd in 1983.

Glen Mhor

Owner:	Region:	Founded:	Status:
Diageo	N Highlands	1892	Demolished

Glen Mhor was one of the last three Inverness distilleries and probably the one with the best reputation when it comes to the whisky that it produced. Glen Mhor was closed in 1983 and three years later the buildings were demolished. Today there is a supermarket on the site.

Glenugie

Owner:	Region:	Founded:	Status:
Chivas Bros	E Highlands	1831	Demolished

Glenugie produced whisky for six years before it was converted into a brewery. In 1875 whisky distillation started again, but production was very intermittent until 1937 when Seager Evans took over. Following several ownership changes, the distillery closed in 1983.

Glenury Royal

Owner:	Region:	Founded:	Status:
Diageo	E Highlands	1825	Demolished

The founder of Glenury was the eccentric Captain Robert Barclay Allardyce, the first to walk 1000 miles in 1000 hours in 1809. The distillery closed in 1983 and part of the building was demolished a decade later with the rest converted into flats.

Imperial

Owner:	Region:	Founded:	Status:
Chivas Bros	Speyside	1897	Demolished

In over a century, Imperial distillery was out of production for 60% of the time, but when it produced it had a capacity of 1,6 million. In 2012, the owners announced that a new distillery would be built. The old distillery was demolished and in 2015 Dalmunach distillery was commissioned.

Inverleven

Owner:	Region:	Founded:	Status:
Chivas Bros	Lowlands	1938	Demolished

Inverleven was built on the same site as Dumbarton grain distillery, equipped with one pair of traditional pot stills. In 1956 a Lomond still was added. Inverleven was mothballed in 1991 and finally closed. The Lomond still is now working again since 2010 at Bruichladdich.

Killyloch

Owner:	Region:	Founded:	Status:
InverHouse	Lowlands	1965	Demolished

Publicker Industries converted a paper mill in Airdrie into a grain distillery (Garnheath) and two malt distilleries (Glen Flagler and Killyloch). Killyloch (originally named Lilly-loch after the water source) was closed in the early 1970s, while Glen Flagler continued to produce until 1985.

Kinclaith

Owner:	Region:	Founded:	Status:
Chivas Bros	Lowlands	1957	Demolished

The last malt distillery to be built in Glasgow and constructed on the grounds of Strathclyde grain distillery by Seager Evans. In 1975 it was dismantled to make room for an extension of the grain distillery. It was later demolished in 1982.

Ladyburn

Owner:	Region:	Founded:	Status:
W Grant & Sons	Lowlands	1966	Dismantled

In 1963 William Grant & Sons built their huge grain distillery in Girvan in Ayrshire. Three years later they also decided to build a malt distillery on the site which was given the name Ladyburn. The distillery was closed in 1975 and finally dismantled during the 1980s.

Littlemill

Owner:	Region:	Founded:	Status:
Loch Lomond Co.	Lowlands	1772	Demolished

Scotland's oldest working distillery until production stopped in 1992. Triple distillation was practised until 1930. In 1996 the distillery was dismantled and part of the buildings demolished and in 2004 much of the remaining buildings were destroyed in a fire.

Lochside

Owner:	Region:	Founded:	Status:
Chivas Bros	E Highlands	1957	Demolished

Most of the output from the distillery was made for blended whisky. One of the owners combined grain and malt whisky production. In 1992 the distillery was mothballed and five years later all the equipment and stock were removed. The distillery buildings were demolished in 2005.

Millburn

Owner:	Region:	Founded:	Status:
Diageo	N Highlands	1807	Dismantled

The oldest of those Inverness distilleries that made it into modern times. With one pair of stills, the capacity was 300,000 litres. In 1985 it was closed and three years later all the equipment was removed. The buildings are now a hotel and restaurant owned by Premier Inn.

North Port

Owner:	Region:	Founded:	Status:
Diageo	E Highlands	1820	Demolished

The names North Port and Brechin are used interchangeably on the labels of this single malt. The distillery had one pair of stills and produced 500,000 litres per year. Closed in 1983, it was dismantled piece by piece and was finally demolished in 1994 to make room for a supermarket.

Pittyvaich

Owner:	Region:	Founded:	Status:
Diageo	Speyside	1974	Demolished

Built by Arthur Bell & Sons on the same ground as Dufftown distillery. For a few years in the 1990s, Pittyvaich was also a back up plant for gin distillation (Gordon's gin). The distillery was mothballed in 1993 and has now been demolished.

St Magdalene

Owner:	Region:	Founded:	Status:
Diageo	Lowlands	1795	Dismantled

The distillery came into ownership of DCL in 1912 and was at the time a large distillery with 14 washbacks, five stills and with the possibility of producing more than one million litres of alcohol. Ten years after the closure in 1983, the distillery was re-built into flats.

James Sedgwick Distillery in South Africa

Distilleries
around the globe

Including the subsections:
Europe
North America | Australia & New Zealand
Asia | Africa | South America

This year, two new countries were added to this section. Both Hungary and Slovakia can now count themselves as malt whisky producing nations. But the club is bound to be expanded already next year. A giant project is underway in China where Pernod Ricard has started the construction of Emeishan malt whisky distillery in Sichuan. The owners will invest $150m in the site over the next ten years and they hope to start producing in 2021. Meanwhile, still in China but on the definitive opposite end of the scale, a whisky enthusiast by the name of Weidong Wei has already distilled tiny volumes in his pilot still and has plans to build a proper distillery. The Chinese company MengTai Group has revealed plans to build a whisky distillery with the help of Scottish manufacturers of equipment in Inner Mongolia and a Scottish whisky consultant is currently working on distilleries both in Macau and Myanmar. The first single malt whisky produced in Singapore was filled into a cask in autumn 2019. For Brass Lion Distillery, a company focusing on gin, it was just a test and we'll have to wait until next year to see if they'll be included as a whisky distillery in this book.

But 2020 will also be remembered as a year when new and often small distilleries around the world were struggling to survive due to the restrictions caused by the covid-19 pandemic. Building a distillery is a substantial investment and few companies can manage that without taking a loan in the bank. As for incomes, especially in the beginning, they often rely on a visitor centre often combined with a restaurant, a bar, a shop and a tasting room. In many countries around the world lock-downs of various degrees forced the owners to cease production at least for a few weeks but when distilling was resumed, their visitor facilities had to remain closed depriving many of them of one of their most important sales channels. A survey made by the Distilled Spirits Council of the United States in April 2020 showed that 43% of distillery employees had been furloughed, a 64% sales decline was reported and two-thirds of the responding distilleries did not believe they would be able to sustain their businesses for more than 6 months. Similar observations were made in Australia and other countries. At the same time both small and large companies in the industry did what they could to adjust to the new situation. Many switched to production of hand sanitizers for a while and there were also plenty of efforts trying to support the on-trade business when restaurants, bars and pubs were forced by the authorities to close. One such effort was Diageo's "Raising the Bar" programme launched in July 2020 where $100m was directed to support the recovery of hospitality centres of all kinds.

The attitude of "we're all in it together" where different segments of the wider drinks business have been working together to mitigate the consequences of the pandemic has certainly been helpful but nonetheless, when the storm has blown over, we expect to see a number of companies that did not survive.

Europe

Austria

Destillerie Haider

Roggenreith, founded in 1995

whiskyerlebniswelt.at

The owners released the first Austrian whisky in 1998. In 2005, they opened up a Whisky Experience World with tours and tastings. The distillery is equipped with two 450 litre Christian Carl copper stills. The main part of the production is made from either 100% malted rye or a combination of rye and malted barley while the rest is from malted barley. Five expressions make up the core range and apart from them there are peated versions as well and limited releases are launched regularly. One of the latest include a special bottling in March 2020 to celebrate the distillery´s 25th anniversary.

Broger Privatbrennerei

Klaus, founded in 1976 (whisky since 2008)

broger.info

The production of whisky is supplementing the distillation and production of eau de vie from apples and pears. The distillery is equipped with a 150 litre Christian Carl still. The current range of whiskies consists of Triple Cask, Medium Smoked, Burn Out and the limited Distiller´s Edition. A new range of four whiskies is Hoamat with the grain coming from neighbouring farms.

Other distilleries in Austria

Dachstein Destillerie

Radstadt, founded in 2007

mandlberggut.com

Apart from production of various spirits from berries, malt whisky is also produced. Their only release so far is the five year old Rock-Whisky which is distilled 2,5 times.

Ebner, Brennerei

Absam, founded in 1930 (whisky since 2005)

brennereiebner.at

Whisky is produced in this combination of a guesthouse, brewery and distillery. Besides a single malt from barley, they have also released whiskies made from maize, dinkel and wheat.

Franz Kostenzer, Edelbrennerei

Maurach/Achensee, founded in 1998, whisky since 2006

schnaps-achensee.at

A huge range of different spirits as well as whisky is produced. Several expressions under the name Whisky Alpin have been released including a 6 year old single malt with a sherry cask finish, a 6 year old single malt rye and a rye with an amarone finish.

Hermann Pfanner, Destillerie

Lauterach, founded in 1854 (whisky since 2005)

pfanner-weine.com

Two core whisky expressions are produced, Pfanner Single Malt Classic and Single Malt Red Wood with a maturation in red wine casks. There are also several limited releases including heavily peated and various finishes, for example Grand Marnier.

Keckeis Destillerie

Rankweil, founded in 2003

destillerie-keckeis.at

Whisky production started in 2008 and today one expression, Keckeis Single Malt is for sale as well as the new make Keckeis Baby Malt. Part of the barley has been smoked with beech and maturation takes place in small ex-sherry casks.

Lagler, Spezialitätenbrennerei

Kukmirn, founded in 2009

brennerei.lagler.cc

One of few distilleries that are using vacuum distillation. Two single malts and a blend are available under the name Pannonia.

Old Raven

Neustift, founded in 2004

oldraven.at

More than 250,000 litres of beer are produced yearly and the wash from the brewery is used for distillation of whisky. The triple distilled Old Raven comes in three expressions – Old Raven, Old Raven Smoky and the limited edition Old Raven Black Edition.

Pfau Brennerei

Klagenfurt, founded in 1987

pfau.at

Focused on production of "Edelbrände" from fruits and berries, the owners also make whisky. The core expression is a 7 year old single malt but recently a limited 15 year old has also been released.

Reisetbauer & Son

Kirchberg-Thening, founded in 1994 (whisky since 1995)

reisetbauer.at

Specialising in brandies and fruit schnapps, a range of malt whiskies is also produced. The current range of whiskies have all been matured in casks that have previously contained Chardonnay and Trockenbeerenauslese and include a 7, a 12 and a 15 year old.

Rogner, Destillerie

Rappottenstein, founded in 1997

destillerie-rogner.at

Producer of a variety of spirits including whisky. The range consists of Rogner Waldviertel Whisky 3/3 (malted and unmalted). Rye Whisky No. 13 and a single malt, Whisky No. 2. A peated 12 year old named Old Power was released in June 2019.

Weutz, Destillerie

St. Nikolai im Sausal, founded in 2002

weutz.at

The distillery added whisky to the range in 2004 when they started a cooperation with a local brewer. Some of the whiskies are produced in the traditional Scottish style while others are more unorthodox, for example based on elderflower.

Wieser Destillerie

Wösendorf in der Wachau, founded in 1996

wieserwachau.com

Traditionally a distillery producing schnaps and liqueur from fruits and berries, they have also launched different versions of a quadruple distilled whisky called Uuahouua; American oak, French oak, Pinot Noir and Smoke on the Water.

Belgium

The Owl Distillery

Grâce Hollogne, founded in1997

belgianwhisky.com

The first commercial bottling of Belgium's first single malt, 'The Belgian Owl', appeared in November 2008 and the core expression today is the 3 year old Belgian Owl bottled at 46% or at cask strength. Recent limited releases include an 11 year old single cask and even a 12 year old has been released. The distillery is equipped with a 2.1 ton mash tun, four washbacks and two stills that had previously been used at Caperdonich distillery. All the barley used for production comes from farms close to the distillery.

De Molenberg Distillery

Blaasveld, founded in 1471 (whisky since 2003)

stokerijdemolenberg.be

In 2010, the brewer Charles Leclef started a distillery at the family estate Molenberg. The wash still has a capacity of 3,000 litres and the spirit still 2,000 litres. The first bottles under the name Gouden Carolus Single Malt, appeared on the market in 2008 and this 3 year old is still the core expression. A limited range called Pure Taste include three different bottlings; Bourbon, Anker and Oloroso and the 6th anniversary edition with 4 years of extra maturation in madeira casks appeared in autumn 2019.

Other distilleries in Belgium

De Graal

Brakel, founded in 2002

degraal.be

A beer brewery also producing whisky. The only single malt currently available is the 5 year old, ex-bourbon matured San Graal.

Filliers

Bachte-Maria-Leerne, founded in 1880 (malt whisky since 2008)

filliers.be

For many years, only gin and genever was produced but in 2007 a blended whisky was launched followed in 2016 by the first Belgian rye whisky. In 2018 two pot stills from Forsyths were installed and malt whisky is now also on the menu.

Pirlot, Brouwerij

Zandhoven, founded in 1998 (whisky since 2011)

brouwerijpirlot.be

Originally a brewery, their distillery is equipped with a German continuous still and the spirit is matured for 18 months in ex-bourbon casks and then another 18 months in quarter casks from Laphroaig. The first batch of Kempisch Vuur single malt was released in 2016 and several releases have followed.

Radermacher, Distillerie

Raeren, founded in 1836

distillerie.biz

In a wide range of products from this classic distillery, there is also single malt whisky to be found. The 10 year old Lambertus has been aged in American oak casks that previously held tequila.

Sas Distillery

Stekene, founded in 2014

sasdistilleries.com

Founded by Benedikt Sas who is a professor in organic chemistry. In a personally designed 200 litre column still, Sas is producing gin, rum, absinthe and whisky according to old recipes. In 2019 the Ignis Templi single malt bottled at 44% was released.

Wilderen, Brouwerij & Distilleederij

Wilderen-St. Truiden, founded in 2011

brouwerijwilderen.be

A combination of a beer brewery with a history going back to 1642 and a distillery founded in 2011. The current core bottling of a single malt is Wild Weasel bottled at 46% and a limited sherry cask finish was released in autumn 2019.

Czech Republic

Svachovka Distillery

České Budějovice, founded in 2016

svachovkadomu.cz

Owned by Vaclav Cvach, this is a combination of a brewery, distillery, hotel, restaurant and spa. Equipped with stainless steel washbacks and copper stills the distillery produces fruit brandy as well as 5-10,000 litres of Svach´s Old Well single malt whisky yearly. The first 3 year old single malt was launched in autumn 2019 and a wide variety of expressions have been released since.

Gold Cock Distillery

Vizovice, founded in 1877

rjelinek.cz

The whisky is produced in three versions – a 3 year old blended whisky, a 12 year old single malt and different versions of Small Batch single malt including a 20 year old. Production was stopped for a while but after the brand and distillery were acquired by R. Jelinek a.s. the whisky began life anew.

Denmark

Stauning Whisky

Stauning, founded in 2006

stauningwhisky.dk

The first Danish purpose-built malt whisky distillery entered a more adolescent phase in 2009, after having experimented with

Svachovka Distillery producing Old Well single malt

two small pilot stills bought from Spain. More stills were installed in 2012. The preconditions, however, were completely changed in 2015 when it was announced that Diageo´s incubator fund project, Distil Ventures, would spend £10m to increase the capacity of Stauning. In 2018, it became evident what the investment had meant to the company. A new distillery with no less than 24 copper stills, all directly fired, was opened. The floor malting were increased to 1,000 m^2 and the total production capacity is now 900,000 litres of pure alcohol (220,000 litres produced in 2019). The most recent releases include a 3 year old rye with a rum cask finish, the 5 year old Peat, the 4 year old single malt Port Smoke and the 4 year old Kaos made from both malted rye and malted barley.

Braunstein

Köge, founded in 2005 (whisky since 2007)

braunstein.dk

Denmark's first micro-distillery, built in an already existing brewery in Køge, just south of Copenhagen. The wash comes from the own brewery. A Holstein type of still, with four plates in the rectification column, is used for distillation. Around 40% of the required barley is ecologically grown in Denmark. The first release from the distillery and the first release of a malt whisky produced in Denmark was in 2010. The most recent releases include Library Collection 20:1, an unpeated whisky matured in rum casks and Edition No: 11, peated and bourbon matured. There is also Danica which is reserved for the duty-free market.

Other distilleries in Denmark

Als, Destilleriet

Sydals, founded in 2018

destillerietals.dk

Built as a combined gin- and whisky distillerie with aid from Henric Molin of Spirit of Hven fame, the whisky is distilled in a 350 litre column still. The first single malt is due in 2021.

Copenhagen Distillery

Copenhagen, founded in 2014

copenhagendistillery.com

The first distillery was situated in a listed building close to the Copenhagen Airport but a few years ago it was moved closer to the city. A bus garage has, by way of ingenious Danish design,

been turned into a combination of a distillery and a creative hot spot including a bar and plenty of space for concerts and other gatherings. A wide range of gin, vodka and liqueurs have been produced as an initial "bread and butter" but this is first and foremost a whisky distillery with some unusual features. The grain is milled using a Skiold plate mill and then mashed in a 0.6 ton mash tun. Following a 7-10 day fermentation on the grain, the liquid is distilled one time in a 1,050 litre copper hybrid still by Müller which has a 2-plate column attached as well as dephlegmator to increase the options while distilling. The spirit is mainly matured in toasted 100-litre casks made of Hungarian oak but more unusual casks are used as well. There are three different ranges; Refine which is a more traditional whisky, Raw where the all the flavours are "dialled up" and the experimental Rare bottlings where sometimes alternative grains (for example malted emmer and spelt) are used. The First Edition was released in February 2020 to be followed by a limited release in late 2020.

Enghaven, Braenderiet

Mellerup, founded in 2014

enghaven-whisky.dk

Producing also rum and gin, the first whisky release, in autumn 2017, was a rye matured in both bourbon casks and port casks and in October 2018, the first single malt from a rum cask was released. This was followed by Single Malt No. 2 in late 2019.

Fary Lochan Destilleri

Give, founded in 2009

farylochan.dk

The main part of the malted barley is imported from the UK but they also malt some themselves. The first whisky was released in 2013 and a number of bottlings have been released since then. One of the latest was a 10th anniversary sherry single cask in late 2019 and there is also a recent bottling from Scotch Malt Whisky Society.

Limfjorden, Braenderiet

Roslev, founded in 2013

braenderiet.dk

The distillery moved to a new location in 2018 and a brewery was added. Apart from peated and unpeated single malt and rye, the distillery also produces gin and rum. The first single malt was released in 2016 and recently a limited range of Lindorm whisky

Henrik Brinks (left) and Lasse Öznek, part of the highly innovative team at Copenhagen Distillery

was launched with the third edition (a 6 year old, peated PX sherry cask) appearing in March 2020.

Mosgaard Whisky

Oure, founded in 2015

mosgaardwhisky.dk

Three alambic stills (two wash stills and one spirit still), were designed by the owners (Gitte and Jes Mosgaard) and made in Portugal. There is also a 150 kilo mash tun and four stainless steel washbacks with a 7 day fermentation. The aim is to produce 20,000 bottles per year, all from organically grown barley and the maturation takes place primarily in small 50 litre casks. The first single malts, matured in oloroso casks and PX sherry appeared in spring 2019. Since then there have been a number of releases including oloroso single cask, PX single cask and Peated No. 3. The distillery also has an extensive range of gin.

Nordisk Brænderi/Thy Whisky

Fjerritslev, founded in 2009 (whisky since 2011)

nordiskbraenderi.dk, thy-whisky.dk

The ecological barley used for the production is grown in fields surrounding the distillery. In the first 8-9 years around ten whiskies have been released under the name Thy Whisky, the first in 2014. One of the latest, in November 2019, is No. 11 Stovt which had been matured in a combination of bourbon, port and stout casks.

Nyborg Destilleri

Nyborg, founded in 1997 (whisky since 2009)

fioniawhisky.com

Opened as an extension to an existing brewery, the distillery moved in 2017 to new premises. The distillery is equipped with two copper pot stills with attached columns. The first release of Isle of Fionia single malt was in 2012. The new range of whiskies is called Ardor with a peated version and a Danish oak finish as some of the latest releases. Another range of special and limited releases is called Adventurous Spirit.

Sall Whisky Distillery

Sall, founded in 2018

sallwhisky.com

Gin but above all, malt whisky made from ecologically grown

barley from the land of one of the owners is produced. New make was launched in late 2019 and the first whisky is expected in 2022.

Trolden Distillery

Kolding, founded in 2011

trolden.com

The distillery is a part of a brewery and the wash from the brewery is fermented for 4-5 days before a double distillation. The first release of a single malt was Nimbus in 2014 and in May 2020, the distillery moved to new premises. One of the latest releases, in 2020, was a peated single malt with a Spanish red wine finish.

Ærø Whisky

Ærøskøbing, founded in 2013

ærøwhisky.dk

Situated on the small island of Ærø the distillation started in stills from Portugal. In 2016, new and larger stills were installed and the production increased. The first bottling was a bourbonmatured single cask released in March 2017 while the current range consists of one whisky matured in American oak and another in a combination of American oak and sherry casks.

England

St. George´s Distillery

Roudham, Norfolk, founded in 2006

englishwhisky.co.uk

St. George´s Distillery near Thetford in Norfolk was started by father and son, James and Andrew Nelstrop, and came on stream in December 2006. This made it the first English malt whisky distillery for over a hundred years. In December 2009, it was time for the release of the first legal whisky called Chapter 5 (the first four chapters had been young malt spirit). This was then followed by several more chapters (up to 17) but the sometimes uncomprehensible range was then exhanged for a range with two core expressions; The English Original and The English Smokey, There are also regular, limited releases in the Small Batch series with Virgin Oak, Triple Distilled, Smokey Virgin and Rum Cask being the most recent. The latter, released in April 2020, was originally known as Chapter 7. A few months later, The English 11 years old was released. In 2017 a new and innovative sub range

Jes Mosgaard filling a cask at his Mosgaard Distillery

was introduced – The Norfolk. The whisky expressions in that range have included Malt 'n' Rye made with malted barley and rye, Farmers where no less than eight different grains were used and Parched, a single grain. The distillery is equipped with a stainless steel semi-lauter mash tun with a copper top and three stainless steel washbacks with a fermentation time of 85 hours. There is one pair of stills, a 2,800 litre wash still and a 1,800 litre spirit still. All the whiskies from the distillery are un chill-filtered and without colouring. The distillery also has an excellent, newly expanded visitor centre, including a shop with more than 300 different whiskies. More than 85,000 people come here every year.

Cotswolds Distillery
Stourton, founded in 2014

cotswoldsdistillery.com

The distillery is the brainchild of Dan Szor, who acquired an estate with two stone buildings and converted them into a distillery with a visitor centre. Production of both whisky and gin started in September 2014. There are three stills; one wash still (2,400 litres), one spirit still (1,600 litres) and a Holstein still (500 litres) for production of gin and other spirits. The rest of the equipment includes a 0.5 ton mash tun and eight stainless steel wash backs. During 2019/2020 funds of more than £4m have been raised to further expand the distillery. The first product for sale was their Cotswolds Dry Gin in 2014 while the first single malt, the 3 year old Odyssey, was launched in 2017. In early 2018, the distillery started experimenting with rye whisky and in August the owners made their first trials producing rum. In December 2018, the distillery's second release appeared. Founder's Choice, bottled at cask strength and with no age statement, had been matured in STR casks. A limited release appeared in spring 2019 when the Lord Mayor's Reserve Single Malt was launched and this was followed in August by a single malt that had matured in port casks, exclusively sold to consumers attending The Cotswolds Distillery Festival. In September 2019, a peated version (from time spent in ex-Islay quarter casks) and bottled at cask strength was launched and in 2020, the first bottles in the Arts & Craft series, matured in casks seasoned with Sauternes, were released.

Lakes Distillery
Bassenthwaite Lake, founded in 2014

lakesdistillery.com

Headed by Paul Currie, who was the co-founder of Isle of Arran distillery, a consortium of private investors founded the distillery. The distillery is equipped with two stills for the whisky production,

each with both copper and stainless steel condensers, and a third still for the distillation of gin. A recent £4.25m investment from Comhar Capital has made it possible to install eight new washbacks thereby trebling the production capacity to more than 1 million bottles per year. The inaugural bottling, The Lakes Malt Genesis, was sold on 29th June 2018 at an auction fetching a staggering £7,900. In September 2019, the first installment in a four-year collection of single malts called The Quatrefoil Collection was released with numbers three and four following in 2020 and 2021. In September 2019, the distillery launched its first limited edition in the Whiskymaker's Reserve series. The owners have expressed their intention of becoming a luxury global brand led by sherry-matured malts.

Spirit of Yorkshire Distillery
Hunmanby, founded in 2016

spiritofyorkshire.com

The distillery, founded by Tom Mellor and David Thompson, is actually situated in two separate locations with a one ton mash tun and two 10,000 litre washbacks standing at Tom's farm which also houses a brewery while the 5,000 litre wash still and a 3,500 litre spirit still are 2,5 miles down the road in Hunmanby. A four plate column is designed to run in tandem with the spirit still and currently 50% of the production is distilled using the column to achieve a lighter character of the new make. All the barley comes from the farm and is malted by Muntons. The distillery produces 80,000 litres of pure alcohol a year and has so far filled well over 2,000 casks. There are plans to increase capacity, perhaps as soon as 2020. The distillery also has a visitor centre with daily tours. In December 2017, the owners released their first malt spirit called Distillery Projects Maturing Malt. The fifth and sixth editions were released in summer 2019 and was followed by the 3 year old Filey Bay single malt in October (and yet another batch in December).

Other distilleries in England

Adnams Copper House Distillery
Southwold, founded in 2010

adnams.co.uk

Adnams Brewery in Suffolk added distillation of spirits to their production in December 2010 and, apart from whisky – gin, vodka and absinthe are produced. The first whisky was released in 2013 and the range now consists of Single Malt, Rye Malt (75% rye and 25% barley) and Triple Malt (wheat, barley and oats).

A picture of Susan - one of Lakes Distillery's pot stills

Bimber Distillery

London, founded in 2015

bimberdistillery.co.uk

The distillery buys its floor malted barley from Warminster Maltings and the spirit is distilled in a 1,000 litre wash still and a 600 litre spirit still. The owners use wooden washbacks with a seven day fermentation and more were installed in 2019. They also recently did trials with peated poduction using barley that they floor malted themselves. Distillation began in May 2016 and the first release from the distillery was a vodka followed by a blended 6 month old malt spirit from bourbon, sherry and virgin oak casks. In September 2019, it was time for the distillery´s inaugural single malt bottling – aptly named The First. In June 2020 a number of new releases were launched including two ex bourbon, one ex peated quarter casks and three different ex bourbon finished in sherry casks.

Chase Distillery

Rosemaund Farm, Hereford, founded in 2008

chasedistillery.co.uk

The main product from the distillery is Chase Vodka made from potatoes and gin has also become part of their range. By the end of 2011, the first whisky was distilled and since then well over 500 casks have been filled with a possible first release due in 2020. The distillery is equipped with a copper still with a five plate column and an attached rectification column with another 42 plates.

Circumstance Distillery

Bristol, founded in 2018

circumstancedistillery.com

The owners idea is to make whisky and rum in a flexible distillery equipped with a pot still with attached columns. The very first bottling in March 2019 was Circumstantial Barley 1:1:1:1:6, a spirit from 100% malted barley that had matured for two months using charred oak spindles and then another four months in ex-bourbon casks. The wash had been fermented for 13 days!

Cooper King Distillery

Sutton-on-the-Forest, founded in 2018

cooperkingdistillery.co.uk

Inspired by a trip to whisky makers in Australia, Abbie Neilson and Chris Jaume decided to build their own distillery. Equipped with a Tasmanian copper pot still, the distillery released its first gin in 2018 while whisky production started in June 2019. The first

malt whisky is expected in 2024. The distillery practises a combination of vacuum distillation and traditional distillation with a strong focus on sustainability and reducing the environmental impacts.

Copper Rivet Distillery

Chatham, founded in 2016

copperrivetdistillery.com

Situated in an old pump house in the Chatham Docks, the distillery is equipped with a copper pot still with a column attached as well as a special gin still. Dockyard Gin and Vela Vodka were released early on and in April 2017, Son of a Gun, an 8 week old grain spirit made from rye, wheat and barley, was released. The first Masthouse single malt was released in June 2020.

Dartmoor Distillery

Bovey Tracey, founded in 2016

dartmoorwhiskydistillery.co.uk

Greg Millar and Simon Crow acquired a 50 year old alembic still in Cognac. The brought it to England, refurbished it and attached a copper "wash warmer" to pre warm the wash and increase the copper contact. Distillation started in February 2017 and the first two malt whiskies, matured in a Bordeaux wine casks and an ex-bourbon barrel appeared in February 2020.

Durham Whisky

Durham, founded in 2014 (whisky since 2018)

durhamwhisky.co.uk

The distillery was founded in 2014 with the aim to produce gin and vodka. In 2018, the owners decided to relocate to larger premises in Durham and whisky was added to the range. Using local malt, the distillery is equipped with a 1,200 litre wash still and a 1,000 litre spirit still.

Forest Distillery, The

Macclesfield, founded in 2014

theforestdistillery.com

Located in a 17th century stone barn in the Peak District National Park, Lindsay and Karl Bond produce gin but also, in a 500 litre pot still, single malt whisky with the aim to release it in 2021

The team at Copper Rivet with Head Distiller Abhi Banik far right

Henstone Distillery

Oswestry, Shropshire, founded in 2017

henstonedistillery.com

Commissioned in December 2017, the distillery has released gin, vodka, apple brandy and (in early 2020) a corn "whisky". The first malt whisky, distilled in a Kothe copper hybrid still, will be released in early 2021.

Isle of Wight Distillery

Newport, founded in 2015

isleofwightdistillery.com

The founders, Conrad Gauntlett and Xavier Baker, have years of experience in wine production and brewing but this is their first distillation venture. The fermented wash is bought from a local brewery and distilled in hybrid copper stills. Another 1,000 litre still was installed in summer 2019. The first whisky was distilled in December 2015 and the owners also produce vodka and Mermaid Gin.

London Distillery Company, The

London, founded in 2012

londondistillery.com

The first release was Dodd's Gin in 2013. In December 2013 they got the licence to produce whisky and production started shortly thereafter. A rye whisky was launched in 2018 and early 2019, it was time for the company's first whisky made from malted barley – the highly limited Cask 109. Early 2020, the distillery was bought by honey-infused spirits brand The British Honey Company.

Ludlow Distillery

Craven Arms, founded in 2014

ludlowdistillery.co.uk

Equipped with a 200 litre still, this tiny distillery in Shropshire just south of Shrewsbury released its first single malt, Young Prince, in November 2018. Mike Hardingham also produces wine, brandy and eau de vie

Wharf Distillery

Towcester, founded in 2015

wharfdistillery.co.uk

Probably the smallest whisky distillery in England also producing gin. Their first release of a malt whisky, Cattle Creep, appeared in January 2019 with one edition bottled at 42.9% and another at cask strength. A second release is planned for 2020.

White Peak Distillery

Ambergate, Derbyshire, founded in 2017

whitepeakdistillery.co.uk

Founded by Max and Claire Vaughn, the distillery made the first distillation in April 2018. By that time, Shaun Smith from Cotswolds Distillery had been hired as the head distiller. Gin, rum, a whisky newmake and an 18 months old malt spirit have been released but the first bottlings of the lightly peated malt whisky are not expected until at least 2021.

Whittaker's Distillery

Harrogate, founded in 2015 (whisky since 2019)

whittakersgin.com

The owners have already had some success with Whittaker Gin but whisky was in their thoughts already from the beginning. In summer 2019, two new, larger stills were installed and whisky production started in the autumn with a plan to make 15-20,000 bottles per year.

Finland

Teerenpeli

Lahti, founded in 2002

teerenpeli.com

The original distillery, located in a restaurant in Lahti, is equipped with one wash still (1,500 litres) and one spirit still (900 litres). A completely new distillery, with one 3,000 litre wash still and two 900 litre spirit stills, was opened in 2015 in the same house as the brewery and today the old distillery serves as a "laboratory" for new spirits. The first single malt was launched as a 3 year old in 2005. The core range now consists of a 10 year old matured in bourbon casks, Kaski which is a 100% sherry maturation, Portti which is a 3 year old with another 1.5 years in port casks and the peated Savu matured in a combination of bourbon and PX sherry casks. Recent limited releases (both released in 2020) include the 7 year old Kulo, matured in a combination of PX and oloroso sherry casks and Lemmon Lintu with an 8 months rum finish.

Other distilleries in Finland

Helsinki Distilling Company

Helsinki, founded in 2014

hdco.fi

The distillery is equipped with one mash tun, three washbacks and two stills. The first gin was released in 2014 and more gin and akvavit but also a one year old malt spirit followed. On the whisky side, the focus is on rye but also single malt made from barley. The first release was a 100% malted rye in autumn 2017 and the latest single malt from barley, a PX finish, appeared in February 2020.

Valamo Distillery

Heinävesi, founded in 2014

valamodistillery.com

The distillery is situated at the Valamo Monastery in eastern Finland. Experimental distillation started in 2011 and began in earnest in 2015 when the distillery was equipped with a 5,000 litre mash tun, four stainless steel washbacks and a 1,000 litre Carl still. A 5 year old, matured in first fill bourbon casks has been released while one of the latest bottlings is a peated 3 year old from 2019.

France

Distillerie Warenghem

Lannion, Bretagne, founded in 1900 (whisky since 1994)

distillerie-warenghem.com

Leon Warenghem founded the distillery at the beginning of the 20th century and in 1967, his grandson Paul-Henri Warenghem, together with his associate, Yves Leizour, took over the reins. They moved the distillery to its current location on the outskirts of Lannion in Brittany. Gilles Leizour, Yves' son, took over at the end of the 1970's and it was he who added whisky to the Warenghem range. WB (stands for Whisky Breton), a blend from malted barley and wheat both distilled in a pot still, saw the light in 1987 and Armorik – the first ever French single malt – was released in 1998. The distillery is equipped with a 6,000 litre semi-lauter mashtun, six stainless steel washbacks and two, traditional copper pot stills (a 6,000 litre wash still and a 3,500 litre spirit still). Around 180,000 litres of pure alcohol (including 20% grain whisky) are produced yearly. In 2019, a second warehouse was built as well as a stunning visiting centre with a beautiful tasting room. The single malt core range consists of Armorik Édition Originale and Armorik Sherry Finish. Both are around 4 years old, bottled at 40%, have matured in ex-bourbon casks plus a few months in sherry butts and are sold in supermarkets in France. Armorik Classic, a mix of 4 to 8 year old whiskies from ex-bourbon and sherry casks and the 7 year old Armorik Double Maturation which has spent time in both new oak and sherry wood are earmarked for export as well as the Armorik Sherry Cask. Warenghem has also distilled rye whisky which was first released in 2014 under the name Roof Rye and in 2018, the first peated expression, Triagoz, was released. At the end of 2018, to celebrate the 30th anniversary of their first single malt, Armorik released its first 10 year old which is now part of the core range. In September 2020, the distillery released its peatiest whisky to date, Yeun Elez and also their first organic whisky, Iroise.

Distillerie Rozelieures

Rozelieures, Grand Est, founded in 1860 (whisky since 2003)

whiskyrozelieures.com

Hubert Grallet and his son-in-law, Christophe Dupic started with whisky production in 2003 and launched the Glen Rozelieures brand in 2007. Five versions are currently available: Original Collection aged in ex-fino casks, the lightly peated Rare Collection matured in ex-sauternes, Fumé Collection (20ppm) matured in ex-fino, Tourbé Collection and finally, the only un-peated in the core range, Subtil Collection. Every year, the distillery also releases single cask bottlings matured in ex-burgundy casks from famous producers. With a production of 200,000 litres, Rozelieures is now one of the largest distilleries in France. Since 2015 they are independent in energy with their own biogas plant a few hundred meters from the distillery. In 2018, Christophe Dupic opened a malting plant, with a capacity of 2,000 tons and they are now supplying many French distilleries with malted barley.

Distillerie des Menhirs

Plomelin, Bretagne, founded in 1986 (whisky since 1998)

distillerie.bzh

Originally a portable column still distillery, Guy Le Lay and his wife Anne-Marie decided in 1986 to settle down for good and the first lambig with the name Distillerie des Menhirs was released in 1989. Shortly after, Guy Le Lay came up with the idea of producing a 100% buckwheat whisky. Eddu Silver was launched in 2002, followed by Eddu Gold in 2006, Eddu Silver Brocéliande in 2013 and Eddu Diamant in 2015. Ed Gwenn, aged for 4 years in ex-cognac barrels, was released for the first time in 2016 and in 2017, the third release in the Collector´s Range (Eddu Dan Ar Braz) appeared. In June 2019, Les Menhirs released a vintage 2004 which was the first whisky distilled from malted buckwheat.

Domaine des Hautes-Glaces

Saint Jean d´Hérans, Auvergne-Rhône Alpes, founded in 2009 (whisky since 2014)

hautesglaces.com

At an altitude of 900 metres in the the French Alps, Jérémy Bricka and Frédéric Revol decided to produce whisky from barley to bottle. Apart from growing their own barley, all the parts of whisky production take place at the distillery – malting, brewing, distillation, maturation and bottling. They are producing the first French single estate whisky and organically too. The cereals are harvested, malted, distilled and aged field by field and without any chemicals. Principium, the first whisky made at the distillery has been available since 2014. Domaine des Hautes Glaces was bought by Rémy Cointreau in 2015 and a second distillery started operating in June 2020. The core range includes two whiskies, Les Moissons Malt (100% malted barley) and Les Moissons Rye (100% malted rye). Single cask bottlings such as Ceros or Secale (rye), Flavis, Tekton, Ampelos or Obscuros (barley) are released from time to time.

Miclo

Lapoutroie, Grand Est, founded in 1970 (whisky since 2012)

distillerie-miclo.com

Gilbert Miclo, the grandfather of Bertrand Lutt, the current manager, founded the distillery in 1970, specialising in fruit spirits. It is equipped with four Holstein waterbath pot stills and since 2012, wort from a local brewery is fermented and distilled into malt whisky. Under the brand name Welche's, three different whiskies were released in December 2016 - Welche, Welche Fine Tourbe, Welche Tourbé. In 2018, Miclo released Welche Cherry Cask Finish, an annual limited edition finished in ex-cherry eau-de-vie casks.

Bercloux

Bercloux, Nouvelle Aquitaine, founded in 2000 (whisky since 2014)

distillerie-bercloux.fr

After many trials, Philippe Laclie opened his own brewery in 2000. In 2007 he decided to diversify by buying some Scotch whisky and finishing it for a few months in Pineau des Charentes barrels. In 2014, Philippe took the next step and invested around 100,000 euros, buying an 800 litre Stupfler pot still. After the first trial runs, regular whisky production started in September 2014. The first two bottlings of Bercloux Single Malt Whisky (peated and non peated) were released in September 2018. In November 2019, the distillery was bought by Les Bienheureux, a company founded by Alexandre Sirech (the founder of Havana Club) and Jean Moueix

Domaine des Hautes Glaces produces organic single estate whisky

(owner of Bordeaux wine Petrus). Their intention was to secure stock and production for their own brand – Bellevoye triple malt whisky which was launched at the end of 2015.

Domaine Mavela

Corsica, founded in 1991 (whisky since 2001)

domaine-mavela.com

The creators of the P&M brand are the Pietra family, also responsible for Pietra beer since 1996, and Venturini family who set up the Mavela distillery in 1991. Distilled in a Holstein still and aged in ex-Corsican muscat casks, the P&M single malt was sold for the first time in 2004 and its unique taste of the Corsican maquis surprised many whisky lovers. End of 2017, the distillery released its first 12 year old and in 2018, Fanu Venturini and his brother Lisandru, who now run the distillery, unveiled a completely new range of three expresions: P&M Signature, P&M Red Oak (aged in ex-red-wine casks) and P&M Tourbé (peated). Recently both a 13 and a 14 year old have been released and the owners are now expanding with a brewery of their own, a second still and a new warehouse.

Glann ar Mor

Pleubian, Bretagne, founded in 1999

glannarmor.com

The founder, Jean Donnay, started his first trials in 1999, then made some changes to the distillery and the process and regular production commenced in 2005. Two small stills are directly fired and worm tubs are used for condensing the spirit. The fermentation in wooden washbacks is long and the distillation is very slow. The full capacity is 50,000 bottles per year but lately, the actual production has been less than 10,000 bottles. There are two versions of the whisky – the unpeated Glann ar Mor and the peated Kornog. Core expressions are usually bottled at 46% but every year a number of limited releases are made including single casks and cask strength bottlings. Since 2016, Kornog Roc'hir (ex-bourbon casks) is the permanent Kornog bottling. Early 2019, Glann Ar Mor released its oldest bottling, a Kornog 12 year old, the first ever French triple distilled single malt called Teir Gwech and a curiosity named Ar Seizh Greun, distilled from a mash of seven malted cereals: barley, wheat, rye, oat, millet, spelt and triticale. In June 2020, it was announced that Jean Donnay had sold the distillery to Maison Villevert, producers of Cîroc vodka.

Hepp, Distillerie

Uberach, Grand Est, founded in 1972 (whisky since 2005)

distillerie-hepp.com

A family-owned distillery with two main expressions without ag statement; Tharcis Hepp (matured in bourbon and sherry) and Johnny Hepp (bourbon and white wine). In 2018, no less than three new bottlings were released from Distillerie Hepp; Ouisky, Tharcis Hepp Tourbé and French Flanker. Hepp is also behind the brand Roborel de Climens, launched in 2019 by Aymeric Roborel. The idea is to present whiskies finished in single grape wine cask. Merlot, Sauvignon, Semillon, Rolle, Grenache and Ugni Blanc have already been released. As well as producing their own whisky, Hepp distils for Meteor, the brewery that supplies the wort to some Alsatian distilleries.

Castan, Distillerie

Villeneuve Sur Vère, Occitanie, founded in 1946 (whisky since 2010)

distillerie-castan.com

In 2010, Sébastien Castan decided to permanently house the portable still that had been in the family for three generations in a proper distillery. The same year, he distilled his first whisky and aged the spirit in ex-Gaillac wine casks. In 2016, a brewery was built to supply the beer. The range consists of five bottlings: Villanova Berbie (ex-white wine casks), Gost (new cask), Terrocita (peated), Roja (ex-red wine casks) and Segala (rye). In June 2019 the construction of a new distillery started which has now been completed.

Distillerie Naguelann

Languenan, Bretagne, founded in 2014

naguelann.bzh

Lenaïck Lemaitre, a former musician and hotel owner, launched Naguelann Company in 2014 as an independent bottler. He sourced malt spirits and whiskies from Distillerie des Menhirs and Armorik, before ageing them in different casks (cider, red and white wine) and blending them. The range includes Mesk, Gran'pa, Ed Unan and Ruz!. While working as an independent bottler, Lenaïck started to build his own distillery fitted with two small stills. Dieil Tantad (rare and peated in the Breton language) released in June 2020 is his first bottling from own production.

Rouget de Lisle

Bletterans, Bourgogne-Franche Comté, founded in 1994 (whisky since 2006),

brasserie-rouget-lisle.com

Rouget de Lisle is a brewery created by Bruno Mangin and his wife. In 2006, they commissioned the Brûlerie du Revermont to distil whisky for them. The first Rouget De Lisle single malt whisky was released in 2009 and in 2012, Bruno Mangin bought his own still. Current bottlings are from the numerous casks he filled during his association with the Tissot family and which lie maturing in his own warehouse. End of 2018, Bruno Mangin renamed the brand BM Signature. The core range consists of two NAS aged in ex-vin de paille and ex-Macvin casks. Apart from that there are a lof of vintages ranging from 2008 to 2015

Other distilleries in France

Bertrand, Distillerie

Uberach, Grand Est, founded in 1874 (whisky since 2002)

distillerie-bertrand.com

The distillery manager, Jean Metzger, gets the malt from a local brewer and then distils it in Holstein type stills. The core bottling is a single malt aged in both new barrels and barrels which have previously contained the fortified wine Banyuls. Being a great wine connoisseur, Jean Metzger started to experiment with ageing and finishing whisky in casks having held a number of different French wines (rasteau, arbois or pupillon), including in ex-casks of the famous burgundy wine from Domaine de la Romanée Conti.

Brûlerie du Revermont

Nevy sur Seille, Bourgogne-Franche Comté, founded in 1991 (whisky since 2003)

marielouisetissot-levin.com

For many years, the Tissot family were travelling distillers offering their services to local wine producers. Relying upon a very unique distillation set-up, a Blavier still with three pots, designed and built for the perfume industry, they have been producing single malt whisky since 2003. Pascal and Joseph Tissot launched their own whisky brand Prohibition in 2011, aged in "feuillettes", 114 litre half-casks coopered specially for macvin and vin de paille french wines.

Brunet, Distillerie

Cognac, Nouvelle Aquitaine, founded in 1920 (whisky since 2006)

drinkbrenne.com

In 2006, Stéphane Brunet made the bold move to start whisky production in the Poitou-Charentes region - famous for its cognac production. His whisky, Tradition Malt, was released in 2009 and was launched in the USA by whisky enthusiast Allison Parc under the brand Brenne. In September 2015 a 10 year old version was released in small quantities in the USA. Since 2015 Brenne Cuvée Spéciale is also available in France. In 2017, the brand was acquired by Samson & Surrey with Allison Parc still being involved.

Castor, Distillerie du

Troisfontaines, Grand Est, founded in 1985 (whisky since 2011)

distillerie-du-castor.com

Founded by Patrick Bertin, the distillery produces both fruit and pomace brandies. It is equipped with two small stills which have been used since 2011 by Patrick's son to distill single malt whisky. The distillate is aged in ex-white wine (sauvignon blanc) casks and then finished in ex-sherry casks. The whisky is sold under the name St Patrick.

Charlier & Fils

Warcq, Grand Est, founded in 2015

facebook.com/laquinarde

Opening up a micro-brewery in 2015, it was Yann Charlier's ambition already from start to create his own whisky from indigeneous yeast and practising long fermentations (7 to 8 days). The first Charlier whisky was released in May 2020. The production will increase in the coming years as Yann Charlier recently bought another still from Gilbert Holl.

Claeyssens de Wambrechies, Distillerie

Wambrechies, Hauts de France, founded in 1817 (whisky since 2000)

wambrechies.com

One of the oldest distilleries in France, it was originally famous for its genever. The first whisky, a 3 year old, was released in 2003 followed by an 8 year old in 2009. In June 2019, the distillery was bought by Saint-Germain brewery/distillery. The is currently mothballed but a new Holstein still is expected to make its appearance soon. The current range consists of Wambrechies 5 year old, Sherry and the peated Tourbé.

Didier Barbe Entreprise

Lusigny Sur Barse, Grand Est, founded in 2012

didierbarbeentreprise.com

Using and old still that hadn´t been in production for the last fifty years, Didier Barbe started producing brandies and gin. In 2017 the first whisky was produced from the wash from local breweries. The

first whisky, aged in ratafia barrels, Barbe & Fils, was launched in May 2020.

Dreumont

Neuville-en-Avesnois, Hauts de France, founded in 2005 (whisky since 2011)

ladreum.com

Passionate about beer, Jérôme Dreumont decided to open a distillery as well in 2005. In 2011 he built his own 300 litre still and has since then been filling only one cask per year. His first whisky, distilled from a mix of peated and non-peated barley, was launched in 2015 and has since then been followed by more releases every year in March.

Ergaster, Distillerie

Passel, Hauts de Frances, founded in 2015

distillerie-ergaster.com

Founded by two friends, one of them being Éric Trossat who founded the Uberach brewery in Alsace. Fitted with a Stupfler pot still, peated and unpeated spirit is slowly aging in ex-Cognac, ex-Pineau des Charentes, ex-Vin Jaune and ex-Banyuls casks. The first whisky, the organic Ergaster Nature was launched in December 2018 and was followed by Ergaster Tourbé in October 2019.

Gilbert Holl, Distillerie

Ribeauvillé, Grand Est, founded in 1979 (whisky since 2000)

gilbertholl.com

In 1979, Gilbert Holl began to distill occasionally in the back of his wine and spirits shop but it wasn´t until the beginning of 2000, that he finally started producing also whisky. His first bottling, Lac'Holl, was put on sale in 2004 and was followed by Lac'Holl Junior in 2007 and Lac'Holl Vieil Or in 2009. In 2015, Lac'Holl Junior was replaced by Lac'Holl Or. The oldest whiskies, 10 and 12 year olds, can only be found at the distillery.

Hagmeyer

Balbronn, Alsace, founded in 2016

distillerie-hagmeyer.com

Originally fruit producers for several generations, Willy and his

Clayssens Distillery was recently bought by Saint-Germain brewery and distillery

brother André started whisky production in 2016, after sourcing beer from Perle brewery. The first edition of WAH (Whiskey Alsacien Hagmeyer) was launched in October 2019, after 42 months in Alsatian wine barrels.

D'Hautefeuille, Distillerie

Beaucourt En Santerre, Hauts de France, founded in 2015

distilleriedhautefeuille.com

Founded by Étienne d'Hautefeuille who took over the farming business of his parents in 2013, and Gaël Mordac, a recognized drink specialist retailer in Amiens. Fitted with an 800 litre Stupfler still, a new warehouse and a filling/bottling room was built in 2020. The first whisky, Loup Hardi distilled at another distillery, was launched in December 2018. The first release from their own production appeared in May 2020.

Laurens, Domaine

Clairvaux d'Aveyron, Occitanie, founded in 1983 (whisky since 2014)

domaine-laurens.com

The wine estate Domaine Laurens was founded in 1983 by two brothers Gilbert and Michel Laurens, assisted by their wives, Martine and Maryse. In 2014, Vincent started a whisky production with the help of a neighbor brewery. The first versions. Red Léon, aged in white dry aveyron wine ex-casks, and Blue Léon, red ratafia ex-casks, were launched in 2017.

Lehmann, Distillerie

Obernai, Grand Est, founded in 1850 (whisky since 2001)

distillerielehmann.com

The story of Lehmann distillery starts in 1850 when the family of the actual owner set up a still in Bischoffsheim. Yves Lehmann inherited the facility in 1982 but decided to move all the equipment to a new distillery in 1993. The first regular bottling from the distillery, aged for seven years in Bordeaux casks, was launched in 2008. The range now includes Elsass Origine (4-6 years) and Elsass Gold (6-8 years), both matured in ex-white wine casks, and Elsass Premium (8 years) matured in ex-Sauternes casks. Florent Lehmann joined his father in 2020 and soon after launched a new range, Birdy, with three bottlings celebrating the legendary French art de vivre: Coup de Foudre, C'est la vie and Rendez-vous.

Leisen

Malling, Grand Est, founded in 1898 (whisky since 2012)

distillerie-leisen-petite-hettange.fr

Since 1898, the Leisen family has distilled fruit spirits but also spirits made from rye and barley. The distillery is equipped with two Carl stills (250 and 350 litres respectively). In 2018, Jean-Marie Leisen released his first bottles under the JML brand.

Meyer, Distillerie

Hohwarth, Grand Est, founded in 1958 (whisky since 2004)

distilleriemeyer.fr

Founded in 1958 to distill fruits, Meyer distillery started producing whisky in 2004. The first bottlings of Meyer's were launched by Jean-Claude Meyer in 2007, just one year before his sudden death. and the two sons Lionel and Arnaud took over the operation. There are only two malts whiskies on sale, Meyer's Pur Malt and Meyer Pur Malt Le Fumé.

Michard, Brasserie

Limoges, Nouvelle Aquitaine, founded in 1987 (whisky since 2008)

bieres-michard.com

Started as a craft brewery, the second in France, Jean Michard began to also produce whisky in 2008. The first whisky, J Michard, was released in 2011. It was followed by a second batch in 2013. Jean Michard has now retired and the still does not work very often but a brand new bottle and packaging design has been launched, announcing a new start.

Moutard

Buxeuil, Grand Est, founded in 1892 (whisky since 2017)

famillemoutard.com

The Moutard and Diligent families are well known in the Champagne area for their wines and spirits. Recently, François Moutard and his sons, Alexandre and Benoit, started buying wash from local breweries in order to make whisky. Their distillery is fitted with five pot stills and production started in April 2017. Matured in Champagne ratafia barrels, the first whisky was released in May 2020.

Ninkasi Distillery

Nalin, Distillerie

La Chana, Auvergne-Rhône Alpes, founded in 1919
(whisky since 2015)

distillerie-nalin.fr

A family distillery for three generations installed in Meys in the heart of the Monts du Lyonnais since 1919. For a long time, the Nalin family distilled mainly pear eaux-de-vie for other companies. In 2015, they started whisky production and the first bottling has been sold under the name of NP since November 2018.

Ninkasi

Tarare, Auvergne-Rhône Alpes, founded in 2015

ninkasi.fr

The whisky is distilled in a 2,500-litre Prulho Chalvignac still and aged in different types of barrels of the most famous wines of Bourgogne and Côte du Rhône areas. A second still, Charentais type and 1,500 litres, was installed in 2019. Track01, a limited edition of 1,000 bottles, was launched end of 2018 followed by Track02 (lightly peated) and Track 03 in 2019.

Northmaen, Distillerie de

La Chapelle Saint-Ouen, Normandie, founded in 1997
(whisky since 2002)

northmaen.com

Originally a craft brewery but later equipped with a portable still. the 3 year old Thor Boyo was released in 2003. the 8 year old Slepinir in 2013, the 5 year old peated Fafnir in 2015 and the 6 year old Kenning in 2018. The still is not portable anymore but now works in a real distillery.

Ouche Nanon

Ourouer Les Bourdelins, Centre-Val de Loire, founded in 2015
(whisky since 2018)

ouche-nanon.fr

Originally a micro-brewery, the owner Thomas Mousseau acquired an old Guillaume still from 1930s. With a capacity of 500 litres, the still is heated with wood. Thomas Mousseau started distilling in May 2015. The first whisky, La Petite Bertha aged in ex-Sauternes casks, was released in November 2018 and was followed in 2019 by the peated Frog´s Peat.

Paris, Distillerie de

Paris, Île de France, founded in 2016

distilleriedeparis.com

Sébastien and Nicolas Julhès installed a still in January 2016 and obtained license No. 1, the first one granted to Paris for over a century. It is equipped with a small 400 litre Holstein still. The first Parisian whisky was launched in September 2019, after 42 months of ageing in a variety of small casks.

Piautre, La

Ménitré Sur Loire, Pays de Loire, founded in 2004 (whisky since 2014)

lapiautre.fr

Ten years after Yann Leroux and Vincent Lelièvre had founded a brewery, they decided to start malting their own barley and to start experiments with distillation. La Piautre is now equipped with two Charentais direct-fire heated stills. The company released their first Loire Valley whiskies in January 2018: Malt, Tourbé and Seigle.

Quintessence, La

Herrberg, Grand Est, founded in 2008 (whisky since 2013)

distillerie-quintessence.com

In 2008 Nicolas Schott took over the family distillery in Herrberg in order to continue the production of fruit spirits (raspberry, pear, plum, quetsche or quince) and also liqueurs (spices or asperule). End of 2016, the 34 year old distiller surprised everyone with the release of his first single malt whisky, Schott's, bottled at 42%.

Roche Aux Fées, La

Sainte-Colombe, Bretagne, founded in 1996
(whisky since 2010)

distillerie-larocheauxfees.com

Gonny Keizer installed a micro-brewery in 1996 and became the first female master-brewer in France. In 2010, Gonny and her husband Henry bought a 400 litre portable automatic batch still. The still is wood-heated and equipped with a worm-tub condenser. The first Roc'Elf bottling, distilled from three malted cereals (barley, wheat, oat), was released in January 2016 followed by a second in early 2017. In 2020, the brewery moved to a new location, in order to have more space for whisky production.

Saint-Palais

Saint-Palais de Negrignac, Nouvelle Aquitaine, founded in 2016

alfredgiraud.com

In 1896, Louis Gautriaud built a distillery, Chevanceaux, which was taken over by his son and grandson. In 1963, a new distillery was built with ten stills to be enlarged in 1990 when the number was doubled. In 2016, Julien Naud built a brewery dedicated to whisky production fitted with a filter press. In 1995, Philippe Giraud who came from a famous cognac house, joined the company to form the Alfred Giraud French Malt Whisky in association with Julien Nau. Two versions of their blended malt have been released, Harmonie and Héritage.

Vercors, Distillerie

Saint-Jean En Vercors, Auvergne-Rhône Alpes, founded in 2015
(whisky since 2019)

distillerie-vercors.com

The distillery is an atypical installation equipped with a Charentais copper still and a steel boiler which works under vacuum for the first run. First distillation is carried out at low temperature (around 50°C). Sequoia Première Impression and Sequoïa Tourbé, two malt spirits, were launched in September 2018 and in April 2020 the first "proper" whisky was launched. All the spirits are certified organic..

Germany

Whisky-Destillerie Blaue Maus

Eggolsheim-Neuses, 1980

fleischmann-whisky.de

The oldest malt whisky distillery in Germany distilling their first whisky in 1983. It took, however, 15 years before the first whisky, Glen Mouse 1986, appeared. A completely new distillery became operational in 2013. All whisky from Blaue Maus are single cask and there are around ten single malts in the range. Some of them are released at cask strength while others are reduced to 40%.

Slyrs Destillerie

Schliersee, founded in 1928 (whisky since 1999)

slyrs.de

The malt, smoked with beech, comes from locally grown grain and the spirit is distilled in 1,500 litre stills. The non chill-filtered whisky is called Slyrs after the original name of the surrounding area, Schliers. The core expressions are a 3 year old bottled at 43%, the 51 which has matured in casks that previously held sherry, port or sauternes and a 12 year old. Limited editions include various finishes including an 12 year old Islay cask as well as Mountain Edition where the whiskies have been matured at a high altitude.

Hercynian Distilling Co (formerly known as Hammerschmiede)

Zorge, founded in 1984 (whisky since 2002)

hercynian-distilling.de

Hammerschmiede´s main products used to be spirits from fruit, berries and herbs but whisky distilling was embarked on in 2002. The first bottles were released in 2006. The core range used to be called Glen Els but following a complaint from the SWA, the name was changed to Elsburn in September 2019. One subrange is called Alrik represented by experimental and smoky whiskies while the Willowburn range consists of whiskies finished in different types of casks and Emperor´s Way is all about peated whisky.

Bayerwald-Bärwurzerei und Spezialitäten-Brennerei Liebl

Kötzting, founded in 1970 (whisky since 2006)

coillmor.com

In 2009 the first bottles bearing the name Coillmór were released. There is a wide range aged between 4 and 12 years currently available. Recent limited editions include the 8 year old Bavaria & Toscana with a finish in Caberlot casks (a cross breed of cabernet franc and merlot) as well as the peated Albanach.

St Kilian Distillers

Rüdenau, founded in 2015

stkiliandistillers.com

St Kilian is one of few German distilleries designated to make only whisky. The distillery has a capacity of producing 200,000 litres of alcohol. The first single malt, Signature Edition One released in 2019, was a 3 year old matured in bourbon casks and the most recent, Edition Four, is heavily peated and matured in sherry casks. The first core bottling is expected in 2022/2023.

Finch Whiskydestillerie

Heroldstatt, founded in 2001

finch-whisky.de

The distillery is one of Germany´s biggest with a yearly production of 250,000 litres and it is also equipped with one of the biggest pot stills in Germany - 3,000 litres. The range of whiskies is large and they are made from a variety of different grains. The age is between 5 and 8 years and included is a 5 year old single malt.

Other distilleries in Germany

Alt Enderle Brennerei

Rosenberg/Sindolsheim, founded in 1991 (whisky since 1999)

alt-enderle-brennerei.de

The first whisky distillation was in 2000 and the owners now have a wide range of Neccarus Single Malt for sale from a 4 year old to a 20 year old! The latest limited release was the 7 year old, smoky Terrador with a finish in rum casks.

Altstadthof, Hausbrauerei

Nürnberg, founded in 1984

hausbrauerei-altstadthof.de

The first German distillery to produce organic single malt. The current range consists of Ayrer´s Red, Ayrer´s PX, Ayrer´s Bourbon and Ayrer´s Ayla (peated). Recent limited expressions include the 5 year old Mastercut bottled at 75,2% and the 5 year old Alligator.

Am Hartmannsberg, Schaubrennerei

Freital, founded in 2011

hartmannsberger.de

Working on a range of various spirits, the owner also produces small volumes of whisky. The first whisky was released in 2015 and the latest was a 5 year old single malt, matured in ex-sherry casks.

Avadis Distillery

Wincheringen, founded in 1824 (whisky since 2006)

avadisdistillery.de

Around 2,000 bottles are released yearly and the oak casks from France have previously been used for maturing white Mosel wine. Threeland Whisky is between 3 and 6 years old and the range also consists of finishes in oloroso and port casks.

Hans-Gerhard Fink and his team at Finch Distillery

Bellerhof Brennerei

Owen, founded in 1925 (whisky since 1990)

bellerhof-brennerei.com

The production of whisky made from barley, wheat and rye started in 1990 and today there is one single malt in the range - the 5 year old Danne´s Gärschda Malt, available at cask strength or 43%.

Birgitta Rust Piekfeine Brände

Bremen, founded in 2011

br-piekfeinebraende.de

A producer of gin and other spirits but also single malt whisky. One of the latest releases is the Van Loon 5 year old single malt with a port finish.

Birkenhof-Brennerei

Nistertal, founded in 1848 (whisky since 2002)

birkenhof-brennerei.de

The first release from the distillery in 2008 was the 5 year old rye Fading Hill. This was followed a year later by a single malt. The most recent bottling (in November 2019) was the first peated expression, matured in a bourbon casks.

Bosch Edelbrand

Lenningen, founded in 1948 (whisky since 1997)

bosch-edelbrand.de

A family company run by the third generation, the distillery produces gin, edelbrände and single malt whisky. The range consists of whiskies (both grain and malt) up to ten years of age.

Brauhaus am Lohberg

Wismar, whisky since 2010

brauhaus-wismar.de, hinricusnoyte.de

The first release of Baltach single malt was in 2013. It was a 3 year old with a finish in sherry casks. The latest edition of Baltach, finished in PX sherry casks was released in November 2019.

Burger Hofbrennerei

Burg, founded in 2007 (whisky since 2012)

sagengeister.de

Apart from distillates from fruits and berries, the distillery also produces whisky made from malted barley. Maturation is in small (100 litres) casks made of American white oak. The first release of Der Kolonist single malt was in spring 2015.

Dolleruper Destille

Dollerup, founded in 1990 (whisky since 2014)

dolleruper-destille.de

A huge variety of spirits from fruits, berries and nuts are produced but also single malt whisky. At least six different bottlings, including peated, have so far been released.

Drexler, Destillerie

Arrach, whisky since 2007

drexlers-whisky.de

Apart from spirits made from herbs, fruits and berries, malt whisky has been produced since 2009. The first release of Bayerwoid Single Malt was in 2011 and has been followed up by more releases including a 100% malted rye whisky. The oldest release of Bayerwoid so far is a 10 year old.

Druffel, Brennerei

Oelde-Stromberg, founded in 1792 (whisky since 2010)

brennerei-druffel.de

A huge variety of different spirits are produced including malt whisky. The first whisky, named Prum, was released in 2013 while the latest (in 2018) was a 4 year old sherry-maturation finished in casks made from plum wood.

Dürr Edelbranntweine

Neubulach, founded in 2002

blackforest-whiskey.com

The first release from the distillery, the 4 year old Doinich Daal, reached the market in 2012. The latest release, batch 5, appeared in December 2019 with three expressions; Moosäcker, Tannenrain and the smoky Krabbawäldle.

Edelbrände Senft

Salem-Rickenbach, founded in 1988 (whisky since 2009)

senft-destillerie.de

The first 2,000 bottles of 3.5 year old Senft Bodensee Whisky were released in 2012 and they were later followed by a cask strength version. The latest limited release, the 6 year old Edition Herbert, appeared in early 2020.

Eifel Destillate

Koblenz, founded in 2009

eifel-destillate.de

Even though other spirits are produced, the focus is on whisky of all sorts. The core range consists of Single Rye, Single Malt and the blend Smoky Malt & Rye. All whiskies are between 3 and 6 years old and they are not chill-filtered or coloured.

Faber, Brennerei

Ferschweiler, founded in 1949

faber-eifelbrand.de

Established as a producer of eau-de vie from fruits and berries, whisky has been included in the poduction during the last few years. The only whisky so far is a single malt that has matured for 6 years in barrels made of American white oak.

Feller, Brennerei

Dietenheim-Regglisweiler, founded in 1820
(whisky since 2008)

brennerei-feller.de

In 2012 the 3 year old single malt Valerie matured in bourbon casks, was released. It was followed by two 5 year olds (sherry- and amarone-finish respectively) and a 4 year old finished in a madeira cask. A range called Augustus is reserved for single grain.

Fitzke, Kleinbrennerei

Herbolzheim-Broggingen, founded in 1874 (whisky since 2004)

kleinbrennerei-fitzke.de

The first release of the Derrina single malt was in 2007 and new batches have been launched ever since including a lightly peated. The different varieties of Derrina are either made from malted grains (barley, rye, wheat, oats etc.) or unmalted (barley, oats, buckwheat, rice, triticale, sorghum or maize).

Glina Whiskydestillerie

Werder a.d. Havel, founded in 2004

glina-whisky.de

The distillery moved to larger premises in 2016, thereby ten-folding the capacity. The first Glina Single Malt was released in

2008. Most of the whiskies are between 3 and 5 years old. The oldest whisky so far is an 8 year old single malt matured in a combination of casks including port and Bordeaux.

Gutsbrennerei Joh. B. Geuting

Bocholt Spork, founded in 1837 (whisky since 2010)

muensterland-whisky.de

The first releases from this distillery, two single malts and two single grain, appeared in September 2013. More releases of the J.B.G. Münsterländer Single Malt have followed, the latest a 3.5 year old matured in sherry casks

Heinrich, Brennerei

Kriftel, founded in 1983 (whisky since 2009)

brennerei-henrich.de, www.gilors.de

The first whisky release was the 3 year old single malt Gilors in 2012. The two core expressions, Gilors fino sherry matured and Gilors port matured, are both 3 years old. Recent limited editions include Gilors Peated (made from peated malt and matured for three years in bourbon casks) and a 7 year old, finished in PX casks.

Höhler, Brennerei

Aarbergen, founded in 1895 (whisky since 2001)

brennerei-hoehler.de

The first whisky from the distillery was released in 2004 as a 3 year old. A couple of the more recent releases of their Whesskey (so called since it is from the province Hessen) include versions made from rye, oat, triticale and pilsner.

Josef Druffel, Brennerei

Oelde-Stromberg, founded in 1792 (whisky since 2010)

brennerei-druffel.de

The first single malt, Prum, was released in 2013 and had matured in a mix of different casks (bourbon, sherry, red wine and new Spessart oak) and was finished in small casks made of plum tree! In 2015, a 5 year old version was released.

Kammer-Kirsch, Destillerie

Karlsruhe, founded in1961 (whisky since 2006)

kammer-kirsch.de

The distillery is working together with a brewery which delivers a fermented wash to the distillery and they continue distilling a whisky called Black Forest Rothaus. The whisky was launched for the first time in 2009 and every year, a new batch is released.

Kinzigbrennerei

Biberach, founded in 1937 (whisky since 2004)

biberacher-whisky.de

The first release was Badische Whisky in 2008 and two years later came the 4 year old Biberacher Whisky, the first single malt, followed by Schwarzwälder Rye Whisky, the smoky single malt Kinzigtäler Whisky and Geroldsecker where peat from Scotland was used. The oldest whisky so far is the 8 year old No. 8 Select.

Kymsee Whisky

Grabenstätt, founded in 1994 (whisky since 2012)

kymsee-whisky.de

A distillery was added to the existing brewery in 2012 and three years later the first bottling of the triple-distilled Kymsee single malt was released. This is still the only expression.

Landgasthof Gemmer

Rettert, founded in 1908 (whisky since 2008)

landgasthof-gemmer.de

The only single malt released is the 3 year old Georg IV which has matured for two years in toasted Spessart oak casks and finished for one year in casks that have contained Banyuls wine.

Lübbehusen Malt Distillery

Emstek, founded in 2014

theluebbehusen.com

The distillery has one of the largest pot stills in the country, where whisky made from peated Scottish malt is distilled. The first release, a 3 year old, appeared in autumn 2017. Rye whisky has also been released and attached to the distillery is a visitor centre.

Marder Edelbrände

Albbruck-Unteralpfen, founded in 1953 (whisky since 2009)

marder-edelbraende.de

The first release in 2013 was the 3 year old Marder Single Malt matured in a combination of new American oak and sherry casks. The latest limited edition was an 8 year old, peated single cask.

Märkische Spezialitäten Brennerei

Hagen, whisky since 2010

msb-hagen.de

The spirit is distilled four times, matured in ex-bourbon barrels for 12 months and then brought to a cave, with low temperature and high humidity, for further maturation. The first whisky, Tronje van Hagen, was released in 2013 and has now been renamed DeCavo.

Mösslein, Destillerie

Zeilitzheim, founded in 1984 (whisky since 1996)

weingeister.de

Originally a winery, whisky production was brought on board in 1996. The first whisky was released in 2003 and the core range consists of a single malt and a grain whisky, both 5 years old. In 2017, the first 12 year old, Ernest 25, was released.

Nordik Edelbrennerei

Jork, founded in 2012

nordik-edelbrennerei.de

A variety of spirits including whisky are produced. Their current single malt expression, peated and matured in oloroso casks, was distilled in 2014 and bottled in September 2019.

Nordpfälzer Edelobst & Whiskydestille Höning

Winnweiler, founded in 2008

nordpfalz-brennerei.de

The first release was in 2011, a 3 year old single malt by the name Taranis with a full maturation in a Sauternes cask while the latest release, in 2020, was a 5 year old also matured in a Sauternes cask.

Number Nine Spirituosen-Manufaktur

Leinefelde-Worbis, founded in 1999 (whisky since 2013)

number-nine.eu

The production was expanded in 2013 to include rum, gin and whisky. The first single malt was launched in 2016 while one of the latest, Peated Breeze madeira finish, appeared in spring 2020.

Old Sandhill Whisky

Bad Belzig, founded in 2012

sandhill-whisky.com

The first whisky was released as a 3 year old single malt in 2015.

Since then a wide range of older bottlings have been launched including single malts matured in port pipes and Bordeaux barriques respectively.

Preussische Whiskydestillerie

Mark Landin, founded in 2009

preussischerwhisky.de

The spirit is distilled five to six times in a 550 litre copper still with a rectification column. Since 2013 only organic barley is used. The first whisky was launched as a 3 year old in December 2012. From 2015, all the whiskies have been at least 5 years old.

Ralf Hauer, Destillerie

Bad Dürkheim, founded in 1989 (whisky since 2012)

sailltmor.de

The first release from the distillery appeared in 2015 with the 3 year old Saillt Mor single malt. The oldest whisky so far is 5 years old and new bottlings are released regularly with a peated single malt matured in oloroso casks being one of the latest (autumn 2019).

Rieger & Hofmeister

Fellbach, founded in 1994 (whisky since 2006)

rieger-hofmeister.de

The first release was in 2009 and currently there are four expressions in the range – a single malt matured in pinot noir casks, a malt & grain from chardonnay casks, a malted rye and a single grain. A peated single malt is due for release in 2023.

Sauerländer Edelbrennerei

Kallenhardt, founded in 2000 (whisky since 2004)

sauerlaender-edelbrennerei.de

The first release of the Thousand Mountains McRaven appeared in 2007 as a 3 year old. One of the latest bottlings (December 2019) was the Peaty PX Sherry Special.

Scheibel Mühle

Kappelrodeck, founded in 2015

scheibel-muehle.de

Distillers of Kirschwasser and other spirits in the third generation, the owners are now also producing whisky. The first single malt was released in 2018 and Emill Kratwerk is now available at 46% and at cask strength.

Schlitzer Destillerie

Schlitz, founded in 2006

schlietzer-destillerie.de

Apart from a range of different spirits and vodka, single malt whisky is also produced. It is available under two brand names; Slitisian Single Malt (both unpeated and a variety matured in ex-Laphroaig casks as well as a single grain) and Schlitzer Single Malt.

Schloss Neuenburg, Edelbrennerei

Freyburg, founded in 2012

schlossbrennerei.eu

Small volumes of single malt whisky are produced with the spirit maturing for two years in new, German oak and then for another year in pinot noir casks. The first release was in August 2016.

Schwarzwaldbrennerei Walter Seeger

Calw-Holzbronn, founded in 1952 (whisky since 1990)

krabba-nescht.de

The first single malt was launched in 2009 and at the moment, the owner has two expressions in the range; Black-Wood single malt matured in amontillado sherry casks and a wheat whisky.

Senft, Gasthof

Gräfenberg, founded in 2007 (whisky since 2013)

gasthof-seitz.de, elch-whisky.de

A combination of a brewery, distillery and restaurant with a heritage going back to the 16th century. Today it is family-owned and apart from spirits from fruits and berries, malt whisky with the brand name Elch is also on the menue. The three year old, smoky Torf vom Dorf has been produced using peat from Germany.

Singold Whisky

Wehringen, founded in 2017

singold-whisky.de

Although founded in 2017, the brand has been produced at another distillery since 2012. Current releases include Singold Malt Whisky including a cask strength version, Singold Sherry Cask and Singold Grain with a port finish.

Spreewood Distillers

Schlepzig, founded in 2004 (whisky production)

stork-club-whisky.com

The distillery, which changed hands in 2016, had a history of producing a wide range of spirits but the new owners decided to focus mainly on rye whisky. The new range is called Stork Club and includes two single malts made from barley.

Steinhauser Destillerie

Kressbronn, founded in 1828 (whisky since 2008)

weinkellerei-steinhauser.de

The main products are spirits which are derived from fruits, but whisky also has its own niche. The first release was the single malt Brigantia which appeared in 2011. It was triple distilled and an 8 year old has followed since.

Steinwälder Hausbrennerei

Erbendorf, founded in 1818 (whisky since 1920)

brennerei-schraml.de

A kind of whisky was made here already in the early 1900s but was then sold as "Kornbrand". When the current owner took over, the spirit was relaunched as a 10 year old single grain whisky under the name Stonewood 1880. Other releases include a wheat whisky as well as two 3 year old single malts, Dra and Smokey Monk.

Stickum Brennerei (Uerige)

Düsseldorf, founded in 2007

stickum.de

The wash comes from their own brewery and the distillation takes place in a 250 litre column still. The single malt is called BAAS and the first bottling (a 3 year old) was released in 2010. In 2014 the owners released their first 5 year old whiskies.

Tecker Whisky-Destillerie

Owen, founded in 1979 (whisky since 1989)

tecker.eu

Apart from a variety of eau de vie and other spirits, around 1,500 litres of whisky is produced annually. The core expression is the 10 year old Tecker Single Malt matured for five years in ex-bourbon barrels, followed by five yers in oloroso casks. There is also a single grain (wheat and barley) aged for 5 years in bourbon casks.

Thomas Sippel, Destillerie

Weisenheim am Berg, founded in 1992 (whisky since 2011)

destillerie-sippel.de

Wines as well as distillates of all kinds are on the menu with whisky being introduced in 2011. The first release of the Palatinatus Single Malt came in 2014 and there are several expressions available, including a 6 year old peated version.

Volker Theurer, Brennerei

Tübingen, founded in 1991

schwaebischer-whisky.de

Located in a guesthouse, they released their first whisky as a 7 year old in 2003 and since then they have released Sankt Johann, an 8 year old single malt and the 10 year old Tammer. Theurer is also selling a blended whisky called Original Ammertal Whisky.

Simon´s Feinbrennerei

Alzenau-Michelbach, founded in 1879 (whisky since 1998)

simon-brennt.de

In 2013 a new Holstein still was installed, raising the whisky production to 3-5,000 litres per year. A single pot still whisky has since been released and the first rye whisky from the new still was launched in 2016 followed by whisky made from rice and emmer.

Wild Brennerei

Gengenbach, founded in 1855 (whisky since 2002)

wild-brennerei.de

Two 5 year old whiskies have been released so far – Wild Whisky Single Malt which has matured for three years in American white oak and another two in either sherry or port casks and Blackforest Wild Whisky, made from unmalted barley.

Zeitzer Whisky Manufaktur

Zeitz, founded in 2014

whisky-zeitz.de

The distillery is equipped with a Lomond still as well as a still built in Germany in 1935. A variety of newmake and 3 year old single malt has been released.

Ziegler, Brennerei

Freudenberg, founded in 1865

brennerei-ziegler.de

The maturation takes place not only in oak casks, but also in casks made of chestnut! Their current core bottling is a 5 year old called Aureum 1865 Single Malt and there is also a cask strength version. Limited releases, also peated, occur regularly and the oldest so far is an 8 year old in three different versions.

Hungary

Gemenc Distillery

Pörböly, founded in 2014

gemencdistillery.hu

Unlike so man other distilleries in Hungary producing pálinka, Gemenc is completely focused on whisky. The owner´s, Lajos Szöke, interest lies mainly in various grain whiskies which are distilled in a 4 plate copper still. Maturation takes place in 55-110 litre casks made from Hungarian oak or acacia and three different levels of charring are used. The current distillery is quite small but the long term plan is to build a larger facility. Since 2017, Szöke has also filled circa 30 casks with both peated and unpeated single malt made from barley. One single malt, made from chocolate malt, has so far been bottled but can only be obtained at the distillery.

Iceland

Eimverk Distillery

Reykjavik, founded in 2012

flokiwhisky.is

The country´s first whisky distillery where only organic barley grown in Iceland is used for the production and everything is malted on site. Both peat and sometimes sheep dung is used to dry the malted barley. The distillery has a capacity of 100,000 litres where 50% is reserved for gin and aquavite and the rest for whisky. The first, limited release of a 3 year old whisky was in late 2017 and more bottlings have followed since then. Two of the latest limited releases are Double Wood Reserve with a finish in stout casks and Birch Finish where toasted staves made of birch were put into the barrels for a few weeks.

Republic of Ireland

Midleton Distillery

Midleton, Co. Cork, founded in 1975

irishdistillers.ie

Midleton is by far the biggest distillery in Ireland and the home of Jameson´s Irish Whiskey. The production at Midleton comprises of two sections – grain whiskey and single pot still whiskey. The grain whiskey is needed for the blends, where Jameson´s is the biggest seller. Single pot still whiskey, on the other hand, is unique to Ireland. This part of the production is also used for the blends but is being bottled more and more on its own.

Until recently, Midleton distillery was equipped with mash tuns both for the barley side and the grain side. After considerable research and trials however, these have now been replaced by mash filters with an astonishing increase in spirit yield from 385 litres per ton of barley to 415 litres. Two major upgrades of the distillery (in 2013 and 2017) means that Midleton is now equipped with 48 washbacks, 6 column stills and 10 pot stills. A new maturation facility with 40 warehouses has also been built in Dungourney, not far from Midleton. More investments were announced in autumn 2018 when the owners revealed that 150 million euros would be spent on more warehouses and an expansion of the bottling and packing facilities. In autumn 2015, a new micro distillery adjacent to the existing distillery, was opened. With a production capacity of 400 casks per year, it will be used for experiments and innovation. However, in spring 2019, a commercial release of Method an Madness Gin made at the micro distillery was introduced.

Of all the brands produced at Midleton, Jameson´s blended Irish whiskey is by far the biggest. In 2019 the brand sold 97 million bottles – an astonishing increase by 60% in the last five years! Apart from the core expression with no age statement, there are Crested (which used to be called Cresten Ten), Black Barrel and an 18 year old. Since 2015, a number of special series have been launched; Deconstructed with three bottlings – Bold, Lively and Round, The Whiskey Maker´s Series with The Cooper´s Croze and The Blender´s Dog and Jameson Caskmates with two whiskies aged in stout barrels and IPA barrels. In spring 2018, Jameson Bow Street 18 years old, the first cask strength release of a Jameson, appeared with yearly batches released since then. In July 2019, the triple-cask (bourbon, sherry and Malaga wine), triple-distilled Jameson Triple Triple was released as an exclusive to duty-free. Other blended whiskey brands include Powers and the exclusive Midleton Very Rare. The latter is also the name of a newly released series of exceptionally old whiskies – Midleton Very Rare Silent Distillery. They have all been distilled at the old Midleton Distillery which closed in 1975. The first installment in February 2020 was a 45 year old single malt and the other four releases will appear with one new bottling every year.

In recent years, Midleton has invested increasingly in their second category of whiskies, single pot still, and that range now includes Redbreast 12, 12 cask strength, 15 and 21 year old as core bottlings. In spring 2020 another expression was added - a 27 year old partly matured in port casks. Limited releases include the sherrymatured Lustau Edition and the Redbreast Dream Cask 32 years old. In May 2019, the limited 20 year old Redbreast Dream Cask Pedro Ximénez Edition was launched. Furthermore, there is Green Spot without age statement, the 12 year old Leoville Barton bordeaux finish and the Chateau Montelena finish, Yellow Spot 12 years old, Red Spot, released in late 2018 and matured in a combination of ex-bourbon, oloroso sherry and marsala casks and, launched in 2020, Blue Spot - a 7 year old matured in a combination of bourbon, sherry and madeira. Powers (John´s Lane, Signature and Three Swallow) and Barry Crocket Legacy are other eaxmples of their single pot still whiskies. The first release of an Irish whiskey finished in virgin Irish oak in 2015, the Dair Ghaelach, was followed up by a seond edition in 2017 and a third (Knockrath Forest) in early 2020. More innovation was displayed in 2017 when a range of experimental whiskeys were released under the name Method and Madness. Included in the range were four expressions with one of them, a single pot still, finished in French chestnut casks. More expressions have been added to the range with two of the latest being two single pot stills finished in acacia wood and wild cherry wood respectively.

In June 2020, Midleton´s Master Distiller Brian Nation who has been with Irish Distillers for 23 years, left the company to take up a position at a new craft distillery in Minneapolis - O´Shaughnessy Distilling Co - which will open in 2021.

Tullamore Dew Distillery

Clonminch, Co. Offaly, founded in 2014

tullamoredew.com

Until 1954, Tullamore D.E.W. was distilled at Daly´s Distillery in Tullamore. When it closed, production was temporarily moved to Power´s Distillery in Dublin, and was later moved to Midleton Distillery and Bushmill´s Distillery. William Grant & Sons acquired Tullamore D.E.W. in 2010 and in May 2013, they started to build a new distillery at Clonminch, situated on the outskirts of Tullamore. The four stills produce both malt whiskey and single pot still whiskey and the capacity is 3.6 million litres of pure alcohol. In autumn 2017, a bottling hall and a grain distillery with a capacity

of doing 8 million litres of grain spirit was opened on the same site. All whiskies at Tullamore are triple distilled. Tullamore D.E.W. is the second biggest selling Irish whiskey in the world after Jameson with 13 million bottles sold in 2018. The core range consists of Original (without age statement), 12 year old Special Reserve and 14 and 18 year old Single Malts. Recent limited releases include Trilogy (a triple blend whiskey matured in three types of wood), Phoenix and Old Bonded Warehouse. As an exclusive to duty free, the Tullamore D.E.W Cider Cask Finish was launched in summer 2015 and this was followed in autumn 2017 by a Carribean Rum Cask Finish.

Cooley Distillery

Cooley, Co. Louth, founded in 1987

thetyrconnellwhiskey.com, connemarawhiskey.com

In 1987, the entrepreneur John Teeling bought the disused Ceimici Teo distillery and renamed it Cooley distillery. Two years later he installed two pot stills and in 1992 he released the first single malt from the distillery, called Locke´s Single Malt. A number of brands were launched over the years. In December 2011 it was announced that Beam Inc. had acquired the distillery for $95m. In 2014, Suntory took over Beam and the new company was renamed Beam Suntory. Cooley distillery is equipped with one mash tun, four malt and six grain washbacks all made of stainless steel, two copper pot stills and two column stills. There is a production capacity of 650,000 litres of malt spirit and 2,6 million litres of grain spirit. The range of whiskies is made up of several brands. Connemara single malts, which are all more or less peated, consist of a no age, a 12 year old and a cask strength. Another brand is Tyrconnell with a core expression bottled without age statement. Other Tyrconnell varieties include three 10 year old wood finishes and Tyrconnell 16 year old with a finish in both oloroso and moscatel casks. Finally, there is the lightly peated Locke´s 8 year old.

Teeling Distillery

Dublin, founded in 2015

teelingwhiskey.com

After the Teeling family had sold Cooley and Kilbeggan distilleries to Beam in 2011, the family started a new company, Teeling Whiskey. John´s two sons, Jack and Stephen, then opened a new distillery in Newmarket, Dublin in June 2015. This was

One of Midleton´s warehouses

the first new distillery in Dublin in 125 years. One year after the opening, an amazing 60,000 people had been welcomed to the distillery. In summer 2017, Bacardi acquired a minority stake in Teeling Whiskey for an undisclosed sum. This is the first time Bacardi gets involved with Irish whiskey.

The distillery is equipped with two wooden washbacks, four made of stainless steel and three stills made in Italy; wash still (15,000 litres), intermediate still (10,000 litres) and spirit still (9,000 litres) and the capacity is 500,000 litres of alcohol. Both pot still and malt whisky is produced. The core range from the distillery consists of the blend Small Batch, the biggest seller, which has been finished in rum casks, Single Grain which has been fully matured in Californian red wine barrels, Single Malt - a vatting of five different whiskies that have been finished in five different types of wine casks and Single Pot Still (50% malted and 50% unmalted barley), the first of the whiskies being entirely distilled at the current distillery. The others had been distilled at Cooley. Recent limited bottlings include the third installment in the Brabazon series, a 14 year old PX sherry finish, and also a 28 year old single malt. The latter had been matured in bourbon casks and then allowed to marry in Sauternes casks. Small batches are released regularly, available either at the distillery or in select markets including one finished in chinkapin oak and one in rye gin casks..

Roayl Oak Distillery (fomerly known as Walsh Whiskey Distillery)
Carlow, Co. Carlow, founded in 2016

walshwhiskey.com, royaloakdistillery.com

With succesful brands such as The Irishman and Writer's Tears (both produced at Midleton), Bernard Walsh decided to open his own distillery at Royal Oak, Carlow. With a back-up from the major Italian drinks company, Illva Saronno, construction began in late 2014 and the distillery was commissioned in March 2016. The capacity is 2.5 million litres of alcohol and all types of whiskey is produced including grain- malt- and pot still whiskey. The equipment consists of a 3 ton semi-lauter mash tun, six washbacks, a 15,000 litre wash still, a 7,500 litre intermediate still and a 10,000 litre spirit still. There is also a column still for grain whiskey production. Apart from producing whiskey for its own brands, the distillery has allocated 15% of the output for a number of international partners. In January 2019, it was announced that Illva Saronno would take full control of the distillery while Bernard

Walsh would continue with the brands Writer's Tears and The Irishman, trading under the name Walsh Whiskey and in the future relying on whiskey from Irish Distillers (Midleton) for his needs.

Great Northern Distillery
Dundalk, Co. Louth, founded in 2015

gndireland.com

In 2013, the Irish Whiskey Company (IWC), with the Teeling family as the majority owners, took over the Great Northern Brewery in Dundalk and turned it into a distillery. When it became operational in August 2015, it was the second biggest distillery in Ireland, with the capacity to produce 3.6 million litres of pot still whiskey and 8 million litres of grain spirit. The distillery is equipped with three columns for the grain spirit production and three pot stills for producing malt and single pot still whiskey. In summer 2019, another two washbacks were added to increase production. The main part of the business is supplying whiskey to private label brands but since 2017, the owners have their own brand of Irish single malt called Burke's Irish Whiskey, which had been distilled during the family's Cooley days.

Waterford Distillery
Waterford, Co. Waterford, founded in 2015

waterforddistillery.ie

Founded by the former co-owner of Bruichladdich distillery, Mark Reynier. In 2014 he bought Waterford Brewery and in December 2015, the first spirit was distilled. The distillery is equipped with two pot stills and one column still and, even though grain spirit will be produced, malt whiskey is the number one priority. The distillery also has a mash filter instead of a mash tun. There is a focus on local barley and Reynier is sourcing the barley from 72 farms on 19 different soil types. The distillery has a capacity of 1 million litres but the owners have plans to go up to 3 million litres in the future. After having distilled Ireland's first organic whiskey in 2016, Reynier decided to also produce the first biodynamic whiskey in 2018. In April 2020, Pilgrimage, the first general whiskey release from the distillery appeared. This was followed in June by Bannow Island and Ballykilcavan, the distillery's first two single farm whiskies.

Ned Gahan, Head Distiller at Waterford Distillery

Roe & Co. Distillery

Dublin, founded in 2019

roeandcowhiskey.com

The opening of Roe & Co Distillery marks Diageo´s return to the Irish whiskey scene which they left in 2014 when they sold Bushmills. A blend named Roe & Co made from sourced whiskies was launched already in 2017 and at the same time plans to build a distillery in Dublin were revealed. The distillery is situated in The Liberties district in the former Guinness Power Station. Three stills made by Abercrombie in Alloa and wooden washbacks make up part of the equipment and the production capacity of double- and tripledistilled whiskey is 500,000 litres. The distillery, which opened its doors to viistors in June 2019, is named after George Roe, a prominent whiskey maker in the 19th century.

Other distilleries in Ireland

Achill Island Distillery

Achill Island, Co. Mayo, founded in 2019

irishamericanwhiskeys.com

This is Irelands first island-based whiskey distillery and it was founded by the IrishAmerican Trading Company, a family owned company with offices both in Dublin and Boston. The founder is John McKay who sadly passed away in February 2020 but before that he took part in the opening of the company´s distillery in summer 2019. The distillery is equipped with two copper pot stills from Forsyths in Speyside and although whiskey from their own stills won´t be released for a while, the owners already have two expressions of sourced whiskey for sale – a blend and a 10 year old single malt.

Ballykeefe Distillery

Ballykeefe, Co. Kilkenny, founded in 2017

ballykeefedistillery.ie

A classic farm distillery growing their own barley and the first to operate in Kilkenny for over 200 years. The distillery is equipped with three copper pot stills and the first distillation was in spring 2018. Gin, vodka and poitin have already been released and the first Ballykeefe whiskey was released in August 2020.

Blackwater Distillery

Ballyduff, Co. Kerry, founded in 2014

blackwaterdistillery.ie

Originally located in Cappoquin, Co. Waterford, the distillery moved in 2018 to Ballyduff. At that time the company was already famous for their gin. In their new distillery, equipped with three stills from Frilli in Italy, whiskey is now also produced. Director and co-founder Peter Mulryan is passionate about single pot still. The current legislation says it must be produced from malted and unmalted barley and that only 5% of other grains can be a part of the mash bill. According to legislators this is the traditional way. Going through hundreds of recipes from the 19th and 20th century Irish distilleries, Mulryan has shown that a substantially higher percentage of other grains were involved. Apart from making some single malt, Mulryan has spent 2019 making single pot still from a huge variety of these ancient recipes.

Boann Distillery

Drogheda, Co. Meath, founded in 2016

boanndistillery.ie

Assisted by the well-known whisky consultant, John McDougall, Pat Cooney built the distillery which is equipped with three Italian-made copper pot stills and a gin still. The first pot still whiskey distillation was in December 2019 but in common with most Irish distillery start-ups, they have already launched a sourced whiskey called The Whistler.

Burren Distillery

Ballyvaughan, Co. Clare, founded in 2019

burrendistillers.com

It´s been a long time coming since the company was granted planning permission in 2015 but in 2019, they finally started distilling whiskey. The owners are using locally grown barley which is floor malted at the distillery, distillation takes place in traditional copper pot stills and for some of the maturation, casks made of Irish oak are used. Bot single pot still and single malt whiskey will be produced.

Clonakilty Distillery

Clonakilty, Co. Cork, founded in 2016

clonakiltydistillery.ie

For eight successive generations, the Scully family have farmed the coastal lands near the resort town Clonakilty in West Cork. Michael and Helen Scully, together with other members of the family, started production in early 2019. With Paul Corbett (former Teeling Whiskey Company) as the head distiller, the main product will be a triple distilled pot still whiskey. The first release is planned for late 2021 with sourced whiskey already in the range.

Connacht Whiskey Company

Ballina, Co. Mayo, founded in 2016

connachtwhiskey.com

The distillery is equipped with three pot stills made in Canada and has the capacity to produce 300,000 litres of pure alcohol per year. The first distillation of whiskey (double-distilled) was made in April 2016 and in 2017, triple distillation started as well. Apart from malt whiskey and single pot still whiskey, the owners also produce vodka, gin and poitin. Releases so far have been made from sourced whiskey including the blend Brothership – a vatting of 10 year old Irish pot still and 10 year old American whiskey.

Dingle Whiskey Distillery, The

Milltown, Dingle, Co. Kerry, founded in 2012

dingledistillery.ie

Equipped with three pot stills and a combined gin/vodka still, the first production of gin and vodka was in October 2012 with whiskey production commencing in December. The first general release of a single malt whiskey appeared in autumn 2016. The most recent bottlings are Batch No. 4 of the single malt and Batch No. 3 of the pot still. In October 2019, Graham Coull of Glen Moray fame was hired as the new master distiller.

Dublin Liberties Distillery, The

Dublin founded in 2018

thedld.com

The birth of this, the third whiskey distillery in Dublin in modern days, and its location in the historical Liberties district, has been a struggle spanning at least eight years. Finally starting the production in early 2019, it is now owned by Quintessential Brands (75%) and East European drinks company Stock Spirits (25%). The master distiller is Darryl McNally who spent 17 years working for Bushmills. The three coper pot stills will produce both double and triple distilled whiskey as well as peated expressions. The mash tun charge is two tonnes of barley, the fermentation time is 60-72 hours and the total capacity is 700,000 litres of pure alcohol per year. The whiskeys currently available in the visitor centre have all been produced at either Bushmills or Cooleys.

Glendalough Distillery

Newtown Mount Kennedy, Co. Wicklow, founded in 2012

glendaloughdistillery.com

For the first three years, the company acted as an independent bottler. In 2015 Holstein stills were installed and gin production began. Apart from gin, the company regularly releases sourced whiskies. In 2016, the Canadian drinks distribution group Mark Anthony Brands invested €5.5m taking over 40% of the distillery and in December 2019 they took over the remaining 60%.

Glendree Distillery

Glendree, Co. Clare, founded in 2019

glendreedistillery.ie

A couple of years ago Alex Loudon and his father Paul started a brewery which has now been expanded with a distillery. Using the wash from the brewery and equipped with a 1,500 litre hybrid copper still with three columns, the distillery will be producing vodka, gin and whiskey. Apart from a lightly peated single malt, they will also make whiskies from rye and wheat. A very unusual feature is that they will be using 100% rainwater for the production.

Kilbeggan Distillery

Kilbeggan, Co. Westmeath, founded in 1757

kilbegganwhiskey.com

Brought back to life in 2007, Kilbeggan is the oldest producing whiskey distillery in the world. The distillery is equipped with a wooden mash tun, four Oregon pine washbacks and two stills. The first single malt from the new production came in 2010 and limited batches have been released since. The core blended expression of Kilbeggan is a no age statement bottling but limited releases of aged bottlings have occurred. There is also a Kilbeggan grain produced at Cooley distillery and in autumn 2018, Kilbeggan Small Batch Rye distilled and matured at Kilbeggan, was launched. In 2020 a single pot still whiskey with 2.5% oats was also released.

Killowen Distillery

Newry, Co. Down, founded in 2017

killowendistillery.com

Founded by Brendan Carty, the distillery started producing gin in 2017. Whiskey was always on the charts however and in early 2019 the first batch of pot still whiskey was distilled. Carty's approach is a bit different compared to many other Irish distillers as the spirit is double distilled and peated and the mash bill contains not only malted and unmalted barley but also other grains (like oats). Furthermore, the two Portuguese stills are direct heated and worm tub condensers are being used. In 2019 the first in a range of sourced whiskeys called Bonded Experimental was launched. The second, in February 2020, was the 10 year old Basque Txakolina Cask which was finished in casks with acacia heads.

Lough Gill Distillery

Hazelwood House, Co. Sligo, founded in 2019

loughgilldistillery.com

A group of investors led by David Raethorne came up with the idea in 2014 to build a distillery adjacent to Hazelwood House, a country house built in the 18th century. Planning permission was secured in 2017 and in December 2019 the distillery was commissioned. Equipped with three pot stills from Frilli in Italy, the distillery is unusually large with a capacity of 1 million litres. Several releases of sourced whiskey have already appeared under the brand name Athrú.

Lough Mask Distillery

Tourmakeady, Co. Mayo, founded in 2017

loughmaskdistillery.com

Equipped with two alambic stills, the distillery started production in early 2018. The Loch Measc malt is double distilled and both

peated and unpeated spirit will be produced. The first whiskey will be released in 2021 but both gin and vodka are already for sale.

Pearse Lyons Distillery

Dublin, founded in 2017

pearselyonsdistillery.com

Dr Pearse Lyons, who passed away in 2018, was a native of Ireland and used to work for Irish Distillers in the 1970s. In 1980 he changed direction and founded a company specializing in animal nutrition and feed supplements. In 2008, he opened a whiskey distillery in Lexington, Kentucky. Four years later he started a distillery in Carlow, Ireland. After a few years, the stills were moved to Dublin where Dr Lyons restored the old St James' church and converted it to a distillery. The first distillation was in September 2017 but the owners already have a range of aged malt whiskies made from whisky produced at Carlow. In July 2019 they also started distilling pot still whiskey.

Powerscourt Distillery

Enniskerry, Co. Wicklow, founded in 2017

powerscourtdistillery.com

The distillery is situated at the Powerscourt Estate, owned by the Slazenger family, south of Dublin. Three pot stills were ordered from Forsyths in Scotland, distillation started in autumn 2018 and a visitor centre was opened in summer 2019. Noel Sweeney from Cooley Distillery is in charge of the distillery which has a capacity of producing 1 million bottles per year. A range of sourced whiskies have been released under the name Fercullen.

Shed Distillery, The

Drumshanbo, Co. Leitrim, founded in 2014

theshedddistillery.com

Founded by entrepreneur and drinks veteran P J Rigney, the distillery is equipped with five pot stills, three column stills and six washbacks. The focus for the owners is triple distilled single pot still whiskey but Drumshanbo gin has been on the market for years. The first whiskey distillation was in late 2014 and in December 2019 the first whiskey was released - a five year old pot still.

Slane Distillery

Slane, Co. Meath, founded in 2017

slaneirishwhiskey.com

The Conyngham family established a whiskey brand a few years ago which became popular not least in the USA. The whiskey was produced at Cooleys but the family decided to start a distillery of their own. After an unsuccesful partnership with Camus Wine & Spirits, Brown-Forman stepped in and took over the entire project in 2015. Equipped with three copper pot stills, six column stills and washbacks made of wood, the distillery started production in summer 2018. Three types of whiskey are produced; single malt, single pot still and grain whiskey.

West Cork Distillers

Skibbereen, Co. Cork, founded in 2004

westcorkdistillers.com

The distillery, equipped with four stills, produces both malt whiskey and grain whiskey and some of the malting is done on site. The whiskey range is quite substantial including also peated whiskey. Among the latest releases is a range of wood finished expressions. In autumn 2019 the founders bought out the majority stake in the business held by Halewood Group and in 2020 the company moved to a new and expanded distillery in Marsh Road in Skibbereen.

Italy

Puni Destillerie
Glurns, South Tyrol, founded in 2012

puni.com

There are at least two things that distinguish this distillery from most others. One is the design of the distillery – a 13-metre tall cube made of red brick. The other is the raw material that they are using. Malt whisky is produced but malted barley is only one of three cereals in the recipe. The other two are malted rye and malted wheat. In 2016, however, they also started distilling 100% malted barley. The distillery is equipped with five washbacks and the fermentation time is 96 hours. There is also one wash still (3,000 litres) and one spirit still (2,000 litres) . The first single malt was released in October 2015 and the current core range consists of Alba (marsala casks with a finish in Islay casks), Sole (two years in ex-bourbon and two years in PX casks), Gold (5 years in ex-bourbon) and Vina (5 years in marsala casks). A recent limited release is the 6 year old Aura, matured in a combination of ex-bourbon and Islay casks and bottled at cask strength.

Psenner Destillerie
Tramin, founded in 1947 (whisky since 2013)

psenner.com

A producer of spirits from apples pears and later also a grappa, tried their hands at whisky for the first time six years ago. Their inaugural release of the 3 year old single malt eRètico appeared in October 2016 and had been matured in a combination of ex-grappa and ex-oloroso casks.

The Netherlands

Zuidam Distillers
Baarle Nassau, founded in 1974 (whisky since 1996)

zuidam.eu

Zuidam Distillers was started in 1974 as a traditional, family distillery producing liqueurs, genever, gin and vodka and is today managed by Patrick van Zuidam. The first release of a single malt whisky, which goes by the name Millstone, was from the 2002 production and it was bottled in 2007 as a 5 year old. The current range is a 5 year old which comes in both peated and unpeated versions, American oak 10 years, French oak 10 years, Sherry oak 12 years and PX Cask 1999. Apart from single malts there is also a Millstone 100% Rye which is bottled at 50%. Limited expressions include the 8 year old Double Sherry Cask (oloroso and PX), American Oak Peated Moscatel, the 4 year old 92 Rye, the 7 year old Peated PX and, not least, a 23 year old oloroso single cask released in November 2019. This was by far the oldest expression from the distillery. The distillery has been expanded continuously over the years and two more stills from Forsyths were commissioned in early 2020. The distillery has also started to grow their own barley and rye at a nearby farm.

Other distilleries in The Netherlands

Den Hool Distillery
Holsloot, founded in 2015

denhoolwhisky.nl

Originally a farm, the owners also started brewing beer in the late 1990s. In 2009 some of the wash was sent to Zuidam Distillers for distillation into whisky. The first release from those early batches appeared as a 6 year old Veenhaar single malt in 2016 and the latest

Lough Gill Distillery was commissioned as late as in December 2019

was an 8 year old in November 2019. Since 2015, distillation is carried out on the farm and they are also taking care of their own malting.

Eaglesburn Distillery

Ede, founded in 2015

eaglesburndistillery.com

The owner, Bart Joosten, is a firm believer in long fermentation and the wort is fermented for at least 10-12 days. The first release of a 3 year old malt whisky (ex-bourbon) was in October 2018 while the latest appeared in October 2020 - a 3 year old with two years in ex-bourbon and a further year in a cognac cask.

Hemel Brewery and Distillery, De

Nijmegen, founded in 1983

brouwerijdehemel.nl

Situated in a 12th century monastery, what started as a brewery has now been complemented by a distillery. The two releases of Anima whisky are technically "Bierbrands", i. e. distilled from a hopped beer.

Horstman Distillery

Losser, founded in 2000

distilleerderijhorstman.nl

Producers of genever and whisky, the distillery released their first bottling in 2016 (a 5 year old matured in port casks). The current range includes both grain and single malt, matured in various casks.

Ijsvogel Distillery, De

Arcen, founded in 2012

ijsvogel.com

A huge variety of different spirits are distilled including malt whisky. The first whisky was bottled in 2015 and the latest, released in 2019, was a 4 year old matured in an oloroso cask.

Kalkwijck Distillers

Vroomshoop, founded in 2009

kalkwijckdistillers.nl

The distillery is equipped with a 300 litre pot still with a column attached. The main part of the production is jenever, korenwijn and liqueurs but also whisky. In spring 2015, the first single malt was released. Eastmoor is 3 year old made from barley grown on the estate. One of the latest releases was the 5 year old 10th anniversary bottling released in 2019.

Lepelaar Distillery

Texel, founded in 2009 (whisky since 2014)

landgoeddebontebelevenis.nl

Joscha and Inge Schoots started a brewery and shop in 2009 and continued five years later by adding distilling equipment. The business is a part of a larger crafts centre. Single malt (both peated and unpeated) as well as grain whisky and genever is produced. A first, limited release of Texelse Whisky was made for the crowd funders in 2018 and was later followed by a general release.

Stokerij Sculte

Ootmarsum, founded in 2004 (whisky since 2011)

stokerijsculte.nl

The distillery is equipped with a 500 litre stainless steel mashtun, 4 stainless steel washbacks and two stills. The first Sculte Twentse Whisky was released in 2014 and this was followed by a 4 year old in 2016. The third release was heavily peated (30ppm) and this has recently been followed by a fourth and fifth batch.

Us Heit Distillery

Bolsward, founded in 2002

usheit.com

Frysk Hynder was the first Dutch whisky and made its debut in 2005 at 3 years of age. The barley is grown in surrounding Friesland and malted at the distillery. The whisky (3 to 5 years old) is matured in a variety of casks. A cask strength version has also been released.

Northern Ireland

Bushmill´s Distillery

Bushmills, Co. Antrim, founded in 1784

bushmills.com

Bushmills is the second biggest of the Irish distilleries after Midleton, with a capacity to produce 4,5 million litres of alcohol a year. In 1972 the distillery became a part of Irish Distillers Group which thereby gained control over the entire whiskey production in Ireland. Irish Distillers were later (1988) purchased by Pernod Ricard who, in turn, resold Bushmill´s to Diageo in 2005 at a price tag of €295.5 million. Since the take-over, Diageo invested heavily into the distillery and it now has ten stills with a production running seven days a week, which means 4,5 million litres a year. In 2014, Diageo took the market by surprise when they announced that they were selling the distillery. The buyer was the tequila maker Casa Cuervo, producer of José Cuervo. Diageo already owned 50% of the company´s other, upscale tequila brand, Don Julio and with the deal, they got the remaining 50% as well as $408m.

The new owners, Casa Cuervo, applied for a planning permission to expand the capacity and also to build another 29 warehouses over the next two decades on adjacent farmland. The approval process proved to be quite difficult due to environmental objections but in April 2019, the local council gave the green light. Apart from the new warehouses, an additional mash tun, eight new washbacks and ten new stills will be installed. The capacity after the expansion will be 9 million litres of alcohol. The total investment will be around £34m and the new distillery is set to open by 2021/2022.

At Bushmill´s Distillery, single malt whiskey is produced - nothing else. For their range of blended whiskies, the grain part is brought in from Midleton Distillery. Black Bush and Bushmill´s Original are the two main blended whiskeys in the range but in December 2017 a third expression was added to the range – Bushmills Red Bush. The first new expression from the distillery for the domestic market in five years, Red Bush is a blend of triple distilled single malt and grain whiskey. Bushmill´s core range of single malts consists of a 10 year old, a 16 year old Triple Wood with a finish in Port pipes for 6-9 months and a 21 year old finished in Madeira casks for two years. There is also a 12 year old Distillery Reserve which is sold exclusively at the distillery and the 1608 Anniversary Edition. In spring 2016, Bushmill´s launched their first whiskey exclusive for duty free, The Steamship Collection, with special cask matured whiskies, So far sherry, port, bourbon and rum have been released. In December 2018, Bushmills became one of the first distilleries in the world to release a whiskey matured in acacia wood. The bottling, only available at the distillery, had been finished in acacia casks for more than a year. Bushmills is the third most sold Irish whiskey after Jameson and Tullamore D.E.W.

Other distilleries in Northern Ireland

Copeland Distillery

Donaghadee, Co. Down, founded in 2016

copelanddistillery.com

In early 2019, the founder Gareth Irvine moved his distillery in Saintfield 20 kilometres south of Belfast to Donaghadee by the coast. Already established as a gin producer, the owners filled their first cask of malt whiskey in November 2019. The distillery is equipped with a still from Arnold Holstein.

Echlinville Distillery

Kircubbin, Co. Down, founded in 2013

echlinville.com

After having relied on Cooley Distillery for his mature whiskey, Shane Braniff decided in 2012 to build his own distillery. Located near Kircubbin on the Ards Peninsula he started production in August 2013. The distillery was further expanded with more equipment in 2015 and in April 2016, a visitor centre opened. The distillery also has its own floor maltings. Apart from single pot still and single malt whiskey, vodka and gin is also produced. Using sourced whiskey Braniff has revived the old Dunville's brand of blended whiskey and included also single malt. So far there has been no release of their own whiskey.

Rademon Estate Distillery

Downpatrick, Co. Down, founded in 2012

shortcrosswhiskey.com

Fiona and David Boyd-Armstrong opened their distillery on the Rademon estate in 2012. Since its inception, their main product has been Short Cross gin which quickly became a success story. In summer 2015 the production was expanded into whiskey and during the first year, around 100 barrels were filled. Through a £2.5m investment, the capacity of the distillery was further increased in 2018 with a new gin still as well as a new still for the whiskey production. No whiskey has yet been released.

Norway

Det Norske Brenneri

Grimstad, founded in 1952 (whisky since 2009)

detnorskebrenneri.no

Founded in 1952 the company mainly produced wine from apples and other fruits. Whisky production started in 2009 and two Holstein stills are used for the distillation. In 2012, Audny, the first single malt produced in Norway was launched. Recent bottlings include Eiktyrne Quadruple Batch 1. It is double distilled while Quadruple refers to the four different types of casks used for maturation; virgin American oak, bloodtub oloroso, brandy and PX.

Other distilleries in Norway

Arcus

Gjelleråsen, founded in 1996 (whisky since 2009)

arcus.no

Arcus is the biggest supplier and producer of wine and spirits in Norway with subsidaries in Denmark, Finland and Sweden. The first whisky produced by the distillery was launched in 2013. Under the name Gjoleid, two whiskies made from malted barley and malted wheat were released. More recent bottlings, some up to 5 years old, include Blindpassasjeren and Praksis 1.1 and 1.2.

Aurora Spirit

Tromsö, founded in 2016

bivrost.com

At 69.39°N, Aurora is the northernmost distillery in the world. The mash is bought from a brewery, fermented at the distillery and distilled in the 1,200 litre Kothe pot still with an attached column. Both non-peated and peated whisky is produced. Apart from single malt whisky, the owners also produce gin, vodka and aquavit. All their products are sold under the name Bivrost and the first malt

whisky, Odin's Share, appeared in May 2020.

Berentsen Distillery

Egersund, founded in 1895 (whisky since 2018)

berentsens.no

A producer of mineral water for more than 100 years, the company started brewing beer 15 years ago and just recently expanded into distillation of spirits (vodka, aquavit and whisky). With stills from Arnold Holstein in Germany and with the aid of Frank McHardy (ex Springbank) as a consultant, the owners hope to be one of the biggest whisky producers in Norway. No whisky released yet.

Feddie Distillery

Island of Fedje, founded in 2019

feddiedistillery.no

An already existing brewery was complemented by a distillery in 2019 and production of organic whisky started in November 2019. The goal for 2020 is to produce 50,000 litres of pure alcohol and the owners have a plan to open a visitor centre. Fedje is the most westerly, populated island in Norway

Klostergården Distillery

Tautra, founded in 2017

klostergardentautra.no

Equipped with two copper stills from Hoga in Portugal (1,000 and 600 litres repectively), this distillery is situated on the island of Tautra in the Trondheim fiord. There is also a brewery, hotel, restaurant and shop. No official bottling has yet been released.

Myken Distillery

Myken, founded in 2014

mykendestilleri.no

This distillery lies in Myken, a group of islands in the Atlantic ocean, 32 kilometres from mainland Norway. The equipment consists of copper stills produced by Hoga in Spain and in 2020 production was increased. Both peated and unpeated whisky is produced. The first launch of Myken Single Malt was in September 2018. Recent releases include Peated Sherry (35ppm) and the 4 year old Octave Symphony, released in March 2020.

Oss Craft Distillery

Flesland, founded in 2016

osscraft.no

Specialising in gin and other spirits made from herbs and botanicals, the distillery has already launched a range of spirits under the name Bareksten. In 2017, production of malt whisky began as well and in 2019 the distillery was expanded. .

Slovakia

Nestville Distillery

Hniezdne, founded in 2008

nestville.sk

The distillery is owned by BGV which was founded in 2001 and focuses mainly on production of ethanol and grain alcohol for industrial use. Whisky production started in 2008 and in 2012 the first Nestville whisky, a blend, was released as a three year old. Currently there are six different blends, all based on 90% grain made with a mash bill of malted barley, triticale and corn and 10% malt whisky. The first single malt was released in 2018 followed by a 6 year old in 2019.

Spain

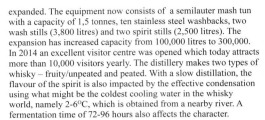

Distilerio Molino del Arco

Segovia, founded in 1959

dyc.es

The distillery has a capacity for producing eight million litres of grain whisky and two million litres of malt whisky per year. In addition to that, vodka and rum are produced and there are also in-house maltings. The distillery is equipped with six copper pot stills and there are 250,000 casks maturing on site. The big seller when it comes to whiskies is a blend simply called DYC which is around 4 years old. It is supplemented by an 8 year old blend and, since 2007, also by DYC Pure Malt, a blend of malt from the distillery and from Scottish distilleries. A new range called Colección Maestros Destiladores was launched in 2018 with a 12 year old blend as the first release. This was followed by a 15 year old single malt in 2019 to commemorate the distillery's 60th anniversary.

Other distilleries in Spain

Destilerias Liber

Padul, Granada, founded in 2001

destileriasliber.com

Apart from whisky, the distillery produces rum, marc, gin and vodka. For the whisky production, the spirit is double distilled after a fermentation of 48-72 hours. Maturation takes place in PX sherry casks that have been previously used in a solera system for 20-30 years as opposed to casks made of new oak and then seasoned with sherry for a few years. Until recently, the only available whisky on the market has been a 5 year old single malt called Embrujo de Granada. Starting 2020, a number of single casks aged 12-16 years have been released in small numbers.

Sweden

High Coast Distillery (former BOX Distillery)

Bjärtrå, founded in 2010

highcoastwhisky.se

Set in buildings from the 19th century, the distillery started production in November 2010. Eventually sales of their whisky exceeded the owners' expectations and in 2018 the distillery was

expanded. The equipment now consists of a semilauter mash tun with a capacity of 1,5 tonnes, ten stainless steel washbacks, two wash stills (3,800 litres) and two spirit stills (2,500 litres). The expansion has increased capacity from 100,000 litres to 300,000. In 2014 an excellent visitor centre was opened which today attracts more than 10,000 visitors yearly. The distillery makes two types of whisky – fruity/unpeated and peated. With a slow distillation, the flavour of the spirit is also impacted by the effective condensation using what might be the coldest cooling water in the whisky world, namely 2-6°C, which is obtained from a nearby river. A fermentation time of 72-96 hours also affects the character.

The first whisky, The Pioneer, was released in 2014. Between 3 and 4 years old, it was the first in a range of four called Early Days Collection. In 2017, the first core expression, Dàlvve, was launched and in 2019 a new core range was introduced; the bourbon matured, heavily peated Timmer, the medium peated Hav with some of the whisky matured in new oak from Sweden and Hungary, the unpeated Älv matured in first fill bourbon and unpeated Berg matured in PX sherry casks. This was followed in 2020 with the limited Cinco, matured in a combination of five different types of sherry casks; oloroso, fino, amontillado, palo cortado and PX. At the same time the first in a range to honour closed saw mills working in the vicinity of the distillery was released, the peated (44ppm) Marieberg was released.

Mackmyra Svensk Whisky

Valbo, founded in 1999

mackmyra.se

Mackmyra's first distillery was built in 1999 and, ten years later, the company revealed plans to build a brand new facility in Gävle, a few miles from the present distillery. In 2012, the distillery was ready and the first distillation took place in spring of that year. The construction of the new distillery is quite extraordinary and with its 37 metre structure, it is perhaps one of the tallest distilleries in the world. Since April 2013, all the distillation takes place at this new gravitation distillery. In 2017 however, the old distillery was re-opened as the Lab Distillery where the company aim to develop innovative spirits. Two different gins have already been released.

Mackmyra whisky is based on two basic recipes, one which produces a fruity and elegant whisky, while the other is smokier. The first release was in 2006 and the distillery now has four core expressions; Svensk Ek, Brukswhisky, the peated Svensk Rök and MACK by Mackmyra. A range of limited editions called Moment was introduced in 2010 and consists of exceptional casks selected by the Master Blender, Angela D'Orazio, who was inducted into the Whisky Hall of Fame in 2019. Three of the latest editions are Skogshallon where part of the whisky had been matured in

Mackmyra's warehouse in Bodås Gruva (an old mine) and their whisky made with the help from AI

casks that had previously held raspberry wine, Lava, a smoky 9 year old matured in a combination of ex-bourbon and ex-oloroso and Moment 22 in August 2020. The latter was a vatting of 1,000 remaining bottles of the first release (Preludium) from 2006. The whisky was emptied into a combination of ex-bourbon and Swedish oak and bottled again after 3,5 years. Seasonal expressions are also released regularly with Grönt Te being one of the latest. Part of the maturation was enhanced by the addition of leaves of four different Japanese green teas into the casks. In autumn 2019, the distillery launched the first whisky in the world where AI (artificial intelligence) had been involved in the creation process.

Spirit of Hven

Hven, founded in 2007

hven.com

The distillery is situated on the island of Hven right between Sweden and Denmark and the first distillation took place in May 2008. Henric Molin, founder and owner, is a trained chemist and very concerned about what type of yeast and grain he uses not to mention the right oak for his casks. The distillery is equipped with a 0,5 ton mash tun, six washbacks made of stainless steel, one wash still, one spirit still and a designated gin still. Apart from that, a unique wooden Coffey still was recently installed to be used mainly for distillation of rye and corn. Part of the barley is malted on site using Swedish peat, sometimes mixed with seaweed and sea-grass, for drying. Apart from whisky, other products include rum made from sugar beet, vodka, gin and aquavit.

Their first whisky was the lightly peated Urania, released in 2012. The second launch was the start of a new series of eight limited bottlings called The Seven Stars released over seven years. The first and so far only core expression, Tycho's Star, was released in 2015. New and innovative bottlings include Sweden's first rye whisky, Hvenus Rye, and Mercurious, the first whisky in Sweden made predominantly (88%) from corn which had been grown on the distillery grounds. One of the latest bottlings (March 2020) was Charlie's Wagon - basically a vatting of all whiskies made during the first ten years.

Smögen Whisky

Hunnebostrand, founded in 2010

smogenwhisky.se

Pär Caldenby – lawyer, whisky enthusiast and the author of Enjoying Malt Whisky – is the founder of this distillery on the west coast of Sweden. Equipped with three washbacks (1,600 litres each), a wash still (900 litres) and a spirit still (600 litres), the capacity is 35,000 litres of alcohol a year. An interesting addition to the equipment setup was made in summer 2018 when Pär installed worm tubs to cool the spirits. Heavily peated malt is imported from Scotland and the aim is to produce an Islay-type of whisky. The first release from the distillery was the 3 year old Primör in 2014. This has over the years been followed by many limited releases, mostly single casks. The Primör casks from 2014 were refilled with new-make and early 2020, the 6 year old Primör Revisited was launched. Summer 2020 saw the release of a 6 year old "100 proof" from sherry seasoned quarter casks and an 8 year old bourbon and sherry maturation is in the pipeline for autumn 2020.

Other distilleries in Sweden

Agitator Whiskymakare

Arboga, founded in 2017

agitatorwhisky.se

The owners of this new distillery have chosen some rather unusual techniques in the production. Water is added during the milling in order to make the mashing more efficient. The same fermented wash is split in half and distributed to the two pairs of stills in order to achieve different characters. The stills, by the way, operate under vacuum which is extremely rare in pot still whisky making. The distillery is experimenting with different kinds of grain apart from barley - oat, wheat and rye. Finally, the maturation sometimes takes place in casks where extra staves have been inserted, some of them made from chestnut. The distillery has a capacity of 500,000 litres of pure alcohol and the first distillation was made in February 2018.

Gammelstilla Whisky

Torsåker, founded in 2005

gammelstilla.se

Built by the owners, the wash still has a capacity of 600 litres and the spirit still 300 litres and the annual capacity is 20,000 litres per year. The first, limited release for shareholders was in May 2017 with a general release in January 2018 of the 4 year old Jern. The latest release, in February 2020, was Isaac Kock with 3 years on bourbon casks and another 1.5 years in new American oak.

Gotland Whisky

Romakloster, founded in 2011

gotlandwhisky.se

The distillery is equipped with a 1,600 litre wash still and a 900 litre spirit still. Local barley is ecologically grown and part of it is malted on site. Unpeated and peated whisky is produced and the

Agitator is one of very few pot still distilleries producing under vacuum

capacity is 60,000 litres per year. The first limited release of Isle of Lime was in early 2017. Recent bottlings, aged up to 4 years, have been a mix of public releases and shareholder's bottlings.

Nordmarkens Destilleri

Årjäng, founded in 2014 (whisky since 2018)

nordmarkensdestilleri.se

The first products to come from this new distillery were aquavit, vodka and limoncello. Sourced whisky has also been released. The first whisky distillation was in December 2018 and both peated and unpeated spirit is produced.

Norrtelje Brenneri

Norrtälje, founded in 2002 (whisky since 2009)

norrteljebrenneri.se

The production consists mainly of spirits from ecologically grown fruits and berries. Since 2009, a single malt whisky from ecologically grown barley is also produced. The first bottling was released in summer 2015 and several limited editions have followed.

Tevsjö Destilleri

Järvsö, founded in 2012 (whisky since 2017)

tevsjodestilleri.se

The owners are primarily focused on distillation of aquavit and other white spirits but whisky production is also included. In December 2019 the first malt whisky and "bourbon" were released.

Uppsala Destilleri

Uppsala, founded in 2015

uppsaladestilleri.se

With a yearly production of 1,500 litres this is currently one of the smallest distilleries in the country. Production started in 2016 with a 100 litre alambic still from Portugal but yet another still has already been installed. Apart from whisky, gin and rum are also produced.

Switzerland

Käsers Schloss (a.k.a Whisky Castle)

Elfingen, Aargau, founded in 2001

kaesers-schloss.ch

The first whisky from this distillery, founded by Ruedi Käser, reached the market in 2004. It was a single malt under the name Castle Hill. Since then the range of malt whiskies has been expanded and today include Doublewood (3 years old matured both in casks made of chestnut and oak), Smoke Barley (at least 3 years old matured in new oak), the portmatured Family Reserve and the 8 year old Edition Käser, the distillery's premium expression. In the last couple of years, Rudi's two sons Michael and Raphael have taken over the running of business and have also changed the brand name to Käser's Schloss.

Brauerei Locher

Appenzell, founded in 1886 (whisky since 1999)

saentismalt.com

Brauerei Locher is unique in using old beer casks for the maturation. The core range consists of three expressions; Himmelberg, Dreifaltigkeit which is slightly peated having matured in toasted casks and Sigel which has matured in very small casks. A new bottle, Föhnsturm, was also introduced in 2019. A range of limited bottlings under the name Alpstein is available. The most recent, the 7 year old Edition XVI, had been finished in casks that had held a Monbazillac wine. Another limited range is Snow

White where edition 7 had been finished in calvados casks. Finally, a new range of limited releases, Edition Genesis, was introduced in spring 2019.

Other distilleries in Switzerland

Etter Distillerie

Zug, founded in 1870 (whisky since 2007)

etter-distillerie.ch

The main produce from this distillery is eau de vie from various fruits and berries but whisky production commenced in 2007. The first release was made in 2010 under the name Johnett Single Malt Whisky and the current 8 year old has a peated touch from ex-Laphroaig casks. In 2016, a limited Johnett with a 12 months finish in Caroni rum casks was released.

Hollen, Whisky Brennerei

Lauwil, Baselland, founded in 1999

single-malt.ch

The first Swiss whisky was distilled at Hollen in July 1999. In the beginning most bottlings were 4-5 years old but in 2009 the first 10 year old was released and there has also been a 12 year old, the oldest expression from the distillery so far.

Humbel Brennerei

Stetten, Aargau, founded in 2004

humbel.ch

With a history going back to 1918, the distillery uses a wash from the brewery Unser Bier in Basel to produce their Glenreuss Whisky

Langatun Distillery

Langenthal, Bern, founded in 2007

langatun.ch

The distillery was built under the same roof as the brewery Brau AG Langenthal. Casks used for maturation are Swiss oak (Chardonnay), French oak (Chardonnay and red wine) and ex sherry casks. The two 5 year old core expressions are Old Deer and the peated Old Bear. Other bottlings include Old Eagle rye, Old Mustang "bourbon" and the organic Old Woodpecker matured in chardonnay casks. Recent limited bottlings include Winter Wedding, Avo Jazz and the distillery's first 10 year old.

Lüthy, Bauernhofbrennerei

Muhen, Aargau, founded in 1997 (whisky since 2005)

brennerei-luethy.ch

Their first single malt was Insel-Whisky, matured in Chardonnay casks and released in 2008. Several releases have since followed. Starting in 2010, the yearly bottling was given the name Herr Lüthy and the 12th release from these had been matured in a combination of chardonnay casks, ex-oloroso casks and ex.bourbon barrels. Whisky from rye, corn, rice and dinkel are also produced.

Macardo Distillery

Strohwilen, Thurgau, founded in 2007

macardo.ch

Built on a former cheese factory, the distillery produces fruit brandy, gin, rum and whisky. The range consists of a core expression without age statement, two 10th anniversary bottlings (bottled at 42% and at cask strength) and special bottlings under the label Distillers Selection

Rugen Distillery

Interlaken, Bern, founded in 2010

rugenbraeu.ch

A brewery founded in 1892 was expanded with a distillery

in 2010. Before that, a cooperation with Zürcher distillery had resulted in a few one-off bottlings of malt whisky called Ice Label. Since the distillery in Interlaken was built, the company does their own distillation. The brand name for the whisky is Swiss Mountain and the core range consists of Classic and Double Barrel. Limited releases include Rock Label with a finish in Swiss oak and the sought after Ice Label where the major part of the 10 year maturation has taken place in the ice of Jungfraujoch at an altitude of 3,454 m.

Sempione Distillery
Brig-Glis, Valais, founded in 1976 (whisky since 2011)
sempione-distillery.ch

A family-owned distillery of fruits and berries making their first trials at whiskymaking in 2011. Current single malts made from barley are Wallisky and Swiss Stone Eagle while Sempione and 1815 - 3 Sterne also include dinkel and rye.

Stadelmann, Brennerei
Altbüron, Luzern, founded in 1932 (whisky since 2003)
schnapsbrennen.ch

The distillery is equipped with three Holstein-type stills and the first generally available bottling (a 3 year old) appeared in 2010. Small volumes of Luzerner Hinterländer Single Malt are released yearly. The first whisky from smoked barley was distilled in 2012.

Z´Graggen Distillerie
Lauerz, Schwyz, founded in 1948
www.zgraggen.ch

Focusing on spirits distilled from fruits and berries, the owners also produce gin, vodka and whisky. The distillery is quite large, with a combined production of 400,000 litres per year. There are three single malts in the range – 3, 8 and the 10 year old Bergsturz.

Zürcher, Spezialitätenbrennerei
Port, Bern, founded in 1954 (whisky from 2000)
lakeland-whisky.ch

The main focus of the distillery is specialising in various distillates of fruit, absinth and liqueur but a Lakeland single malt is also in the range. The current core expression is an 8 year old ex-oloroso maturation while a recent limited edition had matured for 9 years in a port cask.

Wales

Penderyn Distillery
Penderyn, founded in 2000
penderyn.wales

When Penderyn began producing in 2000, it was the first Welsh distillery in more than a hundred years. A new type of still, developed by David Faraday for Penderyn, differs from the Scottish and Irish procedures in that the whole process from wash to new make takes place in one single still producing a spirit at 92% abv. In 2013, a second still (almost a replica of the first still) was commissioned and in 2014, two traditional pot stills, as well as their own mashing equipment was installed. The owners have plans to open two more distilleries - one in Llandudno in 2021 and another in Swansea in 2022/23. Both will be smaller than the original but also equipped with Faraday stills.

The first single malt was launched in 2004. The core range today is divided into two groups. Dragon consists of the Madeira finished Legend, Myth which is fully bourbon matured and Celt with a peated finish. The other range is Gold with Madeira, Peated,

Portwood, Sherrywood and, most recently, Rich Oak which has matured in bourbon casks and then finished in rejuvenated ex-wine casks. The smoky notes from the distillery´s peated expressions comes from maturation in ex-Islay casks. In 2019, the distillery´s first travel retail exclusive, Penderyn Faraday, was launched. Over the years, the company has released several single casks and limited releases and a new range of whiskies called Icons of Wales was introduced in 2012 with the seventh edition, the sherryfinished Rhiannon, being released in September 2019. An excellent visitor centre opened in 2008.

Other distilleries in Wales

Aber Falls Distillery
Abergwyngregyn, founded in 2017
aberfallsdistillery.com

In common with so many other distilleries, Aber Falls started producing and selling gin. Malt whisky, however, is also produced and in spring 2019, they distilled rye for the first time. The first single malt is expected in 2021

Dà Mhìle Distillery
Llandyssul, founded in 2013
damhile.co.uk

Focusing on gin and grain whisky, malt whisky is also produced. Aged, organic single malts, distilled by Springbank back in the 1990s, has been offered for a while and in December 2019, their first organic single malt from own production was released - The Tarian Edition from a single first fill oloroso cask.

Pot still at Penderyn

North America

USA

Westland Distillery

Seattle, Washington, founded in 2011

westlanddistillery.com

Until 2012, Westland was a medium sized craft distillery where they brought in the wash from a nearby brewery and had the capacity of doing 60,000 litres of whiskey per year. During the summer of 2013 the owners moved to another location equipped with a 6,000 litre brewhouse, five 10,000 litre fermenters and two Vendome stills. The capacity is now 260,000 litres per year. In 2017, global spirits giant Remy Cointreau bought Westland Distillery. Sine the start the distillery has been focusing on local barley varieties and also local peat.

The first core expression, Westland American Single Malt Whiskey, was released in 2013. The current core range consists of American Oak and Peated Malt, both matured in a combination of new American oak and first fill bourbon casks and Sherry Wood which has matured in new American oak as well as in casks that previously held Oloroso and PX sherry. All three varieties have been mashed with a 5-malt grain bill and the wash has been fermented for 6 days. Over the years there have also been a large number of different releases of single casks. Apart from experimenting with a multitude of different barley varieties, Westland is also exploring different types of oak for maturation. One of them, Garryana oak, is native to the Pacific Northwest and was used for the first time for whisky maturation by Westland. The fourth release of a single malt partly matured in Garry oak appeared in September 2019. In summer 2019 three expressions made from different barley types (Maris Otter, Golden Promise and Pilsen malt) were released in order to highlight the flavours that the grains impart. Celebrious was finished in a tequila cask while Cask 3204 was heavily peated and matured in an oloroso cask. In January 2020, the 6th edition of the limited Peat Week was released and in February, Coldfoot, a collaboration between Westland and maker of outerwear and workwear Filson was released.

Balcones Distillery

Waco, Texas, founded in 2008

balconesdistilling.com

Originally founded by Chip Tate who left the company in 2014, Balcones celebrated it´s 10th anniversary last year. All of Balcones´ whisky is mashed, fermented and distilled on site and they were the first to use Hopi blue corn for distillation. The core range currently consists of five expressions; Texas Single Malt, two corn whiskies made from blue corn, Baby Blue and True Blue 100 Proof, Texas 100 Rye and Pot Still Bourbon.

Limited but yearly expressions include Rumble, Mirador, Fr. Oak and High Plains Texas Single Malt. In December 2019 two new single malts were released; Juntas matured in virgin French oak and finished in tequila barrels and the 4 year old Staff Selection matured in a combination of American and French oak. All whiskies are un chill-filtered and without colouring. In early 2014, another four, small stills were installed. The big step though, was a completely new distillery which was built 5 blocks from the old site. Distillation started in February 2016 and the official opening was in April. The new distillery is equipped with two pairs of stills and five fermenters and they now distill approximately 350,000 litres per year.

Stranahans Whiskey Distillery

Denver, Colorado, founded in 2003

stranahans.com

Founded by Jess Graber and George Stranahan, the distillery was bought by New York based Proximo Spirits in 2010. Rob Dietrich took over as master distiller in 2011 but left the company in 2019 to work with Blackened whiskey, introduced by the heavy metal band Metallica together with the late Dave Pickerell in 2018. Except for the core Stranahans Colorado Whiskey, the range is made up of Diamond Peak, a vatting of casks that are around 4 years old, a Single Barrel and Sherry cask. The latter is a version where the classic single malt has received a finish in oloroso sherry butts. Every year in December there is the a release of the limited Snowflake edition. In December 2019 it was Mount Bross which was a vatting of Stranahan´s Original aged between 4 and 9 years that had been finished in fresh wine and bourbon barrels. Some of the younger whiskies in the blend had been resting for a year in maple syrup and port casks.

Hood River Distillers

Hood River, Oregon, 1934

hrdspirits.com

Since the foundation, the company acts as importer, distiller, producer and bottler of all kinds of spirits. Some of the products are distilled in-house while others are sourced. The role in the single malt segment came through buying Clear Creek Distillery in 2014. Founded by Steve McCarthy the distillery was one of the first to produce malt whiskey in the USA. The only single malt whiskey produced by the company is the peated McCarthy´s Oregon Single Malt. In December 2017, Clear Creek closed their distillery in Portland and moved to Hood River.

Tuthilltown Spirits

Gardiner, New York, founded in 2003

tuthilltown.com

The distillery, 80 miles north of New York City, was founded in 2003 by Ralph Erenzo and Brian Lee. In 2010, William Grant & Sons aquired the Hudson Whiskey brand while the founders still owned the distillery. In spring 2017, William Grant followed up the deal by buying the entire company. The first products came onto the shelves in 2006 in New York and the whiskey range now consists of Hudson Baby Bourbon, a 2-4 year old bourbon made from 100% New York corn and the company´s biggest seller by far, Four Grain Bourbon (corn, rye, wheat and malted barley), Single Malt Whiskey (aged in small, new, charred American oak casks), Manhattan Rye, Maple Cask Rye and New York Corn Whiskey. One of the more recent limited releases (January 2019) was the single barrel Port Wine Cask Manhattan Rye with a 6 months port finish. There is also gin, vodka and liqueur in the range.

Copper Fox Distillery

Sperryville, Virginia, founded in 2000

copperfoxdistillery.com

Founded in 2000 by Rick Wasmund, the distillery moved to another site in 2006 and in November 2016, he opened up a second distillery in Williamsburg. Wasmund does his own floor malting of barley and it is dried using smoke from selected fruitwood. After mashing, fermentation and distillation, the spirit is filled into oak barrels, together with plenty of hand chipped and toasted chips of apple and cherry trees, as well as oak wood. The first single malts (known as Red Top) were just four months old but the current batches are more around 12-16 months. An older version, Blue Top, has matured for up to 42 months. Other expressions include Peachwood Single Malt and Copper Fox Rye Whiskey. In 2019, Rick Wasmund rebranded the entire range which now goes by the name Copper Fox and at the same time he introduced a 100% malted Sassy Rye which had been made using rye that had been smoked with sassafras wood.

St. George Distillery

Alameda, California, founded in 1982

stgeorgespirits.com

The distillery is situated in a hangar at Alameda Point, the old naval air station at San Fransisco Bay. It was founded by Jörg Rupf, who came to California in 1979 and who was to become one of the forerunners when it came to craft distilling in America. In

1996, Lance Winters joined him and today he is Distiller, as well as co-owner. In 2005, the two were joined by Dave Smith who now has the sole responsibility for the whisky production. The main produce is based on eau-de-vie and a vodka named Hangar One. Whiskey production was picked up in 1996 and the first single malt appeared on the market in 1999. St. George Single Malt used to be sold as a three year old but, nowadays, comes to the market as a blend of whiskeys aged from 4 to 20 years. The latest release is Lot 20 in autumn 2020 and every lot is around 3-4,000 bottles. A fairly new addition to the range is the single malt Baller which has been matured in a combination of ex-bourbon barrels and French oak wine casks. After a filtration through maple charcoal, the whiskey is finished in casks that have held umeshu - a Japanese plum liqueur.

House Spirits
Portland, Oregon, founded in 2004
westwardwhiskey.com

In 2015, Christian Krogstad and Matt Mount moved their distillery a few blocks to bigger premises. The main products for House Spirits used to be Aviation Gin and Krogstad Aquavit but with their new equipment they drastically increased whiskey capacity from 150 barrels per year to 4,000 barrels. In September 2018, Diageo´s "spirits accelerator" Distill Ventures acquired a minority stake in the distillery and the brand which will help expanding the capacity in 2019 by nearly 40%. The first three whiskies were released in 2009 and in 2012 it was time for the first, widely available single malt under the name of Westward American Single Malt. Originally two years old, later releases have been aged for up to five years. A limited release appeared in early 2019 when the Oregon Stout Cask Finish was launched. Westward has recently been released in Australia (currently 30% of their total sales) and Europe.

Corsair Distillery
Bowling Green, Kentucky and Nashville, Tennessee, founded in 2008
corsairdistillery.com

The two founders of Corsair, Darek Bell and Andrew Webber, first opened up a distillery in Bowling Green, Kentucky and two years later, another one in Nashville, Tennessee (followed by a second one in Nashville a few years later). In March 2018 a third site in Nashville was acquired for $6,8m. This will be used for

warehousing, distilling, offices etc. In January 2020, the distillery was expanded with a new and larger mash tun. Apart from producing around 20 different types of beer, the brewery is also where the wash for all the whisky production takes place. Corsair Distillery has a wide range of spirits – gin, vodka, absinthe, rum and whiskey. The number of different whiskies released is growing constantly and the owners are experimenting with different types of grain. The big sellers are Triple Smoke Single Malt Whiskey (made from three different types of smoked malt) and Ryemaggedon (made from malted rye and chocolate rye). Recent releases include Quinoa Whiskey, Oatrage, Hydra, the hickory smoked single malt Wildfire and Tennessee Single Malt finished in a cognac cask.

Kings County Distillery
Brooklyn, New York, founded in 2010
kingscountydistillery.com

This distillery is the oldest in Brooklyn and the founders, Colin Spoelman and David Haskell, have made a name for themselves as being both experimental and yet at the same time true to Scottish methods of distilling whiskey. The wash is fermented for four days in open-top, wooden fermenters and they practise double distillation in copper pot stills. A third pot still from Vendome was also recently installed. In June 2019, they went from small bottles to full-sized 750ml bottles with the ambition to increase their distribution beyond the 20 states and six countries where their products are currently available. The first single malt (60% unpeated and 40% peated) was launched in 2016. It has then been released in batches aged between 1.5 and 4 years. In the product range is also bourbon with the unusual mash bill of 60% corn and 40% malted barley and a rye made from 80% rye and 20% malted barley. Both the bourbon and the rye are available as peated versions as well.

Virginia Distillery
Lovingston, Virginia, 2008 (production started 2015)
vadistillery.com

The whole idea for this distillery was conceived in 2007. The copper pot stills arrived from Turkey in 2008 but following several changes in ownership and struggling with the financing, the first distillation didn´t take place until November 2015. The distillery has the capacity of making 1.1 million litres of alcohol and is equipped with a 3.75 ton mash tun, 8 washbacks, a 10,000 litre

Christian Krogstad - founder and owner of Westward Whiskey (House spirits Distillery) filling the 1000th barrel

wash still and a 7,000 litre spirit still. Their first single malt from own production was a very limited release of Prelude: Courage & Conviction in autumn 2019 followed by a general launch in April 2020. The first bottling of Courage & Conviction is a vatting of whiskies matured in bourbon, sherry and wine casks. In autumn 2020, individual bottlings from each cask type will be available.

Long Island Spirits

Baiting Hollow, New York, founded in 2007

lispirits.com

Long Island Spirits, founded by Rich Stabile, is the first distillery on the island since the 1800s. The starting point for The Pine Barrens Whisky, the first single malt from the distillery, is a finished ale with hops and all. The beer is distilled twice in a potstill and matures for one year in a 10 gallon, new, American, white oak barrel. The whisky was first released in 2012 and was followed in 2018 by a bottle-in-bond version (at least four years old) and later by an expression that is cherrywood smoked. The whiskey range also includes Rough Rider bourbon and rye.

Great Wagon Road Distilling Co.

Charlotte, North Carolina, founded in 2014

gwrdistilling.com

The distillery, founded by Ollie Mulligan, started with a 15 litre still but is now equipped with a 3,000 litres Kothe still in the 15,000 sq foot facility. The mash comes from a neighbouring brewery and the fermentation is made in-house in four tanks. The first batch of his Rua Single Malt was launched at Christmas 2015 and several batches have since followed, including vodka and Drumlish poteen. New releases in 2018 included a straight Rua single malt, two finishes - port and sherry - and a rye whiskey. They were followed in autumn 2019 by their first cask strength release (at 63%) and a Rua matured for nine months in virgin oak and another 20 months in a sherry cask.

Hamilton Distillers

Tucson, Arizona, founded in 2011

whiskeydelbac.com

Stephen Paul came up with the idea of drying barley over mesquite, instead of peat. He started his distillery using a 40 gallon still but since 2014, a 500 gallon still is in place. In 2015, new malting equipment was installed which made it possible to malt the barley in 5,000 lbs batches, instead of the previous 70 lbs! The first bottlings of Del Bac single malt appeared in 2013 and they now have three expressions – aged Mesquite smoked (Dorado), aged unsmoked (Classic), unaged Mesquite smoked (Old Pueblo) and aged unsmoked, bottled at cask strength (Distiller's Cut).

Deerhammer Distilling Company

Buena Vista, Colorado, founded in 2010

deerhammer.com

The location of the distillery at an altitude of 2,500 metres with drastic temperature fluctuations and virtually no humidity, have a huge impact on the maturation of the spirit. Owners Lenny and Amy Eckstein released their first single malt, aged for only 9 months, in 2012. More and older batches (2 to 3 years) of their Deerhammer Single Malt have followed including several different finishes. In autumn 2019, the first edition of a new series, Progeny, was released. In a collaboration with Cultura Craft Chocolate, 2,5 year old single malt was finished for 6 months in barrels that had held cacao seeds and whiskey.

Hillrock Estate Distillery

Ancram, New York, founded in 2011

hillrockdistillery.com

What makes this distillery unusual, at least in the USA, is that they are not just malting their own barley – they are floor malting

it. When Jeff Baker founded the distillery he equipped it with a 250 gallon Vendome pot still and five fermentation tanks. In spring 2019, the distillery was substantially expanded with a new pot still, a lauter mash tun and more fermentation tanks. This tripled the capacity to 20,000 cases of whiskey per year. The first release from the distillery was in 2012, the Solera Aged Bourbon. Today, the range has been expanded with a Single Malt and a Double Cask Rye. Over the years, limited bottlings have appeared such as the peated Single Malt and a Napa cabernet cask finished bourbon

Santa Fe Spirits

Santa Fe, New Mexico, founded in 2010

santafespirits.com

Colin Keegan, the owner of Santa Fe Spirits, is collaborating with Santa Fe Brewing Company which supplies the un-hopped beer that is fermented and distilled in a 1,000 litre copper still from Christian Carl in Germany. The whiskey gets a hint of smokiness from mesquite. The first product, Silver Coyote released in 2011, was an unaged malt whiskey. The first release of an aged (2 years) single malt whiskey, Colkegan, was in 2013. Since then, the range has been expanded to include also a version finished in apple brandy casks and one bottled at cask strength.

Copperworks Distilling Company

Seattle, Washington, founded in 2013

copperworksdistilling.com

Jason Parker and Micah Nutt obtain their wash from a local brewery and then ferment it on site. The distillery is equipped with two, large copper pot stills for the whiskey production, one smaller pot still for the gin and one column still. The whiskey is matured in 53-gallon charred, American oak barrels. The first distillation was in 2014 and the first batch of the single malt was released in 2016. In autumn 2018, to celebrate the distillery's fifth anniversary, they released their first single malt to be fully matured for 38 months in French oak instead of new American oak. One of the latest single malt releases, in December 2019, was batch 24 finished for two months in casks hat previously had held stout beer.

Rogue Ales & Spirits

Newport, Oregon, founded in 2009

rogue.com

The company consists of one brewery, two combined brewery/pubs, two distillery pubs and five pubs scattered over Oregon, Washington and California. The main business is still producing Rogue Ales, but apart from whiskey, rum and gin are also distilled. The first malt whiskey, Dead Guy Whiskey, was launched in 2009. In 2016, it was time for the first straight malt whiskey - the two year old Oregon Single Malt Whiskey. Spring 2018, saw the launch of the company's first 5 year old single malt as well as a 3 year old rye malt whiskey. The latest addition to the range was in February 2019 when Rolling Thunder Stouted Whiskey was released - a single malt aged for one year in new garryana oak and a further two years in casks that had held imperial stout.

FEW Spirits

Evanston, Illinois, founded in 2010

fewspirits.com

Former attorney (and founder of a rock and roll band) Paul Hletko started this distillery in Evanston, a suburb in Chicago in 2010. It is equipped with three stills; a Vendome column still and two Kothe hybrid stills. Bourbon and rye had been on the market for a couple of years when the first single malt, with some of the malt being smoked with cherry wood, was released in 2015. In autumn 2018 a new core bottling appeared when American Whiskey, a vatting of bourbon, rye and smoked single malt, was released. Limited releases include bourbons finished in Italian red wine casks and casks that had previously held American brandy.

Sons of Liberty Spirits Co.

South Kingstown, Rhode Island, founded in 2010

solspirits.com

The distillery is equipped with a stainless steel mash tun, stainless steel, open top fermenters and one 950 litre combined pot and column still from Vendome and is first and foremost a whiskey distillery. In 2011 the double distilled Uprising American Whiskey was launched, made from a stout beer and it was followed in 2014 by Battle Cry made from a Belgian style ale. Both Uprising and Battle Cry have also been released as PX and oloroso finishes respectively. Recent limited releases include Oktoberfest Single Malt in October 2019 and, two months later, two four year old single barrel versions of Uprising and Battle Cry, bottled in bond.

High West Distillery

Park City, Utah, founded in 2007

highwest.com

The founder, David Perkins, made a name for himself mainly as a blender of sourced rye whiskies. None of these were distilled at High West distillery. In 2015, they opened another distillery at Blue Sky Ranch in Wanship, Utah. Even though they consider themselves blenders first and foremost, the 2018 versions of Rendezvous Rye and Double Rye, were the first expressions which included whiskey from their own production. In December 2019, the first single malt made entirely by themselves and named High Country, was released. It was made, using nine recipes, from a combination of crystal malt, chocolate malt, two-row pale malt and imported Scottish peated malt. Fermented on the grain each recipe was then matured in three different types of caks; new charred oak, used bourbon and rye casks and port casks. In 2016 Constellation Brands (makers of Corona beer and Svedka vodka) bought High West Distillery for a sum of $160 million.

Other distilleries in USA

2nd Street Distilling Co

Walla Walla, Washington, founded in 2011

2ndstreetdistillingco.com

Formerly known as River Sands Distillery, the company has been around since 1968 but the distillery only started in 2011. Different types of gin and vodka are produced, as well as a single malt – R J Callaghan. It is aged for 1,5 years in charred American oak and then finished for 6 months in Hungarian oak. In 2016 a 100% malted rye, Reser's Rye, was also released.

3 Howls Distillery

Seattle, Washington, founded in 2013

3howls.com

The malted barley is imported from Scotland including a small amount of peated malt. For the distillation they use a 300 gallon hybrid still with a stainless steel belly and a copper column. Their first whiskies were released in 2013, a single malt and a hopped rye, and these were followed in 2014 by a rye whiskey and a bourbon.

10th Street Distillery

San José, California, founded in 2017

10thstreetdistillery.com

Inspired by a two-week apprentice program on Islay, Scotland, Virag Saksena and Vishal Gauri went on to build their own distillery in California. So far they have released Peated Single Malt and STR Single Malt where STR stands for shaved, toasted and re-charred - the type of casks used for maturing the whiskey.

Alley 6 Craft Distillery

Healdsburg, California, founded in 2014

alley6.com

A small craft distillery in Sonoma county with rye whiskey as the main product. The first bottles were released in summer 2015 followed by a single malt in May 2016. The owners are experimenting with a range of different barley varieties, mainly from Germany and Belgium.

Amalga Distillery

Juneau, Alaska, founded in 2017

amalgadistillery.com

The distillery uses a 250 gallon pot still from Vendome and they are also floor malting their own barley, some of it grown in Alaska. The first single malt will be released in 2020 but both vodka and gin have already been launched.

Andalusia Whiskey

Blanco, Texas, founded in 2016

andalusiawhiskey.com

Focusing entirely on whiskey production, the spirit is double-distilled in a 250 gallon pot still and the first single malts were released in late 2016; Stryker, where mesquite and oak have been

High West's distillery in Wanship, Utah

used to dry the barley and the lightly peated Revenant Oak. This was followed up end of 2017 by Andalusia Triple-Distilled. There is also a special range with cask-finished whiskies with PX sherry being the latest.

Arizona Distilling Company

Tempe Arizona, founded in 2012

azdistilling.com

The first release from the distillery was a bourbon sourced from Indiana. The ensuing releases, which started with Desert Durum made from wheat, have all been produced in their distillery. Humphrey's – a single malt – was first released in late 2014. The distillery is one of few using open top fermenters.

ASW Distillery

Atlanta, Georgia, founded in 2016

aswdistillery.com

The distillery is equipped with two traditional Scottish copper pot stills but with the American twist of fermenting and distilling on the grain. Among the latest releases are Duality, made from 50% malted barley and 50% malted rye with both grains fermented and distilled in the same batch, Ameireaganach Single Malt, the heavily peated Tire Fire, the triple distilled Druid Hill and Maris Otter, released together with Monday Night Brewing.

Atelier Vie Distillery

New Orleans, Louisiana, founded in 2012

ateliervie.com

The first product from the distillery, released in 2013, was Riz - a whiskey made from Louisiana rice, Owner Jedd Haas then went on to distil also malt whiskey from barley. Louisiana Single Malt was first released in April 2019 and a second version (2 years old) appeared in early 2020.

Axe and the Oak Distillery

Colorado Springs, Colorado, founded in 2013

axeandtheoak.com

A combination of a distillery, bar and restaurant, Axe and the Oak have so far released both a bourbon and a rye whiskey but there is also single malt maturing.

Bendt Distilling Co. (former Witherspoon Distillery)

Lewisville, Texas, founded in 2011

bendtdistillingco.com

The main products from this distillery used to be bourbon and rum but they have also did small runs of Witherspoon Single Malt. The distillery recently changed names to Bendt Distilling Co and the current big seller is Bendt No. 5, a blend made from five different types of whiskey.

Bent Brewstillery

Roseville, Minnesota, founded in 2014

bentbrewstillery.com

This combined brewery and distillery produces, apart from a range of beers, also gin and whiskey. A rye whiskey named Punish95 has been released and recently, Double IPA-Skey, made from one of their hopped beers, was released.

Bently Heritage Distillery

Minden, Nevada, founded in 2016

bentlyheritage.com

A true estate distillery, growing their own grains and floor malting it themselves, Bently Heritage is located in an old mill from the early 1900s. The equipment consists of a Briggs mash tun, oak

fermenters, one pair of copper pot stills made by Forsyths and hybrid stills with columns for the distillation of vodka, gin and all whiskies except single malt. The first distillation was in 2018 and the owners have so far released gin and vodka but have also laid down a substantial amount of casks for future whiskey releases.

Big Bottom Distilling

Hillsboro, Oregon, founded in 2015

bigbottomdistilling.com

The company started out as a blender and bottler of sourced whiskey, not least bourbon finished in different wine casks. A distillery was built in 2015 and in June 2018, their first own 2 year old single malt was released.

Black Heron Spirits

West Richland, Washington, founded in 2011

blackheronspirits.com

The owner started out as a winemaker, then decided to sell the company and open a distillery instead. A wide variety of spirits are produced, including bourbon, a corn whiskey and a limited peated single malt which was first released in January 2017.

Blaum Bros. Distilling

Galena, Illinois, founded in 2012

blaumbros.com

The distillery equipment consists of a 2,000 litre mash tun, five 2,000 litre wash backs and a 2,000 litre Kothe hybrid still. Apart from gin and vodka, the first two releases were the sourced Knotter Bourbon and Knotter Rye. The first whiskey from their own production was a rye in 2015 followed by a straight bourbon in 2018. It will be a few years before the first single malt is released.

Blue Ridge Distilling Co.

Bostic, North Carolina, founded in 2010

blueridgedistilling.com

The first distillation at the distillery was in June 2012 and in December the first bottles of Defiant Single Malt Whisky were released. The maturation part is very unorthodox. The spirit is matured for 60 days in stainless steel tanks with oak spirals inserted. According to the owners, this ensures a greater contact between the whisky and the wood which speeds up the maturation process. In autumn 2017, a 100% rye was added to the range.

Bogue Sound Distillery

Bogue, North Carolina, founded in 2018

boguesounddistillery.com

The distillery is equipped with a 500-gallon still and the first spirits released included gin, vodka and rye. Recently the John A.P. Conoley single malt was added to the range.

Boston Harbor Distillery

Boston, Massachusetts, founded in 2015

bostonharbordistillery.com

The distillery concentrates mainly on whiskey but is also making a variety of spirits based on different Samuel Adams´ beers. The whiskies, currently a rye and a single malt (the latest version a 4 year old "bottled-in-bond" from December 2019) are released under the Putnam New England label. Apart from the distillery with its 150-gallon Vendome copper pot still, the facility consists of a shop, tasting room and an event space.

Brickway Brewery & Distillery (former Borgata)

Omaha, Nebraska, founded in 2013

www.drinkbrickway.com

Omaha´s first combined brewery and distillery since prohibition.

All the wash for the distillation comes from their own brewery and distillation takes place in a 550 gallon Canadian wash still, and a 400 gallon spirit still from Forsyth´s in Scotland. The owners are focused on single malt whiskey but they also produce smaller amounts of bourbon and rye as well as gin and rum. Their first whisky was released in 2014 and there is now an aged version under the name Brickway Single Malt Whisky which was complemented in December 2019 by a version aged in oloroso sherry casks. A recent expansion of the distillery made it possible to quadruple the whisky production.

Bull Run Distillery

Portland, Oregon, founded in 2011

bullrundistillery.com

The distillery is equipped with two pot stills (800 gallons each) and the main focus is on 100% Oregon single malt whiskey. First release was the sourced bourbon Temperance Trader. The first release of a single malt under the name Bull Run was a 4 year old in 2016 (now 5 years old). Shortly after that the Oregon Single Malt Whiskey was also released at cask strength (56%).

Caiseal Beer & Spirits Company

Hampton, Virginia, founded in 2017

alley6.com

A combined brewery and distillery where the brewery produces the mash for various distilled products. The first spirits, made in a 1,000 litre copper pot still were released in May 2018 and included vodka, gin, bourbon and an unaged single malt.

Cannon Beach Distillery

Cannon Beach, Oregon, founded in 2012

cannonbeachdistillery.com

The owner´s philosophy about whisky making is never to make the same spirit twice. The whiskies are made in small batches with a new release every 2-4 months. Distillation takes place in a 380 litre Vendome still with a 6-plate column.

Cedar Ridge Distillery

Swisher, Iowa, founded in 2003

cedarridgewhiskey.com

Malt whiskey production started in 2005 and in 2013 the first single malt was launched with more releases being made since then. Other spirits in the range include both bourbon, malted rye and malted wheat. A limited single malt, Murphy´s Solera, matured in a combination of sherry-, port- and cognac-casks and with a hint of peat, was released in November 2019.

Charbay Winery & Distillery

St. Helena, California, founded in 1983

charbay.com

With a wide range of products such as wine, vodka, grappa, pastis, rum and port, the owners decided in 1999 to also enter in to whiskey making. They were pioneers distilling whiskey from hopped beer and over the years several releases have been made including Double-Barrel Release, Doubled & Twisted, Pilsner Whiskey and Charbay R5. The spirit distillation takes place in alambic pot stills with sometimes extraordinary long distillation time (up to ten days!). In spring 2017, the company was split in two with Marko and his wife Jenni focusing on the spirit side while Marko´s father Miles continues with the wine production.

Coppersea Distilling

New Paltz, New York, founded in 2011

coppersea.com

A "farm-to-glass" distillery with the barley malted on site. Open-top wooden washbacks and direct-fired alembic stills. One of the things that make Coppersea stand out is that they don´t dry the malted barley but instead produce a mash from green, unkilned barley. The one year old Big Angus is made from 100% green barley and in the range there is also Excelsior Straight Bourbon, Bonticou Crag Straight Malt Rye and the blend, Springtown Straight Whisky.

Coral Cay Distillery

Cashmere, Washington, founded in 2012

coralcaydistilling.com

An unusual cooperation between a distillery, Blue Spirits Distilling, and the lifestyle brand Tommy Bahama - maker of sportswear, accessories and furniture. When Tommy Bahama decided to expand into spirits, they chose Blue Spirits as their supplier but call it Coral Cay in their marketing. The line-up includes rum, gin, vodka and single malt whiskey.

Cotherman Distilling

Dunedin, Florida, founded in 2015

cothermandistilling.com

All the whiskies are made from 100% malted barley. The mash is brought in from local breweries, fermented at the distillery and then distilled in a pot still and a 3-plate bubble-cap still. First launched in July 2016, several batches have followed since. Apart from whiskey – gin and vodka are also produced.

Cut Spike Distillery (formerly Solas Distillery)

La Vista, Nebraska, founded in 2009

cutspikedistillery.com

In 2010 single malt whiskey was distilled and the first bottles were launched in August 2013. New batches of the 2 year old whiskey have then appeared regularly and recent special editions include one single malt aged in cabernet barrels and another finished in maple syrup barrels. Peated production commenced in January 2020.

Cutwater Spirits (former spirit division of Ballast Point)

San Diego, California, founded in 2016

cutwaterspirits.com

In December 2015, Ballast Point Brewing was bought by Constellation Brands for the staggering sum of $1bn and in December 2019 it was later sold on to Kings & Convicts. The distilling side of Ballast Point, which started in 2008, was never a part of the deal and during 2016, a handful of executives and co-founders started a new company and distillery called Cutwater Spirits. That company in turn was sold to brewing giant Anheuser-Busch InBev in February 2019. The whiskyside of the business consists of Devil´s Share Whiskey which comes in two versions - single malt and bourbon. Lately the range has been expanded with Black Skimmer rye and bourbon.

Dallas Distilleries Inc.

Garland, Texas, founded in 2008

dallasdistilleries.com

The distillery is primarily focused on whiskey. The first products in their Herman Marshall range were launched in 2013. It was a bourbon and a rye and was later followed by a single malt. In summer 2019, a small batch single malt, Herman Marshall Saint Armold Divine, bottled at 50.5% was released.

Dark Island Spirits

Alexandria Bay, New York, founded in 2015

darkislandspirits.com

By way of a device inside the casks, the owners are maturing their spirits with the help of soundwaves created by different genres of music. Musically Matured is trademarked and so far apple brandy, vodka, gin, bourbon, corn whiskey and small volumes of Eleanor Glen Single Malt Whisky have been launched.

Deaf Shepherd Distilling Co.

San Diego, California, founded in 2019

deafshepherddistillery.com

Owned by Josh Christy, a former Navy EOD Operator, the distillery is making bourbon, rye whiskey, rum, gin and a single malt which is due for release in 2021.

Dirty Water Distillery

Plymouth, Massachusetts, founded in 2013

dirtywaterdistillery.com

Starting with vodka, gin and rum, the distillery expanded into malt whiskey in 2015. The first release, Bachelor Single Malt, came in 2016 and was followed by Boat For Sale Malt Whiskey which had been made using a beer from Independent Fermentations.

Distillery 291

Colorado Springs, Colorado, founded in 2011

distillery291.com

Founded by photographer Michael Myers, the distillery now has a core range that consists of seven different ryes, bourbons and American whiskies. In a limited, experimental range Myers has also in 2018 launched two single malts made from 100% barley. In December 2019, the distillery was shortlisted for Craft Producer of the Year in Whisky Magazine's Icons of Whisky.

Dogfish Head Distillery

Milton, Delaware, founded in 1995

dogfish.com

Opened up as a brewery, the company has now expanded into being a distillery as well. Two copper stills and a copper column from Vendome are used to make rum, gin and vodka. On the whiskey side there is also a single malt from malted barley. One of the latest releases had been aged in American oak and then finished in casks that previously aged their own ale, Palo Santo Marron. The company also runs three restaurants in Delaware.

Door County Distillery

Sturgeon Bay, Wisconsin, founded in 2011

doorcountydistillery.com

A winery founded in 1974 was complemented by a distillery in 2011. Gin, vodka and brandy are the main products but they also make single malt whiskey. The first Door County Single Malt was released in 2013 and there are also bourbon and rye in the range.

Dorwood Distillery

Buellton, California, founded in 2014

dorwood-distillery.com

The distillery (which recently changed its name from Brothers Spirits) started producing malt whisky in 2016. The barley is dried using mesquite smoke and the triple distillation takes place in two reflux stills. The vast majority of the releases so far have been unaged but several barrels have been laid down for maturation.

DownSlope Distilling

Centennial, Colorado, founded in 2008

downslopedistilling.com

Made from 65% malted barley and 35% rye, Double-Diamond Whiskey was released in 2010 and it is still the core expression. It was followed by a number of varieties of bourbon, rye and a 4 year old single malt matured in a combination of six different casks. All malt whiskies are made from floor malted Maris Otter barley.

Dry Fly Distilling

Spokane, Washington, founded in 2007

dryflydistilling.com

Several types of whisky have been released – Bourbon 101, Straight Cask Strength Wheat Whiskey, Port Finish Wheat Whiskey, Peated Wheat Whiskey and Straight Triticale Whiskey. A new limited bottling, first released in 2015, is the triple distilled O'Danaghers which is a mix of barley, wheat and oats. A later edition was a single potstill made from malted and unmalted barley. A new 4,500 litre Carl still was installed in 2020 and the distillery moved to a new location.

Eastern Kille Distillery (former Gray Skies Distillery)

Grand Rapids, Michigan, founded in 2014

easternkille.com

In 2014, the owners bought an industrial building for their grain-to-glass distillery and a year later, the first spirit was distilled. The equipment is made up of a 1,800 litre mash kettle, four fermenters and a 2,500 litre pot still with an attached column. The first bottle of Michigan Single Malt, made from a combination of cherry wood smoked malt, peanut butter toast malt and distillers malt, appeared in 2016. In autumn 2019, following a trademark dispute with Campari, the distillery changed the name to Eastern Kille.

Edgefield Distillery

Troutdale, Oregon, founded in 1998

mcmenamins.com

The distillery is a part of the McMenamin chain of more than 60 pubs and hotels in Oregon and Washington. More than 20 of the pubs have adjoining microbreweries and the chain's first distillery opened in 1998 in Troutdale with the first whiskey, Hogshead Whiskey, being bottled in 2002. Limited releases occur every year on St Patrick's Day under the name The Devil's Bit with the 2019 edition having been distilled using winter wheat and barley and matured for seven years in heavily toasted, lightly charred American oak. A second distillery was opened in 2011 at the company's Cornelius Pass Roadhouse location in Hillsboro.

Eleven Wells Distillery

St. Paul, Minnesota, founded in 2013

11wells.com

The distillery is equipped with a 650 gallon mash tun, stainless steel open-top fermentation tanks and two stills. Whiskey is the main product and the first two releases, aged bourbon and rye, were released in 2014 followed by a wheat whiskey in 2015 and finally a single malt made from malted barley.

Fainting Goat Spirits

Greensboro, North Carolina, founded in 2015

faintinggoatspirits.com

First spirits on the shelves for this distillery, as for many others, were gin and vodka. In December 2017, Fisher's single malt whiskey was launched as a 2 year old with the latest batch being released in July 2019. Fisher's Straight Rye has also been released.

Golden Moon Distillery

Golden, Colorado, founded in 2008

goldenmoondistillery.com

Distillery veteran Stephen Gould has built a distillery equipped with six custom designed pot stills as well as four antique stills. Working also as an independent bottler the products from the company are a combination of sourced whiskey (mainly bourbon) and whiskies produced in-house. At least 15 different kinds of spirits are distilled and three single malts whiskies have so far been released, the latest being Principium and Triple.

Grand Teton Distillery

Driggs, Idaho, founded in 2012

tetondistillery.com

The first and foremost product from the distillery is vodka made from potatoes. Actor Channing Tatum has invested in the company and the Born and Bred Vodka. Various whiskies are also produced, including a single malt due for release in 3-4 years.

Hatch Distillery

Egg Harbour, Wisconsin, founded in 2018

hatchdistilling.com

Famous for their spirits made from locally sourced honey, the company also produces bourbon and single malt whiskey (although obviously not made from honey).

Hewn Spirits

Pipersville, Pennsylvania, founded in 2013

hewnspirits.com

Apart from rum, gin and vodka the distillerty produces bourbon, rye and the Reclamation American Single Malt Whiskey. After maturing the malt whiskey in barrels for 1-4 months, it receives a second maturation in stainless steel vats where charred staves of chestnut and hickory wood add to the profile. The distillery moved to a new location in 2020.

High Peaks Distilling

Lake George, New York, founded in 2016

highpeakdistilling.com

John Carr left his job at Adirondack Brewery in 2016 to start High Peak Distilling but he is still very much involved with his old employer. High Peaks obtains all of their fermented wash from the brewery which is then distilled and matured on site. The first release in spring 2018 was the peated Cloudsplitter Single Malt which was followed by Night Spirit Bourbon and Sugar Moon, a maple syrup flavoured bourbon, in spring 2019. All of their bottlings are at least two years old.

Highside Distilling

Bainbridge Island, Washington, founded in 2018

highsidedistilling.com

A family owned distillery which released its first spirit, a gin, in

November 2018. Since then Amaro has also been launched while production of single malt whiskey started in January 2019 with an anticipated release in early 2021.

Hogback Distillery

Boulder Colorado, founded in 2017

hogbackdistillery.com

The distillery founder and owner is the Scotsman Graeme Wallace who moved to Colorado. The focus is to do a Scottish style single malt made from malt from Gleneagles Maltings, some of it peated. While the single malt is maturing, bourbon and rye whiskey has been released as well as Enigma made from four different grains.

Idlewild Spirits

Winter Park, Colorado, founded in 2015

idlewildspirits.com

Production of the first batch of malt whiskey was in June 2016. For maturation they have moved from 5 gallon barrels, via 10 and 30 gallons to the full-size 50 gallon barrels that they use today. Fermentation and distillation being on the grain add to the over-all character. Their Colorado Single Malt was released in 2018.

Immortal Spirits

Medford, Oregon, founded in 2008

immortalspirits.com

A wide range of spirits are produced including gin, rum, vodka and limoncello. The only whiskey made from barley (unmalted) is the 3 year old Single Grain. The Single Barrel range of selected casks has sometimes been represented by a single malt but currently it´s a 4 year old made from barley and corn.

Jersey Spirits Distilling Co

Fairfield, New Jersey, founded in 2015

jerseyspirits.com

Apart from gin and vodka, the owners have two bourbon varieties for sale - Crossroads with a mash bill consisting of corn, rye, wheat and barley and Patriot´s Trail which is a high rye bourbon. The first distillation of a single malt was in summer 2018 and this is due for release in 2020. In 2020, the owners opened a second distillery and tasting room in Brooklyn.

Stephen Gould, founder and owner of Golden Moon Distillery

John Emerald Distilling Company

Opelika, Alabama, founded in 2014

johnemeralddistilling.com

With the wash being fermented on the grain, the main product is John´s Alabama Single Malt which gets its character from barley smoked with a blend of southern pecan and peach wood. The first release was made in 2015 and is currently aged for three years. In spring 2017, the owners also started trial distillations using triticale.

Journeyman Distillery

Three Oaks, Michigan, founded in 2010

journeymandistillery.com

The first release from the distillery (Ravenswood Rye) was sourced from Koval Distillery in Ravenswood. The range of whiskies distilled at their own premises now include bourbon, rye, wheat and single malt. The first release of Three Oaks Single Malt Whiskey was in 2013 and it has been aged in a combination of casks that have previously contained bourbon, rye and rum.

Key West Distilling

Key West, Florida, founded in 2013

kwdistilling.com

The main track is to produce rum but they are also distilling whiskey. The mash is brought in from Bone Island Brewing, fermented, distilled and filled into new barrels or used rum barrels. The first release of Whiskey Tango Foxtrot was in 2015. The distillery moved to new premises in late 2019.

KyMar Farm Winery & Distillery

Charlotteville, New York, founded in 2011

ky-mar.com

Mainly producing wine, liqeurs and apple brandy but a whiskey made from 100% malted barley and distilled in a 300 gallon hybrid and an 80 gallon alembic still, has also been released.

Laws Whiskey House

Denver, Colorado, founded in 2011

lawswhiskyehouse.com

Alan and Marianne Laws released their first 3 year old in 2014 and all of their following releases have been at least 2 years old. The flagship in the range is Four Grain Straight Bourbon but they also have rye, corn, wheat and a single malt called Hordeum Straight Malt Whiskey on the menu. Beginning of 2020, the distillery was closed for a month for a substantial upgrade of equipment.

Liberty Call Spirits

Spring Valley, California, founded in 2014

libertycalldistilling.com

This distillery outside San Diego, uses a variety of barley varieties including caramel malts and the rare Maris Otter. Their single malt is called Old Ironsides and there is also a four grain whiskey named Blue Ridge. In spring 2020, they opened up a second restaurant/distillery in Barrio Logan, south central San Diego.

Liquid Brands Distillery

Spokane, Washington, founded in 2018

warriorliquor.com

Rich and Mary Clemson produce gin, vodka, bourbon, rye whiskey and a single malt made from malted barley.

Liquid Riot Bottling Co.

Portland, Maine, founded in 2013

liquidriot.com

When Liquid Riot opened its doors, it was Maine´s first brewery/distillery/resto-bar. At the waterfront in the Old Port, Liquid Riot produces an extensive range of beers and spirits which include bourbon, rye, oat, single malt, rum, vodka and agave spirit. Distillation is made in a German hybrid still with a 5 plate rectification column.

Loch & Union Distilling

American Canyon, California, founded in 2017

lochandunion.com

A fairly large distillery with an impressive set of two copper pot still for whiskey distillation and a third still designated for gin making – all fabricated by Carl in Germany. The first gin was released in spring 2018 but the inaugural single malt whiskey isn't due for at least another two to three years.

Long Road Distillers

Grand Rapids, Michigan, founded in 2015

longroaddistillers.com

Apart from vodka, gin and aquavit, different styles of whiskey have been released - bourbon, wheat, corn and rye. They also have a continuous collaboration with local breweries, making malt whisky from their beers. One of the latest, released in September 2019, was Vivant Big Red Coq Malt Whisky.

Los Angeles Distillery

Culver City, California, founded in 2018

ladistillery.com

Apart from gin and rum, the distillery is focusing on whiskey. Different versions of bourbon and rye are produced as well as three varieties of malt whiskey from barley; Virgin Oak, Triple Cask and Light Smoked. For maturation, the owners use American and Hungarian oak

Lyon Distilling Co.

Saint Michaels, Maryland, founded in 2013

lyondistilling.com

Focusing mainly on rum but also whiskey, the distillery is equipped with a 2,000 litre mash tun, stainless steel fermenters and five small pot stills. The first, unaged, malt whiskey was released in late 2015 and the first aged release came one year later.

Mad River Distillers

Warren, Vermont, founded in 2011

madriverdistillers.com

The distillery was built on a 150 year old farm in the Green Mountains. Focus is on rum, brandy and whiskey. The only single malt so far is Hopscotch which was first released in late 2016 with batch four launched in autumn 2019.

Maine Craft Distilling

Portland, Maine, founded in 2013

mainecraftdistilling.com

The distillery offers vodka, gin, rum, Chesuncook, which is a botanical spirit using barley and carrot distillates, as well as the Fifty Stone single malt in limited batches. The barley is floor malted on site and both peat moss and seaweed is used to dry the barley.

Maplewood Brewery and Distillery

Chicago, Illinois, founded in 2014

maplewoodbrew.com

A combination of brewery, distillery, taproom and bar, the company has released two single malts; Fat Pug made from pale malt, dark crystal, dark munich, chocolate malt and roasted malt as well as Oaty Otter where Maris Otter barley and oats have been used.

Montgomery Distillery

Missoula, Montana, founded in 2012

montgomerydistillery.com

The owners mill the barley and rye to a fine flour using a hammer mill and the wash is then fermented on the grain. Distillation takes place in a Christian Carl pot still with a 21 plate column attached. The first whiskey was a rye in 2015, followed up by the 3 year old Montgomery Single Malt in 2016 and a 4 year old a year later. In December 2019, a single malt aged between 5 and 6 years and partially aged in oloroso casks was released.

Motor City Gas

Royal Oak, Michigan, founded in 2014

motorcitygas.com

The owners have an experimental approach to whiskey making and use unusual and old grains (Maris Otter and Golden Promise), different yeast strains and unusual woods. The expressions so far have been both unpeated and heavily peated. One of the latest releases was 12 Bolt, distilled from a pale ale.

Nashoba Valley Winery

Bolton, Massachusetts, founded in 1978 (whiskey since 2003)

nashobawinery.com

Mainly about wines, the business has been expanded with a brewery and a distillery as well. In autumn 2009, Stimulus, the first single malt was released. The second release of a 5 year old came in 2010 and a one-off 11 year old was launched in 2016

New Holland Brewing Co.

Holland, Michigan, founded in 1996 (whiskey since 2005)

newhollandbrew.com

After ten years, this beer brewery opened up a micro-distillery as well. The first cases of New Holland Artisan Spirits were released in 2008 and among them were Zeppelin Bend, a 3 year old (minimum) straight malt whiskey which is now their flagship brand. Included in the range are also Zeppelin Bend Reserve, matured for four years and then finished for an additional 9 months in sherry casks, Beer Barrel Bourbon and Beer Barrel Rye.

New Liberty Distillery

Philadelphia, Pennsylvania, founded in 2014

newlibertydistillery.com

The distillery is working with whiskey on two tracks - the Cradle of Liberty which is produced at the distillery (including a Smoked Malt and Dutch Malt Whiskey) and Kinsey which is sourced from other distilleries. On the malt whiskey side, the distillery has a collaboration with Deer Creek Malthouse supplying them with floor malted barley. One of the co-founders of the distillery, Robert Cassell, was also an integral part of the foundation of Connacht Distillery in Ireland 2016. Apart from his distillery work, Cassell has also been working on still designs for the Canadian manufacturer Specific Mechanical and has written two books about distilling.

Noco Distillery

Fort Collins, Colorado, founded in 2016

nocodistillery.com

Using four small hand-crafted copper pot stills, a fermentation of up to three weeks, slow distillation and up to nine different types of woods for maturation, the distillery produces gin, rum, vodka, bourbon, rye whiskey as well as single malt. The latter was first released in March 2019.

Oak & Grist Distilling Co.

Black Mountain, North Carolina, founded in 2015

oakandgrist.com

Inspired by Scotch, the owners are focusing on whiskey made from locally grown and malted barley. So far, apart from a genever style gin, the distillery has released a blended, malted whiskey and have a single malt made from barley maturing in the warehouse. Two of the founders are father and son Ed and Russell Dodson. Ed, with a 40 year plus track record in the Scotch whisky industry, was the distillery manager of Glen Moray until 2005 and was also responsible for getting Ardbeg on Islay back in production in 1997.

Old Home Distillers

Lebanon, New York, founded in 2014

oldhomedistillers.com

The distillery produces bourbon, corn whiskey and New York Single Malt whiskey. The mash is fermented on the grain for 4-5 days, distillation takes place in a 100 gallon hybrid column still and the spirit is matured in charred, new American oak for a minimum of seven months.

Old Line Spirits

Baltimore, Maryland, founded in 2014

oldlinespirits.com

The owners bought the equipment from Golden Distillery when that was about to close down and brought it to Baltimore. Distilling started in 2016 and a couple of months prior, the first Old Line single malt, obviously from the Golden Distillery production, was released. A peated version from their own production was launched in 2017, a sherry cask finish appeared in autumn 2018, a cask strength a year later and Golden Edition (an 8 year old from the first distillery) was released in November 2019.

Old Route Two Spirits

Barre, Vermont, founded in 2017

oldroutetwo.com

Starting with gin and rum, the distillery started making single malt whiskey in November 2018. This, however is not due for release until 2021/2022.

Orange County Distillery

Goshen, New York, founded in 2013

orangecountydistillery.com

The distillery malts their own barley and even use their own peat when needed. Since 2014, they have launched a wide range of whiskies, including corn, bourbon, rye and peated single malt. The first aged single malt was launched in 2015. The latest single malt, in December 2019, was made using Black Dirt Malt from a local malting company and was matured for two years in virgin oak.

Orcas Island Distillery

Orcas, Washington, founded in 2014

orcasislanddistillery.com

What could best be described as a retirement hobby, former journalist Charles West founded a distillery on Orcas Island, 80 km north of Seattle. Apple brandy is the main produce but in 2019 he also won the Best American Single Malt Whiskey award from the American Distilling Institute for his West Island Single Malt Whiskey which was first released in 2018.

Painted Stave Distilling

Smyrna, Delaware, founded in 2013

paintedstave.com

Most of the whiskey production is centered on bourbon and rye but they have also released Ye Old Barley made from 100% malted barley and Diamond State Pot Still Whiskey made from malted barley and rye. In autumn 2019 a limited release, Festskey, was launched made from beer from a local brewery.

Pine Bluffs Distilling

Pine Bluffs, Wyoming, founded in 2018

pinebluffsdistilling.com

Malting the barley themselves, the distillery has been relying on vodka, bourbon, rye and corm whiskey for their first releases. In December 2019, Burly Malt Whiskey made from various roasted malts was released.

Pioneer Whisky (formerly known as III Spirits)

Talent, Oregon, founded in 2014

pioneerwhisky.com

Focusing mainly on single malts, the distillery changed its name in December 2018. Currently there are two single malts in the range; Oregon Highlander made from a grain bill of brewer´s malt, Munich malt and crystal malt and Islay Style Peated Whisky produced from 100% heavily peated malt from Scotland.

PostModern Distilling

Knoxville, Tennessee, founded in 2017

postmodernspirits.com

While focusing on gin, vodka and liqueur, the owners released their first single barrel single malt whiskey in 2018 with the latest being barrel No. 9, launched in January 2020. The distillery gets its fermented wash from the nearby Crafty Bastard Brewery.

Prichard´s Distillery

Kelso, Tennessee, founded in 1999

prichardsdistillery.com

Phil Prichard started the distillery in 1999 and in 2014, a second distillery equipped with a new 400-gallon alembic copper still was opened at Fontanel in Nashville. The main track of the production is rum. The first single malt was launched in 2010 and later releases usually have been vattings from barrels of different age (some up to 10 years old). The whiskey range also includes rye, bourbon and a Tennessee whiskey.

Quincy Street Distillery

Riverside, Illinois, founded in 2011

quincystreetdistillery.com

The distillery produces an impressive range of spirits including

gin, vodka, absinth, bourbon, corn whiskey and rye. So far, single malt whiskey made from barley only forms a small part. The only single malt released so far is Golden Prairie which was launched in December 2015 for the first time only to return in 2020. The malted Steamship Rye in also in the range.

Ranger Creek Brewing & Distilling

San Antonio, Texas, founded in 2010

drinkrangercreek.com

Focusing on beer brewing and whiskey production, they have their own brewhouse where they mash and ferment all their beers, as well as the beer going for distillation. The first release was Ranger Creek .36 Texas Bourbon in 2011. Their first single malt, Rimfire, was launched early in 2013. In June 2019, Heavy Smoke Rimfire made from 85% mesquite hand-smoked barley, was released.

Rennaisance Artisan Distillers

Akron, Ohio, founded in 2013

renartisan.com

Apart from whiskey, the distillery produces gin, brandy, grappa and limoncello. The first whiskey release, The King´s Cut single malt, was made from a grain bill including toasted and caramel malts and new batches appear every 6 months. In autumn 2019 an Islay Style Single Malt and a Blue Corn Bourbon were released.

Rock Town Distillery

Little Rock, Arkansas, founded in 2010

rocktowndistillery.com

Founded in 2010, this is a true grain-to-glass distillery where the grains used for distillation are grown within 125 miles of the property. The backbone of the production is made up of several bourbons, rye, a hickory-smoked wheat whiskey and vodka. For their 9th anniversary in June 2019, they released a 2 year old single malt that had been finished in cognac casks for another year.

San Diego Distillery

Spring Valley, California, founded in 2015

sddistillery.com

A distillery focused almost entirely on whiskey. In March 2016 the first six whiskies were released; a bourbon, a rye and an Islay peated single malt. The next whiskey to appear was a single malt made from seven different types of brewing malt and this was followed in late 2019 by a single malt made from a malted barley called PB Toast. Due to a fire in the distillery in autumn 2017, it was moved, and expanded, to a new location in spring 2018.

Warfield Distillery in Ketchum, Idaho

SanTan Spirits

Chandler and Phoenix, Arizona, founded in 2007 (2015)

santanbrewing.com

With two locations in Arizona, this brewery/restaurant added distilling to its concept in 2015. So far vodka, gin and whiskey has been released. Sacred Stave Single Malt occurs in two versions both finished in Arizona red wine barrels with one being bottled at cask strength. Bourbon and rye are also in the range.

Seattle Distilling

Vashon, Washington, founded in 2013

seattledistilling.com

The distillery produces gin, vodka, coffee liqueur, as well as a malt whiskey. The latter, named Idle Hour was first launched in 2013 followed by more batches. The style is Irish with both malted and unmalted barley being used in the mashbill and the whiskey is matured in barrels that used to hold local cabernet sauvignon wine.

Seven Caves Spirits

San Diego, California, founded in 2016

the7caves.com

Apart from gin and rum, Geoff Longenecker also makes whiskey from malted barley. The first single malt was released in spring 2019.

Seven Stills Distillery

San Francisco, California, founded in 2013

sevenstillsofsf.com

The first releases were made at Stillwater distillery in Petaluma. Since 2016, the owners have been producing their own spirit from a distillery in Bayview, an area in the San Francisco environs. Soon, the concept was expanded with three taprooms and in autumn 2019, the whole production (distillery and brewery) was moved to Mission Bay together with a restaurant, cocktail bar and taproom. The idea is to make whiskey from craft beers and the most recent releases include a whiskey made from Chocasmoke Chocolate Oatmeal Stout and one made from Five Pounds Hazy IPA

Snitching Lady Distillery

Fairplay, Colorado, founded in 2018

snitchingladydistillery.com

The distillery, which moved to new premises in August 2019, has so far released peach brandy, bourbon, rye and blue corn spirit. Single malt made from barley was distilled for the first time in March 2019 but hasn´t been released yet.

Spirit Hound Distillers

Lyons, Colorado, founded in 2012

spirithounds.com

Rum, vodka and sambucca are on the production list, but the distillery´s signature spirits are gin and malt whiskey. The barley for the whiskey is grown, malted and peat-smoked in Alamosa by Colorado Malting and the whiskey released so far is straight, i.e. at least two years old. The first bottles hit the shelves in summer 2015 and the first 4 year old was released in summer 2018 (followed by a second in January 2020). The distillery typically releases 2-3 new single barrels every month.

Spirits of St Louis Distillery (formerly known as Square One)

St. Louis, Missouri, founded in 2006

spiritsofstlouisdistillery.com

A combined brewery and restaurant in St. Louis. Apart from rum, gin, vodka and absinthe, the owners also produce J.J. Neukomm Whiskey, a malt whiskey made from toasted malt and cherry wood smoked malt.

Stark Spirits

Pasadena, California, founded in 2013

starkspirits.com

The first single malt whiskey was distilled in July 2015 and the first release was a barrel of peated single malt in February 2016. The first official distillery release of single malt (both peated and un-peated) came in February 2017. They have two stills with one reserved for all the peated production.

StilltheOne Distillery Two

Port Chester, New York, founded in 2010

stilltheonedistillery.com

Different kinds of whiskey are produced in a 250 gallon pot column still from Arnold Holstein. The only single malts released so far are "287" from a pale ale, "9A" made from a stout and "rt1" using a Belgium style yeast.

Storm King Distilling Co.

Montrose, Colorado, founded in 2017

stormkingdistilling.com

Inspired by a passion for whiskey, the owners have decided to be patient and let their products mature for at least two years which means single malt, rye and bourbon have not yet been released. Currently for sale are gin, vodka, rum and different spirits made from agave.

Sugar House Distillery

Salt Lake City, Utah, founded in 2014

sugarhousedistillery.net

The first release from the distillery in 2014 was a vodka, followed later that year by a single malt whisky. More releases of the single malt have followed and bourbon, rye and rum have also been added to the range. Now working on a single malt made from peated Utah malted barley.

Telluride Distilling

Telluride, Colorado, founded in 2014

telluridedistilling.com

Vodka and malt whiskey is produced in a distillery equipped with open top fermenters and a column still. Maturation is in new charred oak for two years followed by 6 months in port barrels. The first single malt was released in July 2016.

Thornton Distilling

Thornton, Illinois, founded in 2014

thorntondistilling.com

Originally founded as The Well Distillery it recently changed name to Thornton Distilling. The first name came from the historical building they´re operating from which, established in 1857 used to be a brewery. The distillery specialises in the production of single malt whiskey but they also distil gin and rum. A big seller is pecan whiskey made from a sourced bourbon.

Thumb Butte Distillery

Prescott, Arizona, founded in 2013

thumbbuttedistillery.com

A variety of gin, dark rum and vodka, as well as whiskey are produced by the owners, Dana Murdock, James Bacigalupi and Scott Holderness. Rodeo Rye, Bloody Basin Bourbon, Crown King Single Malt and a limited grain whiskey have all now been released. The latest version of the single malt has been made from barley smoked by using Arizona pecan wood.

Timber Creek Distillery

Crestview, Florida, founded in 2014

timbercreekdistillery.com

Fermentation and distillation is off the grain and, surprisingly, they use a traditional worm tub to cool the spirits – a technique that has become rare even in Scotland. Currently they have whiskies maturing made from corn, wheat, rye, barley and oat. The latest batch of Florida Single Malt was released in October 2017.

Town Branch Distillery

Lexington, Kentucky, founded in 1999

lexingtonbrewingco.com

The founder Dr Pearse Lyons, who passed away in March 2018, had an interesting background. A native of Ireland, he used to work for Irish Distillers in the 1970s. In 1980 he changed direction and founded Alltech Inc, a biotechnology company specializing in animal nutrition and feed supplements. Alltech purchased Lexington Brewing Company in 1999 and in 2008, two traditional copper pot stills were installed with the aim to produce Kentucky's first malt whiskey. The first single malt whiskey was released in 2010 under the name Pearse Lyons Reserve and it was later followed by Town Branch Bourbon, Town Branch Malt (currently a 7 year old) and Town Branch Rye. In June 2018, Alltech opened yet another distillery in Pikeville - Dueling Barrels Brewery and Distillery.

Triple Eight Distillery

Nantucket, Massachusetts, founded in 2000

ciscobrewers.com

Apart from whiskey, Triple Eight also produces vodka, rum and gin. Whiskey production was moved to a new distillery in 2007. The first 888 bottles of single malt whiskey were released on 8th August 2008 as an 8 year old. To keep in line with its theme, the price of these first bottles was also $888. More releases of Notch (as in "not Scotch") have followed, aged up to 12 years.

Two James Spirits

Detroit, Michigan, founded in 2013

twojames.com

Equipped with a 500 gallon pot still with a rectification column attached, the distillery started production in 2013. Vodka, gin, bourbon (even a peated version) and rye have been released while a single malt is still maturing in the warehouse. Aged in ex-sherry casks the whiskey has been made from peated Scottish barley. In December 2019, the opened a tasting room in Grand Rapids.

Van Brunt Stillhouse

Brooklyn, New York, founded in 2012

vanbruntstillhouse.com

Part of the Brooklyn Spirits Trail in New York, the distillery made their first release of Van Brunts American Whiskey in 2012, a mix of malted barley, wheat and a hint of corn and rye. This has been followed by a malt whiskey from 100% malted barley, a wheated bourbon, a rye and a smoked corn whiskey.

Vapor Distillery (formerly known as Roundhouse Spirits)

Boulder, Colorado, founded in 2007

vapordistillery.com

Ted Palmer founded the distillery with the ambition to make gin. When he met Scotsman Alastair Brogan in 2014, they decided to change the name of the distillery and also include whiskey making. A 3,800 litre copper pot still was installed in 2015 and now the distillery has three single malt whiskies in the range – an American Oak Boulder American Single Malt Whiskey, a peated version of the same and one that has been finished in port casks.

Venus Spirits

Santa Cruz, California, founded in 2014

venusspirits.com

Production is focused on whiskey, but gin and spirits from blue agave have also been released. The first single malt was Wayward Whiskey, matured in port and sherry casks and released in 2015. This was followed up by a rye and later a bourbon.

Vikre Distillery

Duluth, Minnesota, founded in 2012

vikredistillery.com

Together with whisky - gin, vodka and aquavit are produced at the distillery. Whiskies include Iron Range American Single Malt, Northern Courage Smokey Rye, Sugarbush Whiskey and Honor Brand Hay & Sunshine. The single malt was released in March 2017. The distillery was expanded in 2016 with six new fermentation tanks.

Wanderback Whiskey

Hood River, Oregon, founded in 2014

wanderback.com

The idea for the distillery was inspired by a visit to Boulder, Colorado and a sip of Stranahan's whiskey. The first release of Wanderback single malt (made from four different malts) was in September 2019 as a 3 year old. Since then there have been another two releases, the latest in December 2019. All of the whiskey has been distilled at Westland Distillery and then brought back to Wanderback for maturation and blending.

Warfield Distillery

Ketchum, Idaho, founded in 2015

drinkwarfield.com

Warfield Organic American Whiskey was first released in December 2019 and is distilled from organic pale and crystal malts. Co-founders Alex Buck and Ben Bradley also make gin, vodka and brandy and run a brewery, bar and restaurant. In summer 2020 they expanded their operaton and also installed two new copper pot stills (3,800 litres each) made by Forsyths in Scotland.

Woodstone Creek Distillery

Cincinnati, Ohio, founded in 1999

woodstonecreek.com

Opened as a farm winery in 1999, a distillery was added to the business in 2003. The first bourbon, was released in 2008 followed by a 10 year old single malt. Whiskey production is very small and just a handfull of releases have appeared since.

Wood's High Mountain Distillery

Salida, Colorado, founded in 2011

woodsdistillery.com

Whiskey is the main product at this distillery. The first expression (and current big seller), Tenderfoot Whiskey was a triple malt and so is the latest release, Sawatch, a 4 year old made from malted barley (a mix of chocolate malt and cherrywood smoked malt), malted rye and malted wheat. There is also an Alpine Rye Whiskey in the range.

Wright & Brown Distilling Co.

Oakland, California, founded in 2015

wbdistilling.com

The distillery is focused on barrel aged spirits, i. e. whiskey, rum and brandy. The first whiskey was distilled in 2015 and the first product, a rye whiskey (70/30 rye/barley), was launched in autumn of 2016 followed by a bourbon in autumn 2017. So far, no single malt made from barley has been released.

Canada

Shelter Point Distillery

Vancouver Island, British Columbia, founded in 2009

shelterpointdistillery.com

Founded by dairy farmer Patrick Evans who in 2005 switched to growing crops and four years later added a distillery. The consists of a one ton mash tun, five stainless steel washbacks and one pair of stills (5,000 litre wash still and 4,000 litre spirit still). Distillation started in 2011 and the barley used is grown on the farm. Currently, Evans produces 125,000 litres of spirit (whisky, gind and vodka) per year. In 2016, the first 5 year old single malt was released and this is still the core expression together with a cask strength version. Recent limited releases include Montfort DL 141, made from unmalted barley, French Oak Double Barrel, Single Cask Rye and Smoke Point Whisky which was made from malted and unmalted barley and finished for 8 months in ex-Laphroaig casks.

Still Waters Distillery

Concord, Ontario, founded in 2009

stillwatersdistillery.com

The distillery, on the outskirts of Toronto, is equipped with a 3,000 litre mash tun, two 3,000 litre washbacks and a Christian Carl 450 litre pot still. The still also has rectification columns for brandy and vodka production. The focus is on whisky but they also produce vodka, brandy and gin. Their first single malt, named Stalk & Barrel Single Malt, was released in 2013 and it was followed in late 2014 by the first rye whisky. The current range consists of Blue Blend, Red Blend, Rye and Single Malt. In June 2020 the Three Barrel Whisky, a blend of rye, single malt and corn whisky, was released.

Victoria Caledonian Distillery

Victoria, British Columbia, founded in 2016

victoriacaledonian.com

Founded by the Scotsman Graeme Macaloney who also acquired the services of the late Dr. Jim Swan, one of the foremost whisky consultants in the world. The distillery is equipped with a one ton semilauter mash tun, 7 stainless steel washbacks, a 5,500 litre wash still and a 3,600 litre spirit still. Some of the barley is malted on site and there is also a craft beer brewery. Distilling started in 2016 and in late 2017, the owners released the Mac Na Braiche, a 12 months malt spirit which was later followed by the Peated Mac Na Braiche. The first 3 year old single malt was released in 2020. A visitor centre offers tours of the distillery and the brewery, as well as tutored tastings.

Glenora Distillery

Glenville, Nova Scotia, founded in 1990

glenoradistillery.com

Situated in Nova Scotia, Glenora was the first malt whisky distillery in Canada. The first launch of in-house produce came in 2000, an 8 year old named Glen Breton Rare and a 10 year old is now the core expression. Other expressions have occured - 14, 19, 21 and 25 year olds. Glen Breton Ice, the world's first single malt aged in an ice wine barrel, was launched in 2006 and the latest edition was a 19 year old. A recent limited release is the Ghleann Dubh – a 13 year old peated single malt.

Other distilleries in Canada

Arbutus Distillery

Nanaimo, British Columbia, founded in 2014

arbutusdistillery.com

Situated on the southern part of Vancouver Island, the distillery has so far focused on vodka, gin and liqueurs but single malt whisky is also on the agenda. The first 3 year old appeared in December 2018 and the most recent is Double Barrel launched in November 2019.

Bridgeland Distillery

Calgary, Alberta, founded in 2018

bridgelanddistillery.com

Equipped with an unusual copper pot still from Vendome Copper Works where the lyne arm is extended with a large copper spiral leading to a condenser. The first distillation was in spring 2019 and the distillery is producing brandy, grappa and malt whisky. A single malt spirit was released in August 2019 and the first whisky is expected in 2022

Central City Brewers & Distillers

Surrey, British Columbia, founded in 2013

centralcitybrewing.com

What started as a brewpub has now grown to one of Canada´s largest craft breweries and in 2013 they added a distillery. Apart from whisky they also produce gin and vodka. The whisky is sold under the Lohin McKinnon Single Malt brand including special bottlings such as peated, chocolate malt and one finished in Niagara wine barrels.

Graeme Macaloney - founder and co-owner of Victoria Caledonian Distillery

De Vine Wine & Spirits

Victoria, British Columbia, founded in 2007

devinevineyards.ca

Starting as winemakers, the owners added a distillery in 2014. The first whisky was the 3 year old single malt Glen Saanich which was first released in 2017. Made from floor malted barley it was later followed up by Ancient Grains which had been made from a combination of barley, spelt, emmer, einkorn and kamut.

Dubh Glas Distillery, The

Oliver, British Columbia, founded in 2015

thedubhglasdistillery.com

The whisky is double distilled in an Arnold Holstein still and even though malt whisky is the main focus, gin is also produced. Apart from Noteworthy Gin, Virgin Spirits Barley (a newmake) has also been released. The first release of a single malt was the peated Against All Odds in June 2019 followed by several single casks. In December 2019, four limited bottlings were released; Across the Pond, Godfather, Neighbour and Relocation.

Eau Claire Distillery

Turner Valley, Alberta, founded in 2014

eauclairedistillery.ca

One of the first whisky distilleries in Alberta in modern times, Eau Claire opened in 2014. Their first limited single malt whisky appeared in December 2017 with Batch 3 released in December 2019 and Ploughman's Rye whisky has also been launched.

Last Mountain Distillery

Lumsden, Saskatchewan, founded in 2010

lastmountaindistillery.com

Equipped with two copper stills with columns from Carl in Germany, the distillery produces vodka, gin, rum, limoncello and whisky including rye, wheat and single malt from barley. The current single malt is close to 4 years old.

Liberty Distillery, The

Vancouver, British Columbia, founded in 2010

thelibertydistillery.com

Equipped with two copper stills with columns from Carl in Germany, the distillery produces gin, vodka and a wide range of whiskies all made from organic grain. Sold under the brand name Trust Whiskey, there are two single malts matured in madeira and burgundy casks respectively as well as rye, corn and grain whiskies.

Lucky Bastard Distillers

Saskatoon, Saskatchewan, founded in 2012

lbdistillers.ca

Founded by Michael Goldney, Cary Bowman and Lacey Crocker, in 2012. The first releases were vodka, gin and a variety of liqueurs. In summer 2016 the first single malt appeared and this is now released in small batches.

Maison Sivo

Hinchinbrooke, Quebec, founded in 2014

maisonsivo.ca

Inspired by the family production of fruit brandies in Hungary where he grew up, Janos Sivo founded a distillery producing different kinds of spirit including whisky. Le Single Malt finished in Sauternes casks and Le Rye were both released in early 2018.

Odd Society Spirits

Vancouver, British Columbia, founded in 2013

oddsocietyspirits.com

The first two whiskies from the distillery appeared in late 2018; the Commodore single malt and the Prospector rye. This was followed in December 2019 by Maple - a single malt that had been smoked with maple wood and matured in casks that had previously contained maple syrup.In March 2020 the single malt Blender's Release was launched. Gin, vodka and amaro is also produced.

Okanagan Spirits

Vernon and Kelowna, British Columbia, founded in 2004

okanaganspirits.com

The first distillery named Okanagan was started in 1970 by Hiram Walker but it closed in 1995. In 2004 Okanagan Spirits was established and a distillery was opened in Vernon. A variety of spirits made from fruits and berries as well as gin, vodka, absinthe and whisky are being produced. In 2013 the Laird of Fintry single malt was released with different expressions including a cask strength and a rum barrel finish.

Pemberton Distillery

Pemberton, British Columbia, founded in 2009

pembertondistillery.ca

Schramm Vodka made from potatoes was the distillery's first product in 2009. During the ensuing year, the owner started their first trials, distilling a single malt whisky using organic malted barley. The first release was in 2013 when a 3 year old unpeated version was launched. Since 2015, the owners have a regular expression called Pemberton Valley Organic Single Malt Whisky which is released in batches at an age between 5 and 8 years.

Phillips Fermentorium

Victoria, British Columbia, founded in 2014

fermentorium.ca

Started as a brewery, distillation of spirits was added 13 years later. The first release was gin and this was followed in late 2019 by the 5 year old single malt Small Talk Whiskey which had been matured in a combination of ex-pinot noir wine barrels and bourbon barrels that had been seasoned with the company's own beer.

Rig Hand Distillery

Nisku, Alberta, founded in 2014

righanddistillery.com

Equipped with a 1,100 litre pot still with columns, a Christian Carl still and a gin still, the distillery produces whisky. vodka, rum and gin. Sold in a bottle shaped like an oil drilling rig, the first whisky appeared in 2017. Bar M is a blended whisky made from wheat, barley and rye. This was followed by the Diamond S single malt, the Rocking R rye and, in autumn 2019, the Lazy B corn whisky.

Sheringham Distillery

Sooke, British Columbia, founded in 2015

sheringhamdistillery.com

The distillery, on Vancouver Island, recently moved to Sooke after an initial three years in Shirley. Gin, akvavit and vodka were the first to be bottled while the inaugural release of their Red Fife and Woodhaven whiskies came in 2019. The owners work on different mash bills with malted barley, corn, rye and wheat.

Yukon Spirits

Whitehorse, Yukon, founded in 2009

twobrewerswhisky.com

All of the whisky produced is made from malted grains but not only barley but also wheat and rye. The first 850 bottles of the 7 year old Two Brewer's Yukon Single Malt Whisky were released in 2016 and the current portfolio is based on four styles; Classic, Peated, Special Finishes and Innovative. Their whisky is released in batches using a variety of fermentation techniques and different barrels for the maturation.

Australia & New Zealand

Australia

Lark Distillery

Hobart, Tasmania, founded 1992

larkdistillery.com

In 1992, Bill Lark was the first person for 153 years to take out a distillation licence in Tasmania and he is often referred to as the godfather of modern whisky production in Australia. The success of the distillery forced Bill Lark to bring in investors in the company to generate future growth and since April 2018, Australian Whisky Holdings (AWH) holds a majority of the shares. Late 2019, AWH announced that they would perform a brand transformation of Lark whisky through a three tier price strategy. Including an investment upgrading the production by 350,000 litres, the aim is to turn the whisky from a "local brand to a global hero" with a focus on Asia. The whisky is double-distilled in a 1,800 litre wash still and a 600 litre spirit still and then matured in 100 litre "quarter casks". The old distillery site down in Hobart at the waterfront is now a cellar door and a showcase for Lark whisky. The core products in the whisky range are the Classic Cask at 43% and Cask Strength at 58%. Recent limited releases include Heavily Peated Bourbon Cask, The Wolf Release second edition where casks that had held smoked porter were used to mature the whisky, a rum cask release and the portmatured Distiller´s Selection LD1163.

Bakery Hill Distillery

North Balwyn, Victoria, founded 1998

bakeryhill.com

The first spirit at Bakery Hill Distillery, founded by David Baker, was produced in 2000 and the first single malt was launched in autumn 2003. Three different versions are available – Classic and Peated (both matured in ex-bourbon casks) and Double Wood (ex-bourbon and a finish in French Oak). As Classic and Peated are also available as cask strength bottlings, they can be considered two more varieties. Limited releases also occur with one of the latest being Sovereign Smoke – Defiantly Peated.

Sullivans Cove Distillery

Cambridge, Tasmania, founded 1994

sullivanscove.com

Patrick Maguire was the head distiller (and part owner) since 1999 when in 2018 he was inducted into the global Whisky Hall of Fame. In 2014 the distillery moved to a new building about four times the size of the current facility and in 2016, the distillery was taken over by a company led by Adam Sable who was general manager of Bladnoch distillery for two years. The core range from the distillery, aged for a minimum of nine years, comprises of American Oak, French Oak (where the barrels have contained tawny) and Double Cask. There is also Special Cask where the barrels that are used may vary from time to time, Old & Rare with whiskies that are 16 years or older and Limited Edition. A spectacular bottling was released in October 2019 to celebrate the distillery´s 25th anniversary; the last remaing four casks from 1997 were bottled as a 21 year old, the distillery´s and probably Australia´s oldest malt whisky to date. Recently, the distillery has also launched brandies as well as barrel aged gin.

Old Hobart Distillery

Blackmans Bay, Tasmania, founded 2005

overeemwhisky.com

After years of experimenting Casey Overeem opened up his distillery in 2007. The mashing was done at Lark distillery where Overeem also had his own washbacks and the wash was made to his specification. The distillation takes place in two stills (1,800 litres and 600 litres). In 2014, Old Hobart distillery was acquired by Lark Distillery and is now owned by Australian Whisky Holdings. In summer 2020, the Overeem trademark and part of the whisky

inventory was sold back to Sawford Distillery and Jane Sawford (Casey´s daughter). The range consists of Overeem Port Cask Matured, Overeem Sherry Cask Matured and Overeem Bourbon Cask Matured - bottled at 43% and 60%. Single cask releases occur regularly with a limited PX edition being one of the latest.

Hellyers Road Distillery

Burnie, Tasmania, founded 1999

hellyersroaddistillery.com.au

Hellyer´s Road Distillery is one of the larger single malt whisky distilleries in Australia with a capacity of doing 100,000 litres of pure alcohol per year. The distillery is equipped with a 6.5 ton mash tun, a 40,000 litre wash still and a 20,000 litre spirit still. The pots on both stills are made of stainless steel while heads, necks and lyne arms are made of copper. The first whisky was released in 2006 and there are now more than ten different expression in the range, including 10 and 12 year olds, peated as well as unpeated and various finishes. A range of limited releases called Master Series include whiskies up to 16 years old. The distillery also has a visitor centre with more than 40,000 people coming every year.

Great Southern Distilling Company

Albany, Western Australia, founded 2004

distillery.com.au

The distillery is located at Princess Royal Harbour in Albany. In 2015, the owners opened a second distillery in Margaret River which will is focused on gin production and in autumn 2018 a third distillery, Tiger Snake in Porongurup, started production. In a near future the combined production will be 400,000 litres of pure alcohol per year. The first expression of the whisky, called Limeburners, was released in 2008 and this is still the core bottling. Included in the range are also American Oak, Port Cask and Sherry Cask, all bottled at 43% as well as Peated which is bottled at 48%. Special yet yearly editions include Darkest Winter and Heavy Peat.

Starward Distillery

Melbourne, Victoria, founded 2008

starward.com.au

The distillery, founded by David Vitale, was moved in 2016 to a bigger site in Port Melbourne. The stills (an 1,800 litre wash still and a 600 litre spirit still) were bought from Joadja Creek Distillery. In spring 2020 the distillery was closed for a couple of months for a major upgrade in order to install a new 7,000 litre wash still while at the same time the current wash still became the new spirit still. The first whisky was released under the name Starward in 2013 and the current range consists of Nova (matured in Australian red wine barrels), Solera (matured in casks that had held apera, the Australian version of sherry) and the blended whisky Two-Fold (made from malted barley and wheat). Recent limited expressions include two collaborations with Blackhawks & Sparrows (spirits and wine retailer) and Cutler & Co. (a Melbourne restaurant).

Other distilleries in Australia

5 Nines Distilling

Uraidla, South Australia, founded in 2017

5ninesdistilling.com.au

The owners, David Pearse and Steven Griguol, built their own equipment including a copper pot still and a mash tun and started distilling malt whisky in 2017. Primarily made with local barley, the whisky is still maturing but several gins have been released.

7K Distillery

Brighton, Tasmania, founded in 2017

7kdistillery.com.au

A wide range of gins have been released so far but with whisky being one of Tyler Clark´s passions we may expect the first release of a malt whisky sometime in 2020.

23rd Street Distillery

Renmark, South Australia, founded in 2016

23rdstreetdistillery.com.au

With two used stills, 7,500 litres each, this distillery initially focused on a variety of gin, vodka and rum to start with. In 2019, through a collaboration with Byron Bay´s Stone & Wood Brewing, the first single malt whisky was released.

Adams Distillery

Perth, Tasmania, founded in 2016

adamsdistillery.com.au

After less than two years of production, all the equipment was up for sale to make way for a huge new distillery. The new distillery started production in March 2019 with a capacity of doing 1500 litres of new make daily. Around the same time, the first 2 year old single malt was also released and it was followed by more whisky matured in port, sherry and pinot noir casks.

Aisling Distillery, The

Griffith, New South Wales, founded in 2015

theaislingdistillery.com.au

Since the start, around 400 barrels have been filled at this distillery which is 100% dedicated to producing malt whisky. The first release is expected in mid 2020.

Archie Rose Distilling Company

Rosebery, New South Wales, founded in 2014

archierose.com.au

Apart from producing rye whisky and peated and unpeated single malt, the distillery also makes gin, rum and vodka. In June 2019 Chocolate Rye Malt became their first whisky release and more editions have followed. One was the Ironbark Smoked Rye Malt Whisky in October 2019 where the smoky flavour had been imparted by using water from blocks of ice that had been allowed to melt in a wood-fired oven at a nearby restaurang. The distillery has recently been expanded and the owners have plans to start exporting to the USA.

Backwoods Distilling

Yackandandah, Victoria, founded in 2017

backwoodsdistilling.com.au

The distillery is equipped with a 1200 litre copper ot still with an attached column. The first distillation was in January 2018 and the first release of a whisky is expected in early 2020.

Baker Williams Distillery

Mudgee, New South Wales, founded in 2012

bakerwilliams.com.au

For the first six years, the owners were focusing on producing gin, vodka and schnapps – spirits that are still the base in their business. The first whisky was Lachlan, released in spring 2018 and made from barley, wheat and rye (all malted). A second batch appeared in April 2019 and a third was launched in November that year.

Barossa Distilling Company

Nuriootpa, South Australia, founded in 2016

barossadistilling.com

Located in the historical Old Penfolds Distillery established in 1913, the distillery has focused on gin the first years and have launched a dozen different styles so far. Malt whisky is also produced but is still maturing.

Bellarine Distillery

Drysdale, Victoria, founded in 2017

bellarinedistillery.com.au

Located at the unlikely address Scotchman´s Road, the distillery is equipped with four stills, producing both gin and malt whisky. Gin is in the shops but the first whisky isn´t due for release until 2021.

Black Gate Distillery

Mendooran, New South Wales, founded in 2012

blackgatedistillery.com

Apart from malt whisky, the distillery produces vodka and rum. The first single malt was in 2015 when a sherrymatured expression was released. More bottlings have followed, including hybrid casks (matured in borth red wine and port casks) and peated single malt.

Samples are drawn at Chief´s Son Distillery

Castle Glen Distillery

The Summit, Queensland, founded in 2009

castleglenaustralia.com.au

Established as a vineyard in 1990, Castle Glen moved on to open up also a brewery and a distillery in 2009. Apart from wine and beer, a wide range of spirits are produced. The first whisky, Castle Glen Limited Edition, was released as a 2 year old in 2012 while the latest was a 9 year old single malt.

Chief´s Son Distillery

Somerville, Victoria, founded in 2017

chiefsson.com.au

The distillery is equipped with a 4,000 litre copper pot still which makes it a bit larger than most craft distilleries in Australia. The production is all about malt whisky and the first release appeared in March 2019. They currently have a core range made up of three varieties matured in French oak – the lightly peated 900 Standard, the 900 Sweet Peat and 900 Pure malt – and also the 900 American Oak. Recent limited expressions include Single Cask Sweet Peat Release 2 and Stout Cask Expression.

Coburns Distillery

Burrawang, New South Wales, founded in 2017

coburnsdistillery.com.au

Mark Coburn started production in spring 2017 and has so far released several versions of his gin. The single malt turned two years old in July 2019 but has yet to be released. Coburns is one of very few Australian distilleries with its own peat bog for smoking the barley. Plans for the future include having a set of no less than five 5,000 litre pot stills.

Corowa Distilling Co.

Corowa, New South Wales, founded in 2010

corowawhisky.com.au

Situated in a restored flour mill from 1924, the distillery was founded by Dean Druce and with Beau Schlig as Master Distiller. The distillery is focused entirely on single malt whisky using barley from Dean's own estate. Corowa started distilling in 2016 and the inaugural release from their own production was First Drop (aged in

port barrels) in August 2018 followed by Bosque Verde (also port), Quicks Courage (PX sherry) and Mad Dog Morgan (muscat). In summer 2020, their first peated whisky was released.

Corra Linn Distillery

Relbia, Tasmania, founded in 2015

corralinndistillery.com.au

John Wielstra made the first distillation in his hybrid column still in autumn 2016, using a new, local barley strain that had recently been developed. He is also using his own yeast and smokes his barley using dried kelp instead of peat. The first release of single malt was in December 2018.

Darby-Norris Distillery

Kelso, Tasmania, founded in 2018

darbynorrisdistillery.com.au

A small distillery which started production in spring 2018. Gin and vodka have been released but the first single malt isn´t expected at least until 2020.

Devil´s Distillery

Moonah, Tasmania, founded in 2015

devilsdistillery.com.au, hobartwhisky.com.au

Founded by Rocco Caccavo, the distillery uses only Tasmanian barley for their products. Malt whisky is the main focus but vodka and various liqueurs were the first bottlings to be launched. The first release of their Hobart Single Malt was in 2018 with several wood finishes following (pinot noir, rosé, botrytis, stout). The latest addition in November 2019, was a single malt matured for 3.5 years in casks made from Hungarian oak that had held Tokaji.

Fannys Bay Distillery

Lulworth, Tasmania, founded in 2015

fannysbaydistillery.com.au

The distillery is equipped with a 400 litre copper pot still, a 600 litre mash tun and a 300 litre washback with a 7-8 day fermentation. The first whisky was released in May 2017 and it is now available in three main versions - bourbon, sherry and port.Most of the releases are small batch and ofter single barrels

Devil´s Distillery in Tasmania

Fleurieu Distillery

Goolwa, South Australia, founded in 2016

fleurieudistillery.com.au

A local craft beer brewery was turned into a distillery proper in 2016 but whisky had been distilled already since 2014. Gareth and Angela Andrews released their first single malt in December 2016 and it has been followed by several more, both peated and unpeated with names like Tea in the Sahara, Ecto Gammat, Atlantic Crossing and Whisky Kisses

Geographe Distillery

Myalup, Western Australia, founded in 2008

geographedistillery.com.au

Apart from gin and limoncello, Steve Ryan is also distilling malt whisky. The latest release of Bellwether Single Malt was a 4 year old in November 2018. Medium peated malt from Baird's in Inverness was used and the whisky had matured ex-tawny casks.

Iron House Brewery & Distillery

White Sands Resort, Tasmania, founded in 2007

ironhouse.com.au

Established as a brewery it moved to its current location in 2010 and started distilling whisky as well. The first Tasman Whisky (as the brand is called) was released in summer 2019 and the core range currently consists of Port-, Sherry- and Bourbon Cask - all aged for more than 4 years. There is also a peated whisky in the pipeline.

Joadja Distillery

Joadja, New South Wales, founded in 2014

joadjadistillery.com.au

Equipped with just the one still (800 litres), the distillery was expanded in 2015 with a 2,400 litre wash still and another four washbacks. For the maturation, Joadja focuses mainly on ex-sherry casks from Jerez in Spain. The first whisky was launched in autumn 2017 with a combined bourbon/oloroso maturation in March 2020 as their latest release.

Kangaroo Island Spirits

Cygnet River, South Australia, founded in 2006

kispirits.com.au

Focusing on gin for the first decade, Jon (brother of Bill Lark) and Sarah Lark started distilling also malt whisky in 2018. The first release is expected end of 2020.

Kilderkin Distillery

Ballarat, Victoria, founded in 2016

kilderkindistillery.com.au

The distillery is owned by Chris Pratt and Scott Wilson-Browne and the name Kilderkin refers to the small type of casks they use for maturation. The distillery is equipped with one pair of copper pot stills and have so far released four different gins. The first malt whisky release isn´t expected until 2020/2021.

Killara Distillery

Hobart, Tasmania, founded in 2016

killaradistillery.com

Kristy Booth is the daughter of Bill Lark, often referred to as the godfather of Australian whisky and after 17 years working in her father´s distillery, she opened her own in summer 2016. The first whisky distillation was in August 2016. The succesful Apothecary gin has been on the market for a while and in November 2018 it was time for the first single malt release - a cask strength matured for two years in an ex-tawny port cask. End of 2019, Kristy Booth broke ground on a new distillery.

Launceston Distillery

Western Junction (near Launceston), Tasmania, founded in 2013

launcestondistillery.com.au

The equipment consists of a 1,100 litre stainless steel mash tun, stainless steel washbacks, a 1,600 litre wash still and a 700 litre spirit still – both with reflux balls. The newmake is filled into barrels which have previously held bourbon, Apera (Australian sherry) and Tawny (Australian port). The first release, matured in Apera casks, appeared in July 2018 and whisky matured in ex-bourbon and ex-tawny, also at cask strength, have followed since.

Lawrenny Distilling

Ouse, Tasmania, founded in 2017

lawrenny.com

With a head distiller previously working for Lark and Archie Rose, Joe Dinsmoor, the distillery has initially been releasing vodka and gin. The first distillation of malt whisky was in November 2017 and the first release, initially matured in a combination of ex-bourbon and Australian port casks and with a finish in PX sherry, will appear in autumn 2020.

Loch Distillery

Loch, Victoria, founded in 2014

lochbrewery.com.au

A combined brewery and distillery using the wash from their brewery for the whisky production. The first single malt was launched in 2018 and their seventh and latest release in November 2019 had been matured in ex-bourbon and finished in stout casks.

The McLaren Vale Distillery

Blewitt Springs, South Australia, founded in 2016

themclarenvaledistillery.com.au

The distillery was founded by John Rochfort, the previous CEO at Lark Distillery and is now run by the Rochfort family. Focusing solely on malt whisky, the distillery has a capacity to make 50,000 litres. The only release so far, was the Bloodstone Collection in 2017. Twenty different malt spirits (not yet matured for two years) were launched to showcase different types of oak and how different wines from South Australian winemakers affected the spirit.

Manly Spirits Co. Distillery

Brookvale, Sydney, New South Wales, founded in 2017

manlyspirits.com.au

Equipped with two copper pot stills (1,500 l and 1,000 l), the distillery has already launched gin, vodka and a white dog malt spirit. The first single malt whisky named North Fort is due for release in 2020.

Mt Uncle Distillery

Walkamin, North Queensland, founded in 2001

mtuncle.com

The owners started out by producing gin, rum and vodka - all of which soon became established brands on the market. Their first single malt, The Big Black Cock, was released in April 2014 matured for five years and was then followed by Watkins Whisky.

Nant Distillery

Bothwell, Tasmania, founded in 2007

nant.com.au

The distillery was founded by Keith Batt but was later taken over by Australian Whisky Holdings. The distillery is equipped with a 1,800 litre wash still, a 600 litre spirit still and wooden washbacks. Two more washbacks were added recently, almost doubling the distillery´s capacity. The first bottlings were released in 2010 and the current core range consists of Sherry, Port and Bourbon.

Noosa Heads Distillery

Noosaville, Queensland, founded in 2018

noosaheadsdistillery.com

Equipped with a 2,000 litre copper pot reflux still, the distillery launched its first products in spring 2019 – gin, vodka and a white malt. Single malt whisky is maturing but won't be released until 2021.

Old Kempton Distillery

Kempton, Tasmania, founded in 2013

oldkemptondistillery.com.au

Established as Redlands Estate Distillery in Derwent Valley, the distillery re-located in 2016 to Dysart House in Kempton and later changed the name to Old Kempton Distillery. The first spirit was distilled in 2013 in a 900 litre copper pot still and another three stills have later been installed. The first single malt whisky was launched in 2015 and this has been followed by several more releases including the First Release Solera Cask.

Riverbourne Distillery

Jingera, New South Wales, founded in 2016

riverbournedistillery.com

Located at the head of the Molonglo River, close to Canberra, the distillery started producing whisky, rum and vodka in February 2016. The first two single malts, released in June 2018, were named The Riverbourne Identity and The Riverbourne Supremacy followed later by Ultimatum and Enigma - all matured in a variety of casks.

Sawford Distillery

Kingston, Tasmania, founded in 2018

sawforddistillery.com

The distillery is run by Jane Sawford and her husband Mark. Before Jane was married, her last name was Overeem and she has been deeply involved in the Australian whisky business for more than a decade. She learned distilling at her father's, Casey Overeem, distillery and when Lark Distillery took over the operations she was the Sales and Marketing Manager. The distillery is equipped with two stills from Knapp Lewer (1,800 and 800 litrs respectively) but no whiskies have yet been released even though Lady Jane Whisky has been registered as a trade mark.

Settlers Artisan Spirits

McLaren Vale, South Australia, founded in 2015

settlersspirits.com.au

Until now the distillery has been concentrating on gin but with a new pot still in 2018, whisky distillation has tripled. The only single malt release so far is the port matured Settlers Single Malt.

Shene Distillery

Pontville, Tasmania, founded in 2015

shene.com.au

Damian Mackey started distilling whisky in a small shed already in 2007. In 2016 the opportunity came for him to move his production to the Shene Estate at Pontville. With four stills and a capacity of 300,000 litres this is one of the largest distilleries in Australia. The whisky is triple distilled and the first release of Mackey single malt was in 2017. The fourth release, tawny port matured, appeared in November 2019.

Southern Wild Distillery

Devonport, Tasmania, founded in 2017

southernwilddistillery.com

So far George Burgess, who designed and built his own still,

has released a wide variety of gins but he also has malt whisky maturing in the warehouses with a possible release in 2020.

Spring Bay Distillery

Spring Beach, Tasmania, founded in 2015

springbaydistillery.com.au

A small, family-owned distillery, located on the east coast of Tasmania and equipped with a 1200 litre pot still. The distillery was expanded in June 2019 with a 2,500 litre wash still. The first spirit released was a gin followed in autumn 2017 by the first single malt. More whiskies, matured in port, sherry and bourbon casks, have appeared since then.

Tamar Valley Distillery

Hillwood, Tasmania, founded in 2018

hillwoodwhisky.com.au

Equipped with a 600 litre copper pot still this family owned distillery has a pure focus on malt whisky with no other spirits being produced. Double distilled and matured in a combination of local casks from Tasmanian vineyards as well as ex-sherry and ex-bourbon the first release of Hillwood Whisky is expected in summer 2020.

Timboon Railway Shed Distillery

Timboon, Victoria, founded in 2007

timboondistillery.com.au

Wash from a local brewery is distilled twice in a 600 litre pot still. The first whisky release (and still a signature expression) matured in port barrels, was made in 2010 and some of the latest expressions have been Christie´s Cut and Bailey Street.

Tin Shed Distilling Co.

Welland (Adelaide), South Australia, founded in 2013

iniquity.com.au

The owners, including Ian Schmidt, opened their first distillery, Southern Coast Distillers, in 2004 with a release in 2010. Eventually it was closed and the current distillery started in 2013. The first single malt, under the name Iniquity, was launched as a 2 year old in 2015 and batch 17 was released in September 2019.

Turner Stillhouse

Grindelwald, Tasmania, founded in 2018

turnerstillhouse.com

Founded by ex-Californian Justin Turner, the distillery has so far been focusing on gin. A designated whisky copper still was installed in summer 2019 and the first release of a single malt is expected in 2021.

White Label Distillery

Huntingfield, Tasmania, founded in 2018

whitelabeldistillery.com.au

The distillery is equipped with no less than 16 stainless steel washbacks (4,000 litres each) and one pair of copper pot stills. They work mainly as a contract distiller and brewer. Jane Sawford (nee Overeem) is helping out with marketing and sales and her father Casey overlooks distilling and maturation of the whisky.

Wild River Mountain Distillery

Wondecla, Queensland, founded in 2017

wildrivermountaindistillery.com.au

This is one of Australia´s highest elevated distilleries, located in the Atherton Tablelands in North Queensland at a height of 870 metres. The first single malt, Elevation, was released in August 2019. Lightly smoked it had been matured in a combination of ex-

Tennessee barrels and Australian red wine casks. This was followed by Small Batch, aged in ex-shiraz barrels. Second editions of both followed in spring 2020.

William McHenry and Sons Distillery

Port Arthur, Tasmania, founded in 2011

mchenrydistillery.com.au

The distillery is equipped with a 500 litre copper pot still with a surrounding water jacket to get a lighter spirit. The first whisky was released in May 2016 while the latest edition (spring 2020) is a 5 year old, fully matured in an American oak port cask. This was followed by a number of cask strength releases.

New Zealand

Thomson Whisky Distillery

Auckland, North Island, founded in 2014

thomsonwhisky.com

The company started out as an independent bottler but in 2014, the owners opened up a small distillery based at Hallertau Brewery in North West Auckland. The wash for the distillation comes from the brewery. First release was in February 2018 and the current range is made up by Two Tone (rye and barley), Manuka Smoke, South Island Peat, Four and White Smoke, smoked with manuka, matured in a chardonnay cask and released in March 2020.

Cardrona Distillery

Cardrona (near Wanaka), South Island, founded in 2015

cardronadistillery.com

Building of the distillery started in January 2015 and in October the first distillation was made. The distillery is equipped with 1.4 ton mash tun, six metal washbacks, one 2,000 litre wash still and a 1,300 litre spirit still. The two pot stills were made by Forsyth's in Scotland. Apart from whisky, barrel-aged gin and single malt vodka is also produced. The first 3 year old whisky released were two single casks (sherry and bourbon) in December 2018 followed by another two (pinot noir and bourbon) a year later. Meanwhile a range of 3 year old, cask strength expressions called Just Hatched was introduced with Solera in spring 2019 and has since been followed by another two bottlings.

Other distilleries in New Zealand

Auld Distillery

Scotts Gap, South Island, founded in 2017

aulddistillery.co.nz

For three generations, the Auld family have been growing grain on their farm and for the past few years Rob and Toni have also added distilling. All the barley for the whisky comes from their own land and is also malted on site. First distillation was in 2018 and no whisky has yet been released.

Lammermoor Distillery

Ranfurly, South Island, founded in 2018

lammermoordistillery.com

Founded by John and Susie Elliot who have been farmers at the huge (5,200 hectares) Lammermoor Station for thirty years. What started out as a hobby has now turned into yet another part of the business at the farm. Lammermoor is a true "grain-to-glass" distillery or as it's called in New Zealand "paddock-to-bottle". The Elliots control every step from growing and malting the barley through to distilling and maturation. A gin was released early on and a manuka smoked whisky appeared in 2020.

New Zealand Whisky

Dunedin, South Island, founded in 2020 (cellar door in Oamaru)

thenzwhisky.com

In 2010, Greg Ramsay and partners bought the remaining casks from the closed Willowbank distillery in Dunedin. Owned for a time by Seagrams, the distillery operated from 1974 until 1997 when the stills were sold to a rum producer in Fiji. The remaining stock has been sold over the years under different names; Millford, Lammerlaw and Dunedin with the oldest being the 30 year old Otago, first released in 2017. Since 2015, Greg Ramsay has been distilling small volumes of whisky at the Spirits Workshop in Christchurch but starting in 2020, the company will have its own distillery at Speight's Brewery in Dunedin. The new name of the whisky will be Oamruvian which has already been used for some whiskies coming from the Workshops production, for instance Oamruvian Revolucion.

Spirits Workshop Distillery, The

Christchurch, South Island, founded in 2012

thespiritsworkshop.co.nz

For some time now Doug and Anthony Lawry have been making spirits for others in their two copper pot stills including malt whisky for New Zealand Whisky. This is also where the newly launched Divergence single malt has been made. There are however a few recent whiskies released under their own label, all of them having been matured in what they call "micro barrels" (10 to 20 litres).

Cardrona Distillery

Asia

India

Amrut Distilleries Ltd.

Bangalore, Karnataka, founded in 1948

amrutdistilleries.com

The family-owned distillery, based in Kumbalgodu outside Bangalore in southern India, started to distil malt whisky in the mid-eighties. The equivalent of 60 million bottles of spirits (including rum, gin and vodka) is manufactured a year, of which 1,5 million bottles is whisky. Most of the whisky goes to blended brands but Amrut single malt was introduced in 2004. It was first launched in Scotland, but can now be found in 48 countries. It wasn´t until 2010, however, that the brand was launched in India. The distillery was expanded with four more stills in autumn 2018 and with a total of two mash tuns and 12 washbacks it now has the capacity of producing one million litres of pure alcohol. The fermentation time for the single malt is 140 hours and the barley is sourced from the north of India, malted in Jaipur and Delhi and finally distilled in Bangalore before the whisky is bottled without chill-filtering or colouring. In May 2019, the owner and chairman of the distillery, Sri. Neelakanta Rao Jagdale, passed away at the early age of 66 and was succeeded by his son Rakshit and his son-in-law Vikram Nikam. In summer 2019, distillery manager Surrinder Khumar retired after 33 years with the company and was succeeded by long-time global brand ambassador Ashok Chokalingam.

The Amrut core range consists of unpeated and peated versions bottled at 46% as well as cask strength versions of the two and, finally, Fusion which is based on 25% peated malt from Scotland and 75% unpeated Indian malt. Special releases over the years, often released in new batches, include Two Continents, where maturing casks have been brought from India to Scotland for their final period of maturation, Intermediate Sherry Matured where the new spirit has matured in ex-bourbon or virgin oak, then re-racked to sherry butts and with a third maturation in ex-bourbon casks,

Kadhambam which is a peated Amrut matured in ex oloroso butts, ex Bangalore Blue Brandy casks and ex rum casks, Portonova with a maturation in bourbon casks and port pipes, Amalgam comprising of Amrut as well as single malts from Scotland and Asia (with a peated version introduced in late 2018), Spectrum where the fourth edition had been matured in casks made of four varieties of oak, Double Cask, a 5 year old combination of ex-bourbon and port pipes and finally, the 100% malted Amrut Rye Single Malt. Other recent one-off releases include a Madeira Cask Finish and Port Pipe Peated as well as single casks for select markets. Finally, in August 2020 the first triple distilled Indian whisky was released - Amrut Triparva.

A big surprise in 2013 was the release of Amrut Greedy Angels, an 8 year old and the oldest Amrut so far. That was an astonishing achievement in a country where the hot and humid climate causes major evaporation during maturation with an angel´s share of 10-12%. In 2015 it was time for an even older expression, 10 years old, and in 2016, a 12 year old, the oldest whisky from India so far, was released. Two more releases of the 10 year old (Peated Rum Finish and Peated Sherry Finish) appeared in 2019.

John Distilleries Jdl

Goa, Konkan and Bangalore, Karnataka, founded in 1992

pauljohnwhisky.com

Paul P John, who today is the chairman of the company, started in 1992 by making a variety of spirits including Indian whisky made from molasses. Their biggest seller today is Original Choice, a blend of extra neutral alcohol distilled from molasses and malt whisky from their own facilities. The brand, which was introduced in 1995/96, sold 152 million bottles in 2019. Another brand is Bangalore Malt, a simpler version of Original Choice, which in recent years has been one of the fastest growing spirits in the world. In 2019, however, sales of the brand went down by 18% to 50 million bottles. John Distilleries owns three distilleries and

The new stills at Amrut Distillery

produces its brands from 18 locations in India with its head office in Bangalore and a huge distillery and visitor centre in Goa. The basis for their blended whiskies is distilled in column stills with a capacity of 500 million litres of extra neutral alcohol per year. In 2007 they set up their single malt distillery which was equipped with one pair of traditional copper pot stills but in 2017, another pair of stills were added, doubling the capacity to 1.5 million litres per year. The company released their first single malt in autumn 2012 and this was followed by several single casks. In 2013 it was time for two core expressions, both made from Indian malted barley. Brilliance is unpeated and bourbon-matured while Edited, also matured in bourbon casks, has a small portion of peated barley in the recipe. In 2015 the third core expression was released. It was a 100% peated bottling called Bold, bottled at 46% and in spring 2019 yet another "flagship" bottling was added by the way of the unpeated, bourbon matured Nirvana, bottled at 40%. At the beginning of 2014, two cask strength bottlings were released; Select Cask Classic (55,2%) and Select Cask Peated (55,5%) and since then, more Select expressions have been revealed – Oloroso and Pedro Ximenez. Limited releases also include two 7 year old single malts; Mars Orbiter, a peated whisky matured in American oak and Kanya, unpeated from American oak. In November 2019 Christmas Edition 2019, the second in the limited series, was released and another is planned for late 2020. Bottled at 46%, the slightly peated whisky had been finished in PX sherry casks. Finally, 2020 saw the release of the 6 year old Tula matured in virgin American oak and bottled at 58%.In October 2018, Sazerac, owners of brands such as Buffalo Trace, Pappy van Winkle and Southern Comfort, bought a 23% stake in John Distilleries and in 2019 they acquired another 20%. Paul John, chairman and managing director of John Distilleries still holds a 57% stake in the company.

Other distilleries in India

Khoday

Bangalore, Karnataka, founded in 1906

khodayindia.com

Khoday is a company working in many areas, including brewing and distillation. The IMFL whisky Peter Scot was launched by the company already in 1968 and in spring 2019, the Peter Scot Black Single Malt was launched.

McDowell's Distillery

Ponda, Goa, founded in 1988 (malt whisky)

diageoindia.com

Established in the late 1800s, the distillery produces the best selling whisky in the world, McDowell's No. 1, with 368 million bottles sold in 2019. Owned by Diageo since 2014, the distillery also produces a very small amount of single malt whisky.

Mohan Meakin

Solan, Himachal Pradesh, founded in 1855

mohanmeakin.com

Founded as a brewery in 1820, possibly by Edward Dyer and incorporated as a company in 1855. It was taken over by H G Meakin in 1887 and finally, Narendra Nath Mohan acquired the business in 1949. New breweries were built during the 1970s and 1980s and today, the company is making beer, whisky and rum. Their most famous brands are Old Monk rum and Solan No. 1 whisky. Their first general launch of a single malt whisky under the name Solan Gold Single Malt appeared in 2019 and has matured for at least four years.

Rampur Distillery

Rampur, Uttar Pradesh, founded in 1943

rampursinglemalt.com

This huge distillery, situated east of Delhi, was purchased in 1972 by G. N. Khaitan and is today owned by Radico Khaitan, one of

the biggest Indian liquor companies. The capacity is 75 million litres of whisky based on molasses and 30 million litres of grain whisky. They also have a distillery producing whisky from malted barley. An expansion in autumn 2019 increased the capacity of that distillery to 3 million litres per year. A larger mash tun was installed as well as a new wash still (25,000 litres) and a new spirit still (16,000 litres). On top of that, a refurbished and enlarged visitor centre was opened in 2020. They also own another distillery in Maharashtra with a capacity of 52 million litres. The first whisky brand from Radico (in 1997) was 8PM, which sells around 80 million bottles yearly. The first single malt release, the ex-bourbon matured Select, appeared in May 2016 and since then Double Cask matured in a combination of ex-bourbon and European oak sherry casks and PX Sherry (American oak with a PX sherry finish) have been released in the core range. The oldest whisky so far from the distillery was the limited Signature Reserve. Matured in American oak and finished in PX sherry butts it was bottled at cask strength (44,5%) in autumn 2019. All Rampur whiskies are un-chill filtered and without age statement.

Israel

The Milk & Honey Distillery

Tel-Aviv, founded in 2013

mh-distillery.com

Israel's first whisky distillery, equipped with a 1 ton stainless steel mash tun, four stainless steel washbacks and two copper stills (with a capacity of 9,000 and 3,500 litres each). The current production is 200,000 litres of pure alcohol while the capacity is 800,000. The first distillation was in March 2015 and the first, limited 3 year old single malt, made before the final equipment was installed, was released in August 2017. A Founder's Edition appeared in autumn 2019 and Classic, the first commercial bottling and matured in a combination of ex-bourbon and STR casks, was released in January 2020. Meanwhile, a number of very limited releases appeared during autumn 2019. The distillery has a visitor centre offering a large variety of tours and workshops.

Other distilleries in Israel

Golani Distillery

Katzrin, founded in 2014

golanispirit.com

Founded by Canadian expat David Zibell, the distillery is equipped with two artisanal copper stills and some of the whisky is matured in wine casks from the nearby Golan Heights Winery. In spring 2020, a new, 1 ton mash tun as well as two more washbacks were installed with the aim to install two more and larger stills end of the year. The distillery is focusing on single malt from barley and on grain whisky (51% malted barley and 49% wheat). The first 3 year old whisky appeared in late 2017. A number of different single casks have since been launched. One of the latest releases, in April 2020, was the 5 year old Unicorn matured in an ex-wine cask made of French oak. Meanwhile, David has also opened yet another distillery (Yerushalmi) for peated production and is a part owner of a third distillery focusing on production of corn whisky.

Shevet Brewing & Distilling

Pardess Hanna, founded in 2017

shevet.co.il

A very large and impressive brewery founded by Neil Wasserman and Lior Balmas and partially funded by an investment group in the USA. A distillery equipped with two traditional copper pot stills has also been opened with the idea of distilling the wash from the brewery into malt whisky. A malt whisky by the name Ruach is in the pipeline but has not yet been released.

Yerushalmi Distillery

Jerusalem, founded in 2017

yerushalmidistillery.com

This is David Zibell´s (owner of Golani Heights) second distillery and equipped with a 3,000 litre wash still and a 2,000 litre spirit still it has a capacity of 150,000 litres per year. David´s idea is to concentrate his production of peated whisky to this distillery but also rum and gin is produced. The first whisky distillation was in 2019 and new make has already been offered to customers.

Japan

Yamazaki

Mishima, Osaka, founded in 1923

suntory.com/factory/yamazaki/

In 1923, Shinjiro Torii built the first malt whisky distillery in Japan. A lot of time has passed since Torii took that bold move, almost a century ago, but Yamazaki is still at the forefront of Japanese whisky-making, in terms of quality and quantity. Torii was a pragmatic man, so he decided to build his distillery close to center of commerce at the time, Osaka. The construction of Yamazaki distillery began in late 1922 and was completed the following year. The distillery started out with two pot stills but has been reconfigured and expanded many times over the years, first in 1957 and most recently in 2013, when four pot stills were added bringing the count to 16. There's plenty of variety in terms of heating method, shape, size, lyne-arm orientation and condenser type, but that's typical of Yamazaki at every stage of production. Since 1988, eight of the washbacks are wooden whereas the other nine are stainless steel. With different peating levels for the barley, different yeast strains and a plethora of cask types, the variety of whisky types created at Yamazaki distillery is quite staggering.

Launched in 1984, The Yamazaki was the first generally available single malt in Japan. These days, 'generally available' has to be taken with a pinch of salt. Of the theoretical line-up of NAS, 12, 18 and 25 year olds, the age-statement expressions are well-nigh impossible to find. Yamazaki caught headlines all over the world

with the release of their oldest expression, 55 years old, of which only 100 bottles were available at 3 million yen plus tax. With hardcore collectors eager to get their hands on one of these bottles bottles are changing hands for many times that figure already.

Yoichi

Yoichi, Hokkaido, founded in 1934

nikka.com/eng/distilleries/yoichi/

After leaving Kotobukiya (now Suntory) in 1934, Masataka Taketsuru set up his own distillery. He settled on the town of Yoichi, up in Hokkaido, because the locale and climate conditions reminded him of Scotland, where he had studied whisky making. The first spirit ran off the stills in 1936, with the first product launched in 1940. Initially equipped with a single still that doubled as spirit and wash still, the distillery now houses 6 stills. Coal-heated and featuring straight heads and downward lyne arms, these produce a robust spirit. Although the 'house style' is peaty and heavy, people tend to forget that – like the other big distilleries in Japan – Yoichi is set up to create a wide range of distillates. Between various peating levels, yeast strains, fermentation times, distillation methods and maturation types, it is said that Yoichi is capable of producing 3,000 different types of malt whisky.

In September 2015, the entire Yoichi range (which included a no-age statement expression as well as a 10, 12, 15 and 20 year olds) was axed and replaced with a single option: a new NAS. In March 2020, a limited edition Apple Brandy Wood Finish Yoichi expression was released (6,700 bottles), to commemorate the 100th anniversary of the wedding of Rita Cowan and Masataka Taketsuru.

Mt. Fuji

Gotemba, Shizuoka, founded in 1972

no website

Mt. Fuji distillery (formerly known as Fuji Gotemba distillery) is nestled at the foot of Mt. Fuji, less than 12 km from the peak. The 'mother water' is taken from three bores on site that top into underground streams 100 metres deep. Analysis has shown that the water used today fell on Mt Fuji as snow 50 years ago. The distillery was founded by Kirin Brewery, Seagram & Sons and Chivas Brothers as a comprehensive whisky manufacturing plant

Yamazaki Distillery will be celebrating its 100th anniversary in 2023

where all production processes – from malt and grain whisky distilling to blending and bottling – take place on site. Unlike most Japanese distilleries, which followed Scottish whisky-making practice, Mt. Fuji adopted production techniques and methodologies from all over the world. After Seagram started selling off its beverage assets worldwide, Kirin became the sole owner of Fuji Gotemba Distillery.

The distillery is currently under renovation in order to diversify malt whisky flavor profiles. Two different sets of new pot stills and 4 wooden washbacks will be in operation by the middle of 2021. In addition to malt whisky, three types of grain whisky are made at the distillery using a multi-column still, a kettle and a doubler in a modular way. Understandably, given this production set up, most new products coming out of Fuji Gotemba are blended whiskies and these are put together by Master Blender Jota Tanaka and his team. The flagship Fuji-Sanroku Signature Blend was launched in 2017 but those keen to try a Fuji Gotemba malt whisky should look out for the 17 year old Small Batch or one of the recent 12 year old Red Wine Cask Finish single cask releases. At a visit to the distillery you may also be able to pick up one of the Distiller's Select Single Malt bottlings (there is also a Single Grain) which is put together ever year in the spring.

Hakushu

Hokuto, Yamanashi, founded in 1973

suntory.com/factory/hakushu/

Hakushu was built 50 years after the first Suntory malt whisky distillery and is nestled in a vast forest area at the foot of Mt Kaikomagatake in the Southern Alps. It is often referred to as 'the forest distillery': more than 80% of the site owned by Suntory is undeveloped. The original distillery was equipped with 6 pairs of stills. In 1977, capacity was doubled and another 6 pairs of stills added in a building next to 'Hakushu 1'. With its 4 mashtuns, 44 washbacks and 24 stills, Hakushu (1+2) was the biggest distillery in the world at the time. In 1981, Suntory built a new distillery, 'Hakushu 3' or 'Hakushu East' on the site, and decided to phase out production at #1 and #2 in favor of #3. Distilleries 1 and 2 had big stills, but all of the same shape and size, whereas #3 had a variety of stills with different shapes, sizes, lyne-arm orientations, heating methods and condenser types. What they were after was diversity

and quality rather than quantity. The distillery as it is operative now is Hakushu 3, albeit with the addition of two pairs of pot stills in 2014, bringing the total to 8 pairs, just like at Yamazaki distillery. Since december 2010 there is also a small grain whisky facility at Hakushu.

The Hakushu single malt was introduced in 1994 but spent most of the following decades in the shadow of its bigger brother, Yamazaki. Over the last few years, that has changed. The current range consists of the Distiller´s Reserve without age statement, the 18 year old and the highly awarded 25 year old.

Miyagikyo

Sendai, Miyagi, founded in 1969

nikka.com/eng/distilleries/miyagikyo/

Miyagikyo is Nikka's second distillery and legend has it that it took Masataka Taketsuru three years to find the perfect site. He settled on the valley that brings the Hirosegawa and Nikkagawa (no relation to the company name) rivers together because of the quality of the water, the suitable humidity and the crisp air. Construction started in 1968 and was completed in May of the following year. Originally known as 'Sendai', the distillery was renamed 'Miyagikyo' when Asahi took control of Nikka in 2001. At present, Miyagikyo is equipped with 22 steel washbacks and 8 huge pot stills of the 'boil ball' type with upward lyne arms, encouraging reflux which – given the slow distillation method (steam-heated) – results in a lighter, cleaner spirit. The site also houses two enormous Coffey stills imported by Taketsuru from Scotland. Moved from Nishinomiya in 1999, these are used to produce grain whisky (Coffey Grain) but, occasionally, are used to distill malted barley (Coffey Malt). Since the summer of 2017, they're also churning out Coffey Gin and Coffey Vodka.

In September 2015, Nikka discontinued the entire Miyagikyo range which included a no-age-statement expression, a 10, 12 and 15 year old because of stock shortages. It was replaced with a new NAS expression, which is the only permanently available Miyagikyo single malt until further notice. in march 2020, a limited edition Apple Brandy Wood Finish Miyagikyo expression was released, to commemorate the 100th anniversary of the wedding of Rita Cowan and Masataka Taketsuru.

Mt. Fuju Distillery, formerly known as Fuji Gotemba

Chichibu #1

Chichibu, Saitama, founded in 2007

facebook.com/ChichibuDistillery/

Chichibu distillery may be small but its reputation for consistency of quality is the envy of many. The distillery was established in 2007 and starting producing the year after. There's a 2,400 litre mashtun (manually stirred with a wooden paddle!), eight mizunara washbacks of 3,000 litres each and a pair of 2,000 litre pot stills. Every year, about 10% of production is dedicated to local barley so there is an area for floor malting. There are 5 warehouses and there's also a fully-operational cooperage. Since 2010, Ichiro and his team have been making regular trips to Hokkaido to buy mizunara wood and the two in-house coopers have been perfecting their mizunara-barrel-making skills since 2016. A very small number of casks is made out of local Chichibu mizunara.

Supply and demand is Ichiro's biggest headache. There simply isn't enough to go around. The latest 'big' single malt release (11,000 bottles) was the 2019 edition of On The Way, but that vanished into thin air pretty quickly. Word on the street was that the first official (non-single cask) 10 year Chichibu would be presented in the spring of 2020, but the pandemic had a word to say about that. Keep your eyes peeled in the fall or in early 2021.

Chichibu #2

Chichibu, Saitama, founded in 2019

facebook.com/ChichibuDistillery/

Around 2014, Ichiro Akuto started thinking about setting up a second distillery. Unlike Suntory, Nikka and even Hombo Shuzo, who built their second distilleries in locations that were distinctly different from the environment of their first distilleries, Ichiro wanted to stay in his hometown of Chichibu. His new distillery is just a two-minute drive away from the 'old' one. Construction began in April of 2018 and the first spirit (test production) came off the stills in July 2019. There are many features of the new distillery that are the same as at Chichibu #1 but the new distillery is five times bigger than the first one.

At Chichibu #2, two tonnes of malted barley are processed per batch. The water is the same as at the original distillery. Mashing takes place in a semi-lauter tun. For the fermentation process, Ichiro

is sticking with wooden vessels, but unlike at Chichibu #1 where the washbacks are made of mizunara, the washbacks at the new distillery are made of French oak. There are 5 washbacks at the moment with 10,000 litres of wort going in but there's room for a few more in the future. The stills are the same shape as at #1 and even the lyne-arm descending angle is the same but they are much bigger (10,000 litres and 6,500 litres respectively) and both stills are direct-fired whereas those at #1 are indirectly heated. Ichiro expects this to have the biggest impact on the character of the spirit, producing a more robust, more complex spirit. No products have been released as of yet.

Other distilleries in Japan

Akkeshi

Akkeshi, Hokkaido, founded in 2015

akkeshi-distillery.com/en/

Inspired by Islay and its whiskies, and with equipment and methods imported from Scotland, the goal of the distillery team is to create a whisky that is uniquely shaped by the Akkeshi environment. Production began in the fall of 2016 and relies heavily on peated malt, although non-peated malt is used as well. The distillery has two warehouses on site as well as two near the sea, to explore subtle differences in maturation. Their first single malt, released in early 2020, is Sarorunkamuy, a vatting of whisky distilled in 2016 and matured in bourbon, red wine, sherry and mizunara casks.

Asaka

Koriyama, Fukushima, founded in 2015

sasanokawa.co.jp

The parent company Sasanokawa Shuzo was founded in 1765. Whisky 'making' started in 1946 but don't ask 'how' because the focus was on the lowest grade of blended whisky. Sake production is the bread-and-butter of the company and that allowed them to ride out some of the tougher periods for whisky in Japan. To mark the 250th anniversary of the company in 2015, a proper malt whisky distillery was set up in a disused warehouse on site. By the

Miyagikyo Distillery was founded by the legendary Masataka Taketsuru

end of the year, two small pot stills (2,000 litres and 1,000 litres respectively) had been installed. Production officially started in June 2016. The first single malt expression ('Asaka The First') was released in December 2019.

Eigashima

Akashi, Hyogo, founded in 1919 (whisky since 1984)

ei-sake.jp/en/

This humble producer has been part of the Japanese whisky scene longer than anyone else that is still active today. On paper, it's the oldest whisky producer in Japan – having acquired a distilling license in 1919, four years before Yamazaki. It took them four decades to get their act together, though, and another four decades to release their first single malt (an 8-year-old in 2007). The current distillery was built in 1984. Whisky is made during the warmer half of the year. The old spirit and wash still were retired in February 2019 and replaced with brand new stills made by Miyake Industries in Japan. The first distillation in the new stills took place in March that year. All production is matured on site, near the Akashi strait, in old single-story rickety warehouses in a bewildering variety of cask types. To mark the 101st anniversary of their whisky license, the company released a new single malt expression named 'Eigashima Sherry Cask', a vatting of malt distilled between 2009 and 2014. There is also a blended whisky expression with the same name.

Kaikyo

Akashi, Hyogo, founded in 2017

no website

Kaikyo Distillery is located on the site of the Akashi Sake Brewery, established by the Yonezawa family, which has been brewing since 1856 and distilling since 1918. To mark their first century of distilling, the company decided to replace their old steel stills with new copper pot stills. A new stillhouse was built on site to house the new Forsyths stills and the building was named The Kaikyo Distillery after the Akashi-Kaikyo Bridge that lies in front of the distillery. Together with Torabhaig Distillery (on the Isle of Skye), The Borders Distillery and Mossburn Distillers & Blenders, Kaikyo Distillery is part of a family-owned Swedish investment company. There is a close reciprocal relationship between the distilleries in Scotland and the team at Kaikyo in Japan. The aim is to produce a light, fruity spirit that will age well but show light floral and malty notes at a younger age. The first single malt release is slated for 2022. While they're waiting, the distillery is selling a range of blended and 'pure malt' whiskies carrying the Hatozaki brand name.

Kanosuke

Hioki, Kagoshima, founded in 2017

kanosuke.com

Kanosuke distillery is owned by Komasa Jozo, one of the leading shochu makers in Kagoshima prefecture. Their claim to fame is 'Mellowed Kozuru', a barrel-aged shochu developed by the second president of the company Kanosuke Komasa and launched in 1957. The idea to establish a whisky distillery was born in 2015. Yoshitsugu Komasa, who represents the fourth generation of the family, picked some vacant land next to three warehouses where the company's shochu is matured and had the necessary equipment installed in the summer of 2017: a 6,000 litre mash tun, 5 stainless steel washbacks and 3 pot stills (6,000, 3,000 and 1,600 litres respectively) all with wormtub condensers. Production officially started on November 13, 2017. Following 'Kanosuke New Born 2018 Edition', a 2019 edition was released in the autumn of that year (matured for 16 months in bourbon casks).

Kurayoshi

Kurayoshi, Tottori, founded in 2017

matsuiwhisky.com/en/distillery/

Kurayoshi first emerged on the Japanese whisky scene in 2015 as a brand rather than a distillery, with age-statement releases of 'Japanese pure malt whisky' at a time when age-statement Japanese whisky had become rare. The fact that Japanese whisky-makers don't swap stock together with the extremely lax regulations governing Japanese whisky made it easy for consumers to figure out that the liquid in the bottles was imported in bulk. In 2017, they set up an actual distillery, but all of this happened away from the public eye. They started with three small Hoga alembic-type stills and added two larger stills in 2018 and slowly started to let people into their distillery. At the time of writing, whisky was only produced using the large pair of pot stills.

Mars Shinshu

Miyada village, Nagano, founded in 1985

hombo.co.jp

Mars Shinshu was built at the peak of whisky consumption in Japan, but 7 years into what would turn out to be a 25-year long

Kanosuke Distillery is owned by Komasa Jozo, one of Japan's leading schochu makers

decline, the doors were closed. The distillery was mothballed in 1992 and it wasn't until 2011 that the decision was made to fire up the stills again. Production used to be limited to the winter months, but now it's closer to a typical year-round production schedule with a silent summer season. Since 2014, the distillery has received some much-needed upgrades. The old pot stills were replaced with brand new ones, built following the original blueprints and in 2018, three Douglas fir washbacks were installed. As part of a massive 1.2 billion yen investment, 2019-2020 saw the construction of a new warehouse, a new distillation facility and a new visitor centre. The most recent limited edition coming out of Mars Shinshu was the 'Komagatake Limited Edition 2019', released in autumn 2019.

Mars Tsunuki

Minami-Satsuma, Kagoshima, founded in 2016

hombo.co.jp

Towards the end of 2015, Hombo Shuzo started setting up a second distillery in their homebase of Tsunuki in Kagoshima with the first distillation in October. The distillery is the playground of Tatsuro Kusano, the 32-year old head distiller. Kusano learned the ropes at Mars Shinshu under distillery manager Koki Takehira, and some things are the same as there: the season runs roughly parallel with Mars Shinshu, i.e. September to June) and the barley used is the same, too: non-peated, lightly-peated, medium peated and heavily peated. But there are marked differences as well – not just in terms of the equipment in place, but the approach to making whisky (the use of specialty malts, various yeast types, etc.). The first single malt expression, Tsunuki The First, was released in April 2020, and considered by many Japanese whisky connoisseurs to be the most impressive debut since 'Chichibu The First' way back in 2011.

Nagahama

Nagahama, Shiga, founded in 2016

romanbeer.com/nagahama-distillery/

Nagahama Distillery's motto is "one distillation, one barrel" which suits them well, as they are the smallest distillery in Japan at the time of writing. It was set up in a record time of 7 months as an extension of Nagahama Roman (with the emphasis on the second syllable, as in "romantic") Brewery, which was established in 1996 as a brewpub. The distillery officially started production in November 2016. The first half of the whisky-making process – mashing and fermentation – takes place in the equipment used for beer making. For the second half of the process, a small 'still room' with three 1,000 litre Hoga alembic-type stills was created behind the bar counter. The first single malts were released in May 2020 and all were single casks: Bourbon, Oloroso Sherry (matured in ex-bourbon for one year and finished for two years in a sherry quarter cask) and lightly peated Mizunara.

Nukada

Naka, Ibaraki, founded in 2016

kodawari.cc/en/brewery/nukadabrewry

Nukada distillery was set up by Kiuchi Shuzo in a corner of their new Hitachino Nest brewhouse in 2016. In terms of output, it is the smallest whisky distillery in Japan. Head distiller Isamu Yoneda uses a 1,000 litre hybrid still to make whisky as well as gin. The production volume varies from year to year and is also limited by the fact that the staff is occupied with a multitude of other tasks beside making whisky. The distillery is also used to distil beers to make some of the Kiuchi liqueurs.

Okayama

Okayama, Okayama, founded in 2011

whiskyokayama.com/english/

Okayama distillery, owned by Miyashita Shuzo, is undoubtedly the most under-the-radar distillery. The bread and butter of the company is beer and sake, and whisky is a side-gig. Miyashita Shuzo was founded as a sake brewery in 1915. In 1994, they became one of the pioneers of Japanese craft beer. In 2003, the company started distilling some of their hoppy beer in a stainless steel shochu still and put the spirit in American white oak casks. They acquired a whisky license in 2011 and started double-distilling malt whisky in their shochu still but in 2015 they installed a copper hybrid still. Production is extremely limited and bottlings are rarely seen. The most recent release was 'Sherry Cask Debut', a single cask bottling for Takashimaya department store.

Saburomaru

Tonami, Toyama, founded in 1990

wakatsuru.co.jp/saburomaru/en/

Wakatsuru Shuzo traces its history back to 1862, when they started making sake. Like so many sake breweries hit by the rice shortages following the end of the Pacific War, they turned their attention to whisky-making. Throughout the second half of the 20th

Hombo Shuzo´s second distillery - Tsunuki

century, they produced whisky for drinkers on a tight budget. It wasn't until September 2016 that they decided to start revitalizing their distillery with the aim of producing high-quality malt whisky. Up until 2017, malt whisky was produced using an alumite pot still of the type commonly used in shochu-making. After a successful crowdfunding campaign, the distillery building was refurbished, a brand new mill and mashtun was installed, which increased production efficiency, and the pot still got a copper swan neck. In June 2019, the distillery unveiled its new pair of pot stills: the world's first cast pot stills.

Sakurao Distillery

Hatsukaichi, Hiroshima, founded in 2018

sakuraodistillery.com/en/sakurao/

Sakurao may be a new distillery, but the liquor company behind it is not. Chugoku Jozo was established in 1918 as a limited partnership and incorporated in 1938, when it was given its current name. Their liquor portfolio comprises shochu, sake, mirin and various liqueurs. Chugoku Jozo started 'producing' whisky in 1938 and up until the liquor-tax change of 1989, their field was 'budget' whisky, In 2003, they launched the Togouchi brand, but the expressions in that range are all made up of whisky imported in bulk from abroad. To mark the 100th anniversary of the company, a proper whisky distillery was set up at the company's main site. Half of the production is non-peated and the other half lightly-peated (20ppm). Casks are matured on site as well as in disused tunnels in the town of Togouchi.

Shizuoka

Shizuoka, Shizuoka, founded in 2015

shizuoka-distillery.jp

Inspired by a visit to Kilchoman distillery in 2012, Gaia Flow founder Taiko Nakamura started thinking about building a distillery of his own. He set up a liquor import company to get a foot in the door of the drinks business, and kept working on his distillery project. Shizuoka distillery was officially opened on 25th February 2017. Initially there were 5 washbacks at the distillery: four made from Oregon pine and one made from local, Shizuoka cedar. In 2018, three more Shizuoka cedar washbacks were installed, bringing the total to eight. The stillhouse has three pot stills: one from the old Karuizawa distillery and a new pair made by Forsyths in Scotland. Interestingly, Nakamura opted for direct (wood-fired) heating for the wash still. The old Karuizawa still and the new spirit still are steam heated. The first single malt expression is expected to be released in late 2020/early 2021.

Yasato

Ishioka, Ibaraki Prefecture, founded in 2019

no website

Yasato distillery is Kiuchi Shuzo's second whisky distillery and it is located in the Yasato part of Ishioka city. They designed the distillery based on making a new type of whisky, using various kinds of grain and different types of yeast. There's a four-roller mill, a 5,000 litre cereal cooker for step mashing and rice/buckwheat/corn cooking and a 6,000 litre lauter tun, four 12,000 litre stainless fermenters and four 6,000 litre wooden fermenters. There's a 12,000 litre wash still and an 8,000 litre spirit still, both with a straight head and a downward lyne arm. There are also five yeast propagation tanks. The first official distillation took place in March 2020. The team at Yasato is trying to source casks from small bourbon and rum distilleries and wineries as well as non-oak barrels.

Yuza

Yuza, Yamagata, founded in 2018

yuza-disty.jp

Kinryu, the owners of the distillery, was founded in 1950 and was a joint venture funded by nine local sake producers, initially to make neutral spirit. Over time, they started making and selling shochu made in a continuous still. Overall consumption of shochu (as well as sake) has been on the decline for decades. To mitigate that, the company decided to start producing whisky and set up a brand new distillery in Yuza city. The first distillation took place in November 2018. The set up and the processes are textbook Scottish and the goal is to produce a high-quality single malt.

Pakistan

Murree Brewery Ltd.

Rawalpindi, founded in 1860

www.murreebrewery.com

Started as a beer brewery, the assortment was later expanded to include whisky, gin, rum, vodka and brandy. The core range of single malt holds two expressions – Murree's Classic 8 years old and Murree's Millenium Reserve 12 years old. There is also a Murree's Islay Reserve, Vintage Gold.

Yuza Distillery started their production in 2018

Taiwan

Kavalan Distillery

Yanshan, Yilan County, founded in 2005

www.kavalanwhisky.com/en

On the 11th of March 2006 at 3.30pm, the first spirit was produced at Kavalan distillery. This was celebrated in a major way a decade later when guests and journalists from all over the world were invited for the 10th anniversary. But it was not just to celebrate 10 years of whisky production but also to witness the recent expansion of the distillery which has made Kavalan one of the ten largest malt whisky distilleries in the world! This rapid development may even have surprised the founder, entrepreneur and business man Tien-Tsai Lee, and his son, the current CEO of the company Yu-Ting Lee. Early on, it was decided that expertise from Scotland was needed to get on the right track from the beginning. Dr. Jim Swan was consulted early on and he, together with the master blender, Ian Chang, developed a strategy including production as well as the future maturation. Jim Swan passed away in early 2017 and in spring 2020 Ian Chang left the company for another career.

The distillery lies in the north-eastern part of the country, in Yilan County, one hour´s drive from Taipei. Following the expansion in 2016, the distillery is equipped with 5 mash tuns, 40 stainless steel washbacks with a 60-72 hour fermentation time and 10 pairs of lantern-shaped copper stills with descending lye pipes. The capacity of the wash stills is 12,000 litres and of the spirit stills 7,000 litres. Kavalan only uses a very narrow cut from the spirit run, leaving more foreshots and feints to accommodate a complex and rich flavour profile. The spirit vapours are cooled using shell and tube condensers, but because of the hot climate, subcoolers are also used.

On site, there are two five-story high warehouses and the casks are tied together due to the earthquake risk. The climate in this part of Taiwan is hot and humid and on the top floors of the warehouses the temperature can reach 42°C. Hence the angel´s share is dramatic – no less than 10-12% is lost every year. At the moment, Kavalan are doing experiments aiming to reduce the angel's share to below 10%, hoping for positive results in 2020. The distillery has its own cooperage where the preparation of the STR (shave-toast-rechar) casks plays an important part for the final character of the whisky.

Since the first bottling of Kavalan was released in 2008, the range has been expanded and now holds 26 different expressions. In spring 2020, the core range was complemented by two bottlings being priced competitively to act as an entry level to the rest of the range. One of them was launched already in 2018 and is now called Distillery Select No. 1 while the new expression is Distillery Select No. 2. Apart from them, the core range consists of Classic and an "upgraded" version of that called King Car Conductor. There is also the port finished Concertmaster which was recently supplemented by Concertmaster Sherry. Finally there are Ex Bourbon and Oloroso Sherry, both bottled at 46% and Podium.

The range that first opened the worlds eyes to Kavalan was Solist first introduced in 2009. Matured in different types of casks these are all bottled at cask strength and released in batches. The first two were Bourbon and Oloroso and have been followed by Fino, Vinho Barrique, Brandy, Amontillado, Manzanilla, PX, Moscatel and Port. Another two bottlings are exclusively sold at the distillery visitor centre; Distillery Reserve Rum Cask and Distillery Reserve Peaty Cask. The latter obtains its smoky flavour from maturation in ex-Islay casks. The distillery has produced whisky from peated barley (10ppm) as well and in October 2020 it was released as part of the Solist range. Recent limited releases include two 100 cl bottlings to celebrate the 10th anniversary of the distillery´s first release. Both of them were bottled at 57,8% and had been matured in ex-Bordeaux wine casks from two different regions. After the launch the distillery decided to rename the two expressions and they are now called Sky Gold Wine Cask and Earth Silver Wine Cask. Yet another expression from ex-Bordeaux wines casks appeared in late 2019 to celebrate the 40th anniversary of the foundation of King Car Group and in July 2020, Solist Madeira was released, available only at the distillery.

Whisky is, of course, the main product for Kavalan but production of gin is also carried out in the four sets of Holstein stills that were installed already in 2008. The first release in a series of triple distil-led gins appeared in early 2019. In June 2020, the owners launched a "ready-to-drink" range called The Kavalan Bar and since 2018 they are producing beer at a plant in Taoyuan.

In May 2019, Kavalan opened their first designated 'Cask Strength Whisky Bar' in the busy Zhongshan District of Taipei. Recreating the inside of the distillery´s warehouse, it was the only bar in the world to carry the full range of Kavalan whisky. Guests can order whiskies straight from the cask and the bar also uses special effects to illustrate the environmental impact on the flavour of the whisky. In July 2020, the owners announced that a second bar was about to be opened at the distillery in Yilan. The Kavalan Garden Bar dominates the second floor of the Spirits Castle. The bar is the first phase of a major revamp of the entire visitor centre.

Kavalan is being exported to more than 60 countries and apart from Taiwan, Europe and the US are the most important markets. There is an impressive visitor centre on site with no less than one million people coming to the distillery every year.

Two new bottlings in Kavalan´s core range - Distillery Select No. 1 and No. 2

Other distilleries in Taiwan

Nantou Distillery

Nantou City, Nantou County, founded in 1978
(whisky since 2008)

omarwhisky.com.tw

Located in the central east of Taiwan, Nantou distillery is a part of the state-owned manufacturer and distributor of cigarettes and alcohol in Taiwan – Taiwan Tobacco and Liquor Corporation (TTL). Between 1947 and 1968 it exercised a monopoly over all alcohol, tobacco, and camphor products sold in Taiwan. It retained tobacco and alcohol monopolies until Taiwan's entry into the WTO in 2002.

There are seven distilleries and two breweries within the TTL group, but Nantou is the only with malt whisky production. The distillery is equipped with a full lauter Huppmann mash tun with a charge of 2.5 tonnes and eight washbacks made of stainless steel with a fermentation time of 60-72 hours. There are two wash stills (9,000 and 5,000 litres) and two spirit stills (5,000 and 2,000 litres). The owners are currently looking to expand the distillery with another three pairs of stills. Malted barley is imported from Scotland and ex-sherry and ex-bourbon casks are used for maturation. Nantou Distillery also produces a variety of fruit wines and the casks that have stored lychee wine and plum wine are then used to give some whiskies an extra finish. Initially the spirit from Nantou was all unpeated but in 2014 trials with peated malt brought in from Scotland were made.

The single malt is sold under the brand name Omar and in 2013, two cask strength single malt whiskies were launched – one from bourbon casks and the other from sherry casks. Three years later Sherry Cask and Bourbon Cask, bottled at 46%, were launched and the two now make up the distillery's core range. Another range is called Liqueur Finish and bottled at cask strength they have all been finished in different wine or liqueur casks; plum, lychee, black queen wine and orange brandy. The Cask Strength range is represented by ex-bourbon, ex-sherry and peated ex-bourbon. Finally there are special editions matured in virgin oak, PX solera sherry cask (10 years old) and ex-bourbon (8 year old). There is also a blended malt whisky called Yushan.

Omar from Nantou Distillery

Africa

South Africa

James Sedgwick Distillery

Wellington, Western Cape, founded in 1886 (whisky since 1990)

threeshipswhisky.co.za, bainscapemountainwhisky.co.za

Distell Group Ltd. was formed in 2000 by a merger between Stellenbosch Farmers' Winery and Distillers Corporation, although the James Sedgwick Distillery was already established in 1886. The company produces a huge range of wines and spirits including the popular cream liqueur, Amarula Cream. James Sedgwick Distillery has been the home to South African whisky since 1990. The distillery has undergone a major expansion in the last years and is now equipped with one still with two columns for production of grain whisky, two pot stills for malt whisky and one still with five columns designated for neutral spirit. There are also two mash tuns and 16 washbacks. Grain whisky is distilled for nine months of the year, malt whisky for two months and one month is devoted to maintenance. Three new warehouses have been built and a total of seven warehouses now hold more than 150,000 casks. There is also a highly awarded visitor centre on site.

In Distell's whisky portfolio, it is the Three Ships brand, introduced in 1977, that makes up for most of the sales. The range consists of Select and 5 year old Premium Select, the latter being a blend of South African and Scotch whiskies. Furthermore, there is the 10 year old single malt which was launched for the first time in 2003 and the latest release (Vintage 2007) was launched in June 2020. A range called the Master's Collection was introduced in 2015 with the idea to annually launch something limited in volume and a South African first. Now into it's 5th year and following on from the 10 year old PX finish, a 15 year old Pinotage cask finish, an 8 year old lightly peated Oloroso cask finish, a 9 year old Fino cask finish came this years 11 year old old Shiraz cask finish. Apart from the Three Ships range, the distillery also produces South Africa's first single grain, Bain's Cape Mountain whisky, which has been awarded the world's best grain whisky title on two occasions since its launch in 2009.

The man who tirelessly worked to bring the Three Ships single malt to the market, was Andy Watts. After 25 years as the distillery manager, he has now a role in the company as Head of Whisky where he is primarily responsible for overseeing Distell's South African whisky portfolio as well as being the Three Ships' Master Distiller and Bain's Cape Mountain Whisky Founder Distiller.

South America

Argentina

La Alazana Distillery

Golondrinas, Patagonia, founded in 2011

laalazanawhisky.com

Located in the Patagonian Andes, this is the first distillery in Argentina concentrating solely on malt whisky production. The distillery is owned and run by Nestor Serenelli and his wife Lila. They are both big fans of Scotch whisky and before they built the distillery, they toured Scotland to visit distilleries and to get inspiration. Eventually, Lila also earned a Master of Science degree in brewing and distilling from Heriot Watt University in Edinburgh. The owners are firm believers in the "terroir" concept where local barley, water and, not least, climate will affect the flavour of the whisky. The distillery is equipped with a lauter mash tun, four stainless steel 1,100 litre washbacks with a fermentation time of 4 to 6 days and two stills and there are now plans to increase capacity. A third warehouse was built in autumn 2020 with space for special warehouse tastings straight from the casks. For the last two years, the owners have been growing their own barley and also do the malting using local peat which means a 100% Patagonia single malt is now maturing in the warehouses. The house style is light and fruity but they have also filled several barrels with peated whisky. The first, limited release was made in November 2014 and one of the latest (end of 2019) was an 8 year old matured in a combinationj of ex-sherry and ex-bourbon

Other distilleries in Argentina

Emilio Mignone y Cia

Luján, Buenos Aires province, founded in 2015

emyc.com.ar

Owned by brothers Carlos and Santiago Mignone, this became the second whisky distillery in Argentina. The first distillation was in November 2015 and the distillery is equipped with a 300 litre open mash tun, a 250 litre washback with a 72-96 hour fermentation and two stills, directly fired by natural gas. The first of their Classic Pampa Single Malt Whisky, matured in ex-bourbon barrels, was released in October 2019 and was followed in 2020 by a peated version, matured in PX sherry barrels. The owners are working on a second and larger distillery (10,000 litres) in Lago Puelo which should be up and running during 2022.

Madoc Distillery

Dina Huapi, Rio Negro, founded in 2015

madocwhisky.com

The owner is one of the founders of the first Patagonian distillery, La Alazana. In 2015, he left the company and brought with him some of the equipment, as well as part of the maturing stock to build a new distillery in Dina Huapi. The existing equipment with a lauter mash tun, a washback and a copper pot still was complemented by a wash still and the first distillation took place in September 2016 and a single malt bottled at 40% has been released.

Brazil

Union Distillery

Veranópolis, founded in 1972

maltwhisky.com.br

The company was founded in 1948 as Union of Industries Ltd to produce wine. In 1972 they started to produce malt whisky and two years later the name of the company was changed to Union Distillery Maltwhisky do Brasil. In 1986 a co-operation with Morrison Bowmore Distillers was established in order to develop the technology at the Brazilian distillery. Most of the production is sold as bulk whisky to be part of different blends, but the company also has its own single malt called Union Club Whisky with an 8 year old as the oldest expression.

Muraro Bebidas

Flores da Cunha, founded in 1953

muraro.com.br

This is a company with a wide range of products including wine, vodka, rum and cachaca and the total capacity is 10 million litres. Until recently, the blend Green Valley was the only whisky in the range. In 2014, however, a new brand was introduced. It has the rather misleading name Blend Seven but it appears to be a malt whisky even though it seems that essence of oak is part of the recipe. The main market for the whisky is The Carribean.

ndy Watts - Master Distiller and Head of Whisky at Distell

The Serenelli family from La Alazana Distillery

The Year
that was

Including the subsections:

A perfect storm | The big players | The big brands
New distilleries | Bottling grapevine

The year 2019 will most likely be remembered as the last year of normality before the corona virus spread across the world. Right now it is impossible for anyone to say what the post-pandemic world will look like. Will our consumption and travelling patterns change permanently or do we "just" have to endure a shorter span of time of adjusted behaviour before the world turns back to the way it used to be? Read more about this and other threats to the spirits world on pages 264-266 but let us begin with analyzing the year that passed.

The predominant trend of declining global alcohol consumption continued in 2019 and while consumption of spirits remained strong in 2018, with beer and wine being the losers, Euromonitor International could report a decline in volume also for spirits in 2019 by 2,3%. Some categories were better off than others. Gin, for example, remain strong and was the fastest growing spirits category in 2019 with volumes growing by 12%. Tequila and mezcal came in second with a growing popularity not least in the US and Europe. Whiskies increased overall by 4% (an addition of 185 million bottles) and now accounts for 17% of the global spirits market. Vodka, which has been a cause for concern with six years of declining volumes, seems to be in a slightly better stage at the moment while sales of rum, the category that was said to challenge whisky a few years ago, seem pretty stagnant.

Three indigenous spirits from Asia deserve, as always, there own mentioning. Soju, the Korean national spirit made from rice, wheat, barley or potatoes, is still very popular and the biggest spirits producer in the world, Jinro, alone sold more than 1 billion bottles (plus 11%) of their brand in 2019! In Japan, sales of schochu which is made from a variety of plants including sweet potato, barley, rice and buckwheat, is more or less stable. China, finally, is the home of the largest spirits category in the world - baijiu. Made from fermented sorghum it represents around 40% of global spirits consumption. While it has been the first

choice of domestic drinkers for ages, an interesting aspect is that baijiu now has a growing fanbase in other parts of the world, not least within the bartender community who have found a new spirit for creating novel cocktails.

So what about Scotch whisky? Well, for the fourth year in a row both values and volumes of Scotch whisky export went up to record high levels. While this may seem reassuring, there are practical reasons behind the positive figures. A lot of pre-shipping in anticipation of possible hard exit Brexit "no-deals" in March and October and also ahead of the imposition of a 25% tariff on single malts being exported to the US, definitely inflated the figurs. Despite US importers of Scotch stocking up, exports to the USA fell by 25% in quarter four 2019. The tariff war between USA and the EU originates in differences of opinion regarding governmental subsidies to airplane manufacturers on both sides of the Atlantic (Boeing and Airbus) with other products suffering. Before the 25% tariff on single malt Scotch being exported to the USA, a similar tax was imposed on bourbon going in the opposite direction resulting in a 27% decrease in US whiskey being exported to the EU.

If we look at the two major Scotch whisky categories, the trend continues with single malts surging (both in values and volumes) while blends are struggling to retain the current position. Volumes of single malt exports represent around 10% of the total volume of Scotch whisky exports but the value is now very close to a third (29.7%). And then there is the "newborn" category of blended malt in which both volumes and values were up by 28% during 2019.

SINGLE MALT SCOTCH - EXPORT

Value: +11.8% to £1.46bn
Volume: +13.7% to 138.3m bottles

BLENDED SCOTCH* - EXPORT

Value: +1.1% to £3.16bn
Volume: -1.1% to 836m bottles

TOTAL SCOTCH - EXPORT

Value: +4.4% to £4.91bn
Volume: +2.4% to 1.31bn bottles

* excl. bulk and bottled single and blended grain Scotch whisky.

A record year in 2019 but dark clouds are gathering during 2020

If you're a regular reader of the Malt Whisky Yearbook you will notice that there has been a change of regions in the following figures from the Scotch Whisky Association (SWA). The figures for Asia are now combined with the ones for Oceania while the Africa region has been divided into sub-Saharan Africa and North Africa with the latter also including the Middle East.

The European Union

The European Union continues to be the biggest export market for Scotch whisky both in terms of volumes and value. The region represents more than a third of the volumes (35,4%) which was an increase by 1,2% in 2019 and 30% of the values (+5,6%) and if we look just at single malts, the dominance is even greater; volume 42% and value 36%.

The European Union — Top 3

France	volumes	-8%	values	-2%
Spain	volumes	+2%	values	+5%
Germany	volumes	+9%	values	+6%

France is still the dominant market for Scotch in the EU but in terms of volumes, the figures were slipping for the third year in a row and in 2019 also values were down. It has been suggested that a reason for the slow-down could be the growing interest in whiskies produced in France but even though that has exploded in recent years, it only makes up 1% of the Scotch whisky volumes imported to the country. Spain in second place made a small leap from last year and showed positive figures for both volumes and values. There is, however, a long way to go to match the figures from the mid 2000 when exports were twice as high. Finally, as usual, we find Germany in third place with strong growth as opposed to the year before when figures were in the negative. The total value exported to Germany is slightly higher than that of Spain. In places four to six, we find Latvia (with the majority of the volumes re-exported to other markets, mainly Russia), The Netherlands (with a huge increase in both volumes and values during 2019) and Poland.

North America

The second largest region in terms of values but third (after Asia & Oceania) in volumes. There were fears that the tariff war between the EC and USA would have an impact on the 2019 figures for the entire region. The 25% tax from the US side wasn't imposed until mid October and only concerned single malts. Admittedly volumes for the year were down by 8,5% and values only increased by 2% but worse was to come in 2020.

North America — Top 3

USA	volumes	-7%	values	-6%
Mexico	volumes	-14%	values	-8%
Canada	volumes	+2%	values	+6%

In June 2020 Scotch exports to the USA had fallen by more than 30% since the tariff was imposed and the decline is accelerating. In April exports fell 47% and in May 65% compared to exports in the same months in 2019. Negotiations between the UK and the US governments began in early May where the goal was to agree on a free trade agreement. The lack of progress became evident on the 12th August when the US representative announced that the 25% tariff would be maintained. End of June, there were actually fears that the tariff would be further increased and on top of that also to include gin from the UK. If the situation isn't solved, the 2020 full year figures for Scotch exports to the USA will be devastating. With the same tariff on whiskies going in the other direction (exports of American whiskey to the EU have gone down by 33% since June 2018), the American producers are of course anxious as well to have a free trade agreement in place.

The strong figures from 2018 for the second biggest market, Mexico, changed to a substantial decrease both in volumes and values in 2019. Blended whisky took the hardest blow while single malts were up. However with single malts representing less than 10% of the total value, it wasn't enough to compensate the loss in blends. Canada, finally, was in the positive for the third year in a row.

Asia and Oceania

The new, combined region of Asia and Oceania is the second largest in terms of volumes. A positive trend of increasing exports that started in 2016 continued in 2019 with volumes up 12% and values 10%. The driving force behind these figures were single and blended malts in which both categories grew by 20% while blends showed a moderate growth of 3%.

Asia and Oceania — Top 3

India	volumes	+16%	values	+20%
Japan	volumes	+20%	values	+16%
Singapore	volumes	-2%	values	-6%

The biggest market, at least in terms of volumes, is India. After an off year in 2018, growth figures are back in the positive double digit during 2019 – volumes +16% and values +20%. The interest in bottled single malt and bottled blends in India is definitely growing but one should remember that 84% of the Scotch whisky exports to the country consists of whisky shipped in bulk. This will either be used to be bottled as Scotch in India or to be vatted with Indian-made whisky. The same goes for Japan in second place where the bulk shipment from Scotland is 60% of the totals. The weak legislation regulating the Japanese whisky market admits for Scotch whisky to be bottled and sold as Japanese.

Singapore is still in the top 3 in Asia even though the figures were in the negative for 2019. As always when interpreting the numbers for Singapore, it is important to remember that the vast majority of the whisky is re-exported to other markets in the region, not least to ASEAN countries and China.

Behind the Top 3 we find Taiwan in fourth place (but actually second in terms of value). This country, known for their love of Scotch single malt, actually holds three records in the whisky world; they have the highest single malt Scotch import per capita in the world (if we disregard Singapore and Latvia where most of the whisky is re-exported to other countries) and they have the highest single malt share of total Scotch whisky imports of any country both in terms of volumes (47%) and values (61%).

India is the biggest market for Scotch whisky in Asia and growing

Latin America and Carribean

This region showed an increase in 2019 with volumes up 4,6% and values 2,6%. Not as high as the double digit increases from 2018 but the volatility of the region over the years always creates a degree of uncertainty for the following years's volumes. Single malts were up by 25% but from a very low base. In fact single and blended malt only make up 4% of the total exports. Compared to the year before, blended whisky increased only marginally.

Latin America and Carribean — Top 3				
Brazil	volumes	+10%	values	+6%
Colombia	volumes	+48%	values	+62%
Chile	volumes	-4%	values	-10%

The number one market with more than 30% of the region's import of Scotch is Brazil. The country has been the undisputed leader ever since 2010 when it overtook Venezuela. A surprising number two is Colombia, perhaps not because of the ranking (it was in third place last year) but due to the very impressive increase in both volumes and values. In terms of volume Colombia is now in place 20 globally and has passed for instance a classic importer of Scotch such as Italy. In third place is Chile where very positive figures from 2018 turned into red in 2019.

Sub-Saharan Africa

Export figures used to be lumped for the entire African continent so this is a new region since last year. For 2019, volumes were up by 3,7% while values increased by 11,3%. This was a substantial improvement compared to last year (with adjustments made for the region's new composition of countries) when both figures were red.

Sub-Saharan Africa — Top 3				
South Africa	volumes	+-0%	values	+14%
Kenya	volumes	+8%	values	+9%
Angola	volumes	+104%	values	+40%

South Africa is the shining star representing 61% of the total value of imported Scotch. If 2018 was a disappointing year with both values and volumes down by circa 20%, value improved significantly during 2019 (+14%) while volumes remained unchanged. The country can be found in spot number 10 on the global list of Scotch whisky export. Kenya is in second place in the region just like last year while Angola surpassed Nigeria with an impressive doubling of the volumes and a 40% increase in values. Both countries are still in an early stage when it comes to interest in Scotch whisky and Kenya can be found in place 54 on the global top list with Angola in place 70.

Middle East and Northern Africa

Yet another new constellation since previous years when entire Africa and the Middle East constituted two separate regions. Scotch whisky export to the North African countries is quite small with for example Morocco found in 51st place on the global list. Instead the three top countries are all found in the Middle East. This was the region that showed to weakest figures during 2019 with values down by 13% and volumes by 17%.

Middle East and Northern Africa — Top 3				
UAE*	volumes	-33%	values	-28%
Lebanon	volumes	-21%	values	-34%
Israel	volumes	+7%	values	+22%

* United Arab Emirates

A major share of the sales to UAE are actually destined for duty free sales or for re-exporting to other countries. In 2019, a severe decrease in sales figures caused the country to drop from place seven to sixteen on the global Scotch export list in terms of values. Lebanon, in second place, also had a poor year with double digit decreases in both volumes and values. Israel, on the other hand, bounced back from 2018 with negative figures to an increase in values of no less than 22% in 2019. It is especially the Israelis' interest in single and blended malt that has surged with an increase in values by 33% compared to 2018.

Eastern Europe

The second smallest of all regions in terms of volumes and the smallest in terms of value is Eastern Europe. States traditionally included in Eastern Europe but are members of the European Community are not included here. Instead we are talking mainly about Russia and some of the surrounding countries including the Balkans that are not in the EC. The region had an excellent year with volumes up by 31% and values 20% – in line with a continuation of the equal success in 2018. The increase was all due to single and blended malt while blended Scotch decreased.

Eastern Europe — Top 3				
Russia	volumes	+42%	values	+56%
Montenegro	volumes	+74%	values	+67%
Ukraine	volumes	+17%	values	-3%

The biggest market in the region is Russia with 54% of the total value. The dominance is actually even bigger as large volumes of Scotch whisky destined for Latvia eventually are re-exported to Russia.

Western Europe exc EC

The smallest of the nine regions in terms of volumes, responsible for only 1.6% of the total. Volumes remained unchanged compared to 2018 while values were down by 1,8%.

Western Europe exc EC — Top 3				
Turkey	volumes	+4%	values	+2%
Switzerland	volumes	-8%	values	-3%
Andorra	volumes	-7%	values	-7%

Turkey is by far the biggest market with 56% of the total value and it was the only country that showed an increase in the region in 2019. Both Switzerland and Andorra as well as Norway and Iceland were in the red.

Single malt hot spots

I often get asked the question which countries have a preference for single malt Scotch so let's have a look. In these figures, I have focused on the Top 40 markets and selected the 10 nations with the largest single malt share.

Single malt share of Scotch whisky imports 2019

	Country	Volume	Value
1.	Taiwan	47%	61%
2.	Italy	38%	54%
3.	Canada	35%	59%
4.	Singapore	26%	28%
5.	Sweden	25%	57%
6.	China	22%	52%
7.	USA	22%	35%
8.	The Netherlands	19%	53%
9.	Germany	19%	54%
10.	Israel	14%	23%

If we instead take into account the number of people living in the respective countries, i. e. volume of single malt Scotch per capita, the ranking looks like this (and again we're talking about the Top 40 markets);

Largest single malt Scotch import per capita in 2019

1. Singapore
2. Latvia
3. Taiwan
4. The Netherlands
5. France
6. Sweden
7. Canada
8. Italy
9. Australia
10. Germany

For the two countries in the top, one should remember that both Singapore and Latvia serve as hubs for re-export to other markets.

A perfect storm

The definition of a perfect storm in a non-meteorological sense is when an especially bad situation is caused by a rare combination of unfavourable circumstances and that is what the alcohol industry in general and especially the whisky category is experiencing at the moment.

It started with the tariff war between USA and the EU in 2018/2019 and reached its climax (hopefully) in 2020 with the Covid-19 pandemic. In addition to that the underlying trend of consumers focussing more and more on healthy lifestyles with wellness being a buzzword, a lifestyle in which alcohol is rejected, has also contributed to the producers concern.

Covid-19

Let's start with the biggest threat, not only to the alcohol industry but to many other areas of the economy – Covid

19. In mid March, when authorities around the world realized that we had a pandemic on our hands, a large number of countries decided to lock down their respective societies to varying degrees and one of the implications was a complete shut down of the hospitality business including pubs, bars and restaurants. Initially there were gains to be found in the retail business and e-commerce but not enough to offset the losses made in the on-trade side of the business. Another sales channel that was hit hard when people's movement across the borders was restricted was of course travel retail. A similar impact was seen in 2003 when the SARS epidemic ravaged part of the world. That year sales in travel retail fell by 1,6% and during the financial crisis of 2008/2009 the corresponding loss was 8%. These figures will probably look like a dream scenario when we sum up the year 2020 in spite of the comment made by Julián Dìaz, the CEO of Dufry, the world's largest travel retailer, in March 2020 when he likened the pandemic to a "temporary issue" with "very low impact". He continued saying that there will be a big impact in March, April and first part of May followed by recovery. An optimistic outlook indeed! When I write this (end of July) it is estimated that 30% of the world's 26,000 commercial jets are stuck on the ground and there is limited seating on the ones that fly.

In late May an IWSR report predicted that the alcohol category, which grew by 3,6% in value during 2019, would probably be facing double digit declines by the end of 2020. They also estimated that it will take until 2024 for global alcohol sales to reach 2019 figures. In the UK and US it could even be longer. It was also expected that beer may rebound better than wines and spirits and the outlook for non- or low-alcohol drinks, for instance hard seltzers, is also brighter.

Apart from restrictions on travel and temporary closures of bars, pubs and restaurants there is another cloud on the horizon caused by the pandemic: the effect on people's economy. With a large number losing their jobs it is likely that they will turn their attention to lower priced brands, many times locally produced, rather than expensive bottlings imported from abroad.

The current situation probably affects smaller companies to a higher degree than diversified conglomerates with a wide portfolio of products to sell and also a choice of different sales channels. The number of craft distilleries and breweries has exploded around the world and an already challenging business model all of a sudden became even more risky. A survey conducted end of April by the American Distilling Institute showed that craft distilleries had on average suffered a 64% plunge in sales compared to the previous year. For many of these smaller distilleries, the main part of the sales are made at the distillery or in local stores with both of the channels having been closed for a number of months.

Amongst distilleries in Scotland it was a mixed performance. The majority closed for a number of weeks before re-opening after having complied with the authorities' recommendations for safe production. A quick survey indicated that most producers expected to be able to pick up on lost volumes by reducing the silent periods or increasing the number of working shifts. The strategy seems to be a clear evidence of the long-term perspective of producing Scotch whisky – "what we make today will be sold in ten years time".

Some reports say the alcohol business, due to the pandemic, won´t be back to the 2019 figures until 2024

Production is one thing but the increasingly important visitor side of the business suffered more. All Scottish distilleries stopped accepting visitors in mid March and it wasn't until July that some of the visitor centres re-opened albeit with a lot of restrictions. Similarly, trade shows and tastings all over the world were either postponed or inhibited, cutting off yet another way of promoting your products.

But a crisis like the Covid-19 pandemic also gives birth to a number of innovative ways of keeping in touch with one's customers. Using Teams, Instagram, Zoom and Facebook an unprecedented number of whisky meetings have occurred almost round the clock every day of the week. Whisky enthusiasts have been able to see and hear representatives from the industry explain what they do as well as present their products. This could be one of the good things of the current situation that will stay with us in the future.

Whisky tariffs

The next aspect of this perfect storm is the trade war between USA and the EU and the tariffs imposed from both sides on various products, not least whisky/whiskey. It all started in 2004 when the USA filed a case with the World Trade Organisation against loans for Airbus, the European aircraft manufacturer. The argument from the US government was that these were illegal state subsidies and was damaging to their own airplane manufacturer, Boeing. In the end, the WTO ruled in favour of USA. When the US government failed to see any compliance to the judgement by the EU, the Trump administration imposed tariffs in 2018 on steel and aluminium imported from the EU. That was followed by a 25% tariff by the EU on certain US products including whiskey which has been a huge blow to the bourbon industry. The EU accounts for half of American whiskey exports and since the tariffs came in place, sales to the EU have dropped by a third. Meanwhile the WTO was investigating whether or not there had been state subsidies from the US government to Boeing. In October 2019, the US government made their next move when a 25% tariff was imposed on Scotch single malt (as well as wines from France, Spain and Germany) imported to the US. So far Scotch exports to the US have declined by 25%.

In February 2020, the US government were looking to increase the Scotch single malt tariff to 100% but decided to raise the tariffs on aircraft instead. The EU, on the other hand, is looking for an approval from the WTO to impose tariffs on Boeing aircraft with an approval expected in early July. The WTO however decided they wouldn't give their opinion until September. At the moment both sides are preoccupied with fighting the effects of the Covid-19 pandemic but it seems an escalation of the trade war is possible eventhough the US government decided in early August to stick to the 25% and not rise it any further.

The choice of a new generation

For a producer of whisky the question going back at least a century has been "how do we make the next generation buy our product?" The dominating perception has been that the younger generation is looking for a drink their parents weren't enjoying. That is probably what brought a new generation of drinkers into white wine and vodka in the 1970s and 80s but whereas the rebellious mood is still there, the choice of a new generation could well be no alcohol at all. A recent survey showed that just 15% of generation Z (those who are now 15-25 years of age) are drinking alcohol once a week compared to 28% of the millennials and 36% of the baby boomers. Self-care and wellness is prioritized by the new generation and so is the awareness that everything you do when you're drunk could instantly be shown on social media such as Snapchat and Instagram with little chance of eradication. This doesn't mean that on an average young people today completely discard drinking. To be relevant to generation Z (as it is to some degree with the millennials) means selling an experience based on values rather than a product and knowing that the words and attitudes of their friends mean a lot more than general marketing. This is an area where new and smaller producers so far have been more successful than the major companies. Regardless though, for most spirits producers the lifestyle of many young consumers begs for a review of their product range if they wish to stay relevant to a new generation.

The big players

Diageo

"A year of two halves" – that's how Diageo CEO Ivan Menezes described the company's fiscal 2020 ending 30th June. He was of course referring to before and after the outbreak of the covid-19 pandemic. The first half of the year was described as consistent while the second half significantly impacted the result for the full year. Net sales were down by 8% to £11.75bn while operating profits before exceptional items decreased by 14% to £3.49bn. Exceptional items this year, however, was a staggering write-down of £1.3bn covering impairments in markets such as India, South Korea and Nigeria.

Diageo's business can be divided into five different geographical regions where North America represents 39% of the company's sales followed by Europe and Turkey (22%), Asia Pacific (19%), Africa (12%) and Latin America and Caribbean (8%). All regions showed negative growth in the past year apart from North America which managed to stay in positive growth with 4%. The drivers behind the growth in that market were Crown Royal, Don Julio tequila and Bulleit Bourbon. Johnnie Walker, on the other hand, lost 9% of its sales.

Scotch is the biggest part of Diageo's business with 23% of the net sales followed by beer (15%) and vodka 11%. The majority of the brands are then divided into Global Giants representing 39% of the net sales (Johnnie Walker, Smirnoff, Baileys, Captain Morgan, Tanqueray and Guinness), Local Stars representing 20% of sales (for example Buchanan's, J&B, Windsor, Black & White and Old Parr) and Reserve representing 21% of sales (for example all Scotch malts, Bulleit and Don Julio).

If we look at single labels, Johnnie Walker, the best selling Scotch in the world, the brand's net sales declined by 17% in a year where the owners are celebrating the famous whisky's 200th anniversary. The unfortunate circumstances did not deter them though from releasing four limited anniversary bottlings in July 2020 and work on the huge visitor experience in Edinburgh continues as planned. Other blended Scotch brands also declined – Buchanan (-12%), J&B (-18) and Old Parr (-15%). Even the malts portfolio had a hard time even if the decrease was considerably less. The figures for some of the other, major brands in the Diageo portfolio were Smirnoff (-8%), Crown Royal (+8%) and Guinness (-16%).

Looking forward, Diageo has decided to increase their efforts in the hard seltzer and canned spirits segments with several more whisk(e)y RTD products to be expected. They have also opened a hub in Menstrie in Scotland where a research lab will spearhead the company's innovation and sustainability projects. Finally, a rather unusual situation has developed between Diageo and its rival LVMH. For many years Diageo has held a 34% stake in the French

The vast majority of Diageo's major brands showed decreasing sales in 2019/2020 with Crown Royal as a shining exception (+8%

company's Moet Hennessy division. As they are still waiting for a dividend in the range of €181 m from last year they have started legal proceedings to obtain the money.

Pernod Ricard

Unlike most major companies, having a fiscal year ending in December, Pernod Ricard (together with Diageo) presented a full year result per 30th June where the covid-19 pandemic had impacted the figures during at least four months. The decrease was very much in line with what Diageo presented previously with organic sales down by 9,5% to €8.45bn and profits decreasing by 13,7% to €2.26bn. These were not surprising figures and the company's CEO, Alexandre Ricard seemed pleased given the circumstances but raised a warning for times to come. "For FY21, Pernod Ricard expects continued uncertainty and volatility, in particular relating to sanitary conditions and their impact on social gatherings, as well as challenging economic conditions."

The company has divided their market into three regions where Asia/Rest of the world is the biggest in terms of sales (-13% last year), followed by Europe (-5%) and Americas (-4%). If we look at specific brands only two of their 13 strategic international brands showed growth during the year with The Glenlivet up by 2% and Malibu with a 5% increase. The two that suffered the most were Martell (-20%) and Chivas Regal (-17%). Two other whisky brands, extremely important to Pernod Ricard, are the number two Scotch blend in the world, Ballantine's, which was up by 4% during the calender year 2019 but down by 8% in the financial report and Jameson, the best selling Irish whiskey in the world with an impressive increase of 8% during 2019 but a decrease of 1% in the company's financial year.

Following the sale of Wild Turkey in 2009, Pernod Ricard has in recent years been looking to make a come-back on the American whiskey market. Several acquisitions of smaller brands have been made with Castle Brands (owners of Jefferson' bourbon) as one of the latest.

On the Scotch whisky side, the company launched its "Original by Tradition" campaign for The Glenlivet in autumn 2019, released the tequila-finished Chivas Extra 13 and revealed that they are turning Glentauchers into a carbon-neutral distillery within the next two years.

Edrington

For the fiscal year ending 31 March 2020, the company showed a sales increase of 6% to £699.6m and an increase in profits before tax of 15% to £227m. This was another good year for Edrington but the CEO Scott McCroskie warns for a taxing year ahead due to the covid pandemic. "We anticipate a significant decline in global sales and profits in 2020/2021." The severeness was even further emphasized when the company felt obliged to state in the annual report that "The board of directors have a reasonable expectation that the group will be able to meet its financial obligations for the foreseeable future and have adequate resources to continue to operate for at least 12 months from the date of this annual report."

The positive result during fiscal 2020 can, to a large extent, be explained by increased sales of Macallan single malt, especially in China. Macallan is the world's number one single malt by value and in October 2019 one special bottling was in focus in the media: Distilled in 1926 and bottled in 1986, it was sold at an auction for a record £1.5m!

Another single malt brand in the group is Highland Park which experienced a more difficult year, especially in the US and Europe. Sales in Russia and Asia on the other hand increased by double digits.

After having sold off Cutty Sark at the end of 2018, the company now has only one Scotch blend remaining – The Famous Grouse. A marketing campaign during 2019 led to increased sales in several markets including Sweden, the Netherlands, Russia and Poland.

The biggest news during the year was ownership. The company's principal shareholder is The Robertson Trust which in March 2020 sold 10% of the shares to Suntory Holdings. The two companies have had a relationship ever since Suntory in the early 1990s bought a 25% stake in the Macallan brand. In March 2020, Edrington ceased its operations in South Korea. The reason was the long-term decline for Scotch whisky in the country.

Gruppo Campari

Following the year 2018, when sales decreased by 2.4%, fiscal 2019 proved to be a step in the right direction. Sales rose by 5.9% to €1.84bn while earnings before interest and tax (EBIT) were up by 1.5% to €386m. Similar to last year, it was the company's flagship brand Aperol that performed the strongest. Sales were up by 20,5% while the classic Campari increased by 4,6%. Their biggest brand on the whisk(e)y side is Wild Turkey bourbon which was up by 3%. The brand recently received attention when the owners hired actor Matthew McConaughey as creative director. On the Scotch whisky side, Campari are the owners of Glen Grant single malt. The brand is in a transition where aged spirits will be more in focus. That, however, didn't prevent them from launching a new expression without age statement in May 2020. In the range Arboralis, as it is called, will sit between the 5 year old and the 10 year old.

The company has been known to acquire other drinks companies and in 2018 they bought the cognac producer Bisquit. In the beginning of summer 2020 persistent rumours indicated a considerably larger deal in the making: Campari may be preparing a move to acquire the tequila maker José Cuervo. This would give Campari access to a growing spirits category and not only that. Since José Cuervo owns Bushmills Irish whiskey, yet another category would be added to Campari's list. Whether or not the covid-19 pandemic will be a spanner in the works for such an acquisition remains to be seen. What is clear though is that the Campari CEO, Bob Kunze-Concewitz seems to be slightly less alarmed by the possible consequences of the pandemic than some of his colleagues in other companies. In the end of March he said that the situation was "temporary" and that "the medium- to longterm consumption dynamics will not be affected.

Beam Suntory

Beam Suntory Inc, a part of Suntory Holdings' alcoholic beverage operations which also includes beer and wine, is the world's third largest drinks group after Diageo and

Pernod Ricard. Beam Suntory is responsible for its parent company's non-Japanese spirits operations.For 2019, revenues for the entire division increased by 3.2% to JPY778 billion while operating income grew 8,5% to JPY144.3bn.

If we look at the different brands, Jim Beam, the world's most sold bourbon, and Maker's Mark both showed strong growth in spite of the tariffs imposed by the EU on whiskey imported from the US. Jim Beam increased by 7% selling 125 million bottles and the corresponding figure for Maker's Mark was plus 10% and 29 million bottles. Legent, released during 2019, was especially mentioned in the report. The new brand was a joint-venture between Shinji Fukuyo, Suntory's chief blender and Fred Noe, master distiller at Beam.

Beam Suntory is in the same unfortunate position as Brown Forman where the trade war between the USA and the EU affects them doubly. Scotch single malts, such as Laphroaig and Bowmore, being exported to the US market are the target for a 25% tariff just as bourbon going in the opposite direction. Beam Suntory's CEO Albert Baladi is worried about the future. "Unfortunately, the tariffs that have been imposed on single malts in the U.S. are going to affect growth in that area, where we have the Laphroaig and Bowmore brands." Laphroaig has had a good record of increasing sales in the past four years, up by 20% while during the same time, Bowmore has increased by 8%. Sales of the company's leading blended Scotch, Teacher's, were up by 11% in 2019.

Beam Suntory's mother company, Suntory Holdings, has had a 25% stake in the Macallan brand since the 1990s and in 2020, they notched it up further when they acquired a 10% stake in Macallan's owners – Edrington.

Brown Forman

The initial reaction when going through the report for fiscal 2019/2020, ending on 30th April, is that it could have been a lot worse. Net sales increased by 1% to $3.36bn while net income slipped by 1% to $827m. There are two reasons why these figures could have been weaker. First of all, the trade war between the US and the EU where the latter imposed a 25% tariff on spirits imported from America to the EU in 2018. This came as a retaliation on steel and aluminium tariffs imposed by the US government earlier. However, the decline in sales to the developed international markets (that includes the EU) stopped at 1% and was offset by an increase in sales on the domestic market. The second factor that had an impact on the figures was the covid-19 pandemic. With the fiscal year ending 30th April, there were almost two months where the on-trade market (bars, restaurants and pubs) was severely hit by restrictions globally. The travel retail market also took a blow. For Brown Forman, that particular sales channel decreased by 10%.

If we look at the various brands, the company's whisk(e)y portfolio grew by 2% with Jack Daniel's decreasing by 4% but where Woodford Reserve grew by an impressive 19% and thereby broke the 1 million cases barrier for the first time. In the report no numbers for the company's Scotch whisky portfolio were mentioned, but sales of the three brands (GlenDronach, BenRiach and Glenglassaugh) have increased by 15% since they were taken over by Brown Forman in 2016.

The creation of a new reporting region for Europe in 2020, seems to indicate the company's recognition of the EU as an increasingly important market. Brown-Forman Europe will include major markets such as the UK, France and Germany in it. No acquisitions were made during the year but the intention of selling off Early Times bourbon and Canadian Mist to Sazerac was announced in June 2020.

The big brands
Blended Scotch

What started off as a splendid year for Johnnie Walker thanks to the success of the White Walker launched in connection with the TV series Game of Thrones in late 2018, turned into a decrease in sales volumes for the full 2019 year. The reason was a weaker performance for the brand in the second half of the year due to challenging trading conditions in Mexico and economic disruptions in Peru and Chile. The 2019 result was a loss of 3% to 221 million bottles. Still, these are impressive figures for the best selling Scotch in the world which almost corresponds to the total of numbers 2-5 on the top sales list.

Ballantine's, in second place, can rejoice at being the only whisky among Top 5 that showed sales growth (+4%) during 2019 and a total of 92 million bottles were sold. Ballantine's has in terms of volume been second to Johnnie Walker since 2007.

In third place we have yet another brand from Pernod Ricard – Chivas Regal – which, even though volumes during 2019 were down by 2%, managed to surpass Grant's. The total sales volume was 53 million bottles. Grant's in fourth place carried out a major brand overhaul including new expressions in summer 2018 but a positive effect of that remains to be seen. In 2019, the brand lost 8% of its volumes and landed on 50 million bottles sold. In place number five we find Lawson's, owned by Bacardi, which in 2012 managed to surpass its more well-known stable mate Dewars. The surge in sales for the brand that we could see a few years ago has slowed down and volumes have now during the past five years been stable at around 35 million bottles. During 2019 a total of 40 million bottles were sold which is a decrease by 1% compared to the previous year. Dewar's comes in at 6th place with 36 million bottles (+6%). The owners have done a lot recently in terms of new expressions including Dewar's Double Double for the travel retail market as well as the Cask Finish Series which includes a number of exciting second maturations, for example mezcal.

J&B is just behind Dewar's with around 40 million bottles sold in 2019 (-5%) closely followed by Famous Grouse. In 9th place is a brand that has outperformed most of its competitors in the past five years with an astonishing sales increase of 100%! Black & White sold close to 34 million bottles last year and is especially popular in Latin America and India. Number ten, finally, is Label 5 a brand which made a giant leap during a couple of years around 2010 going from 15 million bottles to 30 million. Since then sales have been pretty stable and during 2019 (when the bottle design and packaging was updated) it increased by 4% to 32 million bottles.

Single Malt Scotch

An otherwise positive trend for the category has been mitigated by the uncertainty created by the 25% tariff on Scotch single malt imposed by the US government in autumn 2019. In 2019, no less than 26% of the values of exported Scotch single malt came from USA. In the past decade, the vast majority of producers have realized that the opportunity of bottling and selling single malts at a substantially higher price compared to blends is one not to be missed. This is no longer a style of whisky for the few aficionados but a spirit that an increasing amount of consumers are intrigued by. More than 25% of the total values of Scotch whisky exports are today made up of single malt.

Number one on the list, and no surprise there, is Glenfiddich. Volumes during 2019 were up by 9% to 18 million bottles and since 2015 sales have increased by almost 40%. The number one spot though is a position that needs to be vigilantly defended and the owners have launched several marketing campaigns the past couple of years, not least targeting young and aspirational drinkers in growth markets such as Mexico, India and South Africa. In second place we find Glenlivet – the only other single malt brand that sells more than 1 million cases per year. In 2019 volumes were up by 4% to 15,6 million bottles and especially the second half of the year was impressive with strong growth in the US, Russia, India, Taiwan and Japan.

For Macallan, very close now to break the 1 million case barrier, and the rest of the malts on the Top 10 list, no sales figures for 2019 were available at the time of printing so what follows here is the position and figures from 2018. There may be changes between them in the ranking but

most likely no new brand has managed to enter the list: Macallan (11.6 million bottles), Glenmorangie (6.3), The Singleton (6.2), Balvenie (4.5), Laphroaig (4), Aberlour (3.2), Cardhu (3) and Talisker (3).

Finally, let's take a look at the top whiskies in North America, India and Ireland.

In North America, Jack Daniel's is the undisputed leader and the sixth most sold whisk(e)y in the world with 161 million bottles. In second place there is the most sold bourbon in the world, Jim Beam, which enjoyed a 7% increase during 2019 selling 125 million bottles. It is followed by the Canadian whisky Crown Royal (95 million) and two bourbons – Evan Williams (36 million) and Maker's Mark (up by 10% to 29 million bottles)

In India, we find seven of the ten most sold whiskies in the world even though they cannot be sold in the EU as whisky since they are made from molasses rather than grain. The top 5 are McDowell's No. 1 (368 million bottles), Officer's Choice (367), Imperial Blue (340 million), Royal Stag (264 million) and Original Choice (152 million). Annual fluctuations in sales volumes can often be dramatic in the Indian whisky category. For instance during 2019 Royal Stag increased by 25%!

No brand is as dominant within its category as Jameson. The world's number one Irish whiskey increased by 8% to reach 97 million bottles. Tullamore Dew, number two on the list, also had a good year with 17 million bottles (+7%) and in place three we find, as usual, Bushmills with 9.8 million bottles

A Macallan 1926, 60 years old was sold for a record sum of £1,5m in October 2019.
The Macallan featured here (inspected by Charles MacLean), sold the year before for £850,000, was the previous record holder.

New distilleries

Scotland

This part of the book deals with the embryonic distillery projects – they haven't started producing yet. In some cases their story is more of a plan where neither funds have been secured nor planning permission has been granted.

Although there has been a virtual explosion of new Scottish whisky distilleries (34 since the new millenium started) I am sensing a recent slowdown in new projects launched and this trend may also be fuelled by the economic uncertainties caused by the current pandemic.

Just one new distillery has started production since last year – Bonnington in Edinburgh and you can read more about that in the New Distilleries chapter, page 179. Another three "new" distilleries that haven't started up yet, are not covered here. They are the closed Brora, Port Ellen and Rosebank – soon to be resurrected. Read more about them on pages 193-195.

Edinburgh, where at one time there were eight operating distilleries, has seen two distillery openings in the last 16 months (Holyrood and Bonnington) but a third is about to open soon. Paddy Fletcher and Ian Stirling are building a distillery beside Ocean Terminal Shopping Centre and the Royal Yacht Britannia. Construction started in late 2019 and, once operational, the Port of Leith distillery will be producing 400,000 litres of pure alcohol per year. The distillery, which will cost £10m to build, is set to become Scotland's first vertical distillery with 9 floors. The top five will hold offices, a shop, bar, restaurant and tasting rooms while the distillery itself will be situated on the four lower floors. Until the new distillery is ready (hopefully in summer 2021) the owners have been producing gin in a temporary distillery, the Tower Street Stillhouse. They are also conducting a two year long study on different strains of yeast together with Heriot-Watt University.

Over on Islay, Ardnahoe became the ninth distillery to open in 2018 and now we are waiting for the tenth. Elixir Distillers, owned by Sukhinder Singh who also operates The Whisky Exchange with three stores in London, filed a planning application already in April 2018 but objections about the exterior design were raised and a new application was submitted in late 2019. At the time of writing (August 2020) it had not yet been approved. Equipped with 16 washbacks and four pairs of stills, this distillery will have the capacity to produce 1 million litres of pure alcohol. It will also feature its own floor maltings with a capacity of producing 75% of their needs. The distillery will be situated just outside Port Ellen on the road to Laphroaig, Lagavulin and Ardbeg.

On the west coast of the Cowal Peninsula, in the west of Scotland (just north of the isle of Bute), the village Polphail was built in the 1970s to house workers on a planned oil rig construction plant nearby. The plans for the oil rig yard were never realized though and the houses that had already been built turned into a ghost town and were finally demolished in 2016. In 2017, Sandy Bulloch, the previous owner of Loch Lomond Distillery, bought the site with the aim to build a distillery named Portavadie. The planning application was approved by Argyll & Bute Council in August 2018 and in autumn 2019, the site, including planning permission and building warrant approval for a distillery, was offered to the market.

Down in the Borders, Mossburn Distillers, owner of Torabhaig distillery on Skye, have plans for two distilleries. One of them, the Reivers Distillery outside Melrose, is more or less ready to start production. Equipped with pot stills as well as columns, they will be producing mainly rye and mixed grain spirits but genever and other spirits are also on the table. This is a fairly small distillery with a capacity of 100,000 litres. Their other distillery is of a

The new Port Ellen distillery and brand home will be ready to open in 2021/2022

Elixir Distillers are still waiting for planning approval for their distillery on Islay

much grander format. It will be built on the site of Jedforest Hotel near Jedburgh and will actually consist of two distilleries – one equipped with three pot stills and a capacity of 1.5 million litres and the other with five columns. The plan is to start with the building of warehouses much needed for the company's other operations followed by the distillery. A possible production start will not take place until perhaps in 2025.

Another distillery planned for The Borders has been postponed for the time being. R&B Distillers, which opened their first distillery on Raasay in 2017, are looking to build it in Peebles south of Edinburgh. One of the owners of R&B Distillers is Alasdair Day who launched a blended whisky named The Tweeddale already in 2010.

Remaining in the south, there are plans to build a whisky distillery in Moffat in Dumfries and Galloway. The whisky blender Dark Sky Spirits, which launched its first spirits in 2019, recently received an approval from the local council to build a distillery with the capacity to produce 60,000 litres of alcohol per year. The submitted plan is for a traditional distillery with wooden washbacks as well as worm tub for the cooling. The company has already been granted £320,000 by the South of Scotland Economic Partnership.

Moving on to the west, The Ardgowan Distillery Company received planning permission in March 2017 to build a distillery on the Ardgowan Estate in Inverkip, 30 miles west of Glasgow. The initial goal was to have the one million litre distillery in production by 2019 but new, revised plans for the distillery were approved by the local council in October 2018 and the hope is now to start production sometime in 2021. Two whisky veterans with an Edrington background have been called in to make it happen: Chairman of the board, Willie Phillips was the Macallan managing director from 1978 to 1996 and Max McFarlane who is the company's whisky maker used to be the Highland Park master blender. In anticipation of whisky

from their own production, a range of sourced whiskies called Clydebuilt has been launched with the blended malt Coppersmith as the first release.

Plans to open a whisky distillery in Loch Lomond national park were revealed in spring 2020. The Glen Luss distillery will open up in the village of Luss which is on the A82 on the western shores of Loch Lomond. An initial round of crowdfunding was initiated in spring 2020 and the owners hope to start producing malt whisky, gin, rum but also beer sometime in 2021.

The third whisky distillery to open up in Glasgow in modern days is not far away. In July 2017 independent bottler Douglas Laing announced that they had plans to build a distillery named Clutha on the banks of the river Clyde at Pacific Quay, just opposite Clydeside Distillery which opened in 2017. The total cost for the distillery will be £10.7m but this also includes a bottling complex, a new corporate head office, a visitor centre, a whisky laboratory and an archive. However, Clutha will not be the company's first distillery. In 2019 Douglas Laing bought Strathearn distillery near Perth.

After several years of planning (the final approval was granted in 2010), the Falkirk Distillery Company has managed to build a distillery at Salmon Inn Road, Polmont but distillation hasn't started yet. Campbell Meyer & Co, blenders, bottlers and exporters of whisky, own a 150,000 square feet bonded warehouse in East Kilbride, just south of Glasgow. In spring 2016, it was announced that the company had plans to add a distillery as well. Whether or not whisky production has actually commenced is still uncertain.

Up in Speyside, The Cabrach Trust plans to build a distillery in the village of Cabrach 15 minutes south of Dufftown. The idea is to convert the old Inverharroch Farm to a distillery and heritage centre including a museum of illicit whisky and smuggling. Planning permission was granted in September 2017 and with £2.1m of the funding in place, the trust applied in 2020 for another £1.4m from the Scottish Government.

A distillery project in Speyside that already has the fundings secured is the one that independent bottler Gordon & MacPhail has launched. The distillery, which will be situated at Craggan, near Grantown-on-Spey in the Cairngorms National Park will have a capacity of 2 million litres once operational. Planning approval was granted in October 2019 and the distillery could be up and running sometime during 2021. Gordon & MacPhail already have one distillery in Forres, Benromach, which they bought in 1993.

Since Dallas Dhu closed in 1983, the distillery has been preserved as a museum by Historic Environmental Scotland. In 2018 the HES sent out an appeal for interested parties to help redevelop the site and ultimately turn it into a working distillery again. They received more than 70 submissions to that plea and have now made a shortlist of six proposals to see which one they will go forward with.

North of Inverness there are a couple of projects worth keeping an eye on. The chance of Heather Nelson becoming the first woman to found a Scotch whisky distillery vanished in 2017 when Annabel Thomas opened her Nc´nean distillery on the Morvern peninsula. Nelson, who has studied at the Institute of Brewing and Distilling, submitted a planning application to build a distillery on the old World War II airbase at Fearn near Tain in March 2017 and it was later approved in just four weeks. The distillery will be equipped with two stills (1,000 and 600 litres respectively) and three washbacks with a capacity of producing 30,000 litres. The start of production has been delayed but the project is still ongoing.

A bit further north, just south of Brora, lies Dunrobin Castle which attracts 85,000 visitors each year. Here, Elizabeth Sunderland, a granddaughter of the former head of Clan Sutherland, and her husband Boban Costin have plans to build a single estate distillery housed in an old powerhouse. Planning permission was granted in late 2016 and the owners are now looking for an investor that can pledge the £6m needed.

As far north as you can possibly get on the Scottish mainland lies John O´Groats and here, Derek and Kerry Campbell have received a £198,000 grant from Highland & Islands Enterprise to build a whisky distillery with a yearly capacity of 60,000 litres. This will be the first distillery in the village since 1837. Planning approval has been granted and a possible opening could take place in 2021.

Plans for a distillery on Barra has been an ongoing theme in this book for many years now. A crowdfunding initiative was launched in early 2019 and in May that same year the distillery received a distilling license. Gin is currently produced and the owners hope to start producing whisky as well as soon as possible.

There are plans for whisky distilleries on a couple of islands in the outer Hebrides. Jonny Ingledew and Kate MacDonald opened a gin distillery on North Uist in April 2019 and in July 2020 they bought the 18th century Nunton Steadings on the island of Benbecula, situated between North and South Uist. The plan is to open a designated whisky distillery within the next couple of years. On South Uist, plans for a community-run whisky distillery were revealed in 2018. The cost for the distillery is estimated at

£10m and with a 300,000 litre capacity, they will also have their own malting floor using local peat to dry the barley.

Finally, one of the latest distillery projects to be announced is being planned on Hopetoun Estate near Queensferry, 20 kilometres west of Edinburgh. A planning application was submitted to the local council in April 2020 and backed by American investors, Julia Mackenzie-Gillanders and Ann Medlock, founders of the bottler Golden Decanters, are behind the project. Ken Robertson, former director of communications at Diageo and former chairman of the Keepers of the Quaich is also involved. The distillery, which will include maltings, will focus on sustainable whisky production. It will be built near the ruined Midhope Castle and there are also plans to restore the 16th century castle.

Ireland & Northern Ireland

The fact that there is a tidal wave of new whiskey distilleries opening up in Ireland and Northern Ireland is nothing new – it has been going on for nearly a decade now. What is surprising though is that the rate of expansion doesn't seem to diminish contrary to the feeling I had when I wrote last year's chapter.

There are 32 distilleries already working (read more about them on in the section Distilleries Around the Globe) and another 18 either being built or seeking funds, compared to ten in the latter category in last year's book.

So, let's go through them all.

In County Mayo, Jude and Paul Davis together with Mark Quick have been working on the construction of their Nephin Distillery for quite some time now. A cooperage has already opened and there is a shop in the village selling Nephin merchandise. Over the years, a total of €3.5m has been raised from various sources and another €2.5m have been added to that from the Davy EIIS Fund in October 2019. Some of the distillation equipment has already arrived at the distillery, which will have a capacity of 1 million litres, and the owners hope to have the distillery up and running during 2020 or 2021. The use of local peat will add to the character of the whiskey to be.

While still on the west coast, we can report on another project. Sliabh Liag Distillers, in southwest Donegal, started as a gin distillery and planned to expand into whiskey production as well. That is exactly what James and Moira Doherty still intend to do but instead of distilling whiskey at the present distillery they will build a new one for that, in the historic town of Ardara, 25 km north east of Sliabh Liag and also move the gin still there. Planning was granted for the new distillery in August 2019. At a cost of €10m Ardara will hold an impressive capacity of 400,000 litres of pure alcohol and production could start sometime around Christmas 2020. The idea is to produce triple-distilled whiskey, both single malt and single pot still, and some of it heavily peated as it would have been in the 19th century. Meanwhile, a sourced blended whiskey named Silkie was released by the owners a few years ago and in summer 2020, the owners distilled whiskey for the first time in their temporary distillery in Carrick.

Remaining in Co. Donegal and located in the former Crolly Dolls Factory, the Crolly Distillery is about to start its whiskey production autumn 2020. Using two old, beau-

James and Moira Doherty hope to have their Ardara Distillery up and running in 2021

tiful cognac stills from France the distillery will be able to produce 50,000 litres of pure alcohol per year.

The island co-op at Cape Clear, six kilometers off the Cork coast, received planning permission in August 2016 to build a €7m distillery on the island. Unfortunately, one of their major investors pulled out along the way and the owners started a Kickstarter campaign in spring 2019 in order to fund parts of the project. A year later their 3 Sq Miles gin has been launched with great success but whisky production has not yet started.

Gortinore Distillers, based in Waterford, launched their triple-distilled Natterjack Irish Whiskey in 2019. The whiskey had not been distilled by them but now the owner, Aidan Mehigan, along with two friends and his father, have acquired The Old Mill in Waterford with plans to turn that into a distillery.

In the south of Ireland, in Kinsale Co. Cork, lies Blacks Brewery & Distillery which started producing beer in 2013. Two years later, Sam and Maudeline Black added the production of various spirits, only to start whiskey production in June 2020. In anticipation of their own whiskey produced on site, a 12 year old sourced whiskey has been released.

Further to the west, in Cahersiveen Co. Kerry, a company has plans to transform an old sock factory into a distillery called Skellig Six 18. The unusual name was inspired by the number of steps (618) to the top of Skellig Michael, an island situated 10 kilometres off the coast of Iveragh Peninsula. Gin was launched in November 2019 and a whiskey distillery is currently being built with a possible distillation start in early 2021.

While still on the Ring of Kerry, the founders of Killareny Brewing Company are planning for a whiskey distillery near Fossa on the northern shores of Lough Leane. Apart from a distillery, the €24m project includes a brewery, a visitor centre and a restaurant. According to the original plans, the distillery could be producing in summer 2021.

Local farmer, Liam Ahearn, and his wife, Jennifer Nick-

erson, chose the Ahearn family farm between Clonmel and Tipperary as the designated spot for Tipperary Boutique Distillery. They also took in Jennifer's father in the business. Stuart Nickerson is well-known to lovers of Scotch after having held the position as Distillery Manager at Glenmorangie and is the mastermind behind the resurrection of Glenglassaugh. While sourced whiskey has already been released, the owners´ planning application for a distillery at Dundrum House Hotel was approved by the local council in summer 2019. Construction of the distillery started the same autumn but has at the time of writing not yet been completed.

In County Longford, west of Dublin, Peter Clancy, in partnership with his brother and siste, is planning for a distillery on the grounds of the old post office in Lanesborough. A gin still has already been installed while whiskey stills have been ordered from Italy. Apart from single malt and single pot still, Lough Ree Distillery will also be producing gin and vodka and the first product, Sling Shot Gin, has already been launched.

Neil Stewart is planning to convert a 200 year old mill in Boyle, Co. Roscommon into a whiskey distillery. The local council approved the planning application in autumn 2017 and around €5m will now be invested in the project. Apparently the celebrity actor Chris O´Dowd, a Boyle native and known from the series The IT Crowd and the movie Bridesmaids, is one of the investors.

In summer 2019, the local council gave the green light to a distillery in the 200 year old Ballykelly Mills near Monasterevin in county Kildare. Behind the project is Jewellfield Ltd with, amongst others, Bono as a shareholder. Monasterevin has a long history of whisky distilling. A distillery was opened already in 1784 and operated until 1934.

Further north in Derrylavan, Co. Monaghan and just west of Dundalk, lies Old Carrick Mill Distillery. Gin has already been launched and production of triple distilled whiskey is about to start.

Finally, in Northern Ireland, there are currently five ongoing projects:

Joe McGirr is the mastermind behind Boatyard Distillery in Enniskillen which began distilling in May 2016. The company has had some remarkable success with their gin and vodka but whiskey production has not yet started.

Michael McKeown, founder of Matt D'Arcy & Company, has been granted planning permission in summer 2018 for a whiskey distillery in Newry in county Down. Around £7m will be invested in the 100,000 litre distillery and a visitor centre. Sourced whiskey from other distilleries (a 10 year old port finish and a 17 year old single cask) were released in spring 2020.

The owner of Chateau de La Ligne in Bordeaux, Terry Cross, is building a distillery within the grounds of Killaney Lodge near Carryduff just south of Belfast. Hinch Distillery including a visitor centre will cost £6m to build and construction is well underway with the main part of the equipment in place. Work was delayed in spring 2020 due to the covid pandemic but was restarted in June with a hope to start production in late 2020 or early 2021. The distillery will be equipped with three pot stills (10,000 l, 5,500 l and 2,500 l). Sourced whiskey (no age, 5 and 10 year old) has already been launched internationally to build the brand.

In Garrison Co. Fermanagh, a couple of kilometres from the Irish border, work recently began on a £5m whiskey distillery where the financial backup comes from a group of investors based in London. Scott's distillery takes its name from the original owner of the farm on which the site is based – Hammy Scott. If everything goes according to plans, the distillery could be producing in late 2021.

A new distillery is underway in Lurgan Co. Armagh. Lough Neagh Distillers already operate Spade:Town brewery and are working on building a whiskey distillery as well but the covid pandemic has caused a temporary hold on.

Bottling grapevine

The covid-19 pandemic has affected the Scotch whisky industry in many ways including the number of new bottlings being launched during 2020. Several producers decided to postpone some of their planned releases while others opted for "business as usual". One of the latter was Diageo who, true to the traditions, came out with their 20th set of Special Releases or Rare by Nature as the range is now called. In the autumn the following expressions were launched; Cardhu 11 year old, Cragganmore 20 year old, Dalwhinnie 30 year old, Lagavulin 12 year old, Mortlach 21 year old, Pittyvaich 30 year old, Talisker 8 year old andThe Singleton of Dufftown 17 year old. But a few months before, Diageo presented a new range named Prima & Ultima. The first set in this new series was put together by the Master Distiller par preference, Dr. Jim Beveridge. The whiskies were sold as full sets of 8 bottles at a price of £20,000 and 238 sets were released. The press release clearly indicated that Diageo is targeting collectors with this new range. The first eight were Caol Ila 1984 (35 years), Clynelish 1993 (26 years), Cragganmore 1971 (48 years and the last remaining cask made when the distillery used coal fired stills), Lagavulin 1991 (28 years), Mortlach

1994 (25 years), Port Ellen 1979 (40 years), Singleton of Dufftown 1988 (30 years) and Talisker 1988 (31 years).

Other distilleries decided to go all-in and presented an entire revamped range. One of them was BenRiach where a new core range of seven expressions with completely new packaging was introduced in autumn 2020. Benromach also presented a new design for their core range and also came out with new versions of their Cissac and Sassicaia wood finishes. Finally, Loch Lomond decided their range should be more comprehensible to their customers and introduced a new core range with several new expressions. It now consists of Classic, Original, 10, 12, 14, 18, 21 and 30 year old. The former brand names Inchmurrin and Inchmoan are still used for other expressions (not least the peated ones) but only mentioned in small letters on the labels under the main brand Loch Lomond.

Dewars launched limited bottlings from four of their distilleries; a 15 year old Aberfeldy finished in Pomerol casks, a 17 year old Aultmore with a finish in several types of casks including palo cortado, a 39 year old Craigellachie and the travel retail range from Royal Brackla was revamped with 12, 18 and 20 year olds – all three with different sherry finishes. Arran Distillers released the 21 year old Kildonan & Padda as the third installment in the Explorer's Series and also a 25 year old was released in October.

The owners of Glenallachie are keen on experimenting with unusual finishes and the three from 2019 were accompanied in 2020 by a 9 year old rye, an 11 year old port and an 11 year old moscatel finish. Glencadam introduced a new member to the core range with the oloroso finished Reserva Andalucia while the sister distillery, Tomintoul, released Seiridh, also finished in ex-oloroso casks. The distillery also honoured their master distiller Robert Fleming who celebrated 30 years in the company by way of a number of limited bottlings in late 2020.

Balvenie released the fourth installment in their The Balvenie Stories in 2020. It was the 19 year old The Edge of Burnhead Wood which had been made from barley grown on the estate and their neighbour Glenfiddich launched the cognac finished Grand Couronne 26 years old and, exclusively for China and Taiwan, the Gran Cortes 22 years old. The third distillery on the same grounds, and also owned by William Grant, is Kininvie. Exciting experiments have been going on at this little known distillery and some of the results were revealed when a 5 year old triple distilled single malt was released together with a 3 year old, partly made from malted rye.

Kilchoman turned a mishap in the filling store into a new release. Am Burach was born when Machir Bay and a port matured Kilchoman were blended by mistake. Remaining on Islay, Bunnahabhain continued to work with some exciting casks with a 2008 manzanilla matured, a 1997 PX finish and a 2005 burgundy finish while Lagavulin presented an 11 year old made in collaboration with the actor Nick Offerman. Laphroaig chose to put the limelight on two of their most important distillery managers/owners from the past when Bessie Williamson Story 25 years old and chapter two of the 30 year old Ian Hunter Story were launched. Ardbeg, delighted their fans with four new expressions; the 5 year old Wee Beastie, the Ardbeg Day expression Blaaack with a finish in pinot noir casks from New Zealand, the 19 year old Traigh Bhan Batch 2 and, to honour the retiring and legendary distillery manager Mickey Heads, a bottling named Arrrrrrrdbeg which was wholly matured in ex-rye casks. Bruichladdich, finally, released Port Charlotte OLC:01 which had matured in three different casks - bourbon, syrah and vin doux naturel before being finished in ex-oloroso. There was also the mysterious Black Art 8 and four new expressions of Octomore.

Tobermory celebrated the re-opening of the distillery, after having been refurbished, with a 23 year old Tobermory oloroso finish and a Ledaig Sinclair rioja finish without age statement. The Distell stable mate, Deanston, came out with no less than five wood finishes; 1991 muscat, 2002 organic PX, 2002 pinot noir, 2007 calvados and 2002 port. The owners of Fettercairn, Whyte & Mackay, continue their efforts making Fettercairn more well-known to the consumers and added a 16 year old made from chocolate malt to the range together with a 22 year old. They also gave another of their distilleries, Tamnavulin, some well-deserved attention with three wine cask finishes – cabernet sauvignon, grenache and pinot noir. The two stars in the portfolio are Dalmore with a 51 year old released in 2020 and Jura where a new series named Cask Editions was launched. The first release was Red Wine Cask.

Glenmorangie has, at least for the time being, stopped with the yearly Private Edition releases that began in 2009. This doesn't mean that they idled during 2020 in terms of new releases. A range of three new expressions destined for duty free was presented in spring 2020 and they were followed by Grand Vintage 1995 and, for the American market, the 26 year old Truffle Oak and The Cadboll Estate. Finally, in October, Bill Lumsden was inspired by his favourite cakes when he prsented the Tokaji finished A Tale of Cake.

From Glen Grant came a new addition to their core range with Arboralis and Glengyle presented their oldest Kilkerran so far – a 16 year old. Meanwhile, the distillery around the corner, Springbank, released the 10 year old Local Barley, a 17 year old madeira finish and this year's Longrow Red – a 13 year old finished in cabernet sauvignon casks.

Macallan took a step back to become even more known as a single malt based on sherry maturation when they discontinued two of their three Triple Cask bottlings and added two new ones (a 15 and an 18 year old) in the all-sherry range called Double Cask. The master distiller for The Glenlivet, Alan Winchester, continued playing games with the customers when he released the fifth mystery bottling. This time it was a set of three single malts called Spectra with very little information on the labels. Having tried them first, the punters can then use a QR code to get more information about the content including maturation.

If anyone was in doubt, Glenfarclas made it clear that they have some old and exquisite whisky in their warehouses when they released two more expressions in their Pagoda Reserve series aimed at the Asian market. This time it was the 62 year old Ruby and the 63 year old Sapphire. Another distillery looking to the east was Pulteney who released a 34 year old sherry finish for China. In anticipation of the re-opening of the Rosebank distillery in 2021, Ian Macleod released two rare single casks from 1993 and from another closed distillery about to come back from the "dead", Port Ellen, came a 40 year old in the Untold Stories series.

Last but definitely not least there were some exciting inaugural bottlings from a bunch of new distilleries. Nc´Nean released their Ainnir, matured in a combination of ex-bourbon and red wine casks, in September and they were later followed by Ardnamurchan, Torabhaig, Isle of Raasay and Dornoch.

Octomore 10 year old, Coleburn 47 year old Gordon & MacPhail, Dalwhinnie 30 year old Rare by Nature, Arran 25 year old, GlenAllachie 9 year old rye wood finish, Fettercairn 22 year old and Cragganmore 1971 Prima & Ultima

Independent
bottlers

The independent bottlers play an important role
in the whisky business. With their innovative bottlings, they increase
diversity. Single malts from distilleries where the owners' themselves
decide not to bottle also get a chance through the independents.
The following are a selection of the major companies.
Tasting notes have been prepared by Ingvar Ronde.

Gordon & MacPhail

gordonandmacphail.com

Established in 1895 the company, which is owned by the Urquhart family, still occupies the same premises in Elgin. Apart from being an independent bottler, there is also a legendary store in Elgin and, since 1993, an own distillery, Benromach. In 2018, the company announced that they had plans to build a new malt whisky distillery at Craggan, close to Grantown-on-Spey and with construction work commencing in 2019, they plan to start distillation sometime in 2021. Gordon & MacPhail's part in establishing the interest in single malt Scotch before the vast majority of producers realised the potential can not be overrated. The company has an incredible variety of casks in their warehouses in Elgin and in 2018, they revamped their portfolio of bottlings. Now there are five distinctive ranges; Connoisseurs Choice is a series well-known to most whisky aficionados. It received a new look and consists of single malts bottled either at 43% or 46%. Some of the latest releases include Bruichladdich 1990, Caol Ila 1988 and Bunnahabhain 1989. Discovery, a new range unveiled in 2018, is grouped under three flavour profiles – smoky, sherry and bourbon. Distillery Labels is a relic from a time when Gordon & MacPhail released more or less official bottlings for several producers. Private Collection, a new range, features old single malts including bottlings from closed distilleries and some of the 2020 releases include Port Ellen 1979, Longmorn 1970 and North British 1962. Generations, finally, was first introduced in 2010. This range comprises the oldest and rarest whiskies in stock, including releases such as Mortlach 75 years old - the oldest single malt ever bottled. To celebrate the company's 125th anniversary, an extraordinary series called "Last Cask" was introduced in September 2020. The first release was a rare 47 year old Coleburn distilled in 1972. The remaining three will all come from closed distilleries or from Lomond stills no longer in use.

Clynelish 2006 13 year old, 54,6%
Nose: Oranges, vanilla, wax candles, walnuts with maple syrup and a hint of cacao.
Palate: Deliciously fruity with notes of ripe peaches and sweet plums, a hint of pepper and cinnamon. Nice, waxy mouthfeel.

Caol Ila 2003 16 year old, 55,7%
Nose: Smoky and ashy with notes of melon, banana, green plants and driftwood.
Palate: Distinctly smoky with sweet notes of butterscotch and vanilla, apples, pears and black pepper at the end.

Berry Bros. & Rudd

bbr.com

The world's oldest wine and spirit merchant, founded in 1698, opened a new flagship shop in London in 2017. The famous address 3 St James's Street, where the company has been since the start, was returned to its appearance of 30 years ago and is now a space for consultations, meetings and events. The new, and much larger store, is just around the corner in 63 Pall Mall. A driving force behind the new shop was CEO Dan Jago who joined the company in 2015. He left BBR in 2019 and was succeeded by Lizzy Rudd, a third-generation member of the Rudd family. Berry Brothers had been offering their customers private bottlings of malt whisky for years, but it was not until 2002 that they launched Berry's

Own Selection of single malt whiskies. Under the supervision of Spirits Manager, Doug McIvor, some 30 expressions are on offer every year. Bottling is usually at 46% but expressions bottled at cask strength are also available. A new series called The Classic Range was released in spring 2018. It´s made up of four bottlings of blended malt; Speyside, Islay, Sherry Cask Matured and Peated Cask Matured. In spring 2019, The Perspective Series was launched including four blended Scotch (21, 25, 35 and 40 years old). Early 2020, a new range of single malts was introduced. The whiskies were selected by and named after the company´s longtime brand heritage director Ronnie Cox. Ronnie´s Reserve consists of seven single malts from 1968 to 1995 and even though the distillery is not mentioned on the labels, these are all from Glenrothes.

The Perspective Series No. 1 35 year old, 43%
Nose: Deep notes of raisins and dark plums, furniture polish, chocolate and treacle.
Palate: Rich with notes of sacher torte, candied fruit, liquorice, cinnamon and oak.

Orkney Islands 2007 12 year old, 46%
Nose: Baked root vegetables, green plants, sunwarm driftwood, heather honey and citrus.
Palate: Starts off with crispy, sweet barley, honey and citrus followed by bitter, ashy smokiness and a hint of white pepper.

Signatory

Founded in 1988 by Andrew and Brian Symington, Signatory Vintage Scotch Whisky lists at least 50 single malts at any one occasion. The most widely distributed range is Cask Strength Collection which sometimes contains spectacular bottlings from distilleries which have long since disappeared. Another range is The Un-chill Filtered Collection bottled at 46%. Some of the latest bottlings released include a Jura 1992, a Mortlach 2007 and a Glentauchers 1997. Finally there is also the Single Grain Collection with a North British 1991 and a Cameronbridge 1984 as some of the latest releases. Andrew Symington bought Edradour Distillery from Pernod Ricard in 2002 and the entire operations, including Signatory, are now concentrated to the distillery in Perthshire.

Ian Macleod Distillers

ianmacleod.com

The company was founded in 1933 and is one of the largest independent family-owned companies within the spirits industry. Gin, rum, vodka and liqueurs, apart from whisky, are found within the range and they also own Glengoyne and Tamdhu distilleries. In autumn 2017 they revealed their plans to resurrect Rosebank Distillery in Falkirk which will be re-opened in 2021. Their single malt range includes The Chieftain´s, which cover a range of whiskies from 10 to 50 years old while Dun Bheagan is divided into two series – Regional Malts, 8 year old single malts expressing the character from 4 whisky regions in Scotland and Rare Vintage Single Malts, a selection of single cask bottlings from various distilleries.

There are two As We Get It single malt expressions – Highland and Islay. The Six Isles blended malt contains whisky from all the whisky-producing islands while one of the top sellers is the blended malt Isle of Skye with five domestic expressions. Finally, Smokehead, a heavily, peated single malt from Islay introduced in 2006, has become a huge success. The range was revamped in 2018 and a new expression was added to the range – Smokehead High Voltage, bottled at 58%. This was followed up in November 2018 with the limited (18,000 bottles) Sherry Bomb and in 2020 with Smokehead Rum Rebel. In 2016, the company acquired Spencerfield Spirit which included Edinburgh Gin as well as the blended malt Sheep Dip and Pig´s Nose blended Scotch.

Smokehead Rum Rebel, 46%
Nose: Meaty and seductive, sweet smoke, canned fruit and quite herbal.
Palate: Smoky, ashy notes go well with delicious fruit from the rum cask. Pears, bisquits and heavy syrup lead to a long finish.

Macleod´s Island, 40%
Nose: Green notes with heather, citrus, vanilla and a touch of seaweed.
Palate: Herbal and earthy with distinct notes of honey and sweet barley, parsnip, vanilla and a light smokiness.

Blackadder International

blackadder.com

Blackadder is owned by Robin Tucek, one of the authors of the classic whisky book, The Malt Whisky File. Apart from the Blackadder and Blackadder Raw Cask (bottled straight from the cask without any filtration at all), there are also a number of other ranges – Smoking Islay, Peat Reek, Aberdeen Distillers, Clydesdale Original and Caledonian Connections. In recent years, two new brands have become increasingly popular; Black Snake which is a vatting of casks finished in a single sherry butt and Red Snake which are single cask malts, always from first fill ex-bourbon. All bottlings from Blackadder are uncoloured and un chill-filtered and most of them are diluted to 43-46% but Raw Cask is always bottled at cask strength.

Duncan Taylor

duncantaylor.com

Founded in Glasgow in 1938 as a cask broker and trading company. In 2002, the company was acquired by Euan Shand and operations were moved to Huntly. Duncan Taylor´s flagship brand is the blended Scotch Black Bull, a brand with a history going back to 1864. Black Bull was rebranded in 2009 by Duncan Taylor and the range consists of four core releases – Kyloe, an 8 year old, a 12 year old and a 21 year old. There are also limited versions such as 40 year old, 10 year old rum finish and 10 year old sherry finish. The Black Bull brand is complimented by Smokin' which is a blend of peated Speyside, Islay and grain whisky from the Lowlands.

The portfolio also includes The Rarest (single cask, cask strength whiskies of great age from demolished distilleries), Dimensions (a collection of single malts and single grains aged up to 39 years), The Tantalus (a selection of whiskies all aged in their 40s), The Duncan Taylor Single Range (whiskies aged 30 years or more from closed distilleries), Battlehill (a range of single malts and single grains) and Rare Auld Grain (a selection of rare grain whiskies bottled at cask strength). The perhaps most popular range in recent years is The Octave. These are single malt whiskies matured for a further period in small, 60-70 litre ex-sherry octave casks. Some of the most recent releases in that range are Laphroaig 2004, Dailuaine 2009 and Dalmunach 2016. In autumn 2019 The Octave Premium with substantially older whiskies, was introduced. Finally, the blended malt category is represented by Big Smoke, a young peated whisky available at 46% and 60%.

Black Bull 21 year old, 50%

Nose: Malt, toffee, sherry, sultanas and spice. Toasted coconut and raisins.

Palate: Rich, sweet and fruity, with soft, sherried spices and glace cherries. Relatively long finish with chilli and ginger.

Black Bull 21 year old, 50%

Nose: Pine needles, vanilla, oatmeal crackers, fennel, chocolate, citrus and nougat.

Palate: Delicious notes of dried fruits, chocolate cake, dry smoke, cherry trifle, tiramisu, clove and cinnamon.

Scotch Malt Whisky Society

smws.com

The Scotch Malt Whisky Society, founded in 1983 and owned by Glenmorangie Co since 2003, has more than 30,000 members worldwide and apart from UK, there is a network of international branches and partner bars in 19 countries around the world. In 2015, Glenmorangie sold the SMWS to the HotHouse Club and a group of the managers. The idea from the very beginning was to buy casks of single malts from the producers and bottle them at cask strength without colouring or chill filtration. The Society has played a significant role for the interest in single cask Scotch that has exploded in recent decades. The labels do not reveal the name of the distillery. Instead there is a number but also a short description which will give you a clue to which distillery it is. Around 500 casks are bottled every year. The SMWS also arranges tastings at their venues in Edinburgh (Queen Street and Leith), London (Greville Street) and, since March 2020, Glasgow (Bath Street) but also at other locations. In recent years, the range has been expanded to also include single grain, whiskies from other countries as well as rum, gin, cognac and other spirits.

Murray McDavid

murray-mcdavid.com

The company was founded in 1996 by Mark Reynier, Simon Coughlin and Gordon Wright and in 2000, they also acquired Bruichladdich distillery. In 2013 Murray McDavid was taken over by Aceo Ltd. and a year later they signed a lease for the warehouses at the closed Coleburn distillery for storing their own whiskies as well as stock belonging to clients. The bottlings are divided into six different ranges; Mission Gold (exceptionally rare whiskies bottled at cask strength), Benchmark (mature single malts bottled at 46%), Mystery Malt (single malts where the distillery is not revealed), Select Grain (single grains), The Vatting (vatted malts) and Crafted Blend (blended Scotch from their own blending). The vast majority of the releases are single casks.

Compass Box Whisky Co

compassboxwhisky.com

John Glaser, founder and co-owner of the company, has a philosophy which is strongly influenced by meticulous selection of oak for the casks, clearly inspired by his time in the wine business. But he also has a lust for experimenting to test the limits, which was clearly shown when Spice Tree, matured in casks containing extra staves, was launched in 2005. Glaser and Compass Box are also advocating more transparency in the industry where the customer is given as much information as possible about the contents of the bottle. The company divides its ranges into a Signature Range and

a Limited Range. Spice Tree (a blended malt), The Peat Monster (a combination of peated Islay whiskies and Highland malts), Oak Cross (American oak casks fitted with heads of French oak) and Hedonism (a vatted grain whisky) are included in the former. A new addition was made in 2018 when The Story of the Spaniard was released. A blend of Highland and Speyside whiskies, it had been partially matured in Spanish red wine casks.

In the Limited range, whiskies are regularly replaced and at times only to resurface a couple of years later in new variations. In autumn 2019, The Myths & Legends Limited Edition series was launched where two of the three releases were single malts and the third a blended malt. These were followed by Juveniles, a collaboration between Compass Box and Paris wine bar Juveniles Bistrot à Vins. In 2020 the blended Scotch Rogues´ Banquet was released, celebrating the company´s 20th anniversary and it was followed in the autumn by Hedonism Felicitas and Peat Monster Arcana. There are also two blended Scotch, Artist´s Blend and Glasgow Blend, with a 50% proportion of malt whisky.

In 2014, Compass Box made a long-term agreement with John Dewar & Sons where the Bacardi-owned company would supply Compass Box with stocks of whisky for future bottlings. In 2015 it was further announced that Bacardi had acquired a minority share of the independent bottler.

Juveniles, 46%

Nose: Elegant and floral with notes of red apples, white wine and a hint of citrus.

Palate: Remains floral with herbal notes, honey, cake frosting, toast and vanilla. Perfectly balanced.

Peat Monster, 46%

Nose: Dry, herbal and medicinal with notes of soot, green plants, aniseed and salted almonds.

Palate: Well balanced with a dry smokiness, eucalyptus, liquorice, dates wrapped in bacon and mango. Lingering finish.

North Star Spirits

northstarspirits.com

Founded in 2016 by Iain Croucher who used to work for AD Rattray before deciding to go it alone. The latest release in his single cask single malt range in 2020 included Bowmore 18 year old, Glenlivet 38 year old, Longmorn 15 year old and Imperial 30 year old. There are also blended malts named Vega with a 22 year old as the most recent. Spica are blended Scotch with a 40 year old released in 2020 while Sirius are blended malts with a 31 year old from 2019. A recent limited edition (from 2020) is the 10 year old Chaos which is a vatting of three Caol Ila casks (two sherry and one bourbon). North Star is not focused on just whisky from Scotland. They also bottle American whiskey as well as rum and gin.

Master of Malt

masterofmalt.com

Master of Malt is an online retailer of whiskies, gins, rums, agave spirits, beer, wine and more. As one of the most innovative whisky retailers in the UK, the company also has its own range of single-cask bottlings, featuring old and rare expressions from the likes of The Macallan, Springbank and Littlemill, to world whiskies like the Paul John 6 year old, and even more unusual expressions, for example, the Croftengea 11 year old 2007 from the Loch Lomond distillery. Every whisky in the range was bottled at both natural cask strength and colour and recent additions include Mortlach 20 year old 1997, Laphroaig 21 year old 1997 and BenRiach 7 year old 2011. In addition, Master of Malt stocks thousands of Drinks by the Dram 30ml sample-size bottles and customers can entirely personalise contents of Drinks by the Dram tasting sets with these. The retailer also offers the Dram Club monthly whisky subscription service, as well as a Blend Your Own option, personalised whisky and has a gift finder to help with special occassions.

Mortlach 1997 20 years old, 54,5%

Nose: Slightly earthy with green/grassy notes, orchard fruits, apple cider, roasted nuts, ginger and wine cellar.

Palate: Dry with some oaky notes followed by ripe fruit, toffee, tobacco, vanilla, brown sugar and a peppery finish.

Atom Brands

Part of the Atom Group which includes online retailer Master of Malt and the UK Distributor Maverick Drinks, Atom Brands is home of their home grown brands as well as their independently bottled whiskies, rums, gins and other spirits from around the world. The brands include Drinks by the Dram with 30ml samples, and the spirit-filled Advent Calendars, as well as Ableforth's Bathtub Gin, That Boutique-y Drinks Company, The Blended Whisky Company, The Handmade Cocktail Company, 1897 Quinine Gin, Darkness, Bitter Bastards, Origin, The 'Hot Enough' Vodka Company and Mr Lyan.

That Boutique-y Whisky Company

thatboutiqueywhiskycompany.com

Established in 2012, this independent bottler is best characterised by its uncompromising approach to flavour and quality and graphic novel-style labels. That Boutique-y Whisky Company has worked with over 160 distilleries to date, creating a range that is a global representation of the whisky category. The brand boasts expressions from some of the most renowned names in Scotch production, as well as whisky from smaller, independent distilleries across the globe, including whisky produced in South Africa, India and Switzerland, and covering blends, blended malts, single grains, bourbons and young ryes.

World Whisky Blend, 41,6%

Nose: Fresh and green with notes of seashore, apples, pears and sourdough bread (or just the dough).

Palate: Sweet notes of sponge cake, eucalyptus, lavender, toffee and honeydrops.

The Character of Islay Whisky Company

characterofislay.com

The Character of Islay Whisky Company offers a range of distinctive whiskies with Islay at their heart. A modern, yet romanticised approach to the Islay whisky category, The Character of Islay Company uses fabled characters to create an imaginary storyline that represent the expressions of Islay whisky, and the regional characteristics of Islay itself. The brand's expressions include Aerolite Lyndsay 10 year old, Grace Île 25 year old and The Legend of Fiona Macleod 33 year old. The makers of The Character of Islay Whisky Company, are also behind the Green Isle, a smoky blended Scotch whisky featuring a core of Islay malt, alongside Speyside malt and Lowland grain whiskies.

Green Isle, 40%

Nose: Green/grassy with notes of vanilla ice cream, coconut, sponge cake, citrus and a whiff of peat.

Palate: Starts off with lightly smoky and sweet barley followed by baking spice, ginger, pears and ever so lightly peppery notes.

Burnt Ends

masterofmalt.com/distilleries/burnt-ends/

The Burnt Ends whiskey brand launched in 2020 and was inspired by the kind of food you'll find in barbecue joints all over the USA. Its core expression, Burnt Ends Blended Whisky, is a meaty, smoky and rich dram made from a combination of Tennessee rye whiskey and sherry cask-finished Islay Single malt Scotch whisky. These two distinct styles were brought together in a complex blend that's housed in what looks like a bottle of barbecue sauce.

Burnt Ends, 45%

Nose: Intriguing with notes of struck matches, cut grass, barbecue sauce and applecider vinegar.

Palate: Dry smokiness with distinct notes of chorizo, chili pepper, vanilla, clove, fennel and distinct spicyness from the rye.

The Whisky Agency

whisky-agency.de

The man behind this company is Carsten Ehrlich, to many whisky aficionados known as one of the founders of the annual Whisky Fair in Limburg, Germany. His experience from sourcing casks for limited Whisky Fair bottlings led him to start as an independent bottler under the name The Whisky Agency, a business that celebrated its 10th anniversary in 2018. There are several ranges including The Whisky Agency, The Perfect Dram and Specials with some unusual bottlings.

A Dewar Rattray Ltd

adrattray.com

The company was founded by Andrew Dewar Rattray in 1868. In 2004 the company was revived by Tim Morrison, previously of Morrison Bowmore Distillers and fourth generation descendent of Andrew Dewar, with a view to bottling single cask malts from different regions in Scotland. One of its best-sellers is a single malt named Stronachie which is actually sourced from Benrinnes. There are currently two expressions, a 10 year old and a 10 year old sherry finish. A peated, blended malt, Cask Islay, became available in 2011 and then again in 2013 but this time as a single malt. It was complemented in 2018 by Cask Orkney 18 year old and in 2019 by Cask Speyside 10 year old. The AD Rattray´s Cask Collection is a range of single cask whiskies bottled at cask strength and without colouring or chill-filtration. In 2020 a new range of single cask whiskies, The Warehouse Collection, was introduced. Bottled at either cask strength or 46% these are a mixture of full or part casks, 'bin ends' and remnants from casks that have be re-racked and they are available exclusively from the shop/online shop. In 2011, the company opened A Dewar Rattray´s Whisky Experience & Shop in Kirkoswald, South Ayrshire. Apart from having a large choice of whiskies for sale, there is a sample room, as well as a cask room. In 2020 the shop was re-branded to become a focused home of A. D. Rattray including personalised own label single cask bottlings.

Cask Speyside Sherry Finish 10 year old, 46%
Nose: Fresh and vibrant with notes of vanilla, toffee, tarte tatin, chocolate milk, cinnamon and sweet barley.
Palate: Jammy notes of plum preserve and then dry and herbal. Shortbread, roasted almonds and a hint of cinnamon.

Cask Islay Bourbon Edition, 58,6%
Nose: A sooty smokiness is followed by notes of orchard fruits, candy and herbs.
Palate: Lovely barbecue smokiness accompanied by sweet notes of apple pie and marshmallows. Some dry tannins towards the end and also nutmeg.

Douglas Laing & Co

douglaslaing.com

Established in 1948 by Douglas Laing, this firm was run for many years by his two sons, Fred and Stewart. In 2013, the brothers decided to go their separate ways. Douglas Laing & Co is now run by Fred Laing and his daughter Cara. Douglas Laing has the following brands in their portfolio; Provenance (single casks bottled at 46%), Premier Barrel (single malts in ceramic decanters) and Old Particular, a range of single malts and grains. The latter has also been expanded with two brand extensions; XOP and XOP "The Black Series". A spectacular release in the latter range was a 40 year old Port Ellen in February 2020.

Six years ago the company started a range that has become highly succesful. The first installment in the series that eventually was given the name Remarkable Regional Malts, was Scallywag – a blended malt influenced by sherried whiskies from Speyside. More versions have followed with Scallywag 10 yer old, Scallywag Chocolate Edition and Scallywag Red-Nosed Reindeer. Regional Malts has been expanded over the years and now also includes Timorous Beastie from the Highlands with no age statement as well as 10, 18 and (since 2019) 25 year old. Rock Island is a blended malt combining whiskies from Islay, Arran, Orkney and Jura and can be found without age statement or as an 18 or 21 year old. In August 2020 a limited Sherry Edition was also launched. The Epicurean represents the Lowlands with a core 12 year old and three limited bottlings released in 2020; the Cask Strength Edinburgh Edition, Rivesaltes Wine Finish and Cognac Finish. The Gauldrons is made from Campbeltown malts and the final regional whisky is Big Peat, a vatting of Islay malts. This was launched several years ago but was later included in the range. The core range is made up of a no age statement bottling, a 10 year old and a 12 year old but older versions (up to 33 years) have been released. In June 2020 the 8 year old Big Peat A846 was launched in connection with Feis Ile. In July 2017, it was announced that Douglas Laing would

also become distillers. Their chosen site in Glasgow is on the banks of the river Clyde just opposite the new Clydeside Distillery and the goal is to have the Clutha distillery operational by 2021.

Timorous Beastie 25 year old, 46,8%
Nose: Fresh, green apples, goose berries, fennel, vanilla ice cream and some earthy notes.
Palate: A virtual fruit cocktail with notes of eucalyptus, sweet barley, ripe banana and a hint off chili pepper. Long and herbal finish.

Rock Island 21 years old, 46,8%
Nose: Lively with notes of grapefruit peel, ashes, seaweed, green apples, minerals and heather.
Palate: Almost prickly on the tongue, sweet vanilla in combination with dry smoke, tropical fruits, pepper and liquorice.

Malts of Scotland

malts-of-scotland.com

Thomas Ewers from Germany, bought casks from Scottish distilleries and decided in the spring of 2009 to start releasing them as single casks bottled at cask strength and with no colouring or chill filtration. The backbone of the assortment is the Basic Line with three blended malts; Classic (18yo), Sherry (15yo) and Peat (10yo). Apart from other ranges of Scotch single malts, Ewers has also added a range called Malts of Ireland. At the moment he has released more than 100 bottlings and apart from a large number of single casks, there are two special series, Amazing Casks and Angel´s Choice, both dedicated to very special and superior casks. Ewers was inducted as a Keeper of the Quaich in 2016.

Hunter Laing & Co

hunterlaing.com

This company was formed after the demerger between Fred and Stewart Laing in 2013 (see Douglas Laing). It is run by Stewart Laing and his two sons, Scott and Andrew. The Hunter Laing portfolio consists of the following ranges and brands; The Old Malt Cask (rare and old malts, bottled at 50%), The Old and Rare Selection (an exclusive range of old malts offered at cask strength), The Sovereign (a range of old and rare grain whiskies), Hepburn´s Choice (younger malts bottled at 46%) and The First Editions. The latter was created by Andrew Laing before Hunter Laing was formed and is now a substantial part of the portfolio. In June 2019, Scarabus, a single malt from an undisclosed Islay distillery, was released as the first in a new range and finally, there are also two small batch blended malts - Islay Journey and Highland Journey.

In January 2016, the company announced their intentions of building a distillery on Islay on the northeast coast near Bunnahabhain. Ardnahoe Distillery, with a capacity of making 1 million litres per year, came on stream in November 2018 and was opened to the public in spring 2019. To celebrate their presence on the island, the company released a range of old and rare whiskies already in 2017 with the label Feis Ile Kinship. This was repeated in 2018 and 2019 and, in 2020, some of the expressions included were a 28 year old Ardbeg and a 30 year old Bowmore.

The Kinship Ardbeg 28 year old, 50,1%
Nose: Lovely dry, grassy smoke with notes of hay, malted barley, vanilla pods, honey and apple sauce.
Palate: Rich and smoky with notes of baked apples, unripe banana, vanilla toffee, dry oak, ryvita and toasted almonds. Beautiful balance and a long finish.

The Kinship Bowmore 30 year old, 58%

Nose: Charming and floral with apple cider vinegar, ripe tropical fruits, milk chocolate, French nougat and sticking plaster.

Palate: A burst of melon, banana and mango with hints of lavender, pepper and blue cheese on a cracker.

Wemyss Malts

wemyssmalts.com

Founded in 2005, the family-owned independent bottler opened up their own whisky distillery at Kingsbarns in Fife in 2014. The company is mainly known for its range of blended malts of which there are three core expressions – The Hive, Spice King and Peat Chimney. These are available at 46% un chill-filtered and also in limited edition batch strength, typically around 55-58%. In autumn 2020 the entire range was rebranded including new packaging. In 2017, the family bottled a new part of their blended malt range called The Family Collection consisting of spirit sourced and fully matured by the family. There were two releases, Vanilla Burst and Treacle Chest and they were followed up in 2019 by Blooming Gorse and Flaming Feast. Two other blended malts are Nectar Grove, released in 2018 and finished in ex-Madeira casks and the oloroso sherry matured Velvet Fig which was relaunched as a 25 year old in 2020 to celebrate the 15th anniversary of the company.

Another side of the business involves single cask single malts, either bottled at 46% or occasionally at cask strength. The names of the whiskies reflect what they taste like although the distillery name is also printed on the label. All whiskies are un chill-filtered and without colouring. In 2019, Wemyss launched a brand new range called the Wemyss Malts Cask Club.
The first two bottlings offered to members were a 35 year old Caol Ila (Smoky Nectar) and a 31 year old, sherried Bunnahabhain. One of the latest, in February 2020, was Black Gold – a 30 year old sherry matured Bowmore.

Black Gold Bowmore 1989, 50%

Nose: Dark and slightly smoky with notes of old Bordeaux wine, cellar, cedar tree, leather and black berry marmalade.

Palate: Dry oak turns into a velvety feeling of dried fruits, raisins, espresso coffee, parma violets, dark chocolate and a whiff of earthy smoke.

Velvet Fig 25 year old, 42,3%

Nose: Charming with notes of liquorice, sweets, marzipan bread, ripe pineapple and blackberries.

Palate: Fresh, vibrant and quite dry with notes of ripe melon, grapefruit, fruit cake, raisins, ginger and a hint of oak and pepper.

Single Cask Nation

singlecasknation.com

In 2011, Jason Johnstone-Yellin and Joshua Hatton, two well-known whisky bloggers, started, in alliance with Seth Klaskin, a new career as independent bottlers. The initial idea with Single Cask Nation somewhat reminds you of Scotch Malt Whisky Society in the sense that you have to become a member (for free) of the nation in order to buy the bottlings. In 2017, the owners decided to develop an alternative way of selling their products and launched a special range of whiskies that could also be found at retailers in a number of states in the USA. This new way of doing business proved succesful and since 2019 their products are available in

Europe and Canada as well. The 6th release of what they themselves call Single Cask Nation Retail Release in spring 2020 included Invergordon 26 year old, Aultmore 30 year old, Milk & Honey 2 year old and Ruadh Mhor 10 year old (peated Glenturret). In order to focus on the new task the owners have stopped arranging (at least for the time being) their popular events, Whisky Jewbilee, in New York, Chicago and Seattle.

Meadowside Blending

meadowsideblending.com

The company may be a newcomer to the family of independent bottlers but the founder certainly isn´t. Donald Hart, a Keeper of the Quaich and co-founder of the well-known bottler Hart Brothers, runs the Glasgow company together with his son, Andrew. There are four sides to the business – blends sold under the name The Royal Thistle, single malts labelled The Maltman, single cask single grains under the label The Grainman and Excalibur with deluxe blended whiskies. A fifth range was recently introduced - Vital Spark focusing on single malts with "a maritime twist".

Elixir Distillers

elixirdistillers.com

The company is owned by Sukhinder and Rajbir Singh, known by most for their three very well-stocked The Whisky Exchange shops in London as well as being the largest on-line retailer of Scotch whisky in the world. In the beginning of October every year, they are hosting The Whisky Show in London, one of the best whisky festivals in the world and for the last four years they have also been involved in the Old & Rare Show in Glasgow and, most recently, in London. In 2005 they started as independent bottlers of malt whiskies operating under the brand name The Single Malts of Scotland. There are around 50 bottlings on offer at any time, either as single casks or as batches bottled at cask strength or at 46%. In addition there are three subranges; Director´s Special which showcases exceptionally old and rare single malts selected by Sukhinder Singh, the accessible Reserve Cask range and the more mature Marriage of Casks.

In 2009 a new range of Islay single malts under the name Port Askaig was introduced. The current range (with limited releases occuring regularly) consists of 100° Proof, 8, 12, 28 and 45 year old. Elements of Islay, a series of cask strength single malts in which all Islay distilleries are, or will be, represented was introduced a few years before Port Askaig. The list of the product range is cleverly constructed with periodical tables in mind in which each distillery has a two-letter acronym followed by a batch number. Two core blended malts, Peat and Peat Full Proof, were released a few years ago but the emphasis is on single malts where the most recent bottlings include Ar_{11}, Bw_8, and Cl_{13}. In 2019, a new range of single casks, single malts, blends or single grain, was introduced. The first release of Whisky Trail was made up of 8 bottles with ages ranging from 9 to 44 years. Sukhinder Singh also has plans to build a whisky distillery on Islay on the outskirts of Port Ellen and at the time of writing he is waiting for a planning approval from the local council.

Port Askaig 12 year old Spring Edition 2020, 45,8%

Nose: Savoury and salty with notes of salami, burnt wood, raw artichoke, celery and green apples.

Palate: A nice texture with notes of peaches and plums, butterscotch, liquorice, lemon tart, mint and a hint of pepper.

Single Malts of Scotland Clynelish 8 year old, 48%
Nose: Charming with icecream made of pears, cut grass, French nougat, heather and thyme.
Palate: Nice and oily, more of the pears but also liquroice pannacotta topped with blueberry jam, digestive and honey. A herbal and peppery finish.

The Ultimate Whisky Company

ultimatewhisky.com

Founded in 1994 by Han van Wees and his son Maurice, this Dutch independent bottler has until now bottled close to 1,000 single malts. All whiskies are un chill-filtered, without colouring and bottled at either 46% or cask strength. The van Wees family also operate one of the finest spirits shops in Europe - Van Wees Whisky World in Amersfoort - with i.a. more than 1,000 different whiskies including more than 500 single malts.

The Vintage Malt Whisky Company

vintagemaltwhisky.com

Founded in 1992 by Brian Crook, the company today is run by his three children, Andrew, Caroline and Kim, supplying whisky to more than 35 countries. The company also owns and operates a sister company called The Highlands & Islands Scotch Whisky Co. In 2018, they acquired a former factory in Port Ellen on Islay where they hope to eventually distill a range of Islay based spirits. The most famous brands in the range are two single Islay malts called Finlaggan and The Ileach. The latter comes in two versions, bottled at 40% and 58%. The Finlaggan range consists of Old Reserve, Eilean Mor, Port Finish, Sherry Finish, Cask Strength (58%) and Red Wine Cask Matured. In 2020, the owners will also add Finlaggan Single Cask Releases. Other expressions in the company´s range are Islay Storm, the blended malts Smokestack, Glenalmond and Black Cuillin and, not least, a wide range of single cask single malts under the name The Cooper´s Choice. They are bottled at 46% or at cask strength and are all non coloured and non chill-filtered.

Finlaggan Cask Strength, 58%
Nose: Fresh, tarry smoke with notes of heather, citrus, artichoke and minerals. Slightly buttery.
Palate: Starts on a sweet honey note and expands into bonfire smoke, barbecued fish, vanilla, green apples and bay leaf.

The Cooper´s Choice Girvan 1992 26 years old, 57%
Nose: Lovely and floral with notes of lilac, rose petals, coconut, arrak and lemon drops.
Palate: Sweet with notes of ripe melon, banana, honey, lemon meringue, nutmeg and a hint of pepper in the finish.

Svenska Eldvatten

eldvatten.se

Founded in 2011 and since the start, more than 100 single casks, bottled at cask strength, have been released. In their range of spirits they have aged tequila and rum and they have also launched their own rum, WeiRon, as well as gin and aquavit. A new, limited range called Silent Swede was launched in 2018. The seven expressions all came from the closed Swedish distillery Grythyttan. Svenska Eldvatten are also importers to Sweden of whisky from Murray McDavid, AD Rattray, North Star Spirits, Sansibar, Hidden Spirits, Claxton´s, Single Cask Nation and, most recently, Spey Whisky.

Wm Cadenhead & Co

cadenhead.scot

Established in 1842 and owned by J & A Mitchell since 1972. The current range consists of Authentic Collection (single cask cask strength whiskies, exclusively sold in their own shops), World Whiskies (single malts from non Scottish distillers as well as from Scottish grain distillers) and Small Batch, a range which can be divided into three separate ranges; Single Cask (single casks bottled at cask strength), Small Batch Cask Strength (2-4 casks of whisky from the same vintage, bottled at cask strength) and Small Batch 46% (same as the previous but diluted to 46%). A fourth range is William Cadenhead Range, which consists of blended whisky as well as single malts from undisclosed distilleries. There are nine dedicated Cadenhead´s Whisky Shops in Europe.

Adelphi Distillery

adelphidistillery.com

Named after a distillery which closed in 1902, the company offers a range of single malts every year where the whiskies are always bottled at cask strength. There are also two recurrent brands, Fascadale and Liddesdale, where the single malt differs from batch to batch. In 2015, the first two bottlings of a new brand saw the light of day. Together with Fusion Whisky, Adelphi launched The Glover – a unique vatting of single malt from the closed Japanese distillery Hanyu and two Scottish single malts, Longmorn and Glen Garioch. This was followed by The Kincardine and the E&K where Amrut single malt from India was blended with Scotch malt whisky, The Brisbane, a combination of Starward single malt from Australia and Glen Garioch and Glen Grant and The Winter Queen where malt whisky from Zuidam distillery in the Netherlands had been blended with Longmorn and Glenrothes. In 2020, Glover Batch 5 was released which was an exciting blend of two casks from Chichibu distillery in Japan and two of Ardnamurchan´s (owned by Adelphi) own casks – all four of them ex-bourbon. Since 2014, Adelphi is also operating its own distillery in Glenbeg on the Ardnamurchan peninsula. Since the opening, the owners have regularly released malt spirit (less than 3 years old) but in October 2020 the first single malt whisky from the distillery was released.

The Glover batch 5, 4 years old, 54,7%
Nose: Charming and citrusy with both tropical and green/grassy notes, almonds, melon, Band-Aid and olive oil.
Palate: Quite dry with a great, oily mouthfeel and good balance. Citrus fruits, fennel and a distant, seaweedy smoke.

Kilchard, 50%
Nose: Warm, smoky and earthy with notes of garden fruit, sea shore and burnt wood.
Palate: Quite smoky with notes of dried fruits and raisins, chocolate chips, leather and salted caramel

Deerstalker Whisky Co

deerstalkerwhisky.com

The Deerstalker brand, which dates from 1880 was originally owned by J.G. Thomson & Co of Leith and subsequently Tennent Caledonian Breweries. It was purchased by Glasgow based Aberko Ltd in 1994 and is managed by former Tennent's Export Director Paul Aston. The Deerstalker range covers single malts as well as blended malt whiskies. Currently there is only one single malt, a 12 year old, and two blended malts - a Peated Edition and a Highland Edition.

Morrison & MacKay Whisky

mandmwhisky.co.uk

An independent bottler with plenty of experience in the company. The Morrison part of the business name is represented by Brian Morrison (as well as his son Jamie) who´s father was the legendary Stanley P Morrison, founder of Morrison Bowmore Distilleries. After leaving Morrison Bowmore, Brian started the Scottish Liqueur Centre and this business has been expanded to also include malt whisky under the name Carn Mor. Currently there are three ranges; Carn Mor Strictly Limited, usually bottled at 46%, Celebration of the Cask which are single casks bottled at cask strength and Celebration of the Cask Black Gold with heavily sherried whiskies in focus. A fourth range of blended malts is called Old Perth.

Edinburgh Whisky Ltd.

edinburghwhisky.com

Two friends, Gordon Watt, a former sales director at Moët Hennessy and Gregor Mathieson with a background in the wine business and partner in the Michelin awarded Andrew Fairlie restaurant at Gleneagles, founded the company in 2013. They were later joined by Iain Hamilton. Single malt single casks are bottled under the name The Library Collection while small batch blended malts are sold under the name New Town. These two were later joined by a third range of blended malts called Whisky Row with Smoke and Peat, Rich and Spicy and Smooth and Sweet.

Sansibar Whisky

sansibar-whisky.com

Started in 2012, this was the brainchild of the current majority owner and CEO Jens Drewitz and Carsten Ehrlich, the organizer of the famous Whisky Fair Limburg. Their idea was to create a range of high quality single malts from Scotland and to market them in connection with the well known Sansibar restaurant on the island of Sylt in northern Germany. Around 60 bottlings are produced per year and the range also includes rum.

Dramfool

dramfool.com

Bruce Farquhar, a whisky fan and collector for 20 years, decided in 2015 to start as an independent bottler. He sources his whisky from private individuals as well as from brokers and has so far released around 30 different bottlings with Lochindaal 10 year old and Illegal Shipyard Riot 13 year old which comes from an undisclosed Islay distillery, as two of the most recent.

Angel´s Nectar

angelsnectar.co.uk

For ten years Robert Ransom worked as the sales and marketing director at Glenfarclas. He left in 2014 and founded Highfern Ltd. There are two main products split into two versions of each; Angel´s Nectar Blended Malt Original and Rich Peat Edition as well as Angel´s Nectar Single Malt Islay Edition and Cairngorms Edition. Highfern is also the UK importer for Smögen single malt and gin and Langatun Swiss single malt.

The Single Cask Ltd

thesinglecask.co.uk

Founded by Ben Curtis who was distributor for a number of Scottish distilleries in south-east Asia before he started as an independent bottler in Singapore in 2010. Since then he has moved back to the UK but the company still runs an impressive whisky bar in Singapore. The bottling side of the business has grown over the years and the brand is now sold in the UK, Europe and Asia. The company also acts as a broker selling casks with both newmake and maturing whisky. A nice feature on their website is a very well written and informative blog.

Selected Malts

selectedmalts.se

A new bottler from Sweden, founded in 2017. Until now, they have specialised in fairly young single malts but with a maturation story that stands out from the ordinary. In 2019, they released their own blended malt, Zippin, which was made up by malts from Tullibardine, Glen Ord, Macduff and Ardmore (peated). They also recently acquired the distribution rights for GlenAllachie in Sweden. The last year, the company has expanded the business into selling casks to private customers.

The Alistair Walker Whisky Co.

alistairwalkerwhisky.com

Alistair Walker, from the Walker family who used to own Ben-Riach, GlenDronach and Glenglassaugh, has spent almost twenty years in the whisky business. When the family sold the distilleries in 2016, he started thinking about what to do next and decided to start up as an independent bottler. The brand is called Infrequent Flyers and the first releases (nine single casks) appeared in August 2019 with a second batch being launched in October..

Skene Scotch Whisky

skenewhisky.com

Founded in 2014 and based in Edinburgh. One of Andrew Skene´s ranges is called Skene Reserve with single cask single malts aged 20 years or more. Younger single casks are sold under the Cask Classics label and finally there is Black Tartan with a blended malt at its core but also blended-at-birth single cask bottlings.

Watt Whisky

wattwhisky.com

When Mark Watt left Cadenheads he decided to start a company of his own together with his wife Kate who has a background working for both Springbank and Glenfarclas. Their philosphy is to mainly bottle single malt Scotch at cask strength and without colouring or chill filtration. The first bottlings to appear in September 2020 were Mannochmore 2008, Caol Ila 2009, Blended Malt 2001, Highland Malt (Clynelish) 2000 and Traveller´s Rum Belize 2007.

The Whisky Baron

thewhiskybaron.co.uk

Jake Sharpe began the business trading casks and eventually started to sell bottled single cask malt to private customers. Some of the latest bottlings include a Glentauchers 22 year old and a Bunnahabhain 16 year old, both bourbonmatured and also a 26 year old Springbank from a first fill sherry butt. An interesting feature is the way Sharpe uses AR technicue (augmented reality). Download an app, scan the label with your phone and The Whisky Baron will become "alive" to tell you stories about the particular whisky.

Lady of the Glen

ladyoftheglen.com

Founded by Gregor Hannah in 2012, the company bottles single cask malts with some of the latest releases being Caperdonich 1997, Jura 1992, a heavily peated Lochindaal 2009 and a Tomintoul 2005 with a 13 months finish in amontillado sherry.

The Islay Boys

islayboys.com

Mackay Smith and Donald MacKenzie are both Islay born and bred and in 2018 they bought the Islay Ales Brewery. Soon after they started as whisky bottlers and at the moment their range consists of Bårelegs single malt (one islay and one Highland) and Flatnöse blended malt and blended Scotch. They are working on moving the brewery to Glenegedale and also integrate a rum- and whisky distillery.

Whisky
shops

AUSTRALIA
The Odd Whisky Coy
25 Anzac Ridge Road, Bridgewater,
SA, 5155
Phone: +61 (0)417 852 296
www.theoddwhiskycoy.com.au
On-line whisky specialist with an
impressive range. Agents for brands such
as Springbank, Benromach and Berry
Brothers and arrange recurrent seminars.

World of Whisky
Shop G12, Cosmopolitan Centre
2-22 Knox Street, Double Bay NSW 2028
Phone: +61 (0)2 9363 4212
www.worldofwhisky.com.au
A whisky specialist which offers a range
of 400 different expressions, most of them
single malts. The shop is also organising
and hosting regular tastings.

The Whisky Company
162 A Fortescue Av., Seaford, VIC, 3198
Phone: +61 (0)434 438 617
www.thewhiskycompany.com.au
One of the largest on-line retailers of
single malt whisky in Australia with
around 500 products currently in stock.

My Bottle Shop
34D Fitzroy St., Marrickville, NSW, 2204
Phone: +61 (0)2 9516 3816
www.mybottleshop.com.au
More than 2,000 whiskies with some of
them being sourced directly from the
suppliers on demand. On-line only.

The Oak Barrel
152 Elizabeh St, Sydney, NSW, 2000
Phone: +61 (0)2 9264 3022
www.oakbarrel.com.au
They have a nice range of 350 different
Scotch whiskies but it is the range of
Australian whiskies (145) that impresses
the most. Wine, beer, cider and other
spirits as well.

AUSTRIA
Potstill
Laudongasse 18, 1080 Wien
Phone: +43 (0)664 118 85 41
www.potstill.org
Austria's premier whisky shop with over
1100 different single malts, including
some real rarities. Shipping within Austria
and to non-EC countries.

Cadenhead Austria
Döblinger Hauptstraße 32, 1190 Wien
Phone: +43 (0)677 622 476 40
www.cadenhead-vienna.at
Focusing on the Cadenhead range but with

a wide range of other whiskies and spirits
as well.

Pinkernells Whisky Market
Alter Markt 1, 5020 Salzburg
Phone: +43 (0)662 84 53 05
www.pinkernells.at
More than 500 whiskies are on offer and
they are also importers of Maltbarn, The
Whisky Chamber and Jack Wiebers.

BELGIUM
Whiskycorner
Kraaistraat 16, 3530 Houthalen
Phone: +32 (0)89 386233
www.whiskycorner.be
A very large selection of single malts,
more than 2000 different. Also other
whiskies, calvados and grappas.

Jurgen´s Whiskyhuis
Gaverland 70, 9620 Zottegem
Phone: +32 (0)9 336 51 06
www.whiskyhuis.be
A huge assortment of more than 2000
different single malts. Also a good range
of grain whiskies and bourbons.

Huis Crombé
Doenaertstraat 20, 8510 Marke
Phone: +32 (0)56 21 19 87
www.crombewines.com
A wine retailer which also covers all kinds
of spirits. A large assortment of Scotch is
supplemented with whiskies from Japan,
the USA and Ireland to mention a few.

We Are Whisky
Avenue Rodolphe Gossia 33
1350 Orp-Jauche
Phone: +32 (0)471 134556
www.wearewhisky.com
On-line retailer with a range of more than
800 different whiskies. They also arrange
3-4 tastings every month.

Dram 242
Rijgerstraat 60, 9310 Moorsel
Phone: +32 (0)477 26 09 93
www.dram242.be
A wide range of whiskies. Apart from
the core official bottlings, they have
focused on rare, old expressions as well as
whiskies from small, independent bottlers.

CANADA
Kensington Wine Market
1257 Kensington Road NW
Calgary, Alberta T2N 3P8
Phone: +1 403 283 8000
www.kensingtonwinemarket.com
The shop has a very large range of

whiskies (more than 1500) as well as other
spirits and wines. More than 80 tastings in
the shop every year. Also the home of the
Scotch Malt Whisky Society in Canada.

World of Whisky
Unit 240, 333 5 Avenue SW
Calgary, Alberta T2P 3B6
Phone: +1 587 956 8511
www.coopwinespiritsbeer.com/stores/
world-of-whisky/
Specialising in whisky from all corners of
the world. Currently there are over 1100
different whiskies in the range including
some extremely rare ones from Scotland.

DENMARK
Juul´s Vin & Spiritus
Værnedamsvej 15
1819 Frederiksberg
Phone: +45 33 31 13 29
www.juuls.dk
A very large range of wines, fortified
wines and spirits with more than 1100
different whiskies (800 single malts).

Cadenhead´s WhiskyShop Denmark
Kongensgade 69 F
5000 Odense C
Phone: +45 66 13 95 05
www.cadenheads.dk
Whisky specialist with a very good range,
not least from Cadenhead's. Nice range
of champagne, cognac and rum. Arranges
whisky and beer tastings. On-line ordering.

Whisky.dk
Vejstruprødvej 15
6093 Sjølund
Phone: +45 5210 6093
www.whisky.dk
Henrik Olsen and Ulrik Bertelsen are
well-known in Denmark for their whisky
shows but they also run an on-line spirits
shop with an emphasis on whisky but also
including an impressive stock of rums.

ENGLAND
The Whisky Exchange
2 Bedford Street, Covent Garden
London WC2E 9HH
Phone: +44 (0)20 7100 0088
90-92 Great Portland Street, Fitzrovia
London W1W 7NT
Phone: +44 (0)20 7100 9888
88 Borough High Street, London Bridge
London SE1 1LL
Phone: +44 (0)20 7631 3888
www.thewhiskyexchange.com
An excellent whisky shop owned by

Sukhinder Singh. Started off as a mail order business, run from a showroom in Hanwell, but later opened up at Vinopolis in downtown London. Moved to a new and bigger location in Covent Garden a couple of years ago and have since then opened two more shops. The assortment is huge with well over 1000 single malts to choose from. Some rarities which can hardly be found anywhere else are offered thanks to Singh's great interest for antique whisky. There are also other types of whisky and cognac, calvados, rum etc. On-line ordering and ships all over the world.

The Whisky Shop
(See also Scotland, The Whisky Shop)
11 Coppergate Walk
York YO1 9NT
Phone: +44 (0)1904 640300

510 Brompton Walk
Lakeside Shopping Centre
Thurrock Grays, Essex RM20 2ZL
Phone: +44 (0)1708 866255

7 Turl Street
Oxford OX1 3DQ
Phone: +44 (0)1865 202279

3 Swan Lane
Norwich NR2 1HZ
Phone: +44 (0)1603 618284

70 Piccadilly
London W1J 8HP
Phone: +44 (0)207 499 6649

Unit 7 Queens Head Passage
Paternoster
London EC4M 7DZ
Phone: +44 (0)207 329 5117

3 Exchange St
Manchester M2 7EE
Phone: +44 (0)161 832 6110

25 Chapel Street
Guildford GU1 3UL
Phone: +44 (0)1483 450900

Unit 9 Great Western Arcade
Birmingham B2 5HU
Phone: +44 (0)121 233 4416

64 East Street
Brighton BN1 1HQ
Phone: +44 (0)1273 327 962

3 Cheapside
Nottingham NG1 2HU
Phone: +44 (0)115 958 7080

9-10 High Street
Bath BA1 5AQ
Phone: +44 (0)1225 423 535

Unit 1/9 Red Mall,
Intu Metro Centre
Gateshead NE11 9YP
Phone: +44 (0)191 460 3777

Unit 201 Trentham Gardens
Stoke on Trent ST4 8AX
Phone: +44 (0)1782 644 483
www.whiskyshop.com
The largest specialist retailer of whiskies in the UK with 20 outlets. A large product range with over 700 kinds, including 400 malt whiskies and 140 miniature bottles, as well as accessories and books. They also run The W Club, the leading whisky club

in the UK where the excellent Whiskeria magazine is one of the member´s benefits. Shipping all over the world.

Royal Mile Whiskies
3 Bloomsbury Street
London WC1B 3QE
Phone: +44 (0)20 7436 4763
www.royalmilewhiskies.com
The London branch of Royal Mile Whiskies. See also Scotland, Royal Mile Whiskies.

Berry Bros. & Rudd
63 Pall Mall, London SW1Y 5HZ
Phone: +44 (0)800 280 2440
www.bbr.com/whisky
A legendary company that recently opned a new shop in Pall Mall. One of the world's most reputable wine shops but with an exclusive selection of malt whiskies, some of them bottled by Berry Bros. themselves.

The Wright Wine & Whisky Company
The Old Smithy, Raikes Road, Skipton, North Yorkshire BD23 1NP
Phone: +44 (0)1756 700886
www.wineandwhisky.co.uk
An eclectic selection of near to 1000 different whiskies. 'Tasting Cupboard' of nearly 100 opened bottles for sampling with regular hosted tasting evenings. Great 'Collector to Collector' selection of old whiskies plus a fantastic choice of 1200+ wines, premium spirits and liqueurs.

Master of Malt
Unit 1, Ton Business Park, 2-8 Morley Rd.
Tonbridge, Kent, TN9 1RA
Phone: 0800 5200 474
www.masterofmalt.com
Online retailer and independent bottler with a very impressive range of more than 2,500 whiskies, including over 2,000 Scotch whiskies and over 1,500 single malts. In addition to whisky there is an enormous selection of gins, rums, cognacs, armagnacs, tequilas and more. The website contains a wealth of information and news about the distilleries and innovative personalised gift ideas. Drinks by the Dram 30ml samples of more than 3,300 different whiskies are available also they also offer the Dram Club monthly whisky subscription service, as well as a Blend Your Own option, personalised whisky and has a gift finder to help with special occassions.

Whiskys.co.uk
The Square, Stamford Bridge
York YO4 11AG
Phone: +44 (0)1759 371356
www.whiskys.co.uk
Good assortment with more than 600 different whiskies. Also a nice range of armagnac, rum, calvados etc. The owners also have another website, www.whiskymerchants.co.uk with a huge amount of information on just about every whisky distillery in the world.

The Wee Dram
5 Portland Square, Bakewell
Derbyshire DE45 1HA
Phone: +44 (0)1629 812235
www.weedram.co.uk

Large range of Scotch single malts with whiskies from other parts of the world and a good range of whisky books. Run 'The Wee Drammers Whisky Club' with tastings and seminars. End of October they arrange the yearly Wee Dram Fest whisky festival.

Hard To Find Whisky
1 Spencer Street, Birmingham B18 6DD
Phone: +44 (0)121 448 84 84
www.htfw.com
As the name says, this family owned shop specialises in rare, collectable and new releases of single malt whisky. The range is astounding - more than 3,000 different bottlings including no less than 465 different Macallan. World wide shipping.

Nickolls & Perks
37 Lower High Street, Stourbridge
West Midlands DY8 1TA
Phone: +44 (0)1384 394518
www.nickollsandperks.co.uk
Mostly known as wine merchants but also has a huge range of whiskies with 1,900 different kinds including 1,300 single malts. Since 2011, they also organize the acclaimed Midlands Whisky Festival, see www.whiskyfest.co.uk

Gauntleys of Nottingham
4 High Street, Nottingham NG1 2ET
Phone: +44 (0)115 9110555
www.gauntleys.com
A fine wine merchant established in 1880. The range of wines are among the best in the UK. All kinds of spirits, not least whisky, are taking up more and more space and several rare malts can be found.

Hedonism Wines
3-7 Davies St., London W1K 3LD
Phone: +44 (020) 729 078 70
www.hedonism.co.uk
Located in the heart of London, this is a temple for wine lovers but also with an impressive range of whiskies. They have over 1,200 different bottlings from Scotland and the rest of the world.

The Lincoln Whisky Shop
87 Bailgate, Lincoln LN1 3AR
Phone: +44 (0)1522 537834
www.lincolnwhiskyshop.co.uk
Mainly specialising in whisky with more than 300 different whiskies but also 500 spirits and liqueurs. Mailorder worldwide.

Milroys of Soho
3 Greek Street, London W1D 4NX
Phone: +44 (0)207 734 2277
shop.milroys.co.uk
A classic whisky shop in Soho with a very good range with over 700 malts and a wide selection of whiskies from around the world. Also a whisky bar within the shop.

Arkwrights
114 The Dormers
Highworth
Wiltshire SN6 7PE
Phone: +44 (0)1793 765071
www.whiskyandwines.com
A good range of whiskies (over 700 in stock) as well as wine and other spirits. Regular tastings in the shop. On-line ordering with shipping all over the world.

Edencroft Fine Wines
8-10 Hospital Street, Nantwich
Cheshire, CW5 5RJ
Phone: +44 (0)1270 629975
www.edencroft.co.uk
Family owned wine and spirits shop since
1994. Around 250 whiskies and also a
nice range of gin, cognac and other spirits
including cigars. Worldwide shipping.

Cadenhead´s Whisky Shop
26 Chiltern Street, London W1U 7QF
Phone: +44 (0)20 7935 6999
www.whiskytastingroom.com
One in a chain of shops owned by
independent bottlers Cadenhead. Sells
Cadenhead's product range and c. 200
other whiskies. Regular tastings.

Constantine Stores
30 Fore Street, Constantine, Falmouth
Cornwall TR11 5AB
Phone: +44 (0)1326 340226
www.drinkfinder.co.uk
A full-range wine and spirits dealer with a
good selection of whiskies from the whole
world (around 800 different, of which 600
are single malts). Worldwide shipping.

House of Malt
48 Warwick Road, Carlisle CA1 1DN
Phone: +44 (0)1228 658 422
www.houseofmalt.co.uk
A wide selection of whiskies from
Scotland and the world as well as other
spirits and craft ales. Regular tasting
evenings and events.

The Vintage House
42 Old Compton Street
London W1D 4LR
Phone: +44 (0)20 7437 2592
www.vintagehouse.london
A huge range of 1400 kinds of malt
whisky, many of them rare. Supplementing this is also a selection of fine wines.

Whisky On-line
Units 1-3 Concorde House, Charnley
Road, Blackpool, Lancashire FY1 4PE
Phone: +44 (0)1253 620376
www.whisky-online.com
A good selection of whisky and also
cognac, rum, port etc. Specializes in rare
whiskies and hold regular auctions.

FRANCE
La Maison du Whisky
20 rue d´Anjou
75008 Paris
Phone: +33 (0)1 42 65 03 16

6 carrefour d l´Odéon
75006 Paris
Phone: +33 (0)1 46 34 70 20

(1 shop outside France)
The Pier at Robertson Quay
80 Mohamed Sultan Road, #01-10
Singapore 239013
Phone: +65 6733 0059
www.whisky.fr
France's largest whisky specialist with
over 1200 whiskies in stock. Also a
number of own-bottled single malts. La
Maison du Whisky acts as a EU distributor
for many whisky producers around the

world. Also run the Golden Promise
whisky bar in rue Tiquetonne in Paris.

The Whisky Shop
7 Place de la Madeleine, 75008 Paris
Phone: +33 (0)1 45 22 29 77
www.whiskyshop.fr
The large chain of whisky shops in the UK
has now opened up a store in Paris as well.

GERMANY
Celtic Whisk(e)y & Versand
Otto Steudel
Bulmannstrasse 26, 90459 Nürnberg
Phone: +49 (0)911 45097430
www.celtic-whisky.de
A very impressive single malt range with
well over 1000 different single malts and
a good selection from other parts of the
world.

SCOMA
Am Bullhamm 17, 26441 Jever
Phone: +49 (0)4461 912237
www.scoma.de
Very large range of c 750 Scottish malts
and many from other countries. Holds
regular seminars and tastings. The
excellent, monthly whisky newsletter
SCOMA News is produced and can be
downloaded as a pdf-file from the website.

The Whisky Store
Am Grundwassersee 4, 82402 Seeshaupt
Phone: +49 (0)8801 30 20 000
www.whisky.de
A very large range comprising c 700
kinds of whisky of which 550 are malts.
Also sells whisky liqueurs, books and
accessories. The website is a goldmine of
information, in particular the videos with
Horst and Ben Luening which are mainly
in German but many English versions are
easily found on Youtube.

Cadenhead´s Whisky Market
Luxemburger Strasse 257, 50939 Köln
Phone: +49 (0)221-2831834
www.cadenheads.de
Good range of malt whiskies (c 350
different kinds) with emphasis on
Cadenhead's own bottlings. Other
products include wine, cognac and rum
etc. Arranges recurring tastings and also
has an on-line shop.

Pinkernells Whisky Market
Boxhagener Straße 36, 10245 Berlin
Phone: +49 (0)30-308 314 44
www.pinkernells.de
An extensive range of whiskies (more
than 700) and they arrange 4-5 tastings
monthly. Also work as whisky consultants
doing corporate events all over Germany.

Home of Malts
Hosegstieg 11, 22880 Wedel
Phone: +49 (0)4103 965 9695
www.homeofmalts.com
Large assortment with over 800 different
single malts as well as whiskies from
many other countries. Also a nice selection
of cognac, rum etc. On-line ordering.

Reifferscheid
Mainzer Strasse 186, 53179 Bonn
Phone: +49 (0)228 9 53 80 71
www.whisky-bonn.de
A well-stocked shop with a large range of
whiskies, wine, spirit, cigars and a delicatessen. Regular tastings.

Whisky-Doris
Germanenstrasse 38, 14612 Falkensee
Phone: +49 (0)3322-219784
www.whisky-doris.de
Large range of over 300 whiskies and also
sells own special bottlings. Orders via
email. Shipping also outside Germany.

Finlays Whisky Shop
Hohenzollernstr. 88, 80796 München
Phone: +49 (0)89 3270 979 140
www.finlayswhiskyshop.de
Whisky specialists with a large range of
over 1,200 whiskies. Finlays also work
as the importer of Douglas Laing, James
MacArthur and Wilson & Morgan.

Weinquelle Lühmann
Lübeckerstrasse 145, 22087 Hamburg
Phone: +49 (0)40 300 672 950

Jacobsrade 65, 22962 Siek (showroom)
Phone: +49 (0)4107 908 900
www.weinquelle.com
An impressive selection of both wines and
spirits with over 1000 different whiskies
of which 850 are malt whiskies. Also an
impressive range of rums.

The Whisky-Corner
Reichertsfeld 2, 92278 Illschwang
Phone: +49 (0)9666-951213
www.whisky-corner.de
A small shop but large on mail order.
A very large assortment of over 2000
whiskies. Also sells blended and American
whiskies. The website is very informative
with features on, among others, whisky-
making, tasting and independent bottlers.

World Wide Spirits
Hauptstrasse 12, 84576 Teising
Phone: +49 (0)8633 50 87 93
www.worldwidespirits.de
A nice range of more than 1,000 whiskies
with some rarities from the twenties. Also
large selection of other spirits.

WhiskyKoch
Weinbergstrasse 2, 64285 Darmstadt
Phone: +49 (0)6151 96 96 886
www.whiskykoch.de
A combination of a whisky shop and
restaurant. The shop has a nice selection
of single malts as well as other Scottish
products and the restaurant has specialised
in whisky dinners and tastings.

Kierzek
Weitlingstrasse 17, 10317 Berlin
Phone: +49 (0)30 525 11 08
www.kierzek-berlin.de
Over 400 different whiskies in stock. In
the product range 50 kinds of rum and
450 wines from all over the world are
found among other products. Mail order
is available.

HUNGARY

Whisky Shop Budapest
Veres Pálné utca 7., 1053 Budapest
Phone: +36 1 267-1588
www.whiskynet.hu
www.whiskyshop.hu
Largest selection of whisky in Hungary.
More than 900 different whiskies from all
over the world. Even Hungarian whisky
and a large selection of other fine spirits
are available. Most of them can be tasted
in the GoodSpirit Whisky & Cocktail Bar
which operates in the same venue.

IRELAND

Celtic Whiskey Shop
27-28 Dawson Street, Dublin 2
Phone: +353 (0)1 675 9744
www.celticwhiskeyshop.com
More than 500 kinds of Irish whiskeys but
also a good selection of Scotch, wines and
other spirits. World wide shipping.

ITALY

Whisky Shop
by Milano Whisky Festival
Via Cavaleri 6, Milano
Phone: +39 (0)2 48753039
www.whiskyshop.it
The team behind the excellent
Milano Whisky Festival also have an on-
line whiskyshop with almost 500 different
single malts including several special
festival bottlings.

Whisky Antique S.R.L.
Via Giardini Sud, 41043 Formigine (MO)
Phone: +39 (0)59 574278
www.whiskyantique.com
Long-time whisky enthusiast and collector
Massimo Righi owns this shop specialising
in rare and collectable spirits – not only
whisky but also cognac, rum, armagnac
etc. He also acts as an independent bottler
with the brand Silver Seal. They are
importer for brands like Jack Wiebers, The
Whisky Agency and Perfect Dram.

JAPAN

Liquor Mountain Co.,Ltd.
4F Kyoto Kowa Bldg.
82 Tachiurinishi-Machi,
Takakura-Nishiiru,
Shijyo-Dori, Shimogyo-Ku,
Kyoto, 600-8007
Phone: +81 (0)75 213 8880
www.likaman.co.jp
The company has more than 150 shops
specialising in spirits, beer and food.
Around 20 of them are designated whisky
shops under the name Whisky Kingdom
(although they have a full range of other
spirits) with a range of 500 different whiskies. The three foremost shops are;

Rakzan Sanjyo Onmae
1-8, HigashiGekko-cho, Nishinokyo,
Nakagyo-ku, Kyoto-shi
Kyoto
Phone: +81 (0)75-842-5123

Nagakute
2-105, Ichigahora, Nagakute-shi
Aichi
Phone: +81 (0)561-64-3081

Kabukicho 1chome
1-2-16, Kabuki-cho, Shinjuku-ku
Tokyo
Phone: +81 (0)3-5287-2080

THE NETHERLANDS

Whiskyslijterij De Koning
Hinthamereinde 41
5211 PM 's Hertogenbosch
Phone: +31 (0)73-6143547
www.whiskykoning.nl
An enormous assortment with more than
1400 kinds of whisky including
c 800 single malts. Arranges recurring
tastings. On-line ordering. Shipping all
over the world.

Van Wees - Whiskyworld.nl
Leusderweg 260, 3817 KH Amersfoort
Phone: +31 (0)33-461 53 19
www.whiskyworld.nl
A very large range of 1000 whiskies
including over 500 single malts. Also have
their own range of bottlings (The Ultimate
Whisky Company). On-line ordering.

Wijnhandel van Zuylen
Loosduinse Hoofdplein 201
2553 CP Loosduinen (Den Haag)
Phone: +31 (0)70-397 1400
www.whiskyvanzuylen.nl
Excellent range of whiskies (circa 1100)
and wines. Email orders with shipping to
some ten European countries.

Wijnwinkel-Slijterij
Ton Overmars, Hoofddorpplein 11
1059 CV Amsterdam
Phone: +31 (0)20-615 71 42
www.tonovermars.nl
A very large assortment of wines, spirits
and beer which includes more than 400
single malts. Arranges recurring tastings.

Wijn & Whisky Schuur
Blankendalwei 4, 8629 EH Scharnegoutem
Phone: +31 (0)515-520706
www.wijnwhiskyschuur.nl
Large assortment with 1000 different
whiskies and a good range of other spirits
as well. Arranges recurring tastings.

**Wine and Whisky Specialist van der
Boog**
Prinses Irenelaan 359-361
2285 GA Rijswijk
Phone: +31 70 - 394 00 85
www.passionforwhisky.com
A very good range of almost 700 malt
whiskies (as well as a wide range of other
spirits). World wide shipping.

NEW ZEALAND

Whisky Galore
834 Colombo Street, Christchurch 8013
Phone: +64 (0) 800 944 759
www.whiskygalore.co.nz
The best whisky shop in New Zealand with
750 different whiskies, approximately
400 which are single malts. There is also

online mail-order with shipping all over
the world except USA and Canada. Owned
by Michael Fraser Milne who became a
Master of the Quaich in 2019.

POLAND

George Ballantine´s
Krucza str 47 A, Warsaw
Phone: +48 22 625 48 32

Pulawska str 22, Warsaw
Phone: +48 22 542 86 22

Marynarska str 15, Warsaw
Phone: +48 22 395 51 60

Zygmunta Vogla str 62, Warsaw
Phone: +48 22 395 51 64
www.sklep-ballantines.pl
A huge range of single malts and apart
from whisky there is a full range of
spirits and wines from all over the world.
Recurrent tastings and organiser of
Whisky Live Warsaw.

Dom Whisky
Wejherowska 67, Reda
Phone: +48 691 760 000, shop
Phone: +48 691 930 000, mailorder
www.sklep-domwhisky.pl
On-line retailer who recently opened
a shop in Reda. A very large range of
whiskies and other spirits. Organiser of a
whisky festival in Jastrzębia Góra.

RUSSIA

Whisky World Shop
9, Tverskoy Boulevard
123104 Moscow
Phone: +7 495 787 9150
www.whiskyworld.ru
Huge assortment with more than 1,000
different single malts. The range is
supplemented with a nice range of cognac,
armagnac, calvados, grappa and wines.

SCOTLAND

Gordon & MacPhail
58 - 60 South Street, Elgin
Moray IV30 1JY
Phone: +44 (0)1343 545110
www.gordonandmacphail.com
This legendary shop opened already in
1895 in Elgin. The owners are perhaps
the most well-known among independent
bottlers. The shop stocks more than 800
bottlings of whisky and more than 600
wines and there is also a delicatessen
counter with high-quality products.
Tastings are arranged in the shop and there
are shipping services within the UK and
overseas. The shop attracts visitors from
all over the world.

Royal Mile Whiskies (2 shops)
379 High Street, The Royal Mile
Edinburgh EH1 1PW
Phone: +44 (0)131 2253383

3 Bloomsbury Street
London WC1B 3QE
Phone: +44 (0)20 7436 4763
www.royalmilewhiskies.com
Royal Mile Whiskies is one of the most
well-known whisky retailers in the UK.
It was established in Edinburgh in 1991.

There is also a shop in London since 2002 and a cigar shop close to the Edinburgh shop. The whisky range is outstanding with many difficult to find elsewhere. They have a comprehensive site regarding information on regions, distilleries, production, tasting etc. Royal Mile Whiskies also arranges 'Whisky Fringe' in Edinburgh, a two-day whisky festival which takes place annually in mid August. On-line ordering with worldwide shipping.

The Whisky Shop
(See also England, The Whisky Shop)
Unit L2-02 Buchanan Galleries
220 Buchanan Street
Glasgow G1 2GF
Phone: +44 (0)141 331 0022
17 Bridge Street
Inverness IV1 1HD
Phone: +44 (0)1463 710525

93 High Street
Fort William PH33 6DG
Phone: +44 (0)1397 706164

52 George Street
Oban PA34 5SD
Phone: +44 (0)1631 570896

Unit 23 Waverley Mall
Waverley Bridge
Edinburgh EH1 1BQ
Phone: +44 (0)131 558 7563

28 Victoria Street
Edinburgh EH1 2JW
Phone: +44 (0)131 225 4666
www.whiskyshop.com
The first shop opened in 1992 in Edinburgh and this is now the United Kingdom's largest specialist retailer of whiskies with 20 outlets (plus one in Paris). A large product range with over 700 kinds, including 400 malt whiskies and 140 miniature bottles, as well as accessories and books. The own range 'Glenkeir Treasures' is a special assortment of selected malt whiskies. The also run The W Club, the leading whisky club in the UK where the excellent Whiskeria magazine is one of the member's benefits. On-line ordering.

The Scotch Malt Whisky Society
www.smws.com
A legendary society with more than 20 000 members worldwide, specialised in own bottlings of single cask Scotch whisky, releasing between 150 and 200 bottlings every year. Recently, the Society has also started bottling whisky from other parts of the world as well as gin, rum, armagnac and other spirits.

Whiskies of Scotland
36 Gordon Street
Huntly
Aberdeenshire AB54 8EQ
Phone: +44 (0) 1466 795 105
www.thespiritsembassy.com
Owned by independent bottler Duncan Taylor. In the assortment is of course the whole Duncan Taylor range but also a selection of their own single malt bottlings called Whiskies of Scotland. A total of almost 700 different expressions. On-line shop with shipping worldwide.

The Whisky Shop Dufftown
1 Fife Street, Dufftown
Moray AB55 4AL
Phone: +44 (0)1340 821097
www.whiskyshopdufftown.com
Whisky specialist in Dufftown in the heart of Speyside, wellknown to many of the Speyside festival visitors. More than 500 single malts as well as other whiskies. Arranges tastings as well as special events during the Festivals. On-line ordering.

Cadenhead's Whisky Shop
30-32 Union Street
Campbeltown PA28 6JA
Phone: +44 (0)1586 551710
www.cadenhead.scot
Part of the chain of shops owned by independent bottlers Cadenhead. Sells Cadenhead's products and other whiskies with a good range of Springbank. On-line ordering.

Cadenhead´s Whisky Shop
172 Canongate, Royal Mile
Edinburgh EH8 8DF
Phone: +44 (0)131 556 5864
www.cadenhead.scot
The oldest shop in the chain owned by Cadenhead. Sells Cadenhead's product range and a good selection of other whiskies and spirits. Recurrent tastings. On-line ordering.

The Good Spirits Co.
23 Bath Street, Glasgow G2 1HW
Phone: +44 (0)141 258 8427
www.thegoodspiritsco.com
A specialist spirits store selling whisky, bourbon, rum, vodka, tequila, gin, cognac and armagnac, liqueurs and other spirits. They also stock quality champagne, fortified wines and cigars. There are more than 300 single malts in the range as well as plenty of whiskies from the rest of the world.

A.D. Rattray´s Whisky Experience & Whisky Shop
32 Main Road, Kirkoswald
Ayrshire KA19 8HY
Phone: +44 (0) 1655 760308
www.adrattray.com
Recently revamped, this is a combination of whisky shop, sample room and educational center owned by the independent bottler A D Rattray. A wide range of whiskies and tasting menus with different themes are also available.

Loch Fyne Whiskies
Main Street, Inveraray, Argyll PA32 8UD
Phone: +44 (0)149 930 2219

36 Cockburn St
Edinburgh EH1 1PB
Phone: +44 (0)131 226 2134
www.lochfynewhiskies.com
A legendary shop and with a second shop in Edinburgh since 2018. The range of malt whiskies is large and they have their own house blend, the prize-awarded Loch Fyne, as well as their 'The Loch Fyne Whisky Liqueur'. There is also a range of house malts called 'The Inverarity'. On-line ordering with worldwide shipping.

The Carnegie Whisky Cellars
The Carnegie Courthouse, Castle Street
IV25 3SD Dornoch
Phone: +44 (0)1862 811791
www.thecarnegiecourthouse.co.uk/whisky-cellars/
Opened by Michael Hanratty in 2016, this shop has already become a destination for whisky enthusiasts from the UK and abroad. The interior of the shop is ravishing and the extensive range includes all the latest releases as well as rare and collectable bottles. International shipping.

Abbey Whisky
Dunfermline KY11 3BZ
Phone: +44 (0)800 051 7737
www.abbeywhisky.com
Family run online whisky shop specialising in exclusive, rare and old whiskies from Scotland and the world. Apart from a wide range of official and independent bottlings, Abbey Whisky also selects their own casks and bottle them under the name 'The Rare Casks' and 'The Secret Casks'.

The Scotch Whisky Experience
354 Castlehill, Royal Mile
Edinburgh EH1 2NE
Phone: +44 (0)131 220 0441
www.scotchwhiskyexperience.co.uk
The Scotch Whisky Experience is a must for whisky devotees visiting Edinburgh with an interactive visitor centre dedicated to the history of Scotch whisky. This five-star visitor attraction has an excellent whisky shop with almost 300 different whiskies in stock. Following an extensive refurbishment, a brand new and interactive shop has been opened.

Tyndrum Whisky
Tyndrum, Perthshire FK20 8RY
Phone: +44 (0)1301 702 084
www.tyndrumwhisky.com
The new name for Whisky Galore at The Green Welly Stop. It was established at a road junction between Glencoe and The Trossachs 55 years ago and is now run by the third generation of the family. Well equipped with a nice range of Scottish single malts, grains and blends but also world whiskies and other spirits.

The Whisky Castle
6 Main Street, Tomintoul AB37 9EX
Phone: +44 (0)1807 580 213
www.whiskycastle.com
A legendary shop that has been selling whisky for more than 100 years. Specialises in single malts (more than 600) and single casks in particular. Also a range of whiskies bottled exclusively for The Whisky Castle. Worldwide shipping.

Whiski Shop
4 North Bank Street
Edinburgh EH1 2LP
Phone: +44 (0)131 225 7224
www.whiskishop.com
www.whiskirooms.co.uk
A new concept located near Edinburgh Castle, combining a shop and tasting room combined with a bar and restaurant in 119 High Street. Also regular whisky tastings. Online mail order.

Robbie's Drams
3 Sandgate, Ayr, South Ayrshire KA7 1BG
Phone: +44 (0)1292 262 135
www.robbieswhiskymerchants.com
An extensive range of whiskies available both in store and from their on-line shop. Specialists in single cask bottlings, closed distillery bottlings, rare malts, limited edition whisky and a nice range of their own bottlings. Worldwide shipping.

The Whisky Barrel
Unit 3, Cupar, KY15 5JY
Phone: +44 (0)845 2248 156
www.thewhiskybarrel.com
Online specialist whisky shop based in Edinburgh. They stock over 1,000 single malt and blended whiskies including Scotch, Japanese, Irish, Indian, Swedish and their own casks. Worldwide shipping.

Drinkmonger
100 Atholl Road, Pitlochry PH16 5BL
Phone: +44 (0)1796 470133

11 Bruntsfield Place
Edinburgh EH10 4HN
Phone: +44 (0)131 229 2205
www.drinkmonger.com
Owned by Royal Mile Whiskies, the idea is to have a 50:50 split between wine and specialist spirits with the addition of a cigar assortment. The whisky range is a good cross-section with some rarities and a focus on local distilleries.

Luvian's
93 Bonnygate, Cupar, Fife KY15 4LG
Phone: +44 (0)1334 654 820

66 Market Street, St Andrews
Fife KY16 9NU
Phone: +44 (0)1334 477752
www.luvians.com
A legendary wine and whisky retailer owned by the three Luvian brothers with a very nice selection of more than 1,200 whiskies (600 single malts).

The Stillroom by Deseo
Gleneagles Hotel
Auchterarder, Perthshire PH3 1NF
Phone: +44 (0) 1764 694 188
www.gleneagles.com
Located in the famous hotel, George Bryers has selected a nice range of both rare and collectible whiskies as well as single malts from a large number of Scottish distilleries.

Robertsons of Pitlochry
44-46 Atholl Road, Pitlochry PH16 5BX
Phone: +44 (0) 1796 472011
www.robertsonsofpitlochry.co.uk
With new owner since 2013, the shop has grown to become one of Scotland's best. An extensive range of both whisky and gin is complemented by single malts bottled under their own label. There's also an excellent tasting room (The Bothy).

Robert Graham Ltd (3 shops)
194 Rose Street
Edinburgh EH2 4AZ
Phone: +44 (0)131 226 1874

111 West George Street
Glasgow G2 1QX
Phone: +44 (0)141 248 7283

9 Sussex Street, Cambridge CB1 1PA
Phone: +44 (0)1223 354 459
www.robertgraham1874.com
Established in 1874 this company specialises in Scotch whisky and cigars. A nice assortment of malt whiskies is complemented by an impressive range of cigars. They also bottle whiskies under their own label.

The Speyside Whisky Shop
110A High Street
Aberlour AB38 9NX
Phone: +44 (0) 1340 871260
www.thespeysidewhisky.com
Opened in 2018, the shop is situated in the very heart of Speyside, in Aberlour. The owners specialise in highly collectable single malts from a variety of distilleries. Also a wide selection of craft gins.

The Jar
33 Ayr St
Troon KA10 6EB
Phone: +44 (0) 1292 319877
www.thejartroon.com
An extensive range of single malts (over 300) and Scottish gins. Specialises in rare and collectable releases.

Whisky Please
24 Heather Avenue, Glasgow G61 3JE
Phone: +44 (0)781 806 1010
www.whiskyplease.co.uk
Online retailer of whiskies and other spirits. A nice presentation of each distillery with a picture and text.

The Islay Whisky Shop
Shore Street, Bowmore, Islay PA43 7LB
Phone: +44 (0)1496 810 684
www.islaywhiskyshop.com
A must for any visitor to Islay, this shop has an impressive range of Islay whiskies, some of them very rare and limited.

Aberdeen Whisky Shop
474 Union Street, Aberdeen AB10 1TS
Phone: +44 (0)1224 647 433
www.aberdeenwhiskyshop.co.uk
A nice selection of whiskies but also other spirits. Free tastings in the shop every Saturday.

SOUTH AFRICA
WhiskyBrother
Shop 16 D Middle Mall,
Hyde Park Corner Shopping Centre,
Johannesburg
Phone: +27 (0)11 325 6261
www.whiskybrother.com
A shop specialising in all things whisky - apart from 400 different bottlings they also sell glasses, books etc. Also sell whiskies bottled exclusively for the shop. Regular tastings and online shop. Recently opened their own whisky bar in Johannesburg with more than 1,000 different whiskies to try. The owner, Marc Pendlebury, is also the organiser of The Only Whisky Show in Johannesburg and Cape Town.

SWITZERLAND
P. Ullrich AG
Schneidergasse 27
4051 Basel
Phone: +41 (0)61 338 90 91
Another two shops in Basel:
Laufenstrasse 16 and Unt. Rebgasse 18, one in Talacker 30 in Zürich and one in Kramgasse 45 in Bern.
www.ullrich.ch
A very large range of wines, spirits, beers, accessories and books. Over 800 kinds of whisky with almost 600 single malt. On-line ordering. Recently, they also founded a whisky club with regular tastings and offers. (www.whiskysinn.ch).

Eddie's Whiskies
Bahnhofstrasse/Dorfgasse 27
8810 Horgen
Phone: +41 (0)43 244 63 00
www.eddies.ch
A whisky specialist with more than 700 different whiskies in stock with emphasis on single malts (more than 500 different). Also arranges tastings.

Angels Share Shop
Unterdorfstrasse 15
5036 Oberentfelden
Phone: +41 (0)62 724 83 74
www.angelsshare.ch
A combined restaurant and whisky shop. More than 600 different kinds of whisky as well as a good range of cigars. Scores extra points for short information and photos of all distilleries. On-line ordering.

UKRAINE
WINETIME
Mykoly Bazhana 1E
Kyiv 02068
Phone: +38 (0)44 338 08 88
www.winetime.ua
WINETIME is the largest specialized chain of wine, spirits and food shops in Ukraine. The company runs 27 stores in 14 regions of Ukraine. An impressive selection of spirits with over 1000 whiskies of which 600 are malt whiskies. On-line ordering. Also regular whisky tastings.

USA
Binny's Beverage Depot
5100 W. Dempster (Head Office)
Skokie, IL 60077
Phone:
Internet orders, 888-942-9463 (toll free)
www.binnys.com
A chain of no less than 42 stores in the Chicago area, covering everything within wine and spirits. Some of the stores also have a gourmet grocery, cheese shop and, for cigar lovers, a walk-in humidor. Also lots of regular events in the stores. The range is impressive with more than 2200 whisk(e)y including 670 single malts, 440 bourbons, 240 rye and more. Among other products more than 600 kinds of tequila and mezcal, 550 vodkas, 480 rums and 260 gins.

Statistics

The information on the following pages is based
on figures from Scotch Whisky Association (SWA), Drinks International
and directly from the producers.

The Top 30 Whiskies of the World

Sales figures for 2019 (units in million 9-litre cases)

McDowell's No. 1 (Diageo/United Spirits), Indian whisky — 30,7
Officer's Choice (Allied Blenders & Distillers), Indian whisky — 30,6
Imperial Blue (Pernod Ricard), Indian whisky — 28,3
Royal Stag (Pernod Ricard), Indian whisky — 22,0
Johnnie Walker (Diageo), Scotch whisky — 18,4
Jack Daniel's (Brown-Forman), Tennessee whiskey — 13,4
Original Choice (John Distilleries), Indian whisky — 12,7
Golden Oak (Himalayan Distillery), Indian whisky — 10,6
Jim Beam (Beam Suntory), Bourbon — 10,4
Hayward's Fine (Diageo/United Spirits), Indian whisky — 9,6
Jameson (Pernod Ricard), Irish whiskey — 8,1
Crown Royal (Diageo), Canadian whisky — 7,9
Ballantine's (Pernod Ricard), Scotch whisky — 7,7
Blenders Pride (Pernod Ricard), Indian whisky — 7,6
Bagpiper (Diageo/United Spirits), Indian whisky — 6,1
Royal Challenge (Diageo/United Spirits), Indian whisky — 5,5
Old Tavern (Diageo/United Spirits), Indian whisky — 5,3
Kakubin (Suntory), Japanese whisky — 5,2
Chivas Regal (Pernod Ricard), Scotch whisky — 4,4
Director's Special (Diageo/United Spirits), Indian whisky — 4,2
Grant's (Wm Grand & Sons), Scotch whisky — 4,2
Bangalore Malt (John Distilleries), Indian whisky — 4,2
Black Nikka Clear (Asahi Breweries), Japanese whisky — 3,4
William Lawson's (Bacardi), Scotch whisky — 3,3
Dewar's (Bacardi), Scotch whisky — 3,0
J&B (Diageo), Scotch whisky — 3,0
Famous Grouse (Edrington), Scotch whisky — 3,0
Sterling Reserve Premium (Allied Blenders & Distillers), Indian whisky — 2,8
Black & White (Diageo), Scotch whisky — 2,8
Label 5 (La Martiniquaise), Scotch whisky — 2,7

Source: Drinks International, The Millionaires Club 2020

Global Exports of Scotch by Region 2019

Volume (litres of pure alcohol)			Value (£ Sterling)		
Region	000s of litres	Change	Region	000s of £	Change
Asia & Oceania	98,117	+11,9	Asia & Oceania	1,238,501	+9,8
Eastern Europe	8,732	+31,2	Eastern Europe	37,120	+20,4
European Community	130,137	+1,2	European Community	1,478,461	+5,6
Latin America & Carribean	39,190	+4,6	Latin America & Carribean	378,202	+2,6
Middle East & North Africa	13,130	-17,2	Middle East & North Africa	239,062	-13,0
North America	53,644	-8,5	North America	1,284,294	+1,9
Sub-Saharan Africa	17,716	+3,7	Sub-Saharan Africa	176,036	+11,3
Western Europe ex EC	5,982	+0,3	Western Europe ex EC	83,142	-1,8
Total	**366,650**	**+2,4**	**Total**	**4,914,850**	**+4,5**

Source: Scotch Whisky Association

Export of Scotch Whisky 2019

= volumes in 000s of litres of pure alcohol   = values in 000s of £ Sterling

Staples in both tables on this page show the Top 10 markets
ranked according to volume and then with the corresponding value.

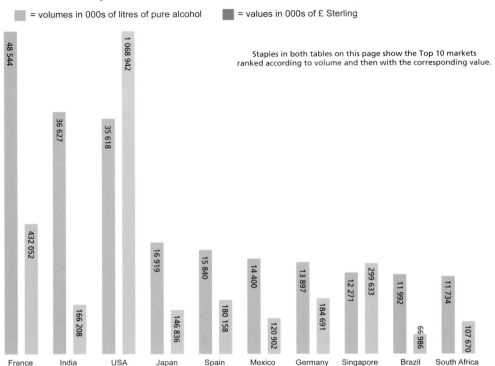

	France	India	USA	Japan	Spain	Mexico	Germany	Singapore	Brazil	South Africa
Volume	48 544	36 627	35 618	16 919	15 840	14 400	13 897	12 271	11 992	11 734
Value	432 052	166 208	1 068 942	146 836	180 158	120 902	184 691	299 633	66 986	107 670

Source: Scotch Whisky Association

Export of Single Malt Scotch 2019

= volumes in 000s of litres of pure alcohol   = values in 000s of £ Sterling

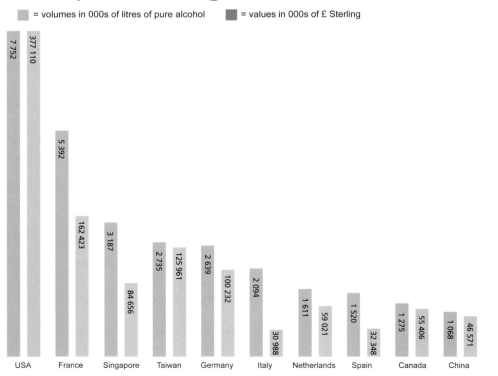

	USA	France	Singapore	Taiwan	Germany	Italy	Netherlands	Spain	Canada	China
Volume	7 752	5 392	3 187	2 735	2 639	2 094	1 611	1 520	1 275	1 068
Value	377 110	162 423	84 656	125 961	100 232	30 988	59 021	32 348	55 406	46 571

Source: Scotch Whisky Association

Distillery Capacity

Litres of pure alcohol - Scottish, active distilleries only

Distillery	Litres	Distillery	Litres	Distillery	Litres
Glenlivet	21 000 000	Ben Nevis	2 000 000	Kingsbarns	600 000
Macallan	15 000 000	Bowmore	2 000 000	Speyside	600 000
Glenfiddich	13 700 000	Inchdairnie	2 000 000	Annandale	500 000
Roseisle	12 500 000	Knockdhu	2 000 000	Ardnamurchan	500 000
Ailsa Bay	12 000 000	Balblair	1 800 000	Bonnington	500 000
Glen Ord	11 000 000	Pulteney	1 800 000	The Clydeside	500 000
Teaninich	10 200 000	The Borders	1 600 000	Glasgow	500 000
Dalmunach	10 000 000	Bruichladdich	1 500 000	Royal Lochnagar	500 000
Balvenie	7 000 000	Bladnoch	1 500 000	Torabhaig	500 000
Caol Ila	6 500 000	Glendronach	1 400 000	Kilchoman	480 000
Glen Grant	6 200 000	Glen Spey	1 400 000	Brew Dog	450 000
Glenmorangie	6 500 000	Knockando	1 400 000	Harris	400 000
Dufftown	6 000 000	Glen Garioch	1 370 000	Glenturret	340 000
Glen Keith	6 000 000	Glencadam	1 300 000	Edradour	260 000
Mannochmore	6 000 000	Scapa	1 300 000	Holyrood	250 000
Auchroisk	5 900 000	Lochranza	1 200 000	Lindores Abbey	225 000
Miltonduff	5 800 000	Glenglassaugh	1 100 000	Arbikie	200 000
Glen Moray	5 700 000	Glengoyne	1 100 000	Isle of Raasay	200 000
Glenrothes	5 600 000	Ardnahoe	1 000 000	Glen Wyvis	140 000
Linkwood	5 600 000	Ardross	1 000 000	Wolfburn	135 000
Ardmore	5 550 000	Tobermory	1 000 000	Ballindalloch	100 000
Dailuaine	5 200 000	Oban	870 000	Eden Mill	100 000
Glendullan	5 000 000	Glen Scotia	800 000	Ncn´ean	100 000
Loch Lomond	5 000 000	Aberargie	750 000	Daftmill	65 000
Tomatin	5 000 000	Glengyle	750 000	Dornoch	30 000
Clynelish	4 800 000	Lagg	750 000	Strathearn	30 000
Kininvie	4 800 000	Springbank	750 000	Abhainn Dearg	20 000
Tormore	4 800 000	Benromach	700 000		
Longmorn	4 500 000				
Speyburn	4 500 000				
Dalmore	4 300 000				
Glenburgie	4 250 000				
Allt-a-Bhainne	4 200 000				
Braeval	4 200 000				
Glentauchers	4 200 000				
Craigellachie	4 100 000				
Royal Brackla	4 100 000				
Glenallachie	4 000 000				
Tamdhu	4 000 000				
Tamnavulin	4 000 000				
Aberlour	3 800 000				
Mortlach	3 800 000				
Glenlossie	3 700 000				
Benrinnes	3 500 000				
Glenfarclas	3 500 000				
Aberfeldy	3 400 000				
Cardhu	3 400 000				
Macduff	3 400 000				
Laphroaig	3 300 000				
Talisker	3 300 000				
Tomintoul	3 300 000				
Aultmore	3 200 000				
Fettercairn	3 200 000				
Inchgower	3 200 000				
Deanston	3 000 000				
Tullibardine	3 000 000				
Balmenach	2 800 000				
Benriach	2 800 000				
Blair Athol	2 800 000				
Bunnahabhain	2 700 000				
Glen Elgin	2 700 000				
Strathmill	2 600 000				
Lagavulin	2 530 000				
Glenkinchie	2 500 000				
Highland Park	2 500 000				
Strathisla	2 450 000				
Ardbeg	2 400 000				
Jura	2 400 000				
Cragganmore	2 200 000				
Dalwhinnie	2 200 000				
Auchentoshan	2 000 000				

Summary of Malt Distillery Capacity by Owner

Owner (number of distilleries)	Litres of alcohol	% of Industry
Diageo (28)	121 370 000	30,0
Pernod Ricard (13)	76 500 000	18,9
William Grant (4)	37 500 000	9,3
Edrington Group (3)	23 100 000	5,7
Bacardi (John Dewar & Sons) (5)	18 200 000	4,5
Beam Suntory (5)	14 220 000	3,5
Emperador Inc (Whyte & Mackay) (4)	13 900 000	3,4
Pacific Spirits (Inver House) (5)	12 900 000	3,2
Moët Hennessy (Glenmorangie) (2)	8 900 000	2,2
Distell (Burn Stewart) (3)	6 700 000	1,7
Campari (Glen Grant) (1)	6 200 000	1,5
Loch Lomond Group (2)	5 800 000	1,4
La Martiniquaise (Glen Moray) (1)	5 700 000	1,4
Benriach Distillery Co (3)	5 300 000	1,3
Ian Macleod Distillers (2)	5 100 000	1,3
Tomatin Distillery Co (1)	5 000 000	1,2
Angus Dundee (2)	4 600 000	1,1
The Glenallachie Consortium (1)	4 000 000	1,0
J & G Grant (Glenfarclas) (1)	3 500 000	0,9
Picard (Tullibardine) (1)	3 000 000	0,8
John Fergus & Co. (Inchdairnie) (1)	2 000 000	0,5
Nikka (Ben Nevis Distillery) (1)	2 000 000	0,5
Isle of Arran Distillers (2)	1 950 000	< 0,5
The Three Stills Co. (The Borders) (1)	1 600 000	< 0,5
Rémy Cointreau (Bruichladdich) (1)	1 500 000	< 0,5
J & A Mitchell (2)	1 500 000	< 0,5
David Prior (Bladnoch) (1)	1 500 000	< 0,5
Hunter Laing (Ardnahoe) (1)	1 000 000	< 0,5
Greenwood Distillers (Ardross) (1)	1 000 000	< 0,5
The Perth Distilling Co. (Aberargie) (1)	750 000	< 0,5
Gordon & MacPhail (Benromach) (1)	700 000	< 0,5
Wemyss Malts (Kingsbarns) (1)	600 000	< 0,5
Harvey´s of Edinburgh (Speyside) (1)	600 000	< 0,5
Adelphi Distillery (Ardnamurchan) (1)	500 000	< 0,5
Annandale Distillery Co. (1)	500 000	< 0,5
Morrison Glasgow Distillers (Clydeside) (1)	500 000	< 0,5
Mossburn Distillers (Torabhaig) (1)	500 000	< 0,5
John Crabbie & Co. (Bonnington) (1)	500 000	< 0,5
Glasgow Distillery (1)	500 000	< 0,5
Others (18)	3 975 000	1,0
Total (126)	**404 715 000**	

ORKNEY ISLANDS

2 3

129

4 Wick

5 6

7 144
8

Isle of Lewis
127
Isle of Harris
140

NORTH HIGHLANDS

151
10 9
11

149

16

18
19 20

21

SKYE

146

73

12 13
14 15
Inverness

SPEYSIDE

23

24

143

139

Kyle of Localsh

17

Loch Ness

26

25

Aberdeen

27

28

30 31
Fort William

29

CENTRAL HIGHLANDS

EAST HIGHLANDS

32

131

72
145

WEST HIGHLANDS

Pitlochry 37
38

34 35
33 134 36

MULL

Oban

40

Loch
Tay

39

Dundee

41
130

42 136

44 Perth 148 137

St. Andrews
43

133

Loch
Lomond

45

Stirling

JURA

70 147
69
68
67 66
71

50

46

47 48
49 Glasgow

53

54

152 153 Edinburgh

55

ISLAY

62
65 63 64

58

51
141 142 52

ARRAN

150

59
60 61 Campbeltown

Ayr

THE LOWLANDS

138

56 126

Dumfries

128

Stranraer

57

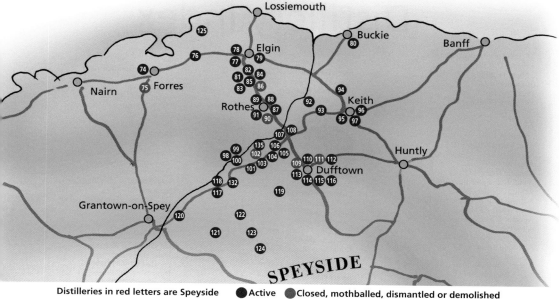

Distilleries in red letters are Speyside ● Active ● Closed, mothballed, dismantled or demolished

c = Closed, m = Mothballed, dm = Dismantled, d = Demolished

Distillery Index

Distillery Index

Distillery Index